For Brett —

SHADOW
THE MAGNIFICENT MACHINES OF A MAN OF MYSTERY

© Pete Lyons 2020

All rights reserved. No part of this publication may be reproduced or stored in a retrieval system or transmitted, in any form or by any means, electronic, mechanical, photocopying, recording or otherwise, without prior permission in writing from Evro Publishing.

Published in July 2020
Reprinted in September 2020

ISBN 978-1-910505-49-6

Published by Evro Publishing, Westrow House, Holwell, Sherborne, Dorset DT9 5LF, UK

Printed and bound in Slovenia by GPS Group

Edited by Mark Hughes
Designed by Richard Parsons

www.evropublishing.com

JACKET PHOTOGRAPHS

FRONT, TOP Jackie Oliver wins the Mid-Ohio Can-Am race of 1974 in the Shadow DN4, securing his title as that year's Can-Am Champion. *Dan R. Boyd*
FRONT, BOTTOM Shadow's splendid single Grand Prix victory came with Alan Jones at Austria's Österreichring in 1977 driving a DN8. *Motorsport Images/David Phipps*
BACK Man of Mystery, Shadowman: Don Nichols during 1975. *Motorsport Images/David Phipps*

SHADOW

THE MAGNIFICENT MACHINES OF A MAN OF MYSTERY
Can-Am • Formula 1 • F5000

Pete Lyons

ACKNOWLEDGEMENTS

WRITING may be a lonely craft, but crafting a book calls for many good helping hands. And I had the best.

I'm equally grateful to you all, but writing is also linear. So I'm sorry guys, but you have to fall into some kind of lineup. I'll start with members of the Shadow team itself, the drivers, designers, mechanics, managers and others who actually made it all happen, not only in the day but also in telling your stories today.

Accordingly, thank you first to Penny Nichols; then George Follmer, Jackie Oliver, Alan Jones, Parnelli Jones, Brian Redman, Stefan Johansson, and Randolph Townsend (apologies to the many other drivers for whom there was just no room); to designer Trevor Harris and wife Linda "Freddi" Fredrickson, and to Peter Bryant and Tony Southgate. Other key players include Jim Mederer, Richard Owen, John Gentry, Mike Hillman, Walt Boyd, Doug Meyer, Jim Spicklemire, Tony Connor, Dennis Muir, Bill Woolridge, Russ Olson, and Gene Lentz. A shout out too for John Simley and Doug Bashear of UOP, plus all the others that I'll probably wake up tonight in a sweat about failing to mention them.

Thanks too to today's faithful Shadowfolk, who keep the cars and the lore alive, including but not limited to Jim Bartel and the Bennett family, the "Big Noise Boys" of RM Motorsports, racers and restorers of the highest degree; to Dennis Losher and his sidekick Roger Lemmel, Shadowfans extraordinaire; Scott Drnek of Virtuoso Performance; Bruce Canepa of his eponymous restoration and preparation firm; Larry Fulhorst, for sharing his knowledge and enthusiasm; Ron Tredway, who knows military insignia along with racecars; George Levy, who in a very real sense made this book possible; David Bull, who initially brought me together with the elusive Shadowman; the late Fred Cziska, who once let this incompetent wannabe loose to drive his Shadow Mk III. What a rocket ship.

Then there are my colleagues, past and present, whose roles have all been vital: D. Randy Riggs of *Vintage Motorsport* magazine, in whose pages this book first took shape; Leon Mandel and my many editors at both *AutoWeek* and *Autosport*, who sent me off to the races; John Zimmermann of *RACECAR* (old) and *Vintage Racecar* (new) for sharing his own interview with Don Nichols; Michael Recca for so thoughtfully passing along a big box of color slides that had come his way; and the many exceptional reporters and photographers whose work breathed life into these pages and are credited individually.

Among them of course is my late father, Ozzie Lyons, who set my feet on this magical road in the first place.

To Eric Verdon-Roe, Mark Hughes and Richard Parsons at Evro Publishing, let me say, "Thanks once again, Mates, working with you is an utter delight."

Nor can I forget the Shadowman himself, Capt. Donald R. Nichols, US Army (Rtd.), founder of Advanced Vehicle Systems and Phoenix Racing, the singular person whose story we tell here. How unexpected it was that he opened his archives and his memories to us, and how crucially valuable our time with him proved to be.

Of course, as always, my greatest gratitude is for the wonderful Lorna, my wife, my life, and my one-time Managing Editor who still, all these years later, somehow manages to keep me on track and powering forward. Couldn't have done this without you, my Love.

Pete Lyons, May 2020

BELOW Lorna keeps the interview going while Pete gets the camera going. *Pete Lyons*

CONTENTS

INTRODUCTION   6

PROLOGUE
THE SHADOWMAN   8

CHAPTER 1
BORN TO BATTLE
A DESTINY RESET IN AN INSTANT   14

CHAPTER 2
THE ENTREPRENEUR
RACE TIRES, RACECARS
AND ONE BIG RACETRACK   28

CHAPTER 3
MOONSHOT
A RACECAR OF THE AEROSPACE AGE   42

CHAPTER 4
THE TINY ONE
AVS SHADOW MK I   62

CHAPTER 5
SHORT AND SAD
THE 1970 SEASON   84

CHAPTER 6
THE MIDSIZE ONE
SHADOW MK II, 1971   104

CHAPTER 7
THE CONVENTIONAL ONE
SHADOW MK III, 1972   134

CHAPTER 8
TAKING ON THE WORLD
SHADOW DN1 (F1), 1973   160

CHAPTER 9
THE BIG ONE
SHADOW DN2 (CAN-AM), 1973   196

CHAPTER 10
FRESH START
SHADOW DN3 (F1), 1974   208

CHAPTER 11
THE BEST ONE
SHADOW DN4 (CAN-AM), 1974   232

CHAPTER 12
FIRST VICTORY
SHADOW DN5 (F1), 1975   266

CHAPTER 13
F1 FOR EVERYMAN?
SHADOW DN6 (F5000), 1975   292

CHAPTER 14
OFF THE BOIL
SHADOW DN5B AND DN8 (F1), 1976   310

CHAPTER 15
A LAST YEAR, AT LAST A WIN
SHADOW DN6B (F5000), 1976   332

CHAPTER 16
FROM BLACK TO LIGHT
SHADOW DN8 (F1), 1977   340

CHAPTER 17
SINGLE-SEAT SPORTS CARS
SHADOW DN6C AND DN10
(CAN-AM II), 1977–78   368

CHAPTER 18
DECLINE
SHADOW DN9 (F1), 1978   378

CHAPTER 19
SCRATCHING TO SURVIVE
DN9B (FORMULA 1), 1979   404

CHAPTER 20
THE ORPHANS
DN11 & DN12 (FORMULA 1), 1980   418

CHAPTER 21
SHADOWMAN'S ACTION ART   430

AFTERWORDS
TREVOR HARRIS   444

DENNIS LOSHER   448

PENNY NICHOLS   453

INDEX   460

INTRODUCTION

"WE'RE PLAYING IT STRONG. We'll either win big, or lose big." That's the attitude Don Nichols presented as he launched his startlingly novel Advanced Vehicle Systems Shadow Mk I "Tiny Tire" Can-Am car for the opening round of the Canadian-American Challenge Cup Series in June, 1970.

It carried a conventional Big Block Chevrolet engine in the back. There ended conventionality.

Colored a flamboyantly in-your-face Tangerine orange for its debut, the AVS Mk I had been imagined, designed and engineered by Trevor Lee Harris, a dauntless young conceptual genius from Seattle whose prior obscurity on the world stage was about to end.

Least possible aerodynamic drag for highest possible speed on straightaways: that's what Harris was going for. To achieve it, he specified the minimum practicable tire diameters for the lowest feasible body profile. This became achievable — or so it seemed — when Firestone agreed to develop special rubberwear some 30–35 percent smaller in diameter than normal tires and wheels of the day, without giving up sidewall height or tread width.

But of course, in engineering one experiment begets another. And another. Smaller wheels and shallower chassis depth meant lower axle lines, new transmission gearing, reconceived suspension geometries and hardware, reduced suspension movement, more challenging springing and damping measures, tighter brake packaging making for reduced braking power, more cramped driver accommodation, crippling cooling issues… as a pitlane saying goes, what was intended to be a racecar becomes "a science experiment."

No wonder a project begun in 1968 for debut in the 1969 season wasn't ready to race until 1970. But "ready" isn't the appropriate word. Unfortunately for Nichols's Advanced Vehicle Systems, Can-Am's once appealingly minimal technical regulations had abruptly become more restrictive. Word came down during 1969 that "moving aerodynamic devices" would be outlawed the next year. Harris was forced to abandon some of his more innovative ideas, especially his intention to deploy air brakes lifting into the slipstream to assist the conventional friction discs, which had to be small to fit the small wheels.

Time drained away. Expenses mounted. Nichols was running out of money. By the time the tiny, nearly exhausted team set out from Los Angeles for Mosport Park, diagonally across all of North America to beyond Toronto, their shop had

BELOW The Shadowman. A man of deliberate mystery — and a wicked sense of humor. *Pete Lyons*

RIGHT "Like a go-kart on steroids!" Shadow's Tiny Tire car made a dramatic debut at Mosport Park. Not in an entirely positive way. *Pete Lyons*

been raided by police seeking assets; there had been court action over an unpaid bill.

Shadow's debut performances in Canada showed some promise, and straightaway speeds were indeed spectacular, but technical problems were still glaringly obvious. Engine overheating, primarily, forced intrepid American driver George Follmer out early at Mosport and again at Saint-Jovite. Worse, on the drive away from the latter circuit the team's transporter rig — a pickup pulling a small enclosed trailer — was hit by a drunk driver and crashed into a ditch. The racecar sustained crippling damage.

Trevor Harris was done. He had to make a living. Nichols could no longer provide it.

So was Don Nichols done as well? Was AVS Shadow about to sink into motor racing's bottomless depths of unfulfilled dreams, unachieved ambitions, bitter disappointments, to become one more barely noticed and scarcely remembered footnote to history?

Nobody but Nichols could have imagined what was to come.

He did not quit. Somehow he scratched more funding together. His team finished a second Mk I, greatly modified from the first. They painted this one black. Shadow entered 1970's Mid-Ohio Can-Am, this time with England's versatile Vic Elford driving. But once again the novel machine dropped out early.

This time Shadow did vanish from the scene.

Until the next year. Incredibly, Nichols found a sponsor, hired British engineer/mechanic Peter Bryant to design and build a new Mk II car, signed Briton Jackie Oliver to drive it, and Shadow raced in most of 1971's Can-Am events. And did it all again in 1972 — showing genuinely competitive speed and, sometimes, reliability.

Ultimately, in 1974, Oliver won the Can-Am championship aboard a Shadow. Called now the DN4, a model designed by another Brit named Tony Southgate, it proved to be one of the best Can-Am racecars ever.

At that point, the team had branched out into other kinds of racing, most notably Formula 1. Where it managed to score two race wins, one of them the Grand Prix of Austria in 1977 (driver Alan Jones of Australia).

Defying further adversities, Don Nichols kept his Shadow Cars racing longer than anyone could have imagined: 10 seasons, 1970 through 1979, plus part of an 11th. From startup late in 1968 to eventual sale and closure in early 1980, the team existed for not quite 12 years. Its participation in F1, from March 1973 to March 1980, exceeds by many years the span achieved by any rival American F1 organization, including Reventlow Scarab, Gurney Eagle, Penske Racing and Vel's Parnelli Jones. Of those Yanks, only Dan Gurney (at the wheel himself) and Roger Penske (John Watson driving) scored singleton GP victories of their own. Today's Haas is a potential challenger to Shadow's record in F1, but they'll have to stay the course for many more seasons.

Bold Don Nichols did play it big. ♠

PROLOGUE

THE SHADOWMAN

"I DON'T THINK THE IDEA ever was to make money. It was to make an art piece, an active art piece which was not only attractive but high performing, and unique, and innovative. Something really innovative in an area where the innovation could be shown and proven, which of course is motor racing.

"I'm a creative of beauty. I like the hardware — I like the artistic aspect of the hardware. That's about all I can say about

BELOW The Wizard at his work, high up in the loft of his cavern at Salinas. *Pete Lyons*

my motivation. It wasn't very well thought out."

It was August, 2013, and Donald Robert Nichols was 88 when he made that remark in quiet, matter-of-fact tones. I remember thinking, well, each of us is multifaceted, and even the most combative, determinedly acquisitive of people may mellow with age.

An aesthetic sensibility, though? This may not be the first character trait mentioned by some who knew this man during his 1970s ventures into international motor racing.

The late American entrepreneur had imagination, drive and daring, of course. Also an air of cultivated mystique mixed with courtly bonhomie, a salesman's glib palaver delivered in rather stately language, perhaps an overly stubborn sharpness of the business pencil.

But an artist's soul?

Yes. Most of his Shadow competition machines were indeed beautiful creations of advanced concept, elegantly drawn and finely crafted by a masterfully talented team — often despite daunting deficits in terms of resources and time. Shadows won races in Can-Am, Formula 1 and Formula 5000, though not many. Nichols claimed to have fathered more than 100 of his beloved objects of action art, and most still survive these long decades later, reverently restored and often enthusiastically shown at speed. For their custodians today, it is mainly about the splendid racecars.

But so many of the Shadow stories such people tell circle around the Shadowman himself. Tall, taciturn, reserved in manner and restrained in emotional expression, he seemed innately enigmatic, even forbidding. Rumors swirled behind him; for many people, he might have been more talked about than spoken to. More myth than man.

Be wary of dealings with him, was the reputation he had gained.

Yet some closer associates found him congenial, even openhearted. Members of his racing team in particular

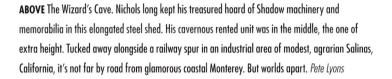

ABOVE The Wizard's Cave. Nichols long kept his treasured hoard of Shadow machinery and memorabilia in this elongated steel shed. His cavernous rented unit was in the middle, the one of extra height. Tucked away alongside a railway spur in an industrial area of modest, agrarian Salinas, California, it's not far by road from glamorous coastal Monterey. But worlds apart. *Pete Lyons*

RIGHT Six days a week Don would arrive early and spend the whole day working with his collection. He wouldn't even break for lunch. As for Sundays, "My wife has things for me to do in the garden." *Pete Lyons*

seemed to rekindle the old camaraderie he had cherished back in his military career. With them he could show an impish, mischievous sense of humor that might have surprised outsiders.

Talking of him now that he's gone, one tends to find that people's opinions are bipolar; some feel admiration, even affection, while others think darkly of him. Expressions this author has heard ranged from "I love the man" to, literally, "I wouldn't piss on Don Nichols if he was on fire!"

Speaking personally, my own impressions of the man never extended to either extreme. I first met him during the Can-Am season of 1970, when our interactions were those of a race reporter speaking with a racer. This continued when Nichols took his Shadow team into Formula 1, so we would have stopped to talk in one pitlane or another around the world through 1976.

Our conversations were almost always cordial. The one exception came after the rain-soaked 1973 Grand Prix of Canada, when we met again at the next GP in the US. His answers to my questions were unusually terse, so I finally asked, "Don, are you mad at me?"

"You could say that," he replied, and explained that in my reports from Mosport I had not mentioned that one of his Shadows briefly led the race.

Surprised, I replied honestly, "This is the first I've heard of it!" I pointed out that the rain had caused such mid-race chaos that seemingly everybody lost track of the running order. I certainly did not deliberately leave out a fact of great significance to this first-year F1 team owner.

But I offered an apology, Nichols accepted it, and there was no further acrimony between us.

When approached in 2013 to collaborate for this book, a book he himself had long intended to write, he was wary but finally welcoming. My wife Lorna and I spent hours that became days with him, immersed in memories.

We would meet of a misty morning at his stored old racer's warehouse, a graceless steel shed of a thing in an unlovely part of plebeian Salinas, over the hill from patrician Monterey, California. The cavernous interior was stuffed three tiers high with treasures: complete racecars or monocoques, body sections, suspension and running gear parts, engines and transmissions or their elements, racks of new metal stock and boxes of old junk, design drawings, pictures, banners, trophies, filing cabinets… thousands of keepsakes of bygone

ABOVE Three stories of stuff. Nichols gradually, reluctantly, sold off many of his heirlooms over the years, but many, many still remained, stacked and crammed and buried on and under rough timber flooring all the way to the bare metal eaves. Chassis, bodies, powertrain parts, rolls of drawings… even the little white minicar prototype he commissioned way back in Fuel Crisis days. *Pete Lyons*

LEFT Nearing 90 and still doing ladders. *Pete Lyons*

times. The Wizard's Cave, I called the magical space.

The old Wizard was lean enough — he denied himself midday meals — to claim proudly that he could still wear his old Army Captain's dress uniform in his closet at home. He would sit with us for hours in his shabby office, his lanky frame bent into a rickety old swivel chair, knitted stocking cap and upturned jacket collar defying the chill of his unheated space, answering our questions or trying to. Ofttimes the memories came hard, sometimes not at all.

But then there would be a sudden spark and he would leap up and dash out across the shop floor to find something he had thought to show us. He knew just where it was and, much spryer than I, the 88-year-old would clamber like a young gymnast up and up through precarious levels of rough timber flooring. He gave me to think that he had erected this scaffold-like structure with his own hands 20 years before.

Way back in my own past, I had been captivated by a painting of a pair of young boys on a jetty, sitting entranced at the feet of an old seaman, who was spinning yarns as he gestured toward fabulous horizons. As our own ancient mariner told his tales, our understanding took shape of the manner of man required to achieve what Don Nichols did, in the ways that he did.

In motorsports history, Shadow is not ranked among the premier teams. It did win races, but seldom regularly; its cars were often fast, but too often fragile; the one drivers' championship, by Jackie Oliver in the Can-Am of 1974, was a worthy achievement by a well-run team, but unfortunately came against thin opposition at the tag end of a dying series.

Asked about his fondest memory from the Shadow days, Nichols paused to consider it. The pause grew long. Finally his agelessly acute eyes refocused and he said slowly, "Maybe winning the Race of Champions with Tom, the first Formula 1 win for Shadow."

Ah, yes. That was at England's Brands Hatch in March of 1975. Despite the event's name — and disregarding promotions of other kinds also dubbed ROC — this early-season sprint for F1 cars, together with a few F5000s, was not a Grand Prix, not part of the World Championship, so not all GP teams and drivers participated.

But the grid did host the likes of Donohue, Fittipaldi, Ickx,

Jarier, Peterson, Scheckter and Watson. Beside Shadow's team of two, there were full-on works entries from BRM, Ensign, Lotus, McLaren, Penske, Surtees, Tyrrell and Williams.

Young Shadowman Tom Pryce out-qualified them all. Then he beat them all.

It was still early in the American team's third season of international F1 racing, a season that started with exciting promise. Shadow's new DN5, its third single-seater model, showed immediate speed. In January, lead driver Jean-Pierre Jarier qualified fastest for both the two opening Grands Prix, Argentina and Brazil. They were Shadow's first pole positions in Formula 1.

Mechanical problems — endemic for everybody back then — spoiled those races and also round three in South Africa, but victory at Brands Hatch was a timely morale booster even if it didn't count for championship points.

But what about Shadow's maiden Grand Prix victory, when Alan Jones came home first in the 1977 Austrian Grand Prix? Did Nichols remember being elated, thrilled, delirious with joy? Once again he had to stop and think way, way back. "I don't remember [any particular emotion]. I guess we were kind of matter-of-fact. We thought we deserved to win, and we were ready to win, so this was it, so Halleluiah. Good." Typical racer. Always looking forward, optimistic there's better to come.

BELOW A work of artist's art, the jewelry-like marque badge made for the nosepiece of the first Shadow. The golden "AVS" ribbon is a Mobius strip. *Pete Lyons*

ABOVE A work of artisan's art, the bent-not-broken suspension rocker that Don proudly showed off to visitors. (The old design drawing underneath is just a stage prop, it doesn't depict this piece.) *Pete Lyons*

Yet in motorsports there's always a worse side lurking, dank underbellies of insecure stepping stones waiting to turn uppermost. Like other teams of the day, small fraternal bands of warriors in the treacherous field, Shadow suffered loss. Two of its drivers died at the wheel in ugly, gruesome crashes impossible to cleanse from the mind.

Is the triumph worth the risk of tragedy? Every racer confronts the question sooner or later. How they answer determines whether they stay in racing.

Was Don Nichols actually a racer, though? Not from boyhood, no. He was in his middle years when the whirlwind caught him up.

But in his youth he had emerged as a born man of combat, a career military veteran who already had endured innumerable grisly World War II experiences of his own — Normandy, Holland, Belgium — without losing his appetite for battle, long before even thinking of auto racing.

So the artistic side seemed incongruous, but it definitely was there. Invited to prowl freely among the countless bits of old competition equipment strewn like timeless treasures in a hoarder's attic, Lorna and I discovered surprising gems of artisanship:

- A beautiful ornament meant as the marque badge of his first AVS car, a finely designed emblem that gave the same feeling as costly jewelry;
- Two expertly crafted aluminum containers meant to showcase books for presentation to wealthy buyers of Shadow racecars;

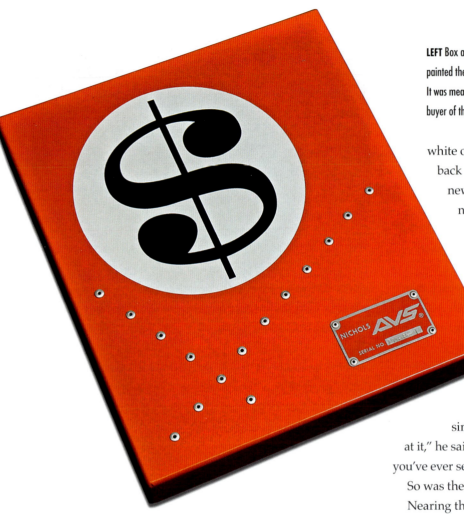

LEFT Box art. A slipcase crafted of the same chassis materials and painted the same Tangerine color as the original "Dollar Car." It was meant to enclose a special book presented to a potential buyer of the vehicle itself. *Pete Lyons*

- A suspension arm of shaped and welded steel, a commonplace component but made with such skill and pride as to stand glistening testimony to racecar metalwork as fine sculpture — but this one savagely bent by some terrible force.

"Look at this, isn't it beautiful," Don murmured with reverence as he displayed the discarded old part. "Bent but not broken! We had the best designers and fabricators in Formula 1."

During one of our several days of interviews, he broke off to lead us to a nearby shop where Dennis Muir, son of Shadow race engine builder Lee Muir and himself a former fabricator with the team, was completing his restoration of a DN8 Formula 1 machine. Don had prepared documents declaring that this chassis was the very one that carried Jones to victory in Austria. (It must be noted that some in the collector world are skeptical of the claim.)

We had visited the shop earlier, during which the old man had pitched in to help by running errands in his small, plain white old Ford Ranger pickup truck. He would come back with a needed item, in one instance a brand-new, in-the-box VW radiator core that perfectly nestled into one of the side nacelles of the old F1, and unload it with a sense of quiet pride that warmed my heart; he was still able to be a useful member of his team.

This time he wanted to witness a grand moment: first fire-up of a freshly installed Ford-Cosworth DFV racing engine. During preparations I noticed Don spending a long while standing in one place behind the glistening machine, simply gazing at it, so I joined him. "Just look at it," he said softly. "Isn't that the most beautiful thing you've ever seen?"

So was the awakened war cry of the long dormant old V8.

Nearing the end of our time together, I asked Nichols how he wished to wrap up our story of his years in racing. This time his words flowed easily, as if the thoughts had long been formed.

"It pleases me," the old warrior told me (I have edited some of our recorded conversation for length and flow), "that we were able to make attractive equipment, [cars] that were extremely well received, and we were able to find sponsors and support.

"It's satisfying to recall that we had an opportunity to do things that we didn't always do well, but we tried to do them in an innovative and creative and, I suppose, exciting and appealing [way]. We tried to make attractive, well-decorated cars and we tried to do programs that appealed to us, or to me personally. It was something I had ability to control — our participation and our expression.

"We thought it was an artistic expression."

What a complex personality, I was thinking as I reviewed my own accumulated impressions of him.

Naturally artistic, but instinctively adversarial. Man of combat, man of fellowship. A face held inscrutably impassive to conceal a mischievous wit and a wicked sense

LEFT A scant mile from his own shop, Don was having an F1 car restored for auction by Dennis Muir, son of former Shadow engine man Lee Muir. Said to be the actual DN8 driven to the team's single GP victory in Austria, it had later become a full-bodied DN10 Can-Am vehicle with an F5000 Dodge engine. Muir, in background, had needed upwards of a year to put it all back to rights. *Pete Lyons*

BELOW Dennis, Don and DN8, done. *Pete Lyons*

of humor. Inspirationally motivational as a promoter of his ambitions, yet ruthlessly avaricious in business, he could be genial in one circumstance, almost breathtakingly greedy in another. Abstemious in his personal habits, he was known not to drink or smoke, yet should wealth fall to him he seemed incapable of frugality. Affectionate with associates and often generous to family, but miserly at other times and seemingly coldly, even brutally indifferent to creditors. The same shoulders that warmly embraced old friends could turn icy against others. The same father of eight who, as age advanced, had great difficulty remembering their names, but who could effortlessly and pridefully rattle off the particulars of every professional driver who ever conducted one of his Shadows… some 37 of them, by his tally. A teller of tales, a holder of secrets. A man loved… and loathed.

Each one of us has such a spectrum, but his extremes seemed to reach far beyond the norm.

How did this Don Nichols fellow, a Midwestern farm boy, High School athlete, wartime paratrooper wounded on D-Day, later career US Army officer and reputed CIA operative, then an entrepreneurial businessman in Japan, a deliberately shadowy man of mystery who was all but unknown in the US racing community… how did such a singular figure pull it off?

Let's see if we can figure him out. ♠

THE SHADOWMAN 13

CHAPTER 1
BORN TO BATTLE

A DESTINY RESET IN AN INSTANT

DONALD ROBERT NICHOLS didn't grow up burning to be a racing driver. Those of us who did should know that about him, I suggest, if we wish to understand how he went about his racing.

He came into life in 1924 in the American rural Midwest, at a small town in a farming community in the middle of the state of Missouri. The earliest competitions he knew of involved school athletics and horse-pulling contests.

According to what he told us about his youth, he did become interested in cars, and came to appreciate ones that performed well, but their primary attraction for him was aesthetic. Their style.

It wasn't until much later and in another, wider world that motorsport caught his interest.

And when the competitive nature of it drew him in, Don Nichols was a mature man whose life had been a war ever since childhood.

ORPHAN

THE MURDEROUS Midwestern tornado struck with sudden terrible violence, ripping apart the flimsy, 1920s-era taxi and hurling the toddler far into the woods. Hours passed and darkness was falling before a search party, holding hands to maintain formation in the thick undergrowth, finally came across his tiny broken body. He was severely hurt, but he would live.

His young mother had suffered fatal injuries. "I don't remember my mother at all," he told us softly, long, long after. The taxi driver survived, which may be why rescuers knew to go searching for a missing child.

Donald Robert Nichols retained no memories of that tragic day when his life so abruptly changed. As he grew he heard the story, of course, and knew it happened sometime in the latter 1920s, but he couldn't say how old he was then, because he was unsure of the year. He presumed it would have happened in the hottest months of a summer, when "cyclones" were most likely. The site would have been somewhere around the small, central Missouri town of Eldon, his birthplace there at the feet of the Ozarks on November 23rd, 1924.

But porous though it had become eight decades later, Don's memory still held his mother's name: "Omah!" he once blurted out during conversation, as if surprised to recall it after so many years. "My mother's name was Omah!"

Our minds may forget, but the Web doesn't. Online searches reveal an outbreak of savage tornados that struck Missouri and surrounding states over a three-day period of May, 1927, reportedly killing more than 200 people. One responsible for four deaths ripped by the Eldon area in the early afternoon of May 9th. A local newspaper archive speaks of extensive damage around the town on that date. Alternative evidence found on a county death certificate suggests it happened the day before, the 8th, but it records the passing of Omah Audra Nichols, nee Clark, on May 10th.

In any case, the family would have just celebrated her 24th birthday.

So Don, her only child, would have been two and a half. For a long while afterward, a year or perhaps more, he remained confined in a rehabilitation hospital while bones knitted and surgeries healed. "My left leg was crooked," he remarked, and gestured toward other parts of his body.

One thing he did recall very clearly, however: the little boy's wagon he received one Christmas. It was a Janesville, he said.

"That was a big thing, that little wagon. It was one of the few in the whole area. It was a beautiful thing. Wooden wagons, you know, they were nicely made in those days. [Later on] they started stamping them out of metal, but the wooden ones were nicely made, attractive.

"By then I had actually recovered to the degree that I was perfectly able to get around and I was able to operate that wagon with great facility. You steered it with a bar, I remember that."

What a pity he didn't still have that fine Janesville wagon, we ventured to jest; it would be the first Shadow Car. The notion made him chuckle. "That's right."

His way of speaking was quiet, deliberate, a mix of courtly with country as he chose elegant words to express himself in a folksy, unhurried drawl that must have echoed the place and times of his youth.

"I'm a Missourian," Don would say of himself with palpable pride, and indeed, that's a group of some distinction. Look up a list of fellow "Show-Me" staters and you'll see military leaders Omar Bradley and John "Black Jack" Pershing, baseball's Yogi Berra and Casey Stengel, Hollywood stars like Betty Grable, Jean Harlow and Ginger Rogers, a writer named Samuel Langhorne Clemens (better known as Mark Twain)… even the famous outlaw, Jesse James. Oh, and President Harry S. Truman, of course. Study our Shadowman and see if you can spot any parallels in his character.

ABOVE What a terrifying sight Don's mother must have seen, roaring down upon her only son. *Alamy*

RIGHT Janesville's finely made wooden wagon, an emblem of prestige in Don's boyhood, remains on the market to this day. *Private collection*

Although he was born at Eldon, upon his release from the hospital the boy was taken in by his paternal grandparents at their farm in the northwest corner of the state. His father, Guy Nichols, was still alive then, but his career as an aviation engineer kept him traveling too much to properly look after his only child. However, farm life suited the boy just fine.

"Grampa's farm was outside Pleasant Hill, which is about 35 or 40 miles from Kansas City, in Cass County," Don told John Zimmermann of *Vintage Racecar* magazine. "That area is kind of a traditional Nichols family homeland. My great-great grandfather Tom Nichols, according to the stories, came from Kentucky at age 15 with his dog and his rifle and took the Ohio River to the Mississippi and then the Mississippi up to St. Louis, and then walked with his dog all the way past Jefferson City to the western part of Missouri, to where some even more ancient Nicholsian had established himself.

"Tom Nichols was legendary. He had four wives — not at the same time, consecutively — and some 30 children, I understand. He was a powerful man. I used to hear stories of him entertaining the Governor of Missouri."

Young "Nick," as he was called, seemed to fit effortlessly into his new family, Don told us. "My grandmother, Grampa always called her Fanny, I called her Mom. She was the only mother I remembered. I was sort of her seventh child, my father being her first. My Uncle Ray, youngest of my uncles, I grew up close to."

Don then added something more about Ray, that he became a Master Sergeant in the Marine Corps. As we will hear, Don's father also had a military background. Influences on the boy's life path?

"My grandfather Nichols, I used to love hearing his stories. When he was first married he left his family's farm and worked for the Railroad on what they called the Section. He did the maintenance of the rails and then went into the train crews. He told me he didn't like wearing a dress-up uniform as a conductor, so he chose to work on the freight trains. You had your caboose on the end and that had all bachelor headquarters. Whatever the engineer wanted, you made him coffee and all that, and you looked after coupling and uncoupling, recombining the train 'snake.'

"He had a terrible accident late in his career. I guess he was possibly 50, and he was climbing what they called grab-irons, the ladder apparatus that's bolted to the sides of the box cars. One pulled out and he fell and he had a back injury. He wore kind of a girdle then.

"But he had tremendous settlement. I think in those days, the '20s, he got almost $100,000, which was big money and he bought the farm where I grew up.

"There was a nice garage on this beautiful model farm. He liked cars, and so did my father, just about everybody in the family did. My aunt, who was the only daughter, always had a rather sporty car.

"My grandfather owned nice cars, but he never really mastered driving them. I remember they'd tell stories about Uncle Bob, as he was known. He'd drive into town and he'd have a crowd of people around to try to help him get the car started. He'd forget to turn the key on, or whatever. He was a master of livestock, but cars sort of mystified him. He always hoped that his guest would know more than he knew about how to drive it.

"His hobby was horses. Actually, those early Nicholses were all horse people. Grampa had Arabian riding horses and Percheron draft horses. At the autumn fairs they would have various horsemanship contests and team pulling contests. It was a big thing in those days, and I was present at many a team pulling contest.

"Grampa would hitch his big, grey dappled Percheron horses to a sled, and they would keep adding bags of cement, making it harder and harder to pull. There was a big fair every year in Kansas City called the American Royal Stock Show and he won that several times.

"So he had a very nice retirement and it sort of compensated for the seriousness of his injury."

On school days, Don attended a very small country schoolhouse at first. "I walked, which wasn't considered a great effort. I think there were about 20 children and one teacher taught all grades, one through eight.

"I continued to walk when I started going to high school. That was in the town of Pleasant Hill, about five miles from our farm. But I was pretty good in track, so I got a good chance to train on the way, running and walking. I played football, too, and other sports, but I liked track best.

"I had my first motorcar at age 13, being a country boy, a Model T Ford with which I violated all kinds of local laws.

"My father would come by when he could, and I liked hearing his stories. As a young guy he was Navy, and he was an aircraft mechanic and a crew chief on Flying Boats. He showed me pictures… I know he was in Panama and a lot of places. He said in those days the pilot would say, 'When you get finished take it up and try it out.' Kind of an incentive to the mechanic to make sure the last nut is tight.

"He went from there into aeronautical engineering, so he had to travel a lot. One day when I was in my high-school years, the war was on, he was on a business trip in Oregon and was in a hotel fire. He didn't survive.

"I never graduated from High School. I was afraid the war was gonna end and I would miss it."

He didn't.

MAN OF WAR

HE JUMPED INTO INKY obscurity. The hour was well before the early midsummer daybreak of northern France. The mission required being first on the ground. First into combat.

The still-infant day was June 6th, 1944.

D-Day.

PFC Donald R. "Nick" Nichols was 19 years of age, six feet two, and trained to fight. He was one of a small team of elite US Army paratroopers of the 101st Airborne Division, a few more than 200 "Screaming Eagles" distributed among 20 lumbering C-47 transport aircraft. Each team in their throbbing "Dakota" plane had spent hours of the night alone, flying their own evasive route south from England, creeping over the Channel and sneaking across the blackened coast of Normandy.

Misty coastal cloud blurred or blotted out most of their assigned drop points. Hardly any crew knew precisely where they were. Hopefully it was well inland from the heavily fortified beachfront. But when ordered to leap out, they leapt.

"I was in the Pathfinders," Don told us, quiet pride still in his voice long decades later, "which was the group that jumped in advance to set up the signal devices so airplanes would know where to drop the paratroopers [as well as land gliders of the mass assault coming along behind]. We went in an hour or so early.

"It was a big deal to be first out of the plane. I always enjoyed hazardous duty-type activities.

"Everybody wanted to be a Pathfinder. You got to wear a badge with a torch with a wing on it. You walked into the Post Exchange or a bar, why, you made sure everybody saw you weren't just Joe Ordinary."

So his boots were among very first American ones on the battlefield that momentous day, but for Don Nichols this particular battle didn't last long. "We were the first down and we attracted the attention and got the artillery coming in. I was one of the first ones hit. So I didn't remember too much about France." A piece of shrapnel slammed into his forehead, concussing him into oblivion.

Lights and radio beacons in place, main body of troops landed and first objectives secured, they fought their way out to the beach and deposited their wounded at a medical tent — where they came under fire again. It was the second day of the invasion, but the German gun emplacements on the Pointe du Hoc bluff above were still in action. Another fragment of steel sliced through the tent wall and into Don's legs. Wounded twice in Normandy.

And again almost precisely a month later, on July 4th. He was still in France then.

In September his 101st jumped once more into the Netherlands, in support of Operation Market Garden. This was the Allied drive to force a route north across the Low Countries, separating the German Wehrmacht from the crucial coastal ports. So ferocious was the fighting for the many river bridges along this road that the Yanks would forever remember it as "Hell's Highway."

"In Holland I was in a couple battles that were pretty intense. I was wounded several times," Don remarked laconically. Pressed for detail, he gestured to his skull, a number of points on his torso, down toward his long, lean legs.

Market Garden may have been where he saw the muzzle of a Schmeisser *Maschinenpistole* swing toward him and burp a string of 9 mm slugs straight at his midriff.

"I was carrying a .30-calibre machine gun on my shoulder, not very heavy, 40 pounds, and I had 20 pounds of Nitramon, nitrous-ammonia

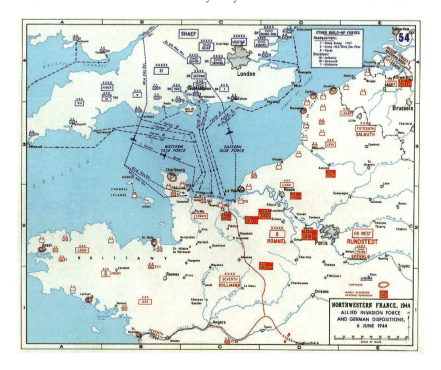

BELOW A reminder of a day that will never be forgotten, this battle map shows how elements of Operation Overlord made their stealthy way from bases across England over The Channel to the beaches of Normandy. Pvt. Nichols was in one of the aircraft. Impatient to jump out.

Private collection

ABOVE D-Day dawn is coming, and "Screaming Eagles" of the 101st Airborne are on their way to war. The Douglas C-47's black and white stripes identified it as part of the invasion force. *Private collection*

BELOW Paratroopers drop en masse into the ferocity of an Operation Market Garden engagement in the Netherlands. But a handful of Pathfinders had gone in first. *Alamy*

explosive, in my jacket," said Don, a Demolition Specialist. "I took the blasting caps out of it and had 'em in my back pocket…"

The enemy rounds impacted squarely on a package of the high explosive in his front pocket. The stuff saved his life. "They went through and I got four little wounds, but I was surprised I wasn't hurt that much. I didn't even get a Purple Heart for it, they didn't write it up."

Well, what's one more? He would end up with two such harrowing distinctions by the end of the war.

One just has to ask, what's it like to get shot? "It feels like somebody hit you hard boxing, you get a punch that sets you back on your heels. There's usually a sound, too, a snap."

His impassive tone suggested that our tornado survivor must have been getting pretty used to this injury business by now.

The young paratrooper had some lighter moments. One of his jumps supposedly ended with a crash through a thatched roof into a lady's kitchen. According to people who heard

RIGHT Livin' the life back in the day. *Courtesy of Penny Nichols*

BELOW One of military history's most significant battles, the Nazi army's "bulge" west through Allied defenses coincidentally took place on ground hallowed by some of the greatest battles in motor racing history. Look for the little towns of Malmedy and Stavelot just north of the German line. Attend a Belgian Grand Prix at Spa and you'll be right there. *Private collection*

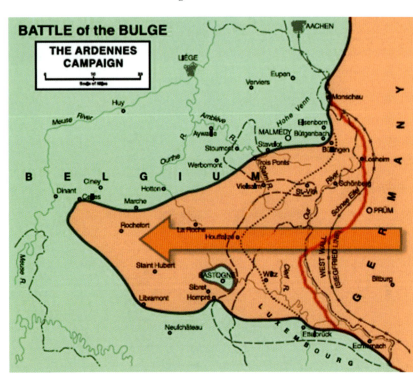

his account (we regret we didn't) he enjoyed describing the expression on her face as she looked up at his combat-booted legs dangling through her ceiling.

During some R&R in northern France near Christmastime, merry thoughts of leave in Paris filling their heads, Don's unit was rousted out abruptly one bitterly cold night, piled into open "cattle trucks" as he described them, and rushed into the snowy, forested Ardennes of eastern Belgium. Hitler had ordered one last, desperate push back through the Western lines to retake the seaports.

Thus began the Third Reich's Winter Offensive, the so-called Battle of the Bulge, and Don found himself in the thick of it at the crucial crossroads town of Bastogne.

"Airborne divisions are the lightest of divisions, they have the lightest-weight equipment and everything, we don't have big guns. Our artillery's little 76 mm toys being towed by Jeeps. So you go up there, and you're facing some of the best that the Germans have.

"They attacked that area because it was poorly defended and it was winter, December. Just suddenly overnight they attacked the least experienced unit, not too well qualified, so the Panzer armored division, von Rundstedt's finest, drove through and made good progress at first.

"When we got there they were only 12 or 14 miles outside Bastogne, so we were sent immediately up closer to a little place called Noville, where one of our tank units was under assault by a ring of Panzers. We went in and we lost two or three hundred men out of 600 in the first 24 hours. Our commander, a Lt. Col., was killed. He was in a house that was hit by artillery.

"We were surrounded and we had to break out. We managed to get back into the main town, but we were running out of ammo, everything. Then the weather lifted and we got some supplies dropped by parachute. So we were able to hold on until we got ground reinforcements and could resist, stop the Germans. That was one of our greatest accomplishments.

"Rundstedt's Winter Offensive didn't 'stop,' we stopped it."

Don received a Distinguished Unit Citation for that engagement. "It's a little blue, gold-bordered thing. I still have it on my uniform, it hangs in my closet." Among numerous other decorations on that Captain's dress coat: a Purple Heart and a French Croix de Guerre (see pages 24–25).

He told these stories calmly, in matter-of-fact tones barren of emotion or judgment. Sure, it all happened many long years before, and he was very old now. But we kept thinking… the man was made for this. Born for battle.

And hardened by it. A quarter century after 1945, during his life in auto racing, Formula 1 was plagued by a period of fatal accidents. Survivors deal with these things by discussing them, so at a subsequent Grand Prix this reporter found himself talking of the matter with the boss of the Shadow team. The tall, dark man's response was… well, chilling.

"You know, in wartime you see a lot of death. You lose a lot of buddies. You just have to go on. And you get used to it.

"You get so you can sit down on a pile of bodies and eat your lunch."

We spoke of that again after a further passage of years, at the twilight of his life. He confirmed the description, and filled it out. He reckoned it had come out of his brutal experiences along "Hell's Highway" in Holland.

"Yeah, bodies are stacked. Sometimes a tarpaulin is over them. It's just an object there that can be leaned on or sat on. Yeah. It's just a fact."

But his Army years weren't all warfare and wounds. The old man smiled as he said, "I remember there was a quiet area after we got out of Holland and Belgium, and we were down along the Rhine river. We had captured the western bank, but the enemy still held the other side. We

LEFT The price of victory. Street scene in Bastogne after the battle.
Alamy

ABOVE Pretty as a picture postcard, handsome old Bastogne snug under her fluffy blanket of snow, her streets filled with happy holiday makers, their hearts at peace in this joyous Christmas season… one day it may again be true. *Alamy*

were living in houses on our side, and on the other side were houses and ships tied up.

"We found a kayak, a two-man Eskimo kayak in this house that we were living in, and we had a good time at night. We'd go take the kayak and paddle across and go through all these German ships over there, looking for souvenirs."

Good Lord, we whispered. He chuckled.

"Heh-heh. Finally we met our Waterloo, though. We backed off from one of our looting sites, and a kayak's a very sensitive vessel. It's only about 12, 14 feet long, and there's just two holes there where you slipped your body in, your feet went straight in. We backed off from one of those ships that we'd been looting and got out in the current and it just turned upside down. We were head-down. And we were wearing our boots and everything.

"The Rhine was pretty wide and we had to swim across. We couldn't go to the closer side, the Germans were there. By the time we finally got to the other side we were a long way down river and it was another unit of our division. So we were strangers.

"We swam up and the sentry yelled out, 'What's the password?' I said, 'I don't know the blankety-blank password, I'm freezing to death.' 'Oh, OK, you must be American.'" Amidst our laughter Don added, "You know, it was a game, a young man's game. We were kids, 18, 19-year-old kids. That's the way we were. It was exciting. I was thinking about having fun and doing the land rush, daredevil stuff."

The war came to its end for Don Nichols by the time his unit arrived in the south of Germany. "We were sent down along the rivers in Austria, and we got into the race to get to Hitler's castle up on the mountain. We were coming down this main highway in Jeeps and any kind of vehicle we could get. We wanted to get to Berchtesgaden and take over the Eagle's Nest.

"But as we got close, a group of French guys, French special forces, I guess, they ran us off the road with some light armored vehicles. We said, you're welcome, go ahead. We didn't know what we were going to get when we got there at Hitler's own facility, so we didn't mind if they got there first.

"When we got there they were looting everything and we helped them and got lots of souvenirs. Weapons. I like to collect weapons."

We almost hesitated to ask… So just how does one acquire them?

"Oh, in combat with the enemy. You'd have various patrol activities, or actually attack with artillery and attack on foot, and when you captured guys, why the first thing you'd do, you wanted to capture the officer because he's the one

22 CHAPTER 1

who had the pistol. He had a Luger or something exciting."

Nearing his discharge date he had amassed quite a collection of various firearms. Around two dozen machine guns mainly, as well as half a dozen Luger pistols. Those especially were valuable on the US market, he knew.

"But I wasn't able to get all those weapons home. When I got off the line in our first bivouac area, the company commander came into the room and all my machine guns were stacked in there. He said, 'Get rid of 'em.' So I ended up with only the little handguns that I'd collected, ones that I could hide."

By November '45 he was out of the Army and back home in Missouri. A civilian once more. Time to catch up on that High School education he'd walked out of.

SPY?

DON NICHOLS turned 21 on November 23rd, 1945. Discharge from the Army made him his own boss once again. Free at last. His future life lay open before him, his to command. What should he do next?

He chose journalism.

"I thought that was an interesting thing to do," he explained to us long decades later. "Writing always appealed to me, and I always threatened to write a book, or books. I did a lot of reportage of events and things like that."

His home state's University of Missouri had a program for that profession, but first there was the little matter of his non-graduation from High School. Passing an exam dealt with that, and he duly enrolled as a Mizzou student, majoring in all the arts involved in becoming a journalist.

But only briefly. This man of action realized that reporting on doings of others was too tame for him. So he signed back into the Army.

"I thought military was where I should be. I liked the military life, the activity. I enjoyed the kind of people, and I was always in, let's say, a

ABOVE Pvt. Nichols's proof of Honorable Discharge, a very small scrap of paper tersely encapsulating untold adversity, pain, danger, loss, achievement, freedom. Sign here, stamp, next. *Don Nichols collection*

BELOW College material? Really? *Courtesy of Penny Nichols*

DON'S DECORATIONS

Army Captain Donald R. Nichols held onto his old dress uniform throughout his life, keeping it fresh and clean in a closet at home. If someone asked, he was pleased to bring it out to display it.

Quite a display. Militaries world-wide hold Insignia and Decorations in high regard (as do racing drivers their trophies), and Don had an impressive quantity of them, awarded for service from D-Day to the Korean War. His array of Service Ribbons, five rows of little patches glittering colorfully from the khaki cloth, and the many individual insignia and badges fastened elsewhere tell many tales to those who can read them.

One who can is Ron Tredway, a racefan as well as an expert in military matters. "Tred" studied photos of Nichols's old uniform and kindly deciphered most of its stories for us.

DECORATIONS DECODED

- Double-bar shoulder badges denote rank of Captain.
- Eagle's head patch on right shoulder: member of 101st Airborne Division "Screaming Eagles."
- Crossed sabers with tanks on both lapels: Armored Cavalry pins.
- Bar on right breast: Distinguished Unit Citation, for Battle of the Bulge.
- On left breast, parachute and wings in white-outlined oval: Army Parachutist Badge.
- Below it, musket on blue background: Combat Infantryman Badge ("A most coveted decoration" — Tredway).
- Block of 14 woven patches: Service Ribbons.
- Braided cord between pocket button and shoulder epaulette: blue and red fourragère of French Croix de Guerre.
- Seahorse in blue-outlined oval patch: Special Engineering Brigade patch ("Don might have been attached during the Inchon landings in Korea; that would [relate to] his Spearhead pin on the Korean Service Ribbon" — Tredway).
- Winged torch on left sleeve: Pathfinder Badge of 101st Airborne.
- Four-bar emblem on cuff of left sleeve: indicates two years of overseas service.
- On cap (not shown), parachute with aircraft: airborne glider parachute cap badge.

SERVICE RIBBONS
From top to bottom, left to right

ROW 1
- Bronze Star Medal, meritorious service, given to most WW2 combat veterans.
- Purple Heart, one Oak Leaf Cluster, wounded June 6th and July 4th, 1944.

ROW 2
- Navy/Marine Commendation Medal with "V" device for valorous action ("Why Navy/Marines is a good question… probably during Korean service" — Tredway).
- Good Conduct Medal, awarded while enlisted.
- American Campaign Medal, WW2.

ROW 3
- Europe-Africa-Middle East Campaign Medal, five Stars for campaigns from Normandy to Berlin.
- WW2 Victory Medal.
- Army Occupation Medal, Europe post-WW2.

ROW 4
- National Defense Service Ribbon.
- Korean Service Medal with two Campaign stars and one Spearhead ("Spearhead denotes lead element of amphibious or parachute landing" — Tredway).
- Armed Forces Reserve Medal.

ROW 5
- United Nations Service Medal (Korea).
- Not identified.
- French Croix de Guerre: honors someone who fought against the Axis enemy; Silver Palm represents five Bronze Stars, each awarded for being Mentioned in Dispatches ("A Unit award, probably while with the 506 Infantry of the 101st Division" — Tredway).

THESE PAGES The Shadowman's secret past unlocked (partially). Thanks to Ron Tredway's knowledge of military history and his diligent research, we can now read the cryptic symbology decorating Don Nichols's old Army uniform. Just as do the stickers adorning a racing mechanic's toolbox, their main message for us is pride in jobs well done. *Don Nichols collection*

ABOVE Portrait of a man who is where he belongs — in uniform. Exactly where or when or why he's standing here is unknown, but neither does it matter. He's an officer in the US Army.
Courtesy of Penny Nichols

distinguished unit, an aggressive unit, and so my military experience was good."

Don served in Korea, where his experiences apparently were good enough to bring new commendations and Captain's bars to wear on his Army uniform. Unfortunately, we came away from our interviews without details of that period.

But he did clarify one point of confusion rampant on the Internet: he was not US Air Force Major Donald Nichols, whose extremely aggressive "positive intelligence" commando exploits in South and North Korea earned both praise and condemnation. Different service branch, not the same age range, wrong man altogether. "I never met the person."

However, as our Donald R. Nichols faced the end of that conflict, he saw Military Intelligence as his best chance to keep up the combative life he craved. He was assigned to learn Japanese at the famed language school in Monterey, California, then sent with wife and first child to Cold War duty in Japan.

And here's the period that Don kept veiled. "There was always something exciting to do that… [long pause] I'm not at liberty to discuss."

Oh joy. A void! How the human imagination rejoices in filling an emptiness of information with abundant speculation!

Especially when the object of inquisition is a person like our Shadowman, the tall, taciturn, innately enigmatic school athlete, D-Day paratrooper, longtime Army officer and (as rumors long have had it) government spy. He has been quoted as laughing about working for "a government agency that didn't have an address." Still, he wouldn't say more.

But on this occasion his interrogator was a journalist (albeit not college trained) bent on writing about him, and after all he had promised his "full cooperation."

So I risked a direct shot. Well, what about that spy stuff? Did you work for the CIA?

The old man gazed back at me, his long, white-bearded face a mask, silent for an extended moment. Finally, in his soft Missouri drawl:

"I can't talk about that. Ah, CIA and military intelligence, counter-intelligence… not proper, I don't think, to discuss it."

Darn it.

Despite his refusal to disclose specifics, he was willing to sketch in some background. He enjoyed intelligence work, but especially the counter-intelligence aspect of it. He described that as "aggressive intelligence against the enemy." From further remarks, essentially he meant taking assertive action to thwart the adversary outside the bounds of an actual battlefield. Shadowy warfare, perhaps one could characterize it.

In Cold War Japan, as elsewhere, the adversary was Soviet Russia. The defeated populace of Occupied Japan was a complicating factor, but presumably they preferred the more benign Americans to be their occupiers. Russia's past actions in Japan had made it no friends there, and the Japanese wanted them out of the country even more than the US did. Open combat was being avoided, but below the civil surface a raw, muscular struggle was going on.

As Don expressed it, "The US sort of owned the country, the government and everything, and there were bases all the way up and down the islands. But there was a very strong Russian population in Japan after the Korean War, and the Russian Embassy, all the Russian subculture in Japan, they were trying to hold on. They wanted a strong presence in Tokyo and the seaports, like Yokohama.

"Our main objective was to make sure it cost 'em a lot. Make them uncomfortable. Our assignment was to get rid of the Russians by anything other than open gunfire. We managed to get their activities in Tokyo shut down, but they were hanging on in Yokohama.

"I had the Goon Squad. Some really salty guys, Chinese and Japanese, Sumo and Judo experts. One was Sargent Soo, a huge Chinese, he was built like a blockhouse. Some of these oriental guys are tremendous. Really large guys, they're dynamite. Compact and really super-strong. Judo-trained or Jujitsu-trained, they're pretty formidable.

"We all went to the Kodokan, the judo school, together." To his Squad it would have been all business, but Don took it more as a sport. "I went from a novice to third grade among six. Not very high, but I enjoyed that."

He remarked on a similar difference in attitude toward their assignment. "With them it was more personal than it was with me. Me, it was just an interesting personal occupation. I was in counter-intelligence and liking the action. But they had the racial and historic feelings of Russians in their country. It was distasteful to them. They were motivated pretty highly."

Also, Don spoke with admiration of a fellow American named Sgt. Rodriguez. "Interesting guy. He lived in Texas. As a teenager he was so — heh-heh — adventurous that the police said, 'You sign up for the Army or you're going to jail.' Ha hah! But he was really a distinguished guy and did so many of those missions with us. He was recommended very highly.

"He was with me in Japan and later he came and was my office manager when we had the racing team. His first name was Ricardo. Yeah, Ricardo Rodriguez, like the race driver."

With the floodgates flowing nicely, I asked Don his rank. Captain usually, he said, although he would be elevated to Major for certain operations. "I remember clearly a mission where we…

"Ah, I don't think it's necessary to talk about this."

My heart sank as suddenly as it had soared. So his old soldier's discipline would hold after all.

Must respect that. Move on. ♠

LEFT On a visit to his boyhood home in Missouri, Don caught the attention of a newspaper writer fascinated by the tall American's mastery of judo. "A Pleasant Hill man is one of the top judo experts in the United States," the story starts. It goes on to explain that Captain Nichols was en route from a year's assignment in Cincinnati, Ohio (where he taught judo in his spare time) to another year of studying foreign languages in Monterey, California — "either Japanese, in which he is already proficient; or, if he can have his choice, Russian."

To earn his black belt after two years at the Kodokan Judo Institute of Tokyo, the unnamed reporter continued, "Twice a day for those two years Don was bounced off the walls [by a 235-lb. world champion]… he had to toss five black-belted opponents in succession without even the hint of a rest between adversaries…

"Don once suffered a broken rib in a bout with a Japanese but his opponent frantically advised him to not go see a doctor 'If you do… he'll make you stop practicing.' Don didn't go to the doctor."

The story winds up with a zinger: "Although Don is a great judo fan he is American enough to believe… 'I doubt if anything can overcome the shock that results from a good old American punch in the nose.'"

Courtesy of Penny Nichols

CHAPTER 2
THE ENTREPRENEUR

RACE TIRES, RACECARS AND ONE BIG RACETRACK

IT WAS EASY to make money, because the Japanese wanted to import stuff and they didn't know how to do it. So I moved to Tokyo and I set up a company.

"We built the Fuji Speedway…"

Don's first marriage had ended during the mid-1950s, while he was in his 30s, and with his new wife he started a second family. For the next several years he was happy to stay on in Japan at his US Army counter-intelligence work, but as children kept coming and years kept going, he began thinking about a better-paying career.

Did leaving the military have to mean leaving the nation, though? He had made a good life in Japan. He thought his kids were getting good educations: "My son went to a Canadian school which taught in English, and my two daughters at the time went to Sacred Heart, the same school Princess Michiko went to. I guess she's the wife of the present emperor. They had Canadian nuns teaching, and they all spoke Japanese of course. I remember going to picnics there."

So he liked the country and its people, and also admired their artistic culture, but beyond that he saw business opportunities for an entrepreneurial westerner fluent in Japanese.

For us decades later, Don's aging memory made it difficult to establish the actual timeline, but he told us that he supported his family for a while by teaching English in Yokohama. At some point he started importing car components, including tires, and even cars. He mentioned Excalibur, the flamboyantly retro-styled specialty vehicle on Detroit underpinnings that debuted in the mid-1960s.

"I remember we had the Osaka Auto Show, and Mercedes-Benz had their car there, and they were furious because we priced the Excalibur at a higher price. It wasn't really, but we put a higher price on it sitting there. [Chuckling] Anyway, we sold quite a few Excalibur cars."

Don's business seemed to grow out of a personal interest in cars as cars, not so much in the racing of them. But his Japanese enterprise put him on track to his eventual deep dive into racing. It began with a Jaguar.

Just when and how this farm-raised Midwestern boy and US Army officer first noticed motorsports isn't clear, but the surge of "foreign" cars into America following World War II was hard for anyone to miss. Nichols family lore tells us that way back at the start of the 1950s, before deploying to Korea, the young veteran bought a Jaguar XK120 roadster; see daughter Penny's memories later in these pages.

But according to her father's own account, that sleek sportster's appeal to Don was more its style than its speed.

"I liked cars," he began, and confirmed that the exotic postwar imports did catch his eye. "MGs came first, but they were not impressive-type cars in my view. Then the Jaguar came out. I remember what a shock it was. It was quite the thing.

"I was at that time at Fort Holabird, which was the National Intelligence Center in Baltimore, and I was doing daily commutes to the Pentagon. I became friendly with a number of the other officers in the lounges and dining rooms. One day I happened to announce to a Lt. Col. there, and I was only a Captain at the time, I told him I'd just bought an XK120 and he never spoke to me again.

"I drove that car to the West Coast on the way to being assigned overseas, and I remember at that time you could drive down Sunset Boulevard, you'd see film stars frequently who were enjoying the popularity of tiny little sleek cars. I think they showed off there. Clark Gable had the first XK120, and Dick Powell and June Allyson, his wife, had one. Mine was white, and it stood out quite a lot."

Penny Nichols tells us what that car's fate was — her Mom said she traded it for a Buick. But in later years her Dad also had a Jag in Japan, which testifies to the success of his business ventures there.

The tall, lean, bushy-bearded American who spoke the language with quick, wry wit

built many friendships in Japan's car circles. One name he kept dropping to us was that of a famous actor.

"I was able to meet people of some prestige, like Mr. Toshiro Mifune, who was very highly respected person, an actor, community leader. I had a Jaguar XK120 in Japan and Mifune-san got an XK120, and we'd go down to the Tamagawa Speedway, which was a little oval track that hadn't had races since before the war, and roar around. We helped get the sports car club of Japan started.

"Mifune opened some doors for me." Returning the favor, "I had gone through the Bondurant school and later I took Mifune there." (Looking at timelines of events and some photographic evidence, we think that Nichols may have confused certain identities, as often happened, and meant the earlier Shelby school at

ABOVE Sporty young blade on his way west, "Nick" swung by his boyhood home to show off his sweet new Jag. And his lovely new wife, of course. Who rode the whole way between coasts in that open cockpit. With their new baby daughter at her feet in that cozy little footwell. *Courtesy of Penny Nichols*

BELOW Capt. Nichols's inspiration? Fellow Jaguarman Clark Gable takes delivery of one of his new XK120s from William Lyons hisownself. *Private collection*

RIGHT Film publicity photo depicts Toshiro Mifune in his iconic Samurai role. Fierce, menacing, mysterious, resolute, a sharp dresser… sound like the secret self-image of anyone we know?
Private collection

FAR RIGHT Mifune-san and family as the family Nichols came to know them in Japan.
Courtesy of Penny Nichols

LEFT Don, standing tall on the far side of the would-be contender for the 1955 Carrera Panamericana that he built in Japan with his friend Bill Stroppe, at far left. Chances are it had one of Stroppe's stout FoMoCo engines inside, but the madly dangerous Mexican road race was cancelled and the burly coupe never ran the event it was made for. That must be why we have found no actual information about this project.
Courtesy of Penny Nichols

Riverside Raceway; driver Bob Bondurant was an instructor there before starting his own business elsewhere.)

As a side note, Toshiro Mifune was already a star in Japan before he played Izo Yamura, the Soichiro Honda-like team owner of the Yamura F1 team in the iconic 1966 racing movie *Grand Prix*. Apparently that was his first major film role outside his own country.

Don denied he aspired to serious race driving, but from time to time he did take part in individual events of various kinds. "I did little sports car things, exhibitions of cars that I imported into Japan." He mentioned a Can-Am style contest with a Lola at Fuji and a small sedan race in Macau — which nearly ended with a swim in the harbor. He added that, on trips back to America, he also participated in the cross-continent Mobile Economy run and Mexico's Carrera Panamericana, both times with Bill Stroppe, the famed Ford racecar preparation specialist. So he was moving in the right circles.

ABOVE & LEFT Oopsy daisy. Nichols never claimed to be a race driver and this could be one reason why. The place is Macau, and the poor little Isuzu Bellel probably was something he was promoting. This incident is unlikely to have made the slightest difference in sales, but it might have boosted local awareness of those "Moon Eyes" stickers on Don's helmet. He was importing product from that Los Angeles hot rod shop to the Asian enthusiast market.
Don Nichols collection

THE ENTREPRENEUR

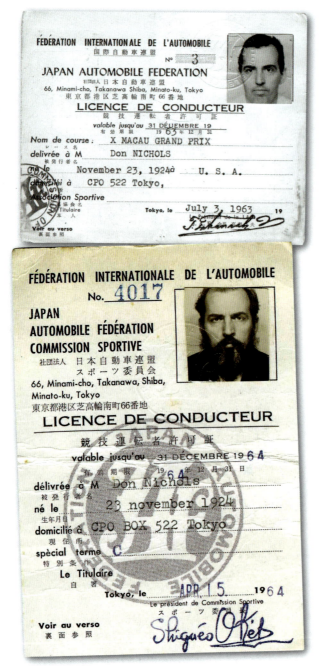

RIGHT Two of the FIA competition licenses Don was issued in Japan. Compare his mugshot on the 1963 document with the following year's version.

Don Nichols collection

Our mystery man's racing tire enterprise is what's most often spoken of, so we asked for details. As Don laid it out:

"I had started Japan Goodyear [as the American firm's distributor] and during the '60s I was going around the world to Grand Prix races, many of them, and buying up all the Goodyear tires that weren't used in the Grand Prix and bringing them back and selling them to the Japanese auto and tire makers. They had no access to competition tires and they were interested in the technology, so any kind of exotic Grand Prix rubber that I could get them, that helped my situation. Such things were totally unavailable in Japan at that time.

"Tire deals were my main source of income."

So let us take note that, long before he burst onto the Formula 1 scene as a team owner, Don Nichols already knew his way around a Grand Prix paddock.

And was himself known there, according to Trevor Harris, Don's first Shadow designer and a longtime friend. "Don ended up with a reputation in certain circles as being the Can-Am Junkman, did you ever know that? Among McLaren and whatnot because he would buy anything." McLaren and others among the Can-Am "whatnots" also competed in F1.

At first, Nichols handled the American tire brand's entire consumer product line. But most of that business was taken away, leaving him with only the much smaller racing tire segment. As he explained it, "I lost Goodyear because I was just one guy. One of the Japanese trading companies, can't remember the name now, wasn't the top one, but they put a lot of pressure into Goodyear in Akron and said, 'You know, Mr. Nichols doesn't have the distribution capability.' So that was taken over.

"So I went to Firestone, and I got the Firestone distributorship." The fighting man fighting back!

As an aside he remarked, "That's when I became very close friends with Bill McCreary, who was Firestone director. Firestone was very active in racing, you know." A relationship that would prove crucial a few years later.

"I did that [Firestone deal] mostly as a business venture. I didn't actually operate the Firestone business very long, because I found a Japanese company who would do like what was done with Goodyear, take over the distributorship.

"I insisted that it be paid in cash. I remember I carried a very large roll of hundred-dollar bills, quite a few thousands of dollars."

Donald Robert Nichols, farm boy and decorated combat soldier, had become an aggressive, industrious wheeler-dealer who was enjoying a halcyon time of his life.

"I enjoyed trading with the Japanese," he told us. "I guess I was interested in doing business with major companies, and I had an opportunity to do so there — not because of any personal background or training, but having access to requirements from the western world. Japan was at that time educating and upgrading their business staffing and business procedures with western technology, business technology. So I could open doors and bring them top-level people and help them progress.

"It was a rewarding business, and I earned more money than I would ever have been able to on my own in the western world. I managed to go from struggling along on a rather modest income — we were living out in the country and I was riding the train in from a low-rent district — to making quite a lot of money. As soon as I made some of the deals, [we moved into] downtown Tokyo.

"I had a nice office in a very high-level new facility near the American Embassy and the Okura hotel, which at that time was the newest posh hotel in Japan."

As Don went on with his story, it emerged that this was the move that resulted in construction of Fuji Speedway — and ultimately in the birth of Nichols's own Shadow racing team.

FUJI SPEEDWAY

ABOUT DON'S involvement at Fuji, the fact that he brought up his Speedway story on several occasions indicates that he was proud of that project, and thought it important. For us, it's further insight into our Shadowman.

International businessman Nichols-san, the Sports Car Club of Japan and a large industrial concern named Marubeni-Ida (which Don described as "the number four industrial company in Japan") joined forces to create a new, modern motorsports facility not far from Tokyo. It was the early 1960s and Japanese motorcycle and automobile companies were maturing fast. Racing was carrying that message world-wide.

The future Speedway's site was some 60 miles southwest along the coast from Tokyo on the eastern skirts of iconic Mount Fuji, an internationally famous resort area attractive to visitors both domestic and international. "We formed a company to design the Fuji Speedway," said Don. "We had the contract with Marubeni-Ida, which eventually did the financing and construction. I set up the office, and got all the publicity going.

"I came over here [the US] and hired Charlie Moneypenny."

Charlie Who?

ABOVE Neither of these happy-snaps in Don's archive carry any information, but it's plain to see that the big, bearded American was having a good time with his Japanese racing buds.
Don Nichols collection

Don explained that Moneypenny was a civil engineer who had designed the Daytona Speedway for Bill France of NASCAR, as well as Talladega Superspeedway and other big banked ovals in stock car country.

Not much is known about this unsung racetrack designer. Mr. Moneypenny had retired from a career with the city of Daytona Beach, where of course fellow resident Bill France anchored his NASCAR organization, so perhaps Big Bill and Charlie already knew each other. In any case, Moneypenny took on the planning and detail engineering of France's new, high-banked Superspeedway, the distinctive triangular facility measuring 2.5 miles around. The job was complicated by having to fit the massive track into a constricted, irregularly shaped property between the airport and a highway. That's at least one reason for the distinctive "Tri-Oval" configuration, rather than the familiar old Indianapolis quad-corner pattern of the same lap length.

To answer France's demand for a "racy" track allowing drivers to run side-by-side, plus an infield extension for sports car racing, Moneypenny consulted with designers of Detroit's proving grounds. He is said to have evolved his own mathematical formulae to calculate optimum radii and angles.

Daytona Speedway opened in 1959, and Don Nichols told us he was on the scene right away. "I was going to races in Daytona and Bill France at that time was building, literally building with a bulldozer, building Daytona. It was a big swamp and Bill was out there driving this thing."

We speculate that Don may have confused Big Bill with his son, Bill Jr., whom history records as having done the actual earth moving, but the bigger question is, why was sports car man Nichols visiting the stock car world that early?

Because his Japanese friends at the big corporation behind Fuji Speedway meant to make a Big Splash. Not only did they want to engage The World's Foremost Circuit Designer, they aimed to partner with The Biggest Players.

Nichols's own company took on both tasks. As he explained, "They liked to have the prestige of international consultants, so it took away any question as to whether they should be respected. So it was my role to bring the authenticity and foreign technology and sporting custom and that sort of thing."

He had a client relationship with the enterprise. "I was actually a member of the Fuji Speedway Corporation for a while, but then it got so big it affected my entire Goodyear business and other businesses."

Styled as Advisory Director, Don accompanied a delegation traveling to Florida for a major announcement by NASCAR on January 23rd,

BELOW Fuji Speedway as first imagined — by a NASCAR track designer before he had seen the property. When Charlie Moneypenny and Don Nichols got there, both immediately realized it was time to go back to the drawing board. *Don Nichols collection*

This type has not yet been constructed anywhere.

Model of a —

1½ mile track with both sides having long radius turns — no tangent sections.

1964, the high-profile day of the Daytona 500. The burgeoning American body was partnering with Japanese motorsports officials and Marubeni-Ida to create Nippon NASCAR, a Japanese organization intending to foster stock car racing at home. To underscore the relationship, that year's Daytona 500 winner's trophy carried an inscription in Japanese.

Also with the delegation was another element of that Big Splash — a pretty lady named Noriko Ando, Miss Japan and a contestant in the Miss Universe pageant. She was a hit at the track, as Don chuckled. (Don recalled a different name, a Miss Tanemoto, which we have taken the liberty of correcting after research.)

"You can't imagine the traffic around [her]. The Chairman of Chrysler corporation, he almost kidnapped her. Everybody wanted to date her. Fabulously beautiful lady. She presented the trophy to Richard Petty for winning the 500.

"Funny story about that trip. When we finished Daytona we came to California, and my friend Mr. Suzuki, who was a supplier to the Japanese auto industry and had a racecar shop that built a lot of stuff for me, wanted to go to Carroll Shelby's racing school at Riverside. [Miss Japan] said she wanted to go too.

"When Shelby heard about us having this beautiful lady with us, suddenly he said, 'Well, I don't think the regular driving instructor can handle this difficult assignment.' So Shelby conducted the driving school while Mr. Suzuki and [Miss Japan] were students. In fact she passed, she was really good, a good driver, and Suzuki, my guy, he flipped a car. [Laughing]. He was trying to out-do her and I don't think he ever did."

Back to Fuji Speedway business. The partners' high-profile approach called for the World's Foremost Speedway Designer to visit the building site. "So we brought Charlie Moneypenny over and put him in the Okura hotel in downtown Tokyo, with an office where he could design the Fuji Speedway. My office was in a building next door.

ABOVE King Richard and Miss Japan at the 1964 Daytona 500. The trophy bears an inscription in Japanese, because plans were afoot to bring NASCAR to the Land of the Rising Sun.
Getty Images/RacingOne

"At that stage I hadn't really been to the site and looked at the land. The Japanese said it was an ideal location that they had bought, just above a famous resort, the biggest seaside resort in Japan.

"Charlie showed up, he already had a plan laid out," Don continued. Indeed, apparently the Daytona man brought along an actual scale model of his idea for Fuji. It showed a fully rounded oval, a sort of watermelon shape with two modestly banked, gently arcing straightaways — like Daytona's front stretch — connecting a pair of steeper, longer curves.

"Naturally, American speedways are on level ground. He and I went down, and the land

THE ENTREPRENEUR **35**

ABOVE Say, why don't we build a beautiful big new international motor racing circuit right here! What a PERFECT spot!
Motorsport Images/David Phipps

was like *this*." Don's long arms indicated a pronounced departure from level. Even on the outer flanks of the majestic volcano the slope is significant.

"He looked at that, and he looked at me and he started laughing. "You're gonna build a Superspeedway *here*? Ha-ha-ha…"

Clearly much rethinking and recalculating had to be done. Maybe the oval track idea itself should be abandoned, and a natural terrain road course designed instead.

"Charlie said, 'Can you get a consultant to help?' I said, 'Yeah, I know a guy that's perfect for a consultant.' Stirling Moss had just had his accident [at Goodwood in 1962, the end of his great driving career]. I hired Stirling to come over. He was like a god to the Japanese."

Our interview entered a mirthful stage. "You hired Stirling Moss!" "Yeah. I've got pictures if I can find them [he did find them], Stirling with Charlie out in weeds this high…

"Stirling was in medium health after his accident, but rambunctious. He spent most of his time measuring his temperature from one side of his body to the other. He said, 'You know, I've got this problem. My temperature on my left side, where I had the accident, is really low, and my temperature on this side is too warm.' But he said, 'It doesn't hurt. When I have contact with the opposite sex it doesn't bother me.' I said, 'I think you'd better activate that circulation!'

"He did. He was with us during the day, trampling around in the tall grass, giving his opinions about how a racetrack should be done, and then hurrying back to Tokyo for the night life."

Back in his luxury hotel office, Moneypenny set to work and construction began in June that same year, 1964. One portion of the originally planned oval track was built, including one long turn banked at 30 degrees, one degree less dramatic than Daytona's.

Western histories say the Fuji track was never completed because the money ran out. Bill France probably did hear back from Charlie Moneypenny and lost interest. As Don Nichols indicated, the impracticality of the terrain and, in hindsight, the area's frequently rainy weather argued against an oval. Road racing was not really NASCAR's thing.

However, the speedway was in fact finished, although as a road racing circuit 2.7 miles around. It boasted an impressive front straightaway just under a mile long, plus at least eight turns or more, depending on how one counts "turns." These included the section of speedway-style banking rising up from the northeastern, lower end of the straight.

Had NASCAR run its planned oval race here, that banking likely would have been "Turn Four," but when the road course opened it was dubbed "Daiichi." This might sound rather romantic to anyone not conversant with the local language, but it simply translates as "Number One."

The designation is of note, because in that case the cars turn to the right at the end of the circuit's long, downhill pits straight. But in fact early races ran either way, with many visitors preferring the counter-clockwise direction.

Fuji International Speedway, aka FISCO, opened in November of 1965, and quickly became a major center of the burgeoning Japanese motorsports world. Future programs would include several Formula 1 Japanese Grands Prix, along with a wide variety of other series. Even NASCAR would turn up on occasion. Fuji

LEFT Huh? You want to build a NASCAR Speedway HERE? Don Nichols, Stirling Moss and Charlie Moneypenny tour the proposed site.
Don Nichols collection

RIGHT OK, fellas, here's what we're gonna have to do.
Don Nichols collection

THE ENTREPRENEUR **37**

International Speedway remains in operation to this day, although much altered from its original lap layout.

Mighty Daiichi still stands too, albeit abandoned and now a weed-grown monument to dreams of grandeur — and, it must be said, to several people who lost their lives there. As built it was a dangerously tricky curve, with the first part of the banking dropping below the level of the straightaway. Drivers hurtling into the turn felt their cars go light just when they wanted to feel planted.

With NASCAR out of the picture, Nichols approached USAC, the body then sanctioning Indycar racing. "Henry Banks was the president [actually the Director of Competitions] of USAC and we brought over [most of] the starters of the Indy 500 race that year and we had a 500-mile [it was 200 miles] race on Mount Fuji. On the road course, there wasn't an oval." Race date was October 9th, 1966, only 11 months after FISCO opened.

GOIN' RACIN'

THE FUJI 200 Indycar event distance actually was 216 miles (80 laps x 2.7 miles), ample for road racing, and it was an "exhibition" outside the regular USAC championship series. Only 22 of 34 entries finally started, after very high attrition in practice. The Indycars ran "the right way around" for them, counter-clockwise, meaning "Number One" was really "The Last" corner. For them, the first turn was another tricky, falling-away plunge, but a more familiar left-hander and not nearly as steeply banked as Moneypenny's masterpiece.

Jackie Stewart came home first in the Lola-Ford he'd driven with less success in May; his teammate at Indy, 500 winner Graham Hill, led nine of the 80 laps at Fuji but placed fifth, four laps back with ignition trouble. Taking second place was Bobby Unser in a Gurney Eagle, the only man behind Stewart to complete the full 216 miles.

It emerged that Fuji's road course posed an unforeseen risk to Indycars of the day. Engines built for American-style left turns were fine around most of the Japanese circuit, but its two longish right-handers starved them of oil. Centrifugal force pulled the precious lubricant away from pickups in the right-hand sides of the sumps. According to a *Sports Illustrated* story of the event, "at least eight of the 11 cars that dropped out during the trials had similar troubles. Since nobody had been allowed to bring a spare engine, the drivers of the disabled cars were through." That's why USAC champion Mario Andretti couldn't even start the race. (He would get his "revenge" ten years later, winning F1's 1976 Japanese Grand Prix at Fuji.)

Digging a little deeper into this oil pickup business, we find that 1966's Fuji event was only the third-ever road race in the then-modern Indycar era. The first had been only the year before, at Indianapolis Raceway Park, a facility several miles from the famous Speedway. The 15 turns on IRP's clockwise layout were indeed mostly right-handers, but evidently they didn't put the stress on oiling systems that Fuji's two did.

Andretti won the '65 IRP race and the subsequent two, three in a row, so his Brawner Hawk-Ford's failure at Fuji in '66 was indeed anomalous.

North America's exciting new Can-Am road racers also came to Fuji, although again not as part of a series championship. The date was November 23rd, 1968, and their race direction was counter-clockwise, the same as for the USAC open-wheelers two years before. American Peter Revson took the event aboard a McLaren-Ford entered by Carroll Shelby. Among the entries were five new Toyota racecars; they all finished, which cannot be said of the 13 Detroit-powered starters.

The "Unlimited" Can-Am machines returned in 1969, again running counter-clockwise, and this time a Toyota did win, with Japan's Minoru Kawai wheeling a turbocharged V8-powered car to defeat Canada's John Cannon in a Ford G7A. The field was even smaller than the year before. Japan's Can-Am experiment ended.

However, a similar local series did develop, called Group 7 for the international racing regulations under which Can-Am was governed. Old videos show them running clockwise around Fuji, bravely tackling the fearsome Daiichi as the true First Turn. Don Nichols must have been referring to this Group 7 series when he told us of participating at Fuji as an entrant and driver. Looking into it, we think this was the so-called Grand Prix of Japan on May 3rd, 1967. In fact it was run for sports cars, a rather thin field of them. Apparently rules required coupe bodywork.

"I remember going to Stardust [in Las Vegas, final venue of the 1966 Can-Am series] and buying three Lola T70s. 'Cause the Japan Grand Prix was coming up. I was living in downtown Tokyo in a ritzy six-story building, it had a parking lot, and I put those three Lolas over in the far corner and built a hasty tent structure over 'em.

"These roadsters all had to have a top, a coupe top. I had to build those with inexperienced labor, and we made frames and we cobbled together a mould for the fiberglass. Stupidest-looking canopy you ever saw, but I managed to get a cover over the cockpit.

"I sold two of 'em to principal Japanese. One was the guy who owned a nightclub in Las Vegas. I can't think of his name. And then the top driver in Japan bought one… don't remember his name either. The last one, I was gonna drive. So I had a team in that race, three Lolas.

"We got to the track and they said, 'You gotta inspect the car.' The inspector says, 'Oh, you have to have seat belts.' Went back and got a belt, but didn't bolt it in. They rolled the car up and I was sitting on the seat belt and it was buckled over my lap, so 'OK, OK.' Of course I was fairly prominent at that time so I could get away with most things.

"I did start the race but I didn't last too long. It was a sequence of amusing instances. But it was a fairly interesting period…"

Don's memory wasn't doing him justice. He did finish that Japanese GP (according to online resources), driving his parking-lot-special Lola T70 with its Small Block Chevy engine to seventh

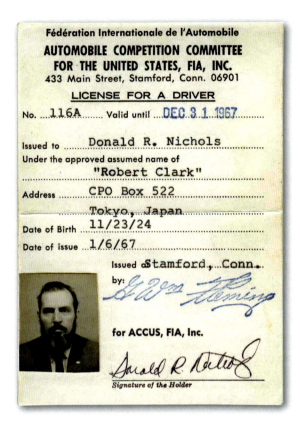

LEFT The Shadowman's undercover identity card. "Robert" was his own middle name, "Clark" that of his mother's family. *Don Nichols collection*

place. He was four laps behind the winning Porsche 906, a two-liter machine. His team-mate didn't finish; Ginji Yasuda dropped out with engine trouble, according to posted results.

The pair ran as Team Toro, and theirs were the only T70s listed. Don's no. 14 seems to have been painted blue and white, while Yasuda's no. 15 was gold (per a kit-built model discovered online, its date labeled as 1966, not the 1967 of the race). We cannot find a record of a third such entry, although that doesn't necessarily cast doubt on Nichols's accuracy. As part of his wider business he was buying and selling these cars frequently,

BELOW One of Nichols's trio of "parking lot specials" for 1967's Japanese Grand Prix at Fuji Speedway was painted gold and driven by local star Ginji Yasuda. Although he didn't finish the race, his was the Lola memorialized by this model. The other Team Toro entry was blue and white, and Don himself kept it running to the end. *Courtesy of Ebbro*

THE ENTREPRENEUR 39

ABOVE Don Nichols, Pedro Rodriguez and Lola T160 before Fuji's 200-mile Can-Am race of 1968. Don owned the car, while Dean Moon's Los Angeles speed shop prepped the Big Block Chevy with its Hilborn fuel injection system. That engine was installed for Nichols in Costa Mesa, California, by someone called Trevor Harris; we are soon to hear more about him.
Dean Moon

and a new owner of "the third one" might not have run it that day.

"Toro" Nichols was back at Fuji again in 1968, although not as a driver. That role fell to Mexican superstar Pedro Rodriguez. The single car was another Lola, but a newer T160 with a Big Block Chevrolet. Don seems to have been the owner, and had rented it to Ginji Yasuda, who entered as Team Yasuda and hired Rodriguez. Unfortunately, the engine overheated after just four laps.

In the accompanying photo we see Don standing with Pedro and the Lola on the Fuji starting grid. The red car carries prominent Goodyear stickers, but Don wears a Firestone jacket. The cartoonish "eyes" emblems seen on both the car and two other garments are the doing of the man holding the camera: Dean Moon. An energetically entrepreneurial American hot rodder, his "Moon Eyes" brand of speed equipment was being imported by Nichols and becoming popular in Japan. Moon's involvement in this Lola venture turned out to play a seminal role in our story of the Shadows. We'll go into detail about that in following chapters.

Unfortunately, Don's fun in the Far East was finishing. As he explained it, his decision to pack up his family and move back to the US later in 1968 came when "the Japan economy in the late '60s just really crashed."

We think he was referring specifically to the local auto racing economy. Fuji Speedway was gaining a sad reputation as being too dangerous. The weight of fatal accidents finally forced the circuit to reduce its operations in 1970, and in 1974 the lap was reconfigured, bypassing the fearsome "Turn One" banking.

All that sent a chill through the wider industry, according to Don, and severely affected his many automotive business ventures. "Without any racing going on my business suffered," was the gist of remarks to us.

In fact racing there did continue, albeit at reduced intensity for a while, so there may have been other reasons for his returning Stateside.

Darker rumors have always swirled about Don Nichols's business life, and it was the nature of the Shadowman that they will continue swirling behind his memory. We chose not to raise such issues during our time with him: this book is about his Shadows, not his shadows. But he did say this:

"My enterprise in Japan was under pressure and [pause] it wasn't advisable for me to go back to Japan. I imagine the company was under some kind of foreclosure or whatever. I had moved back to the States, but we were selling Excalibur cars in Japan. I left [someone] in charge of my business over there and he managed to get into difficulties. I didn't want to participate in those difficulties, so we just sort of severed the relationship."

However it was, Don brought his family back to America as a wealthy man, still in his 40s. So, we suggested, he could have lived out the rest of his life just playing golf, or whatever other idle hobby caught his fancy, right? His response was simple.

"Yes." ♠

ABOVE The wet and wild Japanese GP of 1976, the first conducted as a round of the F1 championship, carried Fuji Speedway's name to the world. That's because, in the most dramatic possible manner, it made a World Champion of British Golden Boy James Hunt. Here we see his McLaren M23 splashing around the sodden road circuit late in the evening, as storm clouds begin to lift over majestic Mount Fuji towering beyond. *Motorsport Images/LAT*

BELOW Remember Daiichi? The steeply banked "Turn 1" engineered by stock car man Charlie Moneypenny killed so many sports car drivers that it was eventually bypassed. But it lives on to this day, abandoned, overgrown, but not forgotten. This photo was made in 2007. *Motorsport Images/Gareth Bumstead*

THE ENTREPRENEUR 41

CHAPTER 3
MOONSHOT

A RACECAR OF THE AEROSPACE AGE

OPPOSITE The Very Beginning: In his little Costa Mesa workshop late in 1968, Trevor Lee Harris is almost overshadowed by tall Don Nichols as the designer demonstrates his radical concept for a "Tiny Tire" racecar. "I bought a Small Block Chevy, put it on the floor of my shop, and built a plywood frame around it to hold four little wheels I made out of wood and cardboard. It didn't have a body. It was just to demonstrate how small a thing you could make. Didn't take long to build — in fact it was terribly simple to make, considering what it led to!" The collaborators included this photo in their sponsorship presentation to a certain tiremaker in Ohio.
Trevor Harris collection

HOW MYSTERIOUS, the delicacy of those zephyrs of chance that distribute the seeds of our lives, govern their gestation and growth, and then sometimes, apparently capriciously, guide our intricate storylines into touch with one another.

We have traced the writhing vine of life that placed Missourian Donald Robert Nichols at a Japanese speedway one day in 1968; but how could his particular odyssey possibly have intertwined with that of a creative hot rodder and inventive racecar designer/builder/driver from Seattle named Trevor Lee Harris?

The crucial intersection point was a racing equipment supply business set up by retiring driver Charlie Hayes in the Los Angeles area. Harris, having relocated to that motorsports hotbed himself in 1966, had a nearby shop of his own, where he was industriously inventing, designing, engineering, fabricating, repairing, modifying and generally resolving whatever other special needs a racer might ask of him. Be it a simple replacement part, a custom-crafted set of exhaust headers, or even fine-tuning handling setups at the racetrack, racers all across his sprawling new town were starting to call on Harris.

Let us also tuck away the information that Trevor was working with driver George Follmer, whose Lola T70s were among the fastest and best handling in the nation. This, and what Harris says was Follmer's special ability to sense and report slight differences in the feel of subtly different tire designs, made him a favorite of Firestone's development engineers to test experimental new rubberwear.

Harris traces his involvement with Hayes and then Nichols this way: "I was buying parts from Charlie Hayes, and also selling him tire temperature gauges I was building, and one day in '68 I got a call from him saying a customer of his in Japan, this Don Nichols character he'd mentioned earlier, who was dealing in racecar parts, rod ends and spherical bearings and stuff,

was coming to Los Angeles and it might be fun to meet him for dinner.

"At the restaurant I gave Don my business card. Well, he called and came over to my little shop in Costa Mesa. He had a Lola Can-Am car that he'd bought, and he needed somebody to shovel a Big Block Chevy into it. The engine already had Hilborn injection on it, I think it had been built by Dean Moon's shop, but it needed to be plumbed, it needed exhaust headers, and it needed a rear spoiler. Then it needed to be shipped to Japan. Pedro Rodriguez was going to drive it."

The race was 1968's Grand Prix of Japan at Fuji on May 3rd; that suggests this conversation could not have occurred later than mid-April.

"Of course, as always there was a time constraint. Of course, as usual I said, 'Sure, I can do that.' I hired a friend to help and we did get it done in time. I test-drove it around the streets in Costa Mesa to verify it ran. Somehow I made it back to the shop without getting a ticket, and Don loaded it up and off it went to Japan."

Nothing remarkable about this racer's story so far, most are like that, but while his new client was visiting his shop Harris showed Nichols concept sketches for a novel racing vehicle, one very, very low to the ground.

"It was an idea I'd been thinking of for a Can-Am car, a lot smaller and lighter than an

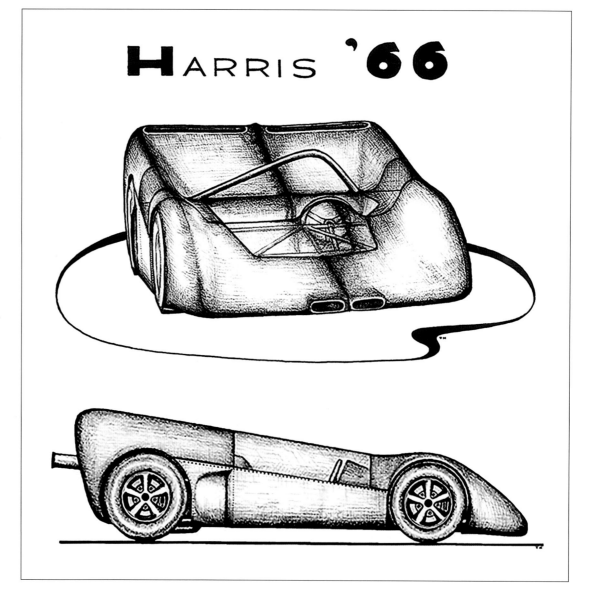

RIGHT Nichols would have seen these sketches of the low-profile "Car X," which Harris started building back in Seattle but lacked the funds to complete. Its pronounced "racer's wedge" body profile with aerodynamic "fences" along the upper edges would be seen again in the eventual AVS Shadow. *Trevor Harris collection*

ordinary racecar with abnormally small tires and a six-cylinder Corvair engine in back. It was air-cooled and flat-opposed, so its weight and profile were both very low. It wasn't a big-inch motor, but I was going to turbocharge it.

"Don said, 'Have you ever considered that kind of a concept with a Chevrolet V8 instead of a Corvair?' I said, 'No, but I'll build a mockup for you of what such a thing might be like.'

"Don came back, looked at this thing, fell in love with it. He asked me, 'How much would it cost to build a racecar like that?' I said something like, 'Oh, I think we can do it for 40 or 50 thousand.' Just a guesstimate! Completely haywire! So far off…

"This was the beginning of the Shadow project. Late 1968, October or November." By the end of the latter month Don Nichols would have turned 44, and Trevor Harris was 30.

As for Nichols's view of it, we've already heard about his two earlier "Can-Am" ventures with Lola T70s in Japan, but it's appropriate now to add further evidence that ambition was stirring to be a racecar constructor as well as team owner:

"Having done the Fuji Speedway, I decided that I wanted to do a car with Bill Stroppe, who ran the Lincoln team in the Mexican road race. I had gotten well acquainted with him, and he and I put together the design for a Mexican road

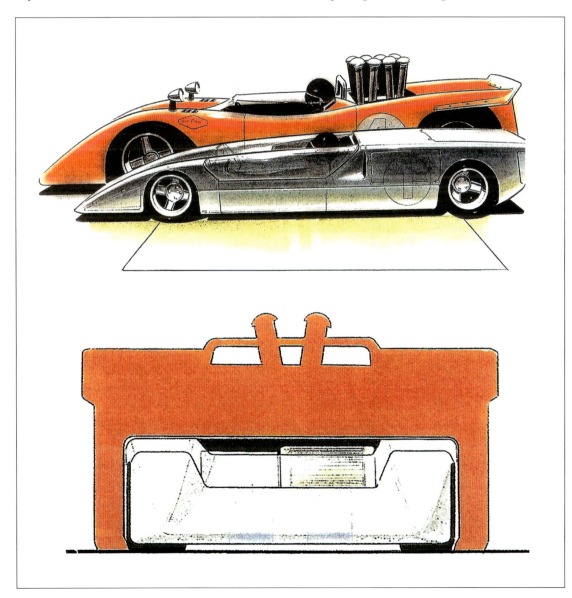

LEFT Harris hoped to put radically small tires under a car with exceptionally reduced frontal area, thus adding speed along straightaways. These sketches suggest how dramatically svelte such a vehicle might look compared to 1968's contemporary McLaren M8A. *Trevor Harris collection*

MOONSHOT 45

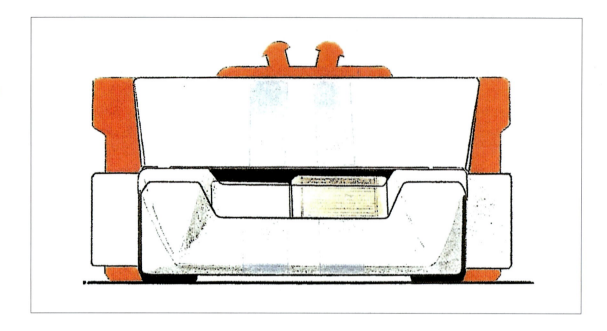

RIGHT Trevor's secret tweak to overcome the handicap of tiny brakes in tiny wheels — a set of air-brakes deployed into the slipstream for an enormous increase in drag. *Trevor Harris collection*

race special car. I built it in Japan, but we never actually got to use it."

Now here at his feet on Trevor Harris's floor lay a second opportunity. An exciting one to an entrepreneurial, risk-taking man of action who had amassed wealth enough to indulge his fancies.

"I bought a house in the Palos Verdes area of Los Angeles — beautiful view of the ocean — and put my kids into school there. My wife was a big tennis fan and she joined a club. I didn't have anything to do. So Trevor and I said, 'Why don't we build a car?'

"We just wanted to do something that was fun. The idea was, we'll build the car and we'll race it and see what happens then."

And his attraction to Can-Am? "It was a free formula. You could do anything. There were no limitations."

Well, that was still pretty much true in 1968, before regulations unfortunately tightened for the 1970 season. This would seriously cripple the new team's first effort.

Don started making daily commutes down the coastline to Trevor's place in his orange Mercury station wagon with his name on the side. He liked to remember that his free-spirited new partner drove "a clunky old Volvo with its headlights aimed two different directions. It looked like it had been crashed at least twice, and he managed to nurse it into mobility every time."

Good-humored needling aside, the more time he spent with Harris the more impressed Nichols became with the younger man's abilities. "You know his family were all full professors at the University in Seattle. His uncle too. Very, very highly educated people. But Trevor was rebellious. I don't know if he ever graduated from anything, but growing up in that family he was exposed to brainwaves! [Laughing] He was naturally brilliant.

"Trevor was always doing weird car projects and made various things. He actually was very skillful with tools and as a mechanic and fabricator. He loved welding. He fancied that he was The Ace Heliarc Welder. [Laughing]

"When we moved into our beautiful new building, 10,000 square feet in Santa Ana, not far from Dan Gurney's, we had 10 or 12 guys working in the shop and Trevor had his own drafting room. He was supposed to be in there designing parts, but we had to keep pulling him off the shop floor. 'Trevor, we've got the best people doing that, you go back and draw pictures.'"

That palace of a workplace still lay in the 1969 future when, back in 1968 at Trevor's little quarters in Costa Mesa, he and Don sat down with Wayne Hartman, a master fiberglass craftsman whose own shop was right next door and who often collaborated with Harris on various racecar jobs.

"So we loosely formed this little partnership," Don continued, "because Wayne had the capability to make things and Trevor could draw pictures. I had a little money. Later we formalized it, when I actually formed Nichols Advanced Vehicle Systems, which was my company, but at first it was just a group that was going to do things."

What things?

Oh, merely the most ambitious, shoot-for-the-moon, mindblowingly innovative competition vehicles on the planet. "We were just trying to think creatively about how to make the ultimate racing machine. Not talk to these guys who had started with covered wagons towed by mules and gotten down to where they put a motor in one end; we were trying to approach this from a space-age basis and see if we couldn't make something that was just totally different.

"First thing we wanted to do was reduce the ultimate frontal flat plate area."

THE KNEE-HIGH

A RECTANGLE's height multiplied by its width gives a number for its area, by which it can be compared to another of differing dimensions. Hold them up in a blast of wind, and you feel the larger experiencing more force trying to push it over, or along. Sailing vessels have been using the principle for thousands of years. More sail area, more "horsepower."

But with racing cars, wind is an enemy. Frontal area — width times height — is a literal drag on the speeding vehicle. One six feet wide and three feet high, for example, will have inherently more wind resistance, or aerodynamic drag, than one that's two feet high — 18 square feet vs. 12. All else being equal, such as body shape and engine power, the lower-slung car with one third less flat-plate area as viewed from the front can be pushed through the atmosphere to a higher ultimate velocity.

Hey, free speed! But how low can you go?

BELOW Harris says he does not recall making this drawing, which is unsigned and undated, but it well illustrates how the Shadow was evolving in his mind. Note the two different body lengths. *Trevor Harris collection*

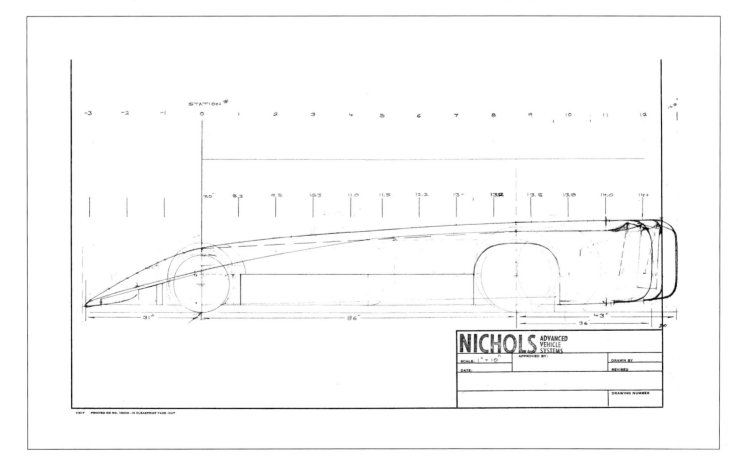

RIGHT Even closer to the finished thing, this professional artwork clarifies the Mk I's long, low profile, wedge nose, enclosed rear wheels and wide airscoops to cool the tail-mounted radiators.
Trevor Harris collection

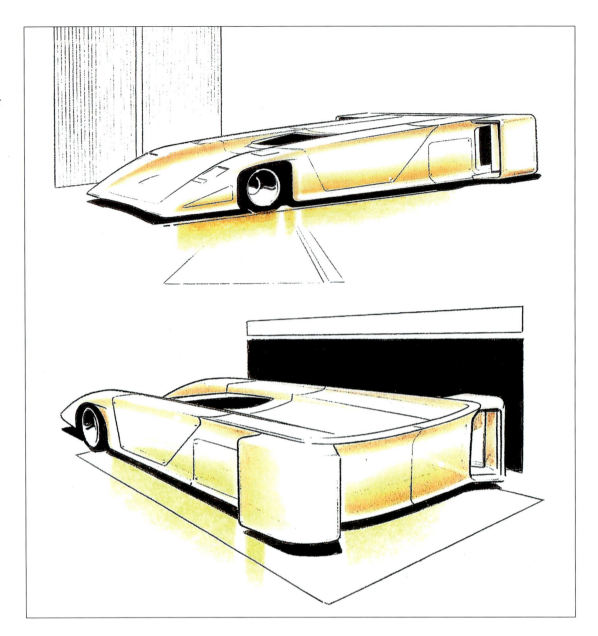

Both Nichols and Harris recalled playing with that very thought during early bench-racing sessions. What's the lowest thing we could make? What object has zero height?

As Don put it, "Trevor and I both argue about who came up with the idea that, since he was always trying to make a low-profile [car], the ultimate low-profile image would be a shadow, which has no third dimension. So that struck everybody as being a great idea [to name the car The Shadow]. It was exactly the way Trevor thought about doing designs." Don delighted in describing this eye-popper as a "two-dimensional car."

It should be noted here that the name also spoke to Don on a personal level. As he said to author Tom Madigan for George Follmer's biography *Follmer*, published in 2013 by ejje Publishing Group, "Very early in the project, Trevor and I discussed what we would call the team… we wanted something that expressed the fact that the car was very mysterious, and I had a rather secretive background. In fact I had worked at one time for an employer who didn't have an address. [Nichols laughs]

"Anyway, in part the namesake goes all the way back to the days of radio and the program, 'The Shadow,' a show about a mystery man who

48 CHAPTER 3

fought crime and beat the bad guys. When I was a youngster I listened to the show, and so we hired a design guy who fashioned our logo with a character that reminded me of that show."

That logo depicted a sinister figure in a black cloak and wide-brimmed hat, and his mysterious face obscured. It was an image that immediately and indelibly seized the imagination of the public. Even decades later everyone remembered it, so naturally they assumed the car's name referenced Nichols's reputation as a one-time "Spy." We've just heard our Shadowman confirming his "secretive background."

But we're talking about his "two-dimensional car" here, and although that's a catchy nickname, of course the whole point of the racing vehicle is to carry a racing driver. But even when the human body lays down as flat as it will go, it still presents a draggy cross section. As for the vehicle itself, 2D drawings are fine to design and build the machine — or to celebrate its engineering elegance as wall decor — but it has to have a third D to function.

Besides, it's hard to sell sponsors on a car that can't be seen from the sidelines, and flat drivers make for dull interviews.

Seriously, no matter the power of vision, it cannot outreach available technology. The dream of an ultra-low racecar depended on ultra-small tires, but dream had to awaken to reality: suitable ones did not exist. Not yet.

To recruit help from a tiremaker, the designer had to work out what to ask for. The smaller the better, but daring must not escalate to danger. Centrifugal force was an implacable opponent. Smaller wheels must rotate more rapidly to cover the same distance at a given road speed. At the time, even high-performance, bias-ply racing tires were "just rubber and bits of string," as an irreverent tireman was once heard to remark. Above a certain rpm they wouldn't be able to contain themselves and could blow apart.

Conventional tires were engineered for the fastest cars, which on the longest straightaways in the Can-Am series — eg. Riverside — might edge above 200 mph. Yet Harris calculated his low-drag car would go 250.

Doing his sums, he decided on tire tread diameters of 15 inches front and 19 rear. Rims of course were smaller; Harris specified 10 and 12 inches respectively. This was a very ambitious goal for a big, powerful machine. Even the smallest-engined racecars usually ran on 13-inch wheels at the minimum.

It is true that smaller wheels did appear in some forms of racing. The contemporary Mini Cooper S came with 10-inch wheels, while karts — basic trainers for so many drivers — ran on 5- or 6-inchers.

But road racers like Can-Am and Formula 1 cars typically wore 15-inch diameter wheels at both ends. Tires wrapping rear wheels tended to be the larger ones, so overall tire heights there often reached above 24 inches. When drawing sports car body lines, allowances had to be made for suspension deflection, plus tire growth with centrifugal force.

Photos establish that when personnel stood next to conventional Lolas and McLarens of the era, the bodywork over the front wheels came to mid-thigh on most people, and over the rear wheels rose nearly to hip level. Roughly the height of a typical office desk.

Harris boldly drew his Shadow's uppermost body lines much lower. Over the front wheels the height was at an average person's knees, even at the bottoms of many kneecaps. Desk chair height at most.

So Trevor's brainstorm would not be exactly shadow-slim, but alongside typical Can-Am machines of the day, track weapons honed to razor-thin minimalism themselves, the "Tiny-Tire Shadow" looked startlingly minute. It settled fondly into patron Don Nichols's memory as the "Knee-High Car."

But who would tackle the tiny tire-making? Such experimental, cutting-edge rubberwear was essential to the radically experimental Shadow concept.

No tires, no car.

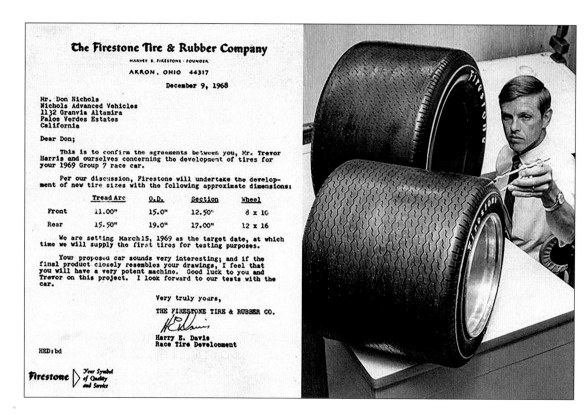

RIGHT The Prize! A press release announcing that Firestone had agreed to work with Nichols Advanced Vehicle Systems to develop small-diameter tires — the keys to making Trevor Harris's dream a reality.
Don Nichols collection

PITCHING AKRON

DUBBED THE "Rubber Capital of the World," the mid-size town of Akron in the northeastern part of Ohio had long been headquarters for numerous tire and rubber companies. These included both Firestone and Goodyear, then the primary tire supporters of American motorsport. Nichols had contacts at both firms from his time importing their products to Japan, but considering both his own and Harris's strong recent links with Firestone, he phoned them first. It turned out to be the only call he needed to make.

Trevor expresses a little surprise at how easy it was to get a meeting, but he and Don put together a sales pitch and early in December 1968 they flew to Akron. There before Firestone executives and many of the tire-development engineers Harris already knew, he presented his photos, drawings, charts, graphs and performance calculations. Nichols then spoke of the promotional potential of such a novel car, and outlined the schedule for making it a reality.

If Trevor thought securing a meeting was surprising, its outcome was even more so. "The guy who could make the decision, the head of race tire development, was Harry Davis. I had never met him before, and I never saw him again," says Trevor. "I remember showing how we would run 250 miles an hour with this very small vehicle, and if the tires adhered properly and if everything worked right, we would have a winning racecar.

"The strangest thing about the promotion was, I got done with the presentation and Harry Davis, who was the guy that could say 'yay' or 'nay' to it, agreed to do it on the spot! We never had a second meeting. We got a written agreement from Firestone, dated December 9th, 1968, that they were going to supply our tires!"

Their hosts shed illumination when they revealed that Firestone already was working on tires of very similar dimensions. Stylists for automaker Oldsmobile, forecasting that passenger car wheels might shrink in size, had asked for tires that would fit completely under the bodywork of a future concept, looking as though the car had no wheels at all.

Firestone's racing department well understood how a competition program could help move such a project forward for their client. But there was something else.

Their passenger car client would not have thought of it, but the racing engineers would have instantly seen the advantages awaiting a tiremaker who could offer open-wheel car racers — Indycar and Formula 1 particularly — a massive reduction in tire frontal area. If cooperating with Shadow bore fruit, in the form of small racing tires that performed as well as big ones around corners while allowing higher straightaway speeds, Firestone would have the jump on a big market.

Once again, mysterious forces had brought together two entirely different story lines: at precisely the right time in history, two guys from California who wanted to build the wildest of racing cars happened to approach a tire company that was already working on a wild-looking future Detroit passenger car.

Well, it was the 1960s. A wild time in society. Incredibly, America was going to the Moon!

Trevor: "We left Firestone that day totally blown away. I remember it hitting us at that point that, gosh, now that they had agreed to do our tires, we really had to do the car!"

DAWN OF REALITY

BACK AT HOME base, there may have come a morning in Trevor's little workshop in Costa Mesa when he and Don sat staring at one another, momentarily speechless, trying to grasp what lay before them.

Their very first sales presentation had landed full manufacturer support for the "Tiny Tires" crucial to their concept. But confronting them now were two new challenges, both equally monumental. Somehow, they had to create the extremely radical new Can-Am racing machine they had promised Firestone. Somehow, they must find commercial sponsorship to cover the construction, testing and racing season expenses that Don had promised to shoulder.

Time was speeding by, both tasks had to be accomplished simultaneously, and both men had to be involved in both efforts.

As December wound down toward the new year, Harris set to work establishing basic dimensions of the car's chassis. Fiberglass man Wayne Hartman, right next door, required this information before he could start building the bodywork. For his part, Nichols set out to find workshop space sufficient for the staff and equipment required to construct the new vehicle.

At the same time, the pair had to refine their sales pitch and start reaching out to more potential sponsors.

Surprisingly, their beginners' luck with Firestone seemed to hold when they arranged a trip to Ford Motor Company. In Trevor's memory, it was still December 1968 when they flew to Dearborn.

The initial meeting was disappointing. They failed to impress two lower-level executives. But before leaving Ford HQ, Nichols paid a courtesy call to one of the many friends he had made in his years of visiting racetracks. Legendary Corvette designer Larry Shinoda was now head of Ford Styling, having come over from General Motors with his own good buddy Semon "Bunkie" Knudsen, whom Ford had recruited as president.

Shinoda was so excited by his visitors' project that he immediately took them to meet Knudsen, and that flamboyant enthusiast also caught the spark. Ford's new president promptly promised corporate cooperation and a supply of the company's big, 427 cubic inch NASCAR racing engine. Hands were shaken, goodbyes were said.

Once again, the rookie racecar constructors headed home not quite believing their luck.

Which in this case did not hold. Nichols had not secured from Ford the same kind of signed document that he had with Firestone. (Trevor recalls that Don had a mysterious aversion to signing his own name on any binding agreement.) In the euphoria of the moment that might have seemed a mere formality, but in the background Ford was in fact winding down its long decade

```
mario andretti, 53 south market street, nazareth, pennsylvania 18064•215/759-5118
```

February 5, 1969

Mr. Don Nichols
Nichols Advanced Vehicle Systems
771 Newton Way
Costa Mesa, Calif.

Dear Don:

It was a great pleasure meeting you and Trevor yesterday and seeing your project.

I am greatly impressed with your facilities and the preliminary stages of the car. I can readily see that you have gathered the talented personnel and the facilities to do a really superior job of development.

As to the car design itself, I can truthfully say that the only word to describe it is "fantastic". I have long dreamed of a car with these performance capabilities. It is certainly within the realm of reality with currently available power plants to reach the speeds that you are planning. The chassis and body size and configuration have been the limiting factors, and I feel certain that your design will overcome the problems and make these speeds possible.

Based upon what I have seen thus far I will commit myself to be your official test driver. After thorough testing, when we think the car has been developed to its full competition potential and we think it is capable of winning races, I will finalize with you our agreement for a Can-Am driving contract.

Please keep me informed as the construction progresses. I would like to drop in periodically and literally let you tailor the car to my body. I feel that my physical size is favorable to the design and that we should take every advantage of this factor.

With best wishes for success, I remain

Very truly yours,

Mario Andretti

MA/plw

ABOVE Mario Andretti, already an Indycar National Champion and with so much more still ahead, tried on Wayne Hartman's Shadow body buck for size, and signed a letter of intent to drive the radical racer should it prove competitive. *Don Nichols collection*

of lavish support of motor racing. More conservative managers soon overruled their president. Knudsen and Shinoda eventually left the company.

By the time Trevor learned that AVS would not be getting the Ford after all, the Mk I's monocoque chassis was under construction and past the point of no return. He had dimensioned it according to engineering drawings Ford had sent him of its big V8 engine. Very big, to Trevor's eye. "All my experience was with Small Block Chevys. This thing looked enormous!"

Indeed, the US auto industry's long-traditional, everyday V8 encompassed displacements ranging from below 300 cubic inches (5 liters) to about 360 (5.9 liters). If we imagine approximately cube-shaped boxes fitted around such engines, each facet would measure about 18 inches (60 cm) wide.

The newer generation of 427s, such as those introduced by Chevrolet and Ford, would need boxes of about 24 inches a side.

Visualize the comparative volumes: 3.375 cubic feet alongside a massive 8.000.

So Harris was confronted by a powerplant vastly bulkier and heavier than what he'd had in mind, the familiar "small" Chev, let alone the little flat-six Corvair that had sparked his original idea.

But there was no time to waste in feeling daunted. No matter how massive the monster he confronted, it had to be caged, and quickly. Waiting next door in his glassfiber shop, Wayne Hartman couldn't get started on the bodywork before knowing the measurements of the chassis it was to clothe.

Meanwhile, Nichols was anxious for Harris to go out with him to chase sponsors. "I had to get the boundary dimensions worked out before I could leave," Trevor remembers. "Width and length of the chassis, cockpit dimensions, seating, etcetera, all had to be settled."

The engine's bulk determined everything else. Its width, length and height established those of the engine bay, the sides of which were the inner walls of the fuel boxes. From there Harris could work out how long the wheelbase and track dimensions had to be.

Track would be shorter and narrower than usual, because the car's center of gravity would be low thanks to the small tires. That meant stability against pitching and rolling could be maintained with a more compact stance between the tire contact patches, the car's four feet.

"Knowing that allowed me to go ahead with designing the complete monocoque. It settled the dimensions very early and there was no going back."

It may have been while he still expected Ford support that Don Nichols thought up his next promotional brainstorm. He reached out to two superstars of the day, America's Mario Andretti (Sebring, Indy 500) and Belgian Jacky Ickx (Formula 1, Le Mans), both of whom had contracts with both Firestone and Ford.

Describing his revolutionary new Shadow in no doubt dazzlingly hyperbolic terms, he offered

ABOVE Ferrari Formula 1 driver Jacky Ickx, pictured with Trevor Harris and Don Nichols, also visited AVS and said he was enthusiastic about the Mk I's potential. *Don Nichols collection*

BELOW With the Shadow project a go, Don Nichols quickly set up this spacious facility in Santa Ana and started hiring the best racecar builders in Southern California. Here from the left rear we see Trevor Harris conversing with Nichols, then Jim Mederer at the worktable, Walt Boyd in the distance, Don Borth at the metal-shaping machine in the middle of the floor, Chuck Noble sucking a pipe, Larry "Silver Fox" Stellings working on the chassis, and Jerry "MagnaCharger" Magnuson more interested in his lathe than the camera. *Don Nichols collection*

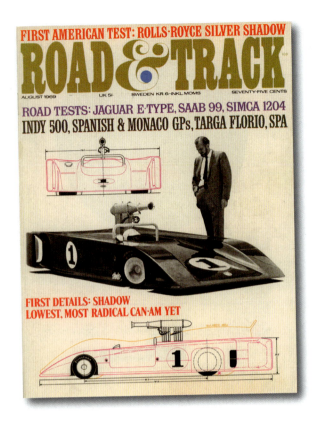

ABOVE The Big Issue: *Road & Track* devoted its August 1969 cover story to the "Knee-High Car." Nichols thus gained an enormous publicity boost.
Trevor Harris collection

RIGHT *Road & Track*'s supposed "exclusive" dissolved with the simultaneous publication of competing articles, to the considerable dismay of editor Dean Batchelor.
Trevor Harris collection

to fly them to Los Angeles to see the project for themselves. If they perceived some potential, perhaps they would declare their interest in driving it.

They came, they sat in the mockup, they were conquered. Both readily signed Don's declarations. (He had no problem with others putting their names on something for him!) These he folded into his sales pitch.

A very effective pitch. Trevor remembers sponsorship negotiations where, as he says, "People had a hard time saying 'no' to us!"

But in the end everyone managed just that. The road warriors kept coming home empty-handed.

Nichols's wallet went on emptying.

But he pressed on with the plan, and in the early months of 1969 the fledgling organization set up its new, much larger headquarters at 1313 East Borchard Avenue in Santa Ana, about eight miles' drive northeast of Harris's former shop in Costa Mesa. Body man Hartman stayed behind in his own place there, but still produced panels for Shadow.

Tucked away in an industrial cul de sac, the 10,000-square-foot AVS building was surrounded by similar properties, rather than family homes. This convenient isolation would come into the story one memorable afternoon.

Quickly, a streamlined group of expert machinists and fabricators hand-picked from around the SoCal racing scene started making real progress on components. But the racecar was still well short of completion when Nichols had another promotional idea.

Back in Costa Mesa, not two miles from where the project all began, former hot rodder, Bonneville speed racer and meticulously ethical magazine editor Dean Batchelor headed up the

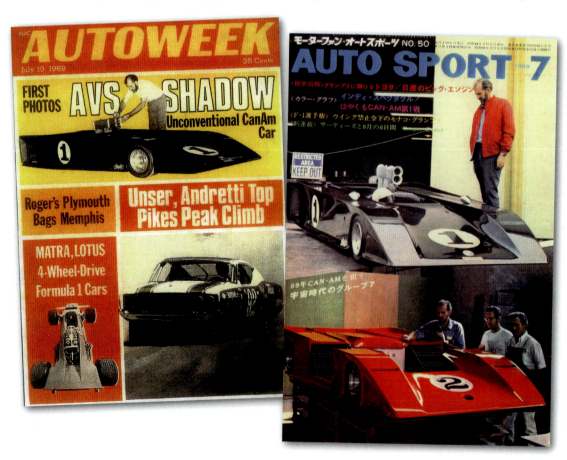

prestigious *Road & Track*. Perhaps his own B-17 bomber service during World War II — and subsequent confinement as a POW — helped the two veterans bond.

In their meeting, Dean and Don agreed that *R&T* would produce an exclusive first look at, and in-depth study of, America's excitingly radical new Can-Am contender. Meaning, this full-blown cover story would appear before any rival's.

Accordingly, the Shadowmen rigged up a photogenic representation of what the final car was to look like; it was actually Hartman's body buck, or mold, painted glossy black to cover unsightly patches of filler, mounted on a wooden frame and standing on dummy wheels. The first iteration of Harris's ultra-narrow fuel injection intake system was set up on top, as if an engine lurked below.

Worming his way down into what looked like a cockpit, Trevor Harris pretended to be a driver while towering Don Nichols was posed to emphasize the vehicle's diminutive height.

The photo made an eye-catching cover, and the magazine's team captured enough information and actual work in progress inside the shop for a feature story no racefan could resist.

Do you think it's possible that this single magazine cover story, which so dramatically depicted the astonishingly low-slung new concept in racecars, might be the primary reason for the marque Shadow living on in our memories to this day? The Mk I established expectations for every model that would follow. It's hard to imagine such an impact by an ordinary, conventional vehicle, particularly one whose racing career suffered a similar "success" rate as Shadow's. Such a brand would have vanished back into darkness.

The piece duly appeared in the August 1969 issue of *Road & Track*.

Unfortunately, so did competing stories that very same month in US rival *Sports Car Graphic*, albeit not with a cover photo, while both *AutoWeek* and Japan's *Auto Sport* did show Shadows right up front — two on the latter.

Batchelor was the opposite of amused. *R&T* was supposed to have had a scoop. He wrote a scathing letter to Nichols about breaking their agreement.

Meanwhile in Santa Ana, craftsmen continued toiling away. The first Shadow gradually took shape. Very gradually. ▲

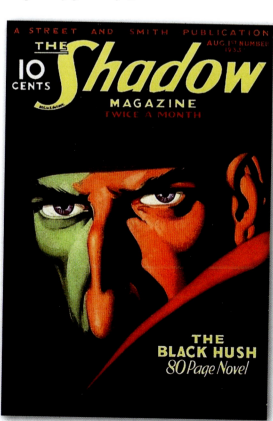

ABOVE *Sports Car Graphic*'s story was the work of their tech editor Paul van Valkenburgh, a former engineer for General Motors and Chaparral with particular expertise in aerodynamics. He was also a racer, and Harris remembers that when Paul came to see the AVS project, he was so excited that he asked for a job. *Trevor Harris collection*

LEFT "Nick" Nichols's inspiration? A fictional crime-fighting character known as "The Shadow" debuted on broadcast radio dramas in 1930, and quickly became so popular that "he" was given his own series of printed pulp novels. Later on films were made, and the mysterious figure lives on today. A secretive detective with the persona of a spy, The Shadow assumed various personal names, but "Lamont Cranston" is the one remembered by most fans — including by Don Nichols, who at one point had it embroidered on his white workshop coat. *Private collection*

MOONSHOT 55

TREVOR HARRIS
DESIGNER

SUPERIOR SPEED on straightaways; that's what the first Shadow was supposed to show. And in fact it did. But…

We've already seen that Daring Don Nichols was ripe to hazard an investment in some such speculative project. But who was this Tempter Trevor Lee Harris, who dangled his own concept for a wildly low-profile racing car in front of the wealthy man's widening eyes?

Born to university professors in Seattle in 1938, Trevor was the youngest of three siblings growing up in settled circumstances. But despite his parents' occupation, and the more studious bent of his older sister and brother, the youngster had zero interest in Academia.

His rebel enthusiasms were for electronics at first, and then mechanical devices of every sort. Figuring out how things worked, making them with his hands, inventing better and newer ones; this was his soul's passion.

"My parents were academics, so they understood its pitfalls and they were perfectly OK with me following my own path. In fact they encouraged me."

He looks back on struggles with polio when he was 11 as a positive influence on his approach to life. "It screwed up several muscles in my legs. I think the challenges of coming back from that were ultimately useful over the years. They just forced me to work a little harder at things."

A year into that bout, at age 12, he mounted a small gasoline motor atop a simple push-scooter and devised a belt-drive system. That's right, Shadow Fans: the first motor vehicle "designed" and crafted by our Trevor Lee Harris rolled on Tiny Tires.

At 15, still short of driver's license age, he acquired two old '37 Lincoln Zephyr coupes, both minus their original V12 engines and desperately cheap. The derelicts lay at the Harris home while they waited for the budding Maestro of Metalwork to meld them into a single chopped-and-channeled masterpiece of some sort. Meanwhile, the youngster taught himself how to weld.

"My future Hot Rod occupied the garage, which put my father's car onto the front street," Trevor remembers. "He wasn't into that stuff at all, but he was extremely

LEFT Before he could legally drive Harris was building his own automobile, a true "Hot Rod Lincoln." Finished, the Olds-powered "Trevarri" became his daily driver through his High School years. *Trevor Harris collection*

understanding, and so was my mother. My folks really supported whatever goofy project I had going on."

While still in High School he finally finished his Hot Rod Lincoln, hopped up an Oldsmobile V8 to overpower it, and was running it on dragstrips as well as around town. But circle track racing resonated with him too, and he kept his eye on sports cars — Ferraris of the '50s inspired some of his massively restyled Zephyr's looks.

Straight after High School graduation young Harris joined Boeing, where he assembled electrical test equipment for the Bomarc missile program, but more significantly a co-worker there gave him a ride in his Austin-Healey. A life-changer, Trevor says.

"All of a sudden, I had a bigger-than-ever interest in doing something with sports cars, rather than drag racing." He left the aircraft industry and his storyline became ever more branched, intricate and fascinating. It wove together:

- enrolling in a university to study Physics, but soon walking away from that career path to get his hands back on something tangible;
- a little shop he called Harris Enterprises, where he custom-fabricated all sorts of specialized competition car components, especially exhaust headers;
- a newer homebuilt racecar with the same souped-up Olds engine, along with old Grand Prix Maserati parts (!), in a Harris-made chassis frame with an independent suspension package, all topped by his own fiberglass body;
- using that homebuilt not only to qualify for his racing license, but for a program of instrumented track tests, using potentiometers to measure body lift and experimenting with spoilers to reduce it;
- a rapidly lengthening client list of northwest road racers, among them future star Jerry Grant, who brought Trevor a Lotus 19 and asked him to install a Chevrolet engine.

Grant and Harris trailered the new Special to Westwood, British Columbia, in 1964 for its debut race. Trevor: "Jerry qualified on the pole, broke the track record, won the first heat, and won the second heat with it.

ABOVE Mom and dad gave over their family garage to serve their budding genius as his first racecar shop. *Trevor Harris collection*

RIGHT The second Harris hot rod took shape around several then-worthless 1935 Maserati Grand Prix parts — including its transaxle — along with other cast-off components. *Trevor Harris collection*

MOONSHOT 57

RIGHT In 1960 Trevor opened his own place of business in Seattle. *Trevor Harris collection*

BELOW One rainy raceday at Kent, Washington, Trevor stepped back to take this snap of his homebuilt Special. Moments later an oncoming driver lost control of his own car and spun into the unprotected pits, destroying the Harris car and badly injuring its designer-builder-driver. "This is the last picture of it," says Trevor dolefully. *Trevor Harris collection*

ABOVE Rising northwest racing star Jerry Grant had Harris add Chevy V8 power to this Lotus 19, which originally came with a much smaller four-cylinder. Engineer and driver then set off to Canada to win the Bardahl Special's debut race. *Trevor Harris collection*

"That was the first race for the car, and it was pretty exciting for me."

Racing's cauldron soon swirled Trevor together with Bruce Burness, another gifted carbuilder who built a Porsche-powered Lotus 23 for hard-driving newcomer George Follmer. Fast and reliable, this hybrid let Follmer win 1965's United States Road Racing Championship (USRRC) — defeating Chaparral's Jim Hall.

When the professional, international Can-Am series began in 1966, Trevor joined Burness in working for driver Mike Goth, who had an older McLaren fitted with a newer-style aluminum body. That led to a Burness-Harris partnership in sprawling Los Angeles.

One new client was fellow traveler Pete Brock, whom Toyota commissioned to design a pair of small, sleek prototypes. Brock styled the coupe bodywork, while Harris designed and fabricated the spaceframe chassis and suspension. Meanwhile, Burness rejoined Follmer. Harris worked with them too, prepping and sometimes crewing Follmer's Lola T70 for the USRRC and Can-Am series.

Trevor's role was chassis development, and among his tweaks were much stiffer sway bars. Rival Lola runners looked askance at this, he laughs. "Mark Donohue called us The Big Bar Guys." But George was scaldingly fast. "At Bridgehampton in '67 he qualified on pole but was protested on the basis of it not being possible. He

58 CHAPTER 3

took the car out again and requalified on pole."

Follmer's USRRC car ran on Firestones, a fact that would become a key element of our main story a couple of years later. Regarding this car's "Big Bars," its Firestones had a fundamental difference compared to rival Goodyear's. Looking across a tread of the latter brand from the inner to the outer edges, one could see noticeably rounded tread profiles, allowing more latitude for camber change. By contrast, Firestone treads looked completely level all the way across. This company's engineers preferred to make all the rubber work all the time. But keeping flatter treads square to the road meant minimizing body roll around corners.

"George and I ran several tire tests at Riverside for Firestone. He was a terrific test guy for them, because George is pretty amazing at it. Test drivers don't know what they're sent out on, the different tires can't be told apart by us, but if after testing several sets the engineers repeated one they'd put on earlier, George could tell just by the feel. 'These are the same compound you gave me three sets ago,' he'd say. He was phenomenal. Firestone loved using him.

"We ended up with a pretty quick Lola T70, so the Firestone field engineers were well aware of what I could do with chassis development and I became friendly with them."

Unfortunately, as Trevor admits, he wasn't similarly adept at cost control. "Bruce Burness and I had to shut down our shop. We were actually totally out of money. The Toyota project, we mis-bid that by tens of thousands of dollars and it was probably more my fault than anybody's, because I worked out the costs of parts and whatnot.

"I went to work for Crown Manufacturing, where I designed a kit to install a Chevrolet V8 in the back of a '65 Corvair. They called it a Corv-8. So I became a little bit

TOP Grant in his Lotus-Chevy started 1964's USRRC at Mid-Ohio in the middle of the front row, splitting the Chaparrals of Jim Hall and eventual winner Hap Sharp. Trevor remembers Jerry leading the Road Runners for 10 twisty laps before his brakes overheated. *Trevor Harris collection*

ABOVE Harris built the huge rear spoiler and also engineered suspension modifications for this McLaren, an early M1A rebodied in aluminum. Owner Mike Goth drove it in 1966 USRRC (seen here at Watkins Glen) and Can-Am races. Trevor remembers it was so quick at Laguna Seca that Bruce McLaren strolled over with puzzled brow to see why. *Pete Lyons*

RIGHT Trevor trying out Pete Brock's coupe bodywork on the chassis Harris and Burness built for Toyota. Two cars were made but are thought not to have raced. Pity. *Trevor Harris collection*

RIGHT Seen chasing Jim Hall's Chaparral 2G at 1968's Riverside Can-Am, George Follmer became one of the most formidable of Lola T70 drivers, thanks in part to engineering work on his own earlier T70 carried out by Harris. During 1967 Follmer raced a team Penske Lola as partner to Mark Donohue — but didn't think it was as good as his own.
Pete Lyons

LEFT All the while Trevor was working to make other people's cars faster, his restless, fertile brain was thinking up his own even faster ones. Before leaving Seattle he built a chassis for what he called "Car X," a very light, very low concept that turned out to be the ancestor of the Shadow.
Trevor Harris collection

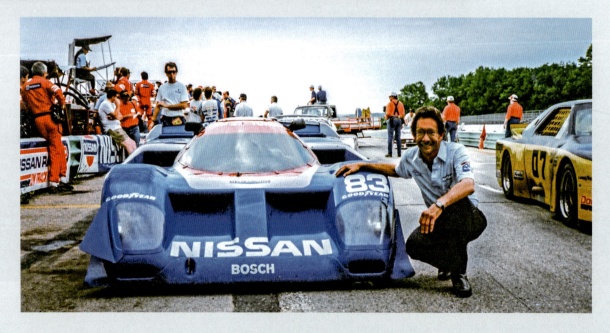

RIGHT Harris designed and track engineered the chassis for Nissan's series of turbocharged GTP cars, winners of IMSA's American sports car championship for four straight seasons, 1988 to 1991. Here at what appears to be Road America Trevor shows pride in "his" winning ZX Turbo.
Trevor Harris Collection

LEFT While out bicycle shopping one day, Trevor's inquisitive mind started thinking, There Must Be A Better Way. The 1973 result was this patented lever-powered transmission system. The idea was to apply torque throughout each leg's entire power stroke, without the unproductive segments of the traditional circular motion. *Trevor Harris collection*

BELOW Not merely a hands-on development engineer, Mr. Harris got his whole body involved in evaluating a Gurney Eagle Indycar he designed for Al Unser Jr. in 1983. This wild ride was at Phoenix, Arizona. *Trevor Harris collection*

familiar with the Corvair engine, and I started looking at the potential for an extremely small Can-Am car based on a highly modified Corvair engine."

Actually this followed on from something Harris had been working up back in Seattle in 1965. He ran out of money before completing the build, but his sketches for this "Car X" show similarities with his Shadow concept three years later. The driver would sit very low in the front of a dramatically wedge-shaped body, the sides of which rose up on either side to form aerodynamic "fences." The intent was to contain air pressure atop the body as it flowed aft to a transverse elevation at the tail; think of a household dustpan.

In Los Angeles he couldn't shake his Car X idea. "I made some drawings and built some mockup tires, everything scaled down from a normal Can-Am car, and it appeared to me that the aerodynamic and dynamic potentials for such a thing might be extremely interesting. That was going on in a little shop I had in Costa Mesa. I was just fooling around with it, but seriously fooling around with it.

"This was before I met Don Nichols, by the way…"

Earlier we learned how Don came into Trevor's orbit, by way of common friend and parts supplier Charlie Hayes introducing them over dinner. That resulted in Nichols commissioning Harris to install an engine in a Lola T160,

which led to the new client seeing the conceptual drawings for a revolutionary new Can-Am car.

"So that was the beginning, the very beginning of the actual Shadow project."

Images of these and the innovator's many other vehicles and inventions can be seen at http://trevorlharris.com/time-line.html

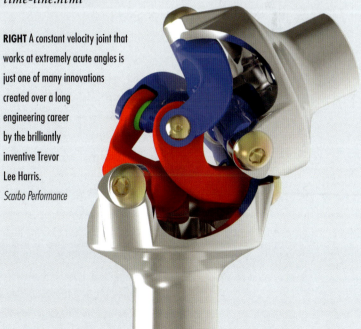

RIGHT A constant velocity joint that works at extremely acute angles is just one of many innovations created over a long engineering career by the brilliantly inventive Trevor Lee Harris. *Scarbo Performance*

MOONSHOT 61

CHAPTER 4
THE TINY ONE

AVS SHADOW MK I

AS RECOUNTED EARLIER in detail, Don Nichols returned to the US from his entrepreneurial years in Japan with ample wherewithal for his next adventure, and an eye out for what it might be. He spotted it in Trevor Harris's concept sketches for a radical new Can-Am racecar.

Slung ultra-low between ultra-small wheels, and wrapped within super-slender bodywork meant to pierce the air like a missile, this "Knee-High" vehicle promised to show straightaway velocities far above the reach of conventional machines of the day.

Would it actually reach them? And would straightline gains make up for any speed sacrificed around corners? Let's try it and see! Back then few race teams had another way to evaluate something new. Only a few of the largest automakers had computers, very big and very pricy number-crunchers that actually didn't do much, not as we see it today. Our effortless, ubiquitous desktop simulation was unimaginable.

Engineering experimentation carried out in the open air, where everybody could watch the craziest brainstorms succeed or fail, was the very thing that made Can-Am racecars so exciting.

But seriously, what a strange-looking contraption. Seemingly the product of an uncontrollably inventive mind, with every detail driven by the myriad challenges of very small tires, Harris's AVS Mk I departed from convention at almost every point.

Looking back these long years afterward, Trevor freely admits that in the heat of youthful enthusiasm he made many problems for himself. His tire choice did yield that marvelously minimalistic body profile, but it carried adverse knock-on consequences affecting braking performance, suspension layout, roadholding and handling, weight distribution, aerodynamic stability, engine cooling, transmission gearing, chassis design, fuel capacity, cockpit configuration, driver comfort and control — just about everything necessary to put a

BELOW This is our plan, boys. Split the wind, go like hell, and win the Can-Am. All we have to do is build it. Fifty grand and six months ought to cover it, right? *Trevor Harris collection*

LEFT Many days and dollars later, the designer stands with one of his concepts come to life — or it would have, had AVS ever finished and fired up the experimental turbocharged V8 Toyota buried within. The Japanese automaker had commissioned them to install and test it, but something went sour with the deal, and the project sat idle until its chassis was needed for something else. This photo does not show the engine, but Trevor Harris tells us "this is the only photo of it that was ever taken." As for the secret engine, when Toyota asked for it to be returned, Nichols told them he didn't know where it was. In truth, he hoarded it under a tarp for decades. We can tell you it looked like a slightly enlarged Cosworth DFV. *Trevor Harris collection*

THE TINY ONE **63**

THIS PAGE From the hand of the master, a few surviving examples of how Harris sketched out his ideas to be made in metal. The X-shaped one is an early iteration of a big plate to mount the engine in the chassis.
Trevor Harris collection

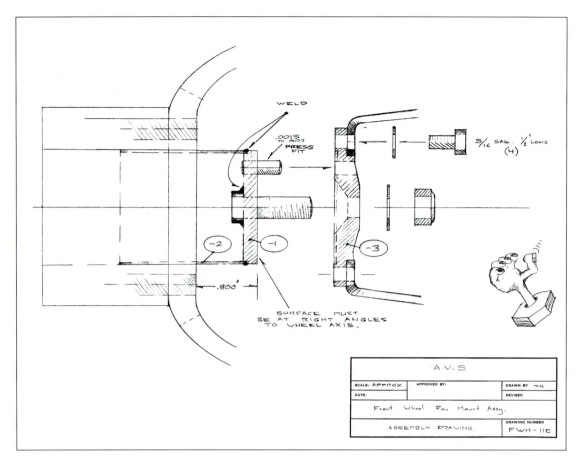

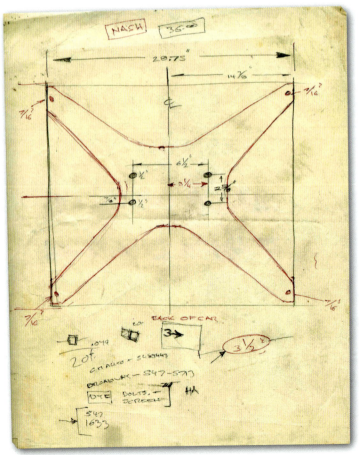

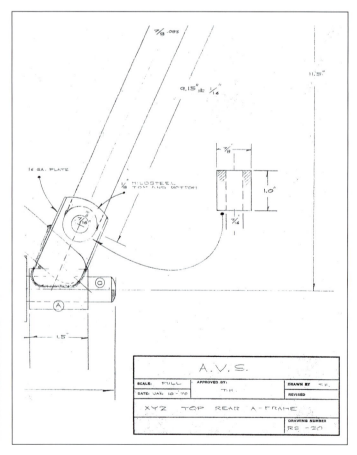

64 CHAPTER 4

competitive racecar on the starting grid.

As problem after problem came to light, Harris was forced to alter just about every fascinating feature of his original design, in some cases even to abandon them.

And that burned up time, along with Don Nichols's money. AVS's original plan was to compete in the 1969 Can-Am season. But as days ticked down toward June's opening date, reality hit the little novice team like a cold wind. The car wasn't even built.

THE MOCKUP

WHAT WAS he thinking?

When the Shadowmen rolled out their mockup for a photo shoot one day in mid-1969, what an arresting sight it was. Ultra-low, long, and lean-lined as a javelin, Trevor Harris's free-thinking conception of a Can-Am competitor looked like a Bonneville streamliner dropped off at a road-racer shop by mistake.

Its long profile was wedge-shaped. The nose section was especially sloped, which of course had to do with making front-end downforce. Yet the very long tail was essentially level and clean. It wore not even a simple "ducktail" spoiler to generate downforce. Had this Harris guy forgotten about aerodynamic balance?

The one "adornment" rising from the afterbody was a "periscope," a tall, slender air-induction system for the Big Block engine hidden inside. But any added drag from the periscope was countered by fairings streamlining the rear wheels, so the tires were visible only where they touched the road.

In plan view the outline was somewhat arrowhead-shaped. This was not really a feature, the designer says. It just worked out that way, as he drew a line from the front corners of his relatively narrow nosepiece back past the front tires to the wider rears.

Right at the stern, air scoops stuck out sideways like angry elephant ears. These brought the car's overall maximum width, according to *Road & Track*, to 79 inches (2,007 mm), something like a foot wider than the front, depending on where along the arrowhead the measurement was taken.

Its lack of height, the fender lines a scant 24 inches (610 mm) on average above the road, made AVS Mk I look very long. In fact it was only a bit longish compared to rivals of the day. *Road & Track* reported that the original Shadow's body extended to 161.5 inches (4,102 mm), though *AutoWeek* gave it as 155 inches (3,937 mm), while records say that McLaren's dominant M8s came to only 154 inches (3,911 mm).

And its proportions were unusual, with a very long tailpiece jutting out a whopping four feet (about 1.2 meters) behind the rear wheel centerline. Accentuating that contrast was the relatively short wheelbase, 86 inches (2,184 mm), only slightly over half the body length; the McLaren's was 94 inches (2,394 mm).

Harris chose the short wheelbase partly

BELOW The Maestro at his Magic Drawing Board. Over many decades Trevor's effervescent mind has created innumerable interesting things, all of them remarkable and many very successful.
Linda "Freddi" Fredrickson (Mrs. Harris)

ABOVE A basic mockup of what the monocoque AVS Mk I chassis was to look like.
Don Nichols collection

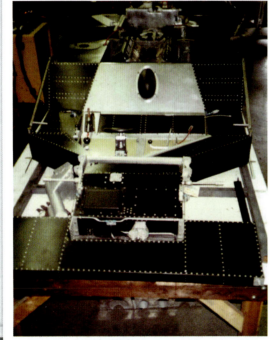

RIGHT & BELOW The real thing takes shape in black-anodized aluminum, its many panels joined with both adhesive and stainless steel "pop" rivets.
Don Nichols collection

because it allowed narrower track dimensions than usual, further reducing the car's frontal area. Because the small car carried its weight low, the stance between the four tire contact patches maintained the same resistance to pitch and roll as a vehicle of conventional specifications.

Visiting reporters were told of grandiose plans for an expansive AVS future. The *AutoWeek* man wrote of Shadows made for Group 6, i.e. Le Mans and other long-distance events; open-wheelers for the Indy 500 and "Formula A," aka F5000; and, yes, Land Speed Record attempts. He mentioned "other non-racing automotive concepts" as well.

Road & Track's Ron Wakefield detailed an array of engines under consideration, including Ford's exotic, four-camshaft Indycar winner and Chevrolet's new ZL1, an aluminum version of its Big Block. But those were never actually in the shop, attests Trevor today. The prototyping work was going on around an ordinary iron Chevy.

Several notetakers noted that Mr. Harris was oddly reticent to describe exactly what he intended for the transmission. This of course sparked stories about secret automatic gearboxes.

One crazy concept? Let's hear what Mr. Harris has to say now.

Firstly, he would like to share his belief that with this car he introduced the concept of lips jutting out around the bottom edge of the body. He was picking up from the "chin-spoilers" used to forestall the frighteningly frequent instances of modern widebody racecar front ends lifting off the track and flipping over backwards, like the "blow-overs" suffered in speedboating.

The cause was high-speed air piling up under the car's floor, a catastrophe the chin spoilers helped avoid. Trevor reasoned that his arrowhead shape also presented the car's flanks to the wind, and powerslides or crosswinds would exaggerate the effect. The side lips were intended to prevent any lifting along there.

"It's something that caught on, and I used it again myself on many cars I did later."

The artist in him couldn't resist continuing the lip around the stern of his Shadow. After all,

a racecar can spin backwards, can't it? That little detail was lost before the car raced.

Another detail of note: the underside of the nose wasn't flat. Supporting the front end of the bodywork was not a tubular structure, as might be expected, but a sort of subsidiary monocoque box bolted to the front of the primary chassis tub. At first glance this box had no other purpose than to hold up the body, but Harris gave it a cunning cant. The bottom surface sloped up at five degrees from front to back. He meant this as a venturi, to create ground effect.

How about that original tailpiece, why so long? Because it housed a pair of water radiators — off-the-shelf, crossflow aluminum rads mass-produced for Corvettes. Farther inside were additional coolers for engine and gearbox oil.

Those "ears" on the sides scooped in air for all these internal radiators. Harris planned to equip each scoop with a pivoting vane, like an oversize carburetor throttle. This would alter position at various points around the track, directing air either through the radiators for better cooling, or straight out the back for lower drag. All the way across the top of the flat body, right at the tail, a slot-shaped opening was meant to draw hot air up and out of the radiators (see next page). But that wasn't its primary function.

Want a clue? See the two slots in the sloping nosepiece, just ahead of the wheels? More air extractors, right? Sorry, no, not in the front.

In Harris's original plan, these three slots — the big one at the rear and the smaller pair at the front — would each house a vertical blade. On command, these blades would rise up into the airstream, the rear one in particular generating enormous drag at high speed. Air brakes.

But wait, there's more. Lift that rear panel only a few inches, and it would become a driver-adjustable air dam, collecting pressure atop the big afterbody to balance front-end downforce. As with Chaparral's flipping wing, the ratio of downforce to drag could be varied around the track.

ABOVE Don Borth turns from the drill press to watch his fellow Shadowman show Don Nichols their progress on the first Mk I. Special points of interest: the mini-monocoque front structure that will not only support the body nosepiece but also generate some venturi-effect downforce; the small, nine-inch steering wheel positioned nearly flat; the swelling after parts of the chassis where the twin fuel cells live; the pair of angled radiators behind the wide rear wheels; and the eight engine intakes fabricated in steel sheet that curve upwards into a single, narrow row to reduce aerodynamic drag.
Trevor Harris collection

THE TINY ONE **67**

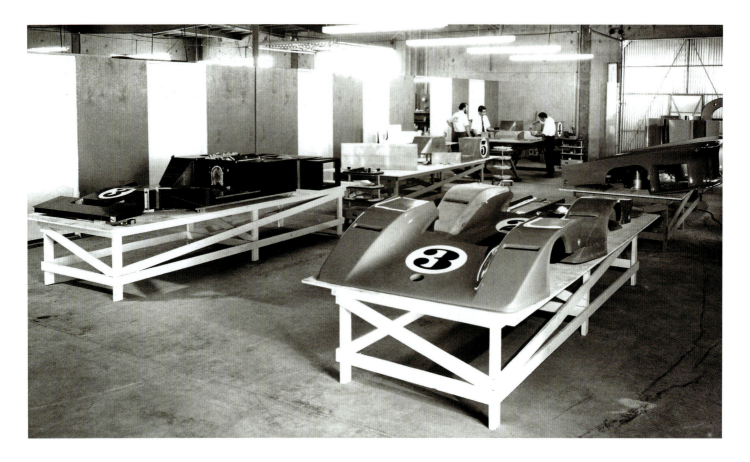

ABOVE Body panels being gathered to clothe what the team seemingly expects to be five finished Shadows. The narrow slots atop the nosepieces would have accommodated front-end air brakes, but new rules outlawing "moving aerodynamic devices" killed that idea. *Trevor Harris collection*

BELOW This scan from *Sports Car Graphic* magazine nicely shows the original Mk I body shape. Note the air ducting meant to cool the rear-mounted radiators, drawing it in behind the wheels and expelling it upwards through the slot across the tail. That slot is where the lifting air brake would have risen, had it ever been installed. Other air-management measures are the body-top fences intended to hold high-pressure air in place long enough to do its downforce job, and the anti-lift lips around the bottom of the entire car. *Trevor Harris collection*

Trevor reprised an idea from his old "Car X" body by adding aerodynamic fences along the edges of the deck. They were shallow, but must have contained at least some of the air pressure piling up ahead of the dam.

We must say "must have," because, sadly, none of these tricks were never tried. But what if all his ideas for dynamic aerodynamics had been finished, development-tested on the completed car, and worked as intended? Mr. Harris might be remembered as that madman who turned out to have method in his madness. His Shadow might have been a revolutionary turning point in racecar design.

Back to reality. A change in rules stopped him cold. The new car was still under construction in 1969 when sanctioning body SCCA announced that, for 1970, Can-Am regulations would adopt a new International FIA ban on so-called "moving aerodynamic devices."

This was aimed at Chaparral-style driver-adjustable wings, which some officials considered dangerous, but for Shadow it

68 CHAPTER 4

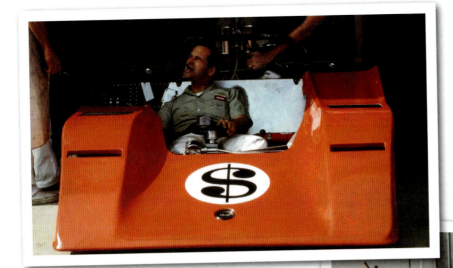

LEFT & BELOW Fresh out of Wayne Hartman's shop, glowing in its Tangerine gelcoat (it's not paint). The tailpiece shown has on either side the "elephant ears" that guide air not used for radiator cooling out into the semi-vacuum behind the moving racecar, again to reduce drag. Originally, Harris meant to incorporate large "butterfly throttle plates" in each duct to control airflow into the rear-mounted radiators. Again, such devices were outlawed before the car raced. *Don Nichols collection*

BELOW Big Block Chevy ready to go to work. Built at Dean "Mooneyes" Moon's famous hot-rod shop, it is a cast-iron Chevy 427 L88 wearing one version of the AVS-fabricated induction system with Hilborn fuel injection. Notice the commonplace electric starter motor at the lower front. *Don Nichols collection*

ABOVE Because designer Harris was determined to install the engine as low as possible, he replaced Chevrolet's flywheel and starter ring gear with a smaller one from the British Motor Corporation. But that meant the American starter motor no longer lined up properly. One of the Shadowmen had to devise a little angled driveshaft.
Courtesy of Dennis Losher

THE TINY ONE 69

outlawed Harris's lifting air-brake system and the pivoting vanes inside the side scoops.

Wording of the rule even nixed the tall air scoop rising from the engine. Its inlet, a "forward-facing air gap," had to be lower.

Harris: "By the time I heard about it, we already had our agreement with Firestone, so I never considered abandoning the project. I just had to keep on with it and hope I could make it work."

RUBBER TROUBLE

Talk about the Tiny Tires, they had issues too. Trevor says that Firestone was months late in delivering its first examples. "We had the car ready to run before the first tires arrived. I was seriously worried."

Clearly the Firestone engineers were running into unanticipated difficulties, the worst of which had to do with the tire profile across the treads.

It wasn't flat. When the car was simply pushed across the shop floor, the wide treads picked up dust in two stripes separated by a virginally clean middle section. Think of a truck with dual rear wheels, but this was happening at both ends of the car. Half the rubber did not meet the road.

"We had to inflate those things to 60 or 70 PSI just to get all the rubber on the racetrack!" complains Harris. "Later on they got better, but we still had to use like 37 pounds. Still way too stiff. They bounced off the road like a go-kart." Besides that, heat build-up in the smaller tires required the rubber compound to be much harder than expected, "like three generations behind what everybody else was running."

At least the small wheels were successful, and interesting in themselves. Rather than have aluminum or magnesium castings designed, made and machined, Harris found a local craftsman who specialized in "spinning" bowl shapes out of aluminum sheet, like forming clay on a potter's wheel. Two of his deep bowls

BELOW Moment of truth: can we get it down into that little thing? The big V8 is a Chevrolet, so it must be that nobody had time to remove the leftover "Ford" emblem from the body panel.
Don Nichols collection

LEFT A pair of original Firestone Tiny Tires, lovingly preserved for half a century and still looking almost fresh enough to run on.
Pete Lyons

bolted together back to back formed the 12-inch rear wheels.

Each 10-inch front wheel consisted of a single inner dish, inside of which the brake and suspension would live, with an outer face of machined aluminum that accepted cooling fans.

Cooling the brakes was going to be hard because, obviously, normal 12-inch racing brake discs of the time could not fit inside 10-inch wheels. What about carrying the brakes inboard, on the chassis, and adding shafts out to the wheels? Not an option, because the chassis was very compact and the driver's splayed-out legs filled what space was available.

So outboard the brakes had to be. To make them as powerful as possible, Trevor bought high-quality, specialty Hurst Airheart racing disc blanks much larger than needed, and had them painstakingly machined down to just eight inches diameter. The same manufacturer's racing calipers also were trimmed down to fit inside the tight little wheels.

Obviously all this massively reduced disc surface area.

That's why Trevor appropriated an idea he had already noted on race-prepped Corvettes: to the outsides of his machined front wheels he attached mass-production engine cooling fans from Chevrolet's air-cooled Corvair. Even trimmed down to fit the 10-inch wheels, they "pulled a huge amount of air through and expelled it to the outside." That did help, but marginally. Any running without the fans quickly faded the brakes to ineffectiveness.

Happily, the rear brakes didn't present that problem. Harris adopted the commonplace practice of mounting them inboard next to the transaxle. Then he spent a lot of time trying to rig forced cooling by means of another Corvair fan driven from the gearbox — which was Hewland's Indycar variant with a protruding starter shaft — but finally gave in to the calendar and simply installed a couple of ordinary air scoops feeding in from above. They worked fine.

FURTHER DRAMA

Because the small wheels had to rotate so much faster than conventional ones, something had to be done about the four-speed Hewland LG500's standard final-drive ratio. By cutting and welding gearwheels to fit shafts they hadn't been made for, Shadow's craftsmen managed to produce the necessary new top gearset. But fitting the larger gearwheel on the lower, "input" shaft required a bulge be welded onto the transmission case.

English manufacturer Mike Hewland must have heard about this hot-rod mod, because he stopped by the Shadow premises and declared it would never work. Although his product did pump gear oil onto the heavily loaded final-drive gears, it relied on splash lubrication for the intermediate gearsets. He predicted failure when these were subjected to significantly higher rpm.

Hot-Rod Harris says he was delighted to have Hewland's criticism of his plan. He took it as an alert to engineer a pressure supply. Laughing, he looks back and declares, "It worked great. We never had any trouble with the gears at all."

Ultra-small wheels also brought suspension consequences. Here too, Harris had to design something unique. At the front, the steerable hub, its associated linkage, and the upper and lower locating arms all had to fit within the 10-inch rims, along with the brakes.

"The front suspension was a huge compromise to me. I like long links, I try to put them in all my cars, but there was no room with the Shadow. And because of the wide tire treads, I was very concerned about camber change. So I took a gamble on parallelogram geometry working through short suspension travel, two or three inches. The ground clearance was 2½ inches.

"My steering kingpin axis was vertical and ahead of the wheel centerline. There was no camber change, and zero bump steer throughout the wheel travel."

Life was easier at the back. The two tubular wishbones also were parallel, but of different lengths and mounting points. The broad-based upper N-frame pivoted on a longitudinal brace atop the gearbox, the A-shaped lower farther out, under the brakes. The difference made for a slight amount of camber change with wheel motion, but Harris says it was only about a degree and a half and he could live with that.

Suspensions need springs, and here too it was necessary to depart from convention. Industry-standard coil spring/damper units were too bulky for the tight space available. Harris turned to short, slender coils that looked like large engine valve springs. Actually they were Die Springs, commonly used in auto plants to separate stamping dies after the formation of a three-dimensional body panel. He packaged trios of these together at all four corners of the car.

Trevor is still enthusiastic about these Die Springs. "You can get them anywhere, and they come color-coded in hundreds of different sizes and strengths, so it's easy to mix-and-match to get just the spring rate you want."

But his choice of dampers (shock absorbers) was not as successful. Not nearly. Thinking to avoid the extra complication of sourcing — or making — very small hydraulic units and working out how to mount them in very cramped quarters, Trevor reached back into automotive history and revived the friction shock. Like a multi-disc friction clutch, this is a hamburger of small steel "patties" clamped against matching "buns" of a fibrous material that resists slipping. Tightening a center nut increases the friction, i.e. the damping. Or it's supposed to.

Even to enthusiasts familiar with friction shocks from the olden days, these looked archaic in 1969–70. Trevor answered raised eyebrows by blithely remarking, "Friction technology has come a long way in 50 years."

But he admits he was blowing smoke. "They were terrible shocks! We had all the old stick-slip problems that made everybody abandon them in the first place. The car just jumped and danced around. People would come in from watching it around the course and tell me they saw inches of air underneath all the tires!

"I think friction shocks were my biggest mistake on that car."

Well, maybe that's challenged by his burying the radiators in the tail. It was a forced decision, though. No other location was workable.

The traditional up-front position was out. Harris was so zealous about low frontal area that the nose of his car was way too shallow to accommodate normal heat-exchanger matrixes. In fact he never intended to put one there. When he and Nichols posed for a photo with his plywood mockup, Trevor casually set a handy rad on the floor just ahead of a rear wheel (see page 43).

That was just a photogenic suggestion, of course, but other designers — Jim Hall with his 1966 Chaparral 2E was a notable early example — were finding that radiators can work perfectly well when integrated into the car's hips or flanks. It's a common layout to this day.

But the AVS Mk I offered no suitable place for radiators anywhere along the entire midsection. The most logical position, either side of the engine, was entirely taken up by fuel tanks. These had to be there, because it was impractical to carry fuel farther forward, alongside the cockpit, as did most cars of the day. Can-Am's rulebook was thin, but it did require doors of certain specified dimensions.

One of the few regulations imposed from Day One had to do with the SCCA wanting to present Can-Ams as sports cars. Therefore builders had to include token doors either side, each offering an unobstructed area measuring at least 30 cm deep (11.8 inches) and 50 cm wide (19.7 inches). With a car of conventional height that was not much of a problem, likely because the rule had been written with them in mind.

But on the low-line Shadow, the mandatory doors took up most of the car's depth. Only a scanty four inches (10 cm) remained for monocoque structure there, not really enough for practical fuel tankage and certainly not for effective radiators.

Some designers manage to incorporate engine coolers in the sides of the body, and indeed Shadows to come would have such a configuration. But Trevor's tiny one left him no room. Making it narrow to harmonize with its low height, he allowed just 62 inches (1,575 mm) of monocoque chassis width between its outer edges, as measured at the rear of the cockpit area. With 40 inches (1,016 mm) devoted to the driver and theoretical passenger, either door sill came to 11 inches (279 mm) wide. Noticeably narrower than with conventional Can-Am cars.

What about sticking rads atop the bodywork somewhere? Anathema! This was Trevor's super-low-drag car! No, the only choice he saw was to tuck them down behind the rear wheels.

ABOVE The best moment in the birth of any new car — getting to sit in it! The man who designed this one looks happy with the "go-kart" driving position; the man who paid for it, not so much. Apparent here is the "duallie" appearance of the tire treads, early examples of Firestone's problems in keeping their profile level. *Don Nichols collection*

OPPOSITE Undergoing restoration, this is an AVS Mk I chassis in original longtail form, but with later conventional steering wheel position. Open access panels reveal the nearly horizontal pedals (the throttle is in darkness but is similar to the visible brake). Stainless steel rivets show nicely against the black-anodized aluminum panels. Nestling between two 25-gallon fuel cell boxes, the Big Block Chevrolet is clamped between transverse aluminum mounting plates. *Pete Lyons*

BELOW In this recent image Harris points to one of four bolts that mate his front suspension module to the monocoque. The package includes the outer half of the 10-inch front wheel, the drastically trimmed-down 8-inch brake disc, and hub carrier plus upper and lower suspension arms fabricated of steel. Seen under Trevor's finger is one of the trio of small, color-coded Die Springs clasped between machined aluminum pods, while tucked in close to the lower pivot point is the Harris Revival friction shock absorber. *Freddi Harris*

Far from an ideal choice. AVS Mk I's engine always ran on the edge of overheating, and although the elephant ears did help, test driver George Follmer seemed unable to remember how wide the scoops were. Or maybe he simply didn't like them. He kept bashing the projections against trackside obstructions. Instantly the water temp soared.

Trevor can chuckle about it now. "Don't ever, ever put your radiators down behind your rear wheels, that's all I've got to say!"

His obsession with low drag also presented challenges with the engine itself. To carry it as low as possible, he had to shrink the size of the flywheel and starter ring gear — which required making up an angled drive from the starter motor — and fabricate the absolute shallowest of oil-sump pans. The rotating crankshaft very nearly scraped the metal.

So there was no depth left for the usual dry-sump system's oil pickup. Pondering this, Trevor visualized the whirling crankshaft throwing all the oil to just one side of the sump, so that's the side where he installed his pickups. It worked perfectly well, he says with satisfaction, and he considers it another Harris innovation that swept through the industry.

He also considers his first-ever monocoque chassis design a success. "I was familiar with them from working on other cars, and it actually was pretty straightforward."

But the man had to do it his own way. After having his thin, 6061 T6 alloy sheet metal panels trimmed, bent, and drilled for rivets, he sent them out to be anodized black. This process stiffened the material, and also hardened the surfaces against inevitable careless scratching.

Then, although shop personnel fastened the panels together in the conventional manner, with both adhesives and rivets, Harris specified not the Bucked rivets commonplace in the racecar and aviation industries, but Blind rivets — "Pop rivets" as he persists in calling them. Bucking rivets is often a two-person operation, but with Blind rivets someone working solo can quickly and easily "pop" long lines of them, especially using a pneumatic tool.

"Don Nichols wasn't very mechanical," Trevor remembers with a grin, "but for some reason he loved pulling rivets. He would come in on Saturdays to do that."

The structure was a success. "We did 3,000 miles of testing and racing with that first one, and we never popped a seam."

The car's weight distribution was a different matter. The radiator-heavy tailpiece, as well as the rearward position of the fuel cells, plus the sad fact that financial shortfalls forced the team to run heavy iron L88 engines (a penalty of about 150 lb over Chevy's aluminum ZL1), all piled a lot of pounds on the rear tires. With the car fully fueled, they might carry as much as three-quarters of its total weight. Other mid-engine designers usually specified a better-balanced two-thirds or so.

The Shadow's imbalance could have been worse. Cramped dimensions restricted each of its rectangular fuel tanks to only 25 US gallons for a total of 50 (182 liters). By stark contrast, McLaren's M8B of 1969 could carry 72 US gallons (272 liters), a quantity this all-conquering team chose so cars could comfortably cover the longest Can-Am race non-stop. Shadow Mk I would have to refuel, if it lasted that long.

Since we have you daydreaming about driving, let's have you step into the original Shadow cockpit. Go ahead, that's a dare. Do you feel comfortable lying practically on your back, your

ABOVE A second chassis photographed on another occasion shows the original single-spoke steering wheel at its initial "bus driver's" position. The knobbed lever at driver's left operates the clutch because there are only two foot pedals, awkwardly angled to fit the very shallow footbox. A combination of cables and rods constitute the shift linkage, which has to thread aft through very tight places. *Pete Lyons*

head cranked up on your straining neck to peer forward over your tummy? Are you happy about that stout steering column standing straight up from your crotch? That tiny nine-inch wheel laying level in your hands? And how about that cramped little footwell, scarcely seven inches deep — how long are your racing shoes? Are you OK with cranking your feet sharply left and right to operate the only two pedals in there?

Ahh… where's the clutch pedal? Stretch out your left hand to the big knob on the long lever next to your leg.

Uhm… what about my right hand? Is it supposed to both steer and change gear at once?

Don't worry. You can still use your left hand for steering once you get good at shifting without the clutch. After all, George could do it.

Fearless Follmer was an adaptable fellow, and he could live with the crazy cranked pedals, but test by test he got Harris to sit him up so he could see better, and to angle the steering column so he could steer better.

What about frontal area, the designer wails? To which the driver retorts, what about driving the racecar properly?

So seating position must rank as another of

Trevor's well-meaning mistakes. By the time he moved his driver into place to do his job, the dream of ultra-low drag was fading. So the centerline of the body could just as well have been high enough to allow three conventional pedals. And inboard brakes. And a front radiator.

But we are nothing but armchair warmers chiming in half a century later. Who are we to criticize the ideas and efforts of those real warriors who created this innovative racetrack weapon as best they knew how?

Think of the adversities they faced and the magnitude of what they accomplished, all with little time and less money, and so much of it with their own hands and minds and stamina as they toiled away through endless dark hours in their own shop.

That first Nichols AVS Shadow doesn't rank with the most successful racers of all time, but that it came to exist at all is an epic saga of stubborn resolve and endless ingenuity. And unending exhaustion.

OK. Tiny Tires fitted to tiny wheels, car bolted together, fluids in, coachwork resplendent in Tangerine gelcoat… let's get outside and test the thing.

WALT BOYD
DEBUTANT DRIVER

RACERS are get-it-done people. And after they finally get a racecar ready to run, they just have to run it. Whether or not there's an actual racecar driver standing around.

Thus it came about that the very first person to try out the newly built AVS Shadow Mk I was one who helped build it.

Walt Boyd was one of Shadow's small bunch of ace craftsmen, a talented fabricator who could make anything out of anything. It was Boyd who drew the job of modifying the Hewland gearbox to accept the larger gearset, for one example of many intricate accomplishments.

But in an earlier life, back East, Walt had raced Midgets and Sprint Cars on short oval tracks. That made him the best man in the shop to see if their new baby felt like a racecar.

Which happened, you guessed it, on the public street. There came a weekday afternoon when the car was finally ready to go, so Walt wriggled down into the cramped cockpit.

"Seems to me I was sitting on the tub, there wasn't a seat," he recalled long decades later. "It was a little bitty steering wheel. The pedals took some getting used to. Of course you had a hand clutch, so you shifted without the clutch. It shifted pretty good.

"I was afraid to really get on it. I didn't want to damage all the hard work so many people put into building it. And I'm an oval racer, I've never raced on a road course. But the Shadow did feel like a racecar. No way I could resist putting my foot down!"

Borchard Avenue was tucked away in a secluded industrial area surrounded by other businesses, not by private homes, but the shattering bellow of a Can-Am racing car blasting by their doors instantly drew people out to watch. Apparently they all enjoyed the show and nobody called the cops. Not even when test driver Boyd — who really was trying to be restrained — locked up the front wheels and slid wildly into a parking lot.

"The thing accelerated like a top-fuel dragster! We didn't have the nosepiece on, and the weight distribution was 30/70 or something, so the front end was very light. It felt like I could have wheelied all the way down Borchard Street.

"Coming back by our shop, the front brakes locked. There was a company near us that luckily had quit early, and their lot was empty. I went flying into there, made a big broadslide."

Chastened, Walt crept back to AVS and shut off the noise.

He kept his new job when shakedown testing began at

LEFT Let me outta here! I'm a racecar, I wanna GO! The new Shadow fidgets at the door of the shop, impatient for Walt Boyd to spring it upon an unsuspecting Borchard Avenue. *Don Nichols collection*

ABOVE Walt comes in from a test run and reports to Larry Stellings, entering from the left, and Jim Mederer in his trademark black hat. Maybe they're discussing the array of makeshift metal tabs tacked onto the tail, latest attempt to nail the rear end to the ground. *Courtesy of Walt Boyd*

BELOW At speed trying another spoiler variant. Note the eight simple, no-nonsense engine intakes that replaced the complex original design. We also see this is now "The Dollar Car," flamboyantly announcing that project costs have wildly exceeded what Don Nichols was told to expect. *Don Nichols collection*

nearby Orange County International Raceway. That was a grand name for a dragstrip that happened to have a road circuit added on, a rudimentary one but good enough for initial systems sorting. Several local teams, including Dan Gurney's, would use OCIR for that purpose rather than haul cars out to Riverside, the nearest proper road course but much farther away.

Orange County was where famed Parnelli Jones, Indianapolis 500 winner and legendary master of every other sort of racecar, became the first big-name driver to try out the Shadow.

As Trevor Harris explains, "At this point Firestone wanted a professional driver's opinion, so they asked Parnelli to come over. He was one of their contracted drivers, but he was supposed to be retired from big-time racing. He still did his off-road stuff, but his partner Vel Miletich wanted him to quit racing entirely and concentrate on their business. He told Parnelli, 'No more racecars!'"

That Jones boy came anyway. OCIR wasn't much of a track, but Firestone only wanted his opinion as to whether the radical, highly experimental Tiny Tire car was worth continuing with. Trevor breaks into one of his gleeful grins.

LEFT Tall Dan Gurney, at right, looks at first glance to have accepted his neighbor Don Nichols's challenge to a drag race at Orange County International Raceway. Alas, his highly modified McLaren M6B "McLeagle" has simply stopped on its way to the transporter to show us the Shadow's ultra-low stance. The AVS is without its front brake cooling fans. *Don Nichols collection*

"He said, 'Yeah, this is a real car. Keep going with it.'

"Vel never knew about that!"

Walt Boyd was there that day, and his assessment was, "I don't think he drove any harder than I did."

Parnelli seemed to back that up when I asked him, because he could scarcely recall anything of that day. He was complimentary about the Shadow team, against which his Vel's Parnelli team competed later, but could pull up nothing to say about testing Shadow's very first car. Memory too full of actual hard racing elsewhere, probably.

But the pace of testing ramped up when George Follmer came into the program. "He had no hesitation to get on the gas hard!" Walt laughs.

Back at his day job, Boyd tackled the job of modifying the Hewland gearbox. "It was quite a project. I had to carve it up so it could take the larger gear.

"I cut a big window in the bottom and back side of the box, and since it was magnesium, I covered the opening with 1/8 or 3/16 magnesium plate welded in place. Not terribly difficult, mag welds pretty easily. But I still wonder why they couldn't just change the ring and pinion ratio."

Walt made these mods to at least two transaxles, both of which still exist, then went on to all the other work awaiting his magic touch. But Nichols's financial state was sinking, and so meeting payroll was a mounting issue. Men with mouths to feed had to leave. Boyd was gone before the wrecked car returned from Canada.

"Leaving was a money thing. We weren't getting paid. I was one of the last two guys, along with Larry Stellings. He and I left and went into business together… [but] I always liked Nichols.

"I think Don Nichols deserves more credit then he ever got. Wasn't he more successful in Formula 1 than other Americans? He was in it longer, and won an equal number of GPs to Gurney and Penske.

"He was a mystery man, I guess he liked it that way. I always got along well with him. He was a good guy.

"One day at Orange County Don challenged Dan Gurney to a drag race. They didn't do it," Walt adds with disappointment in his voice.

In later years Nichols hired Boyd to assemble another Mk I chassis, likely the one that became a museum piece in Germany. "There was some existing old stock, but I had to make a lot of extra parts. Some were hard to make. I used a press brake to cut and bend panels, and had to get them anodized. Then I used the same stainless rivets we did back then."

Though now into his 80s, Walt Boyd is still building racecars. His dream is to create a single design that's suitable not only for road courses but paved and dirt ovals as well, and so inexpensive to manufacture that young talent from anywhere can afford it. Today's computer-operated machine tools make that possible, he says.

Born racer Boyd has his prototype done and it's undergoing track development — by appropriate drivers.

IN ACTION AT LAST

SHADOW'S Tiny Tires first rolled for real at the Orange County International Raceway, the dragstrip/road course a convenient 13 miles from the AVS shop in Santa Ana. There builder/driver Walt Boyd made sure the new machine was ready for serious track work, Parnelli Jones gave Firestone his blessing, and then the team started making the 50-mile freeway drive east to Riverside International Raceway.

That's where George Follmer, Trevor Harris's pro-driver friend, jammed his lead foot onto the awkwardly angled gas pedal and started uncovering problems.

One was speed, or lack of it. The entire rationale for the car's radical design was to reach radical velocities on Riverside's mile-long straightway. Harris had predicted 250 mph.

How embarrassing it must have been for Don Nichols when a speed-measuring crew from the Japan Auto Federation set up their timing equipment on the long straight. The Shadowman had asked them to come and prove his designer's prediction of jawdropping velocity.

Records of the result have eluded us. Possibly because the result was not worth recording. As Trevor remembers it ruefully, "I'm not sure

THESE PAGES As Walt Boyd started lapping Orange County's dragstrip-based road circuit, Firestone's toiling engineers took advantage of their relationship with a somewhat more famous superstar and asked Indy 500 champion Parnelli Jones (in the bright blue shirt) to come out and render his opinion. Did this radically experimental vehicle actually feel like a big-time racecar? Sure, go for it said "Ruf," and he sent Don Nichols an autographed snapshot to prove it. So Trevor Harris recommended that Nichols hire one of Firestone's favorite — and fastest — contracted test drivers, George Follmer. *Don Nichols collection*

what we did. Maybe 162, that seems to pop up in my mind.

"Obviously we had a big problem. Either our drag was way higher than I anticipated, or our horsepower was way lower than we thought it was. It was harder to change the body, so we looked at the engine."

For months, AVS had its Big Block Chevys built by engine guru Fred Larson, who worked at the hot-rod shop owned by Nichols's business partner Dean Moon. It was Larson's dynamometer that guided evolution of the fuel-injection system away from the original tall "periscope" configuration.

Harris had designed that for minimum possible wind resistance. A slender horizontal plenum with a single orifice at the front fed air down through a single row of eight vertical ducts into the V8's cylinders. As their spacing was close together, these were hand-made of sheet metal with rectangular sections to maximize cross-section area.

But it wasn't enough. The dyno said the engine was starving. During further testing, the single tall periscope gave way to a series of shorter twin-orifice designs. Each one seemed better, but it wasn't until the team abandoned all thoughts of streamlining, and simply bolted on eight conventional tubular intakes in two rows, that the engine came to life.

Or seemed to. "It looked good on Moon's dyno, but we just couldn't make it work in the car," Harris explains. "We tried everything we could think of, but we never figured out why."

Eyes fell on the fuel injection itself. At Moon's shop, the default choice was the Hilborn system commonly used in the American speed-equipment industry. Originated for oval speedway racing, it also worked well on drag strips and in speed-record cars. But road racers, a relatively new breed in the US, were finding it lacking in low-speed throttle response and flexibility.

That's when Nichols turned to Can-Am engine builder Lee Muir. He worked for

THE TINY ONE **81**

THESE PAGES Ongoing development at OCIR, Riverside and Laguna Seca resulted in many evolutionary changes, including a Lucas-injected Chevy motor better suited for road racing and, finally, a proper rear wing to tame the tail. *Don Nichols collection*

McLaren during the season but was open to freelance work in the wintertime. Muir replaced the Hilborn setup with the English-made Lucas system that McLaren and others used, complete with the distinctive huge, towering intake trumpets.

Taking it a step farther, AVS replaced the original, restrictive exhaust system. Instead of modestly hidden piping winding down and back between mechanical elements to outlets under the tail, a no-nonsense array of larger headers and collectors rose boldly out of the engine compartment.

"Suddenly we had real horsepower!" exclaims Harris. He was less enthusiastic about adding still more aero drag.

More power highlighted other issues. The tiny brakes easily overheated. So did the engine; the rear-mounted radiators weren't really doing the job. Neither were those Tiny Tires. Firestone's engineers kept working hard, and did make progress over time, but the abnormally high air pressure required to keep the treads flat on the road caused the tiny wheels to bounce off it. Which misbehavior the tiny friction shocks couldn't tame.

Harris describes another weird phenomenon: "The car would come in from running laps with the tires mysteriously flat. I finally realized that, because our small wheels were turning so much faster than usual, centrifugal force was overwhelming the little springs in the tire valve stems.

"The solution was to put on valve caps. Usually I didn't bother. It's a problem I've never had with any other racecar."

The most visible part of the car, its body, may have evolved the most during the months of testing. As had been foreseen, the new aerodynamic restrictions for 1970 badly compromised the designer's original concept. Harris would never learn whether or not his vision had been viable; all he knew was that, lacking the articulating spoilers, rear-end downforce was seriously insufficient.

Test by test, work continued on the afterbody. New openings were cut into the stern. Various crude-looking ducktails were tacked atop the tail. Early on, the airflow-smoothing rear wheel fairings were taken off for the last time — easy wheel-changing was more important.

A day came when Trevor Harris faced facts. He had tried everything else he could think of to nail down his long, wingless car's rear end, with no success. So he gave in. Don Borth fabricated a wing to spoil the clean airflow above the long, sleek tail.

"We took the car all the way up to Laguna Seca [at Monterey, California] and George started driving around with the new wing perched up on top of the longtail body," Harris recounts. "It really worked. The car was fast for the first time. George was throwing it around so hard that he kept knocking those rear scoops into things.

"That's when I decided to just literally chop off the tail. I did it myself."

Of course that required someplace else to put the radiators. Harris being Harris, he came up with something novel: a pair of long, shallow coolers perched atop the wing across its very rear edge. "It worked sort of like a porous Gurney flap, and increased downforce along with cooling the car.

"That's the way we went to Mosport." ▲

THE TINY ONE 83

CHAPTER 5
SHORT AND SAD

THE 1970 SEASON

JUNE 14th, RACE DAY for the opening round of the new Can-Am season, was coming up fast. The venue would be Canada's Mosport Park, almost as far from Southern California as one can drive, a long haul diagonally across all of North America past Toronto in Ontario province.

But the Shadow program, seemingly so comfortable at the outset, was now in serious financial distress.

Despite months of hard work to make presentations nationwide, Don Nichols had not landed a corporate sponsor. He had committed to cover shortfalls himself, expecting to rely on regular payments from his old Japanese business. But the caretaker he left in charge in Tokyo wasn't doing the job. The AVS office telex machine was kept smoking with trans-Pacific queries and assurances, and at one point a promise came through that a check had been sent. But only the promise ever arrived.

Near the end of 1969, Nichols realized that the "$40,000 to $50,000" initial budget that Trevor Harris had casually suggested had swollen monstrously. In later years Don said he had spent a million dollars. A more contemporary source, a 1971 article in *Road & Track*, puts the figure at half that. Either way, it was a fair chunk of change to squander.

To be fair to Trevor, he had been asked for an estimate to build one car. It had been Don's decision to set up a small factory with all necessary equipment, hire the best staff, build several chassis and go professional racing at the top level.

But that's the way the man was. Characteristically, Nichols "celebrated" his financial problem by putting prominent "$" signs in the test car's number roundels. Forever after, he gleefully called this "The Dollar Car."

But by springtime 1970 he was truly running out of money. Key personnel had departed. Only a faithful skeleton staff remained. These included Harris, determined to see it through;

a trained engineer and keen amateur racer named Jim Mederer; and "Teji," short for Noritchka Tejima, a loyal young mechanic whom Nichols had befriended in Japan. Only they would be going to Canada with Nichols.

Pre-race preparations were ongoing when Sheriff's Deputies appeared at the door. Earlier, Nichols had engaged an architect to spruce up his Palos Verdes home, but couldn't (or wouldn't) pay for the job. The lawmen presented a court order to seize two Shadow racecars, and produced a copy of the Japanese magazine *Auto Sport* showing the pair they wanted. One was a partly assembled orange car bearing number 2, the other what looked like a complete, race-ready black one numbered 1.

"Of course that was never a real car," says Trevor with his trademark grin about the black version, which had also appeared on the cover of *Road & Track*. "It was just Wayne Hartman's body buck painted up in black to cover the Bondo and mounted on a fake chassis he made out of plywood. I don't remember how he made the wheels, but they weren't real either."

As fellow Shadow employee Kent Telford would later write in his own *R&T* story, quoted here at the end of this chapter, that black-bodied mockup was on display in the shop, so to the court it would satisfy half the judgement. Apparently nothing else in sight was clearly the orange vehicle, at least to laymen's eyes, so the Shadowman realized they had an opportunity to exercise a little racer's ingenuity. Trevor grins again as he tells the tale:

"We quickly knocked up a crude frame out of square tubing and draped one of our genuine production bodies over it. I did the welding. It wasn't the best job of welding I ever did."

Meanwhile, out of sight, measures were being taken to secure the team's single running, race-ready machine, the same "Dollar Car" used for all the testing. Time was too short to build another — but long enough to worry that the plaintiff would realize he had been conned.

ABOVE & BELOW En route to their race debut at Mosport, Shadow's merry band stopped in Akron to show their friends at Firestone what their tire money had made possible. Walking Raymond Firestone around the AVS Mk I, smooth salesman Don Nichols might have had to reach deep into his long years of practice at wheeling and dealing to explain why the stubby orange machine with its unusual rear wing looked so different from the lean little black streamliner he'd promised 18 months before. *Don Nichols collection*

RIGHT Rolling through the Mosport paddock, the startlingly low-slung Shadow is dwarfed by Peter Bryant's conventionally sized Titanium Car in the foreground. At the time, nobody knew that a year later Bryant would be working with Don Nichols on a semi-conventional Mk II Shadow. *Pete Lyons*

BELOW Japanese mechanic Teji steers the car into its pit, giving an astonished world a good look at the novel rear wing with radiators on top. *Pete Lyons*

There came a mad, dark-of-night scramble to spirit the Can-Am racer out the back door of the shop and into a trailer. Then they bundled a hired driver into a stake-bed truck to haul the precious fruit of a year's work out of California.

Following on by plane, Nichols shepherded Harris, Mederer and Tejima to Ohio, where they reconvened at the Firestone headquarters with their hired driver and their racecar to show their supporters where all their Tiny Tire development money had gone. Then it was on to Toronto to finish building the racecar and spend a hard week of development testing at Mosport.

To properly set the scene, it must be acknowledged that Shadow's troubles were not the only ones darkening the Can-Am mood. For one thing, the new 1970 regulations had unfortunately emasculated a rare form of racing machine once known for its wild and free lack of restrictive rules.

From now on Can-Am would evolve into just one more series offering ever more conventional cars.

Then, just 10 days before the opening race, Bruce McLaren had been killed during a testing accident in England. The man whose bright spirit and natural ability to lead a team had shaped McLaren Racing into the "Bruce and Denny Show" was gone.

At about the same time, team-mate Denny "The Bear" Hulme had suffered nasty burns to his hands during a fuel fire at Indianapolis.

The Kiwis turned to the best man they knew; Dan Gurney would step into Bruce's empty seat.

ABOVE LEFT Caution, mad genius at work. The fertile Harris mind is full of ideas, but sometimes it takes a while to locate them. *Pete Lyons*

ABOVE RIGHT & LEFT "What the heck has he done to it this time?" George may be thinking as he reacquaints himself with the ever-changing Dollar Car. The gigantic engine's towering inlet stacks, plus the twin trumpets that cool the rear brakes, pretty much ruin Trevor's original Knee-High concept. The driver's insistence on sitting upright hasn't helped either. "But at least he can drive it now," mechanic Teji (at right) may be thinking. *Pete Biro*

MOSPORT, ONTARIO (CDN)
Can-Am (R1), June 14th, 1970
1st, Dan Gurney, McLaren M8D
DNF, George Follmer, AVS Mk I, overheating

Your scribe had the good fortune to be present at Shadow's first race. I had been reading about the novel car, but it was the first time I saw it in person. Here's a portion of what I wrote about it for *Autosport* of England:

"Honours for The Most Astonishing Design went to the AVS Shadow… The car is hard to believe even when seen, so tiny is it — literally knee-high. It all depends on the minute Firestone tyres, which have 11ins and 16ins [wide] footprints but are mounted on wheels 10ins and 12ins in diameter. It is said the carcass construction is more flexible than a normal tyre to give a longer footprint, and naturally the rubber compound is harder; pressures in the

region of 37psi are used. Temperatures appear to be normal…

"When this insignificant-looking little 'go-kart' explodes into 7-litre life on the circuit the effect is attention-getting to say the least. [George] Follmer appears to be working very hard in the corners, and admits the term 'go-kart' is not wildly inappropriate. Hand timing indicates that its cornering power is not especially high, and on the straights the rear wheels seem to bound clear of the road, producing a quaver in the exhaust note. This

ABOVE "When this insignificant-looking little 'go-kart' explodes into 7-litre life on the circuit the effect is attention-getting to say the least. [George] Follmer appears to be working very hard in the corners, and admits the term 'go-kart' is not wildly inappropriate" — from the author's race report in England's *Autosport* magazine. *Pete Lyons*

RIGHT Even when they jacked the car up, photographers went low to shoot it. With doors removed along with the nosepiece, we clearly see in the side view the stout struts adding stiffness to the shallow midsection of the monocoque. These are easily removed by the driver, but he doesn't seem to bother about doing so. Note the cockpit ventilation holes in the door, and the rectangular outlet for brake cooling airflow. *Pete Lyons*

problem seems to arise under heavy braking as well, and [as George remarked to me] the little wheels 'find all the holes.'"

To his team, he remarked that the Shadow was so much lower than other cars that sometimes their drivers seemed unable to see him alongside.

On the other hand, even with a large wing now in place Trevor Harris's low-drag concept did yield higher terminal velocities. Official clocking along Mosport's long, uphill back straight reportedly showed the Shadow was easily the fastest car in the field, by some

ABOVE From almost any vantage point, the eye goes to the massive 427 (7-liter) Chevrolet V8 and its imposing array of flared intake trumpets. The manly exhaust headers look they're trying to escape the cramped engine bay. Twin snorkels duct cooling air to the inboard rear brakes. Little doors atop the body show where fuel goes into the two 25-gallon tanks in the flanks. *Pete Lyons*

LEFT Not what the back end of a "normal" Can-Am car looks like. When Trevor Harris decided it was time to abandon his rear-mounted radiators, he simply chopped off several feet of structure and didn't take time to put bandages over the surgery site. There is a normal Hewland transaxle in there, but it's so densely packaged with other things that not even the "normal" shift linkage fits. Instead, a pair of push-pull cables writhe through and around to mate up with Mike Hewland's original hardware. *Pete Lyons*

SHORT AND SAD **89**

RIGHT & BELOW According to the Can-Am rulebook this is a "sports car," because it has space for two seats. But for two people? Even one is challenged to fit, with feet splayed out in a footwell so cramped that there's room only for two pedals. How to work the clutch? That's what the left-hand lever does. At least the manual gearshift lever on the right is familiar. *Pete Lyons*

BOTTOM An access port allows pedal adjustment. *Pete Lyons*

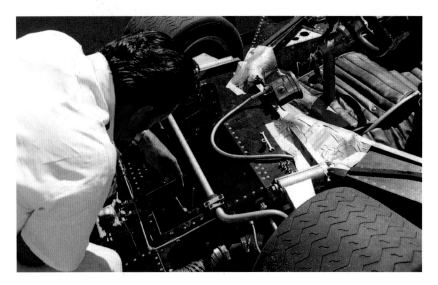

18 mph — 194 mph vs. McLaren's best, 176.

Remarkably, Shadow achieved that despite having the smallest-displacement "Big Block" in the field, Chevrolet's everyday, off-the-shelf, 427 (7-liter) with standard-production iron block — the only engine spec the team could afford.

Soberingly, the Shadow's straightaway speed advantage was more than lost into and around the corners. Front-wheel braking was nearly non-existent, and roadholding frankly terrible. Trackside observers were alarmed to see the Tiny Tires bouncing completely clear of the road.

Yet Fearless Follmer qualified the little 'rollerskate' sixth fastest overall!

The McLaren M8D "Batmobiles" of Dan Gurney, the ultimate race winner, and 1968 series champ Denny Hulme, his paws wrapped in bandages, topped the times. Keep note of who came next: future Shadow Can-Am Champion Jackie Oliver driving the Peter Bryant-built Ti22 "Titanium Car." Then it was Peter Revson's new Lola T220 and Lothar Motschenbacher's McLaren M6B.

Follmer's grid time was a whopping 3.1 seconds slower than Gurney's in the new McLaren. But in fact such gaps were routinely seen in the old Can-Am. It may have been a

FAR LEFT Teji changes a Tiny Tire. But first one has to take off the brake-cooling fan, an item from Chevrolet's air-cooled Corvair trimmed down to fit the 10-inch diameter wheel. *Pete Lyons*

LEFT Trimmed down to eight inches from a much larger original disc, the Shadow's tiny brakes need a lot of help. While we're in here, look for the tiny coil springs that suspend the car. The front friction shocks are not visible from this angle. *Pete Lyons*

ABOVE LEFT & ABOVE At the rear the friction shocks are up top in plain sight. Doesn't mean they work any better.
Pete Biro (above left)
Pete Lyons (above)

RIGHT Tightly packaged, with a lot of Big Car Stuff in a small pot, AVS Mk I was a hard thing to work on. An engine change was a nightmare. It took hours. *Pete Lyons*

SHORT AND SAD **91**

driver's championship, but the bellowing, bestial, wildly individualistic cars were what Can-Am fans came to see.

In the race Follmer passed Motschenbacher into fifth place, but the Shadow's temperature gauge was rising and he eased back to avoid an engine failure. He knew the team couldn't afford another. Their pre-race testing had been badly needed, but it had been hard on their dwindling stock of tired iron engines. After only 24 laps of the scheduled 80-lap race, George finally pitted and switched off. Perhaps he wasn't too bitterly disappointed.

But Nichols and the team certainly were. This opening race was to be televised across North America, giving the distinctive bright orange Shadow novelty car the best possible publicity. That might result in sponsorship. But when the race began, TV was still covering something else. As Harris remembers it, "They didn't start broadcasting our race until lap 25. The one after we dropped out."

LEFT Fearless Follmer drove a gritty race at Mosport, but not for long. The engine was tired at the start and soon died of heat exhaustion. *Pete Lyons*

OPPOSITE If position counts for points, the Shadow looks pretty good starting from the third row. Follmer was headed in qualifying only by the two McLarens of Dan Gurney (48) and Denny Hulme (5), Jackie Oliver's Titanium Car (22), Peter Revson's Lola (26) and Lothar Motschenbacher's older McLaren (11). Gurney would win after Hulme dropped back, struggling with his painfully burned hands. *Pete Lyons*

BELOW In a blow to Nichols's hopes of attracting sponsors, the Shadow's demise at Mosport occurred just before the race began showing on national TV. *Pete Lyons*

SHORT AND SAD 93

RIGHT As Trevor Harris's original "rads-on-top" wing had been declared illegal at Mosport, he produced this "rads-inside" solution for Saint-Jovite. His new aerofoil effectively was split in half, like an opened sandwich, containing long, shallow cooling cores transversely across the span. *Pete Lyons*

BELOW Air flowed in through the leading-edge slot and exited out the trailing edge. Elegant, efficient, clean-looking, nice. *Pete Lyons*

BELOW RIGHT Unfortunately the new trick wing had to be contrived in frantic haste, far from home base, with necessary hardware only available in ordinary plumbing stores. Pipes were too small, joints too crude, testing time nil. When the car came in boiling like a tea kettle, Shadow's second race weekend was over. *Pete Lyons*

SAINT-JOVITE, QUEBEC (CDN)
Can-Am (R2), June 28th, 1970
1st, Dan Gurney, McLaren M8D
DNF, George Follmer, AVS Mk I, overheating

During tech inspection at Mosport, Harris had been advised that his wing-top radiator violated another new 1970 rule. This limited the upper edge of any "forward-facing air gap" to no higher than 32 inches (80 cm) above the bottom of the chassis. This rule, meant to restrict wing height, also outlawed tall scoops ducting air into the engine intakes, as Harris originally planned his car to have. Permission was granted to run the Shadow at Mosport, but the rule would be enforced for Saint-Jovite. Happily, Harris had been told this would happen, and came prepared. He had already fabricated what he still feels is the most elegant aerofoil he ever designed. This relocated slightly shallower radiators to literally inside the wing itself.

But what about air to cool the radiators? A

doubled leading edge formed a slot along the entire width of the airfoil, making an air gap low enough to meet the regulations. A hinged part of the upper surface allowed access to the internal radiators and their plumbing.

This "split wing" novelty had never actually been mounted and tested, because the team had been forced out of its headquarters early, but following Mosport Harris rigged up the necessary plumbing. Then the Shadowmen headed for Quebec's twisty, hilly, very pretty little "Le Circuit" near the mountain resort community of Mont-Tremblant.

They struggled through another miserable weekend. Trevor's trick new wing appeared not to work after all, when after a few slowish laps on Friday the car returned to the pitlane wreathed in steam.

But Harris still denies his wing itself was to blame. He feels the problem lay in the inefficient, restrictive household plumbing he was forced to cobble together with ordinary hardware store parts. "It was the worst plumbing job I ever did in my life. Horrible. A real Rube Goldberg. It bothered me a lot."

Furthermore, the worn-out engine was only firing on seven cylinders. This was the little team's only remaining engine, they lacked personnel and parts to fix it, and Nichols had no money to bring his new engine specialist Al Bartz from California with a fresh one.

Follmer also suffered some gearbox troubles on Saturday, and his grid position was an unhappy 10th, over five seconds slower than Gurney's pole-position lap.

This time Shadow's race was even shorter. After six laps George uncharacteristically spun off the road, and once going again he made it only to lap 13 before retiring. The engine was overheating again.

But the real disaster happened later, on the public road, as the exhausted, unhappy Harris and Mederer were towing the Shadow away from the circuit. It was raining when a drunken local in a stolen car coming the other way lost

control and speared straight at them. Driver Mederer managed to swerve away from a head-on collision, but the wayward motorist slammed into the trailer, knocking it into the ditch.

The precious racecar inside — the team's one and only racecar — sustained crippling damage.

Trevor Harris was spent physically, emotionally and financially. He flew back to Los Angeles with the others, but then walked away from the team. "I didn't even go back to the shop to pick up my tools and stuff. I was done. It was a long time before I could speak to Nichols."

ABOVE The day the Dollar Car died. Heading away from Saint-Jovite, an oncoming car knocked Shadow's trailer into the ditch. The racecar inside was badly damaged. *Trevor Harris collection*

RIGHT Not what Trevor Harris had in mind. With the ultra-low-drag innovator gone from the team, practical Jim Mederer took over a second chassis and built it into probably the highest-drag Can-Am car on the grid. But hopefully higher downforce would make up for it around the twisty, humpy Ohio circuit. *Pete Lyons*

MID-OHIO (USA)
Can-Am (R5), August 23rd, 1970
1st, Denny Hulme, McLaren M8D
DNF, Vic Elford, AVS Mk I, handling

What, the Shadow was back? Amazingly, after missing two rounds of the season, Nichols had somehow found some more money.

This is speculation by outsiders, but it was thought that legal action he had brought in Japan years before, against the party that had taken away his Goodyear distributorship,

ABOVE Mederer's mods began with an original Shadow wing carried at a very steep angle, and with bulky radiator cores plugging most of the air gap below it. It was hardly a wing anymore. Then he made a stab at replacing his predecessor's friction shock dampers with hydraulic units. He only managed this at the rear, bolting the long tubes into place on a central wing-support plate. At the front the friction discs remained, as did the trios of little springs at all four corners. *Pete Lyons*

RIGHT Firestone came back as well, sending a support crew to what was practically a backyard racetrack. They finally found a purpose for the hitherto useless front fender slots, legacy of Harris's original air-brake scheme. *Pete Lyons*

had finally been decided in his favor.

He phoned Jim Mederer, who had quit and was happily (if unprofitably) racing his own two little formula cars. The younger man agreed to talk, because he did need to start earning some money again, but he knew enough now to inquire precisely what his job would be.

Nichols outlined such a long list that Mederer pointed out these were the duties of a crew chief, not a mere mechanic. He held out for more pay. The older man had to agree.

But what would be Jim's duties? The battered old "Dollar Car" had been pushed into a corner, untouched, so a second chassis had to be completed for Mid-Ohio. It is believed that they commandeered the half-done Toyota project and swapped its 5-liter four-cam engine for a 7-liter pushrod Chevy. Toiling day and night, the diminished team got the job done in time for some pre-race testing at the Ohio circuit.

In marked contrast to the original Harris concept, Mederer abandoned all thought of low drag. Downforce would be everything. An original Mosport-pattern wing — minus top-side radiators — was put on the new chassis, but at an extremely steep angle. Big conventional engine coolers sat in the airstream just below it.

To Trevor Harris's enduring distress, the lowest-drag Can-Am car had turned into probably the dirtiest aerodynamically.

Apparently Mederer resurrected Harris's idea for replacing the rear-end friction shocks with convention hydraulics, although during our interview long years later Jim couldn't remember doing that. He said he had become so tired and stressed already that he wasn't sure what he was doing.

George Follmer came to Ohio for the testing, but he judged the new car — this one painted glossy black like the fake vehicle seen in early photos — as no improvement on the old Tangerine one. He declined to race it.

Having foreseen such a possibility, George

ABOVE George Follmer came back to test the new concept, but felt no improvement in overall performance. He decided his time was better spent in other, better cars in other places. *Don Nichols collection*

BELOW Following Follmer's withdrawal, Vic Elford agreed to step in. The tall Brit appeared to enjoy himself. *Don Nichols collection*

SHORT AND SAD **97**

ABOVE Quick Vic duly started the Mid-Ohio race, intending to pit if he felt the unquestionably wayward car's stability was a danger. Retirement seemed to be inevitable. *Jim Chambers*

BELOW Elford did give it a good go for a few laps, including a tussle with fellow Brit Tony Dean's Porsche — what a contrast in aero concepts! *Pete Lyons*

had talked his friend Vic Elford, a British rally and sports-car star, into tagging along. Keen to break into American racing and hoping for just such an opportunity, "Versatile Vic" agreed to give it a go. Over several days of further testing, he was able to tune the Mk I well enough that he said it had begun to behave like a normal racecar (well, he had founded his career by hurling rally cars over the world's roughest terrain!).

Around corners he thought the Shadow wasn't too bad, on speed if not stability, though in a straight line it was nearly unmanageable. One problem was ultra-quick steering; a change from the nine-inch wheel to a 12-inch one helped. Offering a pointer for the future, he suggested that narrower front tires might improve steering response, and be less disturbed by bumps.

Elford felt the parallelogram suspension geometry was an inherent disadvantage, because it required very stiff spring rates to keep the tires from tilting. However, the four inches of total travel didn't strike him as a problem — many older cars of the day had as little.

Summing up, Vic said that whether this particular car would ever come good was one question, but he could see no reason why the small-diameter Firestone tires themselves should be faulted. He was able to qualify seventh, within four seconds of the fastest.

But once again Shadow's race was short — a mere nine laps this time. The team said the driver stopped because a front wheel weight spun off and the vibration made it impossible to hold the steering wheel, but that it was too time-consuming to fit a new wheel.

That's the story most histories have recorded, but my own live report for *Autosport* went on to record that Elford had told his crew before the start that he would pull in if the car's straightaway instability threatened other drivers' safety, and he had decided this was the case.

Afterward, Nichols announced Shadow's withdrawal from the Can-Am series for the year. But he would push ahead to construct a new, more orthodox vehicle for 1971.

Sure. Defeated racers always vow they'll be back.

OUTCOMES

So Don Nichols's bold play did "lose big." A whole year late and many dollars beyond projections, his Advanced Vehicle Systems' ultra-advanced vehicle appeared in only three of the 1970 season's 10 rounds, showing a bit more performance than perhaps outsiders had expected, but a lot less reliability than any team can accept. Racers are risktakers, they always aim high, but bitter experience teaches them not to overreach. Not to allow what was supposed to be a competitive vehicle to become a "science experiment."

Clearly that happened here, but, as always, failing was an education in itself. The Tiny Tire's tale of woe does trace an interesting, exhausting, very steep learning curve for everyone involved.

Trevor Harris would rebound from his overly ambitious Shadow Mk I experience to become one of the most sought-after creative engineers in motorsport. His long resume of successful car designs includes championship winners for Brock Racing Enterprises, Gurney and Nissan; he also holds numerous patents for innovative designs such as bicycle transmissions and high-angle constant velocity joints. Eventually he reconciled with Don Nichols and rejoined him for two further projects; we'll look in on those later.

Jim Mederer left the perpetually overworked, ever uncertain life of a race team mechanic and co-founded Racing Beat, widely known for its high-performance work with Mazda and particularly with the company's rotary engine.

"Teji" remained loyal to Nichols for several more years, before starting his own auto repair business in Los Angeles. And a family member joined Mederer in his Racing Beat enterprise.

Versatile Vic Elford, having shown his eagerness to try something novel, got a call later that summer from Jim Hall, inviting him to drive Chaparral's similarly experimental 2J Ground Effects Vehicle. Unlike the Tiny Tire Shadow, the Chaparral Fan Car was fast.

Tiny Tiremaker Firestone had taken its best shot; now it was time to move on. The expense had probably been higher than anticipated, but any such manufacturer maintains developmental budgets to evaluate new product ideas. Supporting the Shadow experiment had been a normal cost of doing business.

The money was well spent, in fact. The Akron race tire engineers could in good conscience report back to their Detroit client that they really had tried their hardest to make ultra-small tires work in the red-hot crucible of auto racing. Oldsmobile could be satisfied that failure was not due simply to lack of effort or commitment.

And indeed, the automaking industry did not go in that direction. Styling's "hidden wheels" idea was quietly forgotten.

Well… not exactly.

A rival firm did not forget. Six years later, and an ocean away, Goodyear's UK racing tire engineers cooperated with the Tyrrell Formula 1 team to produce Derek Gardner's astonishing six-wheeler. Seeking lower aero drag, he asked for tires to fit rims of only — what, you've guessed? That's right, a tiny 10 inches in diameter. Four of these held up the front of the Tyrrell P34, the two per side running in tandem, with all four hooked to the steering and each carrying their own individual brakes.

Goodyear's version of tiny tires were only eight inches wide, which could explain why they held their shape whereas Firestone's wider ones didn't. But the pair per side gripped the road like one twice their width. They worked well around the racetrack. Well enough to win a Grand Prix in 1976.

Meanwhile, that Nichols fellow… ♠

KENT TELFORD
SPONSORSHIP GETTER

"WHAT HAPPENED to the Shadow?" That's how *Road & Track* titled its second article about Can-Am's radical newcomer. Published in the magazine's issue for May 1971, not quite two years after *R&T*'s introductory cover story dated August 1969, it was something of an epitaph — and also something of a tell-all expose by an insider.

This was Kent Telford, the young man whom Don Nichols hired to find sponsorship and to help with various other business matters. He penned his piece in the aftermath of 1970's three-races-and-out debacle, when Advanced Vehicles Systems appeared to be sinking into history.

Telford did not arrive at the team as a racer, but he was observant and bright, and picked up enough about the sport to understand why enthusiasts had been excited by Shadow's little black missile. He reckoned they would like to know why they probably would never see it again.

In publishing his story back then, he gave to us in the here-and-now details we've not seen elsewhere, and firmed up timelines that are unclear otherwise. Fifty-year-old memories are often sure of many things about racecars and races, but dates become elusive.

In terms of timing, Telford wrote that, "By the end of 1969 two Shadows were nearly complete. Initial tests on one of them started in January [1970]…" This is later than we had supposed.

And of course a painful portion of a year later than Nichols and his men had dreamed of at the outset.

Next we read of "the first real tests" in February at Laguna Seca, then additional sessions at Riverside beginning in March and extending into May.

Telford's account is nicely flavored with technical nuggets; here are key points:

"One of the first problems to emerge was cooling… good enough for only five hard laps before the 14 psi pressure cap blew its stack." Also there was not enough horsepower, nor enough rear-end downforce to keep the tail on the track. Either the body shape or the 60 psi in the tires might have caused the car's skittishness, "But the body could be changed, the tires could not." So an 8-inch ducktail spoiler appeared.

Our reporter understood what that meant: "Aerodynamic defeat. With the spoiler the frontal area — the Shadow's reason for existence — went up nearly 50 percent! Its big advantage was already nearly lost."

February, timeframe of the Laguna visit, is when he says the engine got its Lucas fuel injection. "This had been a backup system in case the AVS-Hilborn induction system didn't work. Harris had hoped for 700 hp, but with the Lucas he'd have to settle for 600–620. But at least now they could reach 170 mph on Laguna Seca's long sweeping section, and that was fast enough to get down to some serious aero testing.

"In the meantime the spoiler had been replaced by the Shadow's first wing, in the usual hope of getting as much downforce as with a spoiler but with less drag.

"After some infuriating minor problems that wasted three days, the car began running fairly respectably, and with adjustments to suspension, gearing, brakes and fuel metering it got down to one minute three second laps, some four seconds off the existing track record."

Back at Riverside, Telford noted that the "the suspension was working better than many of us thought it would, and the tires were working well enough that we thought they would last for a race."

In mid-April he reported that the heavily modified transaxle was a success. "With 19-inch diameter rear tires and available Hewland gearbox ratios, top speed would have been only 165 mph. Chevrolet division suggested planetary overdrive units between transaxle and wheels; nobody at AVS thought the Hewland would stand the sustained high speeds if an overdrive were imposed between it and the engine.

"Harris took a less interesting but more practical way out: modifying the Hewland gears themselves. The first solution was composite gears, three-piece, welded together for a double-setup fifth gear. The final one was to narrow some of the gears, modify the bearings where necessary and use a 48:26 first gear set upside down for a 0.542:1 fifth gear!

"It took a large welded bulge on the rear of the gearbox to accommodate it. Suitable ratios were available from Hewland for first through third, and another gearset was inverted for fourth. An oil pump was added to force-feed the trick gears, as the normal splash lubrication wasn't adequate."

He also wrote about another of Trevor Harris's solutions, this to address the car's chronic cooling problems. After an unsuccessful attempt to scoop air from the top of the tail and force it downward into the still-buried radiators, he tried relocating the radiators to the top of the wing.

"Two 6 x 22-inch sections of Corvette aluminum radiators were added to the fixed (but adjustable) wing, making not only a heat exchanger but a 6-inch high "porous spoiler" that worked approximately like the 4-inch solid one. Oil coolers were there too — two from MGBs. And the system worked. Harris says that if anything it was too efficient."

Telford also shared the difficulties he himself had faced in seeking financial support. "It was becoming painfully obvious that 1970 was the worst possible year to find racecar sponsorship, especially for an untried car. We secured $10,000 for the rights to make a model of the car [from Mattel's Hot Wheels], but otherwise all the more than $500,000 spent was Don's own money.

"AVS desperately needed a sponsor. The Mosport race was the only race of the Can-Am series to be televised; maybe, just maybe, there would be someone out there in the tube's vast wasteland who would see the Shadow and want to be a part of its unique effort. So AVS would go to Mosport, come hell or high water."

But then trouble showed up.

BELOW Compared to its original design, the Knee High's cockpit was a paragon of practicality. But compared to ones George was used to... Hey, is there a bar open around here? *Pete Biro*

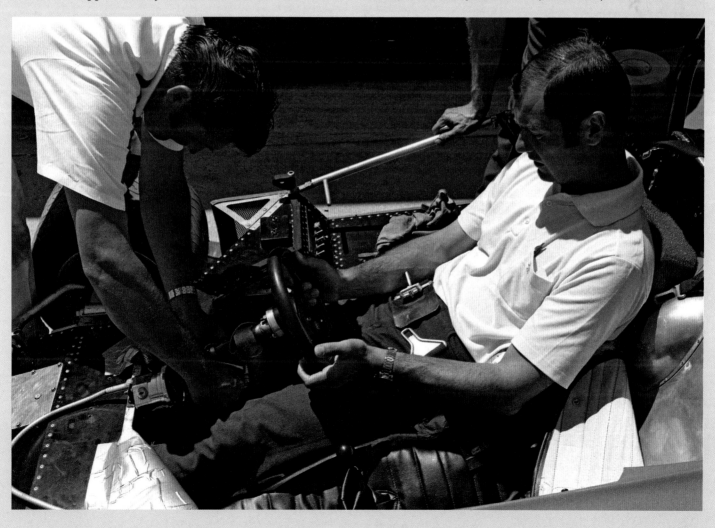

"In mid-May, two law enforcement officers quietly walked into the shop and told the AVS people they had come to issue a writ of attachment for two Shadows.

"This pair of lawmen had seen the new Toyota Shadow [the one carrying the loaner 4-cam 5.0] and the fiberglass mockup for the original car, both in the front of the shop. They hadn't seen the real Shadow behind a wall at the other end, and soon that was being quietly wheeled out the back of the shop and hidden. After two high-tension hours the policeman took pity on the poor racers and allowed that keepers could be hired to come in and guard the attached cars, allowing the shop people to continue work."

Racers are racers; offered a little leeway, the Shadowmen took a lot. They already had hidden away the one functioning racecar, but they needed a second. So it seems the Toyota V8 gave up its chassis to a Chevy.

Meanwhile, as Harris himself has already told us, a dummy frame was knocked up to go under a spare set of body panels, birthing a lookalike sister to the mockup displayed in the front of the shop.

Telford adds that, "An engine was to go along with the two 'cars' and for this they put cast-iron heads on an iron block with absolutely nothing inside it, painted it, stamped a number on it and eventually surrendered it as one of the engines for the racecars!

"The climax came at 7 am on May 16th, when Don took the front half of the spare Shadow chassis wheelbarrow fashion and wheeled it down the street to a secret shop that had been rented for storage. The keeper was engaged in a diversionary conversation. Now the car and crew could be off to Canada…"

Shadow's adventures north of the border are covered earlier in this chapter, but Telford's *R&T* piece tells of a side trip required to make it all happen.

George Follmer, who had done all the team's speed testing and was the right man to debut the Tiny Tire car in the Mosport race, of course also was working other gigs that summer. One had him at Indianapolis with Andy Granatelli's STP team. He'd qualified for the race on May 17th, but stayed on for pre-race testing and was still there on Sunday, May 24th. That was "Bump Day," still six days before the 500. Nichols phoned him that night to ask when he would arrive in Toronto for a couple of midweek days of shaking down the Shadow at Mosport.

"George allowed that he wouldn't. It seems that the head of STP refused to let any of his drivers do any other driving while they were preparing to do Indy for him.

"At 1 am Don Nichols decided that perhaps Firestone could help encourage Mr. STP to let AVS have its driver. After all, Firestone paid a lot of bills in support of STP somehow or other. So off went Don and two other AVS people to Akron in driving rain and a rent-a-racer. No sleep, of course, and Monday there was a full day of meetings at Firestone on how to get the only man in the world who could drive the Shadow into the car at Mosport. It worked, oddly enough."

To our friends overseas, know that it's a drive of about 315 miles (506 km) between Toronto and Akron. At night. In the rain. Without sleep. Don Nichols was a resolute, tenacious man.

We already know the sad outcome of all that work and worry. The car dropped out early, so the coveted TV exposure was, well, not precisely nil. As the team's

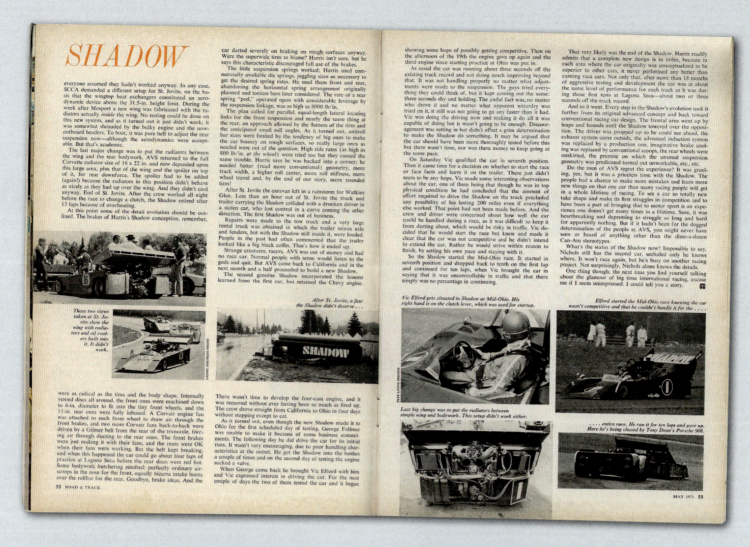

THESE PAGES Telford's piece was richly illustrated with photos (some by this author) showing the AVS experiment at every stage of the machine's short but eventful life. *Road & Track*

sponsor-hunter saw it, Follmer retired on lap 25 [official results say he completed just 13 laps]. National broadcast coverage had begun on lap 20.

"The Shadow appeared once on the tube, and if our Sugar Daddy was watching he would've had to fall in love at first sight."

Kent Telford's five-page article goes on to detail the even less satisfactory Saint-Jovite and Mid-Ohio weekends, but let's fast-forward to his wrap-up thoughts:

"Every step in the Shadow's evolution took it farther from its original advanced concept and back toward conventional racing car design. The frontal area went up by leaps and bounds until the Shadow towered over the opposition. The driver was propped up so he could see ahead, the exhaust system came outside, the advanced induction system was replaced by a production one, imaginative brake cooling was replaced by conventional scoops, the rear wheels were unskirted, the premise on which the unusual suspension geometry was predicated turned out unworkable, etc., etc.

"Do the men of AVS regret the experience? It was grueling, yes, but it was a priceless time with the Shadow. The people had a chance to make more mistakes and learn more new things on that one car than many racing people will get in a whole lifetime of racing.

"To see a car so totally new take shape and make its first struggles in competition, and to have been a part of bringing that to motorsport, is an experience one doesn't get many times in a lifetime. Sure, it was heartbreaking and depressing to struggle so long and hard for apparently nothing.

"But if it hadn't been for the dogged determination of the people at AVS, you might never have seen or heard of anything other than the dime-a-dozen Can-Am stereotypes."

CHAPTER 6
THE MIDSIZE ONE

SHADOW MK II, 1971

AS RIVAL racers do, Don Nichols and Peter Bryant would have developed a circumspect camaraderie at the track, and the Brit took a step toward actual friendship with the Yank early in 1970. After Saint-Jovite, where his first-generation Titanium Car backflipped to destruction, Peter offered Don his superfluous motel room reservations.

As things turned out, Nichols didn't need the rooms either. Still, near the end of that year, when Bryant called to ask for a meeting about a fresh start, the Shadowman readily invited him to his Palos Verdes home. There, with both well aware that the Englishman had wound up the Can-Am season with the fastest American-built car, Peter succeeded in rekindling Don's fire to go racing again.

Indeed, they formed enough rapport that Peter must have thought he had come to know Don rather well. But then they traveled cross-country together.

Bryant's book *Can-Am Challenger* (David Bull Publishing, 2007), explains that Nichols had abandoned the bitterly disappointing 1970 Mid-Ohio Shadow almost on the spot, leaving it on a nearby farm owned by family members. Now he proposed to Bryant that they fly back East to retrieve it. Since Don was in no position — nor in any mood, one might presume — to get back into racing in the same lavish manner as before, his idea was that Peter should economize by incorporating as much of the left-over Trevor Harris racecar as possible in a new Shadow.

Bringing it back West together in a rented truck, as Bryant wrote in his biography, "I soon discovered Don's enthusiasm for *Man of La Mancha*, the Broadway musical. He had brought along some tapes to keep us from getting bored.

"At first, I thought he was trying to imprint the phrase 'to dream the impossible dream' on my mind as a way of spurring me on to greater creativity in racecar design. But later I decided that he saw himself as a kind of Don Quixote, tilting at windmills and trying to reach the unreachable stars."

Sounds about right.

For Bryant that long haul must have been insufferable. But it would have been worse to complain and annoy his benefactor. He suffered in silence.

Lamentably for Nichols, once Bryant studied the Tiny Tire car back in Los Angeles, he found little that would suit the new Shadow Mk II design taking shape in his mind. In fact, he chose only two pieces: the deeply dished inner halves of the two 12-inch rear wheels, which he would repurpose as the inner halves of his front wheels. He tells us that his boss took the costly news calmly.

(In his book, Peter mentions also reusing "the Weismann gearbox," but clearly that was misremembered. The first-generation Shadow never ran anything but Harris's painstakingly modified Hewland. However, Bryant did select the relatively new, American-made Weismann for his own design.)

Bryant described in his book his interesting "trade study" process for deciding characteristics and features of his new vehicle. Compared to his Ti22, he wanted more aerodynamic adjustability to suit a variety of racetracks, which meant more emphasis on aerofoils than spoilers.

He also felt that reducing frontal area was a good idea, but not to the extent that Harris tried to achieve with his ultra-small tires; "…he'd gone a little too far and inadvertently created as many problems as he solved."

Thus Bryant's concept was a sort of halfway step in size, between the ultra-low Harris AVS Mk I and his own conventionally proportioned Ti22. The Shadow Mk II would ride on 12-inch diameter front wheels (later increased to 13-inch) to yield a front fender height splitting the difference between the previous two cars. But overall frontal area depends on body depth at the higher end, and at the rear Bryant specified conventional 15-inch rims.

So where was the advantage? Harris thought existing rear tires were too tall. He wanted lower rear fenders to hold down frontal area, as well as improve airflow effectiveness to the height-limited rear wing. Achieving this required special tires with shorter sidewalls to yield smaller diameters.

So his was the same dilemma that Harris had faced: a supportive tire maker was essential, or the car could not be built.

Unfortunately, Firestone's enthusiasm for tiny tires had run its course; fortunately, Bryant already enjoyed a good relationship with Goodyear. Perhaps a little crosstown rivalry entered into the tiremaker's agreement with the ambitious, energetic Englishman whose Can-Am track record was so impressive. And there was always that tantalizing possible dramatic decrease in drag for open-wheel cars.

ABOVE Different car body designers, different tools. In those CAD-free days of old, some stylists worked with clay, others shaped metal; Peter Bryant's Mk II was done in plywood. This "buck" would shape molds to make final body panels of glass-fiber. The resulting racecar was handsome, but there was no mistaking its humble birth in a woodworking shop. Notice that, right from the first, Bryant left a gap for a small, adjustable aerofoil between the two fenders, or "wings" as the Brit would have called them. Airflow would then split into two channels either side of the cockpit cowl. *Don Nichols collection*

PETER BRYANT
DESIGNER

CAN-AM'S COCKNEY car constructor, Peter Bryant was a child during wartime London's Blitz. Of his million rollicking life stories, he enjoyed telling of evenings in the garden when the family would hear the sudden, alarming wail of air-raid sirens. Whereupon his Mum would jump up nervously and say, "Oh, I'll just put on a pot of tea, shall I?" Especially with American audiences, Peter's droll delivery always brought down the house.

Not born to wealth, but well-endowed with more valuable riches like ambition, determination and ingenuity, the boy left school at 15 to work for a living. A London car garage took him on as an apprentice mechanic, where he began learning his lifelong trade by doing it hands-on.

He was already keen on motor racing, thanks to listening to it on the radio, but never saw an event in person until one of his car-owning clients invited him to come along to Goodwood one Saturday. It was a cool September day in 1953. They drove down in an open Austin-Healey sports car, which was then the latest thing. Peter was 16. And vibrating with excitement.

Goodwood already was a hallowed place in English lore, and the youngster was instantly entranced by the great names and great machines he saw that day. Among a multitude of indelible takeaway memories, he witnessed Mike Hawthorn take a Formula 1 Ferrari to victory in the feature event. Peter studied everything, asked endless questions, and returned home with his career path set in stone.

Following advice from a friendly racing mechanic he approached that day, Bryant improved his prospects by attending a London technical college to learn welding. That paid off with his first job with a racing team — Lotus. A young team then, but destined for greatness. Their new fabricator helped build many of Colin Chapman's important, innovative early Lotuses.

LEFT Proud Papa Peter Bryant enjoys the inquisitive attentions of Denny Hulme, F1 World Champion and Can-Am king. "The Bear" was always interested in the workings of things, and he could not resist studying the Shadow's inboard front brakes. *Pete Lyons*

LEFT Early in his racing career young master Bryant worked for Eric Broadley at Lola, and thus he was at Silverstone on the day in May 1963 when the lovely little Lola GT made its racing debut. This advanced, Ford-powered coupe, of course, would ultimately lead to Ford Motor Company's mighty GT40. Peter is the figure in white; driver Tony Maggs is at the extreme left, debriefing Broadley and another crewman. *Peter Bryant collection*

BELOW Six years later Bryant built a car of his own, a Can-Am racer called the Ti22, and invited Jackie Oliver to drive it. Don Nichols then brought them both to Shadow. *Pete Lyons*

At the same time, he eagerly joined other mischievous lads in blowing off steam with practical jokes. One of his great stories described the Lotus Space Program.

This involved a shop-built rocket put together on the sly out of four-inch tubing. On launch day — carefully chosen as one when "Chunky" Chapman and the rest of the VIPs were away testing a new car — the infernal device duly emitted a deafening boom, soared nobly toward the skies, but then crashed back through the skylight of the team drawing office. Designer Len Terry bolted out with missile fragments in his hands and his face ashen. Police were summoned. The Lotus Space Program came to an abrupt end.

Peter Bryant told about all this and the rest of his fascinating career in his book *Can-Am Challenger*. A good read well worth looking for.

Leaving the shop-bound routine of fabrication for a more adventurous life as an itinerant racing mechanic, young Bryant traveled widely, working endless hours on many cars for many teams, including in Formula 1. He acquired enormous experience — along with an ever-growing fund of fun stories — all while building up his professional resume as a problem-solver-under-pressure. Everywhere he went he made good contacts that would help him later.

His career led him to America, where he stayed on to work with Indianapolis and Can-Am teams before designing and building his own first Challenger in 1969.

Called the Ti22 for Bryant's ambitious use of the advanced, super lightweight metal titanium, and driven hard and fast by fellow Brit Jackie Oliver, the "Titanium Car" had some interesting, effective new aerodynamic features.

At the same time it also suffered some bedeviling problems, especially a frightening "blow-over" crash at Canada's Saint-Jovite. But when the Bryant creation ran right it proved to be a strong contender to the mighty McLarens.

Frustratingly, double-dealing by so-called business partners tore his Ti22 from his hands at the end of 1970. Bryant was left only with his burning ambition — and fresh ideas for an all-new design. Going for him was a reputation for designing quick racing cars, ones that combined a certain ambitious ingenuity of engineering with an experienced mechanic's hard-headed practicality.

What he lacked was financing. Did he know anyone who might help? He phoned Don Nichols.

THE MIDSIZE ONE **107**

SETTING TO WORK

Starting in January 1971 at his own very large drawing board crammed into a very small office that Nichols rented for him, Bryant laid out fundamental dimensions of what would be the second Shadow design.

"The first order of business when designing a new car is to set the specifications according to the desired performance," he explained. Accordingly, he settled on a wheelbase of 96 inches, a normal figure for the day and 10 inches longer than the 1970 Shadow's. Front and rear track widths came to 60 and 56 inches, considerably wider as well. Also unlike the AVS Mk I's extreme weight bias to the rear, the Mk II fell in the range considered conventional, closer to 40/60 front/rear.

As measured by the author at the first race, Goodyear's new front tires for the new Shadow had an overall diameter of 18.8 inches with a tread width of 10 inches, and those 12-inch diameter rims were 11 inches wide. At the rear, the 15-inch rims were 16 inches wide and the tires were 22.3 inches in diameter and of 14 inches tread width. (McLaren's new M8F wore 17-inch wide rear wheels.)

Despite the front tires going up in size, 12-inch wheels were still too small to accommodate 12-inch brakes with their calipers. Rather than follow Harris's lead and trim down the brakes, Bryant elected to mount them inboard on the chassis. Doing so required driveshafts (aka "halfshafts") with articulating constant velocity (CV) joints running from the discs out to the wheels. Although these raised overall weight a little, they removed the dead weight of the brakes from the wheels and improved tire adhesion over bumps.

Bryant's old employer, Lotus, had done this with its most recent Formula 1 car, the type 72, which launched in 1970. Although some severe issues surfaced (a front halfshaft breakage is thought to have caused Jochen Rindt's fatal crash), the Lotus 72 was the most advanced and successful F1 design of its day.

Bryant was committed to the 12-inch wheels, and therefore to the halfshafts, but his book says that from the outset he had misgivings about their lifespan because of the heavy shock loads their CV joints would suffer. He looked around for the most suitable halfshafts/driveshafts on the market, and selected components made for Porsche's 914/6 sports car. Yet these gave constant trouble in Can-Am service, so the team ended up installing new joints just about every time the car ran.

To carry the front wheels Bryant designed and commissioned new castings.

The Mk II was a so-called "front-steer" design, meaning the fabricated steering arms were in front of the wheel centerline. So, of course, was the rack-and-pinion steering mechanism, a Schroder Racing component that bolted to the front of the chassis.

Another drawback of the small wheels was that they required an actual kink in the "toe links" to avoid their rubbing the rims at full steering lock. The entire steering design would change for 1972.

Bryant's life was much simpler at the back end. He just bought the same Gurney Eagle rear suspension setup that he'd used on his old Ti22. And as with that one, his preference for Pete Weismann's American-made transaxle meant the Shadow Mk II's rear brakes would live outboard with the wheels. The Weismann had no provision for mounting them inboard, unlike the Hewland from England.

The Mk II's aluminum semi-monocoque was 10 inches deep front to back, thanks to this model's higher body line, meaning the mandatory doors didn't steal as much space from the chassis depth as before. The tub extended back alongside the engine, so it was long enough to contain a whopping 84 US gallons of gasoline — although it is thought that a lot of that space was left unused, 75 gallons being a more normal quantity for Can-Am cars of the day. But Bryant claims he already

LEFT Bryant had his aluminum monocoque chassis panels black-anodized, like the first Shadow's, but to save assembly time he assigned much of the work to outside suppliers. At this point the tub is fitted with its front-mounted radiator, but little else. Of particular note here, this model's larger, 12-inch front wheels have allowed a higher upper chassis surface, yielding more footroom and ample fuel capacity. *Don Nichols collection*

was thinking ahead to turbocharging, a year before rumors of Porsche's phenomenal Panzer proved true.

As Harris had done, Shadow's second designer specified black-anodized aluminum sheetmetal chassis panels, but assembly was done primarily with conventional bucked rivets. The exceptions were in the footbox area and other subframes, where blind "pop" rivets were needed because the tubing was fully enclosed.

These subframes took suspension loads, and were formed from rectangular tubing, made of steel, because "Titanium man" Bryant found such stock was not available in his preferred material. But he says he had all the suspension linkages made of Ti.

As most rivals were doing, Bryant bolted the Big Block aluminum Chevy engine solidly into the back of the monocoque, making "the lump" a part of the chassis. He stated that his structure's torsional stiffness was "10,000 pounds to no part of a degree." Whatever that actually meant, it sounds impressive for an open car of the era.

It is believed that two complete chassis were made, along with panels and parts for one additional spare. However, only Mk II number 71-1 would race that first year.

Peter plugged in the biggest Chevrolet motor then available, an aluminum-block ZL1 stretched to 494 cubic inches (8.1 liters). Rather than top it off with the towering fuel injection intakes everybody else was using, he sought to improve airflow to the rear wing by shrouding his injection system down under the engine cover. He turned to Jim Hall, who had used this low-line "crossover" Chevrolet design for his 1969 and 1970 Chaparrals, but who was now out of racing.

Chaparral's engine shop was still operating, though, and agreed to supply Shadow with Chevys inhaling through the low-profile intakes (interlace your fingers of both hands to see the "crossover" geometry). A known downside was that the intake duct area was a little constricted,

RIGHT Photo op. Just imagine pulling this small, hard-driven crew away from their urgent real work to tidy the two tubs, spiff themselves up and stand around looking pleasant while the darned photographer fusses with his (or her) lights and camera. What's it got to do with getting ready in time for the first race?
Don Nichols collection

resulting in somewhat reduced power. Maybe lower body drag would compensate.

As mentioned earlier, the Brit went with a four-speed transaxle from Pete Weismann in Los Angeles. This American product should not be confused with a much later German specialty automobile also called Weismann.

Bryant's book implies he was the body designer as well. The overall shape resembled the old Shadow wedge, not quite as low to the ground but with smoother lines. Outer-edge air pressure fences coincidentally contributed a jaunty effect. At a static ride height of 3 inches, the body rose less than 23 inches from the road at the front fenders, and 25.5 at the rear, two inches higher than the Tiny Tire's bodywork. Width was 72 inches. Body material was light but very stiff honeycomb glassfiber, comprising two thin outer sheets sandwiching a hexagonal matrix a quarter-inch thick; the builder's book gives the matrix material as Nomex but other sources say it was glassfiber.

A wing resembling one of the old Shadow's stood on chassis-mounted struts at the rear, its downforce balanced at the front by a smaller aerofoil that formed the top of the radiator air outlet. Forthrightly installing a radiator at the front avoided Harris's problems with cooling.

Don Nichols had set aside his AVS brand in favor of a new company he called Phoenix Racing Organization. Rise-from-the-ashes, get it? The man did delight in starting new companies with clever names.

His new, streamlined, financially more efficient Phoenix operation didn't yet have its own factory, so most fabrication tasks had to be farmed out to various specialist shops. Glassfiber master Wayne Hartman landed another Shadow bodywork project. A former Shadow team member from the previous year, Jerry Magnuson (who was setting up his own supercharger brand, MagnaCharger), got the job of casting front suspension uprights and the outer faces of the front wheels. Chassis and certain suspension work was done by Pete Wilcox, famed as a former Gurney Eagle man who now had his own shop.

Incredible workload, slavish hours, and the

time efficiencies of sub-contracting meant that, unlike the first-generation Shadow, this one was going to be ready to race in June.

In the early stages, Nichols wanted the whole project kept quiet. As Bryant wrote:

"Don insisted on secrecy about the drawings that were going to be sent to our suppliers, so I had to change the name on the drawing title block from the official Phoenix Racing Organization. I just couldn't resist a practical joke, so I changed it to 'Blivet Car Company.' I don't think Don knew what the word meant. It was a very rude old Cockney obscenity, and basically anyone who didn't know, didn't want to know!"

So far, this was a venture based on enthusiastic hope. And then…

"One day," wrote Bryant, "Don came over and said he thought he'd lined up a sponsor…"

MONEY!

HAVE YOU EVER heard of a company called Universal Oil Products? Well, of course you have — by way of all those glossy black Shadow racecars with big white UOP logos all over 'em. But back in the spring of 1971, few if any in the motorsports community had any awareness of such a firm.

UOP was then, and still is, huge in the petrochemical industry. Their specialty is catalytic cracking, the process by which oil producers turn crude into many refined products, including gasoline but much, much else besides. UOP, which dates back to 1914 and is now a division of Honeywell, is a well-known player in the world's oil patch. And only there. The people in the corporation couldn't care less if UOP never rings a bell with you, the motoring public. You're not their customers.

So why did UOP spend so much money to sponsor all those Shadow racecars for five seasons, 1971 through 1975?

Let's call it one of those fleeting moments

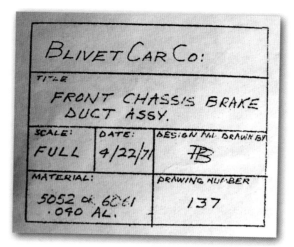

LEFT You thought that "Blivet" business was just a tall tale, didn't you? Here's a corner of one of Peter Bryant's original component drawings. *Dennis Losher collection*

when two tendrils of chance intersect. Or maybe it was just a temporary executive-suite aberration.

Remember Kent Telford from 1970? After Shadow shut down, he wrote his tell-all *Road & Track* story, which one might suppose burned any bridges to Nichols, but when operations resumed in 1971, young Kent got a phone call. Nichols was back on the sponsor hunt.

"I'd like you to get a copy of the Fortune 500 list and start telephoning," is what Nichols said he told Telford. "He says, 'Shall I start with A?' I said, 'Yes. I think there are more names, probably, in the A area than in the Z area.'

"So he started in. And after weeks of canvassing companies about their possible interest in sponsoring a racing team, he arrived at, guess what — U!" Don's listeners always matched his hearty chuckle at the irony.

Chances are the person at the Chicago area's UOP headquarters who fielded the cold call that day was Ben Williams, who handled the corporation's PR. A live wire, he instantly saw an opportunity. At the time, a government campaign was underway to introduce lead-free gasoline, for public health reasons.

Conceivably enough time has passed that we should explain. Basic, pure gasoline tends to pre-ignite at relatively low engine compression ratios, which causes an audible "knock" and limits horsepower. For decades, the easy, inexpensive way to raise gasoline's resistance to pre-ignition, its anti-knock "octane rating," was to add

THE MIDSIZE ONE 111

Tetraethyllead (TEL). Actual lead, to be plain.

But this heavy metal has long been known to be very harmful to the human body, and after many decades of effort to sway public sentiment against TEL, fresh impetus came from rising concern about air pollution. Cleaning the air meant passing engine exhaust through catalytic converters, but these are destroyed by lead in the gasoline. Hence the push to lead-free fuel.

UOP was aligned with it because the potential market for its cracking and catalytic technologies was enormous (as of course was its corporate concern for public health). But equally enormous was resistance. Fuel suppliers and automakers alike were reluctant to take on massive extra expenses for catalytic exhaust converters and specially formulated gasoline, while elements of the motoring public had concerns about possible loss of performance and even engine damage. All sides were vigorously lobbying Congress.

Bryant's book picks up with further details: "The chief of research for the catalyst program at UOP was Ted DePalma, who turned out to be the grandson of Ralph DePalma, the driver who had won the Indy 500 back in 1915. Ted was convinced that if the new Shadow was sponsored by UOP and ran on unleaded gasoline, it would go a long way to dispel the public perception that unleaded gasoline could burn the valves." As allies, DePalma and Williams approached the company's new president, John Logan.

Don Nichols: "John Logan... had been a very successful head of Winchester Repeating Arms company." To be more precise, Logan was a career research chemist who had been executive vice president of Olin Mathieson Chemical, which corporation held what had been the originally independent firearms manufacturer, Winchester. When Logan joined UOP, he apparently brought new thinking for how to expand the company.

"Splendid person," said Nichols. "He and I had a meeting and he decided to sponsor us."

Nichols also told us that, to start with, the agreement was made with Williams's publicity department, and covered just the first three races of 1971. Little Shadow had that long to prove its worth to the corporate giant.

Although still primarily a petrochemical concern, UOP had grown to be a sprawling conglomerate with numerous disparate divisions. According to a company history, "By 1966, UOP had acquired more than 20 businesses in trades as diverse as fragrances, food additives, copper mining, forestry and even manufacturing truck seats and aircraft galleys."

Logan directed each division to contribute equally to the race-team sponsorship fund. They would use race weekends as team-building exercises, setting up hospitality centers and inviting company personnel along with good customers to meet-our-driver parties. Furthermore, some of UOP's many facilities around North America provided on-the-road workspaces for the team.

As for specific specialties directly applicable to the racecar, titanium tubing for the roll bar came from the Wolverine division, filters from Johnson, and Flexonic contributed flexible metal ducting and expansion joints for vibration control as well as fuel, oil and hydraulic lines. In his book, Bryant expressed special gratitude to UOP's large seat-making arm, Bostrom, which offered to make a seat for the racecar custom-fitted to its driver. In the future, Bostrom would help out again in England.

Of course, UOP would also supply massive quantities of lead-free fuel to Shadow. Ted DePalma gave writer Bob Fendel the relevant considerations in an *Automotive News* report dated January 10th, 1972. DePalma said: "There is a false idea around that you need leaded fuel to get really high performance. We think winning performance has many elements. For instance, we expect 7 to 8 per cent better mileage per gallon and more BTUs per volume of gas, which means more energy, and Jackie Oliver... our driver, swears he gets better throttle response."

The story also mentions the corporate stakes: getting out front in the catalytic muffler business,

LEFT Out in the open at last, the Mk II rests for a moment in the Saint-Jovite pitlane having its inboard brakes cooled, while driver Jackie Oliver confers with designer Peter Bryant and crew chief Jim Mederer (black bush hat). Probably that's Mike Lowman's knee at the edge of the frame; the road crew was pretty small. *Pete Lyons*

potentially worth several hundred million dollars a year.

On the other side of a still-bubbling controversy, the cost of upgrading gasoline refineries to make lead-free fuel was put at $2.5 billion. Mere crumbs nowadays, of course, but back in the early 1970s…

Once UOP's cash started flowing, Nichols immediately gave Bryant a big raise, complete with arrears. He found new shop space near his friend Bill Stroppe in Signal Hill, a modest elevation rising above Long Beach, and hired staff to complete and race-prep the car. To drive it, he signed Bryant's friend Jackie Oliver, who had done so well with the Titanium Car.

Gone were reservations about publicity. PR materials were generated and the risen-from-the-ashes Shadow Mk II program was revealed to the world.

With palpable pride, Peter Bryant informs us that "the Shadow Mk II looked very low and fast, and painted in black, even a little sinister. This made Don Nichols very happy. He liked that sort of image. It made for great PR."

SHADOW'S 1971 SEASON

AFTER SUCH a buildup, Shadow's second year was a letdown. Of the 1971 season's 10 Can-Am races, the revived team ran only eight, and showed poorly in most of them.

First race missed was the first of the series, on June 13th at Mosport, where Denny Hulme's McLaren M8F won. This date clashed with the Le Mans 24 Hours, for which Jackie Oliver was contracted to co-drive a Porsche 917L with Pedro Rodriguez. Jackie was a past co-winner of the French marathon, in 1969 with Jacky Ickx, and now in 1971 Oliver and Rodriguez had already won the enduros at Daytona, Monza and Spa, so the English driver had to be at Le Mans. Alas, luck fell against a repeat victory; his car broke down.

The UOP Shadow team did consider hiring a stand-in driver for Mosport, but let it go. "Jackie doesn't like anyone else driving it," Peter Bryant explained to *AutoWeek*. He didn't actually state that the car was ready to race at that point.

THE MIDSIZE ONE 113

ABOVE Testing in Texas, the crew sometimes left the body off — something that Bruce McLaren used to do at Goodwood with brand-new cars. Nothing to do with driver comfort on hot days; it was more about basic, first-cut chassis settings, making adjustments quickly, and maybe also spotting any leaks or other glitches. But, dear modern reader, if you blanch at how exposed the driver looks, know that putting the lightweight coachwork back on would add scarcely any protection. That's how it was in those days. Cockpits designed as "survival cells" was a concept awaiting another time. *Ben Williams/UOP*

After his Le Mans disappointment, Oliver flew straight to Midland, Texas, for a shakedown test of the Mk II. Jim Hall was allowing Chaparral's new engine customer to use his famous personal test track, Rattlesnake Raceway. The team would then drive on to Quebec for the car's debut race at Saint-Jovite.

The Rattlesnake visit went well enough, the brand-new machine giving remarkably little trouble throughout some 250 miles of testing. Beyond a tendency toward oversteer, Oliver found the car handled well, and he didn't expect the small wheels were going to be any problem. He did notice that the 12-inch fronts "snatched" from side to side under braking on bumpy surfaces, which effect he'd encountered on 13-inch F1 wheels.

Aerodynamically, the car's low frontal area did seem to yield good straight-line speed, but Jackie thought the front aerofoil was too sensitive to adjustment. Another issue: cockpit heat there in the West Texas plains.

The only serious problem appeared abruptly at the very end of the test. In fact it ended the test — an unlucky jackrabbit jumped out of trackside "gunch" straight into the path of the speeding racecar.

Consequences were unhappy on both sides, although the survivors were able to joke about the radiator that they sent back for repair getting lost in transit, then being quickly found by its ripening odor. When outsiders heard about the incident, some floated a line about "Shadow got a jackrabbit start to the season." At that point there could be hope that the unsavory incident was not a metaphysical omen for the year to come. Yeah, right.

The team truck continued its long drive northeast, driven by Jim Mederer, whom Nichols had somehow lured away from building his own Racing Beat business, and Mike Lowman, another alumnus of the Dan Gurney University of Racecar Wrenching. Meanwhile Bryant accompanied Nichols in his new Cadillac limousine. As described by the Englishman, "It was black with tinted glass and a radiotelephone, so we had our own sinister look with our new Shadow image." This time he refrained from commenting on his boss's taste in music.

Possibly the onboard phone kept them abreast of a brouhaha concerning the Saint-Jovite race. The Quebec track near Mont-Tremblant in the pretty Laurentians had not paid America's SCCA and Canada's CASC their sanctioning fee.

"OK, we're canceling the event."

"But we don't have the money!"

"No money, no race."

Staredown finally resolved, the event went ahead as planned, but out there on the long American road Don Nichols had ample time to think about it.

According to Bryant's account, the Shadow team knew they had publicity value to the Saint-Jovite race promoter. Their Tiny Tire vehicle had made an impression on fans in 1970, for all the wrong reasons — but an impression is an impression. This gallant second attempt had a

ABOVE Why yes, I am the driver, Mike Lowman might be claiming to Canadian fans at Saint-Jovite. D'you want my autograph? Stoically keeping his face straight behind the wing is the sponsor's PR man, Ben Williams. Happening to be passing by in the background is Brad Niemcek, long a PR rep for Can-Am sponsor J-Wax who later served Shadow in the same capacity. *Pete Lyons*

BELOW A tidy-looking piece, the new Shadow Mk II, low, compact, sturdy and practical — at least as practical as a new compromise can be that involves small, low-sidewall tires and inboard front brakes dependent on aftermarket street-car halfshafts. Maybe that's why we have a lot of photos of Ollie checking the front end. *Pete Lyons*

RIGHT Jim Mederer darts in to do something on the far side of the Chaparral-built Big Block Chevy, which came complete with the low-profile crossover induction system originally made in 1969 for Jim Hall's low-drag Chaparral 2H. Also on view here are the front-mounted water radiator, the aircraft oil cooler atop the left fuel tank area, and a corresponding box on the opposite side containing… nothing. *Pete Lyons*

BELOW It's all about the speed, Oliver might be telling himself, but perhaps also wondering if tucking the engine intakes down out of the airstream won't somewhat stifle the poor beast's breathing. But so far, early during its first race weekend, the new Shadow is looking good. *Pete Lyons*

chance of turning that around, thanks to the reputation Oliver and Bryant had made with the very good Titanium Car — until Ollie's spectacular failure to make an airplane of it provided another reason people might buy tickets.

"The woman organizing the entry had contacted us right after our press conference, to be absolutely sure we were going to have our new car there," wrote Bryant. "I guess Don had played a little game of hard-to-get with her, because she ended up offering to pay starting money if we showed up and raced."

Perhaps it should be explained that Can-Am organizers discouraged the otherwise widely commonplace practice of paying teams to fill starting grids with cars, any cars. Instead, the SCCA's relatively new Pro Racing division felt that paying good prize monies for good race results attracted more serious entries with faster, more durable machines, giving fans better races to watch.

LEFT Several cells distributed the huge load of lead-free racing gasoline around the monocoque chassis. Also visible from this angle is a triangular-looking titanium strut, one of a pair running from the rear faces of the aluminum tub inward to carry the back of the Chevy 494 engine block. *Pete Lyons*

BELOW LEFT Small, 12-inch wheels and inboard brakes make for a crowded front suspension area. Extending out from the front-mounted steering rack, the steering arms have to be kinked a little to clear the wheel rim on full lock. *Pete Lyons*

BELOW One advantage of designing your body in plywood: it gives nice flat panels that can be stiffened with a layer of lightweight honeycomb. *Pete Lyons*

However, starting money had been dangled before Nichols and he wanted it. But getting it from cash-strapped Saint-Jovite "might require a little gamesmanship," as Bryant told the story.

"While we were en route, Don called [the track person] from his radio phone in the Cadillac to make arrangements for collecting the money. Don told her that unless it was paid in cash at the border, we wouldn't go on to the race. It went right down to the wire, but eventually she made the arrangements to pay it. We collected it and drove on…"

THE MIDSIZE ONE 117

SAINT-JOVITE, QUEBEC (CDN)
Can-Am (R2), June 27th, 1971
1st, Jackie Stewart, Lola T260
DNF, Jackie Oliver, Shadow Mk II, fuel starvation

The UOP car showed up well at first. The little black bolide looked sleek, with a graphic presentation that caught the eye. And as always with Shadow, there was something mysterious about it.

Back on May 10th, when the forthcoming UOP Shadow project was revealed to the media, an artist's rendering showed the car number as zero. So why did the real thing wear the bold number 101?

Absent hard information, theorists of numerology rushed to fill the void with speculation. Could it possibly honor former "Screaming Eagle" Don Nichols's wartime service with the 101st Airborne?

What about California's famous Highway 101, "El Camino Real," which ran 600 miles along the long state's coastline and therefore figured in many a Shadow team road trip?

Maybe it was just a clever way to distinguish Shadow's entry from the 90 possible rivals who were backgrounding themselves with mere two-digit numbers.

Or could the truth be as some old timers at UOP believe, that it called attention to the sponsor's impressive feat of chemical engineering: creating unleaded gasoline with a high octane rating suitable for high-performance racing engines?

Unfortunately, all these years later we could find no one at today's UOP prepared to state a specific octane number for that ancient fuel. Some outside sources do claim it was 101, but various others quote values from there through 104 to 107. Quite possibly they're all right, at different points in time. The company's research alchemists probably never stopped experimenting. But their reports cannot be found.

BELOW Low and square-cut, the new Shadow looks distinctively different from more voluptuous earlier cars, like these McLarens trying to chase it. No. 39 is Rainer Brezinka's M6B, while behind Oliver is the blue Tony Dean M8D driven by Chuck Parsons. *Gerald Schmitt*

118 CHAPTER 6

LEFT Generous airspace between rear wing and low-line body is nicely demonstrated here. We also clearly see the end result of that front-end airflow channeling, which was so evident on the original plywood body buck. Farther aft on the far side is the single NACA duct for the oil cooler. *Pete Lyons*

That 101 is one of those insignificant, mosquito-like uncertainties that won't stop pestering the mind.

Mechanically, after about 250 miles of testing in Texas the Mk II could boast more development than many brand-new Can-Am machines, and its track manners showed it. Oliver wound up fourth best on the starting grid, his time of 1:35.4 being 2.5 seconds behind pole starter Denny Hulme in his McLaren. Not as good as was wanted, to be sure, but there were mitigating factors.

One, the Chaparral motor that had been hammered around Rattlesnake died of a burned piston at Saint-Jovite, so Oliver earned his second-row starting spot with a stand-in 427. Meanwhile a fresh 494 was being flown in for raceday. (According to Bryant's memoir, Jim Hall had to administer Don Nichols some of his own financial medicine by requiring it be paid for first. "Don was a master at stretching out accounts payable in those days.")

A second excuse for sub-par speed had more to do with human factors. Frankly, Oliver was wary of repeating his blow-over crash of the year before on the circuit's notorious hump — especially after witnessing someone else nearly suffer the same catastrophe right in front of him this year. So he admitted he was easing the throttle on approach to the take-off point. (In future years this sharp hillcrest would be shaved down.)

Of course, Goodyear's not-quite-so-tiny tires drew a lot of attention. Though not as small as the previous year's Firestones, they were still startling in the Can-Am context. Goodyear engineers said the big problem with such low-profile designs was keeping the bias-ply treads flat; that echoed what their rival colleagues had said the year before. The main measure against that was playing with cord angles across the bias-ply tires. Also, the tires tended to run hot because their footprints met the ground more frequently per mile, but the engineers hadn't

THE MIDSIZE ONE 119

ABOVE The brand new Shadow started its first race from fourth place on the grid, behind Jackie Stewart's Lola and the McLaren pair Denny Hulme and Peter Revson. Jackie Oliver had actually been only fifth fastest, but moved up when Lothar Motschenbacher elected to start from the back.
Pete Lyons

yet felt it necessary to develop abnormal compounds.

It appeared that these new Can-Am tires didn't seem to have any relationship at all to European-produced F1 types. As one Goodyear man at the circuit noted, "We aren't as sophisticated as they are, not yet!"

Stepping back to take in the state of the Can-Am as a whole, a series launched only five years earlier as a uniquely North American form of racing, it was sobering to realize that UOP's little black bullet was the only American-built contender in the 27-car field. On the other hand, mighty McLaren now had its first American driver, Peter Revson.

The race went 75 laps, but the Shadow was out at 20. Despite careful routine precautions to filter the fuel, a small piece of dirt had clogged the pressure-relief valve, causing a misfire.

That fuel, by the way, was not the lead-free product called for in Shadow's contract with UOP. On Monday Nichols and Bryant drove the Cadillac to Chicago to explain why. Forthrightly, Peter says he told management that their gas was not good enough.

It was a matter of octane rating. Given the company's (and government's) goal of healthy fuel for everyday motorists, they had simply supplied everyday Amoco-brand unleaded gasoline. Sold as an option at stations in the eastern part of the US and known to the racing public by its sponsorship of the Sebring 12-hour race, this used aeromatic additives like benzene instead of Tetraethyllead to yield an octane rating of 95.

Bryant pointed out that this could not possibly produce horsepower to match a high-compression racing engine burning 104-octane racing fuel from rival suppliers — and once he got back to Signal Hill he proved it with a dyno test.

The UOP chemists set to work on stronger additives to suppress pre-ignition, but it would take some weeks to develop the right stuff.

ROAD ATLANTA, GEORGIA (USA)

Can-Am (R3), July 11th, 1971
1st, Peter Revson, McLaren M8F
DNF, Jackie Oliver, Shadow Mk II, fuel feed

From still-springtime June in Quebec to Georgia in sweltering July; Road Atlanta was hot, hot, hot. The team painted the topside of the Shadow white in hopes of reducing cockpit temperatures. Additional cooling ducts appeared as well.

Also running a bit hot was Jim Mederer's temper. Already disenchanted with Nichols's business style, and never a man to hold his tongue about engineering decisions he disagreed with (in this case about the inboard front braking system), he and Bryant finally exchanged words sufficient to terminate his employment. His departure left all three men happier.

Unfortunately, it didn't make the overall situation any happier. Goodyear had promised a supply of new, better tires, but they didn't arrive. Oliver's Shadow was neither gripping the track

ABOVE In sunny Georgia for its second race, fresh white topsides give a smart two-tone look. To keep the insides cooler was the practical reason given. *Pete Lyons*

BELOW Simple and sparse, Oliver's office is built for business. But the other seat in this "sports car" is not passenger friendly. One reason is obvious. Another is scalding-hot water piping under the seat. *Pete Lyons*

nor handling well, and once again he failed to muster McLaren-challenging speeds. His fourth on the grid might have looked OK, but the lap time was a full 3.0 seconds behind Denny Hulme's pole position. Shadow's race went no better, an annoying recurrence of the fuel-feed problem dropping the car to 15th place with 45 laps completed out of 75.

WATKINS GLEN, NEW YORK (USA)
Can-Am (R4), July 25th, 1971
1st, Peter Revson, McLaren M8F
DNF, Jackie Oliver, Shadow Mk II, tie rod

Oh dear. This wasn't going the right way at all. Once again the new Goodyears failed to show. But what did show here in New York's Finger Lakes region was a couple of strong new Can-Am cars along with a gaggle of fast endurance-racing coupes from the Glen's Saturday six-hour race. Shadow started a miserable-looking 18th, and dropped out of the 82-lap race on lap 65, this time when a steering rod broke.

Actually, things were worse than that. Filling us in decades later, Bryant wrote of the engine losing a cylinder just before the race. He instructed his unhappy driver to put on the best show he could for the sponsor: "drive it until it melts." That didn't quite happen. A front brake shaft began to fail first, but Oliver, angered by the whole situation, kept on pushing until vibration from the shaking wheel snapped the steering and put the car into a barrier.

Decision time. The next race would be practically a month later, August 22nd at tight, bumpy Mid-Ohio. Team Shadow had no hope of better results there without drastic improvements in terms of tires, handling and overall reliability.

So they withdrew from Ohio, where Jackie Stewart won for Lola. They spent that month and longer testing, testing, testing back home at Riverside, and happily they made a lot of progress. Would missing their second race pay off in better results at Road America?

BELOW She may look spiffy, but under her makeup she's a mess. What she needs is a nice long holiday break in Southern California. *Pete Lyons*

ROAD AMERICA, WISCONSIN (USA)
Can-Am (R6), August 29th, 1971
1st, Peter Revson, McLaren M8F
12th, Jackie Oliver, Shadow Mk II

The UOP Shadow, its snappy white-over-black livery freshly emblazoned with bolder UOP signage, started on the front row of the grid! In front of the sponsor and everybody! A huge turnout of UOP executives, corporate clients and enthusiastic employees enjoyed a beautiful summer's day in the lush Wisconsin countryside near Elkhart Lake village, a comfortable weekend's drive from the company's home office in teeming Chicago.

Plus, UOP had come up with actual high-octane racing gasoline. For the first time what was in the tanks matched what was claimed on the flanks.

According to Bryant, this was a pricy brew, made of a specially made, 100-octane industry test fuel called Isooctane, which itself cost some

ABOVE Rested and refreshed, Shadow Mk II 71-1 is back at work in Wisconsin. See how she brims with confidence in her bolder, more stylish finery. Surely she'll do better here in her sponsor's backyard. *Pete Lyons*

BELOW Exuding confidence himself, Jackie Oliver does a pre-flight walkaround. Soon he'll see if enlarging the front wheels to 13 inches and repositioning the wing more forward works as well at Road America as it did at Riverside. *Pete Lyons*

THE MIDSIZE ONE 123

ABOVE Wow. Just wow. Front row of the grid at Road America, and foremost in the photographer's lens on the pace lap. How could it get any better than this? *Pete Lyons*

RIGHT Hurling uphill through Thunder Valley, ShadowLady shows us her new, tastefully small NACA inlet on the right-side door, and wantonly flaunts her naked crossover fuel injection system. What had that girl got herself up to in wicked California? *Pete Lyons*

four times as much as consumer-grade gasoline. UOP further boosted this to 104 (or 101?) octane by adding enough acetone to nearly double its volume. After pouring in a distinctive green dye, they delivered several barrels to Shadow at every racetrack.

About that octane booster, Bryant's book emphasizes that it was "the same acetone that cleans paintbrushes" and that "if you stood too close to a car's exhausts when it was running on this fuel, it would make you nauseous, and your eyes would water like crazy. It was nasty stuff, but by definition it was unleaded gasoline."

Peter goes on to give us a rollicking account of SCCA technical official John Timanus asking for a sample of the new product so it could be tested. No good declaring it to be free of lead, the claim had to be proven scientifically.

When Bryant went to draw the sample, the nearest empty bottle had contained pale green Gatorade. Because of the UOP product's similar color, before taking it over to the SCCA motorhome he carefully wrote a warning on the label against ingesting it. See where this is going?

It was a sweltering hot day, and the very same Timanus arrived drenched with sweat, spotted the bottle — but not the label — and took a big, delicious, thirst-quenching swig of unleaded green high-octane UOP racing gasoline.

Bryant: "His face turned into a horror-stricken mask. He immediately puked straight across the table, and the fuel caught fire from someone's cigarette on its way to the window drapes. I nearly fell down, I laughed so hard…"

Our Cockney comedian adds that never again was he asked for a fuel sample.

The Shadow also had better tires at Road America. Riverside's intense testing had resulted in a whole new generation of Goodyear at both ends. The fronts were now mounted on 13-inch wheel rims instead of the former 12s. The tire engineers said they had not given up on the smaller size, but their much larger inventory of

LEFT The glory faded at flagfall. Denny Hulme's McLaren speared away out of sight at Road America; his team-mate Peter Revson quickly stormed up from the back row and, briefly, harried Oliver out of Turn 5 and up toward the section called Hurry Downs. Still, could have been worse — at least Ollie avoided another DNF. *Pete Lyons*

13-inch manufacturing equipment made it more practical to do the development at that size.

As for Jackie Oliver's photogenic front-row starting position, McLaren's second driver, Peter Revson, missed Saturday Can-Am qualifying because of an Indycar conflict in California, so otherwise he might have been alongside Denny Hulme on Sunday instead of starting from the back of the lineup.

That said, Shadow showed well. Oliver earned his front-row spot with a time 2.3 seconds slower than poleman Hulme, but that was better than it sounds. Over Road America's long, 4-mile lap, the time difference was a much tighter percentage than back at the shorter Atlanta track.

What's more, Jackie Oliver beat Jackie Stewart (Lola T260) for the first time in the series.

But after all that, tire wear rates during practice suggested the new Goodyears wouldn't last the race distance. What to do — put the old ones back on? Bryant opted for what looked like the best of the new ones. Which duly let him down: after 15 laps a rear went flat. Three miles of slow driving to get to the pits dropped the Shadow to 11th. Later Ollie suffered the same experience again and fell to dead last. At least the new UOP team finally posted an official finish, in 12th place, completing 39 laps of the 50.

DONNYBROOKE, MINNESOTA (USA)
Can-Am (R7), September 12th, 1971
1st, Peter Revson, McLaren M8F
DNF, Jackie Oliver, Shadow Mk II, front CV joint

Four races to go. Here in Land-o'-Lakes Minnesota, at the fast, open circuit known nowadays as Brainerd, the Shadow still did not have the good Goodyears. Using sets borrowed from Formula 5000 this time, Oliver reckoned he was losing 1.5 seconds a lap. He expected it would be yet another month before the next generation of purpose-built tires came along.

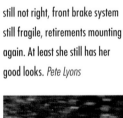

BELOW Back to real life. Tires still not right, front brake system still fragile, retirements mounting again. At least she still has her good looks. *Pete Lyons*

On pole this time was McLaren's Peter Revson, whose 1:26.5 was 3.3 seconds better than Oliver in fifth spot. This meant that if Ollie really had been able to go 1.5 seconds faster, he would have started third ahead of Jackie Stewart's Lola. But that would not have prevented a front brake constant velocity joint failure, which forced another Shadow retirement at a mere 28 laps out of 70.

EDMONTON, ALBERTA (CDN)
Can-Am (R8), September 26th, 1971
1st, Denny Hulme, McLaren M8F
3rd, Jackie Oliver, Shadow Mk II

Never mind, yet another fifth-place start. At this remote but petroleum-rich corner of Alberta, Canada, Oliver finally scored Shadow's first decent finish of the year: third place! And the Mk II looked sharper doing it, if only thanks to a fresh, all-white paint job complete with pinstripes, courtesy of another cooperative UOP division.

Paint did not count toward points, fast driving did, and Jackie did his part. With pole qualifier Revson starting several laps late (a stray bolt had to be extracted from his throttle mechanism) and front-row team-mate Denny Hulme lagging on a track surface dampened by light, chilly rain, third man Stewart forged through to the front while Oliver followed him to seize second place!

Hulme was no fan of rain-driving, but by half distance he caught Oliver and passed to chase Stewart. But then the Lola driver spun off and presented McLaren the lead. The Shadow driver thus regained second place, but then with just 13 laps to go out of 80 he clipped a trackside buried-tire marker, damaging the body. Out came a black flag demanding a pitstop for repairs, which cost two laps. Stewart went on by, but he finished second a whole minute behind Hulme. Oliver had been much closer than that before his pitstop.

ABOVE All white now and pinstriped to boot, California Girl might have expected a warm welcome home. Alas, fame is so fickle. The spotlights are no longer hers. *Pete Lyons*

LAGUNA SECA, CALIFORNIA (USA)
Can-Am (R9), October 17th, 1971
1st, Peter Revson, McLaren M8F
DNF, Jackie Oliver, Shadow Mk II, throttle linkage

This hilly little circuit on the Monterey peninsula was where Peter Bryant had introduced his first Titanium Car two years before, but he was not nostalgically pleased to see the familiar shape reappear now. David Hobbs was now driving Bryant's second-generation Ti22, and he was 1.55 seconds faster in qualifying than Oliver had been in the same car in 1970 — when he made the fastest lap of the race. Such seasonal improvements for individual cars were extremely rare in the Can-Am.

And now, in 1971, Hobbs qualified third fastest compared to Oliver's — you guessed it — fifth. And have you guessed that the Shadow suffered yet another retirement? This time it was due to a broken throttle linkage at just 23 laps out of 90. At least during the race Oliver had briefly passed Hobbs, and by the end of it his gentlemanly fellow Brit had the courtesy to also retire Bryant's older car.

In the chill of the coastal Pacific evening it

ABOVE Brit on Brit. Charging out of Laguna Seca's hairpin, Jackie Oliver in the new 1971 Peter Bryant Shadow finds himself chasing David Hobbs in Bryant's Ti22 from 1970. Hobbs hasn't driven the Titanium Car before, it's now in the hands of a club-level team, and its greater bulk is dramatic — but it's faster. Because its bigger tires are. (Hobbo may tell it differently.) *Pete Lyons*

BELOW Hard scratching gets Ollie ahead in the race, but only briefly. Shortly afterward the damned car breaks down again. *Pete Lyons*

seemed completely irrelevant that Goodyear had at least supplied Shadow a new generation of tires designed for Formula 1. Bryant says they also supplied everyone else with new tires designed for Can-Am. Zero-Sum, that game.

RIVERSIDE, CALIFORNIA (USA)
Can-Am (R10), October 31st, 1971
1st, Denny Hulme, McLaren M8F
DNF, Jackie Oliver, Shadow Mk II, leaking wheels

Where do you suppose Oliver qualified here? Yep, fifth fastest. But it was after a narrow escape during practice. The low-drag Shadow nearly touched 200 mph on the high-speed Riverside straightaway, fast enough for centrifugal force to pull the small-diameter tires away from the rims. Instant flats at terminal velocity!

The only alternative was to go back to 12-inchers — but these had done the same thing

LEFT Last chance at Riverside. Goodyear has some better front tires for the 13-inch rims. Bryant has given up Shadow's long quest for low drag and installed a honkin' big set of vertical intake stacks for more power. Oliver is as keen as ever. It must come right. Mustn't it? *Pete Lyons*

BELOW Fifth on another starting grid, the usual place. Out early, the usual fate. Oh, and sudden high-speed tire deflations left and right. Are we having fun yet? *Pete Lyons*

THE MIDSIZE ONE **129**

RIGHT Bye 'til next year.
Pete Lyons

back in the summertime testing at this circuit.

Bryant knew he could try installing screws in the rims to hold the tire beads in place, but with Shadow's particular rim design this was not simple. Peter credits McLaren's Tyler Alexander for giving him a handful of little sealing washers at the last minute. His book tells the rest of the story:

"By the time we got the last wheel done and back on the car, the grid had left, and Jackie had to start from the pits. He tried as hard as he could, even passed some cars, but after about 12 laps, he felt the tires deflating again and pulled into the pits." (This is a different reason than was given out at the time: "Broken front driveshaft joint." Better to blame a purchased part than a crucial collaborator.)

SHADOW'S 1971 season brought six retirements from eight starts. While champion Peter Revson scored 142 points, Oliver's 12 put him level with privateers Greg Young and Howden Ganley in 14th place. What a dismal year.

By this time designer Bryant was heartily sorry he had tried the low-profile approach. At Riverside he even gave up his low-drag crossover intakes in favor of the tall thunder-trumpets everyone else was using.

Looking for bright sides, he wrote: "We certainly hadn't done as well in the 1971 Can-Am as we would've liked, but we had nothing to be ashamed of. We were the only American team to build and race a new car that year. We'd even put the UOP Shadow on the front of the grid and finished a race in the top three. We were the first car to prove that high-octane unleaded gasoline works in race engines, and we found out a lot more about the aerodynamics of Can-Am cars."

Even better, despite the season's troubles UOP's Ben Williams declared the sponsor happy to continue. The PR man knew company personnel had enjoyed their outings and, as Bryant stated in his book, "He had been told by one top UOP sales executive that he had closed a multimillion dollar deal simply by bringing the client to see the car race."

Whew. It had been hard enough to land this golden sponsor. Even golden-tongued Don Nichols would have struggled to attract another, given Shadow's win-loss record.

Widening our focus, we should acknowledge new Can-Am champ Peter Revson, the first American to top the series standings. He'll enter our story again, but all too briefly. ♠

JIM MEDERER
CREW CHIEF

I came to Advanced Vehicle Systems straight out of the Air Force. I was an aircraft maintenance officer at Davis-Monthan in Tucson, and on weekends was racing my own little Formula Vee and Formula B cars. SCCA's tech inspector was John Timanus, and at one race I went to him and said, "I'm getting out of the Air Force shortly, going back to Southern California, and I want to join a race team. Any suggestions?" And John said, "Well, there's this new organization in Santa Ana…"

So I went down there and they hired me. That was about June of '69.

It was a miracle they hired me. Nominally I was a mechanical engineer, because I went through a five-year engineering school before the Air Force, but I had no engineering ability to speak of as far as AVS was concerned. I was kind of a fill-in guy. I would do mechanical assembly. I would be drilling sheet metal, pop rivet it all together, whatever. I had no machining ability at the time, no welding ability, but I wanted to learn all those things.

Don Nichols brought together a group of people who were frankly very talented. Trevor Harris was extraordinary. I like Trevor very much. He could use a little more humility, perhaps, as can we all. He would go off on tangents. His

BELOW Versatile Vic, they call him, but Elford has never driven anything like this. He ain't gonna like it, might be the thought carefully masked on Jim Mederer's black-hatted face. What's Don Nichols thinking there in the background, hand stroking his beard? Only the Shadow knows. *Pete Lyons*

THE MIDSIZE ONE **131**

Shadow was a tangent and on sober reflection nobody would have thought that some of these things were a good idea.

Let's see, some of the other guys were Walt Boyd, Larry Stellings, Jerry Magnuson, Don Borth… Don was magical, one of the legendary fabricators. It's awe-inspiring to see what they can do. He and I got along very well, and I learned so much from him.

They were already at Borchard Street then, which was pretty big, 10,000 square feet. The shop used only half of it. We actually had another half that was full of Trevor's junk. Some of Borth's stuff, too, his planishing machine and so on. Big heavy machines that they put in there, not in the main shop.

I think actually the one reason Nichols hired me was that he saw me a little bit as an assistant to Trevor. He asked me to go to Detroit to the SAE convention. They were going to have several people involved in racing there giving little talks. So he said, "Go around our shop, look at what everybody is doing, what Trevor is doing, and give a 10-minute speech about the Shadow to the SAE." It was a little daunting. I had to fly back there alone, go to Cobo Hall and stand in front of a room full of engineers.

I had a front tire and set it on top of the podium. The thrust of it was, this is the new direction for high-level racing, going to very low frontal area vehicles. Turned out that wasn't true. I didn't know one way or the other. I didn't appreciate the problems that Trevor was building in.

And Nichols wanted to rule the world. He always had these Grand Ideas for things he wanted to do. And he had a thing about black, oh, a big thing about black. The black hat and the black car, the whole idea of The Shadow, he enjoyed that whole schtick very much.

He was an interesting person. First of all, he was [an officer] in the military in Japan, and was used to giving orders. Apparently while he was there he followed racing. He knew nothing about the mechanics of racing, but he loved racing, was incredibly dedicated to it.

In Japan at that time they were just awakening to automobile racing, the factories were just dipping their toes into it. They would build their own engines, but they needed things from the outside world, Koni shocks and Girling brakes and all that sort of stuff, things that they couldn't invest time to develop themselves.

Don was a go-between. He could speak Japanese, and he would procure for them whatever. He told me a little story once that one of the teams, I think it was Toyota, found they needed little shock absorbers, and they needed them very badly, like in a week and a half. They didn't exist. And Don's like, OK, here's the price.

It was the time in Europe when they take off, August. Don contacted Koni, they called the people necessary in from their vacation, and he paid them I'm sure a scary amount of money. But he delivered the shocks on time as requested.

The Japanese at the time didn't know how to do those things. They didn't have personal friendships with, you know, the head of Koni. Don apparently did. And he would supply them their tires. He was a guy who could get things done.

He did some remarkable things. He had enormous success in Europe. He managed to continue that relationship with UOP for some time, that was a massive accomplishment. He had to have been a pretty good salesman.

On the other hand, most everybody he dealt with ended up not wanting to deal with him.

Now, when I was in the Shadow team, early on, I know money was a major problem. I didn't get paid at one point. I got a check, the check bounced, I called Nichols and said, "I'd like you to take care of this." He took care of it.

But a lot of times, he had no problems stiffing people. If they yelled and screamed I'm sure he'd just forget about it and move on. I don't think Nichols set out to cheat people, it's just that if he didn't have the money, he'd say, "I don't have the money," and deal with it later. It's just how he was.

He didn't invent it. There are a lot of people in racing like that. It's kind of the way of the world, but it's especially that way in racing.

He was a complex guy. I don't bear him any ill will. I'm glad I had a chance to meet people like that, because it taught me a lot about people, but people like that use other people, and it's not a way I would care to operate. You burn a lot of bridges.

After that disastrous trip to Canada in 1970, where we ended up with our racecar unusable and I guess pretty much all of us had left, Nichols somehow came up with more money. He called me and said he was going to race the second car at Mid-Ohio, and would I come back.

"To do what, exactly," I asked.

He said, "I want you to do this and this and this."

ABOVE Crewman Mike Lowman peers from the cockpit as crew chief Jim Mederer supplies the unloading power. Bossman Nichols stands ready as backup brakeman. Shadow's ramp-back truck is the latest thing in racecar transportation. *Pete Lyons*

I said to him, "You're asking me to be the Crew Chief." He said, "Oh no, no, just do..."

I said, "No, if you want me to do all that you got to pay me that money and give me that title.

He said, "OK." Because there was no one else that he could bring in who knew enough to run the car.

Mid-Ohio was horrible. We went there with George Follmer to test it, and Follmer decided he didn't want to race it. Vic Elford got in it and he just didn't like it either.

It was evil. It did nothing right. And there was no one there to direct what to do to make it better, including me. I had so much on my plate just trying to keep the thing in one piece that there was no possibility of making it better.

In 1971 I came back again for a while. That was with the Shadow Mk II, the Peter Bryant car, and Nichols had the UOP sponsorship. We drove to Rattlesnake Raceway to test it. It wasn't a bad sort of test, but Jackie Oliver hit a rabbit late in the day. We had to pry its guts out of the cooler.

We took off immediately for Saint-Jovite. I was not alone, we would swap, but it was a really, really horrible drive all the way up there, day and night. Got there and I came down with some gastroenterology thing. It hit a lot of people at Saint-Jovite. I was incapacitated, I couldn't get six feet away from the toilet. I felt very bad about it, because I felt I was letting the team down.

As soon as I could remotely work I staggered over to the hangar at the little airport where all the Can-Am teams were and did what I could. I seem to recall the race faintly.

From there we drove down to Atlanta, where Peter Bryant fired me. Well, I was very unhappy with what was going on and occasionally would tell them what I thought. I remember saying I thought the constant velocity joints he was using for the front brakes were going to give trouble. I don't blame him at all for wanting to get rid of me.

I wanted to get my own business going anyway.

Jim Mederer went on to found Racing Beat, a large, successful enterprise focused on performance services and products for Mazda vehicles. He did so in partnership with a gentleman from Japan, a family member of AVS mechanic "Teji," who introduced the two. So in that sense a bit of Shadow DNA lives on in Racing Beat today. Jim's remarks here are from a conversation shortly before his passing in 2016.

THE MIDSIZE ONE

CHAPTER 7
THE CONVENTIONAL ONE

SHADOW MK III, 1972

FOR DON NICHOLS's third Shadow model, his second designer had some first-rate news. The boss once again asked for economies, and although Peter Bryant did plan wholesale upgrades, he worked out that he could reuse the existing black-anodized Mk II chassis, along with many other proven components.

Accordingly, for 1972 the 1971 car became a Mk III. The model ID on the chassis plate remained the same, "71-1." But supposedly to clarify things, the SCCA handed out a brass dash tag reading "72-1."

Right in line with the obscure persona of the marque's creator.

Bryant put the number of detail changes at 55, ample to justify a new model designation. But in fact the transformation was not just in substance — Shadow's entire concept had changed.

First of all, he had given up his and Shadow's old dream of revolution. They once hoped to defeat conventional cars rolling on mainstream racing tires by building a radically lower vehicle atop significantly smaller wheels. But the myriad surprises and compromises and drawbacks that lurk in revolution had blocked their every attempt. Bryant decided his Mk III would wear regular Goodyear racing rubber on regular rims, of 15-inch diameter front and rear.

Larger front wheels offered an opportunity get out from under the problems inherent with inboard brakes. Bryant therefore designed and ordered new front suspension components, especially new cast uprights, to accept outboard brake calipers. But for reasons his book does not explain these never came through. Thus the mechanics were doomed to spend another season replacing front brake halfshaft joints almost daily.

Actually, Bryant says that Jackie Oliver didn't seem worried about the front brakes, so the designer didn't see it as a serious issue until another driver tried them. In 1972 Shadow raced two cars at some tracks, where its second driver, promising young Brazilian Carlos Pace

LEFT Same chassis, bigger car. Peter Bryant massively redesigned his original Mk II of 1971 to become 1972's Mk III, while managing to do it all atop the same monocoque tub. At first it seemed promising. By Watkins Glen, however… *Motorsport Images/LAT*

BELOW In this second year of their collaboration, Don Nichols and Jackie Oliver seemed close. In years to come that would change. *Lionel Birnbom*

(pronounced *PAH-say*), complained about brake pedal vibration.

Bryant was puzzled why Oliver never mentioned something that Pace so strongly condemned, so the two Brits had a chat. Peter came away with a story to tell about differences between drivers. Ollie said something like, "Oh, yes, it does get bad. I'm sure it hurts my lap times because I can't completely trust the brakes. But I'm more concerned about not having enough power."

Race drivers are all about going!

To mate up with the larger front wheels and steerable hubs, Bryant raised the upper suspension pickup points two inches, bringing them to the level of the top of the chassis monocoque.

While he was at it, he also changed the "front-steer" layout to "rear-steer," installing a different rack-and-pinion behind the wheel centerlines inside the footbox. This, as well as the larger wheels, meant the steering links could now go

THE CONVENTIONAL ONE **135**

ABOVE For a few races this year Shadow ran a second car. At Road America Oliver gave his team-mate Carlos Pace some driving tips for a vehicle very different from the young Brazilian's regular ride, a March F1. *Tom Schultz*

BELOW As seen here at Mosport's season opener, the frontal aerodynamics of the Mk III split airflow between front wheels and cowl, then down a sloping channel into the hip-mounted engine coolers. This would evolve later on, and so would the rear fender line. The wing atop the nose would disappear. *Pete Lyons*

straight out from the rack to the hubs without a kink.

Bigger rear tire diameters called for lengthening the wheelbase, so a two-inch spacer moved the rear wheels aft to place them 98 inches behind the fronts. The Eagle-sourced rear suspension carried over, complete with outboard brake location at that initial stage, with suitable revisions to mounting points and linkages.

Tire track width remained the same at the front, 60 inches, while wider rear tires meant their track width went up by an inch to 57. The wider tires protruded more, so the bodywork was now 77 inches wide, five more than for the Mk II.

Taller tires meant new, higher bodywork. Bryant laid out the differences in his book: "The rim/tire assemblies on the Shadow Mk III were going from only 18 inches in diameter at the front to the standard 23.3 inches, and the rears were going from 23.5 to 26.8. In my suspension geometry, I permitted the wheels to jounce [rise from their static ride-height position] a maximum

136 CHAPTER 7

of 1.5 inches." He had found that running his cars low to the ground on stiff suspensions often improved lap times. All this determined the height of the bodywork over the wheels, so the math works out to 25 inches front, 28.3 rear.

Some other cars probably offered more suspension travel, so the Shadow might still have been a bit lower than some.

Remarkably, Bryant said the "new" car was 160 pounds lighter than the previous year's version. He did not go into details.

New bodywork offered an opportunity for a revised radiator system. The single front-mounted water cooler disappeared in favor of a pair buried in the car's flanks, one either side of the engine. Farther back sat a pair of oil coolers.

Initially, Bryant channeled air into these through outgrowths of the previous year's extractor ducts. Air rammed through the open space formerly occupied by the bow radiator, then split to either side of the windscreen, then flowed through deep troughs let into the tops of the doors into the coolers in the flanks.

But these design elements evolved as the season progressed. Because of chronically high engine temperatures, as well as his ongoing quest to improve downforce, Bryant reshaped the nose and doors, deleting the channels. On top of the new, flat-top doors he inset more efficient, quasi-triangular NACA ducts.

To start the season the car retained a nose wing in the same place, although it was higher and larger — on one occasion much larger. Mounting troubles eventually led to the wing's disappearance altogether — which evidently did not lower the amount of front-end downforce. Porsche's development team had discovered the same while developing its new, turbocharged 917/10K. It too had a scoop-shaped nose profile like the configuration Bryant adopted for his Shadow Mk III.

A seemingly beneficial upgrade wound up being the opposite. Pete Weismann had revamped his transaxle, which had been bulletproof during 1971 and had a nice shift

LEFT Looking straight down the radiator inlet channel we see the inboard-mounted brake disc lurking below its outlet duct. *Pete Lyons*

action that Oliver favoured, so Bryant was happy to adopt the American gearbox man's newer product. But surprisingly, the "improvement" proved troublesome. Gears kept breaking, which the manufacturer blamed on poor heat-treating by a new supplier, but Bryant noted a further issue — that parts requested never arrived.

BELOW This rear view shows where the oil coolers were carried, in the middle of the tail over the transaxle. See how generously the rear wing is fenced. *Pete Lyons*

RIGHT Body off in the Watkins Glen pitlane, Oliver's Mk III reveals that the upper front suspension wishbones were raised level with the top of the monocoque chassis; a year before on the same chassis the pivot points had been two inches lower, suiting the smaller wheels used in 1971. This view also lacks steering arms, because the formerly front-mounted steering rack has been relocated to behind the front wheel centerline. *Pete Lyons*

LEFT Pity the poor air, first roiled by the front wing, then being asked to change direction twice more before finding its escape through the buried radiator cores. *Pete Lyons*

The Brit finally swapped over to his native land's Hewland. And it was no simple swap: the job required the fabrication of numerous new mounting structures and ancillary components.

However, for the first time there was an opportunity to move the Mk II/III's rear brakes inboard, next to the transaxle, to get their weight off the wheels. Hewland provided mounting points lacking on the Weismann product.

Although Bryant had been able to please Don Nichols in regard to keeping the old chassis, he then had to deny his boss's sudden interest in turbocharging. The racing community knew that 1972 would bring new Porsches packing ultra-powerful, twin-turbocharged 12-cylinder engines. Chevrolet-powered teams, notably McLaren, were trying to counter with similarly boosted big V8s.

But more power would require more fuel. Bryant: "The Shadow Mk II held 84 gallons [for most races it is thought to have carried less, perhaps 75 gallons] and averaged about 2.5 miles per gallon with about 750 hp. I figured that a 1,000-hp turbo engine would only get about 2 miles per gallon, and at that consumption rate, a nonstop, 200-mile Can-Am race would take about 100 gallons.

"There was no way I could get all that extra fuel in the car. If Don wanted a turbo, then we would have to refuel during the race." For the time being Peter let that problem go as his plate was piled high with more urgent matters.

Shadow's sponsor, evidently delighted with "their car's" showing if not its racing, had given Nichols substantially more money for 1972. He used it to move into a larger facility, another building of 10,000 sq. ft. like his old Santa Ana place but still located in Shadow's new base, Signal Hill. Also, a full-sized tractor-semitrailer rig big enough for two racecars took over the hauling duties.

Engine work went back to Lee Muir, who had supplied Shadow's first strong engine two years before. Part of the job now was developing the turbocharged Chevy V8 that Nichols wanted.

And the team hired more staff. One addition

Bryant acknowledged in his book *Can-Am Challenger* was Ronnie Spellman, described as "a first-class mechanic who'd worked with me before." But the author had to add, "I was sad when Mike Lowman, who had come with me to Shadow after working for me on the Ti22, decided to go back to England with his wife." In fact Lowman would rejoin Shadow at its UK location a year later.

Leading the team now was another former mechanic from Britain, Ray Brimble, who had joined Shadow the year before as a helper but now became team leader and logistics man. His job involved interfacing between the bossman and the team, as well as acquiring supplies and externally sourced parts. Far cry from the simple old AVS days when, if a guy on the shop floor needed something, he just picked up a phone and ordered it.

Shadow even had its own PR pro, Brad Niemcek, who had done that job for the Can-Am's former series sponsor.

About all this growth and change, Bryant expressed competing emotions. While glad about having a bigger, stronger team and consequently a better chance of winning races, this up-by-his-bootstraps lad from London missed the mechanic's work he so enjoyed; he was too busy managing. But he had been the one who set it all in motion, back when he first called Nichols.

As in the Trevor Harris days, Peter Bryant's

ABOVE One stuck truck. It is the Friday evening before the season-ending Can-Am on Riverside's road course. But the Shadow transporter is 25 Freeway miles away at Ontario. High-centered while emerging from the Superspeedway's infield access tunnel. Inside is the team's long-awaited turbocharged Mk III. What a good idea it must have seemed: we'll just pop up the road and give 'er a bit of a run 'round the NASCAR oval, make sure all's well before she's introduced out at Riverside tomorra'. And it was a good idea. Once the hauler got hauled out of the tunnel. Crewman Doug Meyer, Engine Expert in the shop but Hauler Herder on the road, confesses that he was driving. But he blames his boss for beaching it. "We looked at the tunnel before I drove it in and I told Don, 'It's gonna hang up.' 'No it won't, just gun it hard.' We had to jack the thing up."
Pete Lyons

ABOVE On the starting grid for the season opener at Mosport, these grinning guys are eager to go. Lee Muir, who builds the engines, car designer Peter Bryant and the man who makes it go, Jackie Oliver, have no foreshadowing of what they'll be feeling at season's end. *Pete Lyons*

new Shadow ran its first shakedown tests at Orange County International Raceway, using the dragstrip for instrumented aerodynamic development. The value of this work was proven later at Laguna Seca, where Jackie Oliver wound up smashing the track record for Can-Am cars. "Fantastic news," Bryant enthused.

"By the time we got the Shadow Mk III to Mosport for the first race of 1972 Can-Am, we did manage to tune the total downforce at 100 mph to over 900 pounds. At full speed, it could push the car down to within ½-inch of the track surface, generating more than 1G of force [ie, artificial weight]. If the track had twisted and gone upside down, the car would have still clung to it."

This same claim had been made two years earlier for Chaparral's 2J "Fan Car," but the new Shadow allegedly was making equivalent downforce without the suction fans and vacuum-sealing skirts.

"As a result, our suspension springing got stiffer and stiffer, and our car went faster and faster."

OLLIE'S INPUT

"OLIVER'S ODYSSEY" was Jackie's first-person column that ran periodically during 1972 in the British weekly *Autosport*. The ambitious English driver also was running several NASCAR and some USAC races in 1972, so he had plenty of anecdotes and insights to share with his countrymen across the great water.

Ollie was truly delighted to report that Shadow had been able to carry out a lot of advanced testing — one of the prime factors behind McLaren's success in Can-Am. "The refinements and things that we've learned in months of testing the UOP Shadow Can-Am car have been translated into a brand-new body and we were anxious to begin final testing at Laguna Seca in California.

"We were all rewarded because it was a real shot in the arm for Don Nichols, Peter Bryant, all the mechanics and myself when everything worked beautifully. I managed to get down to 0.8 seconds under Peter Revson's ultimate qualifying record set last fall in the works McLaren M8F.

"What's more important is that we filled it up with gas and it ran proportionately as well. Last year with lots of gas it was a real pig, like any Can-Am car is. I am really thrilled to bits with it all because last year we went testing and testing and couldn't get within three seconds of a competitive time and all too often the thing would break. We now have indications that the car will work and what's more important, it doesn't break down and for the very first time we're seeing lap times that might even be competitive.

"We've managed to move the rads to the back of the car without encountering the massive overheating problems that many people have experienced. We've got the inboard brakes working perfectly [ahem… with brand new CV joints, one must presume — author], it handles well and right now it is 160 pounds lighter than the 1971 car. Mosport here we come!"

It seems he had no premonition of all the trouble to come.

SHADOW'S 1972 SEASON

MOSPORT, ONTARIO (CDN)
Can-Am (R1), June 11th, 1972
1st, Denny Hulme, McLaren M20
DNF, Jackie Oliver, Shadow Mk III, gearbox

A cold chill struck the Can-Am paddock in Canada. Porsche's long-rumored turbocharged contender was a reality at last, and so was the threat it posed to the Establishment. According to statements at the time, the 917/10K's pair of exhaust-driven "Kompressors" boosted the 5-liter, opposed-12 endurance-racing motor by some 50 percent, out-powering the best of the good old Big Block Chevys by a good 200 hp. In a high-downforce car prepared by Roger Penske Racing and engineered/driven by Mark Donohue, it threatened to crush all opposition.

And, indeed, Donohue duly put it on pole. He was almost a second faster than the

ABOVE Portrait of nearly 4,000 horses about to stampede for almost 200 miles around Mosport Park. Mark Donohue starts from pole in Penske's glistening, whistling turbo-Porsche 917/10K (no. 6); in the McLaren team's new M20s are Peter Revson alongside (no. 4) and Denny Hulme; fourth on this grid is Jackie Oliver in the Shadow Mk III. *Gerald Schmitt*

BELOW Ollie plunges down into Turn 1 just past the pits. Although a little bulkier than before, the Shadow is still more compact than most other Can-Am cars of the new year. But its reliability would prove to be poorer than the general average. *Pete Lyons*

fastest McLaren. Everyone started calling this frightening German war machine "The Panzer."

Without that, Shadow would have looked pretty good, at least for a while. Driving the massively updated 71-1 chassis, Oliver qualified "third in class", within a few tenths of Peter Revson and Denny Hulme in their new McLaren M20s, and a whopping three seconds ahead of fifth-placed Milt Minter in a non-turbo (non-K) Porsche 917/10.

But troubles spoiled the Mk III's debut. The team arrived at Mosport a week before official practice opened to do some quality testing, but most of that time was lost to rain. Therefore not until race week did they discover bedeviling problems that robbed further time and affected qualifying. In the race Oliver thought he could have been faster than the McLarens, but for ongoing problems with the new, "better" Weismann gearbox.

As he detailed the adventure in his "Oliver's Odyssey" column in *Autosport*, "Sometimes at the start of a race you get a feeling that everything is going to be all right. I felt like that at Mosport!

"From the fourth grid position [I] dropped behind Denny and the way I could stay with him for the first half lap I thought that everything was going to be just fine. But from the Moss corner hairpin I came up against our other problem with the Wiseman [sic], first gear wasn't strong enough and I had to use second… [Others] just pulled away. To cut a long story short, the transmission failed for the second time in two days and we were out after only seven laps."

ROAD ATLANTA, GEORGIA (USA)
Can-Am (R2), July 9th, 1972
1st, George Follmer, Porsche 917/10K
DNF, Jackie Oliver, Shadow Mk III, engine

As was becoming a Shadow tradition, the team arrived early for some thorough testing, only to have a thoroughly bad experience. The Mk III's throttle stuck open at high speed.

"I had only done about 20 laps of initial sorting when the throttles jammed wide open," wrote Oliver, "and before I could hit the kill switch and get things slowed down, I hit the earth banking [outside Turn 2] at around 160 mph. Luckily it didn't get upside down and I stepped out of the badly bent Shadow which had to be sent back to California to have the monocoque chassis tub reskinned.

"I must say that Peter Bryant builds a very strong car for that is the second accident I've had in a Bryant car and walked away from it." (The first such incident was his backflip in the original Ti22 at Saint-Jovite in 1970.)

In fact Shadow's was not the only heavy crash that day. On the opposite side of the Road Atlanta circuit, at maximum speed on the long, undulating straightaway, Mark Donohue suffered a savage accident when the engine lid of his Porsche flipped open. Its aerodynamic balance seriously upset, the massive machine literally flew and then smashed down on its nose, ripping away the entire front end of the magnesium spaceframe and exposing Mark's legs to heavy impact with the road.

He survived and would heal, but Roger Penske quickly had to find someone else to race the spare car. He tracked down George Follmer

BELOW Lucky to survive a major testing crash before Road Atlanta, Oliver pressed on with the rebuilt car but all efforts to get a good grid time fell victim to failure after failure. Here he comes into Atlanta's old pitlane outside the last turn to report one more problem. *Pete Lyons*

ABOVE At Watkins Glen Oliver starts ahead of François Cevert's McLaren M8F (2), Milt Minter's Porsche 917/10 (0) and several other worthy drivers — but ahead of the Shadow are five faster cars. *Motorsport Images/ Rainer Schlegelmilch*

and informed him he was going to learn to drive the world's most powerful road racing car, one of the most notoriously tricky to handle, here on a very challenging, high-speed circuit that George had never seen before.

As George recounted the terse instructions he received, "I'm supposed to win the race, and I am not supposed to crash." He fulfilled both parts of the assignment.

Back at the Shadow camp, Bryant accompanied the stripped monocoque back to California to help get it repaired. They made it back to Georgia and the days leading up to the race brought another transaxle failure, engine overheating, and a broken rear driveshaft. Oliver couldn't put a good lap together and his grid position was a demoralizing 14th. Then during race morning warmup, there were yet more broken teeth in the Weismann gearcase, but this was fixed in time for the race.

Soon after the start, the throttle stuck again but this time Ollie was able to avoid another crash and drive back to the pits to have it fixed. This time the gas pedal was found to be fouling on a misplaced fire extinguisher line. He went back into the race — until the engine blew after 20 laps.

"I was beginning to think that Atlanta was not a good place for us," wrote Peter Bryant.

WATKINS GLEN, NEW YORK (USA)
Can-Am (R3), July 23rd, 1972
1st, Denny Hulme, McLaren M20
DNF, Jackie Oliver, Shadow Mk III, crash

Another "killer weekend," Bryant recorded. He had a brainful of tests and alterations in mind, especially to body shape and radiator ducting, but no time to try them. At least he was able to bring a new radiator to The Glen, one with an extension to improve cooling. His team-mates laughed at its L-shaped appearance, but it did seem to work.

Not much else did. Oliver's best lap time earned a not impressive sixth place start, and the race brought an early pitstop because — hold your hat — one of the brake pads had been installed backwards. That was put right, but then the brakes failed totally. Slam, into the blue guardrail after just 18 laps. Pretty much a reprise of 1971's Watkins weekend.

Three races, three debacles. For Nichols it was 1970 all over again. Oliver called a council of war. Bryant remembered Jackie saying, "Well, something is very wrong and it has to be fixed if we're going to have a sponsor next year. I need to finish a race!" To which Peter replied, "In front of Ben Williams of UOP, I promised that if he didn't finish in Ohio, I would resign in favor of any engineer he cared to name. The pressure was on me, then."

MID-OHIO (USA)
Can-Am (R4), August 6th, 1972
1st, George Follmer, Porsche 917/10K
2nd, Jackie Oliver, Shadow Mk III

BELOW Turnaround at Mid-Ohio, where Bryant gave Oliver a new car, new gearbox and renewed determination to finish the race. At last it all came good… against the poorest of odds. *Pete Lyons*

Bryant's determination to turn things around started with a new chassis. The spare tub he had commissioned, never used in 1971 but updated to become "Mk II/III 71-2," had been earmarked for turbo engine development. After two more gearbox failures during practice — despite which Oliver posted fourth-fastest grid time — on Saturday evening the team split into two shifts for the all-night job of swapping to the Hewland.

This had actually been done for the Watkins Glen race, but then the swap was reversed at Mid-Ohio after the California manufacturer shipped a new 'box along with assurances that all problems had been resolved. They hadn't.

As Jackie Oliver put it in his "Odyssey" column, "the Weismann… is a beautiful gearbox but it just won't last… The changeover is quite an operation, because the gearboxes are quite different considering that all the suspension hangs off the transmission housing…" But he worried about the extra load on "our already overworked mechanics." With gratitude he reported that their loyal response was, "Let's have a go."

While they were at it, the boys also exchanged the practice engine for a nice, fresh 494. Bryant had split the crew so everybody could get at least a little rest, except for himself. He toiled sleepless through that entire night. All beer 'n skittles, this motor racing lark.

The work dragged on so long that the team only just made it to the track for Sunday morning warmup. This particular circuit did not allow people to stay on premises overnight, so everyone had to find workshop space elsewhere. Time got so tight that, rather than spend extra minutes loading the finally finished racecar back into its big, beautiful transporter, chief mechanic Ray Brimble simply jumped into Oliver's cockpit and drove the bellowing black beast along the public highway like any everyday racegoer.

Good job, that. The warmup session revealed a gasoline leak. This was fixed in time to send the car to the grid to start the race.

Whereupon it started to rain.

Your reporter was moved to tell the story this way for *Autosport*: "Even as the grid set off on their pace laps, the first minute sprinkles of rain came down the wind like tears of celestial

laughter. We don't have to run our Group 7 cars in the rain very often, but when we do, OH BOY what a joke."

After a half hour of only light precipitation, during which everyone held onto their slick tires while Follmer turbocharged his way into a big lead, "Quite suddenly the track was wet. The brutish big Can-Am behemoths quite suddenly and thoroughly were helpless. They came lumbering down into the turn[s] at a frantic wheel-locking twitch, slowing right down to a crawl, slipping and slithering around the bend[s] with the front wheels rebelling, back wheels frisking saucily. It was all spinning wheels and twirling steering and stumbling, unhappy motors."

Not even the mighty Penske Panzer was invulnerable. Follmer looped it twice. But both times he recovered and rejoined without losing his lead — and he remained on his slicks.

So did Oliver, but he didn't spin. As others did pit, or spin, or both, the man in the Shadow seemed to be reveling in the ever-changing conditions. At one point, the black machine was the fastest thing on the track and was pulling back five seconds a lap on the whistling white one. With one incautious twitch of George's toe, Ollie's second place could have turned into a first-place finish.

At the finish, Jackie was on the same lap as the winner, though George had him in sight ahead, and they were both three laps up on the third-placed car. UOP's Shadow's Mk III had finally finished a race. It might have won it.

Back to Bryant: "When Jackie asked me why the car had handled so well in the wet, I was a bit reluctant to admit to him that the rear anti-rollbar mounting bracket had broken on one side. The bar hadn't been working at all. What a strange thing — something had broken that actually helped make the car go faster in wet conditions!

"But I told Ollie that it had been his fantastic driving that had made all the difference. He was

ABOVE What a race! Too much rain, way too much torque, and on their treadless slick tires either George or Ollie could have chucked it all away with one careless press of the throttle. Follmer did in fact spin the big turbo Porsche twice, though both times he recovered in time to keep ahead of the rumbling Big Block Shadow. In fact, at this moment he was this close to setting Oliver a lap down. *Pete Lyons*

ABOVE Shadow was a two-car team at Road America, where designer Bryant had the second-generation body profile ready for Oliver to try on a second chassis. He even tried a really big front wing, but only until it broke. Driving the original car (in the background here) was Brazilian newcomer Carlos Pace. *Pete Lyons*

BELOW Hey, man, run down to Goodyear and see if they've got our tires mounted up yet. And don't bring 'em back muddy again. *Pete Lyons*

truly magnificent that day at Mid-Ohio."

So had been Peter Bryant's pre-race prep. Jackie Oliver, who had set off the team turnaround with his strong words a fortnight earlier, thanked his hard-working countryman by reaching deep into his own pocket.

Reading Peter's book, we see nothing about other news Ollie might have shared with him then and there. Evidently there was a leak that reached print, but Bryant would not learn of it for another five weeks.

ROAD AMERICA, WISCONSIN (USA)
Can-Am (R5), August 27th, 1972
1st, George Follmer, Porsche 917/10K
DNF, Jackie Oliver, Shadow Mk III, engine
DNF, Carlos Pace, Shadow Mk III, ignition

"A nightmare." That's how Bryant felt about the nine-race season's midway point. Rainy weather handicapped pre-race practice and qualifying, a

special burden for Team Shadow because for the first time they had two cars to deal with.

Carlos Pace, a talented young Brazilian who was in his first season of F1 with Williams, joined Shadow for his first taste of Can-Am. He didn't find it very tasty. His older car, 71-1, suffered constant electrical issues apparently caused by the rain; also, he didn't care at all for the model's inherent, confidence-disrupting brake-pedal vibrations. His grid place was a discouraging 30th out of 34. (Yes, beautiful Wisconsin's Road America tended to attract lots of Can-Am contenders!)

Oliver's newer car, 71-2, had several significant improvements. A completely new nose section was an effort to improve airflow to the waist radiators — which were also new and larger. Rather than the earlier "channel duct" system, which induced air to flow from below the bow wing up and back between the front fenders and then out around the cockpit to the radiators, Bryant now deleted the

ABOVE Poor Carlos Pace didn't get a very good impression of the Can-Am. Early in the weekend at Road America, while it was still sunny, he found himself in a roadside ditch. But gosh, isn't rolling, wooded, bucolic Wisconsin such a pretty shade of green. Almost like Brazil. *Tom Schultz*

BELOW Saturday's rain squalls showed the reason for the countryside being so lush and green. But that happens in Brazil as well. *Pete Lyons*

THE CONVENTIONAL ONE 147

twisting, narrow channels in favor of a much more straightforward flow pattern over the fenders. When air arrived atop the doors, it was welcomed into the rads by more efficient, quasi-triangular NACA ducts. All this worked — the coolant temps now remained within reason.

At first there was a larger nose aerofoil than before, but a failed mount caused its removal for the race. It remained off for the rest of the year.

Pace's older car was as before in all respects, except that, like Oliver's, it had the Hewland. But he still retired — after just four laps the ignition magneto packed up. This was usually a very reliable item.

And Oliver, the hero of Ohio? Jackie made a strong start from another fifth place on the grid, and was in third place by the third lap behind Denny Hulme and François Cevert (in the ex-Revson McLaren M8F of 1971, that year's champion's car). There Oliver stayed as others ebbed and flowed around him, George Follmer in the Porsche whooshing up from the back to win, the McLarens falling out with mechanical issues, but in the end Shadow was denied a second podium.

"We told the press that the problem was a broken exhaust system, but it actually went a bit deeper than that," admitted Bryant long afterward. In Oliver's own description to the press we learned that sometime after the exhaust pipe bounced away on the circuit the engine began to feel like it was vibrating itself to bits and he thought he'd better switch it off.

DONNYBROOKE, MINNESOTA (USA)
Can-Am (R6), September 17th, 1972
1st, François Cevert, McLaren M8F
3rd, Jackie Oliver, Shadow Mk III
DNF, Carlos Pace, Shadow Mk III, ignition

News greeted Peter Bryant here at Brainerd, Minnesota. Which do you want first, the bad news or the worse news? The merely bad was

BELOW By Donnybrooke, aka Brainerd, Shadow had given up on front aerofoils, leaving a prow profile quite like the Porsche's. Minus the 917's huge front-mounted oil cooler, of course. Bryant's new aero package was at last bringing sufficient airflow into the water coolers buried in the Mk III's flanks. *Pete Lyons*

LEFT Brainerd's Bridge afforded a rare overhead viewpoint, nicely revealing the 1972 Shadow's final shape. Of note here, see the scalloped nose, the rectangular inlets and outlets for the inboard brakes, the transverse brace to maintain fender position, and the efficient NACA ducts atop the doors seducing over-fender airflow into the side radiators. The oil coolers still live in the stern, fed by a transverse scoop behind the eight massive engine induction stacks. *Pete Lyons*

that Mark Donohue had recovered well enough from his Atlanta crash to join George Follmer in a second Penske Panzer. Mark stuck his foot hard into his turbos and qualified on pole, four tenths of a second faster than his team-mate.

The Shadows lined up seventh and tenth, Oliver's somewhat the faster but trailing Donohue by a whopping 2.7 seconds. In the race, Pace was first man out with another ignition failure. Oliver's car kept going, and toward the end was looking better and better because the faster cars ahead were falling out left and right. Both Porsches quit (although both completed enough laps to be official finishers), Donohue after a rear tire blew and Follmer when his thirsty turbocar sucked up the last of its gas — at 210 miles, this was the longest Can-Am of the year.

But both the factory McLarens retired of engine failure. Left running at the end was privateer François Cevert in the ex-Revson 1971 McLaren, the very car that won here the year before. Milt Minter lasted to take second aboard the non-turbo Porsche.

And Jackie Oliver rolled in third, his Shadow the only other car to go the entire 70 laps. Finishing another race was something in such a troubled year, and Peter Bryant took some pleasure in his team timers finding that Oliver had set the race's fastest lap. He would have been happier if the track's official lap scorers had caught it too. They gave that honor to Follmer.

But wait, we spoke of worse news for Bryant. On the phone from California, his wife told him she had just read that the UOP Shadow team would be expanding into Formula 1 for 1973, and it didn't sound like Peter was going to be part of the operation.

In fact, as we learned above in the Mid-Ohio story, the news had already broken over a month earlier. But life on racer road makes it hard to keep up with your snail-mailed magazines, so Peter never saw it. But neither had Oliver or Nichols mentioned it to him.

ABOVE As in the pitlane (briefly) so on the starting grid: The Shadowmen were split at Edmonton by David Hobbs in Lola's T310 — the once-dominant constructor's last ever Can-Am car. *Ozzie Lyons*

BELOW Oliver's Shadow 101 gets rolled toward its place nearer the back of the Edmonton starting grid. The second Penske Panzer has yet to roll out. *Motorsport Images/David Phipps*

Here in the parking lot of their motel at Brainerd he confronted the pair about it. The others tried to smooth things over, but Bryant felt betrayed. Harsh things were said. He slept poorly that night. But in the morning he resolved to make the best of his last Can-Am season whatever happened.

After that race Oliver used his *Autosport* column to reveal that UOP indeed would be embracing F1 the following year, and he would be involved. Details to come.

EDMONTON, ALBERTA (CDN)
Can-Am (R7), October 1st, 1972
1st, Mark Donohue, Porsche 917/10K
4th, Carlos Pace, Shadow Mk III
DNF, Jackie Oliver, Shadow Mk III, driveshaft

Canada's Edmonton is nearly 200 miles above Calgary, and that far north even the beginning of October is rather late to be going racing. Once

ABOVE Third-time charmer Carlos Pace had a decent Can-Am race at last, being the one Shadow driver to finish at Edmonton and in fourth overall at that. Not really special, but this team was happy to take it. *Ozzie Lyons*

again the weather was chilly and sometimes wet; once again the group of Group 7 cars was thin, just 22 entries; 21 started.

Only the two pairs of fast cars, the Porsches and McLarens, attracted any real attention. Everybody else looked like spear carriers. But Shadow's new man Pace seemed to be getting into his stride, and out-qualified his team-mate to take seventh on the grid by a mere 0.025 of a second. A tiny margin, but David Hobbs squeezed his white Lola T310 into it and relegated the second black Shadow to ninth. Spear carriers can put on a show too.

In the race Oliver dropped out early with a broken driveshaft — at the rear, for once, a failure of the inboard CV joint. Pace's car took him all the way for the first time, and he placed fourth, best of the supporting cast. At least he came away with one good impression of Shadow in this, his final stint with the team.

Looking for light in his gloom, Bryant noted that "We had now scored three top-four finishes in the last four races. Going into the final two races of the season, I was hoping we had a trend started. I was looking forward to Laguna because Oliver had smashed the lap record there."

LAGUNA SECA, CALIFORNIA (USA)
Can-Am (R8), October 15th, 1972
1st, George Follmer, Porsche 917/10K
DNF, Jackie Oliver, Shadow Mk III, oil leak

Oliver made a good impression at Laguna, according to Bryant: "When qualifying was over, people were coming over to take another look at the Shadow Mark III. The only cars faster were the two Panzers of Donohue and Follmer, and Revson's M20 McLaren. Oliver managed to out-qualify Hulme by nearly half a second to get on the second row of the grid."

He was, however, about a second and a half behind pole sitter Donohue. In fairness, it must be said that rainy weather curtailed everyone's

THE CONVENTIONAL ONE 151

ABOVE Laguna Seca looked like something of a rebound for Shadow, with Oliver splitting the McLarens to start fourth, ahead of Hulme. Nothing was going to touch the Panzers, but as tall Don Nichols (make him out at far right, white cap atop white jacket) watched them all head off onto the pace lap he must have been thinking, if we keep going and Revvie drops out... *Pete Lyons*

BELOW This short but quick little road course on a hilltop behind Monterey was something of a home circuit for Shadow. The team tested its new cars here, and here is where Oliver set some exciting times in practice. *Pete Lyons*

performance during practice, especially Saturday.

There were two UOP Shadows on hand but only one driver, Jackie testing both trying to make up his mind between them. NASCAR star Bobby Allison, well known as a stock-car man interested in other kinds of racing, was at the circuit to drive in a supporting event for 2.5-liter Trans-Am sedans. There was some sort of arrangement whereby he might possibly practice a Shadow, but it did not happen.

Probably that was because of Saturday afternoon's poor weather. After several laps of very hard driving in the newer car, Oliver dropped one side off the edge of a fast corner, which damaged the nose piece. The rain intensified, so everybody packed up and effectively abandoned qualifying.

On Sunday the weather kept looking ominous until suddenly, just before starting time, it turned sunny and warm and, well, Californian. The Porsche pair hurtled away from the Second Class, while Revson tucked into third place.

ABOVE Alas, Laguna Seca brought Shadow another unhappy result when practice promise went up in raceday smoke. But before she goes, notice how trim the Bryant-designed car looks amongst the broader-beamed McLarens and Porsches. *Pete Lyons*

But instead of a team-mate right behind, he had an enemy, Ollie's Shadow Mk III going like absolute hell and for the very first time able to stay right with the McLaren M20. It was electrifying to watch.

But the Shadow was trailing smoke. Oil leak. UOP shoulders sagged. Each lap the smoke thickened. Officials shook out the black flag for the black car.

Apparently the oil tank had punctured. This was patched and Oliver rejoined the fray, but he had lost a lot of laps. And the car was smoking again. When he came in a second time it was to retire with the front crankshaft oil seal leaking. He had managed only 22 laps.

The winner did 90. Donohue had been leading until near the end when he let Follmer by. George was going to be Can-Am champion regardless but underlining it with a win didn't really hurt Mark — not more so than he already had been. Having "your ride" taken over by someone else is painful.

RIVERSIDE, CALIFORNIA (USA)
Can-Am (R9), October 29th, 1972
1st, George Follmer, Porsche 917/10K
DNF, Jackie Oliver, Shadow Mk III, gearbox

An incandescent, ember-red meteor streaking through the night; that was our indelible first impression of Shadow's monster motor. It was long past sunset above 2.5-mile Ontario Motor Speedway, and the darkening sky cast down only just enough light for the giant oval's white-painted walls to be half-seen in the gloom. The speeding black car itself was invisible — except for its turbo exhaust system glowing as bright as overheated brake discs.

The only sound was the engine's, a fascinating sound, a mixture of a nice, crisp rasp from the crossover exhausts and a whistling from the blowers, all heavy and muted. It sounded extraordinarily like a World War II vintage four-engined bomber orbiting the sprawling speedway's grounds.

THE CONVENTIONAL ONE 153

So why was a Can-Am road racer doing laps of an Indycar/NASCAR Superspeedway on a Friday night? Just to reel off system checks. UOP Shadow's long-awaited turbocharged answer to the Porsche Panzer would be introduced formally on Saturday at Riverside Raceway, not far down the Freeway. All being well, it would contest the season finale.

Providing the team could get it back out of the Superspeedway. Their spiffy big transporter had gotten itself stuck in the track tunnel. Getting it unstuck had delayed the test until it was almost too dark for Jackie Oliver to see the road in front of him.

But it all did work out and Saturday sunshine did sparkle down on the new Shadow. And what a sight it was. The two Schweitzer turbochargers were enormous and Lee Muir had packaged them at the very back of the car, hanging off the gearbox. The exhaust plumbing was very complex, like a big bunch of writhing, angry snakes. Or, in the down-home drawl of visiting NASCAR driver Bobby Allison, "It's like puttin' antlers on a canary!"

The famous stock-car specialist, still interested in road racing, was standing by just in case he got a chance to drive the normal Shadow. He

ABOVE At last making its debut at Riverside, Lee Muir's turbocharged Big Block Chevy looked a formidable piece. Indeed, when it ran on the dyno it made more torque than the test rig could handle. No true horsepower peak could be measured. But it never ran for long on the dyno, and it wouldn't last at Riverside either. *Pete Lyons*

RIGHT What a savage smile on Mark Donohue's face! "Captain Nice" has dropped by to check out the new rival to his own turbocharged Porsche, but what he sees must remind him of something visiting NASCAR Good Ol' Boy Bobby Allison blurted out: "It's like puttin' antlers on a canary." Neither Shadowman Mike Lowman, turning away, nor driver Jackie Oliver, studiously absorbed in some task, seem to share the amusement. *Don Nichols collection*

did run some practice laps in it, but his Can-Am hopes were dashed. Oliver was having so much trouble with the turbo engine that he displaced Allison to race the regular one.

Obviously highly stressed, the monster motor had taken five months of work and a claimed $160,000 to reach this point, and was said to have done but five runs on a dyno before arriving at Riverside. During those bench tests it had shown an impressive 708 hp at just 4,000 rpm, a figure conventional 494s didn't offer until 6,000. At 5,000 rpm the Shadow's horsepower reached 800 and the torque reading was a whopping 985 pounds feet! But that was the limit for both dyno and engine. The testbed's torque capacity topped out at 1,000, and the 494's combustion chamber pressures blew gaskets.

Which seems to have been what happened again at Riverside. According to Lee Muir, a piece of a head seal overheated, sparked detonation, melted the spark plug and damaged the piston. It happened twice, in Saturday practice and, despite efforts to retune the system, again on Sunday morning.

Musing about it all long afterward, Peter Bryant wrote this: "I figured the standard Lucas fuel injectors were having trouble passing

ABOVE OK Jackie, says Lee, I put it back together last night and I think I fixed the detonation problem, but get on it easy for the first lap or two, OK? *Pete Lyons*

BELOW Oliver dutifully evaluated the turbocar during morning warmup at Riverside, but when it broke again he thumbed Bobby Allison out of the normal car for the race. To be fair, though, turbocharging was new technology to everyone. As embarrassing to team and sponsor as it was to have the public watching Shadow failures, mighty Porsche had struggled through the same sort of painful development period — but in private. Stuttgart fans mostly got to see success. *Pete Lyons*

THE CONVENTIONAL ONE 155

RIGHT Bobby Allison, already a NASCAR winner but with his greatest career achievements still ahead, also enjoyed road racing and drove anything he was offered anywhere he had time. How he must have been looking forward to his first sports car race ahead of an engine bigger than his own stock car powerplants. How much history might he have made this fine day? *Pete Lyons*

BELOW Under his UOP cap Nichols is at work charming his new man Allison. Bobby and his colleague may not be buying it. At our left, Ray Brimble watches to see how much more work this is going to mean. *Don Nichols collection*

enough gas at the higher RPM, but as it wasn't going to be my concern anymore, I kept that to myself. When anyone asked me what went wrong with the turbo, I told them it was having trouble passing gas."

Back in Old Faithful (?) for the race, Jackie Oliver started from fifth on the grid, behind The Usual Suspects from Porsche and McLaren. Ollie held that position until the third lap, when he spun. Rejoining 12th, his driving became more spectacular than usual, if that seems credible, full of great sweeping tail slides that rapidly brought him up through the field again. A lap from the end he was holding fourth when, of all things with the normally reliable Hewland gearbox, its input shaft sheared. With no power going to its wheels, the black car coasted by the pits, turned sharply into the exit lane and rolled straight into the paddock. But Oliver did retain his fourth-place "finish."

So ended Shadow's third racing season, which had looked promising but, once again, ran into

LEFT Last lineup of 1972, as the pack forms up on Riverside's "Mile-Long Back Straight" for the start, which awaits just around the next corner. *Gerald Schmitt*

BELOW Last sight of the Shadow Mk III, as Oliver flashes by the pits and into fast Turn 1. *Pete Lyons*

THE CONVENTIONAL ONE **157**

ABOVE The pair of Peter Bryant cars crest the rise before descending into Turn 7, his earlier Ti22 giving way to his latest — and unfortunately his last. Now two years old, the "Titanium Car" is in the hands of club racer Nick Dioguardi. Neither he nor factory man Jackie Oliver will be running at the finish. *Pete Lyons*

too many troubles. In some ways Mark Donohue had suffered the same sort of season.

Mark "should have" won the series — he had the car for it. But flirtatious lady luck deserted him to run off with George Follmer. Thus placed to become America's second Can-Am Champion, George did.

LEAVING RACER ROAD

PETER BRYANT too had Shadow troubles ahead, despite being done with the team. He believed that way back before the 1971 season, during their first talks about joining forces, Don Nichols had promised him a ten percent share in the venture. But Nichols now denied this. Evidently it had never been committed to paper.

Bryant considered countering by seizing one of the Shadows, which he happened to have in his possession because UOP asked him to display it at an engineering convention. His wife talked him out of that, but there remained a matter of $500 owed for taking the car to the convention.

"Nichols had one more bullet in his gun, and he fired. He told me he would give me the $500 when I returned the drawing board from my office," Bryant stated in his book. This was a high-end, German-made product that Bryant actually owned and had brought to that office. He continued, "I had just signed up for unemployment, money was tight, and I was looking for work. I knew the board was worth more than $500 and I should tell him to go to hell, but then I remembered that you couldn't eat a drawing board."

The once-friendly relationship between the two men remained bitter as long as they lived.

We don't bring up this sour note to denigrate either man, but rather to cast a little light on their personalities. Cars are creatures of their creators. Peter Bryant was a boisterous, jolly, quick-witted fellow who loved racing and was good at it, but whose talent and desire for building racecars was unfiltered by formal education. Nor, by his own admission, did he have a head for business.

Don Nichols was an injured orphan first in life, became a warfighter, and made himself a sharp-eyed business entrepreneur with a burning drive to acquire wealth. At the same time he enjoyed creating fine things — and he relished the camaraderie of teamwork. Many who knew the American in that context speak well of him to this day; some who dealt with his other persona share feelings more in line with the Englishman he dismissed.

Bryant left motor racing for good, at least on a professional level. Going into engineering of recreational vehicles, he designed a minivan type of RV, was named vice president of engineering for successive motorhome companies, then co-owned a business making buses for sale in developing countries. Later, he spent more than two decades as an independent engineering consultant, during which he gained eight US patents. In the late 1990s Carroll Shelby hired Bryant to design an Oldsmobile-powered production sports car called the Shelby Series 1, though usually Shelby himself is publicly credited for its engineering.

Peter did not turn his back on the sport he loved, though, staying involved with the vintage racing scene by helping competitors track-tune their cars — as well as making sure their evening gatherings were lively and loud with laughter. And of course he wrote David Bull Publishing's 2007 book *Can-Am Challenger*, which details his entire life and career leading up to and through his Titanium Car and Shadow period. Just two years later he died suddenly, on March 31st, 2009. He was 71.

Racers keep his memory in mind through the annual Peter Bryant Challenger Award, by which The Racing History Project celebrates excellence in motorsports engineering. Honorees have included Dan Gurney of Eagle fame, McLaren's Tyler Alexander, and Bryant's predecessor at Shadow, Trevor Harris. 🌲

BELOW Bryant brought Oliver to the Can-Am in 1969, and they often seemed on the brink of breakthrough success. But it never happened. By the end of 1972 they were split. *Pete Lyons*

CHAPTER 8
TAKING ON THE WORLD

SHADOW DN1 (F1), 1973

BELOW Grace, yes. Pace? We'll see. This cutaway shows airflow through the side radiator, and also the innovative rear suspension with single trailing rod and rearward lower link. *Motorsport Images/LAT*

JACKIE OLIVER seems to be the one who directed Don Nichols's attention toward Europe. The Londoner had driven for good Formula 1 teams, including Lotus, but his career there hadn't gelled. In two-seaters he had won Le Mans and other long-distance races, and his Can-Am prospects still held promise, but sports cars don't scratch a single-seater racer's itch.

So Oliver proposed that Shadow invest some of UOP's money to acquire a facility in England, engage an experienced European car designer, and mount a two-pronged effort — F1 as well as Can-Am.

Up to that point Don had no vision of a Grand Prix program, he told us. "We were kind of

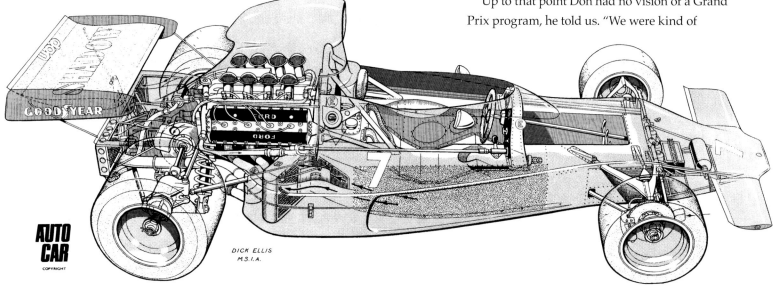

160 CHAPTER 8

LEFT Tony Southgate and Jackie Oliver had worked together at BRM, where they gained faith in each other's abilities.
Motorsport Images/David Phipps

enamored of Can-Am… the big American engine idea. I think when Jackie came along, that's when he brought my focus into Formula 1, saying, 'Why not?' And, 'If you have a good sponsor, Formula 1 is a place where good sponsorship allows you to do development and succeed.'"

Such would have been the Brit's business-case pitch to his American boss. Ollie's personal goal was obvious, but D-Day Don would not have seen a racer's burning ambition as any reason to say no.

Let us remember, he was no neophyte to F1. More than a decade earlier, after he retired as a US Army officer but remained in Japan to build a business, one of his ventures was importing racing tires.

As he described it, "I was going around the world, following the Grand Prix circuit, buying up surplus tires and selling them to the Japanese carmakers, because they loved to have the exotic Grand Prix rubber. Such things were totally unavailable in Japan at that time."

Thus he knew his way around an F1 paddock when he began setting up UOP Shadow's European operation. As a first step, in July 1972 he and Oliver flew to England for the British GP, which that year was at Brands Hatch, just southeast of London. If they needed any cover, they could point to hometown boy Jackie's one-off ride there with his old employer, BRM.

As Don continued the story, "We went over there and talked to several designers. I won't mention the ones I rejected, but when I asked them, what are your plans for next year, they would say, 'Oh, I'm thinking about lengthening this slightly and modifying that and, oh yes, we have a new upright coming.' I didn't see any dramatic changes that promoted roadholding or acceleration."

What he was hoping to find was creativity on par with Trevor Harris's. He put it this way in a 2012 interview with both men filmed by Trevor's wife Freddi:

"Trevor… was a thinker on the exotic dimensions. His design concept was exercising

TAKING ON THE WORLD **161**

ABOVE Shadow's Weedon Road raceshop in April 1973, about the time of Silverstone's non-championship race. Tidy but tight, it was a makeshift encampment borrowed from Bostrom before a proper facility could be set up around the corner in Ross Road. *Pete Lyons*

innovation and creativity into new technology, pushing the envelope. Other designers tended to design minuscule modification of certain features from year to year. Trevor was appealing, because he was that broadest kind of open mind… seeking always for the maximum advantage."

Nichols found his man in Tony Southgate. Then BRM's chief designer, this quiet, thoughtful young Englishman had created some very competitive cars for his employer. As a BRM driver and Southgate admirer, Ollie made sure Tony and Don had a talk.

Don was delighted. "Tony… was much like Trevor. Tony was continually emerging with new concepts and wasn't bound by what other people were doing with their cars. That's what I liked."

During our own conversations not long afterward, Don added this:

"And Southgate had a relationship with a technical college in London, with access to their wind tunnel. He suggested he would like to have a budget that would enable him to have a consultant. We decided on Tony.

"He was very businesslike… and very practical… plus he had fresh ideas, and he was blindingly quick at designing things. He designed some beautiful cars for us right away."

Because the 1973 Grand Prix season would start in January, five months before the first Can-Am contest, the F1 design came first. This first Southgate Shadow received the model designation DN1.

Of course, the letters meant Don Nichols, but don't conclude that the Shadowman's own ego called for it. His new designer says he came up with that on his own, and furthermore, "I was quite happy with it. I later used the same system when I designed a car for Teddy Yip called the TY01."

The technical college mentioned by Nichols was the University of London's famed Imperial College. Southgate enjoyed good relationships with professors there, and they gave him access to its wind tunnel, a facility rarely available to racers in those days. Aerodynamic refinement was becoming increasingly vital in racing, as engineers cut-and-tried their way toward shapes and configurations that balanced the age-old desire for low drag against the new emphasis on downforce.

When Southgate's new 1973 Shadow DN1 rolled out, the F1 community immediately noted its blend of sleek body lines — including then-uncommon panels streamlining the engine bay — with a low-jutting "shovel nose" as Tony termed it, and a markedly rear-set, very large wing at the back. The designer's aptitude for art revealed itself in a particularly shapely airbox, the tall intake scoop feeding the engine.

His very readable autobiography, *Tony Southgate: From Drawing Board to Chequered Flag*, recounts how he began drawing "Don Nichols number 1" in October 1972. At first he worked at a table in his home garage, because Shadow was still establishing its first shop in England, at Northampton, about 15 miles northeast of Silverstone circuit. Coincidentally, the town was the home of Cosworth, manufacturer of Ford's F1 engines of the day, but Shadow came simply because sponsor UOP owned property there. One of UOP's divisions, Bostrom, a manufacturer of cushioned, suspended seats for trucks, had some spare real estate the F1 team could use.

Located in an industrial area on Weedon Road, it was spare because it was derelict. "We went up and looked," said Nichols, "and it was a condemned building. The floor was caving in, it was full of holes. But we managed to locate some places where you wouldn't fall into holes four or five feet deep. That's where we built the first Formula 1 car."

Nichols broke into a chuckle. "That first car, we had to take it out through the toilet. It couldn't go out the front of the building, it was too big, so the thing had to go through the men's room to get onto the loading dock."

The glitz and glamor of Grand Prix racing.

Shadow failed to make January's two opening GPs, but a pair of glossy black DN1s did arrive

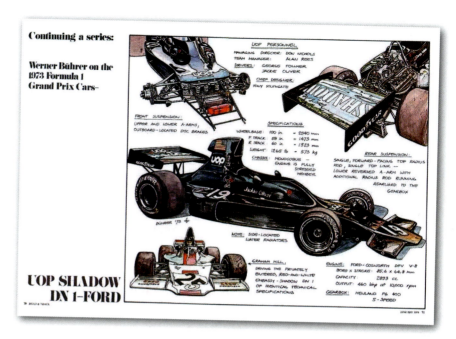

for round 3, held on March 3rd, 1973, around the swooping, high-altitude Kyalami circuit outside Jo'burg, South Africa.

There was historical significance in this. Although numerous American drivers had done well in F1, notably 1961 World Champion Phil Hill with Ferrari, American GP teams had been exceedingly scarce. The most recent had been Dan Gurney's All American Racers, which launched its own Eagles in 1966. The following season Big Dan drove his California-built, British-powered cars to two wins, first in the non-championship Race of Champions at Brands Hatch, then the full-scale World Championship Belgian Grand Prix at Spa. The American driver's GP victory in his own car was a feat that remains unique to this day.

Earlier, Lance Reventlow entered his Scarab team for a few European GPs in 1960, though to little effect. In New York's 1937 Vanderbilt Cup (not actually a GP but featuring European GP teams), Californian Rex Mays wheeled an Indianapolis-modified Alfa Romeo to an impressive third place amidst a quartet of Auto Unions. Way back in the 1921 French GP, Jimmy Murphy trounced Europe's elite with a US-made Duesenberg.

So after 52 years, GP racing's newest American-owned team (strongly flavored by members from other nations) had a modest but distinguished heritage to live up to.

ABOVE Beauty in the Bolide. One of *Road & Track* magazine's handsome presentations of racing car technology by Swiss artist Werner Bührer. In this debut year of Shadow in F1 American hopes burned bright for international success. *Courtesy of Road & Track*

TAKING ON THE WORLD **163**

THE DN1 DESCRIBED

SHADOW'S FORMULA 1 debutant came out very quickly, according to a technical rundown of the DN1 by Cyril Posthumus in *Road & Track*. "Construction… took little more than five weeks from laying down the monocoque tub on the factory floor to rolling the car onto the transporter for the first tests at nearby Silverstone."

As implied by the term "Formula," designers of F1 cars have always been constrained by many regulations. In marked contrast to the freedoms allowed in the contemporary Can-Am, Formula 1 imposed limits on minimum weight, engine displacement, body width at various stations along the car's length, dimensions and positions of aerodynamic aids, and other fiddly restrictions.

And that was before things would get really tight in subsequent years. At least designers in the 1970s still worked with engines of different numbers of cylinders arranged in various configurations, didn't have to fret about how few "power units" they were allowed through the season, weren't prevented from building a whole new car mid-year if necessary, had a choice between tire brands, could attach more than four wheels if they wished and transmit power to however many of them they cared to… they even were welcome to shape and position their nose cones as they thought best.

The most significant new FIA regulation of 1973 concerned fire safety. Fuel tanks now had to be protected from accident damage by cladding the associated areas of the chassis with "deformable structures" made of rigid, crushable foam. Put simply, the car had to wear a crash helmet. The foam was as much as four inches thick, depending on perceived vulnerability. FIA adjusted car width maximums and weight minimums accordingly, giving some cars a bit of a midriff bulge. F1's new minimum weight for 1973 went up by 25 kg, to 575 kg, or just under 1,268 lb.

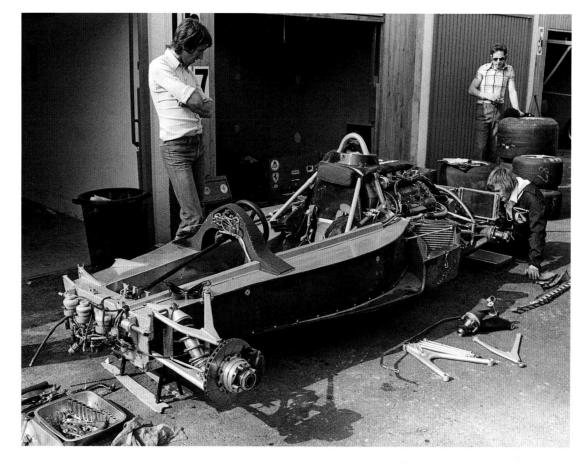

RIGHT Caught undressed in the Zolder paddock, a DN1 shamelessly reveals her elaborately fabricated front suspension linkage, aerodynamically curved side panels leading to the radiator tucked away close to the engine, and the twin oil coolers atop the gearbox at the back. While we're here, store in mind how the instrument panel is made, a sort of mini-monocoque of lightweight alloy. Three years hence new safety regulations will be imposed concerning this. *Motorsport Images/David Phipps*

This rule, along with emphasized concern for fire safety throughout the paddock, helped shape the new Shadow. Southgate drew his basic chassis as a then-typical semi-monocoque core structure made of aluminum sheeting folded, glued and riveted together into a pair of longitudinal torque boxes. These were spaced only just far enough apart to let a lean young race driver squeeze into the "bathtub."

Although the primary chassis pontoons had slab-sided rectangular cross sections, discernible by a line of rivets atop the tub where an interior panel runs lengthwise, to the eye the chassis sides bowed out to form a smooth "coke bottle" arc. The idea was to entice airflow into the hip-mounted radiators. Crushable safety foam filled the empty spaces between visible outer and hidden inner panels.

Although it had been commonplace in years past to employ the "pontoons" either side of the cockpit to carry fuel, this car's chassis torque boxes were effectively empty. In company with McLaren's M23, also built to that year's new rules, the DN1 housed its combustible fluids within the core of the chassis, behind the cockpit. This would have factored into the longer wheelbases of both new cars, but as well as the crash safety aspect the car's balance would be steadier as the fuel load reduced during the race.

UOP's tasty green lead-free fuel rode along in a foam-filled, rubberized safety cell stuffed into that space behind the cockpit. Declared capacity was 40 gallons Imperial of petrol, or 48 of gasoline in American vernacular; in continental liters that's not quite 182. Fuel mileage for F1 cars of the period typically hovered around 5 mpg (US), while in 1973 the longest GP race distance was Kyalami's 202 miles. Monaco was shortest at 159. So cars would not normally carry their full 240-mile capacity.

The sheetmetal portion of the chassis made up only its front two-thirds. It ended abruptly behind the cockpit, where the flat rear face bolted solidly to the front of the lightweight engine castings.

ABOVE Not that we revel in the sight of damaged racecars, but this 1974 snap of Jean-Pierre Jarier's crunched DN1 tub at Interlagos nicely shows the "coke bottle" monocoque shape, as well as the all-in-one bodywork that goes over it.
Motorsport Images/David Phipps

This was the legendary Cosworth-built, Ford-branded DFV, a 3.0-liter V8 that had been designed robustly enough to take on the extra job of being the rear third of a chassis all by itself. Thus none of the main chassis nor any bracing struts extended back alongside the engine, leaving the area free for exhaust headers, suspension links and other necessary systems.

Taking advantage of this open space, the designer directed his hot radiator air inward between wheels and engine and on out the stern. He even pinched the rear of his monocoque inward to ease the flow.

He did admit a miscalculation. Speaking with *Motor Sport* magazine in 2003, Southgate said, "It made for a neat package, except that the radiators proved to be 10 percent too small, so the car was marginal on cooling."

For the Ford DFV's seventh season of racing, manufacturer Cosworth claimed 465 horsepower at 10,250 rpm. It was supposed to be a secret that some teams paid extra to squeeze out a rumored 25 hp more, but at the further expense of shorter engine life.

However, some say the lead-free engines fell just slightly short of the peak numbers achieved by the nasty polluters. "There was a slight

RIGHT Perpetual evolution is a hallmark of Grand Prix racing. This photo shows a DN1 at the Nürburgring, after its first-generation rear suspension changed from the initial "one-link forward, one aft" scheme to the arrangement most other teams used. Angled driveshafts suggest experimentation with wheelbase is going on. *Motorsport Images/LAT*

ABOVE The earlier configuration was snapped in Spain, clearly showing the lower wishbone mounted with its apex under the gearbox, and the rearward extension to keep the wheel aligned. But now there is only one oil cooler instead of the original two. *Charlie Carroll*

difference but not much, and the regulators accepted it," said Southgate. "The fuel used to smell like pear drops, though — it wasn't normal at all. The problem was that, wherever we raced, we had to ship our own fuel in."

Whatever the power, it went to the wheels through Hewland's commonplace LG 400 five-speed transaxle jutting out to the rear.

Shadow's DN1 initially stood on a wheelbase of 100 inches, which was near the upper end of a range between 94 (Brabham and Tyrrell) and 102 (Surtees); all this according to the annual book *Autocourse*. However, mid-season Southgate added a spacer between the engine and transaxle to stretch the DN1's wheelbase out to 104 inches.

His reasons were to move a little of the weight distribution off the rear wheels, and also to steady the handling.

This spacer business is difficult to decipher from old photos, but it came to play a recurring role in Shadow cars as the years passed. Tony kindly described them for us this way:

"The spacers were four inches thick and were silver in colour because they were cast in aluminium and not magnesium. It's quicker to make aluminium and cheap. The spacer would put two percent more weight on the rear wheels if I required it. I would vary the weight distribution from circuit to circuit depending on the balance I was after. It was possible to change the wheelbase in around one hour, so we could do this during a test session or between practices. The clutch input shaft had to be lengthened at the same time."

Southgate was not the only F1 designer at the time who was playing with wheelbases, and for him it would remain work in progress. As he explained in the magazine interview cited above, "As the season progressed I lengthened the wheelbase by four inches and the thing went a lot quicker as a result. It changed the weight distribution — initially the car had had too much weight at the back."

Although the DN1's wheelbase was on the longer side, its track widths were 58/60 inches front/rear, which put them toward the narrower end of that spectrum (March pinched it to 56/58; McLaren's broad stance was 65.5/62.5).

When Southgate was at BRM, he designed his suspensions for Firestone tires, but Shadow's Goodyears had their own particular characteristics. Still, the DN1's suspension was fairly conventional for the day. At the front, upper and lower wishbones fabricated of numerous hand-made pieces cheerfully bathed in the breeze. So did springs coiling around Armstrong shocks, but the Lockheed brakes sheltered inside 13-inch wheels.

At the rear the Lockheeds lived inboard with the Hewland. Here, wheels of 15-inch diameter

ABOVE Jackie Oliver gave Tony Southgate's sleek new Shadow its first runs at Silverstone prior to the team's first race in South Africa. Of special note, look at the "shovel nose" and the fully faired engine bay. Overlook the "101" on the side, this would be a PR photo. *Don Nichols collection*

were each controlled by a single transverse arm and a solo trailing rod up top. There was a reversed lower wishbone — ie, mounted with its apex under the gearbox — to keep each rear wheel from steering, but Southgate departed from convention by eliminating the usual second trailing arm lower down. Instead, he designed a radius rod that led back to a subframe at the extreme rear. *Autosport* magazine declared this N-shaped arrangement to be "new thinking."

At a glance it appears this fore-vs-aft locating system amounts to a Watt linkage, which seemingly would assure perfectly vertical motion of the wheels, thus maintaining the wheelbase exactly. However, Tony explained his real thinking in the 2003 interview with *Motor Sport* magazine: "The lower radius rods ran toward the rear, rather than forward, to free up space for the radiators to nestle closely against the engine and rear tires."

At the time he drew the arrangement, he wanted the weight of metal and liquid well aft. But midway through the season suspicion about poor handling fell on the single trailing rod idea, so the car reverted to the conventional two per side.

Southgate's eye for both aerodynamics and artistry shaped the notably graceful fuselage. The prow's "shovel" shape gave the car's face a distinctive "duckbill" aspect, the sleek lines extended back to include those unusual engine coverings, and the tall engine ram-air scoop was nicely styled, with the Stars and Stripes proudly waving at its top. But Shadow's was a multinational effort, emphasized by American George Follmer and Briton Jackie Oliver as the drivers.

Ollie first tried the first car in the middle of January. It was a damp, wintry day at Silverstone, but there was no thought of escaping to the summertime heat of Argentina and Brazil, hosts for the first two rounds of the 1973 Formula 1 World Championship. This new team had a lot of work ahead.

TAKING ON THE WORLD **167**

TONY SOUTHGATE
DESIGNER

BORN IN COVENTRY in 1940, during that Midland city's wartime Blitz, young master Southgate's gifted engineering mind soon found its challenge in motor racing. While still a teenager he designed and built his own little racecar.

At 21 he presented himself to Lola Cars, then in the southeastern outskirts of London, and convinced Eric Broadley to give him a job. Over the next few years Tony's hands helped design and fabricate such successful Lolas as the T70 sports racers, Graham Hill's 1966 Indy 500 winner and the Honda-powered F1 car that John Surtees drove to victory at Monza in 1967. Dan Gurney then invited him to California, resulting in Eagle's 1968 Indy 500 winner. In 1969 Tony was lured back to England to be chief designer for BRM at Bourne.

One of Southgate's BRMs had just won the 1972 Monaco Grand Prix when he was approached about the Shadow program. As Tony related it in an email to us, "Jackie Oliver was the go-between with the Shadow job.

"I knew Jackie from BRM days, of course, and that he had gone to the US to drive the Shadow Can-Am car. He called me one day to say that Don Nichols, the Shadow owner, wanted to get into F1 with his own car and team. Jackie would be the driver. I did not know Don and had not heard of him before, but Jackie painted a very good picture of him.

"The BRMs were race winners, but the writing was on the wall at BRM. Due to poor engine development there was no chance of any more horsepower, and we were already struggling to keep pace, so the chance to use a Cosworth engine like everyone else was attractive.

LEFT George Follmer struck Tony Southgate as "quite laid-back." Yeah, you sure can see that in the American driver here. You'd never guess he's a hard-nosed, relentless street fighter of a racer, would you? *Motorsport Images/David Phipps*

ABOVE Southgate's admiration of Jackie Oliver's ability came from their time together at BRM. This is Ollie in Tony's P153 at Brands Hatch in 1970. *Motorsport Images/LAT*

"We arranged to meet up. I do not remember the meeting or the general discussions. They were after me, not me after them, so the discussions would have been easy for me: team structure, drivers, my money, when do we start. The location of the new Shadow factory was left to Don and Jackie."

Pending that, in October of 1972 Tony set to work at a table in his home garage to draw what was to be "Don Nichols number 1."

This "was not 'the next BRM'," Tony clarified. "The DN1 was a much more aerodynamically dominated car. It benefited from lessons learnt at BRM, of course, like not going to extremes on the rear axle weight. All the time, irrespective of the team, I would always be pondering and updating my latest thoughts on weight distribution vs. new tyre designs, etc.; all the aspects of the car. The design process would have been ongoing all the time in my head."

For BRM he had tunnel-tested scale models to develop what's called a "shovel nose," a concave or dished upper surface with a forward-jutting lower lip. Tony refined this further for his Shadow because, "I found it fascinating. The shovel was a development of the wedge nose, which was popular at the time on single-seat race cars and sports cars… The front nose splitters fitted to Can-Am cars, etc, in the late 1960s produced a similar effect, but not so efficiently."

By 1972 the dished nose shape was appearing on Can-Am sports cars from Porsche and Lola — and the Bryant-designed Shadow Mk III.

"The shovel nose F1-type bodywork produced very little downforce by sports car standards, but it was better than the normal-shape nose sections. The larger the forward-facing lower lip, the more downforce was produced.

"The BRM P160 ran without a shovel nose to start, then I fitted the shovel nose, which produced 70 lb more downforce [and the car] was quicker.

"The important thing about the shovel was that this increase in downforce was at the very front, at the leading edge of the shovel, which was most effective in nailing the front end down. There was no increase in drag from the shovel shape, a double bonus."

Using his tunnel facility to utmost effect, Southgate tested several variations of the concept. Resulting numbers established that, "There was a maximum limit in the length of the lower edge, or lip, to the shovel in terms of performance. I found that the first four inches were the most efficient, but you could go up to eight inches in length before there was no increase in performance."

Another feature of the DN1 bodywork was full enclosure of the engine, then a rare sight in F1. "I was carrying out more wind tunnel testing than most of the other teams, so I did have the exact aerodynamic figures for such bodywork differences. Even though the drag reduction and downforce improvements were small, they were better, and anything that could produce a better performance in F1 in those days you grabbed.

"Of course I would have been aware of the downside of such bodywork — a little more weight, higher under-bonnet temperature, etc."

However scientific his approach, Tony was blindsided by something he hadn't anticipated. Engine vibration. Spoiled by BRM's smooth-running V12, he didn't appreciate how badly Cosworth's V8 buzzed. Keith Duckworth's beautiful little DFV ranks as one of the greatest F1 motors of all time, but its flat-plane crankshaft made it shake. In the words of writer Ted West in *Vintage Motorsport* magazine, "It was basically two independent 4-cylinders fighting each other for your attention."

This characteristic didn't harm the DFV's scintillating performance, but it was death on anything bolted to it, unless care was taken to absorb the relentless vibration. Early Shadows suffered broken parts and damaged instruments until everything was cushioned with rubber or strengthened.

In due course Tony and his wife moved to Northampton, where Shadow's new digs had been set up. We've heard Nichols's amusing impression of the first building assigned to him, and Southgate agrees to a degree.

"The first Shadow UK factory was a derelict unit waiting to be pulled down, but it was free (that would have impressed Don) and we could move in straight away. It was certainly very tatty and trying to fall down in places, but you could lock it up!

"I do not recall the story of having to take the car through the toilet. Sounds like a pub story much embroidered."

The Brit also has his own view of the Yank's claim that Shadow was a generous provider. "Don may have believed he was the best payer, but generally speaking the boys were paid the going rate plus a bit more as an incentive to move to Shadow. For me it was easy to pay me more than I received at BRM, as BRM were most likely the poorest payers in the business.

"We did have machining and fabricating sections, plus a drawing office, [but] facilities and equipment were nothing special… in fact they were very basic. Don not being there that often to witness some of the manufacturing dramas we had, he likely felt that in his eyes we had all we needed."

Although the two interacted frequently, Southgate describes a superficial relationship. "Don did not spend that much time at the UK factory, he always seemed to be passing through. He was always at the race meetings and that would be where we would talk the most. The conversations were nearly always about the race and the cars, he very, very rarely talked about himself. Don was quite happy to let me get on with the design work, being content to look over what I was doing with a bit of explanation from me. He rarely made any technical comments.

"For me he always had an air of mystery about him, because he was secretive. He was rather a sinister-looking character, being tall and slim with a pointed gray beard and mustache, and invariably dressed in black. I knew nothing about his early life other than he had been in the Army. He wanted to be close and pally with me and all of the crew. He obviously liked being part of a team, his team. He had a good sense of humor."

Asked for any quirks he noticed about his employer, Tony offered these: "Don did not like small European cars. 'Little shit boxes' was his general description of them. We had a large American estate car at the UK factory for general use. The black Cadillac [that Nichols drove around England and the Continent] suited his image of himself very well and helped to maintain the mystique. The mystery about the marque's name suited Don down to the ground. He would play along with it whenever possible. He liked everything black, even wanted the monocoques anodized black, which was not very practical.

"The Shadow name and the shadowy figure… the only comment I got from Don was that there was once a mysterious cartoon figure in a comic called the Shadow, at which point Don got a bit embarrassed and went silent.

"I heard the CIA stories and throwing people out of helicopters, etc, but they were always from Jackie Oliver so may not be true."

About his two drivers, "Oliver had a great deal of

LEFT The men in black hauled their black cars around Europe in a nice big, black transporter. Thoughtfully, just for this photo op their driver puts on an appropriate dark expression. *Pete Lyons*

LEFT Black was the theme of the Shadowman himself. Don Nichols shipped over his big black Cadillac to get himself around Europe in American comfort. As he shows us at Silverstone, its big boot came in handy too. Notice the personalized license plate. *Pete Lyons*

Formula 1 experience and was the team leader," while Follmer "was easy to get on with, being quite laid-back in a very American way. He was not a technical driver, but he was certainly very brave."

About that first season as a whole, Tony's artistic nature was pleased with the team's presentation. "[The DN1] looked quite sleek and sinister, being finished in the all-black Shadow paintwork. The racecar transporter maintained the sinister image because painted on each side was a large figure of a man wearing a wide-brimmed hat and a large black cloak."

Technically, he was less complimentary. "There was no development program in existence at Shadow at this stage, and it began to show. Towards the end of the year, a long-wheelbase update was introduced to put a little more weight on the front wheels, which helped a little, but not enough. We were also suffering from niggling engine problems, accidents, transmission problems and marginal cooling.

TAKING ON THE WORLD **171**

ABOVE One of many Shadows that never emerged from the shadows… Nichols unveils the secret wind tunnel model of a proposed World Sports Car designed by Southgate. The project did not go forward. *Pete Lyons*

"One of the main reasons for the slow development of the DN1 was the requirement from Don Nichols that I design a Can-Am sports-racing car."

Expanding on that, he went on to say this:

"I would like to make a couple of comments about the first Shadow F1 season that help to get a better picture of what it was like from my point of view.

"First, unfortunately Don could not resist the temptation to supply a DN1 to Graham Hill for all the publicity it would bring Shadow. The problem was that the team then had to make another DN1 plus spares when we did not have the time. This made developing the works car harder.

"At the same time I was producing a turbo Chev-engined Can-Am car for Don, the DN2, to race in the USA.

"The combination of both of these projects made development of the DN1 very difficult. It was a case of keeping the show on the road somehow. Obviously the DN2 suffered as well. It was simply too much for a fledgling team."

The team matured, of course, and Southgate remained at Shadow for several years, until financial shortfalls and rising unrest sparked the infamous breakaway that produced rival team Arrows. Still, he and Nichols remained cordial for as long as the American kept his team going. Even afterward, says Tony, Don kept trying to lure him back.

"After the finish of Shadow in the UK [1980] I had no contact with Don until my sports car days in the early 1990s. I was working for Ferrari, looking after the 333SP project and racing in the IMSA series in the US. Don must have heard I was on the IMSA trail and started to appear at the meetings and talked about new race projects that I might be interested in.

"He eventually wanted me to start up an IMSA team with him, using the Ferrari 333SP cars with Andretti driving (wishful thinking most likely). To help Don acquire sponsorship, I gave him a design of mine.

"It was a WSC/IMSA sports car design that I produced after leaving Toyota (when Group C finished) and before starting work for Ferrari. I had intended to sell the design to a new sports car customer, but the offer from Ferrari came about the same time, which I accepted. The design then became redundant.

"I suggested that Don could use my drawings to make a wind tunnel model to impress the would-be sponsor. This he did, but nothing came of it."

Not for lack of effort. In January of 1996 Nichols held a press conference in France to announce a Shadow entry at Le Mans. According to reports, he had partnered with French carmaker Norma to campaign a Tony Southgate-designed car with a Porsche engine. Jean-Pierre Jarier would be the team's lead driver.

It's not clear if this plan is the same as the one described later, in which the Shadowman meant to convert his old DN4 chassis into long-distance machines for World Sports Car competition at Daytona, Sebring and other North American endurance races. In this case, he is said to have approached Ford to supply the horsepower. But such dreams came to nothing.

Nor did he get any takers when he built a new DN4 and proposed selling copies of the breathtaking old racer (at a breathtaking price) to vintage racers. There was even talk of making them legal for the public highway. Although age was advancing inexorably, the old Pathfinder paratrooper just would not quit.

As Tony Southgate recalls, "A few years back Don started to email me a lot about new projects we should do before he got too old, like a Shadow road car, etc. Soon afterwards he started to get very frail, and so it petered out."

SHADOW'S 1973 F1 SEASON

SOUTH AFRICAN GP

Kyalami, F1 (R3), March 3rd, 1973
1st, Jackie Stewart, Tyrrell 006
6th, George Follmer, Shadow DN1
DNF, Jackie Oliver, Shadow DN1, engine

"Debuts can be shimmering, gay, delightful affairs. They can also be disasters. The appearance of the UOP Shadows at the South African Grand Prix was a little of both." That's how yours truly began an *AutoWeek* piece describing Shadow's safari in South Africa.

First of all, the cars went missing. Marooned on a desert island. During the long flight from England their air freighter was forced down with engine trouble. It took five days to fix. Five precious pre-race testing days lost.

Once lapping finally began at Kyalami, the top section of Jackie Oliver's bodywork flew off. Until a new one arrived, he and George Follmer had to alternate track sessions while sharing the single remaining bodytop.

Some might have found that comical, but not what happened later. Oliver arrived at the pits with the first-built DN1 about to break in half. One of the two mounting studs securing the bottom-front of the engine to the chassis had broken, leaving only three to hold the marriage together. The car had only logged about 300 miles.

Replacing the failed part was straightforward, but as a designer for another team watched with sympathy he remarked, "Mind you, every other designer who has had to mount a DFV Ford has had the same problem."

After further delays during practice with balky engines, both Shadows started in the second half of the 25-car grid. Oliver lined up 14th with a time 1.36 seconds slower than top qualifier Denny Hulme aboard another brand new F1 machine, McLaren's M23. Follmer, feeling his way into a world wholly new to him, was 21st.

LEFT Crewman Mike Lowman helps his driver George Follmer on his way to his first day at F1 school. *Pete Lyons*

ABOVE Racers don't expect a lot of rookies. Just drive, learn the car, bring it back in one piece, if you please. This Follmer bloke might be the toast of America, but this is Formula 1, dear boy. Don't even dream of his finishing in the points first time out. *Pete Lyons*

But look where he finished. Although Oliver's unhappy week came to an unhappy end when his engine "just stopped," Follmer's kept going to the checkered flag. He did lose two laps to the winner, but nearly two hours of non-stop running afforded the F1 rookie 77 more laps of experimenting and learning — and awarded him the single World Championship point that came with placing sixth. In the American driver's and team's very first Formula 1 event.

INTERNATIONAL TROPHY (GB)
Silverstone, F1 (non-championship),
  April 8th, 1973
1st, Jackie Stewart, Tyrrell 006
6th, George Follmer, Shadow DN1
DNF, Jackie Oliver, Shadow DN1, clutch

Shadow spent the six-week interval after Kyalami in their new shop in Northampton. They emerged once, for a non-championship test outing in the International Trophy race at nearby Silverstone. A cold, wintry day out didn't yield much information. Both DN1s lined up way toward the back of a mixed grid of F1 and F5000 cars, and after one lap Oliver's quit with clutch slip. Follmer soldiered on through a snow squall to another sixth-place finish, but well behind.

SPANISH GP
Montjuich Park, F1 (R4), April 29th, 1973
1st, Emerson Fittipaldi, Lotus 72
3rd, George Follmer, Shadow DN1
DNF, Jackie Oliver, Shadow DN1, cooling
DNF, Graham Hill, Shadow DN1, brakes

Two-time World Champion Graham Hill came to the Spanish GP with his own Shadow, DN1/3, the first racecar that Nichols had ever sold. The red-on-white color scheme of Graham's tobacco sponsor was a startling departure from Don's Basic Black, but the car did look sharp.

Unfortunately it didn't run that way. As well as being bedeviled by all the new-car troubles racers get used to, Graham himself hadn't driven anything for half a year, so there was rust to knock off. He started the race from a lone position on the back row.

In the Basic Black camp things looked better. After two races and weeks of development work, the drivers, the team and the cars all seemed to be gaining confidence. More efficient hip radiators were keeping the engine cooler, and the "shovel" noses were longer for more front-end downforce to combat excessive understeer. Oliver and Follmer both qualified for the seventh row, Ollie a tick quicker than George and both within three seconds of pole winner Ronnie Peterson's Lotus 72. Oliver managed that despite delays with a broken wing mount and a slipping clutch.

Then… a real scare.

Southgate had spent most of Saturday evening with the mechanics as they slaved away to race-prep the cars, and when they were close to finishing he decided he could safely leave. But hardly had he entered his hotel room when the phone rang. It was chief mechanic Peter Kerr.

"He said that the radius rod mounting on the rear bulkhead was cracked on both cars!" Tony told us by email. "The DN1 utilised only one radius rod to the bulkhead so the loads were a little higher.

"I returned to the circuit straight away. When I arrived Peter had already stripped the back of the cars, engines removed, fuel out, etc. After a close inspection by myself I realised that the only way to fix this problem was by welding up and reinforcing the chassis mounting.

"Sounds straightforward. No. The fuel tank was only one inch away from the mounting and with the fuel drained there was the vapour to worry about, a bigger worry than the fuel itself. It was not practical to remove the rubber tanks entirely in the time available before warm-up the next day, it was already midnight. So I decided to leave the tanks in situ and just push them back

BELOW George came to Barcelona with a championship point in his pocket, and left with three more stuffed in on top of it. On his way to third place he gave Jacky Ickx quite a fight.
Motorsport Images/LAT

TAKING ON THE WORLD **175**

ABOVE Graham Hill, a two-time world champion who just could not turn his back, set up his own team. In future he would build his own Hills, but he started as the first customer Shadow ever had.
Motorsport Images/David Phipps

as far as we could, around 18 inches. I then filled the gap with wet rags and held my breath… remember in those days we used gas welding so there were flames everywhere.

"To get the full picture, the cars were being worked on next to the transporter and our transporter was just one of a row directly behind the pits and very close to each other. One big fire and we would have eliminated all the cars from the grid…"

The designer feigned confidence and calm, but in his book he admitted that inside he was… well, let's render his words as "sweating bullets."

All went well, the cars were back together by 4 am, and Tony could resume breathing.

That Sunday afternoon Follmer had the best race of the three Shadow drivers, a nice, ferocious race against Jacky Ickx in a Ferrari. As I wrote in *Autosport*, "Ickx was very interested in getting by Follmer, and these two were into a fascinating dice for a long time. The American newcomer wasn't giving an inch, and no matter how Jacky came into the braking zones there was George occupying the vital place. The Ferrari even tried lap after lap to get around the Shadow on the outside of the hairpins; once it backfired completely as Ickx found himself shooting off down the escape road with wheels locked!"

This went on for an entertaining 30 laps, enough so that attrition moved their battle up the lap chart. When Ickx finally muscled past Follmer his reward was sixth place. But just five laps later the Ferrari dropped into the pits. The Shadow kept on and on, and up and up.

But wait, there's more. François Cevert was having a battle of his own to stave off Emerson Fittipaldi, until the emerging star of France locked his Tyrrell's brakes and had an escape road visit of his own. Brazil's World Champion breezed on ahead with his Lotus.

Cevert's stop for fresh tires dropped him way back, but then he set the fastest race lap. Slicing by car after car eventually brought him up to Follmer's Shadow. George put up stout resistance,

ABOVE Here I am, standing on a podium alongside Emerson Fittipaldi, the King of Spain at my back, holding the biggest bottle of champagne I've ever seen… F1 is fun! *Motorsport Images/David Phipps*

but François eventually scrambled by and the Tyrrell wound up in second place. Which might have been first if Emerson hadn't succeeded in hanging onto his very wobbly Lotus with only three tires still inflated.

So Shadow's Follmer finished his second GP in third place, and on the same lap as the winner. Shazam, three more points in the championship.

Careful, George, this isn't that easy. The other two DN1s fell out, Oliver's with his temperature gauge going up and up until the engine made nasty noises, and Hill because his brakes "all boiled away."

Wrote Follmer's car designer, "It began to look as though George might possess the mechanical knack of getting his car home, come what may, which does seem to exist with some drivers, Alan Jones being the perfect example of that ability in those days."

And now that we know the story of the night before, we can understand why Southgate often says, "It was magic."

BELGIAN GP
Zolder, F1 (R5), May 20th, 1973
1st, Jackie Stewart, Tyrrell 006
9th, Graham Hill, Shadow DN1
DNF, George Follmer, Shadow DN1, throttles
DNF, Jackie Oliver, Shadow DN1, accident

Here we had a race we shouldn't have. A late resurfacing job at Zolder didn't leave enough time for the new asphalt to cure, so hot racecar rubber soon tore it up. Drivers rebelled, most of them, and a lot of running time went down the drain while arguments raged about cancelling the race. In the end financial muscle won, the cars rolled out to the grid, and the green flag was waved.

And more asphalt came up. Soon the surface looked like it was covered in black snow, with cars plowing a single pair of narrow wheel tracks between long windrows of stinky, oily black gravel. Car after car fell out of the literal groove and went flying off, six of them piling

ABOVE Prepping the cars in the Zolder pitlane, who has a clue about what sort of race this will be? Or if there will be a race at all? *Motorsport Images/David Phipps*

RIGHT A welder's work is never done. *Motorsport Images/LAT*

up in one heap of expensive junk outside one particular turn.

Shadow's part in the story is briefly told. Only Graham Hill managed to finish, but five laps down on ultra-careful, painfully conservative winner Jackie Stewart. Both factory men fell afoul of the foul track conditions, Oliver one of the many to crash and Follmer retiring when his throttles jammed solid in a gooey mess. Let's move on.

MONACO GP
Monte Carlo, F1 (R6), June 3rd, 1973
1st, Jackie Stewart, Tyrrell 006
10th, Jackie Oliver, Shadow DN1
DNF, Graham Hill, Shadow DN1, suspension
DNS, George Follmer, Shadow DN1, accident in practice

Oliver had a new car here, DN1/4, replacing the one terminally damaged in Belgium. Both factory

ABOVE Fixing, fettling, fine tuning… has anyone ever calculated the man hours of labor it takes to keep two Shadow DN1s running through the course of an entire Grand Prix season, against the time they are actually racing? *Motorsport Images/LAT*

BELOW All that work and worry and it comes to this. Oliver's crunched in a catch fence. Follmer's out too. But buck up lads, there's always next week. *Motorsport Images/LAT*

TAKING ON THE WORLD **179**

ABOVE Up until Monaco, Oliver has not seen a checkered flag. A collision at the very start threatens to extend that miserable streak. But here in these mean streets Jackie finally fights his way to a finish. *Motorsport Images/David Phipps*

BELOW The British Lion was once Monarch of Monaco. No more. *Motorsport Images/LAT*

Shadows wore their rear wings several inches farther to the rear. Hill's privateer car was benefiting from recent testing.

None of which benefited their weekend in Monte Carlo. During practice Follmer's relocated wing broke off at speed. Famously, it flew high over the fence and almost fell into the Royal Box near the start/finish line. On Sunday the Prince and Princess of Monaco would have been sitting there.

Oliver's wing might also have broken off, but luckily somebody spotted the incipient failure while Jackie was in the pits. He went on to start from a disappointing 23rd. Hill was two spots farther back on the last row.

But poor Follmer didn't even start. His flying wing episode didn't harm his car, but later in practice a collision with a slowing Ferrari damaged the Shadow to destruction. Two write-offs for the team in as many races.

Amidst the mad scramble of a Monaco start, Oliver's nose fin got bent but he understeered

180 CHAPTER 8

on to finish 10th, his first finish of the year. Hill, once a celebrated King of Monaco, staggered around with ever-worsening handling. After he stopped a rear radius rod was found to have punched into the tub. Shadows of Barcelona.

SWEDISH GP

Anderstorp, F1 (R7), June 17th, 1973
1st, Denny Hulme, McLaren M23
14th, George Follmer, Shadow DN1
DNF, Jackie Oliver, Shadow DN1, suspension and transmission
DNF, Graham Hill, Shadow DN1, ignition

Shadow had another new car, DN1/5 for Follmer. There hadn't been time since Monaco to much alter the other two DN1s.

Follmer's practice got off to a bad start when his brakes failed, and his sparkling new steed hit an improperly installed post in the catch fencing. The impact permanently wrinkled the tub and shoved the left-front suspension back an inch, messing up the handling. Said George, "It turns left real fine, but the other way it doesn't want to turn at all." He qualified nearly at the rear, with the other two.

But it was the other two who ran into trouble in the race, ignition failure in Hill's case, and simultaneous failures of Oliver's rear suspension and gearbox. Follmer's wrestling match went on all the way, although a long pitstop kept him right at the back.

FRENCH GP

Paul Ricard, F1 (R8), July 1st, 1973
1st, Ronnie Peterson, Lotus 72
10th, Graham Hill, Shadow DN1
DNF, Jackie Oliver, Shadow DN1, vapor lock
DNF, George Follmer, Shadow DN1, clutch

Here was another back-of-the-pack qualifying performance for Shadow. Private owner Hill was

BELOW Posed for PR purposes at Paul Ricard, the handsome newcomer seems surrounded by worshipful admirers. Or are those McLarens, Ferraris, Lotuses, Brabhams, Marches and Tyrrells, even that contrarily-colored Shadow, trying to keep the black one penned in the pitlane?
Motorsport Images/LAT

ABOVE For once Graham Hill's Embassy Shadow shows more speed than those in UOP livery. And for once, it maintains good speed all through the Grand Prix de France. *Pete Lyons*

slightly the fastest of the three *this* time, but only fast enough to start 16th. Why were the factory cars so slow?

Apparently because a planned improvement to the rear suspension, repositioning the springs for better roll control, required new brackets (from an outside supplier) that turned out not to fit the car. Having to run stiffer coil springs than optimal for this circuit caused oversteer that couldn't be tuned out. That's even though the rear wings had once again been relocated aft, which should have improved their efficiency.

Ollie's clutch failed at the standing start. George did get going, but stopped alongside the circuit when the engine died. He got out, jiggled some wires and was able to restart, only for it to happen again two laps later. This time he stayed there.

But good old Graham enjoyed a great race, dicing hard with younger men and coming home to a close 10th-place finish.

BRITISH GP

Silverstone, F1 (R9), July 14th, 1973
1st, Peter Revson, McLaren M23
DNF, George Follmer, Shadow DN1, multi-car accident
DNF, Jackie Oliver, Shadow DN1, accident at start
10th, Graham Hill, Shadow DN1, broken chassis subframe

UOP's drivers set identical qualifying times (timed only to a tenth of a second here), a whopping four seconds slower than Ronnie Peterson's pole for Lotus. This despite revised rear suspension geometry reported by the drivers as an improvement.

Raceday brought no better fortunes. At the start Oliver couldn't avoid ramming Niki Lauda, whose BRM broke a driveshaft. Precisely one lap later at the same spot Follmer got caught up in a massive crash triggered by Jody Scheckter spinning his McLaren in front of the pack at

Woodcote corner. Nine cars went no further.

After a long delay the race restarted. Hill dropped out of it before half distance after pitting first for new tires and then again because the entire front end — subframe, suspension, steering and all — had pulled loose from the monocoque.

At least America came away with something: the first GP victory by Peter Revson.

Thirty years afterward, Tony Southgate gave Britain's *Motor Sport* magazine an interview in which he revealed this: "I didn't know initially that Don was not the most popular bloke with Goodyear because of his past dealings in Japan, but I found out at Silverstone. We were very disappointed with our qualifying time there, so soon after the race we went back — with Brabham's Carlos Pace [a Surtees driver that year] secretly driving the car in a plain crash helmet so nobody would recognize him.

"He brought a set of tires along and with those fitted he went 2.5 seconds quicker than Oliver — and Jackie wasn't slow. We were a bit pissed off at that as you can imagine, but there wasn't much we could do. Goodyear gave us 'concrete' tires and that's what we ran on all season long."

A secret test with a secret driver proving they had sub-par tires! If Oliver had taken 2.5 seconds off his Silverstone qualifying time, he would have moved five rows up the grid to start 12th — diagonally just behind Lauda and potentially better placed to know the BRM wasn't moving.

DUTCH GP
Zandvoort, F1 (R10), July 29th, 1973
1st, Jackie Stewart, Tyrrell 006
10th, George Follmer, Shadow DN1
DNF, Jackie Oliver, Shadow DN1, stuck throttle, crash
NC, Graham Hill, Shadow DN1 (insufficient laps, 12th)

This was a dark weekend. A driver died. Roger Williamson's March went off the road

BELOW At Zandvoort the works Shadows appear without the sleek shrouds that had been worn between the airbox and the Cosworth engine. Doesn't seem to make a lot of difference. *Motorsport Images/LAT*

and hit a guardrail, which leaned back in the sandy soil and overturned the car. Fire erupted. Fellow driver David Purley stopped and tried to rescue his friend, but neither the marshals nor anyone else was dressed to wade into open flames to help.

The day before the tragedy, Oliver's Shadow did manage to qualify on the front half of the grid for once, 10th fastest at a mere 1.76 seconds slower than pole man Ronnie Peterson — who was on trick tires. Was Ollie too? Had he strolled over to see his new friend Carlos Pace? But once again he dropped out early, this time when his throttles stuck partway around the second lap and sent him into the guardrail.

The other two Shadows were still way back on the grid, but they did see the checkered flag.

On the bright side, at last the UOP team had been able to build one more new chassis faster than the drivers had been using up older ones, so in Holland they finally had a spare car. It wasn't driven this time, but it introduced revised rear suspension. Thinking that his original single trailing rod might somehow allow the rear wheels to "wind up and release," Southgate added lower trailing rods to make the dual setup that rival cars had. Also, it seems this is the car with its wheelbase stretched to 104 inches, moving the rear wheels aft to increase load on the front tires.

The pair of cars that raced retained their single rods but were missing Southgate's pet engine fairings. Wind tunnel testing had shown better speed without them, but also had suggested ways to design better fairings, once the shop had time to make them.

Hill's DN1/3 also had some aero tweaks, in that the radiator inlet fairings were all but gone. It seemed to improve cooling. There were other departures from "stock" — the independent team was exercising its independence!

GERMAN GP
Nürburgring, F1 (R11), August 5th, 1973
1st, Jackie Stewart, Tyrrell 006
8th, Jackie Oliver, Shadow DN1
13th, Graham Hill, Shadow DN1
DNF, George Follmer, Shadow DN1, accident

Oliver was using the new, four-link car at the 'Ring, but rainy Eifel weather crippled everyone's practice times, so any benefit of the new suspension was unclear. Once again, all three Shadows started well back.

Oliver again suffered a bad getaway with clutch trouble, but once racing he swiftly moved right up the line. He spent the second half of the GP pressing Emerson Fittipaldi and Jochen Mass hard. He was still tight up behind them at the flag, placed eighth. His stirring performance earned him an award named in memory of hard-driving Jo Siffert.

Hill put up a doughty performance too, spending the race holding the gear lever in place with one hand, but he did complete all 14 long, writhing, bumpy and fast Nürburgring laps with

BELOW A winner at last! No, not of the Nürburgring race, but Jackie Oliver's stirring drive up through the pack to finish a fighting eighth earns him the Jo Siffert award.
Motorsport Images/LAT

ABOVE Not a breakthrough, but better: not only do both works cars take the checkered flag at Monza, so does the privateer one. A 100 percent Shadow finishing record! *Motorsport Images/LAT*

the other hand. Follmer had just started his sixth lap when something broke and slammed him into the guardrail.

AUSTRIAN GP
Österreichring, F1 (R12), August 19th, 1973
1st, Ronnie Peterson, Lotus 72
DNF, George Follmer, Shadow DN1, gearbox
DNF, Jackie Oliver, Shadow DN1, fuel leak
DNF, Graham Hill, Shadow DN1, suspension bracket

Hill's Shadow too was now nude of its engine fairing. In the factory team, after his Nürburgring crash Follmer moved into the quad-rod car at the O-ring, while Oliver got his Zandvoort chassis back, repaired.

None of these changes seemed to change anything. All three DN1s took up their usual grid positions well toward the back. How all three fared in the race can be seen in our results listing.

ITALIAN GP
Monza, F1 (R13), September 9th, 1973
1st, Ronnie Peterson, Lotus 72
10th, George Follmer, Shadow DN1
11th, Jackie Oliver, Shadow DN1
14th, Graham Hill, Shadow DN1

ALL THREE FINISHED! Cosmic, considering what had come before.

Not to say their finishing positions were a breakthrough. Practice was unremarkable, the biggest reported problem being engine glitches that cost both Follmer and Hill a lot of time. Qualifying speeds of the trio were typically slow. In the race, Oliver suffered yet more clutch slippage, Hill's boys hadn't yet fixed his engine, while Follmer was just keeping on top of what he thought must be a flexing chassis.

BUT ALL OF THEM MADE IT TO THE FLAG!

And Jackie Stewart made it to his third World Champion's crown, taking it back from 1972 champ Emerson Fittipaldi.

CANADIAN GP

Mosport, F1 (R14), September 23rd, 1973
1st, Peter Revson, McLaren M23
3rd, Jackie Oliver, Shadow DN1
16th, Graham Hill, Shadow DN1
17th, George Follmer, Shadow DN1

Now here was one to remember. Or maybe forget, if you were actually out there, trying to race on a track changing between wet to damp and then dry. At one point everybody charged in for tires all at once, clogging the pits. Not unrelated to that confusion, a shunt so congested the track that officials slowed the pack by deploying a Safety Car for the first time in F1. It picked up the wrong car, a Williams whose driver, Howden Ganley, wasn't actually the leader. This in turn blew up every hand-written, rain-smudged lap chart the length of the pitlane… and so confused the officials that one waved the checkered flag a lap early. Or so others thought.

All this resulted in a long argument about who actually won the Grand Prix. For a while, Don Nichols's team believed it was them.

Not a preposterous concept, given that the pair of black Shadows started the race in a better place than usual, side by side on the seventh row. Follmer was 13th, slightly quicker than his team-mate despite Oliver using the newest car; Hill was two rows back. At flagfall all three got away well, but Ollie got away best. At quarter distance, lap 20, he was… HE WAS RUNNING SECOND!

Drying track conditions had something to do with that, as drivers either crashed or began swapping tires and the sorry Safety Car episode muddled everything. But Shadow's wheel change went well enough that Oliver's men had no trouble believing their lap chart when lap 40 showed number 17 LEADING THE RACE. Other charts saw him falling to third at the end, lap 80 (or 81? 82?), and that's how it's written in the history books.

BELOW Wet and wild race conditions always seem to show Ollie at his best. Mosport turns out to be one of the wildest ever.
Motorsport Images/David Phipps

ABOVE I say, Peter old chap, d'you know who's leading? Hell no, buddy, I thought you were — or Howden, maybe? *Motorsport Images/David Phipps*

LEFT Revson: Sorry, Ollie, maybe you did win but they gave it to me, I don't know what to do about it now. Oliver: Well I'm prepared to let it go, Peter, but you'll come and drive with us next year, alright? Fittipaldi: But Colin, he tell me was maybe me… *Motorsport Images/David Phipps*

RIGHT Together for the last time, in F1 anyway, at Watkins Glen Follmer and Oliver once again score a two-car finish for the factory. Not that nothing is going wrong with the cars, but they do make it all the way to the flag. *Pete Biro*

BELOW Guest driving a third works entry, Brian Redman qualifies the oldest of the cars fastest of the four DN1s at the Glen. Yet he's the only one to drop out. *Pete Biro*

UNITED STATES GP

Watkins Glen, F1 (R15), October 7th, 1973
1st, Ronnie Peterson, Lotus 72
13th, Graham Hill, Shadow DN1
14th, George Follmer, Shadow DN1
15th, Jackie Oliver, Shadow DN1
DSQ, Brian Redman, Shadow DN1, outside assistance

For the second time this season, Grand Prix racing endured a fatal accident. This one happened in practice, when François Cevert, Jackie Stewart's team-mate, suffered a savage crash that killed him instantly. Deeply shaken, Team Tyrrell withdrew from the event, which would have marked new three-time champion Stewart's 100th GP and his final one before his planned retirement.

Going ahead with the remaining teams, UOP Shadow entered three cars this time, making for a strength of four with Hill's private entry. The newcomer was the versatile Brian Redman of Britain, master of any kind of car. Shadow management was already evaluating candidates to join the team in 1974.

Guess who qualified fastest of the four? Redman put up the 11th best qualifying lap, in a DN1 that by now was being called "The Old Nail."

Alas, his race was short. Ahead of him at the very first corner a jostling match between other cars threw up dirt, which jammed his throttle slides shut. Brian coasted to a halt, cleaned the mechanism well enough to run, and restarted. But someone helped him by pushing the car, a rules violation that ended his day.

Less troubled were the other three Shadowmen, all of whom once again completed a race. Follmer was coping with bad handling but did not stop. Oliver did stop to replace a rear wheel, but when a front wheel nut unscrewed itself, the safety pin prevented it coming off so he didn't stop again. Hill also changed a tire, but otherwise was lapping faster than the works cars and finished ahead of them.

Once again, the three season-long Shadow drivers all finished.

ABOVE Poor old Graham has not enjoyed a satisfactory year with his private Shadow, although all in all the team drivers haven't had much better luck. Just think: there was a time when the twice World Champion won three US Grands Prix here in a row. American fans even call one stretch of the Watkins Glen circuit "Graham Hill." *Motorsport Images/David Phipps*

AFTER MISSING TWO GPs, over the remaining 13 races UOP Shadow's team cars made 26 starts, scoring two third places and one sixth. By earning nine constructors' points, Shadow ranked eighth among the year's 11 teams. George Follmer (five points) and Jackie Oliver (four points) were respectively 13th and 14th in the drivers' standings. The team's 14 DNFs, including Brian Redman's, dropped its finishing record to just worse than 50 percent.

Actually, in the day that wasn't as scandalous a number as it looks nowadays. Cars retired a lot back then, almost half of them on average. And George and Ollie did end the year with 100 percent at three races.

As an aside, note that George beat Jackie in the driver standings by one point, albeit for placings that may appear trivial to outsiders. But one wonders if this matter of the Yank trouncing the Brit at his own game informs the ungentle rivalry that would emerge in the following Can-Am season.

So Shadow's first season in F1 had been a difficult learning period, but there had been genuine bright moments. Fans of America's only GP team could hope that continued hard work by its able and faithful personnel would suddenly bring it all into focus. ♠

GEORGE FOLLMER
DRIVER

1970 CAN-AM AVS MK I

THE FIRST TIME I saw the "Knee High" car I should have run out the door! You had to go to the bar for a few minutes to get ready to drive that Shadow.

People tell me it looked frightening. It frightened me! Of course it looked slick. It was so low, so it should go fast and, gee, that part's nice, but whether it will turn and stop and all those other things it has to do as a racecar?

BELOW Forceful Follmer was 25, a family man and an insurance salesman when in 1959 he bought a Porsche Speedster and took up club racing. It transformed him into a ferocious professional, a multi-time champion aboard sports-racing and Trans-Am cars.
Motorsport Images/LAT

Well, the only way to find that out was to go race it.

When I was introduced to the car it was very secret. I mean you'd ask a question like, "Who owns the car?" They'd lower their voice, all mysterious and sinister and whisper, "Only the Shadow knows…"

I didn't know Don Nichols, didn't know much about him. Trevor Harris introduced him as somebody who made money in Japan, and he wants to go race. What Don did before I know little. But Trevor was doing it and I had faith in Trevor.

Trevor has always been enterprising and trying to develop new things and make them work. He and Bruce Burness set up that Lola T70 for me, and I was always half a second faster than Mark Donohue in the same kind of car. We had an experimental oil system that made the engine blow up almost every race, but it was a good Lola. Trevor and Bruce and I were a pretty good team. Every project we went in on together was successful.

The Shadow was a big undertaking. It was not a complete car the first time I saw it — but it never was a complete car! As they were building it, sometimes we'd find things that wouldn't fit, or it would hit something else, and you'd think, this isn't gonna work.

The first version of the car was very difficult to drive. The steering wheel was right up against my crotch. Not very comfortable. Also, the seat had too much of a laydown angle and that had to be changed soon after we started testing.

It had a lot of obstacles. The engine was not a race engine, it was just a Big Block Chevy with some injectors on it. It was OK, but to go Can-Am racing you had to have a pretty good motor. We couldn't afford that, but oh, the thing would run down a straightaway! It was faster than most of the other Can-Am cars in a straight line. But it was a handful around corners.

At Mosport, that turn they call Moss Hairpin at the bottom of that long, uphill run, when I came out of that and got the hammer down, boy! I got up to the other end a lot quicker than a lot of the rest of them.

RIGHT Tackling Shadow's radical, problem-plagued and frankly frightening AVS Mk I required a hard man in its cramped cockpit (here at Mosport). A hard man with a soft spot: George's signature number honored son Jim's 16th birthday. *Lionel Birnbom*

But that corner is bumpy, always has been, so I had to slow down more. The car would hop and you didn't know where you were going, so you couldn't put the power down. I was too busy chasing it all the way around the corner and couldn't pick the throttle up.

If the track had been glass smooth, then it wouldn't have been so bad. It was kind of like a go-kart. If there were any bumps or undulations or ditches in the track it would jump all over the place.

It wasn't the small wheels so much as it was the stiff suspension. The springs were only three inches long, because there wasn't any more room, and they would coil-bind. And it had friction shocks, which left a lot to be desired. At the time there weren't these mini shocks that motorcycles and ATVs have now. It would've made life a lot easier if we had some of the stuff that we have today.

There was never enough air going into the radiators, it would overheat pretty easy. The brakes were small in front, and it took a while to get the balance, but we got those reasonable. To drive it your feet had to point out 45 degrees, because there wasn't enough height. That was a little awkward, but it didn't bother me too much. And the hand-clutch was fine. I only needed it to get out of the pits, after that I never used it. I stopped using clutches to shift after the Hewland came out.

When Don got the second car ready for Mid-Ohio he wanted me to come back. I went there to test it and it wasn't any better. I want to run up front. I couldn't do it with that car. My career was going good in 1970, and I knew I'd hurt it if I stayed with this program. So I told Don I just don't want to race it.

Well, the only guy standing around was Vic Elford. I knew him from Porsche stuff, and I went over and said, "I got a deal for you!" Vic would drive anything, and he's a good race driver. Quick Vic. So I stuck him in that thing and went home.

I felt terrible because Don was a good friend and Trevor was a brilliant designer with a lot of innovations. He wanted to advance the art of car building, and Don wanted something all new and one-of-a-kind.

Yeah, that car was a challenge, but it had good things about it. A lot of the shortcomings could have been overcome if we'd had the kind of budget that you should have to do something like that, so we could go test it. A lot of stuff Trevor was trying to do was the right way to go. A lot of it did show up on cars later. So his Shadow was just a little ahead of its time.

1973 F1 DN1

Formula 1 wasn't the nicest thing I ever did. Shouldn't have gone in the first place, but sure, I always wanted to do it when I was starting out.

I found out there's not a secret science to Formula 1, like they want to think it is. The cars really aren't any different than Indy or Formula 5000. They're just a different kind of racecar chassis, a little smaller here and a little longer there. They're light and quick. They corner well. Of course you gotta keep them wound up on the cam, there's no bottom end. They're different than Can-Am that way.

Making our first race was a real stretch for the team, because they were always behind the curve about two months. They hurried and got the cars on the plane to South Africa so they could make the show.

We had a lot of trouble when we got to Kyalami. After we ran the cars for a few laps they were starting to fall apart. The tub was not stiff enough. The potential was there, and Tony Southgate had done a good job, but he made it too light in some places. So we spent a lot of time, a lot of all-nighters beefing them up so they were somewhat stiff.

It was a difficult time, but the car didn't run that bad when we got it working. And the crew worked real hard. I had a good crew there. I got sixth place out of that one.

That gave us one championship point, and that put our team in the manufacturers' association. That meant that they provided travel expenses for the Shadow team. That one point was a really big deal for a small team.

They took the cars back to England and massaged them some more and mine was running pretty good in Barcelona. Obviously I did pretty well. I would've liked to have gotten second place out of it, but I couldn't hold off François Cevert in his Tyrrell, and of course Emerson had the field covered with that Lotus. Their cars were just too good, they were a lot better than everybody else. They had some tricks that we didn't.

On the podium there Cevert started yelling at me that I was blocking him. I told him, "If you're faster than me, you should have been able to pass me easier." I mean, I'm not going to pull off the track and park for somebody.

So in my second race I was on the podium. Jackie Oliver was not a happy camper. After Spain they took my crew away and gave me Jackie's. I guess they thought my guys were too good for me. I felt that it was political. Jackie wanted the crew I had because he thought they were better than the crew he had. In my opinion, I wasn't sure if there was any difference in the crews.

I was inexperienced in F1 racing, so the team members considered Jackie as the number one driver. He had an impressive record of accomplishments in racing, especially in F1. He had driven for BRM and Lotus, and he was more experienced than I was driving the car and with the politics.

Added to the mix, he and many of them had raced together for years. I was odd man out. The contentious American vs. the established European driver.

As it worked out, Jackie also drove the latest version of the Can-Am Shadow against me in the Rinzler Porsche 917/10. So he and I would be competitors in Can-Am and buddies in F1? It wasn't going to happen.

Throughout the F1 season, the tension between Jackie and me didn't improve. I lost my temper a few times and went after him. That caused more tension. Don didn't want his drivers beatin' the crap out of one another.

My main concern was, I felt that I was not getting the attention I needed to run competitively. But you know, we had a lot of new people, they lacked F1 experience. I wasn't a lot of help on that. Yeah, I could feel the car, but I didn't work on it.

As the season went on we lost our way a little bit and didn't do as well as we had hoped. We scored a few points here and there. Oliver had a pretty good run at Mosport. He was good in the rain, he seemed to have a knack for that. I didn't, I come from California!

But we weren't a big factor. We were at a disadvantage from square one. First problem, we were short on crewmembers and we only had two cars in the beginning. We didn't have backup chassis and body parts to build new cars. True, later on we got up to four cars — then two of them got wiped out so we were back to where we were.

Secondly, we didn't have the best tire deal with Goodyear. The major teams got the best compounds and the latest tire innovations. We were not part of the invitational tire testing program, so we could not qualify as quickly as we could have with a decent tire. That meant that you started in the second half of the field — a breeding ground for crashes. There were plenty of crashes, and my crew would be forced to work day and night just to get the primary car ready. They didn't have the luxury of just pulling out a brand-new machine.

We had the same basic problem with our engine program.

ABOVE The Shadowmen are "happy campers" prior to their F1 debut in the South African Grand Prix at Kyalami. Flanking owner Don Nichols, manager Alan Rees and designer Tony Southgate are drivers George Follmer (left) and Jackie Oliver. Post-race, only one will be happy. *Getty Images/Bernard Cahier*

The high-budget teams had a six-pack of engines available and we didn't. It was a major issue.

So it was a difficult season, we struggled all the way through, but we survived. It was an interesting season. I'm glad I did it. It wasn't very successful as far as I was concerned, not really profitable, but I guess at my age I couldn't really complain too much. I was the oldest man in the field, 39. You know how they feel about that in F1 — you know, if you're not 17 you can't drive.

If you're young and you can live through the first couple of years, you're a pretty good asset to the team. You know the tracks and you know what's what, what it takes. When you come in cold like I had to... I didn't know whether the car was good or bad and I sure didn't know how to fix it.

That's why I really wasn't interested in doing it another year. It's a lot of stress, a lot of pressure, because it's unfamiliar territory, a lot of tracks that you probably have never been on before. And there's that whole scenario of you're an American, and they don't give you a lot of slack.

That's why when Mark Donohue was saying he wanted to come back and go F1, I told him don't do it.

At Shadow I was the outsider. I just came in to drive. There was Don Nichols, Jackie Oliver and Alan Rees, that was the clique. I wasn't in that clique. If there was a test, Jackie did it even if I was standing there. I could have done it too, get the benefit, but no, Jackie did it.

No, I didn't want to go back. I had my niche here. I'd had a lot of success in Trans-Am, and I knew the tracks here, and I knew the people, knew the crews, and that's a big asset.

And it was hard on my marriage. Hard on my kids. I was old enough to know better, I guess.

TAKING ON THE WORLD 193

MY OWN DN1

I wanted to keep the car I drove over there as sort of a trophy for me. I've heard some story that I seized it from Don, because he had stiffed me on pay or something, but that's not true. I purchased the car from him. I bought it.

I found out he wasn't happy about it when I had to go back up to Salinas to Don's shop and try to find pieces for it. I had to have a front upright. Nichols had one but he said, "Oh, I don't want to let any of those pieces go." But we knew each other pretty well, and he finally let me have the part. I finally got the car done and ran it a few times.

1974 CAN-AM DN4

I've always said the Shadow DN4 was one of the best racecars I ever drove. It was light, it was quick, it would stop and so on. Yeah, it was a Formula 1 car with a big block. It truthfully was — Tony put a lot of stuff on that DN4 that was right from the F1 car.

I went faster in qualifying at most of the tracks with that Shadow in 1974 than I did with the Porsche in 1972, when I won the Can-Am championship. I mean it was quicker through the corners. On the straightaways it wasn't quite as fast, but it handled extremely well and it would get off the corners real good, and it had plenty of horsepower. If it had come along a couple of years earlier nobody could have touched it. It was really a great car.

That crash I had at Mosport set me back a little while. It was just an engineering problem that they had. If you pushed the throttle pedal all the way it would catch on a pop rivet down there and hook the throttle open. I tried to make the corner and I almost made it, but I slid off and went into the wall, or whatever they had there. That's racing I guess, but yeah, it was pretty scary.

It screwed up my back and my shoulder was bad, but the worst thing was, I had two cracked ribs. You know, you don't jump around very much for a while. Cracked ribs, they take time and there wasn't time. The next weekend was the race.

I remained in terrible pain for the rest of the season. The

BELOW The DN4 he's hurling around Watkins Glen to win the post-season "Grudge Match" will stand as one of the best cars George ever drove. And he still feels he was the best driver of it. But he denies the "grudge" was real. *Motorsport Images/David Phipps*

two DN4 cars were the class of the field and I wanted to beat Jackie at every race, I just wasn't very effective. Jackie drove very well and won his races fair and square. Jackie won the title, I finished second.

I guess that my personality was not suited for that situation. In Mid-Ohio, I was running hard and Jackie and I tangled and my car spun into the dirt. I just climbed out and headed for my rental car. My back hurt, my ribs were killing me and I was tired of Oliver's crap. I was pissed to the point of no return. I remember tossing my helmet in the back seat and leaving, still wearing my fire suit.

Over the years, Jackie and I have come together and neither of us holds a grudge. It was all just a racing thing. Heck, back when Parnelli and I were beatin' on each other in the Trans-Am Mustangs all the Ford brass were goin' nuts and the press was sure we were gonna kill each other. But he and I would go in the motorhome after and have a good laugh. It was just good racing.

But Nichols didn't like that.

"TEAM ORDERS"

This is a touchy thing to talk about. Some people don't believe me. But Don and I had been together at races for quite some time, and yes, I knew what he was saying when he told me, "I don't want the cars racing."

But that's understood anyway, in any team, that you don't crash your team-mate. So when he said, "Don't push it," when everybody knew I was quicker than Oliver, to me it meant I wasn't supposed to win. I said, "Well, I wish you told me that before."

In that race at Mosport Oliver had some problem and I was way out ahead, but I had a lot of push. There wasn't enough downforce in the front end and those little 13-inch wheels, the left front tire wore out. I came in for a pitstop.

They just stood there and looked at me. The crew, they're like just watching the race go by. I was sitting there waiting for them to change the tire. Then when they finally came over, they had to go get the jack and get the wrench and this and that. I went back out, but Oliver was gone by that time. I wasn't happy.

Oliver was supposed to win, that's all there was to it. I can say that now. I mean I'm not looking for a job, so it's not like I don't want to piss off a car owner. I'm 86. I don't give a damn at this point.

ABOVE One rare, fleeting moment of levity brightens the usually somber, strictly business mood of all racetrack paddocks. Kudos to normally severe manager Mike Hillman (right), who just this once can feign a suggestion of a smile. For poor George's sake. *Dan R. Boyd*

DON NICHOLS

Everybody knows Nichols was kind of an aloof guy. He never said much. At times he didn't communicate very well. You never really knew where the money came from. He was just secretive. He was so damn secretive about that little-wheeled car that you almost had to get a federal pass to get into the shop. Well, he was trying to protect his investment and I don't blame him for that.

Don did a lot for my career. He had a past that he kept close to the vest, but he was also a brilliant thinker and had a fantastic imagination to create state-of-the-art racing machines. He did a lot with very little money and he ended up having many of the world's best drivers run his cars.

Don was always a straight-shooter with me, and for that I will always respect him.

Compiled from in-person interviews, as well as quotes borrowed with permission from George's website and his own book, Follmer *(ejje Publishing Group, 2013), co-authored with Tom Madigan.*

CHAPTER 9
THE BIG ONE

SHADOW DN2 (CAN-AM), 1973

"A BIT MIND-BLOWING." Such was Tony Southgate's first impression of the fresh Can-Am challenge that Don Nichols handed him in 1973.

An 8.1-liter Big Block Chevrolet V8 engine twin-turbocharged to a projected 1,200 horsepower and 1,000 pounds-feet of torque. Transmission components tough enough to handle that. Enough fuel capacity to run wide open for 200 miles at two miles per gallon. A radiator system up to cooling the monster.

Oh, and it had to be designed and constructed and developed in time to start racing in June. All while not letting up in the wrestling match with a Formula 1 machine that was proving recalcitrant.

"The problems were immense," Southgate dryly wrote in his book.

He did have something going for him: this wasn't his first Group 7 rodeo. While at BRM he had designed and race-developed a Can-Am vehicle for 1970 called the P154. The car was clever and elegant and quick, although fragile and not really a contender, but it was a start. A literal start — Tony sketched his first body lines for the new Shadow right on drawings of his old BRM.

"Once again I used Imperial College, London, for all the wind tunnel work. The finished body shape was advanced for the times, with a sharp, 'chisel' nose section that required good pitch control from the chassis. The water radiators were side-mounted and low down, and the high, stubby tail section was complete with a very large rear wing section. Actually the aerodynamic performance was very good for its day."

Massive fuel capacity made the DN2 big and heavy. Compared to the 1972 Bryant car, Tony stretched the new one's wheelbase by five inches to 103, widened the track dimensions to 62 inches front (from 60) and 61 rear (from 57), and the gasoline tanker of a chassis sprawled out to 82.5 inches wide. Dry

weight was given as a hefty 1,650 pounds.

Southgate's chassis design broadly followed recent F1 practice, where the engine block acted as the rear third (approximately) of the structure, thus saving weight and freeing space either side. It was an idea pioneered in 1967 by the Lotus 49, with the sheet-metal monocoque terminating at the back of the cockpit. Keith Duckworth specifically designed his Ford-sponsored Cosworth DFV V8 to handle the extra job of holding up the back of the car.

But General Motors probably never foresaw such a use for its mighty Chevrolet Big Block, so McLaren and other Can-Am designers hedged their bets by adding various tubular braces from back of tub to back of engine.

Southgate's preference was to forget the tubes and reprise his 1970 BRM idea, which extended the shallow tub in the form of a fork along either side of the engine, ending with a pair of tapering, tusk-like pyramids bolted securely to a transverse casting carrying the back of the engine. The Chevy was still part of the chassis, but it had help (see page 199).

For his suspension and running gear, Tony decided he could borrow certain components from his comparatively small F1 DN1, helping to speed the job along while he concentrated on a knottier problem: how to package the turbos. He had looked at 1972's "canary with antlers" solution but balked at hanging all that weight so far back and so high up.

Studying his own car, a penny dropped: there was ample real estate atop that vast acreage of monocoque to plunk down a turbo either side of the engine. A straight shot for headers out from the cylinder heads, an equally easy run for exhaust outlets either side ahead of the rear wheels… tidy, efficient, logical. Southgate's solution would be widely copied in years to come.

If only Shadow's turbo project had been successful, the story of this car might have been happy. But it wasn't. Despite periodic promises

ABOVE Big, Burly and Baaaad … but not in a good way. Don Nichols wanted to meet the Porsche Turbo Panzers head-on by bolting blowers to a Big Block Chevrolet. But the solidly established German automaker had the budget and engineering resources to pull it off. A handful of California hot rodders didn't. So Oliver usually raced with a non-turbo engine, seriously underpowered for the DN2.
Pete Lyons

THE BIG ONE 197

RIGHT & BELOW The DN2 chassis going together at Shadow's Northampton premises in April, just steps away from the already-completed Formula 1 cars. Although an outwardly much different sort of machine, the sports car does incorporate elements of the same designer's DN1. *Pete Lyons*

of an imminent debut, the super motor only raced three times late in the season, and never ran well.

Built for a claimed 1,200 hp, for most of its races the DN2 was seriously underpowered at, according to Southgate's book, a mere 735. Nor did it handle. Jackie Oliver complained all season of heavy steering and gross understeer. He also suffered numerous mechanical breakdowns. Well before the end of a disappointing season, onlookers felt Shadow had abandoned Can-Am to focus on F1.

SHADOW'S 1973 CAN-AM SEASON

ALL PORSCHE all the time. That was the story this year. After the German turbocar's near-dominant performance in 1972, and McLaren's departure from the series, the 917/10K became a customer car and everybody wanted one… although not everybody could buy one.

One who could afford two of them bought the Penske pair that won the championship and

LEFT Once the two monocoques were fabricated in England, they were shipped to Chicago's O'Hare airport for completion by Shadow's American facility.
Don Nichols collection

BELOW Southgate's DN2 chassis was something of a hybrid design, a traditional full-length monocoque that also brings loads down to single points at the rear of the engine, thus asking the block to help carry the car, as with contemporary F1 cars (including the DN1).
Don Nichols collection

hired 1972 Can-Am champ George Follmer to step back into his '72 ride. George's team-mate in the ex-Mark Donohue car was Charlie Kemp. Other names painted on Porsches included Hurley Haywood, Brian Redman and Jody Scheckter. Jody said of his stubby flexi-flier, "It's like riding a bicycle with an afterburner on the back. It's too fast on the straights, and too slow in the corners. If it's wet tomorrow, they can get someone else to crash it."

Meanwhile, Donohue was once again all by himself at Penske, and enjoying a much-improved edition of the Panzer named 917/30. Longer, sleeker, and far better-mannered, it had two special tweaks: a driver-adjustable boost-control knob that could summon as much as 1,500 hp, and a driver-adjustable rear anti-roll bar to help keep it all in line.

The lone factory driver going against all this Stuttgart muscle was one Keith Jack Oliver, a lad with an F1 physique looking rather dwarfed by the vast UOP Shadow DN2.

As did his engine, actually. Its eight tall intake stacks were impressive in a nostalgic Can-Am way, but under the black powerplant

THE BIG ONE **199**

ABOVE Snap quick, it's only gonna last two laps. Oliver's new Can-Am Shadow arrived at Mosport still incomplete, and not surprisingly it was neither quick nor reliable. But it did run long enough to display Southgate's distinctive hand at body design. Developed in a wind tunnel, it combined low drag with massive downforce, not only from the broad "shovel nose" but also the generously sloping rear body line. The giant square intakes in the bow are to cool the brakes only; the water radiators low in the body sides just behind the front wheels are fed from the underside and wheel wells.
Simon Lewis Transport Books

cover were no turbos and consequently no horses. Though Shadow's US engine arm was still working on its turbo Chevy, it was no nearer being race ready now than the original had been eight months earlier.

Similarly underwhelming, the Can-Am series itself was falling short of promise. The year before it had lost its series sponsorship, and now mighty McLaren was gone. So were Lola, Chaparral and some of the other marque names that had helped make the series magical. Crowds were thinner, and track promoters were losing interest. The 1973 calendar offered only eight rounds, one fewer than in '72.

At the same time the wider automotive world was undergoing harsh changes, as manufacturers, legislators and racing organizations faced restrictions on petroleum fuels and regulations intended to improve air quality and driving safety. Powerful, fast racing cars were losing their appeal to the public at large.

MOSPORT, ONTARIO (CDN)
Can-Am (R1), June 10th, 1973
1st, Charlie Kemp, Porsche 917/10K
DNF, Jackie Oliver, Shadow DN2, gearbox

The normally aspirated DN2 was still unfinished when it arrived at Mosport. Oliver's initial debugging laps had to serve as his qualification runs. He took the grid in 11th place, nine yawning seconds behind Mark Donohue on pole. The Shadow raced just two laps before its gearbox broke.

ROAD ATLANTA, GEORGIA (USA)
Can-Am (R2), July 9th, 1973
1st, George Follmer, Porsche 917/10K
DNF, Jackie Oliver, Shadow DN2, suspension

Mosport had been so desultory that series administrators split remaining events into two heats. They hoped that fixing cars retired from

ABOVE By Watkins Glen the nose has grown some fences to persuade air into the brake ducts. The Shadow seems to be going a little better. But it's still no Porsche beater. *Motorsport Images/David Phipps*

the first heat would make for a better show in the second. At least the crowd would get to watch two opening laps, apparently the only moments when cars would bunch together.

Shadow was showing better, Oliver earning fifth-best grid place for the first heat, but he went out early with front suspension failure. He was one who couldn't start heat 2.

WATKINS GLEN, NEW YORK (USA)
Can-Am (R3), July 22nd, 1973
1st, Mark Donohue, Porsche 917/30
NC, Jackie Oliver, Shadow DN2, running but not classified

Mark's super-supercar finally gave him a win at The Glen, starting his string of six unbroken runs to the championship.

And Oliver's UOP Shadow at least managed a finish, finally. That didn't seem likely to begin with, as it took the crew most of practice to fix a leak from the water pump. In the first heat, as recounted by *Autosport*'s Gordon Kirby, "Oliver had been trying to contain the vicious twitches of the Shadow… when the water pump pulley fell off and sprayed water all over his back so that he spun to the back of the field before packing it in after four laps."

That landed Ollie a long way back on the grid for the main race. But this time the repaired DN2 stood up to his hard-charging style, and he worked his way up to sixth place. After losing so many laps of the first heat his final 17th place overall was not official, but at least the car was still running.

MID-OHIO (USA)
Can-Am (R4), August 12th, 1973
1st, Mark Donohue, Porsche 917/30
8th, Jackie Oliver, Shadow DN2

Shadow's own turbocar was on the scene at

THE BIG ONE 201

ABOVE Engine builder Doug Meyer, with beverage, watches his boss Lee Muir plumb the depths of the turbocar's, er, plumbing. Nicely revealed here is Tony Southgate's packaging solution, mounting the two blowers either side of the engine to discharge laterally. Also seen, the water radiators just behind the front wheels. Shadow's team is something of a family affair: waiting behind the wing is regular mechanic Jim Spicklemire's cousin John Spicklemire, while Lee Muir's son Dennis perches in the truck doorway. Dennis Muir will continue working with Shadow on and off for years, eventually restoring a DN8 F1 car for Don Nichols. *Doug Meyer*

last, but it went unused. Oliver was having quite enough trouble with truly evil handling to bother with extra power on this writhing course. Still, during the first race he was able to involve himself in a battle for fifth place until the car ahead, a Porsche turbo driven by Willi Kauhsen, broke a driveshaft and wobbled side-on into the Shadow. Its external radiator piping squashed, the DN2 overheated and Oliver backed off to finish 12th.

His crew replaced the pipes for the second race, but they also had to work on the clutch and the race was underway before Oliver roared out to join it. As Kirby called it, "Ollie began a scythe through from the back of the field… with unrelenting energy, catching the midfield runners by half distance and then working through them.

"All the time the Shadow looked rough and harsh, understeering off under braking, and then lurching into apexes before it would roll over into a nasty oversteering twitch as Oliver tried to put the power down. It seemed a waste of considerable talent."

On aggregate he was placed eighth, six laps behind the winner. But this time Shadow posted its first official finish of the Can-Am year.

ROAD AMERICA, WISCONSIN (USA)
Can-Am (R5), August 26th, 1973
1st, Mark Donohue, Porsche 917/30
DNF, Jackie Oliver, Shadow DN2T, engine
DNF, James Hunt, Shadow DN2, fuel leak

At last Jackie Oliver debuted the turbo model here on RA's long straights. Guest-driving the normal model was meteoric Formula 1 driver James Hunt. Neither had a pleasant time.

The twin Schweitzer turbochargers had never before spooled up other than on a dynamometer. Everything was ready for action until one of the wastegates acted up. Oliver didn't get out until the last minute of practice. Without having set a time, or completed anything like a test, Oliver had to start from the back of the grid.

Hunt had a longer session in the normally aspirated Shadow, long enough to affirm the car was difficult, but before much could be done about it the 494 broke.

Sunday was douse-me-with-a-bucket hot. In the Sprint race Ollie had his 1,200-hp launch from way back on the grid, having not posted a qualifying time. The massive machine soon dropped out with a blown head gasket — sound familiar? — so it did not contest the Cup heat.

Hunt, as Kirby expressed it, "drove forcefully with the ill-mattered Shadow, slithering and sawing his way around the circuit." He did finish the preliminary race in seventh place a lap behind the winner, that man Donohue, but a fuel leak prevented his starting the second one.

James had a column in *Motor*, an English weekly, where he shared impressions of Can-Am: "I had expected 750 bhp to be rather exciting, but the car seemed rather gutless… Not being a racing engine, it's not very lively and thus the only hint I had of any power was that every time I put my foot down the back wheels let go and I got violent wheelspin."

RIGHT James "Superstar" Hunt got a taste of Can-Am at Road America. He found it not to his taste, although to be fair to the series, this car was not its finest example. James came to race the normally aspirated DN2, but this photo proves he was at least strapped into the turbocar at some point. Nobody who drove it liked it, but Shadow's turbo Chev did not die there and then. In later years Lee Muir and Doug Meyer further developed this car engine into an aircraft powerplant. Carrying the brand Thunder Engines, it was test flown, certified as airworthy, and put on the market. *Don Nichols collection*

BELOW James races the normally aspirated car at Road America, making plenty of thunder up through Thunder Valley, but not caring for the experience at all. *Rich Zimmermann*

THE BIG ONE 203

As the *Autosport* man reported, when the engine resisted all attempts to start it for the final, Hunt was "secretly relieved… Driving that car was like doing press ups in a steam sauna for an hour!"

EDMONTON, ALBERTA (CDN)
Can-Am (R6), September 16th, 1973
1st, Mark Donohue, Porsche 917/30
3rd, Jackie Oliver, Shadow DN2

From sweltering Wisconsin to wintry Alberta. Oliver, back in the normally aspirated Shadow, found its handling much improved thanks to development work with springs. He finished the Sprint third, still on the winner's lap. He scored the same result in Sunday's Cup race. Quite a breakthrough. Never mind that Oliver was two laps behind Donohue and second man Follmer; surely these F1 team-mates exchanged a cheery wave each time the Porsche lapped the Shadow.

LAGUNA SECA, CALIFORNIA (USA)
Can-Am (R7), October 14th, 1973
1st, Mark Donohue, Porsche 917/30
2nd, Jackie Oliver, Shadow DN2
DNF, Vic Elford, Shadow DN2T, brakes

Again Oliver chose the unblown Shadow, while the boosted model had a run in the hands of Mr. Versatility, Vic Elford, who had once briefly raced the Tiny Tire car. Quick Vic had already tested here, managing to turn the black car a warm shade of desert tan. In the race it was the brakes that put him out.

This time Oliver started a decent fifth in the first heat and kept on going all the way, posting a nice third-place finish. This was despite nearly running out of UOP fuel, which explained his vigorous swerves during the last three laps. Topped up for the final, he ran the whole way and finished second, only a lap behind Mark Donohue's Panzer. A rousing result, actually.

RIGHT Vic Elford was the turbocharged car's victim at Riverside. *Motorsport Images/Rainer Schlegelmilch*

RIVERSIDE, CALIFORNIA (USA)

Can-Am (R8), October 28th, 1973
1st, Mark Donohue, Porsche 917/30
DNF, Jackie Oliver, Shadow DN2, accident
DNF, Vic Elford, Shadow DN2T, engine

Oliver tested both DN2s in practice, and once again chose the regular one as his Sunday driver. His 10th on the grid reflected the DN2's still-difficult handling. In Kirby's words, "his Shadow [was] looking decidedly vague and discouraging through the slower twists where its heavily unresponsive steering made the car react in delayed and unpredictable lurches. Yet Ollie could get the thing through some faster portions of the track almost as well as anybody."

He dropped out of this season finale after clouting Charlie Kemp's Porsche and hitting some of Riverside's notorious buried-tire apex markers, which ripped off the Shadow's entire nosepiece.

Elford retired as well, this time of issues

ABOVE Turbo installation borders on elegant. Small exhaust ports on the sides of the body, near the number 102, indicate that the pair of turbochargers are just inside, perched atop the broad aluminum monocoque. Tony Southgate considers this setup his own innovation, one that became commonly used by others. Pitlane personnel considered the lateral blasts of fire a bit menacing. *Pete Lyons*

BELOW Pack of Porsches pace the Riverside finale, Donohue on pole with the blue-and-yellow 917/30. Four rows back is Oliver in the normally aspirated black Shadow, and in the far distance Elford in the turbo version. *Motorsport Images/Rainer Schlegelmilch*

RIGHT Pardon us, coming through. Charlie Kemp, winner of the first race of the season, and Jody Scheckter in another 917/10K, muscle their way by Oliver into Turn 7. *Jim Chambers*

variously reported as throttle linkage trouble and overheating.

Only one man had a good day: Mark Donohue in the 917/30. He was having a great time whooshing around the high-speed circuit, a driver-engineer happily playing with his boost control and his sway bar adjuster. His only concern about other drivers was when he came up to lap them.

SCCA officials who still harbored hope that their two-heat system would spice up the events must have been deeply disappointed. So was everyone else. The original "no rules" Can-Am had been a spectacular showcase of excitingly ingenious machinery. Now it was just a clutch of old and tired also-rans droning along far behind one excitingly perfect Porsche.

This listless season finale truly showed the series was on its way out.

So was champion Mark Donohue. He promptly announced his retirement from driving.

But Don Nichols soldiered on. ♠

RIGHT Taken during Saturday practice, Elford in the DN2T catches a brief glance of Donohue's 917/30 showing how turbocharging has to be done. Porsche's ability to show it is greatly due to Mark's engineering prowess. Together they created a car that the new Can-Am champ was calling "a monument to my career." *Pete Lyons*

BELOW Yes, that's "the wrong" helmet in that turbocar. During development the engine team trucked its DN2T to Indianapolis Raceway Park, a dragstrip-plus-road circuit out in the quiet countryside west of the famous big Speedway. Joining them in solitude there was a certain George Follmer, whose weekend job that season was racing a turbocharged Porsche 917/10K for the Rinzler team. Hmmm… thinking back on Parnelli Jones's secretive run in the AVS Mk I at Orange County, and Carlos Pace bringing the good Goodyears to Silverstone, it looks like stealth operations weren't all that unusual *chez* Shadow! *Doug Meyer*

THE BIG ONE **207**

CHAPTER 10
FRESH START

SHADOW DN3 (F1), 1974

AS 1974 OPENED, Shadow Cars UK had just moved house, from its decrepit old place on the Weedon Road, Northampton, into spiffy new headquarters. It was a short move, just around the corner along Ross Road.

A new factory, a new season and two new drivers kept shop life lively enough, but outside the walls things were really boiling. Challenges bubbled in such areas as regulations, technology, economic adversities and, especially, deep concerns about fuel and energy in general.

Middle Eastern petroleum producers had abruptly shut their supply valves, and the world went into shock. Reactions ranged from reasoned to ridiculous, from limits on gasoline purchases to outright bans on using motor vehicles.

In South Africa, totally dependent on imported oil, the clampdown was so draconian that police arrested car builder John Surtees for the crime of trying to test his Formula 1 car on the private Kyalami racing circuit.

One hopes it was a PR stunt.

Around the globe, races and race series were postponed or cancelled outright. Race teams toiling to prepare for the season had to wonder if they would be allowed to go racing at all.

Resolutely oblivious to all the turmoil outside, Tony Southgate kept his mind on two new Shadows he was to design, replacements for the DN1 Formula 1 and the DN2 Can-Am.

The new F1 would be the DN3, and of course it had to be done first, in time for the opening Grand Prix in January. And it was no mere update. Its basic concept was similar to the DN1, but the new car required a new structure differing in almost every part.

Outwardly, the DN3 could be distinguished from its older sibling by, first of all, its bigger, squarer, not-so-handsome engine intake "airbox." At least the good ol' Stars 'n Stripes stood prouder. The body's prow was a further refinement of the "shovel" configuration, with twin nostrils feeding an oil cooler now living up front, instead of the extreme rear. Also the

ABOVE Preparing to race at Brands Hatch, designer Tony Southgate and the usually merry Shadowmen are all business. This year's bigger, blockier airbox is the quick way to identify the DN3, but this is an all-new Formula 1 car in almost every part. *Motorsport Images/LAT*

BELOW Isn't she lovely? Don't you just yearn to slip down inside, touch her, feel her… *Pete Lyons*

rear wing was different, and the chassis sides had been reshaped without the former outward bow. This better suited hip radiators that were located farther forward and appeared larger.

Front suspension retained the principle of outboard coil-overs with A-arms, but mounting points, geometries and parts themselves were all altered. In particular, the spring mounts appeared to be moved back along the chassis by several inches, freeing space ahead of them for simple tubular A-arms rather than the complex, "bent" fabrications of before.

These changes had the effect of moving the driver's position forward, so the foot pedals appeared to be on the front axle line, not a little behind as before.

While at it, Southgate completely redesigned the front suspension mounting brackets to better spread their loads into the aluminum tub, which itself was stiffened with additional internal bulkheads. If published figures are truthful, the new monocoque itself weighed

FRESH START **209**

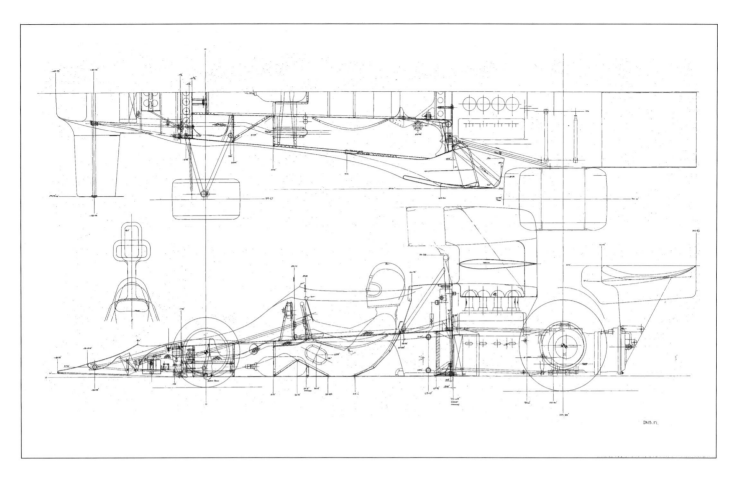

ABOVE From the hand of the master, this drawing lays out how all the multitude of separate components are to come together into one cohesive, balanced, scathingly quick Grand Prix car — while staying just within the boundary lines set by F1's multitude of rules. Notice two alternative orientations of the airbox inlet. *Don Nichols collection/ Dennis Losher*

20 pounds more than the old, at 90 vs. 70. The whole car was reportedly up by 25 pounds, 1,295 compared to 1,270.

At least a new type of gearbox saved a little weight. Compared to the earlier Hewland FG400, a 100-pound item that the team had modified to suit its own ideas, Southgate gave his new car a new TL200, which supposedly weighed just 90 pounds. Impressive if true, as the new gearcase was stronger and its whirling internals were bigger and heavier. Hewland was thinking of endurance for Le Mans, while Southgate was mindful that Cosworth kept making its DFV more powerful. The TL200 was still experimental, and Shadow was the only F1 team using it, although Matra also was trying it on its long-distance sports racers. After early driver comments about sluggish shifting, Hewland looked into shaving weight from the gears. Then they dropped the whole idea.

Curiously, today the famed transaxle firm seems to want its short-lived TL200-series wiped from memory. No reference can be found on the corporate website, and owners of the Shadows built to use it — the DNs 3, 5, 7 and 8 — say replacement parts are almost impossible to find. A small industry exists to reproduce original spares and/or to modify the TL cases to accept FG internals. Not for the casual hobbyist, these old F1 cars.

Shadow's DN3 stood on a wheelbase of 105 inches, slightly longer than the 104 of the older model when it had its gearbox spacer in place. No spacer was used this year, Southgate reckoning the car didn't need to be any longer. Conversely, he narrowed both track widths by an inch, to 58 front, 61 rear.

Every team was working on such individual detail issues of their own, but one big technical challenge faced everyone equally: the Firestone/Goodyear tire war. Intensely heated, it had the rival American firms constantly bringing new rubberwear. Goodyear even borrowed a concept from US drag racing and introduced "wrinkle

LEFT Straight-sided where the previous model was bowed out, the DN3 also has different radiators, more forward driving position and pedal placement, and while the front suspension is the same basic layout it has been thoroughly rethought. Engine oil now runs through a cooler mounted in the nose, instead of the tail. And isn't the craftsmanship beautiful? Almost too nice to risk in a race.
Pete Lyons

RIGHT Rationalizing the relationship between spring perch and suspension linkage made it simpler to fabricate the DN3's A-arms — not a small consideration for a car bound to crash occasionally. New brackets spread suspension stresses more widely into a stronger chassis. While we're here, have a look at the dual-rate coil springs, where the lower, more tightly wound element closes first, effectively stiffening the spring under severe compression loads. *Pete Lyons*

THIS PAGE Back at the loud end, the DN3's rear suspension is the more commonplace setup, with parallel bottom links and two trailing arms either side; the left upper one is visible here, running diagonally forward to the front of the DFV engine. Disc brakes mount inboard on the transmission final-drive case, as they do on just about every F1 car. But Shadow used a different model of Hewland gearbox than other constructors did, an experimental TL200. Center-mounted on a large plate, the two-element wing is kept from wobbling by two slender stays. Somehow the twin exhaust pipes writhe through all this, while leaving wiggle room for all the other tubes and hoses and linkages and wires necessary. *Pete Lyons*

wall" tires 28 inches in diameter.

The company explained that they improved acceleration. While powering out of corners these floppy rubber bags would "wind up and release, wind up and release." With each cycle came a spike in traction, resulting in greater adhesion overall.

This also resulted in the "Bronx Cheer," a rude-sounding rubbery vibration out of the corners that plagued mechanics by savaging rear-end components.

All this kept the teams scrambling to adapt. As Brabham designer Gordon Murray put it to this reporter during a paddock conversation: "The variations among different kinds of tires is now so great that you can go through the entire range of suspension adjustments available to you just to accommodate changes. The diameters can be different, the construction can be different, the sidewalls can flex differently — the whole geometry works completely differently. I'd say that's the one main problem facing the designer today, to accommodate changes in tires."

SHADOW'S 1974 F1 SEASON

NEW YEAR, new car, new drivers. Shadow went into its second Formula 1 season with two world-class, proven winners on the loud pedals. As early as January the team took on young Frenchman Jean-Pierre Jarier, who had dominated 1973's Formula 2 series with a March-BMW 732 to win the championship. Then the team signed Peter Revson, an American who looked like a movie star but was achieving genuine stardom on the stages of Indycar, Can-Am (1971 series champion) and most recently F1. Revvie had already scored two GP victories in '73 with McLaren.

That left Jackie Oliver to concentrate on Shadow's 1974 Can-Am program, while George Follmer turned back to the several other kinds of racing in which he had a good career going.

LEFT Goodyear's "wrinkle wall" tires are truly floppy. *Pete Lyons*

BELOW The new American driver for the only American team (at this point) is Peter Revson, an heir to wealth and lucky on top of that with his charm and lady-killer good looks, but able to put all that behind when he strapped on a racing car. Revvie's ability there was world-class. *Motorsport Images/David Phipps*

ARGENTINE GP

Buenos Aires, F1 (R1), January 13th, 1974
1st, Denny Hulme, McLaren M23
DNF, Peter Revson, Shadow DN3, accident
DNF, Jean-Pierre Jarier, Shadow DN1, accident

Argentina was all about 'Lole'. Carlos Reutemann, that is, the local lad who became a national hero on the third lap, when he majestically swept into the lead. The crowd's cheering literally drowned out the racecars' screaming. And even when his Brabham BT44 ran dry of fuel and stopped on the grass, Lole was still Argentina's darling.

For UOP's Shadowmen, not so much. Peter Revson, expressing himself delighted with his new DN3, seized a splendid fourth spot on the grid — directly ahead of Reutemann — despite several buggy problems during practice. Jean-Pierre Jarier, in the previous year's DN1, could do no better than 16th.

But at the start neither man made it a mile. A multi-car kerfuffle in the first corner slammed the innocent Shadows together hard enough to end both their races.

BRAZILIAN GP

Interlagos, F1 (R2), January 27th, 1974
1st, Emerson Fittipaldi, McLaren M23
DNF, Peter Revson, Shadow DN3, overheating
DNF, Jean-Pierre Jarier, Shadow DN1, brakes

Revson qualified the DN3 sixth this time, despite troubles with water temps and ignition misfires. Jarier's very hastily prepared replacement DN1, based on an old monocoque flown over from England, grudgingly granted him 19th place on the grid.

For neither Shadowman did the misery go on for long. Revson's continued overheating retired him after 11 laps, while Jarier lasted precisely twice that distance before his brakes died.

BELOW Revson started his first race with Shadow from fourth spot on the grid. His two Grand Prix victories with McLaren the year before stirred hopes for debut glory in Buenos Aires — until the first turn of the race.
Motorsport Images/David Phipps

214 CHAPTER 10

ABOVE Jean-Pierre Jarier of France, who had been driving with March in F1 and was an ace in F2, had to run both the South American GPs with a year-old DN1 — two of them, actually, as Argentina's first-turn pileup required a replacement tub for Brazil. *Motorsport Images/David Phipps*

BELOW Revvie's last ride: Brands Hatch in the wet. Days later he was gone. *Pete Lyons*

RACE OF CHAMPIONS (GB)

Brands Hatch, F1 (non-championship), March 17th, 1974
1st, Jacky Ickx, Lotus 72
6th, Peter Revson, Shadow DN3
DNS, Jean-Pierre Jarier, Shadow DN3, shunt in practice

Before the third GP came a pair of non-championship races. Shadow didn't stay in Brazil for the Emilio Medici GP in Brasilia, the country's newly built capital, but did turn out for the Race of Champions sprint at Brands Hatch, a little southeast of London, their two entries making it 16 up-to-date Formula 1 machines to face assorted Formula 5000s.

Jean-Pierre Jarier finally got his own shiny new DN3 like Revson's. Unfortunately for the lad from France, during a rainy Friday practice one of battered old Brands Hatch's bumps caught him out, crunching him into the rail hard enough to wrinkle the front of his shiny new tub.

FRESH START **215**

ABOVE THE DARK SIDE. Peter Revson's fatal accident came when a defective component of the front suspension failed under heavy load in the high-speed second turn at Kyalami. *Motorsport Images/David Phipps*

"Although by our standards it isn't much of a shunt," muttered one of his crewmen. However, it was too much to fix in time for the race.

But guess who set the fastest time that rainy Friday? Peter Revson.

That didn't hold on sunny Saturday, when James Hunt in the new Hesketh dominated to seize pole. America's pride only managed ninth on the grid.

Sunday… wasn't sunny. Entirely the opposite: splashy, spumy, slippery wet. Once again Revson's DN3 looked at home in the atrocious conditions, and rather than falling behind the breakaway bunch up front he stuck with an eight-car dogfight for the lead. Revvie seemed to be reveling in the rain and spray and murk. Others were going off left and right, crunch, crunch, crunch. Polesitter Hunt was one of them.

In the end a fabulous nose-to-tail battle between Niki Lauda's Ferrari and Jacky Ickx's Lotus gave the cold, soaked, utterly enchanted British enthusiasts an electrifying moment: Jacky made a spectacularly bold move around Niki on the outside of the very fast, falling away Paddock Bend and drove on to his only victory of the year.

Revvie in his Shadow was not drawing quite the same attention, but he kept it on the road and splashed on to finish sixth, losing a lap on the way when his engine seemed to lose power.

SOUTH AFRICAN GP
Kyalami, F1 (R3), March 30th, 1974
1st, Carlos Reutemann, Brabham BT44
No Shadows

That rainy day at Brands was Peter Revson's last race. Five days later, on March 22nd, he was testing on South Africa's Kyalami circuit when his car speared off the outside of a very fast, downhill sweeper into the barrier. The impact was so savage that the car punched through the steel guardrails and Revvie was killed. In shock and sorrow his team withdrew from the following week's GP.

Post-crash investigation revealed a front-suspension failure, specifically the ball joint at the outer end of the left-front upper A-arm. It was made of titanium, and apparently the machining process left a tiny, undetected imperfection, which spread under load and caused the piece to snap. The car's designer, struggling with his emotions, did what he could and discontinued use of titanium for such components.

INTERNATIONAL TROPHY (GB)
Silverstone, F1 (non-championship),
  April 7th, 1974
1st, James Hunt, Hesketh 308
3rd, Jean-Pierre Jarier, Shadow DN3

Back in England the weekend after South Africa, Jean-Pierre Jarier gave his Shadow team a small measure of solace by running well in the year's third non-championship event. He was finally racing his new DN3.

An oiled-down Silverstone track held him to 10th starting spot, but raceday presented him with a wonderful dice with his countryman Henri Pescarolo's BRM. Jean-Pierre ultimately scratched by to take third place by inches.

That evening Shadow announced its choice for new second driver.

SPANISH GP
Jarama, F1 (R4), April 28th, 1974
1st, Niki Lauda, Ferrari 312B3
7th, Brian Redman, Shadow DN3
NC, Jean-Pierre Jarier, Shadow DN3,
  insufficient laps

Brian Redman, the F5000 ace who had driven Shadow's spare F1 car late the previous year, rejoined the team here outside Madrid. His new DN3 was set up with a shorter wheelbase for this twisty little circuit, but Jarier's remained at full length. It was good to see the Shadow team

BELOW THE LIGHT SIDE. Jean-Pierre Jarier (left) to Brian Redman: "*Réellement*, Breean, I find zem most responsif to ze gentle touch, almost — 'ow you say? — *une caresse…* zey seem to come alive under your 'ands…" *Dan R. Boyd*

RIGHT Jarier's first GP in a DN3 is the Spanish at Jarama, where he qualifies faster than his new team-mate. So at first "Jumper" looks like having a reasonably good day. But then... *Motorsport Images/LAT*

BELOW New boy Brian Redman, eyed warily here by younger boy John Watson in a Brabham, struggles with poor grip, forcing him to hurl the Shadow in hard just to make the back of the grid. But at the end of a difficult, palm-blistering raceday he saw the checkered flag. *Motorsport Images/LAT*

218 CHAPTER 10

moving forward, and yours truly was happy to relate this: "The morale... was extraordinarily high, with smiles everywhere and an intoxicating spirit of going-ahead in the air."

Redman was finding his new car heavy work: "It's so much more competitive than Formula 5000! I am a second slower than I ought to be, and I can't understand it — but I have to, here, whereas in 5000 perhaps it wouldn't matter quite so much. I can't seem to get any traction, the car understeers through the corner unless I really hurl it in."

Brian qualified over a second slower than his young team-mate to line up near the back. Jarier was 12th on the grid. The race began in light rain, but then the track started to dry, and as in Canada the year before a flood of tire changes blew up many lap charts.

Jarier had already brought his Shadow in to deal with a nose fin bent and bent again in two separate nerfing matches, but then he had a third man attack him from the rear. That sent Arturo Merzario's Iso (an early Frank Williams car) flying over a guardrail into a cluster of photographers, reporters and miscellaneous other onlookers. By some miracle, injuries were few and minor. Jean-Pierre's Shadow carried on from his third incident of the day, battered but unbowed.

Meanwhile, Redman was driving as hard as he could — so hard that the heavy gear change of the Hewland TL200 raised a blister on his palm. He said it was the first time such a thing had ever happened to him. But mechanically the car was perfect, and in fact both Shadows reached the checkered flag to score the team's first Grand Prix finishes of the year.

BELGIAN GP
Nivelles, F1 (R5), May 12th, 1974
1st, Emerson Fittipaldi, McLaren M23
13th, Jean-Pierre Jarier, Shadow DN3
DNF, Brian Redman, Shadow DN3, engine

At this artificial new track in the countryside south of Brussels, both Shadows were identical, both on the long wheelbase. The adjustment did not cure Redman's chassis of its difficult-looking handling problems. After a curtailed, crowded qualifying period, during which amateurish official timing differed hilariously from the professional people doing it in the pits, the two DN3s were awarded the ninth row all to themselves, exactly 0.2 second apart.

Jarier raced on to finish 13th, three laps behind the winner, but five laps from the end Brian Redman went by the pits with his Shadow trailing a huge plume of smoke and drizzling oil. What happened, Brian? "Electrical failure," he said with a straight face. Then he burst out laughing. "The conrod coming out the side of the block cut the main electrical buss!" More laughing all around.

MONACO GP
Monte Carlo, F1 (R6), May 26th, 1974
1st, Ronnie Peterson, Lotus 72
3rd, Jean-Pierre Jarier, Shadow DN3
DNF, Brian Redman, Shadow DN3, multi-car accident

Brian Redman came to Monte Carlo with furrowed brow. He had accepted Shadow's invitation back to F1 because he understood the US F5000 series was to be cancelled and he would lose his very successful Lola ride there. But on the eve of Monaco came word the US series was on again and Carl Haas wanted him back. Decision time.

His DN3 was performing properly through the Principality's cramped old streets, but he just didn't look a happy man. When only one set of soft tires was obtainable and went first onto his team-mate's car, he decided more flogging around was pointless and settled for the eighth row.

French drivers often do well at Monaco, and the man with the soft tires was five rows ahead. Fifth fastest overall. A great spot to start this particular GP.

RIGHT Points scored! Who can say why French nationals so often show special inspiration in the independent Principality of Monaco, but this year Jean-Pierre adds the Jarier name to another scintillating race performance here. *Dan R. Boyd*

The pack had only just flooded through the first corner when… *Carambolage! Drapeau Rouge!*

Sixth-row starters Denny Hulme and Jean-Pierre Beltoise, having got away side by side, were still side by side up the rise toward the Casino. They banged wheels. And instantly created a midstream logjam between the guardrails. Oncoming cars splashed like crashing surf in all directions.

Eighth-row man Redman sauntered back down the street from his wrecked Shadow, swinging his helmet and remarking pleasantly, "Oh well, it was me last race anyway." When some busybody journalist conveyed this to UOP's Ben Williams, the PR man's normally smiling face turned to stone.

Meanwhile, Jarier had been ahead of the melee and when the race restarted he drove his Shadow with the special fire that often inspires French drivers at Monaco. He admitted later to making "a couple of mistakes — I knocked off the ignition switch two times!" His rousing third-place finish was on the same lap as the winner.

SWEDISH GP
Anderstorp, F1 (R7), June 9th, 1974
1st, Jody Scheckter, Tyrrell 007
5th, Jean-Pierre Jarier, Shadow DN3
DNF, Bertil Roos, Shadow DN3, gearbox

Swedish driver Bertil Roos was Shadow's second entry this time. He and Jarier tested the new, shorter-wheelbase DN3 around Anderstorp the week before, and both found it so much quicker that they asked for their race chassis to be reconfigured that way. Only enough bits were on hand to convert one, so Roos had to make do with the slower setup.

"This one is under-steering too much, and so to make the tail come out I have to throw it out. I know it doesn't look very smooth," academically remarked the future driving school proprietor. He started almost at the back of the grid, only to stop after one lap when the

ABOVE After Monaco Redman has stepped out of F1 in favor of F5000, so for the Swedish GP Shadow gives the ride to Swedish driver Bertil Roos. Unfortunately it is short ride. *Motorsport Images/Rainer Schlegelmilch*

BELOW The Dutch GP brings yet another replacement driver, and third time is indeed the charm. Tom Pryce is one of those rare newcomers who really do seem destined for greatness. *Dan R. Boyd*

transmission jammed itself in second gear.

Jarier launched from eighth, and despite fading brakes he stayed on the leading lap to finish fifth.

DUTCH GP
Zandvoort, F1 (R8), June 23rd, 1974
1st, Niki Lauda, Ferrari 312B3
DNF, Jean-Pierre Jarier, Shadow DN3, clutch
DNF, Tom Pryce, Shadow DN3, accident

Zandvoort 1974 is where Shadow introduced the new driver who would become their inspiration and pride going forward. Tom Pryce of Wales, just turned 25, had risen rapidly through single-seater ranks from Formula Ford to F5000. Just four weeks before Holland he came out on top of Monaco's prestigious Formula 3 support event.

At that point he was already an F1 driver, albeit with only two brief appearances in an uncompetitive car called a Token. His hope of

ABOVE Tom Pryce pulls on a racing car like a leotard. His driving is like a dance. Performed on a high wire. At dazzling speed. Watching him make his Shadow debut in the Dutch Grand Prix at Zandvoort can stop your breath. *Motorsport Images/LAT*

BELOW But the magic runs dry at the first turn. *Motorsport Images/Ercole Colombo*

driving that at Monaco was refused for "lack of experience," which is why his car owner plugged Tom into the F3 entry instead. The move made Pryce an international name.

Maybe it also made it easier for Shadow team principal Alan Rees, himself a Welshman and former driver, to sell Don Nichols on signing the new sensation.

Tom's debut was not as desired. It started out well enough, his driving style showing a lot of strength-of-hand, reflecting a general confidence. The tall, friendly, always-smiling young man's willing attitude was making him very popular with his new team, too. His starting grid place was decent for a rookie, 11th, just two rows behind his more experienced team-mate's seventh.

That said, Jarier was not really up to speed. His DN3 benefited from revised front-suspension geometry and bigger brakes, but Jean-Pierre was nursing a wrist sprained in a collision at Le Mans the weekend before. This cost him what he estimated as half a second of pace. Making that up might have put him on the second row.

Hopes and dreams… then reality. As the pack dived into the very first corner after the start, the long "Tarzan Hook," both Hunt and Pryce went for the same gap and collided. Rear suspension broken, Tom found himself in the catch fence. Jarier had a somewhat longer race, but troubles with throttle linkage and clutch finally retired him.

FRENCH GP
Dijon, F1 (R9), July 7th, 1974
1st, Ronnie Peterson, Lotus 72
12th, Jean-Pierre Jarier, Shadow DN3
DNF, Tom Pryce, Shadow DN3, accident

Oops. Two races, two accidents, both at the start. Not quite the way to get off on the right foot with your new team. Happily for Tom Pryce, his footwork during practice had been spectacular.

His DN3 now updated like Jarier's had been in Holland, Shadow's rookie was the fastest man in France midway through Saturday practice. Goodness, what a stir that raised! You see, if that sort of speed had come from a Peterson or a Lauda, nobody would have thought much about it, but whoever is this fellow Pryce? Why, he hasn't even done his apprenticeship! He can't be quick. Can he?

The young Welshman was certainly more than spectacular to watch. The black Shadow was always on opposite lock, always sliding wildly, almost everywhere outside the normal line on the gray matter at the exits; to use an expression, he looked like an accident about to happen anywhere around the fast, swooping Dijon circuit. But he was clear in his own mind about it.

"Yes, other people have said I look wild, but honestly I feel quite comfortable. The car is handling magnificently and I have total confidence in it. As for going wide of the line, well, the car really seems to get a good bite out there."

He qualified third fastest, straight behind Lauda on pole and diagonally behind Peterson's Lotus. Other big names surrounded him, Ferrari's second man Clay Regazzoni just to his left and the likes of Emerson Fittipaldi, Jody Scheckter, Carlos Reutemann, James Hunt and Denny Hulme behind. Jarier was back there somewhere too, on the outside of the sixth row.

It started going wrong just before the start. As this writer reported in *Autosport*, "There was an overlong delay between the order to start engines and the eventual drop of the *Tricolor*. Drivers began getting edgy about temperatures, and Tom Pryce there on the second row with the bulk of the Grand Prix behind him was especially edgy. He was actually watching the temperature gauge when the flag waved. He was caught out. Everyone moving off around him, he dumped the clutch with too few revs on the clock. The Shadow lagged. Fittipaldi squarely behind instinctively swerved to the left, actually shutting his eyes, but slipped by unscathed. Reutemann, however, charging up from the left side further back, swerved to the right as if to avoid Fittipaldi, and rammed Pryce. Tom's steering was whipped out of his fingers, and the Shadow veered across the track to the left, heading diagonally toward the steel rail. But before he could get that far it ran into the path of Hunt's Hesketh.

"It was quite an unbelievable sight. Two weeks ago there was the black car and the white car crunched together. Here it was again. Nobody writes even bad novels like that."

So it was Jean-Pierre Jarier who gave his team another finish.

BRITISH GP
Brands Hatch, F1 (R10), July 20th, 1974
1st, Jody Scheckter, Tyrrell 007
8th, Tom Pryce, Shadow DN3
DNF, Jean-Pierre Jarier, Shadow DN3, suspension

A promotion-minded London newspaper put up a prize for the best lap of the first session of practice, and winner was none other than one T. Pryce, Esq. He staggered back to his team with 100 bottles of champagne — all in one gigantic bottle, to judge by photos. A fine way to cement the good opinion his boys had of him anyway! Tom went on to improve steadily throughout the rest of practice, and ended up on the third row of the grid.

Quietly pleased with his performance, but careful not to appear big-headed, the young Welshman remarked that, "Because we have to run a lot of wing the steering is very heavy, and the worst bumps try to knock the wheel out of your hands. I don't think I'll be keeping up this kind of speed in the race…"

In fact the two DN3s looked very badly affected by the bumps of Brands, cavorting across certain patches like rocking horses. That under these conditions Jean-Pierre Jarier was not as outstanding as his team-mate was understandable, for his wrist could not yet have healed. But, he said tersely, "I can drive."

ABOVE Poor Jean-Pierre's injured wrist is hurting over the Brands bumps, but he's soldiering on.
Motorsport Images/LAT

LEFT Tom's "gift" of champagne pleases his crew at Brands Hatch, but they'll be happier with a trophy. One day, boys.
Motorsport Images/LAT

ABOVE First finish — and first championship point! Around the Nürburgring, F1's longest, most complex, gnarliest of circuits. Driving one-handed. Hard not to see something special in this quiet kid from the wild hills of Wales.
Motorsport Images/LAT

This time the young Frenchman was not the better finisher of the team. In fact he did not finish at all because of a broken suspension mounting point. His Welsh team-mate did get to the checker, his first time to see it from a Shadow, although he had to drop away from an interesting pursuit of Fittipaldi's McLaren with both rear suspension and gearbox trouble. For the last laps he was getting only fourth and fifth gears and having to hold them in with one hand, while muscling the car's heavy steering with the other. Pryce endured to wind up eighth overall, amongst the pack that had fallen a lap behind the leaders.

GERMAN GP
Nürburgring, F1 (R11), August 4th, 1974
1st, Clay Regazzoni, Ferrari 312B3
6th, Tom Pryce, Shadow DN3
8th, Jean-Pierre Jarier, Shadow DN3

Jarier had a lot of seat time in Formula 2 and fast sports cars around the fabulous old 'Ring's 14-plus miles of twists and jumps and evil deceptions, including co-driving a Matra to a 1,000-kilometer victory earlier the same year. Pryce's experience of this most difficult of GP circuits came from a small amount of small-bore formula racing.

Yet the novice qualified ahead of the veteran, 11th to 18th, and went on to place sixth — thus bagging his first World Championship point. Jarier came eighth. Their team was relieved to see both Shadows run all the way.

AUSTRIAN GP
Österreichring, F1 (R12), August 18th, 1974
1st, Carlos Reutemann, Brabham BT44
8th, Jean-Pierre Jarier, Shadow DN3
DNF, Tom Pryce, Shadow DN3, spin

In typically very hot Austrian weather the Ö-Ring surface began to break up, and it caught out Pryce when he was practice-testing the short-wheelbase Shadow. Crunch, yet another bent tub to repair. Back in his regular car along with his team-mate, they both had delays with some engine trouble and qualified well back among the backmarker bunch.

On raceday Pryce went off again, stalled the engine and couldn't restart it. Jarier had been going extremely well, until with about 10 laps to go a malfunctioning fuel valve forced him stop for gas.

ABOVE Sore wrist or not, Jumper keeps on leaping around every 14-plus mile Nürburgring lap to make both Shadows finishers for the first time this year.
Motorsport Images/LAT

ITALIAN GP
Monza, F1 (R13), September 8th, 1974
1st, Ronnie Peterson, Lotus 72
10th, Tom Pryce, Shadow DN3, spin
DNF, Jean-Pierre Jarier, Shadow DN3, engine

Jarier qualified better than his team-mate this time, ninth on the grid, while Pryce was way back in 22nd. On another very hot practice day in Italy he was having gear-selection difficulty.

This time Tom chose to race the T-car, now fully converted to the latest spec in terms of front suspension and wheelbase length. But after only eight laps he came into the pits pointing to his left-front tire. Crewmen quickly changed it and he charged out again, but a mere ten laps later the new tire started losing air pressure. Instead of stopping again, he nursed the understeer until the end. Meanwhile, Jean-Pierre made a stop at 17 laps, this because he felt his engine seizing. He was sent back out, but after a few more laps he retired the car.

CANADIAN GP
Mosport, F1 (R14), September 22nd, 1974
1st, Emerson Fittipaldi, McLaren M23
DNF, Tom Pryce, Shadow DN3, engine
DNF, Jean-Pierre Jarier, Shadow DN3, driveshaft

From heat to chill; time seemed to have a piece missing. The sounds of the racing engines moaned and crackled with a new sharpness in the dense, cold Canadian air, and the shoulder-huddling wind made everyone keenly aware that end-of-season was upon them. There was no more time to await a better day, it was imperative to make the best of this one. Right from the start of practice drivers could be seen grasping their racing animals firmly by the scruffs of their metaphorical necks and forcing them, kick and scream as they would, round the circuit on the limit.

Perhaps the overseas circus felt new pressure from the glistening presence in their menagerie

FRESH START **227**

ABOVE Jarier earned fifth-best grid position for the start in Canada! Stellar. After the start the starlight faded. *Motorsport Images/David Phipps*

of long-anticipated entries from Penske and Parnelli. Both machines, and indeed both teams, looked as superbly finished as everyone had expected. The sheer quality of the twin American newcomers (both with a great deal of English input, just as at Shadow) made even the best prepared of the Europeans look suddenly aware of their season-battered age.

Pryce's Ford Cosworth blew on Saturday morning, and the afternoon replacement — a very quick job of work by the Shadowmen — wasn't worth very much. So once again Tom had to start behind his revitalized team-mate.

Jarier took fifth on the grid, straight behind polesitter Fittipaldi, who was alongside Lauda. Surrounding Jean-Pierre on all sides were Scheckter, Reutemann, Regazzoni, Depailler, Hunt, Pace and Peterson.

Disappointingly, Jarier was not long able to hold his good starting position and was running eighth mid-race when a halfshaft broke. Pryce was 10th when another engine went 15 laps

short of the 80. By awkward contrast, both newcomers saw the checkered flag, Mario Andretti in the Parnelli coming home seventh, Mark Donohue in his Penske 12th.

But look at the drama at the front: Emerson Fittipaldi and Clay Regazzoni were heading into the season's last Grand Prix dead even on championship points.

UNITED STATES GP

Watkins Glen, F1 (R15), October 6th, 1974
1st, Carlos Reutemann, Brabham BT44
10th, Jean-Pierre Jarier, Shadow DN3
NC, Tom Pryce, Shadow DN3, insufficient laps

Last chance of the year for the pioneer American team. A chance missed. Shadow's best grid spot was 10th for Jarier on the fifth row, with Pryce a further four rows back. This time the Welshman's troubles included a broken exhaust pipe and gross understeer.

Meanwhile Mario, who at one point had been the fastest man of all, started fourth in the Parnelli. Mark's Penske split the two Shadows.

Jarier finished in that same 10th place as he started, but his race was more complicated than it sounds. Stopping in the pits to change front tires and crank up the front wings to cure understeer lost him two laps to the many who stayed on the leaders' lap. Pryce saw the flag as well, but after two pit stops — one to change eight spark plugs to cure misfiring, and then again to shore up a dragging nosecone — he was 12 laps behind the winner and therefore not classified.

Fortuitously, this was the meeting where Don Nichols had already arranged for three Shadow DN4s to come and emit some Can-Am thunder. At least UOP's guests could see that one of their lavishly sponsored teams had been successful that year.

Sadly, we must acknowledge another Formula 1 fatality here. Young Austrian driver Helmuth Koinigg slammed head-first into a steel rail and died instantly.

Happily, Emerson Fittipaldi, 1972 World Champion with Lotus, this year won his second title in his first season with McLaren, doing so in the finale at The Glen. He was driving with a picture of his infant daughter in the pocket of his racing suit.

SO ENDED SHADOW's second F1 season. A bitter season, with the tragedy of Peter Revson's death. Nor was it better in terms of results. From 28 Grand Prix starts there were only 11 official finishes, plus two when a car was running at the end but too far behind to be classified. Retirements totaled 15: a 53.6 percent failure rate. Best race placings: a third, a fifth and a sixth for a total of seven championship points. This ranked UOP Shadow eighth among the 12 constructors. So no real progress over 1973.

There was a bright spot: Shadow had found Tom Pryce. ♣

BELOW Mixing and mingling with his midfield friends in the USA, former champs Graham Hill and Denny Hulme among those in this shot, Pryce drives through another trouble-plagued race to yet another outcome far worse than he deserved. *Dan R. Boyd*

BRIAN REDMAN
DRIVER

I drove four Formula 1 races for Shadow. The first time was towards the end of 1973, when Don Nichols invited me to race their spare DN1 car at the Watkins Glen US Grand Prix along with his regular drivers, Jackie Oliver and George Follmer. I qualified way ahead of them both, heh-heh!

But at the start, leaving the grid at full throttle, I got dirt in the throttle slides and they jammed. When I arrived at the first corner, the engine was coughing. I had to pull off; I didn't spin it, contrary to what was reported. We got it going again with the help of some marshals, but because of their assistance I was disqualified.

Afterward Don asked if I'd like to do F1 the next year with Shadow, but I had just done my first year in Formula 5000 with Jim Hall, which was a first-class team. My four years with Jim were my four best years in racing. So I turned Don down then.

The driver who took my place in 1974 was Peter Revson, and of course he was killed in practice for the South African Grand Prix. One can't help thinking, if I had been in that car it would have been me.

Almost immediately after Peter's accident, I heard that F5000 in America was off for the year. So I had nothing! Didn't have a drive of any kind. But Don Nichols rang and asked if I would reconsider F1.

People ask, did I have any reservations about accepting, but no, never thought about it. Because if you start thinking like that, you'd never get in the car. And of course the problem with Peter's Shadow would have been changed. It was a Tony Southgate car. Tony was great to work with. He's quiet, he downplays himself, but he's a brilliant guy.

After Don asked me to rejoin in 1974, my first Grand Prix was the Spanish at Jarama. I qualified 21st there, and although I came seventh in the race I was three laps behind the winner. In Belgium at Nivelles I was all the way up to 18th on the grid! In the race I was running eighth when the engine blew with five laps to go.

We went to Monaco next. I qualified 16th there, then on Sunday morning there was a call from America. Formula 5000 was back on!

I thought, would I rather be in the middle of the field in Formula 1, or somewhere in the points in Formula 5000? And there was very little difference moneywise. So before the race I told Don it was going to be my last one, I was going back to America.

And of course that's the Grand Prix where there was a huge accident on the opening lap and my car got caught up in it. I retired from Formula 1 on the spot.

So I didn't drive the Shadows very long, but I thought they were good cars. They were very nice to drive, a typical Tony

BELOW That lively lad from Lancashire, Brian Redman, who might have had a good, quiet career in catering had motor racing not stolen his heart, logged eight GPs in five different cars over a four-year span before the Shadowman gave him a call. First result: best qualifying time over three regular Shadow drivers for his first race with the team. Half a season later he walked away. *Dan R. Boyd*

RIGHT Redman retired from his fourth Shadow race at Monaco — after the first corner of that race — and simultaneously retired from F1. Our loss, not his. *Pete Lyons*

Southgate design with relatively soft suspension, which is especially good in the wet. And I thought it was a good team, well run, a first-class effort.

The one time I raced against the Shadows was in 1974, that wet-dry Can-Am at Mid-Ohio. I was driving Penske's Porsche 917/30, with which Mark Donohue had won the Can-Am championship the year before. But he had promptly retired, so he was at Mid-Ohio as the reluctant team manager. We hardly spoke. He was uncommunicative.

We were pretty fortunate to win the heat race when it rained. For the main race it was still wet, but it looked like it might dry, so I asked if we could run the slick tires but carve grooves into them.

I started ahead of the pair of Shadows, the DN4s with Oliver and Follmer driving them, but that turbocharged Porsche had lots of throttle lag. Timing when and how you opened the throttle in relation to where the car was on the track wasn't easy. On one lap I opened a fraction too soon and it went sideways. Both Shadows passed me.

As I followed them, I saw George trying to overtake Jackie on two or three occasions, not making it, completely on the grass, dirt flying. I'm happy, there's quite a bit of the race yet to run, maybe they'll take each other off.

At the end of the long straight is a 90-degree right-hander. There's no way you can pass there unless it's a slower car, and I see George go straight into the side of Jackie! Well, George broke the nose on his Shadow and he was out, but although Jackie went sideways he kept going. I'm still behind.

Unfortunately, as the track dried out my handling went off. It had been very nice, but it lost that fine balance and started pushing like a mad thing. I nearly went off on the grass on the right-hand hairpin before the pits.

If we hadn't grooved the tires we'd have been in good shape.

Don Nichols should have been a 17th Century pirate! With his tall boots and pointy beard, all he needed was a patch over one eye. But his ability to put that team together was very impressive. It takes a lot to make a good team.

Of course his past was somewhat "shadowy," heh-heh! All sorts of rumors flying around, as they do in the racing world, but I have no stories. I didn't discuss business with him. We never spoke about Jackie Oliver and Arrows.

I'd say Shadow's legacy is pretty good. I see a lot of enthusiasm for them, posts all the time on Facebook and quite a few cars being vintage raced. I think they should be remembered with considerable honor.

Brian Redman, best known for his great record in sports cars and F5000, also raced a few times for several F1 teams. His stint with Shadow was brief, but busy, as he describes here in his own words from our recent interview.

CHAPTER 11
THE BEST ONE

SHADOW DN4 (CAN-AM), 1974

QUICK AS A swerving racecar, Shadow changed course for Can-Am 1974. For one thing, the team's 1973 Big Boy approach hadn't worked. Reason enough to try another path. But also, late that year Middle Eastern oil producers abruptly choked off that vital lifeblood of modern life. This panicked the rest of the world into draconian conservation efforts.

Can-Am series administrators reacted with yet another rule, imposing "Energy Measures" that restricted fuel consumption to at least three miles per gallon (US). Not a number that would impress motorists waiting in endless lines at gas stations and fretting about buying economy cars, but the SCCA could point out that 3.0 mpg is a healthy improvement in percentage terms from 2.5 or 2.0. At least we're doing our part, they could say.

But Porsche managers found this forced emasculation of their supercar unattractive. Not what our marque is all about, they would have said. Having already proven their prowess, they pulled out.

Shadow went the other way. Clearly chances of doing well were better with the Panzers gone, so why quit now? Also, the year-old, two-heat race format was continuing and now fuel use was being curtailed. So why not build an entirely new car, smaller, lighter, and more efficient.

Key factor: with the longest 1974 heat race distance being 123 miles (at Mosport), there was no need to tank up for the non-stop, 200-plus of the good old days.

In fact, one of those new rules fixed maximum fuel capacity at 37 gallons US. Do the math: cars actually would need to average 3.3 mpg to run the new season's longest heat race — not allowing for pace laps and cool-off.

Tony Southgate succinctly summarized his design for the all-new Shadow DN4 Can-Am car this way:

"As requested by both UOP and Don Nichols, I rejected the DN2 concept, and we all agreed that the way to go was a dedicated design around a naturally aspirated Chevy V8. The DN4 was

much smaller than the DN2, and had 13-inch diameter front wheels in place of the normal 15-inch. This gave the car a very low, 'wedge' look and minimal frontal area.

"The front suspension was effectively the same as on the Formula 1 DN, but with large brake calipers and very wide ventilated discs. I realized that the air ducting for these brakes was going to have to be superb to survive Can-Am racing in North America, where the circuits were (and still are) more stop-and-go than in Europe. So I engineered-in very large brake ducts in the nose section — so large that most people mistook them for the air intakes for the water radiators.

"Aerodynamically, the DN4 was a development of the DN2, but on a smaller scale and much sleeker; I thought it looked great! As it turned out, the brakes were perfect, and the car was very, very quick."

He pulled off this excellent design despite having spent most of his time on the Formula 1 project. To assist with the DN4 design work and also handle its build program, he recruited Mike Hillman, a close friend ever since they met at Brabham a decade earlier, when Southgate briefly worked there.

Hillman and the Shadow team detailed and constructed the DN4 "in exactly 90 days" in his words, and by the first week of March Jackie Oliver was taking the prototype for a shakedown run at Silverstone.

There on a cold, wet day a few stalwarts of the local press had a look at it. *Autosport*'s March 14th report was polite and encouraging, but scanty on information, and with only three photos the coverage was hardly lavish. Possibly that parsimony was related to a larger item on the same page: "Riverside Date Change."

Ominously, the SoCal circuit had asked the SCCA's permission to move its April Formula 5000 meeting to October, when it would be the third major attraction joining the regular Can-Am finale along with a round of the popular new

ABOVE Jackie Oliver hammered the prototype DN4 through some 2,000 miles of private development testing well before the first race, honing the new Shadow into a battle-ready weapon as sharp as the McLarens of old. Here at Laguna Seca above Monterey Bay it's getting late in the day, but Ollie's still hard on it as he climbs to the Corkscrew. *Dan R. Boyd*

BELOW Ghosted atop its older sibling, a side view of the new DN4 shows how much lower it is, with smaller front wheels yielding a significant reduction in frontal area at that station. The partial plan view at the top reveals that, while the car's body width is narrower, the monocoque is even slimmer thanks to 1974's reduced fuel capacity. Consequently room is created for radiators either side of the cockpit, moved aft from behind the front wheels.
Don Nichols collection

inter-disciplinary series called International Race of Champions.

The item reminded us that NorCal's Laguna Seca had already made the same calendar adjustment. Chilly winds for Big Block fans? Triple-header major events must be costly affairs with crowded paddocks and constrained track time. Hard to think these circuits were not hedging their bets in case the weakened "Million Dollar Can-Am" didn't last as long as October.

As *Autosport* put it, "Our American correspondent reports however that this Can-Am will probably not take place at Riverside at all if it does not look healthy during the year."

From wintry Silverstone the prototype DN4 went to sunny Los Angeles for a full-scale launch ceremony, complete with sponsor brass and a stellar new driver, Peter Revson, lured away from McLaren to race for Shadow in both F1 and Can-Am.

This year Shadow meant to field two cars from the outset, for Revson and Jackie Oliver. Perhaps Nichols looked at all those empty Porsche places on the grid and felt he should do his bit to fill them. Hillman would stay on in the US as team manager, working out of Shadow's well-equipped shop near its sponsor in metro Chicago.

AutoWeek's issue dated March 16th reported the Los Angeles event economically, with just one photo of the glossy new racer posing with palmettos along with a short caption. Two lines stand out: "Last year the car was still being built in the pits at the first race. This year, with the car completed and ready for testing well before the season starts, look for the UOP team to win some races."

The UOP team was spooled up to do just that. Over the next three months Oliver logged some 2,000 miles of development work at Riverside and Laguna Seca aboard the car shown to the media. Meanwhile, Northampton constructed two fresh DN4s to be raced in June. The well-

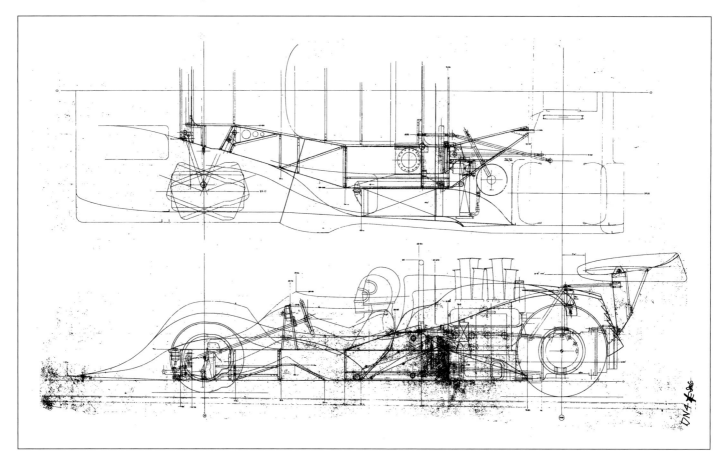

tested prototype would stand by as a spare.

Visually, the easiest way to tell the new car from its older sister was by the DN4's pair of rounded brake-cooling openings in the nose, rather than rectangular as on the DN2. Also, the front wheels were noticeably smaller in relation to the rears, and the whole body line looked less lumpy. Slimmer. Prettier.

This year's monocoque tub and body were narrower, thanks to tanks made only large enough to cram in a just-in-case 45 gallons in all. The wheel track widths were a little narrower as well, but wheelbase went up by two inches to 105. Further to Southgate's description of the suspension as being "effectively the same as on the Formula 1," both models did use the same wheels as well as uprights front and rear, the same hubs and bearings, even the same brake rotors. Differences were found in locating links, ie wishbones/A arms and trailing rods, to suit different overall widths or mounting points.

So satisfactory did these common components prove to be that Southgate carried them forward to his later open-wheelers, the DN5 (F1) and DN6 (F5000).

Tires of course are at least as important as suspensions. Southgate specified small front wheels and tires, but asked Goodyear for some real monsters for his rears. He wanted these "meats" to measure a whopping 28 inches in diameter — nine taller than the 19s called for in Firestone's original agreement for Shadow's Tiny Tire car. Together with improved compounding, the 28s promised to give the Big Block Chevy some mighty dig out of the turns.

However, Goodyear made Shadow begin the season on the back foot, make that the back "Wing Foot," until it built up enough stock of smaller, conventional rubber worn by all the older cars that year. Mechanics had to temporarily alter the DN4's rear suspension to suit.

The DN4's radiators remained in the body sides, but moved from behind the front wheels to just ahead of the rears. Long and narrow, they

slanted back at a steep angle to direct incoming air downward. That air came into them through strikingly small openings atop the doors, then vented out just in front of the rear tires.

Behind the left-side door, where the rear fender started its long, high slope, a third inlet fed the engine oil cooler.

Perhaps surprisingly, given the constraints on fuel use, engine man Lee Muir kept the big Chevy at 494 cubic inches (8.1 liters). He explained to the author that assembling the Lucas mechanical injection system with greater precision not only yielded the necessary improvement in fuel consumption but unleashed an additional 35 horsepower as well. Team literature continued to claim the same 735 hp as the year before, but team members

TOP A DN4 chassis reveals how its hip-mounted water coolers recline at a sharp angle, helping hot air on its way out just ahead of the wheels. An oil cooler sits just above, with the cylindrical dry-sump oil tank close behind. Notice the lightweight "mini-monocoque" instrument panel, as on the contemporary F1s. *Don Nichols collection*

ABOVE Although the Can-Am front suspension layout is similar to that on F1's DN3, the Can-Am wishbones are robust fabrications rather than simple tubing. Brakes are beefier. *Don Nichols collection*

ABOVE Dropping out of Laguna Seca's Corkscrew, the prototype DN4 invites us to admire her athletic grace, with smooth body lines over a tidy, compact package of raw Big Block muscle. The snow-shovel shaped prow that Tony Southgate favored is pierced with two large, round openings for brake cooling. Radiator air enters farther aft, through triangular NACA ducts in the doors. Next, on this side only, is a third inlet for an oil cooler. Behind, the long lift of the afterbody both generates downforce and delivers airflow to the rear wing. *Dan R. Boyd*

said the true number could approach 800.

Years later they also said that one time a Shadow raced with a bigger motor. We'll pick up that story a bit farther along.

SHADOW'S 1974 CAN-AM SEASON

PETER REVSON, the rising American star who had driven to impressive performances at Indianapolis, the 1971 Can-Am championship and two 1973 victories in Formula 1, all with McLaren, became a Shadow driver for 1974. He was going to race in both F1 and Can-Am, partnering Jean-Pierre Jarier in the open-wheeler and Jackie Oliver in the sports car.

Until the tragic, shocking day of his death in South Africa.

Shadow's F1 team in Europe started looking for someone to replace him. The American Can-Am team just called George Follmer.

MOSPORT, ONTARIO (CDN)
Can-Am (R1), June 16th, 1974
1st, Jackie Oliver, Shadow DN4
2nd, George Follmer, Shadow DN4

THIS YEAR the Shadowmen under team manager Mike Hillman had their cars ready to go when their drivers were. One of the drivers, anyway. While testing earlier at the Canadian circuit, George Follmer suffered a scary high-speed crash that wrote off the prototype DN4, hurting his back and cracking two ribs. He made it through the rest of the year with pain-numbing injections before driving.

Shadow's foresight in building a second racecar paid off, if just in time, so Follmer had something to roll onto the front row despite limited setup laps. Team-mate Oliver's pole position was his first in a long time, and his time, 1:14.5, beat his "partner" by 0.6 second, although 0.4 short of Mark Donohue's 1973 Porsche pole.

Poised at the head of the grid, the glossy black

LEFT Oh oh, this is bad. The prototype Shadow had treated Oliver amiably in California, but in Canada she turned vicious on George Follmer. Throttles jammed wide open, the car charged at very high speed into a very slow corner. The savage impact rendered the machine undriveable, and almost did the same to the man. *Dan R. Boyd*

BELOW Follmer would need a new DN4 and nerve-blocking injections before the next several races, but by Road America two months later he was limber enough to perch on the grass to watch Jim Spicklemire doing all the work. Monitoring the operation from on high is team manager Mike Hillman, and that's Don Nichols in the background. *Dan R. Boyd*

machines with the gracefully athletic bodies stood out as the only new cars in this year's Can-Am. Oliver's car retained the number 101 now associated with him, but seeing number 1 alongside was a novelty for Shadow. Rather than applying 102 as with previous second cars, and also eschewing the 16 familiar to Follmer fans over his career, the team painted a number that reminded us of his 1972 Can-Am championship. No doubt '71 champ Revson would have carried the same number.

Either way, the contrasting digits made a graphically interesting composition for the pair, and perhaps also proclaimed that there was no number 2 driver here, but rather two number 1s. Although one of them disputes that to this day.

Third fastest qualifier, albeit a lot slower at 1:17.8, was California star Scooter Patrick in a two-year-old, ex-factory McLaren M20. Originally Revson's ride in 1972, now it was repainted somewhat incongruously in a soft baby blue. At just 18 cars in all, the grid looked rather

THE BEST ONE **237**

emaciated as it formed up for the preliminary Sprint race.

From the rolling start the beauteous black bolides charged away side by side, Follmer looking determined to get in front, but Oliver was on the inside line and came out of the long, downhill first turn first. He held that for three laps, George hunting him hard, until Ollie found a backmarker in his way and had to give up a win. Follmer's number 1 car romped on to win the 30-lapper, while the 101 dropped back with a fuel-system fault.

In the pits between heats the combatants picked up what they had left out on track. Both told their sides years later during interviews for yours truly's book *Can-Am*.

Oliver: "It was a tremendous competition between Follmer and myself. Great rivalry, like always when you've got team-mates with the same cars. George chased me around the garage once, at Mosport. I said some smart-ass remark, I suppose. You know, when you're in front you

ABOVE Instant dominance! The Shadows have not actually reached the green flag but they're already leaving every other car behind. The blue McLaren with Scooter Patrick aboard is the best of them. This is at the start of the weekend's shorter preliminary heat race, called the Sprint. After a break there's a longer Final to establish the overall results. *Lionel Birnbom*

RIGHT Can-Am used to be the "Bruce and Denny Show." Then there was a Mark and George year. In this last-ever season it was all about Oliver against Follmer. It was not a "show," nor was it gentle. *Pete Biro*

always come up with a quip to make someone look ridiculous. He was going to pop me one. My major defense was to run like hell!"

Follmer: "I asked Oliver what happened to his car in the first heat, because I didn't know at the time. And he took offense to it. He says, 'Mind your own damn business,' or 'Get out of my face,' whatever. And I didn't appreciate being talked to like that."

So George took a swing at him?

"He ran, the little, little bastard. Because I probably would've killed him… [chuckling] I'd still be beatin' on him."

And all that happened before George went out for the Final race. Jackie would be starting from the back. Easy peasy.

Follmer: "So I'm sitting in the car on the grid, and Don came up and told me I had to let Oliver win.

"I didn't like that…"

Had George understood that would be part of the deal?

"No. Not originally… the politics was frustrating. Terribly frustrating. You know, everything was controlled. They were going to give Oliver that championship whether he earned it or not. They didn't care where I qualified, but I had to let Oliver win."

Team manager Mike Hillman's take on this accusation is included in the section about him at the end of this chapter.

It sure didn't look like Follmer had any intention of giving up the win as he blasted away into the second race. On his first lap he pulled out two seconds on second man Patrick. But Oliver had his foot in it too: he started the lap on the eighth row, but 2.46 miles later he was fourth overall!

Shortly Ollie reached third place, eight seconds behind the leader, but then eased his foot. It was a 50-lap event, so he had time to be patient with slower traffic, but he also had an actual problem. He could feel something vibrating when he used high rpm, and he saw his

BELOW Follmer starts the Mosport Final hard, knowing Oliver is many places back but won't stay there. Alongside here (momentarily) is Scooter Patrick in 1972's McLaren M20, driven then by Peter Revson and in 1973 by David Hobbs. By 1974 it's definitely Best of the Rest. But no match for a new DN4. *Dan R. Boyd*

THE BEST ONE 239

oil pressure fluctuating. He let the gap to Follmer grow until it was half a minute at half distance.

But then it was George's turn for trouble. Either a tire punctured, as was reported, or simply wore out (see his story, page xxx); in any case the wheel change dragged on for over a minute. By the time Follmer was up to speed again, Oliver was 50 seconds up with 20 laps left.

Team orders be damned. Hurling his Can-Am sports car around the hilly, swoopy circuit like the F1 single-seater he had raced the season before, setting lap record after lap record, Follmer closed up and up. Going into the 50th and final lap he trailed the leader by four seconds, and at the flag he was just two seconds away. Third-placed Patrick finished a whole lap behind.

ROAD ATLANTA, GEORGIA (USA)
Can-Am (R2), July 7th, 1974
1st, Jackie Oliver, Shadow DN4
2nd, George Follmer, Shadow DN4

This time Follmer took pole, his 1:14.9 beating Oliver's time by 1.2 seconds. But Ollie did have "yes buts" to point out: a spin in a sudden rain shower that banged up the back end, then damaging the nose by hitting a loose animal. Again Patrick was best of the rest.

In a blast of black thunder, the Shadows hurled away over the hills to the far end of the track, where Oliver snatched the lead when Follmer seemed to fumble. In fact he was fumbling for gears — the shifter had broken. Limping all the way back to the pits and having the linkage fixed dropped him to the very back of the race. He did forge forward to finish fifth in that heat.

That's where George started the main heat, but halfway around the first lap he was already second behind Oliver. At the end of that first 2.52 miles the Shadows were nose-to-tail again, and all alone. The third-placed car hove into view seven seconds later. Such was the shape and substance of Can-Am 1974.

That, and the George and Jackie Show, of

BELOW Road Atlanta: heat one and number 1 is first into the first turn! *Dan R. Boyd*

ABOVE Heat two, turn 2, Follmer has already disposed of two cars that started ahead of him at Road Atlanta. Not even Canadian ace John Cordts in a McLaren M8F will stave him off for long. Next up, his good mate Oliver. *Dan R. Boyd*

LEFT Number 1 takes the checkers at Road Atlanta in place number… well no, not first here either. *Dan R Boyd*

course. Like the McLarens of old, the Shadows sped around in a race of their own. Would it actually be a race? Was Follmer just biding his time, waiting until the end to defy instructions?

We'll never know. An exhaust pipe broke off, George became sickened by fumes, and his car lost touch with Oliver's. Jackie won by half a minute. Lothar Motschenbacher came third with his McLaren, two laps back. Patrick hadn't run that heat at all, because of transmission failure.

WATKINS GLEN, NEW YORK (USA)
Can-Am (R3), July 14th, 1974
1st, Jackie Oliver, Shadow DN4
2nd, George Follmer, Shadow DN4

The UOP boys turned up late here at the Glen because their hauler's engine broke on the way. Their hard work got the Shadows ready to run anyway, complete with the intended original rear suspension to suit the newer, larger Goodyears that had finally come through. Not that all this toil made any visible difference on the grid sheet. The black cars qualified one-two again, George's pole margin to Jackie this time a second and a quarter.

Oh, we might mutter, that's right, the Brit knew he was going to beat the Yank to the checkered flag regardless. Well, no, that's not why Ollie posted such a slow time. During practice he had a frightening moment when a front tire blew at high speed. Then toward the end his fuel pump started leaking.

Follmer's flat-out mood carried him into Saturday's 20-lap sprint, and once again he maintained the lead over Oliver, until a shock absorber broke.

George went on to drive a different car in a support race, and afterward his Mosport-injured back was seriously painful. As a precaution, Nichols asked David Hobbs to stand by to take over for Sunday. But ferocious Follmer was no man to give up his seat that easily, and in the 33-lap Final race he stormed from the fifth row

RIGHT What do they want from me? In F1 last year I gave them more points than he did. Year before that I was Can-Am champion. This year they put a 1 on my car. So how do they think I'm gonna drive? *Dan R. Boyd*

LEFT Gee, Jackie, don't take it that way, I just thought I should tell you what he said…
Dan R. Boyd

BELOW Watkins Glen's pace lap offers an opportunity to see if this year's Can-Am looks better in color. You can think about it while George and Ollie lead the privateer likes of Scooter Patrick (8), John Cordts and Lothar Motschenbacher (11), all in McLarens, then the white Lola of John Gunn, Mike Brockman's blue McLaren and Herbert Müller in a Ferrari. There's about a dozen more coming along behind. All older than the Shadows, and all a lot slower. But hey, it's the Glen and it's a nice day, so enjoy the *basso profondo* of the Big Blocks. *Dan R. Boyd*

THE BEST ONE **243**

ABOVE Watkins Glen: third race, third win. Starting to look good for a championship. Ollie hasn't taken one of those before. *Motorsport Images/LAT*

RIGHT A broken shock absorber during practice is only one of George's troubles at the Glen. At least fixing this doesn't involve sticking a needle in his back. *Motorsport Images/LAT*

to second place on the opening 3.377-mile lap.

Oliver kept a vigilant eye in his mirrors, but no need. After a while Follmer slowed, visibly fatigued, obviously in pain. His Lidocaine injection was wearing off. He finished half a lap back. Patrick was third by a whole lap.

MID-OHIO (USA)
Can-Am (R4), August 11th, 1974
1st, Jackie Oliver, Shadow DN4
DNF, George Follmer, Shadow DN4, body damage

A real race! Just like in the years of McLaren or Porsche dominance, when every so often a truly competitive car came along, Team Shadow actually had to break a sweat this time. And the challenger was actually faster.

Porsche was out of the Can-Am as a factory, but Penske still had Panzers in-house and one of Donohue's year-old 917/30s arrived with

ABOVE & BELOW Shadow's transporter, queen of the Can-Am paddock, was Don Nichols's idea but race engine builder/car hauler driver Doug Meyer made it happen. That's him on the ground, controller in hand, as one of the DN4s emerges from the upper deck of the big semi-trailer into a misty Mid-Ohio morning. As Doug tells the story, "We were the first to have a lift-gate, so we could carry three cars. Nobody had done a double-decker. Don said, 'I want the biggest, baddest truck. I want us to arrive in something that blows people's minds.' So I went out and found a nice used Kenworth with a Cummins turbo diesel. Then I called up a company that made lift-gates for moving vans. We painted the whole rig black like the cars. We had the biggest truck in the paddock. This was the definitive Don Nichols. 'Go Big. See if we can do that.' As an old hot rodder I loved that!" *Dan R. Boyd*

THE BEST ONE

Mark himself in attendance. Yes, he had retired from driving, but while managing Roger's other programs he thought about Mid-Ohio's tight, twisty track and how little fuel he had burned up the year before. It would be interesting to tune the turbocar for this year's Economy Run and try its luck against the Shadows.

Porsche ace Brian Redman, who had been a Ferrari guest driver the race before, tenderly guided the long, blue, quietly murmuring machine to pole position.

Not that the Shadowmen weren't trying. The body shop molded new front sections to trim off some 10 pounds, the engine shop tried a new fuel injector setup, and Goodyear whipped up new 13-inch front tires with stiffer construction to counter Oliver's blowout at the Glen.

Shadow's drivers were hard on it as well, Jackie and George swapping fastest practice laps until Follmer's DN4 suffered a broken rear shock. That was replaced, but then Oliver's sister car broke its rear subframe, so the Brit had to stand by and watch his team-mate try to out-qualify his countryman. Finally turned loose by the cautious Donohue, Redman won the pole by 1.2 seconds over Follmer. Huge.

Raceday's pace only ratcheted up. Redman won the preliminary race, Penske's team having made a better guess on tires for changing conditions.

The twin Shadows had to start the Final from the second row, with Patrick's McLaren up alongside the Porsche. But Follmer simply muscled Patrick aside through Turn 1, leaving black paint on Scooter's blue body as a courtesy card, and charged off after Redman's Porsche. Oliver quickly came up too, and the trio embroiled themselves in the best race of the season — one of the best Can-Ams of any season. On the first lap Follmer out-braked Redman at the end of Ohio's longest straight to make it Shadow-Porsche-Shadow, the poor old blue McLaren already three seconds behind.

They raced on like this until Follmer lost

BELOW Looking "Bad" itself, Oliver's car is rolled out for the Big Day by his faithful Shadow crewmen, Tony Connor (left) and Chris Jackson. *Dan R. Boyd*

ABOVE It falls to Follmer to have a truly bad day. *Dan R. Boyd*

momentum when lapping traffic and Redman seized the opening to blow by. Next lap Oliver repeated the move and Follmer was third, but a nose-to-tail third.

They were into the thick of the backmarkers now, and the Porsche appeared to carve through them more easily, but once the road cleared the Shadows closed right up again. Follmer wanted to get back ahead of Oliver, and on lap seven did fastest race lap, just a fifth of a second off his qualifying time. But it was still the Brian-Ollie-George Show until lap 18. Then Redman made a mistake.

Cresting a hill through a right-hander, he dialed up the turbo power just a fraction too early and the Panzer snapped sideways. Brian caught it, but the Shadowmen seized the opening and were by.

By, but not done racing. Follmer was not letting Oliver run away, and nearing the bottom of one blast down the long straight… let's ask *Autosport*'s Gordon Kirby to tell us:

"He waited until the last minute then, with his nose inside Jackie's, he stomped on the brakes, bobbled for an instant, tapped the side of Oliver's car in a scuffling moment, each Shadow refusing to give way to the other, each banging against each other before they separated and Follmer spun into the grass."

His bodywork visibly damaged, Follmer was called into the pits for a checkup. He obeyed, but had misinterpreted the signal. Unaware at that point of body panels looking ready to fly off, he thought he was being penalized for trying to pass Oliver. Seething, he erupted from the car and stomped away.

Here is George's side of the story: "Oh, I just got pissed off, because he kept blocking me, so I wound up sustaining damage. Well, what did I have to lose? I was supposed to let him win anyhow, so what difference did it make? People thought I took myself out of that race. Well, yeah, I probably did, but I would just as soon have taken him off and let Brian win! [Bitter laugh]"

THESE PAGES Slicing through the rain in the Can-Am's last great cars, Jackie and George put on the last great race the once-great series will ever see. *Jim Chambers*

ABOVE Brian Redman, a former Shadowman himself, puts the Penske Porsche smack into the middle of the Oliver/Follmer feud. *Jim Chambers*

BELOW The turbocharged 917/30, dominant with Donohue the year before, is still the fastest qualifier in Redman's hands, but as the race wears on and his tires wear out it all slips from his grasp. *Dan R. Boyd*

And Jackie's take: "I did try to psyche him out in the races. At Mid-Ohio, tight circuit, that race was pretty closely fought. George, try as he will, couldn't get on top of me. He was completely frustrated by me. He just kept hitting me from behind, crashing into me. All he succeeded in doing was damaging his own car, actually destroyed all the radiator ducts and the thing overheated. He came into the pits halfway through the race, and he was blowing steam. He got out of the car and left without saying a word to anybody. Ha ha!"

Meanwhile, Redman was losing pace and dropping back from Oliver. Brian took the blame. Before the race the weather looked like it could turn either way, from damp to wet or dry, so he hedged his bets: he asked for a set of slick tires to be grooved into handmade intermediates. The day stayed dry, meaning the reduced contact areas overheated, resulting in ever-worsening understeer. He finished 47 seconds behind. So ended the last great race of a once-great series.

LEFT & BELOW Can-Am's new King Jackie takes his full measure of pleasure with wife Lynne and their son Jason, just three but maturing rapidly. *Dan R Boyd*

THE BEST ONE **251**

ABOVE The Shadowmen have no particular reason to think the Road America race, which turned out to be the last of the series, will have results much different from those of the four before. *Dan R. Boyd*

BELOW The final finish — albeit this is the Sprint. The Road America Final will not bring finishes. *Dan R. Boyd*

ROAD AMERICA, WISCONSIN (USA)
Can-Am (R5), August 25th, 1973
1st, Scooter Patrick, McLaren M20
DNF, Jackie Oliver, Shadow DN4, engine
DNF, George Follmer, Shadow DN4, driveshaft

Both Shadows out. Even mighty McLaren could have told them they would have days like this.

It started out as usual, Follmer on pole with Oliver alongside. The gap was 1.1 seconds on the 4.0-mile circuit. Scooter Patrick's two-year-old McLaren was back in its usual third spot on the grid, but long, long seconds behind.

And so things went on through the race, right up until the opening lap of the Final heat when Follmer spun off. A driveshaft had sheared. Oliver cruised on, and on, and… BANG! Pieces of 494 everywhere.

When a surprised Scooter Patrick popped up the hill onto the finishing straight, his ecstatic crewmen greeted their pretty, baby-blue Batmobile with a board reading "P 1 1 1 1!"

252 CHAPTER 11

ABOVE Formed up for the Road America Final, Sprint race winner Oliver on pole. *Dan R. Boyd*

BELOW Don Nichols has delivered a championship to his good sponsor, John Logan (right), who has brought along a massive turnout of UOP employees and associates from Chicago to enjoy a triumphant day. *Dan R. Boyd*

ONE FURTHER RACE remained on the 1974 Can-Am schedule, at Riverside. The series was originally supposed to have eight rounds, but Edmonton and Laguna Seca had already cancelled. Riverside boss Les Richter had threatened to make the same decision, and after the lackluster Road America round he dropped the axe. Public interest just wasn't there. Fans now thought open-wheel Formula 5000 racing was more worth watching.

So Can-Am's season of '74 died at five.

The SCCA worked for some months to plot various ways forward into 1975, but on November 19th they waved the flag on the entire Can-Am. The noble experiment in "no-rules racing" was dead.

Jackie Oliver duly won his championship, having finished first in all four races he finished. His 82 points were almost twice the 45 accrued by George Follmer, who beat Scooter Patrick by a scant single point. Not that 1972's Can-Am champ would have much cared either way. ♠

CAMEO APPEARANCES

Don Nichols still had a sponsor to please, a sponsor who originally signed on for a full-length series of eight races. So nearing the end of 1974 he organized two promotional events to showcase UOP branding.

At Watkins Glen in October, three roaring DN4s shattered a quiet period between practice sessions for F1's US Grand Prix. It was a glorious exhibition of raw Big Block power. George Follmer, free of the chains that held him down in the Can-Am series, exploded away from Jackie Oliver and Jean-Pierre Jarier. George's dominance of his black beast was a joy to watch. So was his exuberant, grinning, sweating face afterward, when he blurted out, "Nobody can drive a Group 7 car like I can!"

Reminded of that years later he said, "Oh, yeah, I could actually go and win a race! It was a new experience." Asked how the Shadow compared to his championship-winning turbocharged Porsche, he said of the DN4:

"That was an awful good car. Docile. Quick. It cornered well, and it was slippery, clean, fast. We had good power — we didn't have near what the Porsche had, but it was normally aspirated, so you could get on it real quick in traffic.

"I think the Shadow was a better car than the Porsche. The car complemented me, or I complemented it, or whatever, but it felt good. I was comfortable in it, and I

BELOW Shadow threesome lined up abreast for the "grudge match" inserted into the schedule for October's US Grand Prix weekend. Nearest the camera Jackie Oliver is already settled in; George Follmer is still milling around in the middle; hidden beyond is Jean-Pierre Jarier, about to drive his first Can-Am car. *Pete Lyons*

ABOVE Blasting up "Graham Hill" Follmer is already ahead at Watkins Glen and on his way to a runaway win — boosted by his clandestine engine advantage. Oliver is driving steadily, he has nothing to prove. Jarier already looks unhappy, he must already miss his lighter, handier F1 Shadow waiting for him back in the pitlane. *Motorsport Images/David Phipps*

enjoyed running it. It was a fun car to drive. Still one of the best I ever had."

Actually, George's crew had slipped him a trick motor. Size was either 540 cubic inches, as claimed by some, or 510 according to the man who built it ("That Reynolds block couldn't go any bigger"), compared to his unsuspecting team-mate's 494. It doesn't really matter, all's fair in no-rules racing, and besides, the season's over. Let's go get 'em.

A week later the whole Shadow team appeared at Laguna Seca, where one of the cancelled Can-Ams had been replaced with an F5000 event. For this Jarier stepped back into his familiar single-seat DN3, joined for the occasion by James Hunt in another F1. Challenging these two were Oliver and Follmer in their DN4s.

Can-Am vs. Formula 1. Intriguing.

Not for long. The light, agile, highly strung Grand Prix cars seemed born to this circuit. They made the Group 7s look clumsy, sluggish, ineffective. Jarier romped around to finish first, six seconds ahead of Hunt. Both Oliver and Follmer spun off trying to stay with them, and Ollie dropped out when his clutch failed.

Can-Am's big bruisers weren't done yet. Two years later, in 1976, on a sunny August 22nd, Canada's Mosport Park tried pitting leftover Group 7 machinery against contemporary Group 6 long-distance cars, the slippery speedsters made for Le Mans. The latter were supposed to be the stars of the show, a 200-mile round of the World Sports Car Championship, but entries were thin — and not very inspiring with their well-mannered little 3- and 2-liter enduro engines. So the promoter also welcomed eight bellowing Lola, McLaren and Shadow V8s.

Good friends Oliver and Follmer met once more here, Jackie in a single black Shadow DN4 understood to be chassis 4, which had been a spare in 1974. George drove the baby blue McLaren M20 that Patrick had run that year. Shadow's man qualified fastest of all, with the former Shadowman alongside him on the front row. Their stiffest opposition lined up behind, Jacky Ickx in a turbocharged Porsche 936, then two Alpine-Renaults and a Mirage-Ford.

THE BEST ONE 255

LEFT James Hunt was still on Don Nichols's wish list. The reverse was not the case. Laguna Seca's F1 outing with Shadow was no more satisfying for James than his Can-Am experience the year before. *Private collection*

Strength beat stealth. It was a Can-Am blowout. Oliver led every one of the 80 laps, despite his undermanned pit crew — reportedly including Don Nichols himself — making a hash of the mid-race refueling stop. Nonetheless the Shadow won by eight seconds over Follmer's McLaren, with Le Mans ace Ickx's Porsche the only other finisher going the full race distance.

Mosport never repeated that format, but in 1977 the track did try a different matchup. This came courtesy of the SCCA, which had ordered F5000 owners to drape full-coverage bodywork over their single-seaters and call them "Can-Am cars." Alternatively, owners of genuine two-seat Group 7 vehicles could participate as well, providing they installed 5-liter F5000 engines.

Nichols bit. Doing a deal with automaker Dodge, Shadow

RIGHT Back in his F1 element, Jean-Pierre Jarier and Laguna Seca just gelled. George Follmer and his Can-Am car didn't. *Private collection*

BELOW Shadow Showdown! Which kind of car is quicker around Laguna Seca? Doesn't take long to find out. Leading pair are DN3s, Jarier (17) and Hunt; trailing come the DN4s, Oliver (101) and Follmer. *Autosport*

THE BEST ONE 257

LEFT Mothballed for two years, in 1976 this DN4 comes out to play with the small-fry Le Mans machinery at Mosport. She still has what it takes. *Private collection*

RIGHT The Jackie and Jacky Show — celebrated winners of the 1969 Le Mans 24 Hours reunited on the Mosport podium seven years later. *Private collection*

dropped a 5.0-liter version of Chrysler's midsize V8 into the cavernous engine bay of chassis DN4-5a. Thus underpowered for its weight, this hybrid called a DN4B ran only three times in 1977, retiring each time. Aspiring pro Randy Lewis drove it in June at Saint-Jovite (aka Mont-Tremblant), starting fifth fastest but placing a non-running 12th. He did not make the start at Laguna Seca, where he crashed in practice — twice.

That June 26th weekend has become rather infamous in Shadow circles. Poor Lewis suffered his first crash on the Friday, when he had already set a time good enough for second position on the grid next to Tom Klausler in a crowd-pleaser of a quasi-coupe called a Schkee. But as aspiring pros do, he went out again to try for pole, lost the car and it was heavily damaged.

As Laguna Seca was literally just the other side of the hill from the team's workshop in Marina, they had a second DN4B for him on Saturday. He was trying again when, just ahead, Warwick Brown went off heavily, throwing up a plume of dust that blocked Lewis's vision. All he could do was guess which way to go, and he guessed wrong. Crunch.

The driver felt that this time the damage was minimal enough to be fixed by raceday, so he went off to dinner and then drove out to Marina to see how the job was going. It wasn't going at all. The shop was dark, quiet, locked. Lewis finally reached a crewman at his home and learned that Nichols had pulled out of the race. And from subsequent ones that year.

With one exception: two months later Nichols had his F1 hero Alan Jones try his luck with the DN4B at Mosport, where the Aussie qualified eighth and went out with a failed fuel pump.

Not impressive. The underpowered, obsolete two-seater approach wasn't working.

Despite all that, never-say-die Don Nichols launched a fresh attack on Can-Am II, this time using genuinely single-seat chassis tubs from his F5000 and F1 programs. We cover these so-called DN6C and DN10 models in another chapter.

BELOW Mosport a year later, in 1977, but driver and engine have changed. It's Shadow hero Alan Jones struggling to get anything at all from a Dodge V8 less than five-eighths the capacity of the Chevrolets a DN4 was born to run. *Dan R. Boyd*

THE BEST ONE **259**

MIKE HILLMAN
TEAM MANAGER PART 1

JUST AS A racing machine cannot perform without a human at the controls, so a racing team must be guided by someone with experience, understanding, and strength. Don Nichols found such a person in Mike Hillman, an Englishman who managed the American's 1974 DN4 program to Shadow's most successful season.

It was Tony Southgate who brought them together. Tony calls Mike "my oldest and dearest friend." They met ten years earlier, when Southgate left Lola for a brief while and joined Jack Brabham and Ron Tauranac to design a car for "Black Jack" to drive in 1964's Indy 500. This was the Offy-powered BT12 known as the "Zink-Urschel Trackburner Special."

"We shared this tiny drawing office and we got along very well," says Hillman. "We enjoyed each other's company. We had a good relationship, Tony and I."

Hillman himself had recently joined Brabham's burgeoning race team at age 21, looking to make more exciting use of the experience he had gained at Rolls-Royce in an engineering training program. Working as a draftsman under designer Tauranac for seven years, Mike was part of the team's historic F1 championships in 1966 (Brabham himself) and 1967 (Denny Hulme). Moving on to Ford of Europe, Mike had been with Advanced Vehicle Operations for three years when his friend Tony phoned.

It was late in 1973, when Shadow's DN2 was failing

BELOW Pastor Hillman giving his blessing for the Shadow Showdown about to get underway at Laguna Seca. *Dan R. Boyd*

miserably to stop Porsche's domination of the Can-Am. Don Nichols finally accepted that he needed a new car, in fact a new approach.

As Mike tells it, "I first came over to the States in October 1973. UOP paid for a plane ticket from Germany, where I was with Ford of Europe at the time, to sunny California and you don't turn that opportunity down.

"Tony had contacted me and said he was having trouble with that Can-Am program. They had to have somebody who knew what he was doing, and would I be interested in joining them. I said I certainly would like to look them over.

"So I came to Riverside for the last race of the season, and I couldn't believe it. Vic Elford was driving the turbocharged DN2, and every time he came into the pits the car was on fire! The mechanics would pick up this extinguisher and... *fwoof*."

Said mechanics would have been used to that with certain turbo cars of the day, where after shutdown residual oil leaking past turbocharger bearings could pool inside the still very hot blower and ignite. No big deal to battle-hardened crewmen, perhaps, but maybe to English engineer Hillman the sight of the big black machine cruising the crowded pitlane emitting gaudy cannon blasts at everyone and everything was all too much like Admiral Nelson's flagship at Trafalgar, firing broadsides out both sides at once.

"John Logan was president of UOP at the time, a really nice guy — for a chief executive. A really cool chap. He and Don interviewed me, and I said, 'Well, to be quite honest I wouldn't be much good to you if I came over here as an engineer, because the organization is so bad.' Don said to me, could I handle that as well? I said, 'No fear, I can do that.'

"We agreed on a salary and I went back home to Germany, moved my family from Germany to England and found a place in Northampton to stay, and we jumped on the design of the DN4 straight away.

"Tony of course was in charge of the design of the product. I helped out with the drawings…

"What I liked most about Tony's work is that not only was he a natural engineer, but he's quite artistic. Look at the cars that he's drawn, there's not a dull one amongst them.

"I think the DN2 was horrific, but he did his best to do something with it."

As experienced racers, both men understood the wisdom of that age-old saying, "simplicate and add lightness." To achieve it with the DN4 meant nearly a 180-degree turn away from Southgate's unsuccessful DN2.

ABOVE Viewed over the tops of DN4 inlet trumpets, legendary US newsman Chris Economaki interviews Jackie Oliver at Watkins Glen. *Pete Lyons*

One of the first features evaluated was turbocharging. Yes, the lure of massive power and torque was hard to give up, but Shadow's troubles with the large, heavy, ill-handling, complex and unreliable DN2 made the decision easier.

"You know what happens when you supposedly have a thousand horsepower, and I never believed that for a minute, but when you've got that kind of horsepower everything goes to a new scale. The brakes have to be bigger, gearbox has to be bigger. But that's not my philosophy, and certainly not Tony's — and it wasn't Brabham's either. That's why we came together so quickly on deciding what the spec of the DN4 would be.

"Tony and I were of one mind. We ought to do it as clean and simple as possible. We were told we could get

THE BEST ONE **261**

a lot of power out of the basic engine package without a turbocharger. So we decided we were going for lightness and drivability and reliability," explains Hillman, adding:

"The DN2 was like an aircraft carrier. There was a monocoque fastened to the wall and it just spread everywhere. I mean, you could land an F-16 on it. When the DN4 came out of Tony's head it was such a beautiful car, one of the nicest Can-Am cars ever designed. It was so sleek, and the design took out all our worries.

"We had committed to build the car in exactly 90 days. Which we did. It was quite an effort. We had it in California in March."

Mike remembers meeting new star driver Peter Revson there, at a press conference in a Marriott hotel near Los Angeles airport.

"He showed up with Miss World! He said some nice things about Tony, he had some nice things to say about me. He said he was always impressed with people who have managed to keep their commitments, and we met this 90-day commitment and now he was going to enjoy working with the car.

"When it came my turn to speak, I gave him 20 bucks and said, 'Thanks a lot.'"

Revvie then flew away to South Africa, while Hillman, his road crew and Jackie Oliver took the sparkling new Shadow out for a rigorous testing and development program.

The prototype DN4 had already run a few shakedown laps in the UK, and Hillman can't resist chuckling over the first thing that had gone wrong at Silverstone. "This beautiful car goes out of the pits, Ollie does a lap, comes in and the door falls off!"

So reliability was the big thing on everyone's mind, and they achieved it through "more than 2,000 miles testing" at both Riverside and Laguna Seca. "It doesn't sound like a lot now," says Mike, "but in 1974 it was a lot of miles."

So confidence was high when the crew trucked back to their Chicagoland home base. A two-story building at 420 Lively Blvd. in Elk Grove Village, it was leased property about five miles from UOP's HQ in Des Plaines. It offered ample workshop space on the street level, with offices upstairs. Shadow even had its own engine dyno there.

Hillman worked closely with Nichols, both in the office and on the road. "He was a very interesting guy, to me anyway. He was very strong on the military. I think he hid behind having been in the Intelligence. He would never talk about it, he just allowed that to sink in.

"He knew everybody in racing, because he had been a tire supplier in Japan, and apparently he carried that relationship over when he came back to the United States.

"There was a bunch of people that didn't like him, and to this day I think that the Riverside Can-Am race [of 1974] was canceled to piss Don off. Les Richter was the manager there, and there wasn't a close, loving relationship between those two.

"Then I noticed when we went to Indy there was another chap who didn't want to have anything to do with Don."

Just possibly this animosity had to do with Nichols's notoriously tight financial fist. "Don was in charge of the money, and he didn't like to part with it. He got the sponsorship [through] his relationship between Shadow and UOP, and he was a bit parsimonious with it. Bills would be paid at the last possible minute."

What's this about Indianapolis?

"I think it was 1975. Don and I went to Indy for one of the practice days, and he invited Ronnie Peterson over. Don was in love with the idea of getting Ronnie to drive a Shadow in the 500.

"It didn't go anywhere, but it was certainly a good demonstration of how Don would go about romancing somebody and putting an idea in their head."

Of course the 1974 Can-Am season, short as it was, put Hillman close to both Jackie Oliver and George Follmer, Revson's replacement.

Jackie was a good test driver, Mike feels. "He drove every lap that I ever asked him to do, and he could go for hours about half a second off the quickest time. And that's very useful when you try to develop a car and get rid of some of those lumps and bumps. And I don't recall ever seeing Ollie spinning a DN4.

"He was well respected by UOP, and he had a private contract to represent them at functions. It was on top of his contract with Don.

"I don't think he thought much of Follmer."

To both Englishmen, perhaps, George was another American enigma. As Mike puts it, "I mean he was in some ways a very, very good driver. The great thing about George was, he was on the money straightaway. Go out for an exploratory lap, another lap, and then he'd do the quickest lap of the grid. Whereas Ollie liked to sort of work his way gently into it.

"George was usually half a second quicker. That was

RIGHT Romancing Ronnie at Indy: along with Don Nichols, the management pictured here — Mike Hillman, Jackie Oliver and possibly Alan Rees — tried their best to convince SuperSwede that Shadow could make him a 500 winner. The team photographer, Dan R. Boyd, went along for the ride from Chicago:

"We picked him up and the group of us drove down to Indianapolis in a car driven by Don. I sat in the front seat between him and Ronnie. I guess he got bored. I felt him nudge me, and very gently and quietly he put his foot across me to the top of the gas pedal and pushed it down. Dandy Don was stunned. He took his foot off the pedal but the car kept on speeding up. I thought he was going to vapor lock!

"Ronnie kept the pressure on until finally he could not keep from laughing. Everyone else was in a serious panic, we were going way too fast.

"I don't know why it fell through, we didn't do Indy, but that's one of the moments I remember clearly." *Dan R. Boyd*

probably the source of the aggravation between George and Ollie at Mosport.

"Oliver was the driver who had done all the testing, and we go to Mosport and here comes George and in two laps he's quicker than Ollie. All that hard work…"

The other part of it was Follmer's dual-sided personality. "George was a nice guy socially. You went to dinner, you had a very pleasant time. In a racing car he was like Mr. Hyde. He would get the red mist descending over his eyes and he was terrible, like a little boy."

That's not what happened during the team's pre-season test at Mosport, when Follmer suffered his huge crash. Nothing to do with frame of mind, just apparently a stuck throttle.

"George went out on his exploratory lap, then he went close to the lap record on his next lap, and then we didn't see him for a while.

"So we jumped in the rental car and we went around the track and it looked like a garage sale. There were bits of car all over the racing line and down the track, in the bushes, all the way to Toronto.

"And in the midst of all this mayhem is George sitting on a little tussock on the left side of the track, chewing on a piece of grass.

"I said, 'My God, George, are you all right?' and he said, 'You know, I think fifth gear is a little long.'"

After laughing, the manager goes on to say, "He had been hurt. He really had a nasty crash, and I think it affected his driving the rest of the year.

"Maybe it was Watkins Glen, we were on the start line waiting to go, and Ollie was in his car being strapped in, but George was not to be seen. Burdie Martin, who was the SCCA man in charge of the FIA American wing, was anxious to get his big show to go, and there's no George. He said, 'Where is he?' I said, 'He's in the medical building. They're removing the stake from his heart.'

"The reality is he was in there having an injection."

Though Follmer was a cool shoe normally, his emotions could indeed boil if the racing turned heated. Confrontation was frequent between the two team drivers. Most infamously, probably, was that between-heats tussle in 1974's first round at Mosport that Hillman mentioned earlier.

"I didn't actually see that. One of the mechanics came rushing up to me and said, 'You've got to come to the garage, Ollie and George are in a fight.' I'm not sure whether they came to blows, but Ollie said that he ran like blazes and managed to shake George off. They weren't good friends from then on."

Then there was Mid-Ohio. "Oh, that was one of the most fantastic races I have ever been associated with! It was a misty kind of day and there was a little rain coming down and then it would blow away, so you had to choose whether you would go on wet or dry tires.

"And I saw Mark Donohue chiseling the rubber off a slick tire and I thought, 'I gotcha!' [Laughing] I couldn't believe he threw away the race.

"Because he was caught between a rock and hard place. If it was going to stop raining he was going to want to use slicks, but if it starts to rain really hard he's gonna need wets. He left himself no room in the middle.

"Mark was a very capable mechanic, but cutting [intermediates] with what looked like a wood chisel…"

Was seeing the vaunted Penske operation just along the pitlane a bit daunting? "I was a little worried, because that Porsche was supposed to have a thousand horsepower. I hadn't the slightest doubt that Porsche gave the wrong number, so even if he's running a fuel-consumption race he could turn on the power and do the overtaking, and then settle on cruise for the rest of the race.

"That actually didn't happen. The DN4 was quite competitive with the Porsche, and George actually took the lead quite early in the race. I really loved the thought of the competition, [and] this was a real race. There was honor on the table."

Oliver won that race, his fourth victory in a row, but Follmer's day ended in red rage.

"George and Ollie were bumping and banging into each other quite a lot during that race, and one time part of George's rear bodywork came adrift. We could see it in the pits that it was likely to fall off, so we put out a sign to him to come in.

"And George thought he was being brought in because he was dicing with Ollie. That's why he stormed off. But he was brought in because the car looked dangerous and we wanted to fix it."

Which brings up Follmer's contention that Nichols had ordered him to let Oliver win the championship. Team manager Hillman calls that "fiction."

"I've never spoken up about it, but it's kind of ticking me off every time I see it. I know it's a story that George promulgates. Bullshit. And I would know.

ABOVE Mike and his merry Shadowmen man the Watkins Glen pit rail, their spirits rising as the laps keep winding down and nobody's stopped. Yet. *Dan R. Boyd*

"Halfway through the season it became evident that we were well clear of the rest of field. George and Ollie were going through this thing where they were banging into each other. In order to try to stop that, or to bring some sense to it, I said that we must have rules. I told them that so many laps from the end, 20 laps, 30 laps, whoever is in the lead at that time keeps it.

"Now if that can be translated into 'Don told me that I should let Oliver win' I'd be amazed. You would think that Don would have passed that strategy on to his team manager, who could actually implement such a plan! We certainly wouldn't have had to come up with a strategy that we'd finish our race at a certain point and be sure the cars came home."

We heard Follmer's side of this story earlier, on page 195.

Hillman meant to institute this strategy at Road America, but both cars went out before it was needed. Nothing to explain it other than blind bad racing luck, he says, then comments:

"It was actually pretty embarrassing, because UOP had about 20 buses to bring employees up to the race to watch us ruin the opposition. To not win in front of those people who were so excited to be there…

"Fortunately the next year, when we went up there with the Formula 5000 car, at least we won one of the heat races."

Inevitably, because Shadow's 1974 Can-Am championship was its only such success throughout 11 seasons of racing, and was achieved against weak opposition in a curtailed calendar, there are critics who discount its significance.

But it is unfair to denigrate the quality of this team's effort. Under Mike Hillman's guiding hand, Tony Southgate's superb DN4 was always properly prepared, well presented and ably driven.

In all ways, the quality of Shadow's approach to the Can-Am matched those of the legendary McLaren and Penske Porsche organizations. It was hardly the fault of the Shadowman that theirs was the only strong team that final year.

As Mike observes, "It's a pleasure to win, whether as an engineer or driver or team owner, but your opportunities to win a race are fairly limited. So to win a championship is fantastic, no matter what the background to it was."

THE BEST ONE **265**

CHAPTER 12
FIRST VICTORY!

SHADOW DN5 (F1), 1975

Why was Tony Southgate's third Formula 1 Shadow so fast? Because his friends at Imperial College in London installed a rolling-road wind tunnel.

Resembling a giant belt-sander upside down on the floor of the testing chamber, this provides an artificial, miniature racetrack surface zipping along under the experimental car model at the same speed as the air rushing over it. The benefit is more accurate simulation of airflow interactions under and around a real vehicle.

First indications of its value to Shadow came in December 1974, when Jean-Pierre Jarier tested the new 1975 DN5 at Paul Ricard in the south of France. "Jarier… was able to take the fast esses at the end of the pits straight flat out in top gear, for the first time. That's approaching something like 165 mph. This hasn't been done before," reported *Autosport* from the car's official unveiling in Paris a few days later.

Speed with stick. The Holy Grail of racecar design. And Southgate's new tunnel toy gave him the power to test and refine, test and refine, again and again until he had an aerodynamic package that best melded low drag with high downforce.

Here's how he explained the value of the tunnel in his book *Tony Southgate: From Drawing Board to Chequered Flag*: "Shadow was the first UK team to use this facility and it showed on the track. The DN5 definitely had more downforce than any other Formula 1 car in 1975 — up to 750 pounds at 150 mph. This downforce came from very well-developed multi-section wings on both the front and the rear. The sleek engine ram-air box was particularly effective in enabling the air to reach the rear wing with the minimum of flow loss."

He was particularly pleased with his "very efficient" low-slung, twin-nostril nosepiece with lip-assisted oil cooler exit ducting, together with the twin-element, adjustable canard wings either side.

"The importance of the rolling road was that it allowed us to produce much more accurate aerodynamic data. In fact, the center of pressure

LEFT Demure debutant, DN5-1 poses on the carpet for her formal introduction in London. Shadow's Alan Rees, Tony Southgate, Mike Hillman and Jackie Oliver take center stage. Their mere star driver Tom Pryce hides in the background, behind Southgate. Off in the wings are the creme of England's motorsports press, Chris Witty, Alan Henry, and Ray Hutton.
Courtesy of Jackie Oliver

— the point at which the aerodynamic load acts in relation to the car's road wheels — was no less than 20% different when compared with the readings in the static tunnel. This is a massive variation when you are trying to establish exactly what your car needs to be quick, and what you actually have."

Yet as new as this latest Shadow seemed, it was very recognizably a third-step evolution of Southgate's previous DN1 and DN3. Visually, the DN5 is distinguishable in several ways. To relieve the inky blackness of the overall presentation (dark cars look great to the eye but disappear in a camera), bold swatches of color appeared on the nose and sides. Ranging from red through orange and yellow to white, these were dubbed "re-entry colors." Recalling the fiery displays from spacecraft returning from orbit, the nickname lent the team a nice aerospace vibe.

Also distinctive was Southgate's efficient, elegant new engine induction airbox slanting forward with eagerness, while further work with radiators resulted in a wider, more forthright presence but also tidier appearance.

Not quite so eye-pleasing were the massive suspension rocker arms atop the front of the fuselage. These allowed the coil spring-damper units (aka "coil-overs") to be housed inboard, out of the airstream for drag reduction.

"I know it looks a bit rude," the designer acknowledged to *Autosport*'s reporter, referring to the rather bulky ironmongery appearance of the rockers. "But these things bend under 2,000 pounds strain and with our car having a considerable amount of wheel movement, something like 7 inches, it needed to be strong."

These inboard springs were tucked into the monocoque boxes either side of the driver's feet. To fit the rockers, the top of the tub in that area had to be recessed.

Fuel now lived in a pair of rubber bladders either side of a collector tank behind the seat. Wheelbase was 105 inches, one inch up from before. Southgate also refined the suspension

ABOVE Jean-Pierre Jarier luxuriates in his new bathtub whilst one of his servants tops up the bath salts, er, brake fluid. As well as its new rocker arms, another DN5 distinction is the aggressively larger rad scoops either side of the engine. Don't want the bathwater *too* hot.
Motorsport Images/David Phipps

geometry both front and rear, and included a modest degree of the "rising-rate" effect that had been something of a fad for some years. That is to say, as the car sank on its springs, the springs resisted in a non-linear fashion, becoming stronger at an increasing rate. But designers who took this too far found themselves struggling with mysteriously intractable handling problems, so Southgate was cautious. He used two coils in tandem, a linear-rate one as well as a smaller variable one, making fine tuning simpler.

Goodyear was helping to relieve stress about suspension tuning by simplifying its tire options. Now the only supplier in F1, the company dropped the incessant experimentation and customization of past seasons, allowing everybody to become familiar with standard compounds and constructions.

Evidently Southgate hit the DN5's design just right. At the Ricard test, not only was the new car faster through the turns, its roll angles were less. Tony noticed that both his drivers were powering out of the corners "with feet to spare, rather than running up all over the curbs like they have done."

Later in the racing season, when preparing for the British Grand Prix at Silverstone, Southgate conducted a test there to scientifically evaluate his wheelbase theories. As before, cast spacers sandwiched between engine and clutch/gearbox housing could be changed or removed to adjust the distance between front and rear tire contact patches.

"These spacers could be as much as four inches (100 mm) in thickness, thereby changing the weight borne respectively by the front and rear wheels. Over the previous two seasons I had built up a list of long-wheelbase and short-wheelbase circuits, based on first theoretical and then practical experience of running various Formula 1 cars with and without those spacers. Not all of the tests had been conclusive, so for our preparations before the British Grand Prix I decided to run the Silverstone test again.

"Tom [Pryce] was doing the test driving and we had the DN5 in long-wheelbase form for the first few runs. We established a competitive control lap time, and then set about converting the car to short-wheelbase form. The car would be four inches shorter, which I calculated would put 2% more weight onto the back wheels. The change took about 45 minutes. The car returned to the track set up exactly the same in every other respect.

"After Tom's first flying lap I heard Alan Rees, the team manager, tut-tutting and muttering that he had been a bit quick with his stopwatch finger (hand-operated stopwatches were used in those days). The next lap, and there was another 'quick finger!' It was not a quick finger at all. It was a very, very quick lap time. Tom was 1.25 seconds quicker — a fantastic improvement.

"The additional weight on the rear wheels allowed the car to drift more, and produce the type of balance that suited Tom's driving style. We knew we could win the British Grand Prix if only we could finish without any mishaps."

SHADOW'S 1975 F1 SEASON

SHADOW WON A POLE! Twice! And then won a Formula 1 race! Let Shadowfans exult in those encouraging factoids for a moment, before we let all the "yes buts" knock us down.

Actually, most of the "buts" aren't so bad. The team did better in its third Grand Prix season than in both prior years, scoring more points and finishing higher in the constructors' ranks — sixth instead of 1974's eighth — against a field swelled by one new marque to 13. The new Shadow-Ford DN5 was faster, and more often able to let the drivers race competitively. Indeed, Jean-Pierre Jarier was fastest qualifier at both of the first two Grands Prix!

Racing all the way to the checkers did remain a problem, though. In an era when driver points rewarded only the top six finishers, Tom Pryce accrued but eight, making him 10th in the standings. Jarier's mere 1.5 points — because the single race in which he scored ended early, thus cutting his score in half — put him 18th.

But there was one more "but" and it was bad. Shadow's corporate sponsorship ended at the end of this year.

The Grand Prix schedule was one round shorter than in 1974, because Canada dropped out to leave 14 races. Three shorter, non-championship events filled some gaps, and it

ABOVE & BELOW Front-end views taken at Zandvoort (above) and Monza further illustrate rocker-arm suspension and oil cooler in its ducting. (Perhaps the headset was left there to warm it up on a cold day.) Seen also is the dished, pierced, center-lock front wheel design, something of a Shadow hallmark. *Motorsport Images/Ercole Colombo*

FIRST VICTORY! 269

was in one of these that Pryce scored his first victory with an F1 car.

Tragically, the "cruel sport" claimed more lives. Four were spectators mowed down by a crashing car at Barcelona. In Austria another accident took the life of American driver Mark Donohue, along with that of a trackside marshal.

At season's end, Austria's pride, Niki Lauda, took his first World Championship title aboard Italy's Ferrari.

ARGENTINE GP

Buenos Aires, F1 (R1), January 12th, 1975
1st, Emerson Fittipaldi, McLaren M23
DNS, Jean-Pierre Jarier, Shadow DN5, transmission
DNF, Tom Pryce, Shadow DN3B, 12th but not running, transmission

Jean-Pierre Jarier qualified his new UOP Shadow fastest at a new record speed! What a way to open the new season. Fate granted the team 24 hours to revel in it.

Bolstering their joy would have been a remark by a puzzled Ronnie Peterson, the blindingly quick driver with Lotus, who tried to keep up with Jarier only to pit and mutter, "That car is so fast. He only just lifts for the Esses, and in the long loop at the end he must be flat."

It seems that Ronnie had a particular reason to be watching the Shadow. That would come out a few days later.

Saturday night the Shadowmen prepped their beautiful new DN5 with devoted care, including installing new gearbox internals. On Sunday afternoon, as he left the pits to drive around to his pole position on the starting grid, your scribe was watching as "Jumper" Jarier fine-tuned his throttle-and-clutch reflexes.

"Doing one of the flat-out practice starts he does, charging out of the pits with wheels spinning and engine screaming from nearly dead cold, he felt the final drive fail behind him.

BELOW Jarier jumped to the forefront in Argentina, seizing Shadow's first F1 pole position! Jacques Laffite watches to see how he did it from the Williams just behind (its sponsorship is that of a supposed health product; there is no relationship to a future Shadow associate). *Motorsport Images/LAT*

ABOVE Jean-Pierre charges away from pole again in Brazil, only to once again drop out before the checkered flag. Launching alongside are Reutemann in his white Brabham BT44, reigning champion Fittipaldi's McLaren M23 and Lauda's Ferrari 312B3. But the winner will be Pace in the other white Brabham.
Motorsport Images/LAT

A new crownwheel-and-pinion had been fitted to his TL200 the night before, for supposedly reliability, but it didn't last 100 yards now." The grid formed up with pole position left empty.

Later that year gearbox maker Hewland threw itself under the bus, taking responsibility for this and other recent gear failures because of improper heat treating.

That left Tom Pryce the lone Shadow driver, way back in the 12th starting spot with one of the previous year's DN3s. This had been brought up to "type B" specification thanks to a number of little mods, and they seemed to be working. He said the car was good in the fast parts of the track, although it didn't feel comfortable in the fast Esses.

Once the race was underway, Tom held his own with the second-fastest pack of cars, and was driving with noticeable steady maturity in 10th place when, just two laps from the finish, he rolled into the pits with his transmission gone. It dropped him to 12th on the results sheet.

BRAZILIAN GP
Interlagos, F1 (R2), January 26th, 1975
1st, Carlos Pace, Brabham BT44B
DNF, Jean-Pierre Jarier, Shadow DN5, fuel metering
DNF, Tom Pryce, Shadow DN3B, accident

Fortune, so cruel to Jarier two weeks before, seemed to be making it up in Brazil. Again he took pole by a wide margin, despite his first engine scattering fragments all over the track, and this time he actually started the race. Quickly clearing a challenge from Brabham's Carlos Reutemann, Jarier's Shadow simply vanished into the distance, building up a lead of more than 25 seconds by three-quarters distance.

But fortune's smile was a false face. With but eight laps to go J-P's fuel injection malfunctioned and stopped him at trackside. Disconsolately he had to sit and watch his race being won by Brabham's "Other Carlos," Pace that is, a Brazilian performing before an adoring Brazilian crowd.

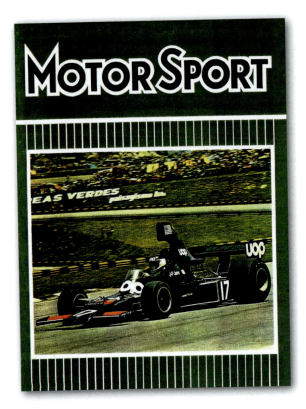

ABOVE Shadow didn't come home from South America with trophies, but Jarier's speed there did grab the attention of magazine art directors. *Motor Sport*

As for Pryce, he was still driving the older model and still buried in the back half of the pack. At the start he did move up a few positions, but late in the going a worsening case of understeer sent him wide onto marbles and on into a barrier.

That left another black car in action, a Lotus driven by Ronnie Peterson. But it could easily have been a Shadow.

Those rumors flying around Argentina turned into photos at Brazil — a newspaper ran shots of Ronnie trying out Tom's Shadow seat in the pits at Interlagos. It emerged that SuperSwede was unhappy with the cars he was getting from Lotus, and also with Colin Chapman's proposed solution. Hamstrung by a significant cut in tobacco sponsorship this year, The Guv'nor was unable to adequately fund the usual intense Lotus development program. So he suggested that Ronnie accept a cut in salary to help pay for the new car he demanded. Ronnie found this unappealing.

Seeing a chance to get the established driver he had long wanted, Don Nichols offered a straight swap, Pryce for Peterson. This probably would have gone through except that Chapman countered by demanding money to release his star driver. Such a deal would have got stuck in the Nichols throat.

So Ronnie raced on for Lotus, and as his black-and-gold car came by the two broken-down black Shadows there might possibly have been a small smile hidden inside that bright blue helmet. Peterson finished last that day, but at least he finished.

SOUTH AFRICAN GP
Kyalami, F1 (R3), March 1st, 1975
1st, Jody Scheckter, Tyrrell 007
9th, Tom Pryce, Shadow DN5
DNF, Jean-Pierre Jarier, Shadow DN5, transmission

A month after Brazil, fate's fickle smile had moved on from Jarier to the next sensation of the moment, local boy Jody Scheckter. This time fate kept smiling. Tyrrell's new star went on to win his national race.

South America's two-time pole man managed a mere 13th on the South African grid, with Pryce back in 19th. Neither Shadow figured in the race. At least Tom finally got his DN5 and finally finished a GP, placing ninth, a lap behind, after struggling with imbalanced handling and fading brakes. Poor Jarier scored his third DNF of the year, parking in the pits after a couple of broken exhaust primaries made the engine run very badly and finally overheat.

With a dry spell now of nearly two months before the fourth GP of the year, England's F1 fans again had a pair of non-championship sprints to slake their thirst.

RACE OF CHAMPIONS (GB)
Brands Hatch, F1 (non-championship), March 16th, 1975
1st, Tom Pryce, Shadow DN5
8th, Jean-Pierre Jarier, Shadow DN5

YES! You read that right! Shadow won a race! What's more, both Shadows finished a race. Pryce seized pole with his DN5, alongside Scheckter and straight ahead of third man Jarier.

But at the start Pryce wheelspun away his advantage and found himself chasing Scheckter and Ickx through the opening laps. Tom did find his way by Jacky, and was all lined up to pounce on Jody when the Tyrrell's Ford engine blew up. And that was that.

Let's say it again: scarcely into its third season

LEFT VICTORY at last! In a photo long cherished by Shadowfans the world over, Tom Pryce boils away his pole position start, but will make it up to WIN the Race of Champions! *Motorsport Images/David Phipps*

BELOW How we remember him. Gifted with uncanny car control, the quiet young man from Ruthin in Denbighshire, Wales, expressed his joy of driving in a way that we all could enjoy along with him. And along with us, Tom struggled to accept that chucking it sideways wasn't the best way to get the best out of the latest F1 tires. *Mike Hayward Collection*

FIRST VICTORY! **273**

ABOVE Despite his early-season speed, Jarier takes his only GP points of the year in Spain's half-race, the disastrous day at Barcelona's poorly prepared Montjuich circuit. *Motorsport Images/Ercole Colombo*

of Formula 1, the American team won a race. A moment that Don Nichols would cherish for the rest of his days.

INTERNATIONAL TROPHY (GB)
Silverstone, F1 (non-championship),
    April 13th, 1975
1st, Niki Lauda, Ferrari 312T
9th, Tom Pryce, Shadow DN5

By agreement only one driver came from each of the F1 teams, and Brands boy Tom Pryce got that nod. This time his best pre-race lap earned only fourth-best grid place, behind James Hunt (on pole) Carlos Reutemann, and Emerson Fittipaldi. Tom also would have had Peterson squarely in front, but Ronnie's engine seized solid just before the race. Just think: that might have been Tom's engine…

Right from flagfall the Shadow started lagging, and presently pitted with a tire gone soft. Charging back out, Pryce tried his mightiest to recover, but the team's best takeaway from Silverstone was that he was within a second of Reutemann at the finish, the last driver to avoid being lapped.

SPANISH GP
Montjuich Park, F1 (R4), April 27th, 1975
1st, Jochen Mass, McLaren M23
4th, Jean-Pierre Jarier, Shadow DN5
DNF, Tom Pryce, Shadow DN5, collision

From a great, short race to a really bad, sadly shortened one. The entire weekend was a debacle, because the essential steel guardrail erected all around the beautiful Barcelona city park atop a hill was poorly assembled. Drivers, to whom these things matter, found that myriad bolts were loose or entirely missing. They refused to drive until the circuit was brought up to spec.

No, said the local officials, our circuit has

passed official inspection, so you must drive or we will impound your cars and equipment.

Drivers who tried to take their appeal to the international inspectors known to be on the scene couldn't seem to find them.

Very late on Saturday, threats of financial force broke the drivers' will and they finally set some qualifying times, and Sunday's race went ahead as planned.

It shouldn't have. At the very first corner the pair of Ferraris took each other out along with a crowd of following cars. Minor mayhems continued until a big one finally hit just short of half the scheduled distance. Rolf Stommelen's rear wing suddenly broke off the Graham Hill car he was driving, sending him into and over a guardrail. The driver suffered injuries, but four onlookers just behind the rail suffered death.

It took several laps before do-nothing officials — who were in sight of the catastrophe — thought of showing a red flag. Jochen Mass's McLaren happened to be the first straggler in the running order, so he "won" this non-race.

To fill in the Shadow blanks: the team had a third, brand-new DN5 along as a spare, though it wasn't used; Pryce for once out-qualified his team-mate, taking eighth on the grid, straight ahead of Jarier on the 10th spot; but Tom ran into trouble on this troubled day, pitting after a collision that damaged a nose fin and his exhaust system; Jean-Pierre was actually third on the road at the red flag, but was penalized a lap for overtaking under a yellow flag.

Sure. Now they cared about safety.

MONACO GP
Monte Carlo, F1 (R5), May 11th, 1975
1st, Niki Lauda, Ferrari 312T
DNF, Jean-Pierre Jarier, Shadow DN5, crash
DNF, Tom Pryce, Shadow DN5, crash

Tom Pryce out-qualified his team-mate for the second time this year, taking second place on the

LEFT Pryce being Pryce, hurling his Shadow sideways through the streets of Monte Carlo. Grand to watch. But once again neither he nor his team-mate are there at the end. *Pete Lyons*

staggered 2x2 grid diagonally behind Lauda's Ferrari, and diagonally ahead of Jean-Pierre Jarier, who was third. Alas, both suffered ill fortune this time. Jarier took himself out on the first lap. Pryce's crash came partway around lap 40, when he chose to hit a barrier rather than a car blocking his path.

For those keeping technical score at home, both DN5s were set up for this tight city circuit with their rear tracks narrowed by two inches. However, the gearbox spacer was left in place, retaining the normal wheelbase. On Jarier's car only, driveshafts came straight from the Shadow Can-Am parts bin to improve chances of surviving this tight, humpy track's severe torque reversals.

BELGIAN GP
Zolder, F1 (R6), May 25th, 1975
1st, Niki Lauda, Ferrari 312T
6th, Tom Pryce, Shadow DN5
DNF, Jean-Pierre Jarier, Shadow DN5, crash

For this stop-and-go little circuit, not unlike a Monaco without the claustrophobic guardrails, the two Shadows retained their slightly narrower rear-track dimension. Jarier did try the spare car with the normal width, but could not feel a difference so the race cars stayed narrow. In his DN5 Pryce was unhappy about the handling balance, and what's more his engine was getting tired, so his fifth spot on the grid was impressive. His team-mate lined up 10th, but only by a very small margin on a tightly competitive grid.

As the pack jostled into the first turn, Pryce dropped back a little to stay clear of the pushing and shoving going on ahead — a smart move, because several tangled and two went out immediately! But Jarier was moving up the line fast. There came a moment when Jean-Pierre tried to out-brake his team-mate and went off into the sand instead. The engine stalled, and there the Shadow remained.

The remaining DN5 wasn't free and clear, because its left-front tire was overheating, a ring of blisters forming all around the tread and causing ever-worsening understeer. Tom's efforts to compensate by inducing pitching oversteer were spectacular to watch, but not enough to overcome the relentless advance of a Ferrari. It wasn't Lauda's — he was well away in front — but Regazzoni's. The Swiss driver had started ahead of the Welshman only to fall behind, but then capitalized on the Shadow's tire trouble to snatch away fifth place. At least Pryce stayed on the winner's lap.

SWEDISH GP
Anderstorp, F1 (R7), June 8th, 1975
1st, Niki Lauda, Ferrari 312T
DNF, Jean-Pierre Jarier, Shadow DN5, engine
DNF, Tom Pryce, Shadow DN5, spin (unable to restart)

Another out-of-the-ordinary circuit, where good balance was elusive. Of the two Shadow drivers, Jarier looked smoother and not as fast, but he ended up significantly quicker than Pryce despite Tom's much more impressive-looking style. The Welshman was hanging his tail out so far it seemed impossible, and there was often a haze of blue smoke from the back tires.

Near the end of one session Tom was coming through a long, long right-hand sweeper called the Karussel at such extreme angles and with his boot so hard down that blue smoke was left hanging in the air all the way around. Immediately then it was jam on the brakes and pitch into the sharp left-hander before the pits. As the Shadow powered out of that, its back wheels absolutely dissolved in smoke and left black rubber streaks for a hundred yards. No, not quick, but way, way keen!

For all his fire and fury Pryce wound up seventh on the grid, two rows behind Jarier's third. As the pack hurtled away into the race, enough dirt flew that Tom's throttle slides stuck. Coming in to have them cleared cost exactly a lap, so upon rejoining he found himself right behind the race leader.

ABOVE IT'S THIS CLOSE! In Sweden Jarier turns it all around, and is racing a close second to leader Reutemann, looking for a way by, until…
Motorsport Images/Ercole Colombo

Who at that point was Vittorio Brambilla in his March. But Brabham's Carlos Reutemann was chasing hard, so Pryce let him by — and then extended the courtesy to his Shadow fellow Jarier. As Vittorio began to slow, both Carlos and Jean-Pierre whisked by and there it was: one of the Shadows holding a close second place in a Grand Prix.

And it got closer! Black Shadow was within a second of white Brabham, Frenchman obviously sniffing for a chance to pass Argentinian, when abruptly the DN5's screaming engine mutinied.

"Suddenly the oil pressure dropped," said the really disgusted Jean-Pierre. It happened squarely in front of the pits and other people thought it dropped with a very audible clang…

At least that left Tom running, right? Nope. He locked up the rear brakes and half-spun down the road. The engine stopped with the wheels, because the clutch refused to disengage, so the driver had to watch the rest of it from right there.

DUTCH GP
Zandvoort, F1 (R8), June 22nd, 1975
1st, James Hunt, Hesketh 308
6th, Tom Pryce, Shadow DN5
DNF, Jean-Pierre Jarier, Shadow DN5, puncture

Horses for courses, they say, and for the second year running Ferrari's Cavallinos were the favorites for Zandvoort. The Shadows? Not in it at all. Jarier's best lap earned a mere 10th-place start, with Pryce straight behind in 12th.

That was on a dry track, but raceday turned rainy. Everybody started on knobblies, which threw up balls of spray so dense that the entire field strung out in a long, single-file string. It gradually turned dry, though, bringing everybody in to swap tires. Coming out of that best was James Hunt in his Hesketh, and obviously aboard the right horse for the conditions he simply drove on and on to his first Grand Prix victory.

Amazingly, in his mirrors was a black horse. Jarier's. His DN5 now mysteriously suiting the

FIRST VICTORY! **277**

ABOVE And here he is again! When the weather turns wet at Zandvoort Jarier's DN5 comes alive and he chases leader Hunt until… *Motorsport Images/ David Phipps*

RIGHT Some days go so wrong you've just got to laugh. *Motorsport Images/Ercole Colombo*

changed conditions, he raced along the second row of the lap chart from lap 16 all the way to lap 43. Then…

Bang! He ran a little wide, his left rear tire found some debris, and the huge mass of rubber instantly exploded with incredible violence. At the end of a lurid trip across the middle of the corner, Jarier picked himself out of a car that was, amazingly, damaged only mildly.

Pryce ran into brake trouble at the end, the pedal going to the floor and spoiling an otherwise decent run.

FRENCH GP

Paul Ricard, F1 (R9), July 6th, 1975
1st, Niki Lauda, Ferrari 312T
8th, Jean-Pierre Jarier, Shadow DN5
DNF, Tom Pryce, Shadow DN5, transmission

On this long, fast circuit overlooking the Mediterranean, all three Shadows had shorter wheelbases. And for once both racecars were pretty reliable all during practice. Jean-Pierre Jarier, a Frenchman visibly tweaked up for the French Grand Prix, was quickest of all on Friday. He couldn't quite match that speed on Saturday, although he still lined up fourth on the grid.

But his team-mate Tom Pryce was the interesting story. For several meetings past the young Welshman had been relying on his magic hands rather than his head. The sight of him scrambling desperately around corners had been one of the most spectacular acts of the GP circus, a grand entertainment — however, the results in terms of lap times hadn't been there. And yet here he was, his times at Ricard improving until they were below Jarier's by the close of Saturday.

Approached for his comments, Shadow team manager Alan Rees, himself a former driver and a fellow Welshman, offered this:

"Well, I may have had something to do with it, talking to him, but they all have to learn it themselves, you know, even if it takes them a couple of years. But the good ones always do learn it. Even Ronnie…"

The lad himself was asked whether this "new leaf" he had turned over affected his sheer enjoyment of driving. Tall Tom's perpetual smile sagged into a rare frown. "Oh, it's no fun at all! It feels like you're just pootling around. You keep wanting to put the old boot in it and get going. But as the lap times are better…" He lined up sixth on the grid, directly behind Jarier.

Sunday morning warmup was when Shadow's luck turned back to normal. Jarier's engine was leaking oil around a rear seal, and fixing it required taking off the gearbox. Then as Pryce lined up on the pre-grid he found the car creeping forward no matter how hard he pushed the clutch pedal down, so he arrived at his starting position pressing the brakes and with the clutch already slipping. His start ruined, he was last away, and his engine revs could be heard wavering on around the circuit.

Tom did seem able to nurse his clutch back to life, but then something must have broken entirely, because abruptly all drive to the wheels ceased and he walked home. Meanwhile Jarier had a better start to his race, but his result was ruined by his rev limiter creeping down to 9,500 rpm, a fat thousand under peak power.

BRITISH GP
Silverstone, F1 (R10), July 19th, 1975
1st, Emerson Fittipaldi, McLaren M23
DNF, Jean-Pierre Jarier, Shadow DN5, crash in rain
DNF, Tom Pryce, Shadow DN5, crash in rain

"Jarier, accident, spun and hit barrier. Pryce, accident, spun and hit barrier." Oh dear. Even Shadow's days weren't usually this dark.

But then we always did get grand value out of the British Grand Prix. Crashes, pitstops, lead changes, disaster, controversy — a splendid show, year after year.

And this one had everything: 16 drivers

BELOW Tom's turn… to start with, anyway. Qualifying fastest of all for his second F1 race in a row on home soil, Pryce again brings some bubbly back to the boys.
Motorsport Images/David Phipps

FIRST VICTORY! 279

ABOVE Blasting away from pole at Silverstone, as he had at Brands Hatch, Pryce once again is spearing along with clear air in front, a first Grand Prix victory almost in sight ahead… say, what's that shimmer in the air just around the bend… *Motorsport Images/Rainer Schlegelmilch*

crashed, 19 made pitstops, seven different ones exchanged the lead nine times. Multiple shunts at two different corners wrote off cars, caused injuries, and forced the race to be red-flagged to a premature end. Then for hours there was a dispute about who finished where.

This time it was all thanks to the English weather. From a dry start it began to rain after about 20 laps, stopped briefly, then turned into a sudden new deluge. A lovely Midsummer's day in the Midlands.

Oh, one more special thing: Thomas Maldwyn Pryce started his UOP Shadow DN5 from fastest qualifying position! From the gleeful grin on his face, maybe race driving was still fun after all, even though he wasn't flinging it about with abandon any more.

Team-mate Jean-Pierre Jarier looked a bit overshadowed in 11th place, but in fact he was one of 12 drivers who all qualified within one second — not bad for the period. Both DN5s were in their usual configuration and running unusually well.

Raceday started off well too, with Pryce making a good launch toward the first corner. However, Carlos Pace alongside made an even better start, and the white Brabham drove around the outside of the black Shadow to steal the lead. But then Clay Regazzoni's red Ferrari powered by them both. On lap 18 the Swiss driver was leading by 3.3 seconds from Pryce… but then disappeared on lap 19. Oh, there he was, very late and straggling into the pits with his rear wing knocked askew. Rain had begun blowing across the wide-open old airfield and the Ferrari had slid into a barrier.

Pryce led! But the squall was intensifying. Tom knew it, and bent into a turn at what he thought was a sensible speed — only to plunge into a wall of rain moving the opposite way. Waggling viciously, the Shadow slammed hard into the catch fences, throwing bits of itself and wooden fence posts in a great bomb-burst of debris. A post gave Tom a heavy rap on the skull, which did his faculties and memory no good at all for

some minutes, but he was not actually injured.

The weather kept changing, so did people's ideas about what tires they wanted, and somehow the Shadow crew got their second man Jarier out on the right rubber at the right time to… why, stone the crows, he's leading the race!

That's right, Shadowfans, both DN5s held first place during the 1975 British Grand Prix at Silverstone. Not 15 miles down the road from their place of birth in Northampton.

But nothing lasts long in motor racing, and J-P's moment of glory ended in a crash just about identical to Tom's. Again catch fencing seemed to explode, and a wooden post shot into a grandstand, causing facial injury to a spectator. The driver himself took the butt end of another post full on his forehead, which split his helmet open and his skin with it.

With seemingly most of the rest of the field piled up in soggy wet heaps, a man with a red flag stopped the madness.

Told'ya it was fun.

ABOVE & BELOW Happily Shadow has two quick runners at Silverstone, and when Pryce crashes out Jarier takes over the job of leading. Right up until… Since we have some space left, let us remember that this is the era of the catch fence; steel chainlink clipped to poles driven into the ground, "soft" nets to rein in wayward racecars. Seems like a good idea, no? *Motorsport Images/David Phipps*

FIRST VICTORY! **281**

ABOVE She flies fine, but can she stick the landing? If watching a fast car leap and bound around the gloriously Wagnerian old 'Ring brings our hearts to our throats, what's it like to be inside the thing. Trying to make it go faster. *Motorsport Images/ Rainer Schlegelmilch*

GERMAN GP
Nürburgring, F1 (R11), August 3rd, 1975
1st, Carlos Reutemann, Brabham BT44B
4th, Tom Pryce, Shadow DN5
DNF, Jean-Pierre Jarier, Shadow DN5, puncture

It wasn't rain that caused trouble here on the mountainous Nürburgring, but little sharp stones. Out of 24 starters at least nine suffered a total of 12 punctured tires, this factor alone causing the retirement of six — two of them in massive crashes.

Few escaped drama of some sort, but Carlos Reutemann from far off Argentina avoided all the stones and mechanical troubles to achieve his first GP victory of the year. His Brabham was all alone on the long track, over a minute and a half ahead of the next car, the Williams of French driver Jacques Laffite. Of the nine still running, only these two went the distance trouble-free.

Despite Shadow's pair of spectacular shunts in Britain, neither of its cars needed drastic repairs and they were simply prepared with spacers giving a longer wheelbase for stability on this circuit. But it didn't seem to help much: the starting grid showed Jarier on the sixth row, Pryce on the eighth.

Jarier went out at half distance with a puncture, the flopping rubber wrapping itself around the halfshaft. Pryce managed to keep going, despite a loose fuel filler allowing green lead-free UOP petrol to splash all over him. The nasty stuff got into his mouth and his eyes, and while trying to see where it was coming from he let the Shadow bump a rail.

Tom kept going without losing what had become second place at this point, but when his skin really began to burn he unfastened his belts to raise himself out of the stingy bath. This meant that he was slacking off over every humpback so as not to fly out, and toward the miserable end he dropped two positions.

AUSTRIAN GP

Österreichring, F1 (R12), August 17th, 1975
1st, Vittorio Brambilla, March 751
3rd, Tom Pryce, Shadow DN5
DNF, Jean-Pierre Jarier, Shadow DN7-Matra, engine

Another bad one, no use sugar-coating it. Legendary American racing champion Mark Donohue suffered severe cranial trauma here when a tire failed during the race morning warmup period, throwing him helplessly into barriers. He died two days later.

Before we knew that, the race itself was amusing. It was the "Half-Prix of Austria," the second GP of this peculiar season to be stopped in the middle so that half points were awarded. This time it was because of rain, rain that grew so heavy that merely driving around the streaming wet high-speed circuit was impossibly dangerous, let alone trying to race.

It ended when, famously or perhaps infamously, Vittorio Brambilla was so surprised to see the checkered flag pronouncing him first that he lifted off the power, lost control of his March and spun across the road into the guardrail, crunch.

Before the non-sunny Sunday, the awning at the UOP center shaded four Shadows against the anticipated fierce heat of Styria in August. Three were familiar Ford-Cosworth DN5s, which showed subtle mods to improve radiator efficiency. The fourth was something new: a V12-engined version of the DN5 chassis called a DN7.

The long, handsome powerplant was a French-made Matra MS73, the most recent iteration of an engine originally designed in the late '60s for that aerospace firm's own Formula 1 and endurance sports cars. Jean-Pierre Jarier also being French, and Don Nichols an American entrepreneur always looking for a good deal, it was hoped that the French V12 would have an edge over the English V8.

BELOW Another race in the rain, another good Tom Pryce drive in it, and this time his Shadow is still holding a place in the points when it's called off early. *Motorsport Images/David Phipps*

FIRST VICTORY! 283

Allegedly, the V12 screamed out 500 hp at 11,600 rpm, up from the 470 at 10,600 claimed for the Ford-Cosworth product as used by Shadow. After trying the Matra, Jarier said, "It's a very smooth engine to drive. It will pull strongly from the middle of the range, from about 6,000 rpm up to the maximum, which is 11,900. It is extremely good in acceleration from the slower corners."

Maybe so, but on the Ö-ring's real-life dyno the DN7's grid speed was as near as makes no difference to Tom Pryce's normal car. Jarier achieved a mere 14th with the V12, precisely 0.02 second quicker than Pryce on the next row. But in fact neither car was running at its best, so the comparison was hardly definitive.

As for the race result, the DN7 failed to make it to even the early finish, going out after just 10 laps with fuel-system troubles. The DN5 was placed third when the checkered flag was suddenly waved at lap 29, 26 short of the scheduled 55.

BELOW That chap in the middle is called Brambilla. Or sometimes The Gorilla. A tough man, but perhaps a little too tough on his cars. He has never won a Grand Prix before. Never will again. But today he's in the right place at the right time. *Motorsport Images/David Phipps*

SWISS GP
Dijon, F1 (non-championship),
   August 24th, 1975
1st, Clay Regazzoni, Ferrari 312T
7th, Tom Pryce, Shadow DN5
DNF, Jean-Pierre Jarier, Shadow DN5,
   transmission

Nearly another great Shadow day! Nearly.

Jarier gave his dream of Matra glory the weekend off, and look how that turned out: his DN5-Ford put him on pole! Granted, this being a non-championship sprint not all the GP regulars were there, but defending World Champion Emerson Fittipaldi was, and his McLaren fell short of the Shadow by 0.02 second. Third fastest was Clay Regazzoni's Ferrari.

Pryce's Shadow wasn't nearly as quick as the other DN5. He was struggling with excess oversteer — yes, Tom complaining about oversteer! — as well as spongy brakes. He couldn't lap within a second of the pole winner's time.

But why was this very rare "Swiss Grand Prix" being staged a good two hours by road from the nearest corner of Switzerland? Because that nation had banned motor racing 20 years before, forcing Swiss fans to mingle with their fellow speed-crazed heathens across the border. Coming with them to Burgundy country was a trio of stalwart Swiss mountain men, who opened the ceremonies with a long, poignant herald on *Alpenhorns* (such a long way from any Alp) and then the cars rolled to the grid.

Jumper Jarier got a perfect, tire-smoking start, but Champ Fittipaldi got nothing but clutch slip. Left free and clear, Jarier made the most of it, and by the end of lap 2 he had a three-second advantage on the next man, Regazzoni. By the 10th lap the gap was a comfortable five seconds plus.

The black car with its rainbow-like "Re-Entry" colors was being driven very hard, bumping over curbs and sliding across the road, wheels waggling. It cannot be described as a clockwork performance, but J-P was still adding to his clockwork advantage over the Ferrari man. On the 30th lap, half distance, the gap behind the Shadow was about nine seconds and on the 33rd lap it had grown to 10.4 seconds.

But then there was no gap at all. That is, Regazzoni popped into sight first. Apparently Jarier's transmission had sheared its input shaft, a part of the Hewland that takes torque from the clutch into the gearcase. So Swiss driver Regazzoni went on to score victory in his "home Grand Prix."

Tom Pryce's troubles carried on throughout the race. Somehow his front tires were overheating and blistering, even though the car was still oversteering mightily. And the brakes were still spongy. He was asked, did you have any bad moments? "Yeah — lots of them!" But he hung on, and in fact the dice of the race was the closing struggle between John Watson, Carlos Pace and Pryce as they flashed across the line 1.01 seconds apart, positions 5–6–7.

ABOVE Jean-Pierre's turn in the spotlight. From pole position he absolutely shoots away, swooping and sliding and dancing around Dijon in delight… Yup. Here's the place for another of those damnable "untils." *Motorsport Images/Ercole Colombo*

The very severely disappointed Jarier went on French radio later and said some harsh things about the ability of his team to prepare racing cars. Team manager Alan Rees thought this critique was uncalled for, especially in reference to a proprietary part that came ready-assembled as a part of something else. Later in the season, contract discussion time, it was noted that Jean-Pierre was being much more polite.

ITALIAN GP
Monza, F1 (R13), September 7th, 1975
1st, Clay Regazzoni, Ferrari 312T
6th, Tom Pryce, Shadow DN5
DNF, Jean-Pierre Jarier, Shadow DN7-Matra, engine

For UOP's team, the best parts of 1975 were about over. The pair of Shadows started side-by-side, but way back on the seventh row. Jarier's time in the Matra-engined DN7 beat Pryce's with the DN5-Ford by precisely a tenth of a second. The French V12 wasn't picking up fuel in Monza's long, right-hand bends, but adding an extra pump seemed to fix that. The Welshman with the English Ford struggled with

ABOVE At Monza Shadow number 17 is the Matra-motored DN7, which Jarier hopes to prove is faster than the powered-by-Ford DN5. He did so in qualifying, by a tenth of a second. But will the aging V12 last the race distance this time? *Motorsport Images/Ercole Colombo*

BELOW All colors flying, Pryce drives the full GP distance in Italy to score one more point. *Motorsport Images/David Phipps*

poor handling on his initial shorter-wheelbase setup until his crew split gearbox from engine and inserted the cast spacer. Tom said that made all the difference.

Both evaded a mass pileup right after the start that looked like another Silverstone but in summery Italian sunshine. Pryce drove on to finish sixth, the last man to complete every lap. Jarier retired, the V12 running erratically because its own internal mechanical drive to the fuel pump sheared. This time the Frenchman was not heard to criticize the French engine maker.

For Italy's Ferrari, their home race was the "rubber-stamp GP." Lauda only needed half a point more to secure his first World Championship. He did so, driving circumspectly in Regazzoni's wake until Fittipaldi challenged him for second place, which Niki graciously handed over with his compliments. Along with his drivers' title, his employer finally earned another constructors' championship after 11 years of disappointment.

UNITED STATES GP

Watkins Glen, F1 (R14), October 5th, 1975
1st, Niki Lauda, Ferrari 312T
DNF, Jean-Pierre Jarier, Shadow DN5, wheel bearing
NC, Tom Pryce, Shadow DN5, not classified under 90% rule

Last race of a long year. Shadow brought three cars to upstate New York, but only raced the two with Ford engines. Both DN5s were back in short-wheelbase configuration. Jarier did spend all of Friday running the inherently longer Matra DN7 and ended with a time as close as makes no difference to Pryce's with the Ford. Next day Jean-Pierre tried the Ford car and lapped 1.36 seconds quicker. It put him third on the starting grid. Tom's time placed him eighth.

Asked about the Matra V12 experiment, team manager Rees thought it was probably a dead issue. "It just doesn't show any advantage."

For Shadow the best parts of the weekend ended Saturday. On Sunday neither car scored an official finish. Jarier dropped out from his good third place on lap 19 when a wheel bearing failed. Pryce did manage to keep running, but a mid-race misfire took two trips to the pits before a bad electrical connection was found and fixed. Crossing the finish line seven laps behind Lauda left Pryce "unclassified."

ALTHOUGH SHADOW'S third Formula 1 season ended quietly, this was its best season. Results had been improving. A first victory had been achieved. The marque ranked higher as a constructor. The future looked promising…

Well, sorry, no. Back on May 1st, 1975, Universal Oil Products sold itself to a larger petroleum firm. The new management's new broom swept out all thought of supporting a racing team.

At the end of the year, Don Nichols would be back on his own. ♣

BELOW Shadow's swansong for '75 is Jarier's third place run at the Glen… before yet another component breaks. Pryce does keep on but can't cover enough laps to qualify as a finisher. Fade to black. *Motorsport Images/David Phipps*

FIRST VICTORY! 287

FRENCH CONNECTION
SHADOW DN7-MATRA

PATRIOTISM, POLITICS and Parsimony; all played a part in this one-off, short-lived project.

Between Grands Prix, Shadow's French driver, Jean-Pierre Jarier, had been doing long-distance races with his own nation's Matra sports cars. Matra was an industrial firm producing military missiles, along with aerospace and telecommunications products, plus a line of sporty automobiles. Racing arm Matra Sports was active from the 1960s into the '70s, bringing victories and championships in Formula 1 (Jackie Stewart won his 1969 world title aboard a Matra campaigned by Ken Tyrrell) and the World Championship for Makes, including three straight victories at Le Mans (1972–74).

At that point the company closed its Matra Sports factory campaign, leaving its MS73 V12 engines unemployed. But Jarier remembered them fondly and thought they had more life left in them. Their displacement was 3.0 liters, same as Ford's Cosworth, but the stated 490 hp was more muscular, so "Jumper" lobbied his GP team to switch.

As Tony Southgate put it in his book, Jarier was "totally convinced he would be significantly quicker… and become the toast of France." The designer wasn't so sure, preferring the team to stay focused on improving the existing car.

But the man they all worked for was focused on luring a potential engine sponsor. Don Nichols happened to be romancing Dodge at the time, specifically for his Formula 5000 effort, and no doubt he knew that umbrella company Chrysler held a 50 percent stake in Matra. So Don asked Tony to try the V12.

It wasn't a simple hot rodder's yank-and-drop job. Compared to the compact little Ford DFV, the Matra MS73 was several inches longer, about 25 pounds heavier (390 vs. 365), and its mounting points to the chassis were different.

BELOW Towering Mr. Phipps assumed the lowest of positions to capture the length of the V12-powered DN7. Adding four cylinders and 20-to-25 horsepower also added weight and taxed the cooling system. Call it a wash, that's what the stopwatch did. Lovely car, though, and unique. There's only one DN7. *Motorsport Images/David Phipps*

RIGHT Although Matra's V12 was a multiple winner at Le Mans, it could never be made at home in a Formula 1 car. Shadow designer Southgate felt he had to add massive diagonal bracing struts to keep the long, slim power unit in line with a chassis designed for Cosworth's V8.
Motorsport Images/LAT

Also, because it made 20-odd more horsepower at 30 percent higher rpm, according to Southgate, it drank more fuel and expelled more heat.

Modified accordingly, what began as a DN5 chassis earned a new designation, DN7. Bolting the V12 to the back of the tub lengthened the wheelbase by an inch, to 106.

Also, rather than rely entirely on the Matra engine block to take on the shorter, wider Cosworth's extra function as the back of the chassis, Southgate added stout lateral bracing struts, bars running from the rear of the V12 diagonally forward to the shoulders of the monocoque.

The need to carry six more US gallons of gas, 57.6 in all, could not be met with the Shadow's central tank alone, so he fitted supplementary cells into the monocoque's hollow torque boxes either side.

Then, to compensate for a fore-aft imbalance introduced by the necessarily longer, heavier radiators as well as the weightier engine in the back, Southgate relocated the rads more forward, to either side of the driver's thighs. To fit the available space he turned the longer units to 90 degrees from the direction of travel, and shrouded them in sidepods to properly duct cool air from between the front wheels and expel it outward. The resulting car looked wider, but was still within the specified minimum.

Finished and given a shakedown test the last week of July, the DN7 then went straight to the German GP. But it never left the paddock there at the tortuous Nürburgring, the team thinking it was better suited to "power circuits" with long straights — like the next two venues.

But was it? At Austria's Österreichring, Jarier qualified two hundredths of a second ahead of Pryce. Jean-Pierre could not finish the race because of a fuel-system problem. Tom placed third.

At Monza, the DN7 again utterly obliterated its less powerful sibling by a massive one tenth of a second! OK, your sarcasm alarms are going off and rightly so. Both cars lined up way down on the sixth row, and sixth was where Pryce finished this time. Jarier? Out again with a fuel-pump issue.

So poor J-P would not be "the toast of France." Just toast.

The designer of both cars — and of all the DN cars so far — had suspected all along that the V12's extra power would not overcome the DN7's extra weight. Said he, looking back, "End of argument; the Cosworth had won… we should have spent the extra money on making the DN5 quicker, rather than pursuing politics."

But gosh, isn't she pretty.

THE 'SPY' WHO WENT BACK TO THE COLD

DON NICHOLS SAID he was blindsided. As he told it long years afterward, he learned that his friend John Logan, UOP's head man at the time, had approached "his old chum, can't remember his name" about funding to expand the company's holdings.

"They said, 'Sure, John, just sign here, and oh incidentally, John, since we have this investment temporarily we'll have to have full chairmanship.' Well, that lasted a few months, then they called John. 'Looks like this isn't the way we want it to be,' and John retired."

The story is given differently by what is now UOP Honeywell. From the corporation's website:

In 1975, UOP had been a broadly diversified independent company for a decade and a half. But the diversification campaign that was intended to bring growth and insulate it from hostile takeover had the opposite effect.

Meanwhile, the Signal Companies, a longtime UOP customer whose business was built on the rich oil fields of Signal Hill south of Los Angeles, sold its oil and gas properties to the Burmah Oil Company leaving it with more than $400 million in cash. After an arduous search, Signal settled on what it decided would be the best way to invest that money: acquiring a controlling interest in UOP.

Signal's overture was anything but hostile. In April, after months of cordial and friendly talks, UOP's board approved Signal's acquisition of a 50.5-percent interest in UOP. The deal was completed May 1, 1975. Also on that date, the company formally changed its name from Universal Oil Products, the name it had held since 1919, to simply "UOP."

LEFT Is this the moment Don Nichols heard the news? His friend John Logan's face suggests he and his wife would rather not be having this conversation. UOP was a good sponsor, vital for Shadow and beneficial for the corporation. To make known its place in the lead-free movement, and not incidentally its expertise in all the other areas of petrochemical engineering, UOP supported racing with enthusiasm for five years, stamping its petroleum-black identity indelibly into motorsports memory — despite some in management who saw no need for any of it. In the end they prevailed. *Dan R. Boyd*

ABOVE Stairway to the Stars, Road America 1974. UOP's transporter roof doubled as a prime vantage point for corporate guests across North America. *Dan R. Boyd*

Don: "After John left I was told to come into the office and this chap I had never seen before said, 'Well, we've decided that we no longer need a racing team.'

"I said, 'We have a contract and a joint-venture agreement.'

"He says, 'No, those were all tentative things. Come over here to the window. See that chap down there mowing the lawn?'

"I said, 'Yeah, I see him.'

"He says, 'Well, when I tell him we no longer need his services, he disappears. And I'm telling you, we no longer need the services of a racing team.'

"We got a few million dollars to continue racing, but that doesn't last long in Formula 1."

People close enough to Don to know say that he never signed anything for a term of more than one year. If that was meant to maintain his flexibility, apparently his caution now turned and bit him.

By Nichols's account, his disappointment went beyond the racing team.

"At the time we had about five different things going with UOP. Not only F1; F5000, an electric car, military programs, lead-free research for petrol fuel, all kinds of things. It was essentially that we were moving into the company as a major subdivision of their research department.

"There was a division of UOP called Automotive Products, which a retired Army Major General was running, and the plan was already in effect that Shadow would become a division of Automotive Products.

"Then suddenly this expansion sort of overwhelmed John Logan's balance in the company, he retired and that ended the honeymoon.

"You know, we had a two-or-three-million-dollar-a-year racing program. We had fast cars and fast drivers and a good designer — we had the best of everything. We were spending more money than most. Tyrrell was still workin' out of a wood yard.

"So there was a chance we could have won the World Championship, I think."

Instead, at the end of the season Nichols found himself in much the same financial fix that Colin Chapman had faced at the beginning of it.

CHAPTER 13
F1 FOR EVERYMAN?

SHADOW DN6 (F5000), 1975

WITH CAN-AM gone, Shadow's beautiful Big Block DN4 two-seaters had nowhere to race. But Don Nichols still had commitments to his sponsor UOP, and both would have wanted to do right by their new champion of the old series, Jackie Oliver. So Mike Hillman's North American team took on Formula 5000, the production-engined, single-seat series that the SCCA was trying to position as its new headliner.

The sports car club happened to be in rare cooperation with the Indycar establishment, resulting in a short-lived joint venture called SCCA/USAC Formula 5000 Championship. This encouraged household Indy 500 names like Mario Andretti and the Unser brothers, Al and Bobby, to join confrontations between such road-racing stars as Brian Redman, Jody Scheckter and David Hobbs. The 1975 schedule of nine events would be the longstanding F5000 series' second year under the SCCA/USAC banner.

In this case the term "formula" implied not only a displacement limit, but further restrictions to maintain engines' origins as off-the-shelf passenger car units. Carrying household names like Chevrolet, Dodge and Ford, they were all V8s cast in iron, and their single camshafts employed pushrods and rocker arms to operate only two valves per cylinder.

With many tens of millions mass-produced over decades, these everyday V8s were abundant and inexpensive, and their displacements made them powerful even in street going applications. When souped up with a bewildering variety of high-performance aftermarket parts from the robust speed-equipment industry, such "stock blocks" were the very heart of North American motorsports, beating hard inside innumerable dragsters, stock cars, dirt trackers, off-road trucks and buggies, some Indycar open-wheelers, most early Can-Am sports racers and a long line of Trans-Am "Pony Cars."

Naturally these ubiquitous powerplants were also the basis for what had started as Formula A but was now called Formula 5000. So long

ABOVE Ready to go at Mosport, Jackie Oliver's DN6-Chevrolet looks like an F1 bulked up on steroids. Taller and heavier than a Cossie, and pumping out more torque, the stock-block Chevy has turned a sensitive creature into an unfeeling brute. But "it's the same for everybody." *Revs Institute for Automotive Research/Geoffrey Hewitt*

as displacement was not over 5 liters/305 cubic inches (the same as in Trans-Am), and any higher-performance aftermarket cylinder heads maintained the stock design concept, the sturdy beasts could be hotted up to within an rpm of their lives.

Affordable, challenging and loud, F5000 gained popularity worldwide. It was sort of a poor man's F1.

Competitors could purchase cars from commercial racecar manufacturers like Lola, but because F5000's basic chassis concept and rules were similar to F1's, in earlier years McLaren had produced a winning stock-block variant of its Grand Prix car.

Some time had passed since, but the precedent was enough for Nichols to ask his ace designer Southgate to knock out some suitably altered Shadow DN5s.

Tony was annoyed to be pulled away from his fast but finicky F1, but he dutifully re-engineered the basic tub's rear face, adding fixtures to accept

BELOW In days of yore, people with old racing cars often replaced their expensive, temperamental old pure-blooded engines with, well, "junkyard dogs." Hey, it kept a lot of old chassis alive until someone appreciated them again. Shadow came into F5000 with new F1 chassis suitably modified by professionals, and the stock-block V8 engines were fresh, but the principle was the same. And Dodge saw a chance to beat Chevrolet. *Don Nichols collection*

F1 FOR EVERYMAN? 293

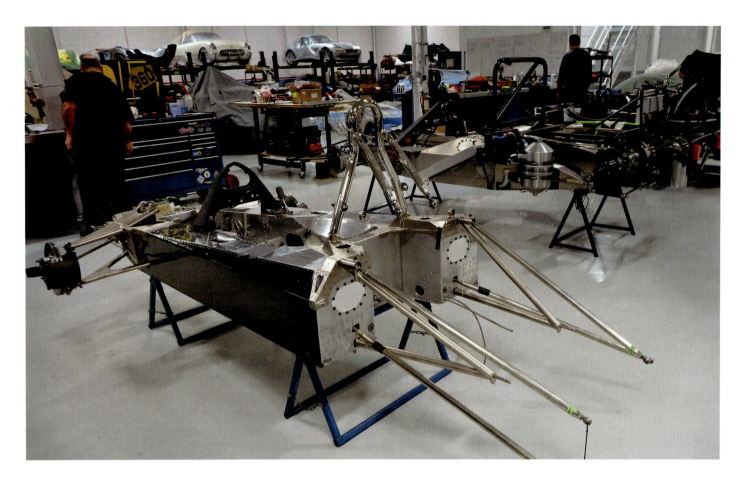

ABOVE & BELOW Pictured while under restoration in recent times, the DN6 chassis were new but revised from Shadow's DN5 Formula 1 design. Most significantly, they incorporated extra bracketry on the backs of the tubs to accept series-production Detroit engines, along with bracing struts extending rearward. The Chevrolets used initially during the 1975 season gave way to similar ones from Dodge. Also changed, repeatedly, were concepts for the side radiators. (In the upper photo, the chassis alongside is a DN4 Can-Am.) *Jim Bartel/RM Motorsports*

a Chevrolet V8, F5000's nearly universal choice of the time.

Compared to the 3-liter Cosworth, Chevy's 5-liter Small Block could produce similar horsepower, more torque, and wasn't materially different in bulk.

Of course it was heavier because it was mostly iron, but more weight didn't necessarily translate to structural strength equivalent to the light-alloy DFV. That very specialized British unit was designed from the outset to shoulder the extra loads.

Not so with Chevrolet's engine. When Small Block designers laid out their built-to-a-price, everyday utility appliance way back in the early 1950s, they could never have imagined that 20 years later some mad soul would think of making such a proletarian lump into an elemental, highly stressed structural component of a blue-blooded, tautly strung racecar chassis.

So the DN5 monocoque's alterations had to include bracketry and bracing struts to help

RIGHT As set up by Shadow engine men Lee Muir and Doug Meyer, Chevrolet's cast-iron, pushrod-valve V8 displaced the 305 cubic inches/5,000 cubic centimeters allowed by F5000 regulations. The package occupied much the same volume as F1's 3-liter Cosworth, but taller fuel injector apparatus made the rear half of the car look a lot more muscular. Overall performance wasn't much different between the two types of engine, and on a good day a well-tuned, well-driven F5000 could mix it up with the F1s. But the less costly car lacked the same fine handling, and the heavy engine's origin as a "stocker" didn't endow better reliability.
Revs Institute for Automotive Research/Geoffrey Hewitt

ABOVE OK, Ollie, you've got your Dodge, go get 'em!
Don Nichols collection

carry bending and torsional loads back to the rear suspension area. The resulting hybrid became model DN6.

When finished, the new chassis went off to the team's North American base and Southgate went back to his F1.

Across the Atlantic in Elk Grove Village, quite near Chicago's main airport, Tony's old friend Mike Hillman, successful manager of the last Can-Am season, was getting his boys spooled up for F5000.

Although the DN6 was set up for F5000's near-universal Chevy engine, Don Nichols was always looking for that elusive engine sponsor. Later that year he secured a deal with automaker Dodge, a brand of Chrysler Corp., for Shadow to carry out development on its own "small" V8.

Once again, Southgate found himself dragged away from his DN5 work to help with the DN6 swap. He wrote, "We were told that the Dodge had more horsepower, but it was also 50 pounds heavier, and that extra weight came with a higher center of gravity, which hurt the handling. 'Here we go again!' I thought."

This mirrors Mike Hillman's perspective. "Well, it irritated me, because the Dodge engine was a bad engine. The car was a good car, but the engine just was simply too heavy. Of course there wasn't much we could do about it."

The Dodge's actual weight penalty was 72 pounds, according to a contemporary report by Gordon Kirby in *Autosport* — and that was after machinists shaved off a reported 100 pounds of excess iron! The block's extra beef arose from its being physically larger than the Chevy. When Chrysler introduced its "B-block" family of engines in 1958, three years after GM's "Small Block" appeared, its displacement was 350 cubic inches (5.7 liters); eventually it was offered at 400 cubic inches (6.6 liters).

Compare those numbers to the Chevrolet. On launch in 1955 the Small Block displaced 265 cubic inches (4.3 liters), and only many years later did it grow to match Chrysler's initial 350.

With significant casting redesign, the Small Block Chevy could get to the 400-cubic-inch level, but similar work raised the Chrysler to 440 (7.2 liters).

So reducing the Dodge B-block internal components to 305 cubes did nothing to shrink the exterior bulk.

As developed through a joint venture between Shadow and Chrysler, the F5000 Dodge started as a standard production block sized at 340 cubic inches. As used in NASCAR vehicles such as Richard Petty's, its piston diameter was enlarged to 4.04 inches to meet that series' maximum of 355 cubic inches. For applications limited to 305 cubic inches, the same pistons stroked through a shorter distance, 2.96 inches. These choices were very slightly different from Chevrolet's, which were 4.0 and 3.0 inches respectively.

Whereas a strong Chevy was said to pump out around 520–530 hp at 7,800 rpm, reported Dodge numbers were 550 at between 8,000 and 8,500.

So Shadow's engine shop wrung good power out of the Dodge, but reliability was a continuing problem. Not that Chevies or other stock-block brands were free of issues of their own.

Shadow's Dodge first raced in the sixth round, at Road Atlanta at the end of August. In the meantime, Chevrolets powered the DN6 as originally intended.

ABOVE & BELOW Shadow engine builders Doug Meyer, caught checking a cylinder, and Gerald "Stump" Davis, fettling a fuel-injection system, at their good work in Shadow's Elk Grove Village facility. Once done this Dodge stock-block V8 will come to life on the team's in-house dynamometer testbed. Shadow's earlier Big Block Chevrolets came from these hands too. *Don Nichols collection*

SHADOW'S 1975 F5000 SEASON

THIS SECOND SEASON of the SCCA/USAC series consisted of nine events around North America, from June through October. The usual weekend format presented three races. First, after qualifying came a pair of short preliminary heats, the first between drivers who had qualified first, third, fifth and on down, the second for the second, fourth, etc. These sprints established starting grid order for the longer Final, where the top ten finishers earned championship points on this scale: 36–24–16–12–8–5–4–3–2–1.

F1 FOR EVERYMAN? **297**

LEFT Nichols and Oliver, still on good terms at this stage, snapped by hardworking team photographer Dan Boyd during what looks to be a test day out at Laguna Seca. For the Shadowman F5000 is the best program to keep his team and its still-loyal sponsor in the North American public eye. For the Shadow driver, it's probably his last best chance of another championship. *Dan R. Boyd*

POCONO, PENNSYLVANIA (USA)
F5000 (R1), June 1st, 1975
1st, Brian Redman, Lola T332-Chevrolet
3rd, Jackie Oliver, Shadow DN6-Chevrolet

Third place first time out. Not too shabby, especially considering the multitude of new-car issues that Jackie Oliver and his team had to tackle. Plus the intermittently rainy weekend that everyone faced at the Pocono Int'l Raceway road course.

Shadow's custom was to arrive at a circuit early for testing, but little could be accomplished on a wet and windy racetrack. On the official weekend they did manage to find that a new idea about radiators didn't work, plus the gearbox began leaking oil — perhaps due to extreme loads generated on the part of the road course that incorporated the Pocono speedway banking — and then a differential failed. Nonetheless, good laps that Ollie managed to do between rain squalls ranked him third fastest, resulting in his Shadow lining up alongside fastest man Andretti's Lola on the front row for the first heat.

Oliver and his friends faced light rain, which caught him out as he tried to beat Andretti around the first corner. Bang, into the rail. Poor Ollie had to climb out and watch the rest of it go on without him.

As a consequence he had to start the Final from the tenth row — the last. Once again the black skies opened, with wind driving rain onto parts of the circuit while other sections stayed dry. The attrition that resulted, plus his own hard driving in conditions the Brit was raised to think were perfectly normal, moved him up as far as third place.

By that time he was well behind the leaders, Andretti vs. Redman, and wasn't gaining on them. But his pace was fast enough that his rear wing began to buckle — again, possibly because of the banking. Then the Shadow's tall, rather ungainly engine intake scoop fell off. Final

BELOW Oliver feels for grip through a tight turn on the infield portion of the Pocono road course, which is completed by flat-out blasts around wide Superspeedway bankings. As at Daytona and other such hybrid circuits, chassis setup here in the rolling mountains of eastern Pennsylvania is an unsatisfactory compromise between two extremes. Then there's rain. *Dan R. Boyd*

blow: he hit a rubber tire corner marker and tore off a canard wing.

Oh, and the throttle had stuck open back in his first-heat shunt, resulting in the pushrod stock-block Chevy buzzing to something like 10,000 rpm. Nine grand would have been enough to worry those who built it.

Yet, wrote Gordon Kirby in *Autosport*, "Ollie reported that the engine never missed a beat throughout the race. That's certainly a tribute to Shadow engine man Lee Muir."

MOSPORT, ONTARIO (CDN)
F5000 (R2), June 16th, 1975
1st, Mario Andretti, Lola T332-Chevrolet
6th, Jackie Oliver, Shadow DN6-Chevrolet

Here in the pastoral hills outside Toronto, the Mario and Brian Show treated F5000 fans to the series' closest finish in history, the two masters of the season battling nose to tail all the way.

Meanwhile, Jackie Oliver again started from the back, because his heat race ended with ignition failure. In the Final he was working his way up through the midfield when a tire exploded. Changing it cost two laps to the leaders, but when Ollie rushed back out he set the second fastest lap of the race. At least the Shadow was showing potential.

Autosport's Kirby watched all this and was moved to express these thoughts: "There is something which is brutally exhausting in simply watching Formula 5000 machines driven to the ragged edge. They lack the nimble finesse which is so much the mark of a Grand Prix car, instead they use every inch of the road in broad, sweeping maneuvers, their front tires squealing out from beneath the coarse roar of their exhaust note and the drivers' arms visibly straining to maintain the tenuous, understeering balance of all that distorting torque." Just what F5000 fans came to see.

BELOW Dan Boyd climbed high into Mosport's control tower for this prized, but restricted-access viewpoint of the final turn onto the pits straight. That high-rise induction box is probably the most unmistakable way to distinguish a DN6 from its little F1 sister. Next would be the simple pressed-steel covers over the plebian valve rockerboxes. *Dan R. Boyd*

ABOVE Team portrait at Watkins Glen with two DN6-Chevys, both asparkle in their fine new designer livery. Oliver's temporary team-mate Jean-Pierre Jarier will drive the 00 car, gaining experience that may or may not give him a leg up on the F1 opposition at this racetrack come October. *Dan R. Boyd*

BELOW Ollie seizes an empty spot on the Watkins Glen starting grid and heads winner Redman for more than a dozen laps. But the Shadow Chevy doesn't stand up to it. *Dan R. Boyd*

WATKINS GLEN, NEW YORK (USA)

F5000 (R3), July 13th, 1975

1st, Brian Redman, Lola T332-Chevrolet

DNF, Jackie Oliver, Shadow DN6-Chevrolet, engine

DNF, Jean-Pierre Jarier, Shadow DN6-Chevrolet, oil line

In the month since Mosport, Shadow had completed a second DN6, and brought it to the Glen along with the first one. Both still had Chevy power, and both wore fresh, much more colorful livery featuring a lot of white.

It was said the new car was only a spare for Jackie Oliver, but since the marque's F1 man Jarier was there for the weekend's other event, a Group 5 enduro with Alpine-Renault (he and co-driver Gérard Larrousse finished third), the Frenchman checked out the new F5000.

"Yes, Jean-Pierre will probably practice it, but he won't race it. A backup car is a backup car," the press was told. But the flamboyant

ABOVE "It's a very nice car, very easy to drive," says Jean-Pierre Jarier to *Autosport* reporter Gordon Kirby at the Glen. But it refuses to let him drive it for long. *Dan R. Boyd*

Frenchman took only 14 laps to get the brand-new machine down to third-best qualifying time. "It is a very nice car, very easy to drive," he said. So Don Nichols invited him to join the F5000 fun.

For his 10-lap heat, Jarier held a comfortable second to Brian Redman until the Shadow began to slow, and Jean-Pierre placed third. He drove straight to the garage for a new engine. In the other heat, Oliver came second to Mario Andretti despite struggling with excessive oversteer.

That put Ollie straight behind pole man Mario for the 30-lap Final. But on the pace lap Andretti's Lola abruptly disappeared, so as the pack came to the man in the lavender suit with the green flag, Oliver saw a vacant space alongside Redman and immediately filled it. The Shadowman managed to hold the lead for several laps, but Lolaman Redman finally scratched by.

In fact the DN6's stock-block Chevy was blowing out water because a head gasket had blown, and when his cockpit suddenly filled with vapor Ollie parked. He got applause from the crowd as he walked back to the pits.

Jarier went off the road, damaging an oil line, and dropped out.

ROAD AMERICA, WISCONSIN (USA)
F5000 (R4), July 27th, 1975
1st, Mario Andretti, Lola T332-Chevrolet
2nd, Jackie Oliver, Shadow DN6-Chevrolet

Shadow's Jackie Oliver won a F5000 race! OK, just a heat race (better was to come the following year), and victory fell into his lap because Redman's Lola broke a rear hub — the Haas/Hall team's first mechanical DNF in 37 races. From Jackie's viewpoint, he was looking at clear air on the front row of the Final, legitimately this time.

This time his opposition was Andretti, whose Vel's Parnelli Lola immediately pulled out ahead. Oliver was 16 seconds behind when he finished a lonely second. Redman trailed home fourth, now suffering with gearbox problems.

LEFT Oliver evaluates both cars prior to Road America, and whatever is found yields a first-place finish. Just in the heat race, but it's a start. *Ben Williams/UOP, courtesy of Michael Recca*

BELOW Raceday's Final event brings a second-place finish. A lonely one, but again it's a step forward. *Ben Williams/UOP courtesy of Michael Recca*

ABOVE Debuting its Dodge at Road Atlanta, the DN6 can light up its tires in top gear! And that's even before raceday's rain.
Courtesy of Jackie Oliver

MID-OHIO (USA)
F5000 (R5), August 10th, 1975
1st, Brian Redman, Lola T332-Chevrolet
4th, Jackie Oliver, Shadow DN6-Chevrolet

Tragedy struck the series here, when a first-lap accident fatally injured promising newcomer B.J. Swanson.

Finishing third in his heat put Jackie Oliver's Shadow on the third row of the Final. Thus he was just ahead of poor Bernie Swanson, whose throttle apparently jammed wide open as the pack raced into the first turn, slamming his Lola into the far end of the pitlane guardrail hard enough to tear four posts out of the ground. The engine kept roaring at redline until someone reached into the red-hot wreckage and pulled wires out of the magneto.

A pace car sobered the procession for several laps, then Andretti and Redman hurtled away on their own. Oliver settled into fourth place behind Al Unser, which became third when Andretti retired with jammed shifter forks. But then the Shadow faded its brakes, so Ollie succumbed to a stern challenge from David Hobbs.

ROAD ATLANTA, GEORGIA (USA)
F5000 (R6), August 31st, 1975
1st, Al Unser, Lola T332-Chevrolet
4th, Jackie Oliver, Shadow DN6-Dodge

Dodge-powered for the first time, Shadow's pair of DN6s looked competitive right out of the transporter. The B-blocks seemed reasonably reliable as well. If the team had a spare, backup Chevrolet V8 hidden away, it never had to be brought out.

Oliver tried both chassis during practice, and chose the newer one to race. His only negative comment sounded like a positive: there was too much torque. He was getting wheelspin in all five gears. Jolly good, his mechanics may have replied, but have a care for the gearbox.

A thin field of 21 prompted officials to forego the usual two-heat format, so everybody fought as one for their grid places. Andretti went out early with gear-selector trouble, leaving Redman to place first ahead of Unser. Oliver was running third until an electrical fault stopped him, so Jackie would join Mario on the ninth row for the Final.

The morning's weather had been sunny and hot, but by the scheduled starting time a rainstorm was soaking the circuit. Officials held their schedule for an hour, and the rain did ease, but it wasn't stopped yet. So the race began under yellow flags and behind a pace car, with five laps lopped off the scheduled distance. All this made the impatient men on the ninth row a little antsy.

Once released, Redman and Unser vanished ahead in balls of spray, leaving Andretti and Oliver to do their anxious best to carve through traffic to catch them. But the sun came out, and as the track began to dry, concern grew about the rain tires fitted to the cars. Redman and Andretti were racing hard enough to rapidly use up their soft knobblies. Unser eased his pace, thinking to make them last. Oliver gambled that a quick stop for slicks would work out best in the end.

It might have, if the stop had been quick. It wasn't. And then he thought he felt a wheel coming loose, so he stopped again.

It was Unser's solution that worked. As the two cars ahead fell off their hectic pace, Big Al overtook first his team-mate Mario and then, just two laps from the end, squeezed by F5000 ace Redman to score his first F5000 victory. Fourth-placed Oliver in his Shadow-Dodge was a lap behind.

LONG BEACH, CALIFORNIA (USA)
F5000 (R7), September 28th, 1975
1st, Brian Redman, Lola T332-Chevrolet
DNF, Jackie Oliver, Shadow DN6-Dodge, crash
DNF, Tom Pryce, Shadow DN6-Dodge, gearbox

For the second time Shadow entered two cars, and for the second time both failed to go the distance. That dour report leaves out considerable action and interest, but most of it happened to others.

But on this inaugural Long Beach Grand Prix weekend, precursor to many years when F1 raced in this seaside city's streets, UOP Shadow did win something: an award for best team presentation at a Concours d'Elegance across the harbor at the proud old *Queen Mary* ocean liner.

Oliver's team-mate this time was Shadow's other F1 driver, Tom Pryce. Jackie was delighted to out-qualify the stellar newcomer, taking fourth grid place by more than three-quarters of a second. Tom was driving the DN6 with all the style and spectacle that Yanks had been hearing of, but he wasn't as impressed as they. Compared to his familiar DN5, he found the outwardly very similar DN6 to be "clumsy" and heavy. Besides, he didn't fit the cockpit and was flopping around like… well, his words were rather too rude to print here.

ABOVE Yet another new livery for this new circuit, future longtime home of F1's US GP West. Basking on the balmy shoreline of Southern California, Long Beach presents a tough, gritty street race just like the one on the Mediterranean's French Riviera… NOT! Unhappily, Shadow's all-too usual luck has returned. Ollie might as well have gone to the movies just along the gritty boulevard. *Don Nichols collection*

ABOVE Double-Zero's guest driver at Long Beach is Tom Pryce. He finds the F5000 less to his liking than did his F1 team-mate Jarier. Both Pryce, leading here, and temporary team-mate Oliver manage some strong laps, but both cars let them down.
Don Nichols collection

Yet his 12-lap heat had a better outcome than his team-mate's, Pryce seeing the checkered flag in third place after struggling with handling.

Oliver started the second heat on the front row next to Al Unser, and in the tight first corner between all those concrete walls he muscled ahead of the Indy man and led the race. Alas, doing so flat-spotted a tire and the Shadow couldn't hold off Unser's Lola. Fighting ever worsening handling, Ollie then had to let Redman and Scheckter by. But he didn't give up, and was making a banzai braking move to get back by Jody when it all went wrong and Jackie crunched the barrier. He was OK, but his chassis wasn't. Oliver's weekend was over.

In the 50-lap final Pryce held sixth place for a dozen laps until he began losing gears. Consequent overrevving bent valves in the Dodge, but it didn't stop until the Hewland finally jammed itself solid.

Brian Redman's overall victory clinched his second F5000 championship in a row.

LAGUNA SECA, CALIFORNIA (USA)
F5000 (R8), September 28th, 1975
1st, Mario Andretti, Lola T332-Chevrolet
4th, Jackie Oliver, Shadow DN6-Dodge

Oliver ran this second California race solo, but had no joy from it. Suffering with bad handling that his hard-working crew couldn't make better, he qualified only 12th. That meant a sixth-place start for his heat, and he only made it to fifth to settle where he would start the Final.

For Ollie that main race of the day was a stern struggle against David Hobbs, and it wasn't until the Lola driver tangled with lapped traffic late in the race that the Shadow took over fourth place.

RIVERSIDE, CALIFORNIA (USA)
F5000 (R9), October 26th, 1975
1st, Mario Andretti, Lola T332-Chevrolet
DNS, Jackie Oliver, Shadow DN6-Dodge, engine
DNF, Jody Scheckter, Shadow DN6-Dodge, engine

South Africa's Jody Scheckter was Shadow's guest driver for this last round of the series. Don Nichols wanted him to join the team for 1976.

But "Baby Bear," his nickname at McLaren when he partnered Denny Hulme, might have been less than impressed with his DN6's tendency to wheelspin and erratic oversteer. Plus, the Dodge had issues with overheating and fading oil pressure this weekend. The South African started his heat race alongside pole sitter Andretti, but dropped out on the fourth lap with the engine boiling — a hose had disconnected itself from one of the side radiators.

In his heat Oliver started from fourth place, but soon began to slow until he finally pulled into the pits with no oil pressure. So both Shadows would have to start the Final near the back of the grid.

From there Jody lifted his car as high as eighth place, but the oil pressure was dropping again and seven laps from the end of the scheduled 40

ABOVE Jody Scheckter is Don Nichols's guest at Riverside, and "Baby Bear" starts his heat race right up front alongside polesitter Mario Andretti. But that's as good as it's going to get. *Don Nichols collection*

RIGHT So Brian, I know we're meant to be bitter competitors and all that, but we've been mates for a long time and I can't help but wonder, might you share a secret or two you've winkled out of your Lola...? *Dan R. Boyd*

he followed Oliver's first-heat example and quit in the pits.

And Oliver himself? He finished the Final nowhere — because he never started. When the Shadow crew completed the chore of exchanging his exhausted Dodge with their last remaining spare and fired it up to check, this one filled its cylinders with water.

"Somehow it's the right kind of way to finish this season," said Ollie.

Said Tony Southgate, "I felt that we might have done better had we stuck to the Chevy."

Oliver ranked fourth in the season's points standings with 77 to champ Redman's 227. ♠

MIKE HILLMAN
TEAM MANAGER PART 2

THE FORMULA 5000 escapade in 1975 was both a lot of fun and a lost opportunity. I got to meet and talk to some of my heros, like Jim Hall and Bobby Unser. On the other hand, as a team we didn't do as well as we should have.

The DN6 was a pretty good car, as you would expect from Tony Southgate. His DN5 Formula 1 was quick, and our F5000 had basically the same chassis. Incidentally, the DN6s were mostly built in Elk Grove Village, not Northampton. An exception would be the bodywork. I would guess that only two DN6s were ever built, maybe three.

Our competition was well ahead of us in F5000 experience, so we had a bit of a late start. Then, just as we were getting the car sorted and more reliable, we were saddled with a motor that was overweight and under-powered. Not a good combination when you are trying to compete with Brian Redman in the works Lola and Mario Andretti from the Parnelli team. Mario could be on a bicycle and still be quick!

Jackie Oliver spun our car a lot, which was unusual, and was not as dominant in the rain as he normally was. This suggests he was having trouble keeping the torque curve under control.

Even when we were still using the Chevy in the first part of the year, the extra weight on the rear did not help. I experimented during practice at Mid-Ohio with moving the radiators forward to improve the weight distribution, but the stopwatch didn't seem to notice.

When you think about it, the DN6 had the same wheelbase as the F1 car, maybe 75 pounds more weight on the rear, a higher center of gravity, and a completely different torque curve. I would also guess that the polar moment of inertia was radically different between the two cars. Couple that to the first race being on a banked tri-oval [Pocono Speedway] and we were off to a rocky start.

Through the beginning of the season we started to make

LEFT Although he's listening courteously to his boss, Hillman will be formulating his own plans of action. He's that sort of bloke. *Dan R. Boyd*

some progress, then we got distracted by the Dodge motor, which was not exactly as promised.

That was the year when Shadows became more colorful. I remember speaking with John Logan about this. He was UOP's CEO, a great guy who had rescued the company some years before Don Nichols hooked up with them. John was a low-profile kind of guy and very sharp as you might imagine. He told me that the reason the company had a black-and-white corporate color scheme was because it was the cheapest!

So in 1975 UOP decided to go for a change and they started introducing color. I can't speak to "re-entry colors," I've never heard the term, but I do know that to come up with a new color scheme, UOP hired Robert Miles Runyan, one of the most talented graphic artists in the country. He later designed the iconic Los Angeles 1984 Olympic "Stars in Motion" logo.

I thought the best feature on the Shadows was a sticker that just had a pair of maniacal eyes. Brilliant!

Our F5000 cars got the full treatment at Watkins Glen in July, and they were quite attractive. When we got to Long Beach in September the team won the Concours. There was a big prize, $10,000. I had promised the crew they would get all of it if they were able to win. Amazing, the power of money!

That first race at Long Beach was surreal. Traffic lights swinging in the wind. Triple-X movie houses opposite the pits. Bumps you could lose a Volkswagen in. The Long Beach Grand Prix has since done a lot for that city.

Tom Pryce drove the second DN6 to prepare him for the Formula 1 GP that was scheduled for the next year. Tom didn't like the F5000 car or the circuit, and I'm not surprised.

The loss of UOP as a sponsor was cataclysmic. The company was in trouble, but the country was moving to unleaded fuels and catalytic converters were already mandatory, so when Signal Oil was looking around to invest some cash, they saw UOP as a gold mine.

They were not interested in motor racing! I never saw the contract between UOP and Shadow — actually the holding company was called Phoenix Racing — but it clearly had a very swift termination clause.

We learned of it early in 1976, around January or February. What money there was left was directed immediately to the F1 program. Don clipped 20 percent off everyone's pay in the US. I had a family, and so I had to leave.

So I missed the second season of the DN6, when they

ABOVE Mike monitors setup progress at Road America, where Jackie will score Shadow's one first-place result of the F5000 season. Not the overall first place that is really wanted, but at least the sponsor is still on board to see it. *Dan R. Boyd*

won the Road America race outright, but to the best of my recollection the "6B" models they used in 1976 would have to have been refurbished 1975 cars. It would be uncharacteristic for Don to build new cars, particularly as we were supposed to be broke!

Hillman left Shadow in March of 1976, and three months later joined Harley-Davidson as an engineer and manager handling advanced projects and strategic planning. After 21 years with that famous motorcycle manufacturer, the last 10 as a Vice President, he took early retirement to launch business ventures of his own. He is now a partner in FX Bikes, inventor and developer of a line of "super-lightweight" all-purpose, all-terrain motorcycles.

CHAPTER 14
OFF THE BOIL

SHADOW DN5B AND DN8 (F1), 1976

This is the epic season told of in the film *Rush*, when James Hunt waged a year-long battle for the World Championship against his strongest rival and good friend Niki Lauda. But compared to the cartoonishly oversimplified Hollywood version, the real thing was much more complex, intense and exciting. Unfortunately, our Shadowmen played no role in that story. Hamstrung by their abrupt loss of sponsorship, Don Nichols and his dwindling team were facing their own epic battle just to survive.

They managed to make fleeting cameo appearances when enough things went right, but too often too much went wrong. Regulation changes as well as tire and technical evolution made the DN5 too old. Its replacement, the DN8, was too young. Finances were too tight to allow enough development testing, let alone an adequate stock of spare parts. Most races, drivers Tom Pryce and Jean-Pierre Jarier struggled.

But real racers never give up hope. They don't want the movie to end.

SHADOW'S 1976 F1 SEASON

OBLIGINGLY, THE FIA made its 1976 Grand Prix season longer, adding a 16th main event with two non-championship sprints squeezed into early gaps in the schedule. The US got two GPs, and the long haul to faraway Japan made Formula 1 truly a World Championship.

The title decision hung in breathless suspense right up to the very last lap.

BRAZILIAN GP
Interlagos, F1 (R1), January 25th, 1976
1st, Niki Lauda, Ferrari 312T
3rd, Tom Pryce, Shadow DN5B
DNF, Jean-Pierre Jarier, Shadow DN5B, crash

One Shadow qualified third on the grid! And the other Shadow came home third in the race! OK, things would go downhill from there, but Brazil

ABOVE So nearly a great day! Jean-Pierre Jarier starts Brazil from third position, almost as impressive as the previous year's pole. The Frenchman's car is a revision of the existing DN5 to suit new tires and rules, although it still wears the original tall airscoop that is to be outlawed later in the season. Absent, of course, are the bold colors of the lost major sponsor. Still, by working away at fast men Hunt and Lauda, "Jumper" sets fastest race lap, and with the end looming his Shadow is pressing the leading Ferrari when…
Motorsport Images/David Phipps

'76 was something for a beleaguered team to hold on to.

Jean-Pierre Jarier was Shadow's qualifying hero. He actually lapped faster than anyone else in open practice but couldn't repeat that during the qualifying session. His DN5B sat on the row behind James Hunt's McLaren and Niki Lauda's Ferrari, whose all-but-identical lap times (scarcely 0.01 second apart) gave early warning of who would be the year's two prime protagonists.

Both Jarier's and Pryce's Shadows were new chassis, with front track width narrower and suspension geometry altered so they could fairly be dubbed "B" models. They now wore an array of vanes or slats on the angled faces of their side radiators to help with cooling. But still in place were the familiar tall engine intake scoops, because new 1976 rules banning them weren't coming into effect until the Spanish GP in May.

Goodyear's tires were new this year, supposedly more conservative in compound but also quite different in behavior, so Pryce carried out an interesting experiment. After getting down to a good time on this year's suspension settings, he tried ones taken from last year's Interlagos notebook. He succeeded only in proving this year's same-for-everybody tires called for completely different chassis characteristics. The ramifications would shadow Shadow's whole season.

Tom wound up four rows behind Jean-Pierre on the grid, 12th.

In the race Jarier continued to lift his team's hearts by hounding Hunt and getting by to second place, then closing in on Lauda. With nine laps to go Jean-Pierre set the fastest lap of the race, three quarters of a second faster than Lauda. Your scribe was watching, and wrote it like this:

"The Ferrari seemed to be faster along the fast parts of the lap, but the Shadow was quicker in the slow sections and was gaining by leaps and bounds — literally in some places! It might be another thing to get by the Ferrari, as it had

ABOVE Meanwhile, not far behind, Tom Pryce is also having an Interlagos drive to remember. The Welshman forges forward from 12th on the grid until, late in the going, he takes over from his French team-mate as another black nemesis chasing Lauda. Until… *Motorsport Images/David Phipps*

been the McLaren, but if trying could accomplish anything Jean-Pierre was going to give it the best shot of his young life. What a finish this looked like turning into!

"Then, following Lauda by two seconds, he went straight off on oil dropped by James Hunt's blown-up engine. Into the guardrail, bang."

The heavy impact crumpled the strong Shadow footbox a little, but the uninjured driver got out as rapidly as he could move. Then, without a backward glance, he strode away, brushing by all the marshals inquiring after his wellbeing, and sat down in the shade behind the guardrail to be alone.

The Frenchman's misfortune looked like benefiting his Welsh team-mate, for Tom now held second to Lauda, but with his back tires worn down and rear brakes locking he had to slip back behind Patrick Depailler's Tyrrell six-wheeler.

Hold this one in your hearts, Shadowfans. Sadly, it doesn't get better. Not this year, anyway.

SOUTH AFRICAN GP
Kyalami, F1 (R2), March 6th, 1976
1st, Niki Lauda, Ferrari 312T
7th, Tom Pryce, Shadow DN5B
DNF, Jean-Pierre Jarier, Shadow DN5B, damaged radiator

During the six-week gap following Brazil the team managed some intensive testing at high-altitude Kyalami. Only Jarier was there for it, because Pryce stayed in wintry England sweating out a case of flu.

Did that play into another four-row discrepancy in their qualifying times? No, because this time Tom was faster, eighth best to Jean-Pierre's 16th. Their DN5Bs now wore an array of vanes or slats on the sloping tops of their side radiators to help with cooling. For this event only, the all-black cars also carried emblems of a cigarette sponsor. Both cars were on short wheelbases.

After the start Pryce moved up well, going

from the fourth row to fourth place, only for a rear tire to puncture. Back out on track Tom found the new tire created some oversteer, which combined with a tendency for the front brakes to lock. All this cost a lap to the leader for a no-points seventh-place finish.

Jarier, never happy throughout the weekend, had to drop out when somehow a large, hard object bashed a radiator and all his coolant leaked away.

RACE OF CHAMPIONS (GB)
Brands Hatch, F1 (non-championship),
 March 14th, 1976
1st, James Hunt, McLaren M23
6th, Tom Pryce, Shadow DN5B

The team brought one driver but two cars to this grey and cold weekend, and Pryce needed both. When the "1976 spare car" blew its engine he swapped into his Kyalami race car, but not

ABOVE Shadow picks up a new sponsor here in South Africa, but only here. Another brand in the same area of commerce will sign on later in the season. *Don Nichols collection*

BELOW Pryce, so fast just a year before, starts this Race of Champions from the fifth row, nearly four agonizing seconds slower than fastest qualifier Jody Scheckter. The DN5B is only marginally quicker than Carlos Pace's Brabham BT45 alongside. *Private collection*

OFF THE BOIL 313

before its wheelbase spacer was installed; even so he complained that "it isn't nice, it's twitchy." Starting ninth, he made a pitstop to try to cure a misfire, and 1975's runaway winner of this event wound up an unhappy sixth.

UNITED STATES WEST GP
Long Beach, F1 (R3), March 28th, 1976
1st, Clay Regazzoni, Ferrari 312T
7th, Jean-Pierre Jarier, Shadow DN5B
DNF, Tom Pryce, Shadow DN5B, driveshaft

For this inaugural event of what was to become an American classic, Pryce again edged his teammate in qualifying, lining up fifth directly ahead of Jarier.

Initially both Shadows overheated, but swapping to larger radiators nicely dealt with weather that was warmer than expected. Then front wing endplates started peeling away from both cars. That was handled by reducing the aero effect by substituting a different wing profile.

Sounds like Shadow came to California well prepped, doesn't it? And next time poor Tom would know not to chug down so much ice-cold fruit juice as to make him ill.

In the race, Pryce stopped on the course when a driveshaft failed, while Jarier struggled long and hard before losing all his intermediate gears three laps from the end. He kept going, but wasn't racing any more.

INTERNATIONAL TROPHY (GB)
Silverstone, F1 (non-championship),
   April 11th, 1976
1st, James Hunt, McLaren M23
4th, Tom Pryce, Shadow DN5B
5th, Jean-Pierre Jarier, Shadow DN5B

Shades of Shadow's 1971 test at Rattlesnake Raceway: Pryce collected a rabbit at Silverstone. Unlike Jackie Oliver's incident in Texas, which

BELOW Rain or shine, brollies are always useful in motor racing. Pryce will start fifth for this first-ever Long Beach Grand Prix, but won't finish it.
Motorsport Images/LAT

only impacted the radiator, the Northants "hunt" resulted in a shunt, but light enough that the car was ready again that afternoon. But then a valve broke in one of the cash-strapped team's mere seven Cosworths. Off it went to Shadow's contracted engine rebuilder in Swindon, while its replacement held up well enough for Tom to qualify third.

Pryce's driving had been notably tidy, especially in contrast to team-mate Jarier's. Normally the lad from France was the less wild-looking of the two, but here he was hurling his DN5B into slides and up curbs. Jean-Pierre said it was the only way he could find any speed in the thing this weekend, and at that he could only manage sixth place on the grid.

Yet the faster Pryce was envious. "Cor, I wish I could do that, but it's no good on these tires. I hope they hurry up and change them, I don't want to drive smoothly for the rest of my career."

It was a short and very sharp race. Pryce spent most of it tight up behind Jody Scheckter, trying hard to pass the six-wheeler Tyrrell but never making it. Jarier was constantly in his mirrors, driving more neatly than the day before, although he had to keep fending off fierce attacks from behind.

SPANISH GP
Jarama, F1 (R4), May 2nd, 1976
1st, James Hunt, McLaren M23 (after protest resolved)
8th, Tom Pryce, Shadow DN5B
DNF, Jean-Pierre Jarier, Shadow DN5B, electrics

At this first European GP new 1976 F1 rules came into force. The starkly visible result was loss of tall "airboxes," the scoops that had risen high above the engine to feed it with cool air somewhat pressurized by "ram effect." Whatever their banishment cost in horsepower, there was also a price in poorer aerodynamic flow to

BELOW Spain brings a major change in car profiles, because of new limits on the height of formerly towering engine induction scoops. *Motorsport Images/David Phipps*

OPPOSITE Stylin' in Monte Carlo, Pryce shows his team-mate the quick way round Upper Mirabeau, named for the grand old hotel rising above. A hotel of distinction: it also "owns" Lower Mirabeau directly below. Can there be another hostelry in the Grand Prix world so honored? But back to business: Jarier's only thought is, "*What is ze Eengleesh guy theenking, zat's not ze quick way 'round!*" *Motorsport Images/ David Phipps*

the rear wing. Tony Southgate's painstakingly tunnel-tested DN5 airbox profile had been particularly efficient at this.

The wings themselves had to be brought forward by about eight inches (20 cm), further degrading their ability to make downforce. What's more, minimum width restrictions all along the car were toughened; inflexibly stringent enforcement at Jarama would cause much angst.

Two provisions of the new regulations most likely to actually improve safety were not readily visible from outside. Small tubular hoops like miniature rollover bars had to be installed just in front of the steering wheel, and driver footwells had to be strengthened against collapse.

None of this was good news for people racing Shadow DN5s. Their basic concept dated to the DN1 of 1973, an eon ago in F1 circles, and too much had changed in regulations and tire technology for mere updates to work any more.

Southgate had a new DN8 model all designed and ready to be built, but Nichols hadn't the money to proceed any further. As of May, the new chassis wouldn't be on its wheels for another two months. In fact four months would go by before the 8's race debut.

By that time Southgate would have been four months gone. He had accepted an unrefusable offer from Colin Chapman to be Lotus chief engineer for 15 months, helping to sort out troublesome new models. Tony would return to Shadow in 1977, but immediately the checkers waved over Jarama '76 Colin came and snatched him away.

What those checkers waved over wasn't happiness, neither at the front nor the back. Tech inspectors — and Lauda's second-placed Ferrari team — questioned Hunt's victory after his rear tire sidewalls were found to bulge a fraction of an inch wider than the new limit; it took months of dispute before James got his win back.

Meanwhile, the Shadow team got no joy at all. The ongoing money problem meant they couldn't come to Jarama early to test their solutions to the new rules and, sure enough, the new low-profile air intakes and relocated rear wings didn't play well with each other. As they lined up a miserable 15th (Jarier) and an even worse 22nd (Pryce), the soon-to-depart designer said through a rueful smile, "At least I've been able to leave them with a pretty comprehensive job-list!"

Starting way at the back meant Pryce's new airbox was well placed to scoop up billowing grit and jam his slide-throttles shut. By the time he got them cleared he was last man on the road.

Jarier had a better start, and in fact enjoyed quite a strong run all the way up to fifth place on the lap chart, but only until his ignition failed.

BELGIAN GP

Zolder, F1 (R5), May 16th, 1976
1st, Niki Lauda, Ferrari 312T2
9th, Jean-Pierre Jarier, Shadow DN5B
10th, Tom Pryce, Shadow DN5B

Qualifying put the Shadow boys precisely side by side on the seventh row, Pryce 0.01 second faster than Jarier. Under the direction of new designer Dave Wass, who had been Southgate's assistant, the team was trying not only their usual variations in wheelbase but also several aero tweaks: a new longer nosepiece, a new V-shaped rear wing, and back-to-back runs with and without the low-line airbox.

This time both drivers were able to race with their fellow backmarkers all the way, though both cars began to fade by the end.

MONACO GP

Monte Carlo, F1 (R6), May 30th, 1976
1st, Niki Lauda, Ferrari 312T2
7th, Tom Pryce, Shadow DN5B
8th, Jean-Pierre Jarier, Shadow DN5B

During practice, Jarier was visibly driving a restrained Monte Carlo. Not for him a repeat of his first-lap nonsense of the previous year. Both

Shadow drivers were well aware that their aging cars were not competitive, and that both — but Pryce's especially — had a tendency toward sudden violent oversteer.

Tom chose to fight back, and he was grand to watch. His driving was all whirling arms and bootfuls of power and missed gear changes because wheels were bouncing in the air. "You're seeing the old Pryce now, give me a good car and you'll see the new Pryce again!" he cracked.

Jean-Pierre, by contrast, hardly attracted any notice at all in the same places. His whole demeanor was thoughtful, methodical, careful. He was also quicker, by 0.3 second and two rows, 10th on the grid vs. 15th.

The race turned it around. A sprinkle of rain wet the track around mid-distance, slowing cars noticeably, but then the Mediterranean sun came back, the street surfaces dried and nothing was different. Except for Pryce's position: he had moved up and overhauled his team-mate.

"Tom, you certainly go very quickly in the wet!" Jarier said to him in their debriefing session afterwards. "Wet?" replied Pryce. "Uh, did it rain today?"

SWEDISH GP
Anderstorp, F1 (R7), June 13th, 1976
1st, Jody Scheckter, Tyrrell P34
9th, Tom Pryce, Shadow DN5B
12th, Jean-Pierre Jarier, Shadow DN5B

It was good to see both the aging DN5Bs finish, as they did at Monaco. "It was handling well," said Pryce, "it just wasn't holding the road." He wound up 11th on the grid, 0.1 second faster than Jarier's 13th. In the race Jean-Pierre got ahead of his team-mate and was spiritedly attacking Jochen Mass's McLaren until he took the Shadow down an escape road. So Tom finished on top, although his chance of finishing on the same lap as the winner — Jody Scheckter's Tyrrell six-wheeler — drained away as his fuel did over the last eight laps.

FRENCH GP
Paul Ricard, F1 (R8), July 4th, 1976
1st, James Hunt, McLaren M23
8th, Tom Pryce, Shadow DN5B
12th, Jean-Pierre Jarier, Shadow DN5B

Here in his home country it was clear that "Jumper" hadn't given up his dream of driving a French car. He had been at Ricard testing the V12 Matra-engined Ligier normally raced by Jacques Laffite. Yet when he came back to his regular job it was interesting to see him doing very similar times with his V8-powered Shadow, slow and obsolete though it was.

Restless tweaking of the DN5B's rear suspension geometry didn't cure severe oversteer, and Pryce in particular was seen sliding everywhere. But once again the black cars were quite reliable, and the major drama seemed to be Jarier smashing his nosepiece against another car in the pitlane. Once again both drivers lined up on the same row of the grid, the eighth, with the French patriot just a tiny 0.15 second quicker than the pride of Wales. But the gap way up to Hunt's McLaren on pole was a massive 2.23 seconds.

Team Shadow found no more speed on raceday. Pryce knew the new DN8 was coming and that he would be getting it. Jarier knew he wouldn't be. No wonder he was chafing to leave.

BRITISH GP
Brands Hatch, F1 (R9), July 18th, 1976
1st, Niki Lauda, Ferrari 312T2
4th, Tom Pryce, Shadow DN5B
9th, Jean-Pierre Jarier, Shadow DN5B

As ever this year Shadow's problem was lack of grip, despite hard work to come up with a fix, any fix. One tweak tried was an effort to stop air going under the car from the sides. Other teams had been experimenting with various strips of metal or plastic hanging down just clear of the road, but Dave Wass used sets of long-bristle brushes that wouldn't be harmed by rubbing the tarmac.

Alas that didn't really work, nor did rejigging the front track three inches narrower — an idea from the forthcoming DN8 — to get better front-tire bite and to cure initial understeer. But here in his own home nation Pryce could qualify no better than 20th, on the very circuit where he scored a victory just a year and a bit earlier. Jarier was two further rows behind, saying, "The front tires grip so badly you must put on very much front wing, which makes it impossible to steer!" Having to operate without a major sponsor to pay for detailed development has that visible an effect on a car's performance.

The outer world remembers this British GP for its infamous first-turn crash, which resulted in a restart and then the season's second long legislative dispute as to who won. Team Shadow had nothing to do with any winning. Both engines started dying, so both drivers kept the

ABOVE Tail-out Tom's driving style is grand to watch, but neither he nor his more restrained team-mate find any grip here at Brands, where Shadows used to be quick. *Motorsport Images/Ercole Colombo*

BELOW Shadows are supposed to be black, you say? But in fact not all have been been so, and more colorful liveries lie ahead. Seriously, doesn't Mike Wilds's DN3 — normally a contender in Britain's *Formule Libre* series — look splendid in scarlet during its World Championship one-off at Brands? *Motorsport Images/David Phipps*

OFF THE BOIL 319

revs down to nurse them home. Poor Jarier was a very unhappy last on the road, six laps down.

As a footnote, one car that didn't qualify nevertheless made Shadow history. Mike Wilds, who had raced an Ensign at Watkins Glen the previous year and BRMs early this season until that constructor closed down, tried his luck at Brands with a bright red DN3 entered by P.R. Reilly. This made Mike the first privateer in a Shadow since Graham Hill's 1973 season with a DN1. Wilds's failure to make the 1976 British GP with a 1974 car was hardly surprising, considering that rules and tire changes kept the much newer DN5Bs off the pace even with the Pryces of this world hurling them around.

GERMAN GP
Nürburgring, F1 (R10), August 1st, 1976
1st, James Hunt, McLaren M23
8th, Tom Pryce, Shadow DN5B
11th, Jean-Pierre Jarier, Shadow DN5B

Indelibly, this is the event where Ferrari's Niki Lauda suffered a huge, fiery crash that almost killed him. His miraculously courageous recovery and return to the cockpit, eventually to win two more World Championships for three in all, is forever etched into Grand Prix lore.

All but unnoticed, the slow Shadows now wore plastic skirting like other cars. To address Jarier's complaint about heavy steering, his wheelbase was set at the shorter dimension, which reduced the effort required. Pryce kept his longer, and once again out-qualified his team-mate despite handling he described as so unsteady over bumps that he had to back off through sections he should have been taking wide open. Both drivers once again started from deep in the slower half of the grid, but at least both cars kept going to the end of the race again. An achievement in itself on the long, mean, gnarly old 'Ring.

BELOW See, what did we tell you about color making a comeback? Bursting over the brow of Nürburgring's *Pflantzgarten* jump is the first liveried appearance of a new sponsor who will be helping Don Nichols for the next few years. *Motorsport Images/Rainer Schlegelmilch*

AUSTRIAN GP

Österreichring, F1 (R11), August 15th, 1976
1st, John Watson, Penske PC4
DNF, Jean-Pierre Jarier, Shadow DN5B, fuel pump
DNF, Tom Pryce, Shadow DN5B, brakes

Feel-good moment: John Watson scored Roger Penske's one and only GP victory at the very place where Mark Donohue heartbreakingly lost his life the year before. Not a cure, but at least some consolation.

Chez Shadow, feelings could genuinely be upbeat, because Tom Pryce was sixth on the grid. "It feels really good, like it does at Silverstone. It seems to like smooth, fast circuits," he said. Its wheelbase short this time, his DN5B also was wearing an older-pattern rear wing for less drag. Jean-Pierre Jarier also enthused about the handling. "It's fantastic — it's the first time it's been good since Spain." He said that despite braking troubles that held him to 18th on the grid.

Shadowboss Nichols said he had a good feeling that his team had turned a corner. That was before the race, when his cars spoiled a six-race reliability streak by both dropping out.

DUTCH GP

Zandvoort, F1 (R12), August 29th, 1976
1st, James Hunt, McLaren M23
4th, Tom Pryce, Shadow DN8
10th, Jean-Pierre Jarier, Shadow DN5B

Goodness, will you look where that Pryce kid qualified — third fastest! To find his team-mate we have to go all the way back to 20th — the region we had become accustomed to seeing both of them. What had changed?

Tom's car. He was racing Shadow's new DN8 for the first time. Visibly reveling in its handling and traction, he was throwing it around with spectacular abandon. "It brakes far better

BELOW New car at last! Shadow's new DN8 debuts in the Dutch GP, where all of a sudden Pryce is competitive again. *Motorsport Images/David Phipps*

than the old one," he enthused, "and it doesn't scrub speed off when you put it sideways."

The main difference, seemingly, was that the new car carried more of its weight forward thanks to the fuel and driver being relocated. The weight distribution was more like that of other fast chassis that season. Rival teams with stronger funding had already enjoyed months of development for the new rules and tires.

The Shadow's speed was all the more creditable as it was only some 300 miles old when it arrived in Holland. Since its unveiling only a few days earlier, an attempt to cure a suspicion of overheating took the form of a "stair" of scoops up each of the slanting side radiators but, as the weather during the meeting wasn't all that hot anyway, these were finally removed. So was the original airbox arrangement in the engine cover, and the car raced with simple gauze screening over the intakes. The loss of engine performance was minimal and not as great as the gain in handling due to better rear wing airflow.

"I think you could say we're back," said Don Nichols, smiling broadly and continually. "Did you realize that Tom's quick time was done on only one flying lap? On the next one his rear wing lost its endplate and he had to come in and we didn't get him out again before the end. He says he thought he could go another few tenths faster." A quarter of a second improvement would have put the new Shadow on pole.

In turn that might have put him ahead of a traffic jam that developed off the grid, which he escaped at the cost of two places. Then Regazzoni's aggressively driven Ferrari dropped the DN8 to sixth, after which Tom fell prey to Scheckter's Tyrrell. That's right, the one that rolled on 10-inch front wheels, same diameter as on Shadow's AVS Mk I six years before…

Tom's four-wheeler then developed a fuel-pickup problem and he finished with a high-speed misfire. But he finished within seven seconds of the winner. His drive had been something special.

ABOVE Racing minus its new airbox, Pryce's DN8 starts the Dutch GP from third on the grid. That lasts only meters before traffic interferes, but Tom's pace and final place is a long-awaited relief. *Motorsport Images/ Rainer Schlegelmilch*

OPPOSITE Tom's new toy is unmistakably a member of Shadow's Southgate family, but distinctively different. Its front rocker arms are more refined, its driving position is more forward, and the twin-inlet airbox is another new way to tackle the new rules. But while the twin coolers seem novel to F1, they have the same narrow configuration as the ones hidden inside the Can-Am DN4. *Motorsport Images/David Phipps*

ITALIAN GP
Monza, F1 (R13), September 12th, 1976
1st, Ronnie Peterson, March 761
8th, Tom Pryce, Shadow DN8
19th, Jean-Pierre Jarier, Shadow DN5B

Amazing what a show of speed can do for sponsorship. Both Shadow cars proudly bore big new logos at Monza. The name had been discernible at some races earlier, but writ small. Now it was dominant: Tabatip, a brand of cigarillo made by a Swiss tobacconist named Heinrich Villiger. "A splendid person," Don Nichols was still calling him 35 years later.

Cringe not, gentle modern reader. In those days the demon weed was still one of our sport's major and most loyal supporters.

The gentleman from Switzerland didn't get much exposure this time. Most setup time was lost to wet weather, and the new Shadow was barely faster than the old, Pryce's new DN8 gridding 15th to Jarier's 17th with the old DN5B. Motor racing can be like that.

Tom's car at least ran well in the race, and he kept moving up the charts to place eighth, on the winner's lap albeit nearly a minute behind. Jean-Pierre fell victim to a brief mid-race rain shower, when his car was one of several to pit even though it proved unnecessary. He was five laps down by the end.

CANADIAN GP
Mosport, F1 (R14), October 3rd, 1976
1st, James Hunt, McLaren M23
11th, Tom Pryce, Shadow DN8
18th, Jean-Pierre Jarier, Shadow DN5B

Another disappointing qualifying result, with Pryce starting 13th, Jarier 18th. The new DN8 looked good to the outsider, with Tom's driving visually on par with Hunt and several others of the elite clique. His car was set up with the short wheelbase, which turned out not to be the best choice for swooping, bumpy Mosport, but the crew was loath to change it before Watkins Glen only a week later. More meaningful development continued with a new airbox design along with fences added to the sides of the sloping radiator inlets, parts which served both to increase downforce and improve cooling.

Pryce said his main handicap was understeer in the slow corners, and the DN8 had no mechanical delays. Which was exactly the opposite experience of his resignedly unhappy team-mate. The DN5B driver's engine locked up after three laps of the first session, and the new one was fired up only in time for 15 minutes of the second. On Saturday Jarier suffered persistent fuel-pressure trouble, making the car absurdly slow on the straights.

But according to a driver from another team, "He's really trying incredibly hard in the corners." J-P's lowly grid place wasn't all that bad, considering. He could only hope that potential employers understood.

Neither man's race turned magical. Pryce said his car started handling badly as the fuel load lightened, while missing a gearchange cost him a couple of places. Jarier, as in practice, still had no power up the long, rising straight.

UNITED STATES EAST GP
Watkins Glen, F1 (R15), October 10th, 1976
1st, James Hunt, McLaren M23
10th, Jean-Pierre Jarier, Shadow DN5B
DNF, Tom Pryce, Shadow DN8, engine

Tom Pryce was fastest! At the close of the first Friday practice session the Shadow DN8 topped the time sheet.

Ah, but there's more to the story. The session was wet and misty, and Tom's time was a dozen seconds off the one James Hunt would turn for pole position. But after a season like theirs, the Shadow team would be happy to wave any paper that showed them up front!

Later paperwork was harsher. Poor Pryce wound up ninth on the grid. "It just understeers

LEFT Watkins Glen's Tech Center offers comfy shelter from the October weather as Shadow's DN8 is preened for this next-to-last race of the year. With the cowl removed the mandatory new dash hoop is visible, a stout mini-roll bar protecting the driver's extremities. Somewhat. *Revs Institute for Automotive Research/ Geoffrey Hewitt*

and understeers in the dry, we can't figure it out. I think we'll be needing a different front suspension," he said. His race didn't go well, not only because of the numb handling but also because an exhaust pipe fractured and then something even more critical broke inside the Cosworth. When hot oil and water started showering into his cockpit he stopped.

Jarier fared no better from his 16th-place start. In fact he didn't start, not when everybody else did. His engine dead, he waved his arms frantically as a river of metal went roaring past. As the sound level died away he did get the engine going and joined the back of the race. An hour and three quarters later he reached the checkered flag in 10th place, but two laps short of full distance.

JAPANESE GP
Mount Fuji Speedway, F1 (R16),
   October 24th, 1976
1st, Mario Andretti, Lotus 77
10th, Jean-Pierre Jarier, Shadow DN5B
DNF, Tom Pryce, Shadow DN8, engine

And so to the year's last round of the World Championship, the first Formula 1 Grand Prix ever hosted by Japan — at the circuit Don Nichols helped to create just the decade before. In that mere breath of history this nation had lifted itself from importing expertise to contributing to it. The entry list included four Japanese drivers, one Japanese-made racing tire brand, and an F1 car constructed literally just outside the speedway's main gate. A good car: Masahiro Hasemi drove Kojima's KE007-Ford to the fifth row of the grid.

And once again in this extraordinary, tumultuous season, this race turned out to be unforgettable. After a long delay while officials tried to wait out drenching rain, as evening began to loom and anxiety ramped up someone unleashed the race regardless.

It was madness. Visibility was practically nil and tire adhesion worse. After two laps of it Niki Lauda, the man who came so close to death at the Nürburgring not three months earlier, rolled into the pits and abandoned his quest to be champion for the second year running. He had already fought his life's hardest battle. Risking death again was not worth one more trophy.

OFF THE BOIL 325

RIGHT Sunshine is not how anyone remembers the Fuji race, but conditions were more pleasant in practice. From the team's sponsorship this weekend, we presume Shadowfolk are sleeping and dining well. Days at the track go not so well. *Motorsport Images/ Ercole Colombo*

BELOW During the still-rainy middle of this peculiar race Patrick Depailler in Tyrrell's six-wheeler is running second, but Pryce is harassing him hard and will finally overtake on the 40th lap (of 73). Second place! Two positions ahead of eventual winner Mario Andretti at that point. But hope holds for only another six laps before Tom's engine loses it. *Private collection*

Shadow was not a team anyone thought had a realistic chance of winning any trophies. In practice Jarier had an engine blow and then a tire blew too, left rear exploding violently and dropping the DN5B so hard that it put a kink in the back of the tub. Jean-Pierre wound up 15th on the grid, one place back from his team-mate. He pretty much spent the race back there.

Pryce, though, put on a show. In the dramatically changing conditions he actually got up to second place — at a point in the latter half of the race when the eventual winner was fourth. But then Tom's engine seized and he had to walk back through the mud to the pits.

JAMES HUNT of McLaren became World Champion, with 69 points compared to Niki Lauda's 68, but by scoring 83 Ferrari won the Constructors' Cup. Shadow's Tom Pryce ranked joint 11th with Ronnie Peterson; Jean-Pierre Jarier scored no points, so Pryce's 10 made Shadow eighth among constructors. ♣

TOM PRYCE DRIVER

There follows the author's interview with Shadow driver Tom Pryce, published originally in *Autosport* magazine on September 23rd, 1976.

Q: Compare the new Tabatip Shadow DN8 with the DN5.

Pryce: The DN8 is a very much better car because it responds more effectively than the old one. The DN5 was very good with the old wing settings and so on, but the new regulations don't suit it at all.

The DN8 is built with the new regs in mind, and it does all the things the DN5 used to do but a little bit better. It's a much steadier car to drive. It brakes more steadily, and it's more stable turning into corners than the DN5 ever was. The new one seems to be a better car all round, and it's far easier to drive.

The only drawback is the traction — not as good as the DN5, but I suppose that's because of the wings, because the weight is further forward.

At Monza, we didn't have the time to set the car up due to the rain, and we had a lot of understeer, so we were slow through the chicane. That is really the only problem we've had with the new car, and that was just lack of testing, really.

Q: Have you done any proper testing of the DN8?

Pryce: No. Nothing except the shakedown tests just before its first race.

Q: Is the problem money? The withdrawal of the team's former sponsor?

Pryce: Yes. You know, we can't risk engines, things like that. We just can't afford to jeopardize the race program, so "no testing" seems to be the rule just now!

Anyway, we are doing the last three races, and I understand that the financial position should be better for next year. I'm very keen to stay with Shadow, because the team really is 100 percent and I get on with them very well. The mechanics really are super. They've been under a lot of pressure recently, and they've responded with maximum effort. I reckon they're about the best crew in Formula 1 at the moment. They do a really good job, and they've built up a fantastic reliability record recently.

And the new car has been dead reliable from the word "go," no problems whatsoever apart from sorting ones. Despite the financial problems of the team, and the fact that J-P has lost a bit of interest recently, the morale is amazingly high.

BELOW In the autumn of 1976 Thomas Maldwyn Pryce, the pride of little Wales, is 27, and the F1 world is coming to see him as a future champion. He has that rare graceful speed that seems effortless, and he seems to be learning fast how to apply it. *Dan R. Boyd*

Q: How have they been able to keep up their morale?

Pryce: Effort. Everybody has really been putting everything into it, Alan Rees, me out on the track, everybody. We've all been very keen to keep the thing going, except J-P perhaps. When you've got problems, and you're not getting the results, you half expect the mechanics to lose heart, but the opposite has been the case. They're just concerned with getting the car finished and as competitive as we can make it, and when we get a good race finish they're thrilled to bits.

My main concern has been about their side of things, as it were, hoping that they wouldn't get fed up, so I'm very happy about it. They don't have any kind of down-in-the-dumps attitude at all, they just keep themselves busy and get on with the job.

Q: How has your own driving been this year? Do you feel you've lost ground because of not being able to test?

Pryce: No I don't think so. I believe I have gained a lot of experience this year, because although we've been struggling a bit, it doesn't really affect my driving. I mean, if you start backing off, accepting that you've got no chance of actually winning, maybe, then your driving will certainly change. So you can't afford to do that, and I've been trying as hard as ever, as if the car was fully competitive. I haven't been in Formula 1 long enough to get blasé about it, and I'll try hard in anything.

When we first raced the DN8, people came up to me and congratulated me on "going better." Now that really annoyed me. Because the DN5 went downhill compared to the new cars coming out, they must've thought that I went downhill too. That's just not the case. It's very rare that a driver loses his ability, it just doesn't happen often, and certainly my driving, in my opinion anyway, has stayed about the same. The car is better, and perhaps even my driving is a little bit better too, because I've gained a lot of experience over the past year or so.

Additionally, as the DN5 became less competitive I had to try all the more in order to get the maximum out of it, and my driving must've benefited from that. If you're up at the front — so I'm told! — it's often the case that you don't have to drive 100%. In the midfield, of course, you do, to try and claw your way up there.

Like at Brands Hatch in the Race of Champions last year, I had to drive hard at first, but as soon as I was in the lead I backed off straightaway. I was able just to watch my pit signals and know that if a challenge came, I had something in reserve. It was a nice feeling, but I don't think it taught me much.

Mind you, in Formula 1 that's been the only time I've been in that position, and I must say that I could see a danger of losing my rhythm and perhaps some of my concentration. I felt I had to keep concentrating hard even though I wasn't trying as much as before, so that I could quickly get back into my rhythm if the challenge ever did materialize from behind.

Q: Tell me about the change in your driving style. You used to be kind of on the ragged edge of disaster all the time. Then, at last year's French Grand Prix, you sort of "came down." Now you seem to be throwing the car around a lot again.

Pryce: Well. I don't think I throw it sideways as much as I used to. At Zandvoort I did, but that was just because we were understeering a lot in the slow stuff, and I had to. In the old days I used to get it sideways and really enjoy myself, and scrub off speed until I almost came to a stop. Now I try to strike a sort of happy medium.

It's something I have learned for myself and which Alan Rees has been telling me all along. It was difficult to make myself stop doing it, but it became easier as I got to get into the feel of a Formula 1 car, as I got to know where it was losing time. Experience, if you like.

Q: It's a matter of sacrificing the pure fun you get out of it for the sake of getting results?

Pryce: Yes. But when it's wet, you can throw it about, and it's fantastic then. I really enjoy it. You can do almost anything you like with the car.

Apart from the wet races, I must say that I don't enjoy racing as much as I used. The way Formula 1 is at the moment the car has to be just right, and it doesn't matter how good the driver is, if the car isn't absolutely "so" it will slip down the field. At present, the driver is less important than the car.

It's always changing, of course. Next year or the year after, driver ability might be all-important again, you can never tell what's going to happen. I hope I'll still be racing when that time comes!

Q: What changes do you think will have to occur for that to happen?

RIGHT Shadow put its new DN8 into Pryce's hands at Zandvoort, and instantly a fresh breeze seemed to sweep the team. Finally they had a car designed for the changed realities of the time. *Getty Images/Bernard Cahier*

Pryce: Tires, probably. Tires are very delicate things at the moment, you've got to have just the right kind of tire for the car or you're nowhere. Ten years ago, the tire side of things was that much more flexible, and so the car was too, and driver ability could make the car a winner or not. Now, tire development has reached the stage where you have to drive very delicately, if you like, to get the maximum out of the car, and if you drive the car any harder, it just gets slower. You've got to find a very fine edge of driving.

It's probably almost as hard physically, but mentally I think it's harder now than it was, keeping on that fine edge and showing the restraint to keep the car just right.

It's not all tires, course. There are so many little things which make the car fractions faster, and fractions are so important, because if you're a second off the pace these days it's very bad news indeed. Shock absorbers and spring rates, camber angles, wing angles, whatever you like, they are all very finely critical, and a hell of a lot of minute adjustments go in to make up that vital second. It's incredible, really.

Certainly it's something I'd never dreamt about when I came into Formula 1 two and a half seasons ago. You can't get away with anything! Bloody nuisance, really. When I was driving Atlantic or Formula 2, even if things were a bit out of shape it didn't matter quite that much and you felt, to hell with it, you could get away with things. And if you tried really hard, it was all right, you could get away with the little things.

Q: Are you a good test/development driver?

Pryce: I've got a lot better than I was. It didn't take me long to realize that it is absolutely essential, and I've tried hard to make sure that things are done properly. I don't think I'm the sort of test driver who says, well, we need this kind of spring on this circuit, and this kind of wing angle on that, but I can talk with the designer and tell him precisely what the car is doing. From there it's up to the designer.

If there is really a big problem, probably that's where we go wrong, because just yet I don't always feel that I can say that the car is, say, completely wrong on its front suspension geometry, something like that. All I can say is that the thing is understeering absolutely ridiculously, for example.

Q: Where do you feel you rank among other Formula 1 drivers, and what would it take for you to become a Grand Prix winner on a regular basis?

Pryce: Well! I don't know. I reckon I'm as good as anybody else, I suppose! Otherwise I wouldn't be doing it. I'm in there to win, and I think I can beat anybody in the race. If I didn't think that, I'd be at a psychological disadvantage straightaway, wouldn't I? I'm sure in my own mind that I'll be winning races as soon as we've got the Shadow done up properly and we start getting the breaks. If I don't win races next year I'll be very disappointed indeed.

Q: What does it take to win races?

Pryce: Teamwork. It's all down to team effort. That's why I think it's a bit dodgy changing teams, that's why I hate the idea of leaving Shadow, because you build up a valuable understanding with everybody in the team, and you get to know how everybody works and how they work best. If you've got a good relationship going, you're halfway there. Then you've got to get the car just right, and then it's down to the driver. If there's any one element of the team effort missing, and you win a race under those conditions, it's got to be something of a fluke.

Q: Do you have the ability to think coolly and analytically when you're in a racing car?

Pryce: Whenever I'm racing, even in a dice, I feel completely at ease. I can't tell you why, but I always feel that there's plenty of time, and I never get irrational about any situation.

Monza was very satisfying for me because, although I knew I had an understeer problem with the car and I was very far back, I was catching up slowly. James Hunt was behind me, but he had a problem getting past John Watson, and he wasn't catching me as quickly as I had thought he would. I could see them in my mirrors and I thought, well, there's going to be a bit of a dice on here, we might be able to tow each other further up towards the front. But after James did get by John he was a bit faster than me down the straight, so he got past me.

But after that, after he came off, I caught up to Stuck and Andretti. After Mario had passed Hans, I was right up behind and he was looking in his mirrors all over the place, didn't know where he was. When he hit Mario, it was because of my presence just behind. He made the mistake because of the pressure I was able to put on to him. So then I had a clear road in front of me — great! Reutemann was way, way in front of me and I thought, hell, this is going to take forever, but I plugged away at it and eventually I got him. Just tenths and tenths, very satisfying, even though I knew that I could never catch the leaders.

Q: Have you had other races as satisfying this year?

Pryce: Oh yes. The thing is that I always seem to go better in the races than I do in qualifying. In practice, I change the little things on the car as much as I can, but the result is often that we don't have the time to do our really fast lap. Alan Rees tells me we spend too much time getting the car just right. As I've said it is so important, but we must make more effort to get our good time. Alan is absolutely right, because although we have passed people and made up places, we started races too far back to make a proper showing.

Q: What are Alan's strengths as a team manager?

Pryce: Oh, he's good. He's taught me a lot. He pushes the

BELOW Fellow Welshman and former fellow driver Alan Rees was just the man to coax the best out of the brilliant Tom Pryce. *Dan R. Boyd*

important things forward until you're sick of hearing about them, but that's terrific, and he's perfectly right about all of them. I've been trying to change myself to fit in with those things, and it's worked out. Every time I used to drive sideways and had a good laugh, I was told off roundly. I refused to believe what he was saying for a while, but now it's got through I realize he's been right all the time. So he's got determination.

And he works very coolly under pressure, and can take the right decisions calmly. These sort of things go to make up the ideal manager, and of course he's been a very fast race driver himself. That's a help, but Alan can also keep pace with the changes in racing and the different demands on driving. We talk about the car, and it's as though he's been out there too, he understands everything I say about it.

Q: How are you getting along with your new designer, Dave Wass?

Pryce: Dave has done a lot recently. We had a lot of problems with the old car because it wouldn't work under the new regulations, so he changed the rear suspension and it worked much better straightaway. He's been making the DN8 better all the time, and I'm looking forward to finding out what he can do with an all-new car when the time comes. He certainly works well on modifications to the DN8.

Q: You think the DN8 is going to be good next year?

Pryce: It needs to be lighter, and we need the proper financial backing for it. But if we do get the backing, and Dave carries on like he's been doing, we're going to be OK.

Q: What is Don Nichols's role in the team?

Pryce: He's the boss!

Q: You mean he tells you what to do?

Pryce: No, nothing like that! He comes to the racing because he loves it. His team seems to be everything to him. Don doesn't interfere on team decisions with Alan, but he looks after the financial side of it, things like that, together with Jackie Oliver. Don only involves himself in major decisions, like new cars, that sort of decision.

ABOVE Dave Wass stepped into Tony Southgate's shoes when the DN8 designer temporarily moved to Lotus. His primary expertise was in gearboxes, but his attention now turned to aerodynamic development of the new Shadow. *Revs Institute for Automotive Research/Ove Nielsen*

Q: Have you had any particularly disappointing races this year?

Pryce: Well, yes, all of them! The whole year has been disappointing to me, because I really expected to win one or two races this year. As it has been, everybody has tried very hard, and we finished seventh or eighth. That's very disappointing. It doesn't affect my enjoyment of actually racing, but I want to win. I'm fed up, now, with being a midfield runner.

Q: Do you actually enjoy racing for the sake of it? When you get into the car, do have a sense of enjoyment?

Pryce: Oh yes. That's why I do it. Because it's very exciting, and can be very satisfying. It's fantastic, and I couldn't do anything else and get so much pleasure.

CHAPTER 15
A LAST YEAR, AT LAST A WIN

SHADOW DN6B (F5000), 1976

DESPITE BRAVE HOPES at the outset, the SCCA couldn't get its sports car public enthused about open-wheelers. Nor was the partnership with USAC bringing much to the road circuits, apart from the impressive presence of Al Unser.

So looking into the next year, the club decided to try something else. We'll talk more about that later. Meanwhile, ironically, this final year of the F5000 championship gave road racing fans some terrific races! As well as Unser and Oliver, series strongmen Redman, Jones, Ongais, Schuppan, Brown, Gethin, Pilette, Lewis, Lunger, Kroll, McKitterick, Posey, Cannon, Tambay and others figured in the results.

Still, not enough fans came to watch. Low crowd counts early on discouraged other promoters and some cancelled their events. Road America slightly alleviated that by stepping up with a second race weekend, but when all was done the 1976 championship embraced only seven rounds. At least they were action-packed.

POCONO, PENNSYLVANIA (USA)
F5000 (R1), May 9th, 1976
1st, Brian Redman, Lola T332C-Chevrolet
DNF, Jackie Oliver, Shadow DN6B-Dodge,
   insufficient laps

When Shadow's primary sponsor shut off its "money pump," the American operation may have been hit harder than the one in Europe. Don Nichols was never one to just quit, but as in Northampton, he had to put Elk Grove Village on short rations while he and Jackie Oliver beat bushes for benefactors.

Payroll cuts cost the team its able manager, Mike Hillman, along with several other important people, but at least long-time engine man Lee Muir stayed on, working with remaining financial supporter Dodge. So did chief mechanic Ed Stone, who had joined late the previous year and immediately made significant improvements to the car. That work continued into the new year, resulting in enough

ABOVE Striking car strikes a pose: a freshly fettled Shadow-Dodge on a patch of grass outside the raceshop in Elk Grove Village. Although under new livery, it's still the F1-based DN6 chassis of the year before, but the team feels detail improvements warrant calling it a 6B. One that's apparent is the shroud enclosing the flank-mounted engine cooler. *Don Nichols collection*

alterations to warrant adding a "B" to the DN6 designation.

Short on people, parts and time, the Shadow-Dodge F5000 team rolled into Pocono with one driver, one car, and one fresh engine. Wearing his race driver's hat, Oliver performed well: he qualified fourth and was holding third place in his heat when a connecting rod failed. The sole replacement Dodge on site had only been assembled; there hadn't been time to test it on the dyno.

The midday engine swap went well enough, but with the black-and-white-and-multicolored machine in place on the back of the grid fuel started leaking out. Fixing a failed fuel pump seal made Ollie five laps late in starting. Though hopelessly behind when he joined the race, he found himself in company with the leaders, Lola drivers Danny Ongais and Brian Redman, and was able to stay with them. Unfortunately, he couldn't rack up enough laps to be an official finisher.

BELOW At first glance Dodge's engine could be mistaken for Chevrolet's, given that in both cases the center exhaust ports are adjacent and the ignition/fuel injection modules are at the backs of the blocks (Ford engines wear theirs at the front, and their exhausts are evenly spaced). But the Chrysler product is physically bulkier and heavier than GM's. *Dan R. Boyd*

A LAST YEAR, AT LAST A WIN

ABOVE Pace lap at Mosport is led by Brian Redman on pole (white Lola entered by Carl Haas and prepared by Chaparral) and Alan Jones, who will win this round (red Lola of Teddy Yip's Theodore Racing). Oliver's Shadow starts fourth, alongside Danny Ongais (black Interscope Lola). *Motorsport Images/LAT*

RIGHT In a brilliant drive Ollie passes Brian (trailing here at Moss corner) and forges on up to lead the race until nearly the end. *Dan R. Boyd*

MOSPORT, ONTARIO (CDN)
F5000 (R2), June 20th, 1976
1st, Alan Jones, Lola T332-Chevrolet
2nd, Jackie Oliver, Shadow DN6B-Dodge

Nearly two months' worth of work in the Shadow shop resulted in a much fresher look at Mosport. The DN6 now justified its "B" designation, thanks to numerous mods including revised suspension settings, springs and roll bars, plus relocation of the hip radiators a little forward to fine-tune weight distribution. The stock of race-ready Dodge V8s was strong now as well.

Oliver again qualified fourth fastest, and actually speared into the race lead early on. Then, racing luck: just five laps from the finish Ollie got caught behind slower traffic, and the lurking Alan Jones snatched away the win.

WATKINS GLEN, NEW YORK (USA)
F5000 (R3), July 11th, 1976
1st, Alan Jones, March 76A-Chevrolet
DNF, Jackie Oliver, Shadow DN6B-Dodge, engine

Oliver qualified third this weekend, and once again led the race — by more than a minute at one point. But he didn't finish it this time. On a day of ever-changing weather, wet to dry to full flood, conditions that had seemingly everyone spinning, including rainmaster Oliver, he ran over an aggressive curb bordering an awkward new chicane. The impact cracked the engine's sump and all the oil bled away.

ROAD AMERICA, WISCONSIN (USA)
F5000 (R4), July 25th, 1976
1st, Jackie Oliver, Shadow DN6B-Dodge

Yes! Savor it: the Shadow finally won overall! And it was a good win, especially so after Oliver's heat race was ruined by two problems.

ABOVE The Shadow is looking good at The Glen until the rains begin. *Dan R. Boyd*

BELOW AT LAST! It all comes together at Road America. *Dan R. Boyd*

ABOVE Glistening in the summer sunshine, the DN6B's F1 pedigree shines bright. Fundamentally a DN5 from 1975, it retains the original sheetmetal dash structure subsequently outlawed for GP racing. But the compact Cosworth that was meant to nestle neatly in the back has been muscled aside by a honkin' great Detroit V8. *Tom Schultz*

BELOW What perfect timing for the engine brand, finally writ large on the car that breaks a certain rival's long domination of F5000. *Tom Schultz*

One was poor traction coming out of turns, which handicapped his chase of "The Flyin' Hawaiian" Danny Ongais. Trying hard anyway caused Ollie's second problem: the front tire he deflated by bashing a curb. That meant he was a distant 14th on the grid for the Final race.

He didn't stay back there. Miraculously, with one of those last-minute, desperate fixes race mechanics shouldn't do, crew chief Stone tried pouring in a different grade of gearbox oil. Magic. Its previously slipping differential locker now driving both tires as it should, the Dodge V8 could get all its power down to the road and the Shadow could charge away from the turns strong and true.

Methodically moving up the line on Road America's long straights, Oliver reached third place on lap 16. Just nine to go. He only needed three of them to roar past Lola men Al Unser and Brian Redman into the lead. And there for once he stayed. His cushion over Unser was five seconds at the checkered flag.

LEFT Hang on a minute, lass, that's meant to be shaken and sprayed! Happily, Vern Schuppan may yet reach in and save the day. *Dan R. Boyd*

As Big Al watched Ollie go away ahead, the Indy champ from New Mexico might have rued a friendly remark he made to the Englishman before the race. "Hey, looks like your locker isn't locking."

It was the first time in five years that anything other than a Chevrolet had won a US F5000 race. And less than a year after a certain locally based sponsor had ripped its logo off the Shadows.

MID-OHIO (USA)
F5000 (R5), August 8th, 1976
1st, Brian Redman, Lola T332C-Chevrolet
2nd, Jackie Oliver, Shadow DN6B-Dodge

Using his spare car, which the team had set up to suit the endless swerves of this writhing, hilly circuit, Oliver started fifth in the Final. Poleman Redman pulled away on his own, while a tight battle developed for second place between Unser, Oliver and Ongais. So hot was their pace that 11 laps from the end Al went a little wide over a hillcrest and touched the grass. Jackie jumped on his brakes, just missed the Lola by inches, then hit the throttle in time to stay ahead of Danny O to the flag.

BELOW Those Spy Eyes! Mid-Ohio's different car wears different livery along with slight differences in its side radiator placement and ducting. *Revs Institute for Automotive Research/ Geoffrey Hewitt*

ABOVE Shadow again races the newer car at Road America's August race. Although it's hard to make out in this picture — see, black really can disappear in a camera — the coolers are not wearing the shrouds so evident in June. (Thanks to our photographer for pointing it out.) *Tom Schultz*

ROAD AMERICA, WISCONSIN (USA)
F5000 (R6), August 28th, 1976
1st, Brian Redman, Lola T332C-Chevrolet
DNF, Jackie Oliver, Shadow DN6B-Dodge, ignition

What a waste of a weekend. Yes, kudos to the circuit for filling one of F5000's yawning schedule gaps by offering a second race, but in fact it was a secondary race. Held on Saturday, it was only 20 laps long. Redman scored his third victory of the six races so far. Oliver suffered his second retirement when of all the silly things the ignition switch shorted out on lap 7. Until that instant he had been in the running for the series championship.

Jackie was still aboard the Mid-Ohio car, because the team decided his regular one, winner here in July, was "getting old and worn out." Forthrightly, the mechanics also admitted that racing the old DN4 sports car at Mosport the weekend before — successful though it had been — stole away much of their F5000 prep time (see pages 255–258).

The prep problem was only proven again on Sunday, when Oliver participated in the weekend's Main Event: this was a strange, rather desperate attempt to boost spectator interest in F5000 by staging a "handicap" race that counted nothing for the championship. So another Shadow retirement didn't really count against its series record.

About this "handicap," Australian Vern Schuppan came out tops with a Lola entered by Dan Gurney.

RIVERSIDE, CALIFORNIA (USA)
F5000 (R7), October 17th, 1976
1st, Al Unser, Lola T332-Chevrolet
2nd, Jackie Oliver, Shadow DN6B-Dodge

Two months later, near enough, the Circus gathered one last time to find out who was

ABOVE That's the stuff. Big Al may be a cowboy from Albuquerque, but he knows how to show proper reverence to a bottle of bubbly. *Motorsport Images/David Phipps*

going to be champion, Redman or Unser. Though Oliver was out of that running, his faithfully hard-working team at least gave him a good-looking runner. For its last-ever important race, the Shadow was refurbished, repainted and polished to gleaming magnificence. And for once the transporter was well stocked with fresh engines.

During his heat race Oliver was chasing Redman hard, so hard that with two laps to go Brian missed a gearchange and Jackie slipped by to win. That put the Shadow on the front row of the Final alongside Unser. The Vel's Parnelli Lola man turned out to be uncatchable, though, leaving Ollie to take second place a dozen seconds behind. That's right, yet another race finish for the DN6B-Dodge, and the driver's third second place of the series.

Shadowfans could only look at their man's several good performances gone down the drain to mechanical failures and shake their heads.

By carefully taking third place, Brian Redman clinched his third series championship, with 132 points to Unser's 112 and Oliver's 108. Let's save a cheer for Big Al. As noted by *Autosport*, "In many ways one could regard Unser as the moral champion of the series, for having missed the opening two rounds the American ace has accumulated more points in the remaining five events than anyone else."

SO ENDED THE SCCA's two-year attempt to rekindle the glory of its dearly departed old Can-Am by replacing those big, powerful, technically exotic and spiritually unlimited sports racing machines with tightly restricted open-wheel Formula vehicles with much smaller engines. Loud, fast, close racing, yes, but not the same thing at all.

The Club's next idea? Drape F5000 single-seaters with ersatz "sports car" bodies and call it Can-Am II. Sure, it's all about the style with road-racing enthusiasts. Substance doesn't matter. Does it? ♣

CHAPTER 16
FROM BLACK TO LIGHT

SHADOW DN8 (F1), 1977

Though its birth was delayed and its youth troubled, this machine would turn out to be Shadow's most significant racing car. Designed by Tony Southgate and further developed by his able assistant Dave Wass, it's the one that presented the marque its one and only Grand Prix victory.

When Nichols and co. abruptly lost their major sponsor for 1976, they had to drastically scale back plans for Shadow's fourth F1 season. A new car was needed, mostly because of evolving tire requirements, and Southgate had been working one up, but funding shortfalls delayed construction of what was to be called the DN8.

While waiting for it, as explained earlier, the struggling team updated the previous year's cars into DN5Bs to meet new safety and bodywork regulations, but budget constraints meant the alterations could rarely be tested outside of actual race meetings.

Meanwhile, the DN8 taking shape on the drafting table was a further step in evolution of Southgate's line of prior Shadows, but quite significantly so. The driver sat noticeably farther forward, the front suspension now had swept-back rocker arms (although this could be altered), and the pair of radiators, still riding outdoors on the sides of the chassis, were oriented differently, almost lying down flat on first impression.

In contrast, the nose of the car looked the same, with twin nostrils admitting air to cool the engine oil.

Here's how Tony has described the vehicle long years afterward, first in a quote from his own book:

"The front end of the DN8 was virtually the same as the DN5, the main differences being the side water radiator layout and the aerodynamics. The water radiators were turned through 90° and then angled downwards at the front in a stepped-wedge configuration, the idea being to produce a low-pressure region behind the water radiator for ground effect while providing water cooling at the same time. It worked, but only produced modest improvements in downforce. It needed

ABOVE Life can be lonely at the front, and glad of it Alan Jones is. What a majestic day, the first Grand Prix victory for both himself and his employer Don Nichols. And in fact AJ is hardly "alone" as he sweeps down around the Österreichring's final curve on his way into history.
Motorsport Images/LAT

a full skirt system, which had not been invented then, so I had settled for sheets of polypropylene bolted to the lower edges of the ducting panels." This was prior to Tony's time away at Lotus, where he would really learn about ground-effects aerodynamics.

Subsequently, he kindly answered our request for further information:

"The cockpit was the same on the DN5 and DN8. The big difference was that the fuel tank behind the driver was much longer. The DN5 had fuel in the sides and a small tank behind the driver, the DN8 had its fuel behind the driver. This meant that the wheelbase was increased. The F1 cars were getting longer for this very reason (nowadays they are massive).

"This meant I had to move the side-mounted water radiators, etc., to correct the weight distribution. I did not want to use gearbox spacers on this car as the wheelbase was quite long, so changed the front rockers instead. I angled the outer part of the rocker forward or backwards by 2 inches to increase or reduce the wheelbase. This would achieve the same effect as the old gearbox spacers, up to 2 percent weight distribution change.

"The standard [ie DN5] rockers were symmetrical, not leaning forward or backwards."

While redesigning the front end of the chassis, he also repositioned the transverse steering rack from the front face of the monocoque, where it had been on his previous DN chassis, to the top of the tub behind the new rockers, above the driver's ankles.

In the American circle-track jargon we've heard in connection with Peter Bryant's Shadow Mk III, this made the DN8 a "rear-steer" car.

The basic wheelbase came out at 107 inches, same as the DN7, although Southgate has told us he could vary this by swapping front suspension components. Also, photos show the rear wheels were behind the final drive centerline, meaning the halfshafts swept back a little.

Tracks measured 58 inches front, 60 rear.

FROM BLACK TO LIGHT **341**

BELOW Naked and unashamed at Watkins Glen, the final iteration of Shadow's DN8 bares her inner beauty to once-and-once-again Shadow driver Jean-Pierre Jarier. Compared to the DN5 he used to drive, this one is longer, fuel capacity is larger and all centrally located, and radiator positioning is refined for efficiency. This Tech Center shot also is a good look at the relatively new front-cockpit mini-roll bar structure holding Jean-Pierre's instruments. *Revs Institute for Automotive Research/ Geoffrey Hewitt*

Wheel widths were similarly different, 16 and 18 inches respectively, but their diameters were 13 inches all round. As seemed to be the trend, the car's weight was up again, to 1,335 pounds (according to *Autocourse*) while stated capacity of that centralized fuel tank was 50.4 US gallons (42 Imperial gallons or 191 liters). The Ford-Cosworth DFV would drink it at a rate between 6½ to a little over 7 mpg (US).

Southgate remained faithful to Hewland's experimental TL200 gearbox; in that, he remained alone among his colleagues.

In the DN8's debut iteration, during the latter part of 1976, at first glance it looked like a top-heavy DN5. The twin-nostril, scooped nosepiece was familiar, but because the driver sat more forward the rise of the cockpit cowl was more prominent. Behind the cockpit, two scoops looking like mouse ears peeked out either side to invite air into the engine. Down below, the appearance of Southgate's "stepped wedge" radiators took some getting used to.

By that time, of course, Tony was 120 miles away in Norwich as chief designer of Colin Chapman's forthcoming Lotus 78 — the first "wing car." Back in Northampton, through that fall and winter Dave Wass kept toiling away on the DN8. When the car came out to race again in 1977, at Argentina and Brazil, it looked quite different.

SHADOW'S 1977 F1 SEASON

This was a season of sadness for Shadow, brightened by a single moment of joy. For the second time Don Nichols lost one of his great drivers. But another earned the team's first Grand Prix victory. Its only one.

Then at the end of the year most of Shadow's key personnel walked out to form their own competing team, Arrows.

Nichols, a flawed man but an unflagging one,

LEFT Posing now in the pitlane, the DN8 reveals the all-but-level front oil radiator, and the stout steering rack housing across the driver's footwell. Harder to make out from this angle is the swept-back angle of the suspension rockers, but the deep air conduits between fuselage and radiator pods are plain to see. *Revs Institute for Automotive Research/ Karl Ludvigsen*

carried on through an ever-darkening storm, with challenges mounting on every side and his small, dwindling team coping with ever too few resources. Sponsors changed, drivers changed, designers and crew changed, the cars changed — again and again. What didn't seem to change was luck. Or not often enough.

When the same Shadows used in 1976 first rolled out in South America to start 1977's campaign, their black paint made them look familiar, even if a second glance showed many changes. Only team leader Tom Pryce's car still bore the red-and-blue upper body colors of its tobacco sponsor — but the company name itself was missing. On the pair of old DN5Bs available to his new team-mate, one Renzo Zorzi, those colors were gone entirely.

All three cars in South America wore only one corporate name, Ambrosio. Franco Ambrosio was a businessman from Naples who made his fortune in the Italian pasta industry, where he was known as the King of Grain. In later years his fraudulent business practices would send him to prison, and his life would end by murder, but all that lay in the unknowable future when he made a deal with Nichols to sponsor a seat for an Italian driver.

In future years the Shadowman did not recall his new benefactor with the same warmth he expressed for his friend Heinrich Villiger, but he did take the extra money.

Ambrosio's first driver, Zorzi, had won Monaco's prestigious Formula 3 race in 1975. To team managers at the time this suggested he had promise for F1, but a handful of subsequent drives with Williams and Wolf didn't really show it. Nor was Shadow any step up for Zorzi. His career would rise no higher.

Pryce, of course, was widely thought to be on his way to superstardom.

As the GP circus gathered at the Galvez circuit in Buenos Aires, Nichols was once again the only American F1 team owner. Both Parnelli and Penske were gone after a mere three years.

FROM BLACK TO LIGHT **343**

ABOVE At season's start in Argentina, Tom Pryce's DN8 is still in its 1976 color scheme. Its original ducted front oil cooler remains as before, but the formerly exposed side radiators have grown enclosures.
Motorsport Images/Ercole Colombo

Expanded to 17 Grands Prix, the 1977 F1 calendar offered only one non-championship outing, the annual Race of Champions at Brands Hatch.

ARGENTINE GP
Buenos Aires, F1 (R1), January 9th, 1977
1st, Jody Scheckter, Wolf WR1
NC, Tom Pryce, Shadow DN8
DNF, Renzo Zorzi, Shadow DN5B, gearbox

Over winter Dave Wass had narrowed the rear track on Tom Pryce's DN8, and also deleted the engine airscoop "ears" behind the cockpit. The Ford-Cosworth DFV now lay exposed to the world, breathing through an air filter atop the injector horns. Guiding air into the side-mounted, lay-back engine coolers were long, boxy ducts rather than the various arrays of vanes and fences tried the year before.

Tom was pleased with his familiar car's upgraded suspension, but during practice its revised radiator layout wasn't doing the job on this hot weekend, and misfiring led to an engine change before the race. His grid place was a lowly 12th, more than two seconds behind new world champ James Hunt's McLaren on pole. Three further rows back was Renzo Zorzi, also slowed with overheating in both of the DN5Bs he drove in practice. These cars retained the old radiator style, so the temperature gremlin must have lurked elsewhere.

Pryce's race started strongly, and he was up to seventh place two laps from the start. But abruptly he lost three spots trying to overtake local hero Carlos Reutemann, who was racing for Ferrari this year. Mid-race the DN8 pitted for a gear-shifting problem to be investigated, and by the time Tom rejoined he had lost eight laps. That rendered him Not Classified as a finisher, though he took the flag ninth. Poor Zorzi's day was even shorter. His gearbox refusing to shift, he was first to retire after just two laps.

BRAZILIAN GP

Interlagos, F1 (R2), January 23rd, 1977
1st, Carlos Reutemann, Ferrari 312T2
6th, Renzo Zorzi, Shadow DN5B
DNF, Tom Pryce, Shadow DN8, engine

Holy smokes! Pryce started a mediocre 12th again, but soared up the chart and was running along in second place late in the race!

In the two weeks since Argentina his DN8 had had its front suspension arms swapped, changing their sweep angle to bring the wheels forward about an inch. This seemed to improve the car's handling balance, and Tom's qualifying time actually beat the previous year's fastest, set by James Hunt for McLaren, by a quarter of a second. So even though Hunt, on pole again, was even faster by more than two seconds, the Shadow lead driver reportedly was looking forward to a good race.

As for Zorzi, having gotten a (short) race under his belt, he looked more at home, although the aged DN5B was sticking its throttles as well as handling poorly. Renzo took the grid 18th, four and a half seconds slower than Hunt.

Under another ferociously hot sun, the race got underway on a very abrasive track surface thanks to rain washing it overnight. Immediately Pryce started moving up the charts, soon reaching eighth and continuing to advance as faster cars broke down or crashed out. With just seven laps to go the black-and-blue-and-red Shadow was holding second place. If race leader Carlos Reutemann, his Ferrari way out ahead by 40 seconds, happened to join the list of retirements…

But it was Pryce who retired, his Ford-Cosworth DFV blowing a mere seven laps from the end.

On the other side of that coin, Zorzi's all-black car kept going all the way and placed sixth, giving himself, Don Nichols and Shadow a World Championship point.

BELOW New Shadowman Renzo Zorzi is driving an older DN5B in Brazil, but a return to Basic Black lends an oddly nostalgic-yet-updated air.
Motorsport Images/LAT

BELOW Brand-new B-spec car stands waiting for Pryce in South Africa. New designer Dave Wass has further developed the aerodynamic concept originally penned by his predecessor, Tony Southgate. Seeking lower drag, he has replaced the single oil cooler in the nose with a pair behind the front wheels, completely altered the water radiator positioning and ducting, and designed a new pattern of induction airbox atop the engine. Also of note is the long, flexible air skirt along the bottom. The chassis has been lightened as well. Right now, all this looks promising. *Motorsport Images/David Phipps*

SOUTH AFRICAN GP
Kyalami, F1 (R3), March 5th, 1977
1st, Niki Lauda, Ferrari 312T2
DNF, Tom Pryce, Shadow DN8B, fatal accident
DNF, Renzo Zorzi, Shadow DN8B, engine

Two DN8s appeared for the first time, now revised into "B" specification. First thing to strike the eye was their bright new livery: gone was Nichols's Basic Black "color scheme" in favor of glistening, gleaming white. Artfully draped over a new, fuller, more curvaceous aerodynamic shape, ribbons of blue set off the single primary sponsor's name, Ambrosio.

Dave Wass had developed the new bodywork in a plumper but smoother, more bullet-like style, aiming to make the car faster on straights. The front-mounted engine oil cooler was gone, meaning the twin-nostril nose inlets and top extractor vents had vanished as well, leaving only a slightly curving wedge like an axe blade. To replace the single cooler, two were located in the swelling bodywork just behind the front wheels and positioned to exhaust laterally, rather like the configuration on Southgate's DN2 Can-Am car. Of course that fed some hot air directly into the engine radiators a few feet aft, but racecars are all about compromise.

The body swell carried on past the cockpit cowling, making that look smaller while also forming a smoother, more streamliner-like overall shape. An engine cover with twin-eared induction scoops was back.

Water radiators still lived either side ahead of the rear wheels but now stood upright on one edge and turned lengthwise, with the flat sides facing outward, nearly but not quite parallel to the direction of motion. A combination of inlet duct shaping and high-pressure build-up in front of the tire induced airflow to veer 90 degrees into these radiators. Lest we imply this was a Shadow novelty, we'll point out that the idea appeared in 1975 with Hesketh's 308, designed by Harvey Postlethwaite, then the following year March

346 CHAPTER 16

ABOVE White is not an entirely new look for a Shadow, but it's the first time on a works car since 1971's Mk II. Mr. Phipps's camera angle nicely displays all the DN8B bodywork alterations in aid of airflow. *Motorsport Images/David Phipps*

BELOW Tom's race began slowly, but he recovered and began making up ground. He had time to move up two places from his lowly starting position. *Motorsport Images/David Phipps*

used it on the 761, and by 1977 several other constructors, including Ferrari, had adopted it.

Zorzi stepped into the DN8 that Pryce had been racing, number 1. The team leader took over number 2, a brand-new chassis said to be significantly lighter.

This is the car that Tom drove to the fastest lap on the first day of practice. Encouraging, sure, but it all happened in drenching rain and nobody questioned the friendly Welshman's brilliant car control. When the next day was dry and Tom's engine was soft, his best effort resulted in another lowly grid position, 15th this time. With numerous mechanical troubles of his own, Zorzi was 18th. They were 1.15 and 2.46 seconds back from repeat pole starter Hunt.

On raceday, a Saturday, under threatening skies Pryce had a slow getaway and finished the first lap 22nd with only one car behind. He did immediately begin to make up lost ground, but it was lap 14 before he regained his starting position and could aim to move further up. On

FROM BLACK TO LIGHT **347**

lap 19 he passed the Ligier-Matra of Jacques Laffite to take 13th.

Four laps later he was hot on the tail of Hans Stuck's March as they powered uphill out of Lion's Head turn and on up the steeply rising pits straight.

Moments before, Pryce's team-mate had pulled his white DN8 off the track opposite the pits, at the crest of the hill on the left-hand side. A fuel line had broken. As Renzo climbed out, there was a quick burst of fire from under the car that hastened his departure. The flames went out immediately, but as the driver went back to the car and reached into the cockpit, apparently to trigger the onboard fire-suppression system, there was a second, quick, temporary burst of fire. As shown in television footage, Zorzi remained alone at the scene up to to this point, with no safety personnel nearby.

So it is understandable — albeit foolish — that across in the pitlane a pair of safety workers impulsively snatched up fire extinguishers, jumped the low wall and ran across the track. One narrowly made it. The other didn't.

Cresting the rise at full throttle came Hans Stuck and Tom Pryce, intent on their duel but probably also glancing at signaling boards to their right. Even if Tom ever saw the human figure pop up in front of him, there was no time to react. The winged prow of the Shadow killed the worker instantly. His heavy fire bottle struck the driver's head.

Unguided, DN8/2A hurtled on down the hill toward Crowthorne corner, veered off track to the right, and rebounded into the path of Laffite's Ligier. Both cars ended up as one heap of junk in the catch fences around the outside of the corner. Laffite was able to get out. Poor Pryce, of course, was lifeless.

Niki Lauda, the winner, was informed of the tragedy literally on the victory rostrum. He and the lost man had been friends. Thus it was impossible find any joy in his first win since his incredible return from the brink of death not eight months before.

RACE OF CHAMPIONS (GB)
Brands Hatch, F1 (non-championship),
    March 20th, 1977
1st, James Hunt, McLaren M23
5th, Jackie Oliver, Shadow DN8B

Two weeks after the Kyalami tragedy, Shadow gave Jackie Oliver a break from team business to drive this sprint event with the only raceable DN8B. Starting seventh of 17, Ollie had *Motor Sport*'s Denis Jenkinson using words like "bravely" and "valiantly" to describe his spirited tussles in the midfield against the likes of Clay Regazzoni and Vittorio Brambilla. The Shadow finally came fifth, one place higher than it would have been if Mario Andretti's otherwise dominant Lotus had not shut off its own electrics six laps from the finish.

UNITED STATES WEST GP
Long Beach, F1 (R4), April 3rd, 1977
1st, Mario Andretti, Lotus 78
DNF, Alan Jones, Shadow DN8B, gearbox
DNF, Renzo Zorzi, Shadow DN8B, gearbox

This was the 20th Formula 1 Grand Prix of the USA, and it marked the day when an American driver finally won America's premier international race. Mario Andretti seized it with relentless desire tempered with patient maturity, keeping the fangs of his Lotus clamped remorselessly on the gearbox of Jody Scheckter's Wolf even as the Ferrari of Niki Lauda came howling at his heels. For 76 laps the wily winner of the Indy 500 and the previous year's Japanese GP waited and watched, refusing to make any mistakes of his own, until with four laps to go he saw his opening and pounced. Lauda followed him through and the trio crossed the finish line nose to tail.

Local observers credit Andretti's stirring victory for making this street race the talk of the nation, thereby saving it from what had looked like certain financial collapse.

Elsewhere in the pitlane, America's only Grand Prix team was facing money problems. Sponsor Villiger's name was missing this weekend. Shadow had spent the month since Kyalami selecting and signing a strong new shoe in Alan Jones. A second-generation racer from Australia, Jones had two prior years in F1 with three different teams resulting in four points-paying finishes, his best a fourth in Japan with Surtees in 1976. Aged 30, he had the experience needed to step into a team seeking stability.

As a prospect for future stardom, though, it must be said that Jones was not regarded at the time as a future World Champion. Wrong.

"AJ's" DN8B was a new car, chassis 3. To prepare him, the car and the mechanics for Long Beach, Shadow accompanied the Wolf team out to Riverside, where they set up artificial turns mimicking the tight going of the city's street circuit. Once at the real place, Alan uncovered troubles with the fuel system,

ABOVE Ollie gets his groove on one more time at Brands, guiding Shadow's single raceworthy DN8B to a result that probably gives himself as much of a lift as it does the grieving team. *Motorsport Images/LAT*

LEFT Fresh car, fresh driver, rather too familiar result. Settling into his new office at Long Beach, Alan Jones must privately nurse the ambitions that all racers do, but first there's the matter of organizing his workspace, getting to know the staff, seeing what can be done with the resources at hand. Too early to think of winning a race, of course. Yes, silly thought. *Motorsport Images/LAT*

FROM Black TO LIGHT **349**

the transmission and the handling, winding up 14th on the grid, 1.4 seconds slower than Lauda's Ferrari. Team-mate Zorzi qualified a further 1.3 seconds and four rows back.

It's speculation, but as they all lined up to start the race, former Shadowman Jean-Pierre Jarier may have taken some little satisfaction in seeing them both in the mirrors of his secondhand Penske car.

On the opening lap all of them escaped a chain-reaction crash that sent James Hunt flying into stardom on front pages all around the world. As things returned to normal, Jones got a good scrap going with Emerson Fittipaldi in his family's Copersucar, and finally overtook into sixth place. But the burly Aussie's potential grasp on a championship point was ripped from his fingers by gearbox failure just after half distance. The same malady had already struck down Zorzi just after quarter distance.

Jarier? He finished sixth.

BELOW Hurtling over the sharp drop from Pine Avenue, Jones moves from his entirely expected 14th starting position all the way up to sixth. Not expected at all, and there's still half the race to go. Plenty of time to move up further. Or not.
Motorsport Images/Ercole Colombo

SPANISH GP
Jarama, F1 (R5), May 9th, 1977
1st, Mario Andretti, Lotus 78
DNF, Alan Jones, Shadow DN8B, accident
DNF, Renzo Zorzi, Shadow DN8B, engine

"It is a long time since one man so completely dominated a Grand Prix meeting as Mario Andretti at Jarama," began the *Autosport/Autocourse* account of this race, when the American launched his Lotus from pole and led every lap to win by almost 16 seconds from Carlos Reutemann's Ferrari.

Our Shadowmen were not so impressive. Villiger's Tabatip branding was back, but there was no obvious improvement in speed. Gridding 14th again, Jones was over two seconds slower than Mario in his revolutionary ground-effects Lotus 78. Yet Alan seemed happy, noted the report. "The genial Australian was thoroughly enjoying life with his new team. 'This year, I actually find myself looking forward to

350 CHAPTER 16

ABOVE Shadow's "Streamliner" makes its one and only appearance in Spain, eyed by a fellow at the left who looks a lot like actor Gene Hackman — an enthusiastic friend of the team. Compared to Jones's regular car beyond, 17T carries both its oil and water radiators toward the rear, while the engine breathes air ducted from the front of a reprofiled cockpit cowl. Nothing will come of this experiment, other than more work toward a better solution. *Grand Prix Photo (Peter Nygaard)*

practice sessions!'" He added that the team had improved the handling, and now was looking for more traction.

A new DN8 variant dubbed the "Streamliner" briefly appeared, but Jones ran only a single practice lap in it. Dave Wass had relocated the engine oil coolers farther back along the body sides, just forward of the water radiators. From the shaping of the surrounding bodywork it appears air was to blow inward, the opposite of the way it went in their former location behind the front suspension. This change appeared to clean up airflow between front wheels and fuselage.

There was also a new engine cover devoid of scoops, leaving the airflow over it unmolested. How was the engine to breathe? Via a pair of triangular openings near the front of the cockpit cowling. Ferrari used the same notion on its contemporary 312T2.

Meantime the hapless Zorzi was seen to be working very hard for his lowly 24th starting slot. Worse for his morale, it was already known that he was driving his last race. Franco Ambrosio wanted to try another Italian prospect.

Poor Renzo only had to endure the humility for 25 laps before his engine died. Alan, meanwhile, was boosting himself up to eighth place and trying to make it seventh by passing Ronnie Peterson in the Tyrrell six-wheeler. But SuperSwede's defense was as resolute as the Aussie's attack. It ended on lap 56 with a collision that sent the Shadow into the fence.

MONACO GP
Monte Carlo, F1 (R6), May 22nd, 1977
1st, Jody Scheckter, Wolf WR1
6th, Alan Jones, Shadow DN8B
9th, Riccardo Patrese, Shadow DN8B

AJ finally scored that elusive point in Monte Carlo, where in fact both DN8Bs made it to the finish flag for the first time this year.

RIGHT Nichols's new driver Riccardo Patrese joins up at Monaco and immediately boosts the no. 16 car to speeds it hasn't seen before. *Motorsport Images/David Phipps*

BELOW New boy Patrese has bent his canard but still he keeps old boy Ickx at bay thoughout the entire grueling GP. *Motorsport Images/David Phipps*

ABOVE Jones takes his first GP championship point in the mean streets of Monte Carlo. *Motorsport Images/LAT*

Riccardo Patrese was Shadow's new driver. Just turned 23, he had already won championships in karting and Formula 3, and in 1977 was racing F2 when Shadow's opening also came his way. Monaco's cramped street circuit has always been a tough place to learn about F1, and at the time starting grids were limited there. The cap was 20 this year, meaning half a dozen drivers wouldn't qualify for the Grand Prix.

So it was immediately impressive to see the young Italian make 15th best time, only half a second slower than his team-mate's 11th and 1.66 seconds behind the Brabham-Alfa Romeo that John Watson put on pole.

Both Shadowmen went on to race solidly, Jones staying on the winner's lap to finish sixth despite having to nurse fading brakes. Patrese did go one lap down, but showed skill and confidence while holding off an Ensign in the vastly experienced hands of Jacky Ickx through the whole 79 laps.

BELGIAN GP
Zolder, F1 (R7), June 5th, 1977
1st, Gunnar Nilsson, Lotus 78
5th, Alan Jones, Shadow DN8B
DNF, Riccardo Patrese, Shadow DN8B, accident

In Patrese's second foray with Shadow he qualified higher than Jones, their 15th and 17th respectively being separated by a mere 0.2 second. Again, reporters remarked on newcomer Riccardo's confidence in the cockpit as well as the precision of his driving. But Old Man Alan was happy, for once offering no complaints about the car. "No, really I'm entirely happy with it, handling, traction, everything," he was quoted. Both Shadows had slightly revised suspension geometry at Zolder.

Raceday was a miserable experience: dark, cold, windy and wavering between streaming wet through drying and then back to even wetter. It was one of those races where people keeping lap charts were working as hard as those in the cars

FROM Black TO LIGHT 353

just to keep on top of things. For crew, who of course had no radio communications with their drivers, it was not quite two hours of watching, wondering and waiting to see if they suddenly had to spring into action to change tires or whatever.

Another historical benchmark for today's racefan: in rainswept Belgium the 1977 Ferrari mechanics changed Niki Lauda's tires in 18 seconds. One reporter called that "truly fantastic." (Red Bull would astound the world 42 seasons later by swapping Max Verstappen's four wheels in 1.82 seconds.)

At the end of the race it's the driver's performance that matters. While several big names crashed out early, new boy Patrese was doing another good job, getting his DN8B up to eighth place and holding off the likes of Peterson, Regazzoni and Jones, right up until lap 13 when he spun into a guardrail.

Meanwhile, that quiet Jones boy soldiered on with only seven cylinders firing, finished fifth, and did so while staying on the winner's lap — the last man to do so.

SWEDISH GP

Anderstorp, F1 (R8), June 19th, 1977
1st, Jacques Laffite, Ligier-Matra JS7
9th, Jackie Oliver, Shadow DN8B
17th, Alan Jones, Shadow DN8B

Jackie Oliver again got his hands on an F1 car in Sweden, because Patrese had an F2 commitment in Italy. With the new driver came a new rear-wing treatment, the aerofoils fitted with much larger, deeper sideplates to better corral airflow trying to be truculent.

As at Brands Hatch earlier in the year, Ollie did well for one who now raced so rarely. His 16th grid place lined him up alongside Niki Lauda's Ferrari, and he brought the Shadow all the way through the full distance of the race. Alan Jones's GP started better, from 11th grid place, 1.125 seconds slower than fastest man Andretti, but a faulty ignition module cost him five laps in the pits. Mario's day turned out even worse: he was running away with the race when his Lotus ran out of fuel.

But it was a delirious day for winner Jacques

BELOW Well the Race of Champions went alright, let's try a full GP. Oliver stands in for Patrese in Sweden and stands in well. Designer Wass's aero tweak of the week is extended rear wing sideplates. *Motorsport Images/LAT*

Laffite. The French driver came through for French constructor Ligier, sponsored by a French cigarette brand and powered by a French-made Matra V12. This was — amazingly — the very first all-French victory since the very dawn of Grand Prix racing. Which happened way back in 1906. In France.

FRENCH GP
Dijon, F1 (R9), July 3rd, 1977
1st, Mario Andretti, Lotus 78
DNF, Alan Jones, Shadow DN8B, driveshaft
DNF, Riccardo Patrese, Shadow DN8B,
　clutch/engine

Once in France Andretti got back on top, once again starting his Lotus from pole and this time going all the way to the checkers, beating Watson to it on the last lap when the Brabham ran out of fuel. Our own men, Jones and Patrese, started 10th and 15th this time, 1.35 and 1.66 seconds back respectively. Again, Alan's row mate was Niki. Both Shadows were still wearing the big sideplates on their rear wings.

Raceday here in Burgundy wine country was fiercely hot. Both Shadows started wilting, Jones getting left behind by Lauda but fending off Scheckter for eighth until the DN8B broke a driveshaft at three-quarter distance. Patrese was gone long before, having lost his clutch at the start then stopping six laps later with oil spewing from the engine.

BRITISH GP
Silverstone, F1 (R10), July 16th, 1977
1st, James Hunt, McLaren M26
7th, Alan Jones, Shadow DN8B
DNF, Riccardo Patrese, Shadow DN8B,
　fuel pressure

Britain's Golden Boy, the reigning World Champion, had not so far won a Grand Prix this year. James Hunt finally redressed that in fine style here at home, starting his McLaren-Ford from pole and winning by 18 seconds.

However, supporters of Ulster's John Watson will want it remembered that the Brabham-Alfa driver with the soft Irish brogue started from the front row, immediately took the lead of the race, and was maintaining that with apparent equanimity until the Italian flat-12 died of thirst.

Although Shadow was practically a local team, based only 15 miles away in Northampton, it didn't draw quite so much attention. During practice both DN8Bs looked twitchy and also were slow in a straight line — evidently the big rear sideplates weren't achieving desired results. That latter fault was the most crippling, said Riccardo Patrese. "Really, is the main problem. It's oversteering, sure, but balance is not bad. In the straight is slow, and this is a very quick track." By the end of the day the young Italian had only made 25th starting place out of 26. But Aussie Alan Jones took 12th a mere 1.11 seconds slower than Hunt's pole time.

From the start Jones gained or lost one or two places as fortunes fell one way or another, but methodically he stayed the course and wound up seventh. Patrese too stair-stepped up the lap chart early on, but his day's fortunes dropped away along with his fuel pressure after just 20 laps.

GERMAN GP
Hockenheim, F1 (R11), July 31st, 1977
1st, Niki Lauda, Ferrari 312T2
DNF, Riccardo Patrese, Shadow DN8,
　lost wheel
DNF, Alan Jones, Shadow DN8, accident

From the Wagnerian heights of the Nürburgring to the flat expanse of the Upper Rhine Plain, the formerly epic flavor of the German GP was muted. Hockenheim was mostly long, long straights along which a lot of engines screamed their last.

Not Shadow's engines, interestingly. The DN8Bs were fast, close to fastest — but it was artificial speed. To achieve it the mechanics

RIGHT *Fast-forward to Austria. Where Alan Jones is fast. And finally first. Motorsport Images/ David Phipps*

backed the wings down, and the drivers paid the price with skittish handling through the relatively few corners. Their overall lap times were three whole seconds behind fastest qualifier Scheckter's Wolf. By a slight margin the faster Shadow this time was Patrese's, car number 16 forming up 16th on the grid. Jones in 17 was next.

AJ went no further. A starting-light failure caused a start-line pileup, which put no. 17 out on the spot. No. 16 lasted until nearly the finishing flag, but lost a wheel. Patrese was thus stationary when he was placed 10th.

However, amidst the general darkness *chez* Shadow there shone a glimmer of something better — a new DN8 so extensively revised that it was in order to call it a C-model. It was trialed in pre-race testing at Hockenheim as well as one session of practice, but wasn't raced. Not this time.

One alert journo noted that a certain Mr. Southgate seemed to be associated with Shadow at this meeting, although Tony's agreement with Lotus didn't officially conclude until the next day.

AUSTRIAN GP
Österreichring, F1 (R12), August 14th, 1977
1st, Alan Jones, Shadow DN8C
DNF, Arturo Merzario, Shadow DN8B, gearbox

The Big Day! Don Nichols and his troubled team woke up to a dark, rainy morning in the forested mountains of Styria, once again facing the numbing prospect of racing as best they could from the back of the grid.

But that afternoon in dazzling sunshine they celebrated the marque Shadow's very first victory in a World Championship Grand Prix. Along with the first for their new Aussie recruit.

Alan Jones was racing the new C-spec car for the first time, chassis DN8C-4A, understood to be the former "Streamliner" seen briefly in Spain. The energetic Dave Wass had further altered his aerodynamic concept and two novel elements attracted attention.

At the front, a rectangular opening above

FROM BLACK TO LIGHT 357

ABOVE With Patrese away again, Shadow offered his seat to Arturo Merzario. Fitting rain tires for the race works well for him at the start, but a change in the weather spoils that, and mechanical failure ends his day altogether. *Motorsport Images/ Rainer Schlegelmilch*

the axe-blade nosecone showed the oil cooler had come back home — although its bedroom had changed. This lay-flat configuration was also seen on other cars in that period, such as McLaren and Lotus. Toward the rear of the body, its formerly generous swell had given way to deep channels between engine cover and lateral side radiators. This reduced frontal area, and therefore drag, while also improving flow to the rear wing.

What a lot of work was going on within a team struggling to survive hard financial times. Attaboy, boys.

Many reporters and historians have attributed this aero change for the Österreichring — and the apparently consequential victory there — to Tony Southgate, only just returned from his sojourn with Lotus. But the man himself denies it, telling us that he already was focusing primarily on an entirely new Shadow model for the following year.

"There was no miraculous change to the DN8 before going off to the Austrian GP [just ten days after his return]. Dave Wass had spent a lot of time changing bodywork shapes to try and achieve a better straightaway speed, the area the DN8 was weak in [initially]. It was now better in this area, so I could have a closer look at the chassis setup to see how it compared to my latest thinking. I revised the setup a bit and adjusted the aerodynamic setup to suit Austria, that's all.

"Dave, who had taken over as chief designer, was not an aero man. His best area was mechanical design and he was particularly good at gearbox design. [In aerodynamic matters] He would have been pushed quite a bit by Jackie Oliver to follow the trend of other F1 cars that he thought were good. Jackie was like that."

In addition to the drastically revised aero package on the new car, in Austria all the Shadows ran without the big rear-wing sideplates in use since Sweden.

How did aerodynamic theory work in practice? Hard to know, because Jones's attempts to set a best time in the C-spec car kept being foiled by ignition faults, prompting him also to try a previous B-model. Once again he was invisible on the starting grid, 14th. Way up ahead by 1.68 seconds, the host nation's hero, Niki Lauda, would launch his Ferrari from pole. Alongside sat championship rival James Hunt, while third right behind them was the season's third contender, Mario Andretti.

But if it was hard to see Jones, team-mate Patrese wasn't there at all. Apparently team sponsor Ambrosio had been neglecting his sponsorship payments, and Nichols finally ordered the man's brand off the cars. Nichols was still happy with Ambrosio's driver, Patrese, but that duo also had a personal support arrangement and the Italian businessman instructed his Italian protege not to drive in Austria. Riccardo thought he'd better comply.

It wasn't hard to find a stand-in. Italian Arturo Merzario was there with his own March, but he jumped at the chance to give it the weekend off while he got paid to drive a factory car. His new crew had to work to adapt the cockpit to his small physique, but he acclimated readily enough to qualify Patrese's B-spec car 0.92 second and seven grid spots behind his new team-mate.

Drenching rain on Sunday morning lifted by race time, but puddles remained on a surface still damp enough that everyone worried about what kind of tires to select. At the last minute most chose slicks and crossed their fingers. As did those who went for wets.

Austrian Lauda made a heroic start and his Austrian crowd rejoiced loudly to see the red Ferrari in front — but only until halfway around the opening lap. Then in a very long U-bend called the Bosch Kurve Niki's car slithered sufficiently wide for Hunt, right behind, to try to squeeze his McLaren by before James thought better of it. But Andretti pressed harder and his Lotus slipped by both of them. Mario quickly raced off into the distance, his model 78 "wing car" making good use of its ground

BELOW In the wet opening stage of the race Jones's new DN8C is just one of the midfield runners. But then both the conditions and his luck change. *Motorsport Images/Ercole Colombo*

FROM BLACK TO LIGHT **359**

ABOVE DANCE OF JOY!
Motorsport Images/LAT

effects around the long curves, despite slippery conditions that had driver after driver falling off the road. Lauda didn't, but his car was so wayward that he briefly dropped back all the way to 10th.

One going the opposite direction was Merzario. He had gambled on rain-treaded tires, and as early as the end of lap 1 he was all the way up from his 21st starting spot on the tail of team-mate Alan Jones, who was only 13th. Lap 2 and Merzario came by ahead, in 11th place, and on succeeding laps he forged up as high as sixth. At the same point Jones held eighth, having overtaken Lauda to get there.

Unfortunately for Little Art, the track was drying. He had to break off for a set of slicks. But later it all went for nothing anyway when his transmission stopped changing gears.

Meanwhile, Big Al was all set to go to the end. And he was going to get there fast. In the morning warmup he had told his team, "It feels fabulous, don't touch anything," and now everything was falling his way. "The Australian was pulling off some heart-stopping maneuvers," *Autocourse* reported, describing a "very brave" move around the outside of Ronnie Peterson's six-wheel Tyrrell. The Shadow driver kept doing that right up though lap 15, when he passed Scheckter's Wolf into second place in the race!

That seemed likely the best Jones could do, as at that point Hunt was 13 long seconds ahead. But after a season like Shadow's, taking second place in a Grand Prix would be rather acceptable.

Then the World Champion's Ford-Cosworth engine blew!

As Jones reeled off the final 11 laps, pit signals and crowd enthusiasm warned him that Lauda was now in second spot and just 11 seconds back. The math was simple. But Niki wasn't making the numbers. In fact the Austrian was losing more time to the Australian. When the white Shadow slipped under the flag, a further 20.13 seconds ticked by before the red Ferrari did.

"A hard, gritty, brave drive under a variety

LEFT "I can't believe it," he keeps saying. Well believe it, mate. You're on your way.
Don Nichols collection

of track conditions," said the *Autocourse* man of Alan Jones's virgin victory. For the American publication *Formula*, correspondent Jeff Hutchinson added this:

"I just can't believe it," exclaimed Alan Jones in euphoria as he climbed out of the Shadow. "I almost panicked when I saw James pulling off and realized I was leading! I kept thinking, 'My engine's going to blow up or something…' But his pit crew had steadied him with 'EZ' signs, and the Australian settled down to the string of perfect laps that took him to the first Grand Prix victory so richly deserved — and so desperately needed — by both himself and Don Nichols' team."

The returning Tony Southgate was fulsome in his judgement of the driver's part in this success: "Alan Jones deserves a lot of credit here because he was very good at looking after a car, keeping out of trouble, whilst not abusing the car and engine at the same time. The result was that Alan achieved the best championship points ever for Shadow."

What Franco Ambrosio may have said was not reported.

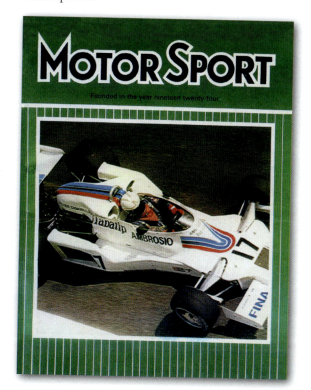

LEFT By the time the Austria winner gets to Monza, Shadow's C-spec aerodynamics are suddenly the focus of every lens in the Autodromo. Even magazine art directors catch Shadow fever.
Courtesy of Motor Sport

FROM BLACK TO LIGHT 361

DUTCH GP
Zandvoort, F1 (R13), August 28th, 1977
1st, Niki Lauda, Ferrari 312T
DNF, Riccardo Patrese, Shadow DN8C, engine
DNF, Alan Jones, Shadow DN8C, engine

The glow of victory lasted one fortnight. Then it was as if it all had been a dream.

Jones qualified 13th at Zandvoort, a second and a half off Andretti's pole. Ambrosio was back along with Patrese, who was three places back by a gap of 0.2 second. Riccardo's white Shadow was now DN8C-5A. Neither car finished the race. Jones had a scuffle with Jochen Mass at the first turn that sent the McLaren into the catch fence but let the Shadow go — for the time being. Alan's race was a little up and down the lap chart, and on lap 32 he was seventh. Partway around the next lap he parked trackside with the engine broken. Patrese also made a promising start, rising to 15th before a pitstop dropped him to the bottom, then he too lost the engine.

ITALIAN GP
Monza, F1 (R14), September 11th, 1977
1st, Mario Andretti, Lotus 78
3rd Alan Jones, Shadow DN8C,
DNF, Riccardo Patrese, Shadow DN8C, accident

Shadow's Italian driver, Patrese, had a very good Italian practice period. The *Autocourse* man wrote it this way: "The sensation of Saturday was Riccardo Patrese, driving a Formula 1 car in front of his home crowd for the first time. With the Shadow's wing screwed back to a point where its downforce was negligible, Patrese made the most of the resultant straight-line speed and scrabbled the car through the turns. By the end of practice, he was sixth, only 0.1s from Niki Lauda.

"'And it wasn't a fluke time, either,' said Jackie Oliver. 'He did it three or four times.'"

Sunday went worse. Right from the start Riccardo lost a lot of ground, stopped to

BELOW Patrese is also drawing attention at the Italian GP, not so much for the C-type he's now driving as for how well he's driving it. *Motorsport Images/ Rainer Schlegelmilch*

362 CHAPTER 16

change a tire, then failed to spot oil on the road and crashed.

His team-mate's Italian holiday was entirely the opposite. Tire troubles hurt Jones's qualifying speeds, but as our trusted source wrote, "as we have seen so often before the Australian becomes a different person on Sunday. The Shadow moved smoothly and quickly up the leaderboard to finish an eventual third a matter of seconds behind second man Lauda's Ferrari." A matter of 6.6 seconds, to be precise. But at least AJ could savor a place on the podium.

However, Niki Lauda was 17 seconds behind winner Andretti. Born in Italy, Mario achieved this third GP victory of the season at the very place that had pulled him in as a child, when he watched Alberto Ascari win the Italian Grand Prix and dreamed of one day…

It was palpably more prosaic for Lauda. On points he was now all but assured of his second championship. It was equally sure that, should he ever win another, it would not be with Ferrari. The iron-willed Austrian had been in a head-on collision with the iron-hard Enzo Ferrari and Niki had already announced his departure at season's end. As he came into the Autodromo, furious Ferrari *Tifosi* hurled rotten fruit at him. He laughed.

UNITED STATES EAST GP
Watkins Glen, F1 (R15), October 2nd, 1977
1st, James Hunt, McLaren M26
9th, Jean-Pierre Jarier, Shadow DN8C
DNF, Alan Jones, Shadow DN8C, accident

Not a great Grand Prix, unfortunately, and positively not for Jones. Once again starting from nowhere, or more precisely 13th this time, he was up to 10th by the end of lap 1, and by lap 3 the white Shadow was seventh — but that's as far as the car climbed. Trying to pass a resistant Peterson on a rain-soaked surface, Jones tapped wheels with the Tyrrell (lots of wheels to tap there). Bang, the first retirement.

His team-mate had a better run, but once again Shadow's second driver was a stand-in — former team-member Jean-Pierre Jarier. Patrese had another F2 conflict, while Jarier had turned up without a ride, so stars aligned. "Jumper" plugged himself into yet another brand-new Shadow DN8C, chassis 6A, this replacing the 5A that Riccardo had mangled at Monza. For a team in dire financial circumstances, this new-car-a-week business was getting expensive.

Asked his impression of the car, Jarier said he liked it. He qualified 16th, half a second slower than Jones, but this car went to the finish.

So did new second-time world champ Niki Lauda. He needed three more points to clinch his title, and finishing fourth in America provided them. But it looked like that's all he wanted. The calendar held two more races, two final chances to win more trophies and money and secure his renown in history, but Lauda wanted nothing to do with them. He wouldn't race again this year.

CANADIAN GP
Mosport, F1 (R16), October 9th, 1976
1st, Jody Scheckter, Wolf WR1
4th, Alan Jones, Shadow DN8C
DNF, Riccardo Patrese, Shadow DN8C, accident

Regular man Riccardo Patrese was back, and by lapping within 0.088 second of Jones's time he put the pair of Shadows side by side on the fourth row. Better.

The Australian driver went on to have a good race, coping with heavy understeer but staying on the leader's lap to finish fourth by three-quarters of a minute. Better yet.

His Italian team-mate's race started out looking really good. Patrese launched strong and completed the first lap in fifth place, three up on Jones. During the balance of the race he went up and down a little, but was again running fifth with just three laps to go.

That's when Andretti, comfortably leading

ABOVE Mosport is not a winning day but it's a decent day for Jones. For Patrese it looks like an even better day — until it all slips away.
Motorsport Images/David Phipps

the race, suffered an engine catastrophe that spewed a lot of oil squarely in Patrese's path. Thump went the Shadow into a guardrail. Then there was another thump as Vittorio Brambilla's March also hit the oil and then hit the Shadow. Two thumps made one write-off. Yet another DN8 destroyed.

Lost with it was Riccardo's potentially best finish of his rookie season. Two of the four cars ahead were going to drop out before the end. He could have placed third.

JAPANESE GP
Mount Fuji Speedway, F1 (R17),
   October 23rd, 1977
1st, James Hunt, McLaren M26
4th, Alan Jones, Shadow DN8C
6th, Riccardo Patrese, Shadow DN8C

What a way to wind up a tightly wound year! This 17th and final event of Grand Prix racing's longest season to date seemed to have everything — bad as well as good.

Andretti, the previous year's winner in Japan, started from another pole position. Hunt started from another front row. James outdragged his rival away from the start. Mario lagged and was passed by several other cars, finishing that first lap eighth. Partway around the next lap he tried passing Laffite's Ligier around the outside of a turn, the two banged wheels and a Lotus steering link snapped. Crunch, into the barrier, taking two other cars along into retirement.

Three laps later, Lauda's replacement, Gilles Villeneuve, was hurtling downhill into the tight first turn when the Ferrari's brake pedal went to the floor and the flat-12 machine rammed Ronnie Peterson's Tyrrell. The six-wheeler was out on the spot, but the red car left the scene in a wild cartwheeling tumble over a guardrail into an area forbidden to spectators but full of them. Several were hurt, one died, and so did a marshal who had been trying to clear them out of the danger zone.

Meanwhile, Shadow was enjoying a good weekend for once. Never mind Jones and Patrese qualified a second and a quarter behind Andretti, that was pretty much routine by now. What was remarkable is that they had qualified incredibly closely, a scant 0.02 second edging the Australian into 12th grid place just ahead of the Italian. That was despite Riccardo being in the team's older spare, 3A, after he had wadded up his shiny new 6A in Canada.

The near-identical cars both suffered plowing understeer throughout the race, but it didn't prevent their moving up and up the thinning line of rivals. Nearing the finish Jones passed Gunnar Nilsson's Lotus and the Shadow was fourth, but it was under attack from Patrick Depailler's Tyrrell. The six-wheeler's braking power finally got it ahead with five laps to go, but the Shadow driver wouldn't let it go. Around the last turn of the last lap Patrick's oversteering car ran wide and Alan made a banzai last-try dive through the inside. He didn't make it, but a car ahead retired so Jones still came fourth.

Meanwhile, just two spots behind, Patrese had been driving a calmly intelligent race, looking after his tires on this track's abrasive asphalt. His seeing the checkered flag made Japan the first time all year that both Shadows finished in the points.

Points that placed the Shadow team seventh among the constructors. The same place as the year before. In fact, looking back over the American-owned team's five-season assault on Fortress Europe, it cannot be said to have improved. In 1973 Shadow came eighth, then eighth again, up to sixth in 1975 but now two sevenths in a row.

No doubt this hard reality had something to do with what was about to happen to Don Nichols's outfit.

In the drivers' points placings, Jones also finished seventh with 22 points to Lauda's 72; Patrese and Zorzi, each on a single point, were joint 18th. ♠

BELOW Fuji is the last race of the longest GP schedule to date, and at long, long last both Shadow drivers finish in the points. True, it's not another win, not even a podium, but Don Nichols has a solid season to point to. For a little while.
Motorsport Images/David Phipps

ALAN JONES
GRAND PRIX WINNER

After two seasons of Formula 1, Alan Jones was sitting out 1977 rather than endure another year with a team owner he found deeply frustrating. After 22 Grands Prix with three different cars, only four races had resulted in championship points — just nine points in all.

The burly Aussie knew he was better than that. But he'd never been able to prove it.

Son of Australian star Stan Jones, winner of their native land's Grand Prix in 1959, Alan went to Europe in 1972 and worked to support himself while building up seat time in single-seaters and sports cars. He came close to winning a Formula 3 championship, but in the deciding race the car let him down.

By April 1977 he was 30. Not quite too old for an F1 driver of the time, but neither was he looking like a bright young prospect. Certainly not many observers saw a potential Grand Prix winner in him, let alone a future World Champion.

BELOW Friendly Aussie smile, ferocious Aussie competitor. AJ was on the brink of obscurity when Shadow called and turned his career around. *Motorsport Images/David Phipps*

I remember a moment in the Austrian race when I thought, bloody hell, what's going on here! I'm in the lead! I'm going to win!

That's the year when I wasn't even going to drive.

I did have a contract to continue with Surtees, but after '76 I actually said, "If the only way I can do Formula 1 is with Surtees I would rather not."

I had a look at USAC racing. I went out to Ontario Motor Speedway and drove one of Bill Simpson's McLaren Indycars around the oval there. I thought, this is not for me, I don't like it. So I came back to Australia. Missed the first two GPs.

Then poor old Tom Pryce got killed at Kyalami. I got a phone call from Jackie Oliver saying we'd like you to take Tom's place. I said, "I have a contract with Surtees. I don't know what I can do about it." And Jackie said, "Well, he fancies himself a bit of a bush lawyer; if we give him enough rope maybe he'll hang himself." And that's exactly what happened!

Jackie got me out of the contract and I flew over to Heathrow, signed with Shadow at a hotel there, then went up to Northampton to have a fitting in the car. And then Long Beach was my first race.

The first time I drove it we went out to, what's the raceway out the back there? Springs-something. Willow Springs, that's it. We did some laps there just to try to acclimatize me to the car before the race.

I did like driving for Shadow, I got on very well with everybody there. Alan Rees, he was very nice to drive for.

Jackie Oliver was good. There is nothing better than driving for a team where everybody's got the same goal, we all want the same result, and everybody works together. Not all teams are like that.

Don Nichols, he was a bit of an enigmatic character, wasn't he? The cape and the hat and all that sort of gear. Maybe that wasn't that strange in California, but it was from a bit of a different era than I was used to.

But I found him a very nice guy. Very easy to get along with. He never wanted to interfere too much, or try to tell you how to drive the car, like some people I drove for.

What happened in Austria, I think I was fortunate as far as she was a bit of a soft, heavy old girl and that just suited the conditions rather well. It was sort of wet-dry, and I was probably in the right car at the right time and took advantage of it.

It helped that I finished ahead of Niki Lauda. Being as it was his home Grand Prix and he was a bit of a superstar, it helped me get noticed. In your racing career you want to do things like that, hopefully, so you come under the nose of the right people.

I was actually contacted by Montezemolo at Ferrari about a possible drive for '78. That fell through in the end, so I went with Frank Williams and look what happened!

After Austria Don came up to me and said, "Will you come over and drive the Can-Am car?" He flew me first class to Canada. That was Mosport, wasn't it, and they had the two-seater with the Dodge engine. I think the car had probably been around for a little while, it wasn't like a brand-new thing. Don't remember much about it.

But Don did have a new one and he wanted me to come back and do a couple more races. That was good for me, because I enjoy racing in America anyway. I always used to like getting over there, and it was more miles under my belt. So I said yes.

The first was up north of San Francisco [Sears Point] and the new car really was new. That had the aluminum body and I can remember it sort of scraping at the front. I thought it could probably do with a bit more development. It didn't lack any horsepower, though.

They got it better for Riverside, and I think I put the thing on the front row. Didn't I lead Tambay for a while in the Lola? I gave Tambay enough troubles for Carl Haas to notice. Obviously he thought, "Well, he's got that thing up there where it shouldn't be," because he invited me to drive for him

ABOVE Jones joined the team at Long Beach. They had found a good man. He had found a good home. *Motorsport Images/Ercole Colombo*

the following year. That led to another good outcome.

I'm not the bloke to ask about engineering details, though. I wasn't, and still am not, really technically minded. I know the F1 Shadow went through a lot of development that year, particularly aerodynamically. It was a bit bulky at first, and then it got slimmed down by Austria. I sort of reckoned Dave Wass knew what he was about.

But don't expect me to give a whole speech on what they did and what were the results scientifically. All I know about cars is, here's the seat, there's the steering wheel, give it a go.

It was all positive. I can't say a bad word about the time I had with Shadow. They were good to work with, and they presented me with a well-prepared car. I won't say it was the most competitive chassis on the grid, but in the end it was good enough to advance my career.

I'd just like to say that I think Don Nichols was a great contributor to Formula 1. Because he was a very colorful character. I don't think he did motorsport any harm at all. We need more characters like him today.

CHAPTER 17
SINGLE-SEAT SPORTS CARS

SHADOW DN6C AND DN10 (CAN-AM II), 1977–78

When the once beloved old Can-Am died in 1974, the SCCA tried replacing it with Formula 5000. These rude weapons were loud, brawny and scary-fast, and they put on a lot of good racing, but the club soon realized that open-wheel single-seaters just weren't drawing the sports car crowds that race promoters fondly remembered from Can-Am's heyday.

Say, here's an idea: why not drape full-width bodywork over an F5000 chassis and call it a Can-Am II?

For once a quick-fix brainstorm seemed to work, and the new series achieved popularity that continued for several years. But all this would lie outside our concern here, except for Don Nichols's attempts to participate over two seasons with three different vehicles.

Working as ever with inadequate budgets, his Shadowmen had to construct these as hybrids, amalgamations of existing chassis with plugged-in Dodge F5000 motors.

As recounted on pages 257–259, the first of the trio was a so-called DN4B, a Can-Am leftover missing three of its original eight liters and thus seriously underpowered. It was driven in races only twice in 1977, by Randy Lewis and Alan Jones. Neither saw a finish flag.

Shadow's second Can-Am II was a genuine center-seater, a F5000 DN6 (chassis number 3A, for you anoraks) wearing a one-off "sports car body" hand-made of aluminum in Shadow's new western shop at Marina, near Monterey, California, where Nichols now lived. The craftsmen responsible had good eyes: the DN6C was quite nice looking.

But not as quick as it looked. When debuted by Alan Jones at California's Sears Point (now called Sonoma) north of San Francisco on September 25th, one month after he had run eastern Canada's Mosport with the DN4B, the DN6C gave away eight long seconds to fastest qualifier Patrick Tambay's Lola to line up 12th on the grid.

Actually, that wasn't as bad as it sounds, if we

ABOVE *Formula* magazine's art director was perfectly positioned at Riverside to capture the climatic moment of the DN6C's best race. Alan Jones has spurred the black Shadow into an early lead, but fellow F1 cavalryman Patrick Tambay's Lola T333 is pushing up hard behind. Push becomes shove here atop Turn Seven. The cars are about to actually "rub" and Jones will wobble on ahead, but only momentarily. A good moment, though. *Larry Roberts*

BELOW Stripped of its Dodge for service, the "sports car" shows us how its underlying F5000 DN6 chassis is actually a modified F1 DN5. Substantial substructures grafted onto the rear of the monocoque include triangular struts that bolt to the back of the V8. Sprawling side bodywork shelters radiators repositioned laterally. *Don Nichols collection*

consider the all-too-typical racer's thrash that got it to the track only just in time. As *Formula* magazine executive editor (and thus my boss) Jim MacQueen described it in our January 1978 issue, "The car was literally finished in the back of the huge truck while towing up from the shop in Monterey, and Jones had to bring his Formula One seat over with him from Europe as personal baggage — which the airline promptly lost! Wondering how the North American Shadow operation could be so woefully different from its European counterpart, Jones was not expecting much more than a long testing session from the weekend.

"The stubby little nose on the car wasn't producing much downforce, so the team lost most of qualifying to fitting side plates; however, in three fast laps the Grand Prix driver took 12th spot on the grid. By the time the yellow flag came out on lap two, he had moved up to sixth place behind Follmer. That would have been fine except that Sears is a very

SINGLE-SEAT SPORTS CARS **369**

TOP Debuting at Sears Point (Sonoma) Shadow's Can-Am II looks quite graceful in its handmade aluminum bodywork. Alas, it's only superficial. Mechanically the modified machine lacks not only grace but pace, balanced handling, development, reliability and, worst, enough time for it all to be made right. Its one big asset: Alan Jones at the wheel.
Jim Bartel collection

ABOVE Some of the bugs are sorted by Riverside, and Jones (entering from the right) will show the black beauty to better advantage in this race. Briefly.
Don Nichols collection

rough racetrack, and insufficient ride height was allowing the pop-riveted side plates to catch and bend back. Jones eventually had to call by the pits to have one pulled off the car, ran well enough the rest of the way to get back up to fifth place, and then saw the oil pressure go away with only two laps remaining." AJ was classified 11th.

Next up was the season finale three weeks later at Riverside, east of Los Angeles. Here's what MacQueen had to say about that one:

"In qualifying Patrick Tambay was again uncatchably quick, almost 1.4 seconds faster than Alan Jones in the Shadow. But in fact Jones was second quickest, and that seemed to be a remarkable achievement for a two-race-old car. Between events, the ride height had been raised and more permanent side plates installed on the nose, along with a small aerofoil. Stiffer springs seem to calm the car down a bit and Lee Muir's Dodge seemed to be pumping out the old horsepower with the most satisfying guttural growl."

Mac called Dodge's outlier engine the "UFO factor" at mostly-all-Chevrolet Riverside. "Out-torquing Tambay at the start, Jones actually took the lead — and began building it to a maximum of four seconds by lap five.

"Of course, the Shadow wasn't really winning. Jones knew the car wouldn't last and was just giving it a good run while he could. Showmanship. Fun. That sort of thing. Also, he lost second and third gears on the second lap and the resulting over-revs were tearing up the insides of the engine. Meanwhile Tambay had lots in reserve and was just sort of testing the waters…

"Still it looked exciting. The Shadow and Lola actually touched once in Turn Seven before Tambay got by. A couple of laps later, the Dodge went on to seven cylinders and Jones brought it into the pits rather than walk back from some far corner of the circuit." (Other sources give the trouble as "transmission." According to marque expert Dennis Losher, an engineer who restores and races vintage Shadows, the F5000-based powertrain still used its F1 Hewland TL200 transaxle, which was strong enough for 3-liter Ford-Cosworth torque but severely stressed by the 5-liter Dodge.)

The end of that season didn't end the tale of the Shadow DN6C, for it would race the first few rounds of 1978 alongside a new model, the DN10. That project was underway across the sea in the team's familiar Northampton works, funded by an enthusiastic American named Randolph Townsend.

Townsend's family had prospered through its large forest products business in Oregon, but Randolph was a California native and at the time he began racing he was teaching at the University of Nevada. He also was becoming active in politics, and eventually would serve many years as a Nevada state senator.

LEFT Five liters of stock-block Dodge easily boost the Shadow by one of Can-Am II's two-liter contenders. Staying ahead of other 5.0s, that's a different matter. *Criag Libuse/Riverside International Automotive Museum*

BELOW Designer Richard Owen's own drawing of his bodywork for the DN10. To be made in glass-fiber, the shape is very different from the 6C's metalwork, but so is the chassis it is to clothe — one of Shadow's now-obsolete F1 DN8s. *Jim Bartel collection*

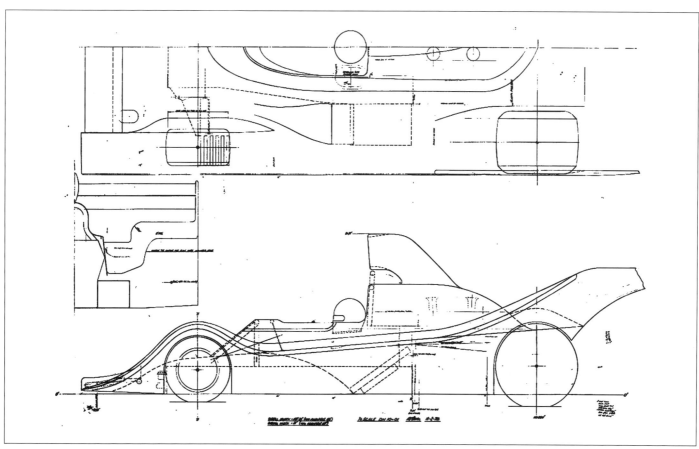

SINGLE-SEAT SPORTS CARS **371**

ABOVE Seizing a moment of sunshine at Silverstone, American Randolph Townsend takes the new car he commissioned from England out for its first exploratory laps. He will not be a satisfied customer. To be fair, his crew wound up with a like view of their client. Racing teams are uneasy associations of strong-willed, success-driven individualists, and they're quick to judge one of their number they view as holding them back.
Don Nichols collection

Shadow designer Richard Owen drew the DN10, including lofting glass-fiber bodywork very different in appearance from the aluminum paneling on the 1977 car. Instead of erecting the 1978 model on the older F5000 chassis, he based the DN10 on the more recent F1 DN8 — actually chassis 4, Alan Jones's Austria winner of 1977. Sentiment was not as highly regarded as expediency.

In fact there would be a pair of DN10s, but only one was finished in time for the 1978 Can-Am II season opener on May 14th. Randolph Townsend came to shake it down at Silverstone, then it was shipped to Road Atlanta in Georgia, where it joined the leftover DN6C that Jean-Pierre Jarier would handle.

Neither Shadow driver was able to set a qualifying time. Starting from the back of the pack, both stopped for reasons described only as "mechanical." In fact, neither man was at all happy with his car, nor the team, nor his employer. Sadly their opinions were not going to improve.

Would you care to know who won that race? A certain Australian named Jones, who was a Lolaman now.

Surely things would pick up for round two on May 27th at Charlotte Motor Speedway, North Carolina? Well, yes, but only very slightly. This time Townsend did manage to eke out a qualifying time, albeit one falling short of poleman Jones by 16 seconds. That's right, sixteen. This achievement earned him 18th place on the grid. One place better than pro driver Jarier, who once again didn't get a timed lap with the DN6C.

Their race was on the day before the banked oval's annual NASCAR 600-miler, but using an associated road course. Jarier completed one lap before retiring; "engine" was put down in the record. Townsend spun out of it when an oil leak lubricated his rear tires in one of the speedway bankings. Thus the second Shadow also wasn't running at the end, although Townsend was scored as finishing 11th, 17 laps short of the winner — who was Elliott Forbes-Robinson driving something called a Spyder but based on a Lola.

Mid-Ohio on June 11th clashed with Le Mans, where Jarier was driving for Renault (he would retire), so Townsend was alone. He started from 22nd place and placed 12th, 10 laps down. Jones won again.

"Jumper" did jump back into the DN6C at Quebec's Saint-Jovite on June 25th. Here he actually qualified for the grid and in seventh spot at that. Gap to pole was only 3.2 seconds. But overheating of the engine retired him from the race. Meanwhile Townsend qualified only 17th, but kept going all the way and finished fourth. Four laps down, but fourth. Saint-Jovite would remain the team's high-water mark.

Oh yes, remember that Follmer fellow? George was the winner this time aboard another Lola-based design, this one called a Prophet.

Jarier finally received his DN10 for race five at Watkins Glen on July 9th. It didn't do him a lot of good. His grid place was sixth by a margin of four seconds, and he went out with gearbox trouble. Townsend started 17th, over 10 seconds slower than the fastest, and he too retired with a broken transaxle. This time the race winner was Warwick Brown, who was driving a Lola like most everybody else.

LEFT At rest in Road America's grassy paddock, a DN10 reveals its DN8 chassis and front suspension, including the F1-mandated "dash hoop" structure of steel tubing. Radiators lay back in the wide but doorless bodywork. *Tom Schultz*

BELOW A big iron Dodge has moved into this house built for a compact alloy Cosworth. This better view of the side rads also shows the smaller aircraft oil cooler above the Hewland TL200 gearbox, as well as the extended roll bar to accommodate the new owner. *Tom Schultz*

SINGLE-SEAT SPORTS CARS **373**

ABOVE Jarier's DN10 displays an extra side cooler not evident on the sister car. *Tom Schultz*

BELOW Townsend's number 00 car is no DN4, but it does reprise that championship winner's frontal treatment, with a somewhat shovel-shaped profile and a pair of prominent inlets. Notice the 'Spy Eyes' below the windscreen that Shadows now wear. *Tom Schultz*

Let us now cut short the second half of the 10-race season.

Race six, Road America, Wisconsin, July 23rd: Jarier, Q9 +5.6 seconds, DNF gearbox; Townsend Q23 +14.5 seconds, DNF fluid leak. Winner, Jones (Lola).

Race seven, Mosport, Ontario, August 20th: Jarier Q9 +4.0 seconds, DNF gearbox; Townsend absent, campaigning for the Nevada legislature. Winner, Jones (Lola).

Race eight, Trois-Rivières, Quebec, September 30th: Jarier Q6 +3.0 seconds, DNF ignition; Townsend missed this one too. Winner, Forbes-Robinson (Spyder).

Race nine, Laguna Seca, California, October 8th: Shadow skipped this one for the second year running as the date clashed with the Canadian GP at Montreal, where Jarier showed so well with Lotus. As for Townsend, he was still on the campaign trail. Al Holbert won the Laguna event with yet another Lola. And then it was on to the season finale.

ABOVE Shadow has only the one entry for Jarier at Mosport, but results are no better for it. *Ron Kielbiski*

BELOW Townsend's sad season with Shadow is about to come to a crashing conclusion at Riverside. *Kurt Oblinger*

Race 10, Riverside, California, October 15th: Jarier Q17 +6.8 seconds, DNF gearbox; Townsend Q24 (of 24) +9.4 seconds, DNF crash. Winner, Jones (Lola).

SO ALAN JONES made himself the 1978 Can-Am II champion by winning five of the nine races he contested (he too missed Laguna in favor of his F1 job at Williams), after starting from pole position in all nine. His advantage in equipment helped: Jones was the year's headline driver for Carl Haas, Lola's US importer, so in effect he was driving the works car, as had the previous champion, Patrick Tambay. Once again it was prepared and campaigned by Jim Hall's superb Chaparral team.

Runner-up was Jones's countryman Warwick Brown, making it an Aussie lock on North America's championship.

Shadow did not enter the Can-Am II series a third time. All three of the center-seaters have since been converted back to their open-wheel configuration. ♠

SINGLE-SEAT SPORTS CARS **375**

RANDOLPH TOWNSEND
RACING SENATOR

Driving the Shadow was easily the worst experience I've ever had in a race car.

It was purely accidental. I had fallen in love with racecars and was doing what every little boy dreams of doing. I was a Porsche guy from the beginning, and was putting together a couple of guys and we would go out running endurance races in SCCA and IMSA. My first Pro race was the 24 hours at Daytona in 1975, with a 3-Liter 911.

A friend told me Don Nichols — whom I had never heard of — was putting together a Can-Am team and wanted a driver. Of course the Can-Am was a big deal, it just touched everyone viscerally, and Shadow was this wonderful branding. The black and white and the design of the car, the thundering hundreds and hundreds of horsepower that just rattled your bones. And the great drivers like Follmer and Redman.

I met Don and he was very charming. He told me the cars were being built in his Formula 1 factory in England, they had Formula 1 chassis, there was going to be a European driver on the team, and this and that. So I did the deal.

The next thing you know I'm in England in a driving rainstorm with this Formula 1 car from 1977 that they had put a body on to create a Can-Am car. We were supposed to test it at Silverstone, and it's a torrential downpour. Finally we got about half a day on a wet track and the car was absolutely undriveable in the wet.

I certainly wasn't qualified to test that car and make some kind of determination about what to do, but I had no option. I mean it's not like they hired a test driver to come out and make it work. They had Hans Stuck, one of the best wet drivers probably in the history of motor racing, and we could have really used that.

We get back to the States and ultimately Jean-Pierre Jarier became the first driver. I'm the second. He drove it and came in and he said, 'What are we going to do with this car? The thing is crap. I'm a Formula 1 driver and it's a Formula 1 car with a body on it and it still doesn't run. I can't race it.' I said, 'You're the experienced guy, not me. So whatever you can come up with to make this thing work as best we can, let's do that.'

It never got any better the whole season. We were at Road America, which was a terrifying track in a good car, but you drive that Shadow there, you were really putting your life on the line.

We went to Charlotte Motor Speedway. Not the world's greatest idea. In the race, one of the covers started to loosen on the motor, and oil spilled on those huge, wide tires as I went down the back straightaway. So suddenly as I start into Turn Three the rear end comes around, I'm now going backwards, and the smoke is coming into the cockpit and

BELOW A young man of ambition and drive, Townsend did not find what he was looking for in Don Nichols and his team. *Revs Institute for Automotive Research/Geoffrey Hewitt*

ABOVE "Taking his life in his hands" at Road America doesn't pay off on the track, but his parallel path in politics will bring him to career success. *Tom Schultz*

now it's starting to burn. The only good news was that instead of going into the wall I just kept spinning down off the bank and into the infield. I came to a stop right at the fire truck. They literally didn't have to get off the truck. They emptied everything they had into the car.

So here's an all-black car and it's now all white. And when I got back to the pits — this is when I knew we had trouble — no one cared how I was. It was, 'It's gonna take forever to clean this car up.' That was the team attitude.

The guys Don brought over from England were very nice guys. I don't know how competent they were. I mean… let me put it this way. I think we had plenty of money. I just think Don took a lot of it himself, and didn't put it into the team, and didn't have the most competent people. That car was…

I'm not saying it was one of the great Formula 1 cars, but when you take a year-old [DN8] and you kind of milk the company for all the money and you haven't updated it and you're using parts that are showing their age, maybe are not necessarily appropriate for safety reasons, and then you throw a Can-Am body on it and hope it can compete? You're kidding yourself.

I met Randy Lewis and talked with him about driving for Don Nichols the year before. Unfortunately I didn't meet him before I made my deal with Shadow, otherwise I probably never would have.

Don was very charming, very cerebral, very smart, he talked about a lot of things outside of racing, but he was very mysterious. You kinda didn't know where the money was going and how it was allocated.

He was the kind of guy you would love to sit and spend three or four hours having dinner with, and even though he invited you, he'd stick you with the bill. That's the kind of guy he was.

Don had made Shadow a great name, but he was living off that name.

It was so disappointing. I almost said, I'm not gonna go looking for money to continue to do this if this is the kind of experience you have. But I talked with Bill Freeman, who had the Can-Am team with Paul Newman, and he said, 'Oh my God, if you can drive for Don Nichols and put up with those crap cars, let's see if we can put something together.'

That was one of the great experiences of all time. I drove with Keke Rosberg and Elliott Forbes-Robinson, great drivers, and the cars were always well prepared. Those guys were real racers.

Compiled from a recent interview.

CHAPTER 18
DECLINE

SHADOW DN9 (F1), 1978

Let us evade tedium. We need not call out every detail of the next two and a fraction years. Shadow's time of promise had passed. Austria 1977 was the high point, and our story from now on must trace sad diminishment. Don Nichols was a tenacious man, but his goal had slipped from his grasp. His team would achieve nothing more of historic significance.

However, human effort counts too. The Shadowman and the stalwart souls still with him kept racing as best they were able in the face of ever-diminishing resources. We should honor their valiant struggle by telling of what they did accomplish.

Shadow's DN9 of 1978 was its own creature, but in fact it carried Lotus genes.

Tony Southgate came back from his year and a half with Colin Chapman brimming with new understandings of aerodynamics and fresh ideas about how to apply them. New machines called "wing cars" were entering Formula 1, and Tony had helped invent them.

The term was not meant for cars wearing actual aerofoils. These appendages had been familiar for a decade. Advanced conceptualists considered them bandaids, though. They had long dreamed of shaping the whole car as an inverted aerofoil, transforming to downforce the lift that keeps an aircraft in the air, thus loading tires with artificial weight so they adhered more firmly to the road.

This was a problematic notion for a vehicle like a sports car, where cockpits take up most of the width and the underbelly must be essentially flat. Some gains were made by carefully setting the car's pitch angle and cunningly sculpting the undersides of its nosepiece and afterbody, and of course the broader the upper surface the greater the effect of high pressure there.

These measures brought less benefit to narrow single-seaters — but look at all the empty airspace either side of the fuselage. What about sticking wings out there?

LEFT Dolled up for her formal launch portrait, Shadow's new DN9 shows off her snappy sponsorship livery as well as several points of interesting design by the now-departed Tony Southgate. In a departure from all his previous F1 Shadows, this has a single engine water radiator inside the nosecone; the engine oil cooler that formerly lived there is now aft, alongside the engine compartment. But this car's big novelty concerns the "side wings." Unlike everyone else's car — apart from the new Arrows by the same designer — the DN9 uses a two-element aerofoil configuration. Under the oil cooler inlet back along the car's flank, the second, narrower slot ducts air downward to the split floor of the side-wing pod.
Motorsport Images/LAT

It didn't work. March tried stubby side-wings in 1970 and abandoned the idea. The shorter the aerofoil, the more potential downforce is lost to air escaping the higher pressure above by curling over the sides and down to replenish the relative vacuum underneath. Tip vortices, such curls are called, and they are ruthless robbers of aerofoil efficiency for both automobiles and aircraft.

Alright, but what about endplates? They're fixed to the tips of wings on both planes and cars, to block the vortices. Fences along the racecar's body itself work the same way. Can't we stick a couple to the outsides of our experimental side-wings, drooping down to the road?

Yer daft, mate. You forget, the car rises and falls over the road. Your fence-plates would have to be trimmed so short they would do no good.

Racers. They race for fun, they'll go for a trophy, they do like money, but if you really want to motivate them, say they can't do something. Better jump back.

WING CARS

Working in the wind tunnel with aerodynamicist Peter Wright, a former colleague at BRM now at Lotus, Southgate helped develop solutions. The all-important aerofoils, very short in span to meet rules limiting body width, but as long in chord as would fit between the front and rear tires, were tipped on their outside ends by large panels that gave the car a slab-sided look.

To seal the air gap below the slabs, Southgate's first idea was to affix rows of stiff bristle brushes along their bottom edges, seemingly sweeping the track but really fencing air out from the underside. Tire grip did increase, and Lotus launched its type 78 so equipped. Testing showed these long "push brooms" leaked air, though, and by the time Mario Andretti won the 1976 Long Beach GP, the Lotus wore rigid polypropylene skirts that rubbed the surface.

"It feels like it's painted on the road," he famously said.

RIGHT Flanked by his boss, Shadow's new team manager is Bert Baldwin, a longtime veteran of the pitlane thanks to his previous role with Goodyear.
Motorsport Images/David Phipps

What of bumps? The Lotus 78's rigid skirts were cleverly pivoted laterally and spring-loaded, so they rose and fell in relation to the heaving car so as to stay in touch with the tarmac. Durable rubbing strips, eventually made of ceramic, defended the skirt material from wear.

The basic idea had been seen in 1970 on Chaparral's 2J Ground Effect Vehicle. That generated its underbelly suction with extractor fans and its skirts did not quite touch the ground, so Lotus was forging its own way to the same end.

That end proved to be Andretti's Formula 1 World Championship in 1978 with the Lotus 79. Which in turn sparked a total transformation of the look and performance of racing cars worldwide.

Jim Hall so liked the idea that he had Briton John Barnard design an Indycar that looked like a duplicate of the champion's Lotus 79 resprayed bright yellow, but was really the Chaparral 2K. Johnny Rutherford drove it to a 500 victory in 1980.

Longtime enthusiasts are likely to already know all of this, and to them we apologize for our pedagogy. But perhaps some younger ones won't know the history, because — of course — racing's pettifogging rules writers soon outlawed the whole concept.

And perhaps in this case they were right. The forces the revolution unleashed were overwhelming.

From the outside it was hard to see, and even the most experienced pitlane personnel may not have truly understood the invisible power of air, but drivers suddenly were feeling crushing, breathtaking g-loads in every direction. We've heard Tony Southgate's pride in achieving 750 pounds of downforce with his DN5 of 1975 — about half the car's racing weight. By the end of the decade builders of "wing cars" — more commonly called Tunnel Cars, for the channels inside their sidepods — were talking of downforces greater than the car's weight. Meaning, theoretically, they could race upside down on the ceiling of a highway tunnel.

Theory is one thing. Reality confronted workers in every racing specialty as they abruptly found themselves dealing with consequences of enormously magnified tire adhesion: much higher cornering speeds, braking loads, structural and physical stresses, driver fatigue, crash impact.

Tires had to be redesigned. Engineers and mechanics had to deal with ultra-critical handling setups, which required stiff, short-travel suspensions on cars that must hug the ground — but not drag on it.

The ground-effects revolution was one of the most significant in motor racing history. And one of the hardest to grapple with.

Why go into all this here and now? To emphasize the battle the Shadow team faced.

When Lotus developed its wing cars, Colin Chapman's organization enjoyed generous budgets, top-flight design and engineering talent, comprehensive fabrication facilities, deeply experienced crew, its own private testing circuit at its Hethel aerodrome premises, and a driver of exceptional ability, sensitivity and determination who eagerly piled up testing mileage. The team had even entered the computer age. By the time they raced the boss's new brainchild, his people had built up a deep fund of knowledge of it.

Also, crucially, Lotus's stature among established top entrants conferred an advantage in tires. It so happened that a war was going on between Goodyear and Michelin, whose development focus was on teams that gave the best chance of besting their opponent. Those outside that top tier had to struggle without the latest rubber — a massive handicap.

All in all, Shadow's disadvantages were many. Southgate gave them a good car, but he was gone to Arrows before it was finished, along with most of the staff that Nichols expected would be working with it. Also departed were his two strong drivers, plus one of his two prime sponsors.

Some crew remained faithful, including shop manager Jim Eccles. Swiss sponsor Heinrich Villiger stepped up by doubling his car count, decking the pair in a snappy new red-and-white livery. In one was the tough veteran Swiss driver Clay Regazzoni, a winner in his Ferrari days. His team-mate was Germany's friendly but fiery Hans-Joachim Stuck, who had been in F1 since 1974 and in the same period had scored several F2 victories.

Among other newcomers were designer John Baldwin (formerly of Lotus and Parnelli) and famed crew chief Jo Ramirez (Eagle, Tyrrell, Fittipaldi) as team manager. So Shadow wasn't devoid of able personnel. Just thin with them. And desperately underfunded.

These born competitors were charged with making sense of the racecar that Southgate had left for them, but without his background knowledge of it.

ABOVE New chief mechanic Jo Ramirez, caught sharing information with driver Clay Regazzoni (and others), comes from a long, impressive career with such teams as Ferrari (where he worked with compatriot and friend Ricardo Rodriguez), JW Automotive/Ford, Eagle, Tyrrell and Fittipaldi. *Don Nichols collection*

THE DN9

Fresh from his work to make the Lotus 78 a race winner, Tony Southgate drew up a machine he intended to be superior. Like the Lotus, it wore shrouded aerofoils on the sides of a long, rigid monocoque chassis designed to tuck the suspension and other components out of the interior airstream as much as possible. As at Hethel, in Northampton he devised a system of plastic air seals along the bottom edges of the flat sides. Also similar were radiators inside the sidepods, although they were for oil not water.

Where Southgate departed was his wing configuration. The Lotus sidepods concealed single aerofoil profiles, dropping from the leading edge down close to the road — but not too close — and then sweeping smoothly up and back to the trailing edge.

Tony's improvement for Shadow was to split the wing into two elements, one leading the second with a small gap between. As with the trailing-edge flaps we see deployed on aircraft to increase lift at slower speeds, the mid-chord gap would introduce fresh air to the second element through a duct from the higher-pressure surface, the upper one on racecars.

Southgate's thinking here was that windtunnel data showed the airflow starting to separate from the lowermost point of the inverted aerofoil, meaning the "lift" was beginning to fail. Adding more air at this point would re-energize the flow.

Evidently Lotus was aware of this too, because on the even more advanced type 79 of 1978, a further step in the ground-effect revolution, the bottom of its inverted, enclosed aerofoil wore small vortex generators that had the same re-energizing effect.

Of course the most significant advance on the Lotus 79 was "sliding skirts." These were rigid panels that rose and fell within the outer walls of the sidepods — think of "pocket doors"

BELOW Shot from the photo tower at Monza's Parabolica, Regazzoni's DN9 gives another view of the two-element side wings and the overall chisel shape of their enclosure, a manifestation of designer Southgate's affection for leading edges like "shovels." The original twin-snorkel engine airbox has been abandoned.

Motorsport Images/LAT

ABOVE Drapes atop the sidepods shield them from damage — and prying eyes — in the pitlane at Brands Hatch. But the rocker-arm front suspension is open to all to see. Not quite as apparent from this angle is the forward-leaning water radiator in the nose.
Motorsport Images/David Phipps

in a house — to follow the road and provide improved sealing.

This innovation came after Southgate had returned to Shadow, and like other designers he was working from the earlier Lotus 78 concept and its hinged skirts. Trying to improve on that is why he devised the ducting inside his twin-element sidepods, and he reshaped the sidepods themselves while he was at it.

His DN9's topside inlet ducts received air forced up by the shovel-shaped leading edges Tony liked, their profiles probably endowing added downforce. Associated with these ducts were engine coolers housed inside the rearward aerofoil elements.

Otherwise, the DN9 "wing car" was a Formula 1 racer in the style of Southgate's previous DN cars. Its fuel nestled behind the driver, who sat well forward, his foot pedals in line with the suspension springs. In the DN9, the pedals were well ahead of the wheels, because the suspension rockers swept back more severely than on the preceding DN8. At 106 inches, the wheelbase was a little longer, while track dimensions were wider, up to 64 and a fraction front and rear (published data indicates the rear track width was widened during the model's life).

Instead of the trick transaxles Southgate liked on his prior DNs, the DN9 drove through a more commonplace, much more available Hewland FGA400 five-speed.

Before Shadow built the car Tony laid down for them, he left for the new Arrows operation, where a very similar machine was quickly constructed (see "The Sharrows Affair" overleaf). As both rival versions of his design evolved through the process of construction and development by rival crews, some variations did appear. One distinguishing point is their differing arrangements of the water radiators inside nosecones that looked all but identical, but whereas the Arrows FA1 continued the lay-back orientation seen with the later DN8s — and the Lotus 78 — Shadow canted it forward.

THE SHARROWS AFFAIR

We racefans are gentle, simple souls. We like racing, period. Sure, we know many things must happen behind the scenes to put our show on stage, but it's the performance itself that we've come to see.

Sometimes, though, what goes on backstage turns so sordid that it sours our racing. So we cannot ignore it.

Just that happened to our friend the Shadowman as 1977 closed. Don Nichols's team had just scored its very first Grand Prix victory, thanks to Alan Jones achieving his own first, thereby bringing Shadow's seasonal constructor points total to 23 — a giddy improvement on the previous best, 10.

Also better was Shadow's rank among constructors, up to seventh from eighth. True, that didn't match the sixth place achieved in 1975, but those had been halcyon days of comfortable sponsorship. The subsequent two years had been much tougher. Would Austria '77 prove to be the turning point in Nichols's dogged battle to attract commercial backing?

No. Jones left him after the last race. So did his other driver Riccardo Patrese, along with former driver-turned-organization man Jackie Oliver, team manager Alan Rees, designer Tony Southgate and his number two, Dave Wass, plus the majority of the expert, seasoned staff. Important sponsor Franco Ambrosio too.

Jones moved to rival team owner Frank Williams — with whom he would eventually win the World Championship — but the others departed en masse to form their own carbuilding enterprise. Their name for it was ARROWS, derived from their various initials.

Phoenix Racing, Nichols called his team. It celebrated his rising from his racing debacle of 1968–70. Now, once again, he found himself in figurative ashes.

Thus began the "Sharrows Affair." It kept motorsports papers aflutter for months.

Unlike most of the juicy scandals so fascinating to British tabloids, this one wasn't about sex. Clearly the root cause was money, or lack of it, but it's no secret that Mssrs. Oliver and the others were by now totally disenchanted

LEFT Arrows top brass in Austria: Jackie Oliver, Alan Rees, Riccardo Patrese and Tony Southgate — plus Riccardo's girlfriend Susie. *Motorsport Images/ David Phipps*

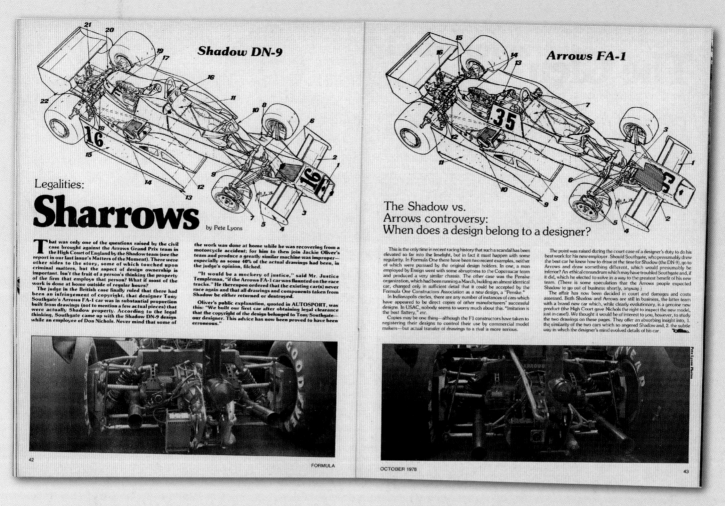

with Mr. Nichols. Tony Southgate's book gives us his own caught-in-the-middle view:

"Things were not going to plan. The money was getting scarce, there had been no sign of the promised James Hunt [mentioned earlier in the book], and the build of the new DN9 was going very slowly. This was not what Don Nichols had promised.

"Jackie Oliver was unhappy with the whole situation. He had become the main sponsor-getter, but it didn't seem to be appreciated by Don. Jackie was now looking to the future after race driving and wanted to be part of the team, a shareholder. Don and his wife, who wholly owned Shadow, would have none of this, which was a pity — a 10 or 15 percent stake in the company might have made all the difference. Instead, this was the start of a load of aggravation for the Shadow team.

"Jackie tried to buy out Shadow Cars, but that didn't work out either. So Jackie indicated that he was going to start a new team of his own…"

Tony goes on to say that he was reluctant to join them at first, because he'd nearly finished designing the DN9 and half the parts were already made. And Don asked him to

ABOVE The author's story about the "Sharrows" scandal in *Formula* magazine for October 1978. Giorgio Piola's fine drawings make stark the similarities between the Shadow and the Arrows — both designed by the same man. The rear suspension comparison photos were shot by the author. *Pete Lyons collection*

dinner, where he actually begged him to stay. "At one stage, he even had tears in his eyes, which was a very impressive plea from such a man."

When he came home, Southgate continues, and told his wife that he was departing after all, she told him he had made a big mistake. Subsequently he came to agree with her.

Nichols's eyes quickly dried and hardened. There had been injury to his firm, but anyone in business knows such things happen. Had the tale concluded there, Shadow's boss might simply have put on his most confident face and moved forward as best he was able.

But also there had been insult.

When Arrows unveiled its new FA1 racing car for 1978, after what was claimed to be an extraordinarily short gestation period of 57 days, it was obvious to every observer that it almost exactly copied Shadow's new DN9, which had been underway for half a year — ever since Southgate

DECLINE **385**

ABOVE Darn, knew we shouldn't have put her on slicks. Begun later but finished first, the Southgate-designed Arrows FA1 makes its debut on a crisp January morning at Silverstone. Not to fear, it's soon jetting off to summery Brazil, just possibly courtesy of that nation's airline. *Motorsport Images/LAT*

returned from Lotus. It could not be coincidence.

Intellectual property is highly prized in any competitive industry, and Don Nichols decided he must have been robbed. No stranger to legal proceedings, he brought charges in London's High Court against his former team-mates for copyright infringement.

"I knew we had trouble," Jackie Oliver said to *Motor Sport* magazine interviewer Simon Taylor in 2007. "It was an infringement of copyright. Tony Southgate brought a handful of initial drawings from Shadow; he should have brought the information in his head. There's a difference."

Southgate himself discussed the matter forthrightly in his own book. To begin with, he explained that, "I had decided to keep the design very similar to the new Shadow because I was quite happy with most of the DN9, and I would not normally change my design philosophy overnight."

He went on to say that he did indeed bring over most of the critical design data — specifications, geometries, dimensions — "in my head." Of the detailed drawings he carried along, his view was that, as a freelance contributor, he owned the rights to his own work, and a lawyer he consulted agreed. But that advice was "totally incorrect," the High Court decided.

In any case, the relatively few Shadow drawings that benefited Arrows mainly involved suspension uprights and a few other components to be crafted by outside suppliers. To save crucial time Tony simply sent his Shadow material to them.

This was enough to ignite the legal fire. After endless

BELOW OK, here you go: what differences can you spot? Patrese's once-white FA1 is now gold. *Motorsport Images/Rainer Schlegelmilch*

386 CHAPTER 18

days of turgid presentations in an expansive, wood-paneled, intimidatingly hushed hearing room of the High Court's Chancery Division in the City of London, Arrows was found to be in the wrong.

A summary of the judgement found online (http://www.5rb.com/case/Nichols-Advanced-Vehicle-Systems-Inc--Ors-v-Rees,-Oliver--Ors) reads, in part,

(1) The drawings were produced with skill and were beyond argument artistic works in which copyright subsisted. (2) The drawings were made by S in the course of his employment under a contract of service, and as such the copyright was vested in the Plaintiffs. (3) The F.A.1 car was plainly a reproduction of the drawings. While some modifications had been made, these were not sufficient to afford the Defendants a defence under s.9(8). (4) S.18(2) required defendants to have believed they were not infringing. Here the Defendants (bar one who was merely an employee) had hoped, rather than believed, that they were not infringing. The infringement was flagrant and additional damages would be awarded under s.17(3). An inquiry as to damages was ordered, along with the relief by way of injunctions and orders for delivery up of the infringing material.

Bottom line, Arrows could no longer race its FA1s. They had to be destroyed or given to Shadow; it is thought Don received five monocoque tubs. But by that time, the second half of the 1978 season, Arrows already had a new car ready, one wholly its own. To assure Nichols of that, he had been granted the right to inspect Southgate's all-new Arrows A1.

Don might have smiled to see that the "F" had been dropped. The original copy-cat car's "FA" stood for Franco Ambrosio, just as DN meant the American's own name, but the Italian was now in serious legal trouble of his own and gone from the team.

Everybody went on about their racing, and with the passage of years even the main protagonists of the infamous "Sharrows Affair" seemed to mellow. In remarks Oliver made to us, he spoke of it as if it were any everyday divorce, saying simply, "Don kept the house, I got the kids" and, "We've reconciled."

When we asked Nichols for his feelings about Oliver's defection, his quiet answer was, "I don't blame him. I couldn't pay him."

Nevertheless, Shadow had suffered a crippling blow.

BELOW Arrows vs. Shadow in Monaco's Mirabeau corner. Even the bottom-edge air skirts look the same. *Motorsport Images/Rainer Schlegelmilch*

ABOVE Guys, guys, you're Formula 1 drivers, this is supposed to be fun! What is it, long-haul flights to Argentina getting too hard on old bones? Three lovely ladies, three! What's wrong with… oh, never mind, take the photo.
Motorsport Images/David Phipps

SHADOW'S 1978 F1 SEASON

This season's Grand Prix calendar again offered 16 races of championship status, but only a single extracurricular extravaganza. And that's the right word, because Silverstone was… well, patience, we'll come to it.

As a marque Shadow actually had three DN9 entries this year, its own pair emblazoned by Villiger plus a third by an outside party. It stirred memories of that 1973 season with Graham Hill, but this arrangement was with an entity called Interscope. This was a sprawling American media enterprise founded by an extremely wealthy racing enthusiast named Frederick "Ted" Field. His Interscope Racing team engaged in several forms of the sport, including USAC Indy, IMSA GTP and SCCA F5000. Field's primary driver was Danny Ongais, aka "The Flyin' Hawaiian," a former US drag racing National Champion who also showed speed on everything from motorcycles to F1 machines. In F1 he had twice raced a Penske in 1977, placing seventh in Canada, and he began 1978 with Mo Nunn's Ensign team, although to no effect.

It's impossible to imagine that the acquisitive Mr. Nichols didn't dream of bigger things resulting from his 1978 relationship with the fabulously well-off Mr. Field. Also, Don's taste in colors would have drawn his eye to Interscope's black paint, and the old paratrooper in him would have liked that the spectacular Danny "On-the-Gas" had been one as well. But it all came to nothing. The Interscope car would be seen at GPs just twice in 1978, without making it through qualifying to either race.

The factory team did take cars to every race for both Hans-Joachim Stuck and Clay Regazzoni. But not with new cars at first, because the DN9s weren't done in time to start the season. Instead, the boys dusted off and shipped familiar old DN8Cs to South America, number 16 for Stuck, 17 for "Regga."

ARGENTINE GP
Buenos Aires, F1 (R1), January 15th, 1978
1st, Mario Andretti, Lotus 78
17th, Hans-Joachim Stuck, Shadow DN8C
15th, Clay Regazzoni, Shadow DN8C

Shadow's first results of the season were utterly unremarkable, but at least they finished. Arrows was not in the country at all. Way up front, Mario Andretti and Lotus were off to a rousing season, although still employing the year-old type 78.

BRAZILIAN GP
Rio, F1 (R2), January 29th, 1978
1st, Carlos Reutemann, Ferrari 312T2
5th, Clay Regazzoni, Shadow DN8C
DNF, Hans-Joachim Stuck, Shadow DN8C, fuel system

Arrows did make it to this round on a new circuit, a flat autodrome along the coast from Rio at a place called Jacarepagua. Their solo FA1 placed 10th in the hands of former Shadowman Riccardo Patrese. We're confident new Shadowman Clay Regazzoni gave him a cheery wave from his points-scoring fifth place aboard a DN8C. A fuel problem forced out Stuck.

SOUTH AFRICAN GP
Kyalami, F1 (R3), March 4th, 1978
1st, Ronnie Peterson, Lotus 78
DNQ, Hans-Joachim Stuck, Shadow DN8C
DNQ, Clay Regazzoni, Shadow DN8C

Both rivals were now at full strength. Against Shadow's old cars the new Arrows proved stronger, if not to great ultimate effect: Patrese actually led for many laps until his engine blew, while his team-mate Rolf Stommelen finished ninth. Neither Shadow DN8C even qualified at Kyalami; this was a season that frequently had more entries than available grid places.

BELOW Regga at Rio. Shadow's new DN9 isn't ready yet, so the aging DN8Cs enjoy the summer sun one more time. Aero evolution has continued under Dave Wass; see the different nose inlet compared to last year's. This is a good view of the side skirts, which improve downforce by discouraging external air from degrading low pressure under the car.
Motorsport Images/David Phipps

DECLINE

INTERNATIONAL TROPHY (GB)

Silverstone, F1 (non-championship), March 19th, 1978
1st, Keke Rosberg, Theodore TR1
NC, Hans-Joachim Stuck, Shadow DN9, ignition
DNF, Clay Regazzoni, Shadow DN9, shunt with Hunt

What was it about Good Olde Silverstone that made for chaotic races? Here once again was a little event crammed full of big drama.

Taking their regular pre-spring break from the hard grind of Grand Prix racing in sunny southern climes, many of the F1 circus traveled to Silverstone amidst the bucolic fields of central England for a pleasant afternoon sprint in the rain.

Lots of rain. Torrents of it. A veritable deluge of rain and mud and spray as thick as London fog.

Really, like Fuji a year and a half earlier, it was a race that shouldn't have started. Conditions were worse, said a man who knew — James Hunt, who had clinched his World Championship that soggy Sunday in Japan.

On this rain-drenched Sunday in Northamptonshire James started from pole position, only to aquaplane off the outside of fast Abbey Curve three quarters of the way around the first lap.

A moment later he was joined by Clay Regazzoni. Who was then hit by similarly helpless Mario Andretti.

At that point it looked like the lucky ones were Niki Lauda and Ronnie Peterson, both of whom had slid into glutinous mud on the warmup lap and never got to the grid.

Of those who did start, so many experienced so many shunts and offs and drowned electrics that fully 12 of the 17 qualified starters failed to see the finish line.

Among them was Stuck, who came along with his team-mate Regazzoni to give their

BELOW Shadow leads a race! Hans-Joachim Stuck in his Shadow DN9 has five laps of glory in front of the field. OK, it's a rapidly thinning field in horrid conditions, and it won't last long. But he'll take it. *Motorsport Images/David Phipps*

spanking new Shadow DN9s their baptism. In chassis no. 1, Hans-Joachim managed a good getaway from the middle of the sparse grid, and so many cars ahead abruptly vanished that there came an amazing moment when his bright red-and-white DN9 came slithering through the spray leading the race! And it kept on leading for five laps.

But water started to cause a misfire that cost the Cosworth its speed. Stuck did keep plowing on, and he was in fifth place as he crossed the finish line, but he was the last to do so. He had lost so many laps that he couldn't be counted as a finisher.

Who won? Had you heard before of someone from Finland called Keke Rosberg? You would in years to come.

Regazzoni was in this race only to systems-check the brand new DN9, chassis no. 2, that was meant to go to Interscope for the next GP. That's why it bore Interscope's glossy black bodywork like the Shadows of yore. But Andretti's glossy black-and-gold Lotus hit it so hard that ever afterward Don Nichols would refer to Mario as "The Destroyer."

UNITED STATES WEST GP
Long Beach, F1 (R4), April 2nd, 1978
1st, Carlos Reutemann, Ferrari 312T2
10th, Clay Regazzoni, Shadow DN8C
DNS, Hans-Joachim Stuck, Shadow DN9, crash in practice
DNQ, Danny Ongais, Shadow DN9

California was where Shadow's first DN9 ran its first GP. In fact two arrived, but brand-new chassis no. 3 was for customer team Interscope, whose "The Flyin' Hawaiian" Danny Ongais failed to qualify. The single works car, chassis no. 2, was handed to Hans-Joachim "Strietzel" Stuck. Caught out was Gianclaudio Regazzoni, who had expected to be driving no. 3 but had to make do one more time with the good ol' DN8C.

ABOVE Interscope's spanking new black beauty must please the Shadowman's artistic eye in the Long Beach pit lane. But he won't get to see it in the race. *Don Nichols collection*

BELOW But neither will Shadow's own DN9 make it to the starting grid. The California beachside city's streets are a bit more spacious than Monaco's, but no less savage. *Revs Institute for Automotive Research/John Blakemore*

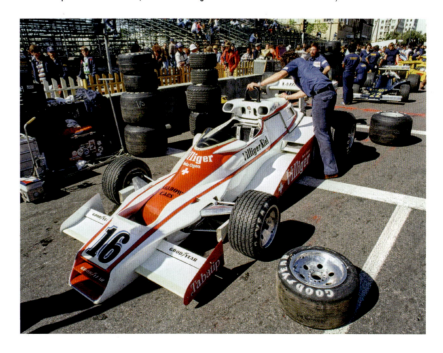

ABOVE "Danny on the Gas" Ongais is one of America's fastest drivers of the day in or aboard anything on wheels, but the entirely unsorted black Shadow won't let him show it. Interscope misses the show.
Revs Institute for Automotive Research/John Blakemore

Good ol' "Regga" made do reasonably well, scoring 10th. Stuck failed to start because of a crash in practice. Meanwhile, those other guys from Arrows placed sixth and ninth.

MONACO GP

Monte Carlo, F1 (R5), May 7th, 1978
1st, Patrick Depailler, Tyrrell 008
DNF, Hans-Joachim Stuck, Shadow DN9, steering
DNQ, Clay Regazzoni, Shadow DN9

Monaco in May, how marvelous. Especially for France's Patrick Depailler, who scored a heartwarming first victory. Down the back things were less joyous. Regazzoni finally got his own DN9, no. 4, but wasn't able to push it hard enough to qualify. Stuck did race his no. 1, but problems with its steering put him out. Arrows again came out ahead, with Patrese sixth, though Stommelen retired of illness.

BELGIAN GP

Zolder, F1 (R6), May 21st, 1978
1st, Mario Andretti, Lotus 79
DNF, Hans-Joachim Stuck, Shadow DN9, spin
DNF, Clay Regazzoni, Shadow DN9, gearbox

Here is where Mario Andretti debuted Lotus's space-age type 79 by scoring its first victory, and his second of the year.

For Shadow, this is where both new DN9s finally made a Grand Prix grid. But not the finish. "Stuckie" went out after he spun, "Regga" after his differential failed. Both Arrows retired as well.

SPANISH GP

Jarama, F1 (R7), June 4th, 1978
1st, Mario Andretti, Lotus 78
15th, Clay Regazzoni, Shadow DN9
DNF, Hans-Joachim Stuck, Shadow DN9, suspension

Andretti duplicated the result of the previous round, becoming the first man this year to win three GPs. As for the friendly rival teams with duplicate cars, they almost had duplicate results. Regazzoni placed 15th (despite fuel injection issues) and Stuck retired (suspension trouble), while Stommelen finished 14th but Patrese dropped out again.

SWEDISH GP

Anderstorp, F1 (R8), June 17th, 1978
1st, Niki Lauda, Brabham-Alfa Romeo BT46B
5th, Clay Regazzoni, Shadow DN9
11th, Hans-Joachim Stuck, Shadow DN9

The fresh, woodsy air of Sweden seemed to break the monotony a bit.

There was a fresh winner in a fresh car, Niki Lauda in a Gordon Murray-designed Brabham powered by an Alfa Romeo flat-12. Which powered a large fan in back, shrouded so it looked like a jet fighter. The fan wasn't to push it along, but to suck it to the ground. Yes, Can-Am Chaparral 2J style.

Powered ground effect went over about as well in 1978 as it had back in 1970. Howls of outrage arose from other pit stalls, protest papers waved furiously, and the car was soon outlawed. Naughty Niki could keep his win, but Mr. Ecclestone must never, ever pull such a stunt again.

Meanwhile, obscured by all the fuss, the fellow on the second step of the podium was — goodness! It's young Riccardo Patrese.

Let me see, doesn't he drive… heavens above! He's earned six championship points for Arrows!

Those miffed sniffs one heard from the Shadow compound meant: a) we scored points as well, our Clay placed fifth; b) our Stuck was 11th, three up on your Rolfie; and c) don't forget what's going on in the High Court… we have confidence in winning that one.

BELOW Clay Regazzoni has had to wait a long while to get a DN9 into the points, but he finally manages it in Sweden. Notice that by now the induction scoops are gone from behind his head.
Motorsport Images/David Phipps

OPPOSITE Together for the last time at Hockenheim, the Arrows and Shadow "brothers from another mother" still have to rely mainly on paint to hide how little they differ. Except in results. Rolf Stommelen in the gold FA1 will be disqualified from the race; Clay Regazzoni in the red-and-white DN9 won't qualify for it. *Motorsport Images/LAT*

FRENCH GP
Paul Ricard, F1 (R9), July 2nd, 1978
1st, Mario Andretti, Lotus 79
11th, Hans-Joachim Stuck, Shadow DN9
DNF, Clay Regazzoni, Shadow DN9, ignition

Paul Ricard's French GP opened the second half of the season. Mario got back on top again in his Lotus 79, a legal ground-effects car unlike Brabham's, so he had four victories from the nine races so far. Shadow's Stuck placed 11th, but Regazzoni retired. Both Arrows finished, Patrese eighth and Stommelen 15th.

BRITISH GP
Brands Hatch, F1 (R10), July 16th, 1978
1st, Carlos Reutemann, Ferrari 312T3
5th, Hans-Joachim Stuck, Shadow DN9
DNF, Clay Regazzoni, Shadow DN9, gearbox

Hans-Joachim Stuck doubled the DN9's points tally, finishing fifth. True, his team-mate retired, but so did Patrese's Arrows. Stommelen's? Didn't even qualify to race.

GERMAN GP
Hockenheim, F1 (R11), July 30th, 1978
1st, Mario Andretti, Lotus 79
DNF, Hans-Joachim Stuck, Shadow DN9, crash
DNQ, Clay Regazzoni, Shadow DN9

Mario-guess-who-Andretti scored his fifth win. Yes, that was definitely a pattern you sense forming. Not so much down in our half of the field. Stuck failed to finish because of an accident, Regazzoni failed to make the grid. The Other Guys did bring Patrese to the flag in ninth place, but Stommelen was disqualified for entering the pits via a route not approved.

And right after that, the Arrows FA1 itself was disqualified. Flagrant copyright violation, declared the judge. Don't race those cars ever again. So the Sharrows Affair was over.

AUSTRIAN GP
Österreichring, F1 (R12), August 13th, 1978
1st, Ronnie Peterson, Lotus 79
DNF, Hans-Joachim Stuck, Shadow DN9, crash
NC, Clay Regazzoni, Shadow DN9, insufficient laps

If Don Nichols expected never again to see Mssrs. Rees, Oliver, Wass and Southgate (the man of the letters "FA" was already put away), he must have been a bit nonplussed upon his arrival in Austria. Arrows had been busy in the workshop as well as the courtroom, and they appeared at the O-Ring with a pair of sparkling new cars. Genuinely new. Designed by Southgate and built in great secrecy, and at impressive speed, the new A1 had nothing to do with any old Shadow.

Mr. Nichols now had many old Shadows. Mr. Oliver had been instructed to send his five viable FA1s to Northampton, where in the fullness of time they would become additional DN9s. Which, to be brutally frank, would do Shadow little good.

Austria gave Hans Stuck his second consecutive retirement, because of his second consecutive accident. Unfortunately that only started a chain of frustration that stretched to the end of the 16-race season — his car wouldn't again reach a checkered flag.

Clay Regazzoni's luck would be even worse — except once.

DUTCH GP
Zandvoort, F1 (R13), August 27th, 1978
1st, Mario Andretti, Lotus 79
DNF, Hans-Joachim Stuck, Shadow DN9, differential
DNQ, Clay Regazzoni, Shadow DN9
DNQ, Danny Ongais, Shadow DN9

"Once again Clay Regazzoni failed to qualify the Shadow DN9," wrote Jeff Hutchinson for *Formula* magazine. "His first day was spoilt with gearbox problems, and Regga made little secret of the

fact he was not happy with the way things were going… the rumor is that he will be back in the seat of an Ensign before the end of the season."

Hutch didn't even bother to report the futile second-time presence of Interscope with Ongais. At least Stuck's gearbox lasted for 56 laps of the 75.

ITALIAN GP
Monza, F1 (R14), September 10th, 1978
1st, Niki Lauda, Brabham-Alfa Romeo BT46
DNF, Hans-Joachim Stuck, Shadow DN9, multi-car accident
NC, Clay Regazzoni, Shadow DN9, insufficient laps

This was one of the black days everyone dreads. At the start a number of cars tangled en masse at the absurdly tight entry to the first chicane. An enormous billow of searing flames obscured the scene for long fearsome moments.

Worst injuries were to Ronnie Peterson, whose Lotus sustained savage impact and burst apart. Both Shadows were caught in the pileup, with Stuck's so heavily damaged it retired on the spot. Regazzoni was also involved, but was able to get out of his DN9 and rush with several other drivers into the flaming wreckage to rescue poor Ronnie. Taken to hospital with severe leg injuries, the brilliant Swedish driver lost his life there to an embolism.

"Regga" participated in the restarted, shortened race to end it 15th on the road, but brake problems cost him too many laps to be counted as a finisher.

By finishing sixth Mario Andretti clinched his World Championship. Eerily, the Italian-born American's day of triumph here in his native land came on a day made somber by the same tragic circumstances that tarnished the achievement of America's first F1 title holder: 17 years earlier at the same circuit, Phil Hill was forced to "celebrate" his title despite the loss of a team-mate, Ferrari's Wolfgang von Trips.

BELOW Disaster at the first corner of the Monza race takes the life of Ronnie Peterson, and with it any joy from his team-mate's championship.
Motorsport Images/David Phipps

UNITED STATES EAST GP
Watkins Glen, F1 (R15), October 1st, 1978
1st, Carlos Reutemann, Ferrari 312T3
14th, Clay Regazzoni, Shadow DN9
DNF, Hans-Joachim Stuck, Shadow DN9, fuel pump

Your scribe might have sounded a bit snarky back in Holland by noting that *Formula* magazine's report didn't mention one of the Shadows… but here in the US said scribe's role as *Formula*'s editor allowed him to assign himself to cover the US Grand Prix. At which glorious event he didn't bother to mention the Shadow team at all. Mesmerized by the Mario magic, apparently. The new World Champion and his Lotus were in another world in Upstate New York.

Thanks to the more diligent work of others, all these years later I can tell you "Hanschen" qualified 14th and "Regga" 17th, but the German's fuel pump only gave him one lap of the race, leaving it to Clay to finish 14th, three laps behind winner Carlos Reutemann — who profited from Andretti's advantage in practice falling away along with a rear wheel in Sunday's warmup session.

CANADIAN GP
Montreal, F1 (R16), October 8th, 1978
1st, Gilles Villeneuve, Ferrari 312T3
DNF, Hans-Joachim Stuck, Shadow DN9, crash
DNQ, Clay Regazzoni, Shadow DN9

At least yours truly did write the names Stuck and Shadow here at Montreal, but only to mention that, after a remarkable wet-weather qualifying session put the tall German eighth on the grid, it all went for nothing because of an unremarkable collision on the first lap.

That only helped a certain former Shadow driver named Jarier, who had filled the sadly empty second seat at Lotus. To the joyous acclaim of the French-Canadian crowd he started from pole position (Andretti's car was giving the champ a miserable weekend) and came around the first lap four seconds ahead of anyone else. Which grew to six seconds on the second lap. And seven next time around.

The next man at that point was another former Shadowman named Jones, while a local boy making good named Villeneuve was a close third. Which position turned into a huge lead when mechanical troubles cut down both drivers ahead.

Young Gilles cruised his Ferrari on to his first career GP victory, accompanied by delirious rapture expressed through tens of thousands of hoarse French-Canadian throats. It was like a movie.

BOX SCORES: Shadow model DN9s appeared 14 times at 13 Grands Prix during 1978 (the team used DN8Cs at the earlier ones), where they finished in the points twice (fifths in Sweden and England), were classified 11th twice and 14th once, retired 12 times, and failed seven times even to qualify.

Drivers Stuck and Regazzoni ranked 18th and 16th respectively; neither would stay on. As a marque Shadow ranked 11th among constructors with a total of six points, two of them achieved by a DN8C.

Twenty miles down the M1 at Arrows, the constructor score was 11 points and joint ninth in the championship, despite racing one fewer time while having to introduce two different cars. Advantage Mr. Oliver.

Oh, and yes, despite the heartbreak at Monza, Mssrs. Andretti and Chapman did come out on top, champion driver and constructor respectively. A team with a secret weapon: the Lotus 79, an even better ground-effects racecar than the previous year's, and therefore well ahead of any rivals who had tried to copy the 78.

But nobody could forget it came at the cost of fellow Lotus man Ronnie Peterson. ♠

SHADOW'S CHAMPION, SHADOWMAN'S RIGHT HAND

JACKIE OLIVER and Don Nichols raced together for seven seasons. The British driver earned six of the American team owner's eight competitive victories, and the marque's only series championship. But Ollie contributed much more.

In the car he had the right foot; outside, he was the right hand to guide and implement a cascade of enthusiastic ideas from an ebullient but inexperienced racing neophyte.

Oliver's contributions included a relentless, hard-nosed, bluntly businesslike management style aimed squarely at success; also an innate gift for suave salesmanship that garnered millions in sponsorship; and the social cachet of a Formula 1 driver and Le Mans 24 Hours winner who represented the American team with European charm and English wit.

Conversely, Don's ambitious but amorphous desire to be a player on the world stage provided an opportunity for Oliver to develop and demonstrate his own abilities as a team principal as he looked ahead to a time when he would no longer drive.

Growing disagreements and a consequent split left hard feelings, but eventually these proud men were able to reconcile. Each has said of the other, "I couldn't have done it without him."

To us, Oliver has expressed these thoughts:

BELOW Keith Jack Oliver, age 30 here at Kyalami in 1973, had raced F1 with Lotus and BRM and won Le Mans along with other sports car classics. *Motorsport Images/David Phipps*

I'D LIKE to see Don get credit for being a major racecar constructor from the United States. Everybody talks about Dan Gurney, everybody talks about Chaparral, but they don't seem for some reason to talk in similar terms about Shadow. That may be because of Don, I don't know.

But I have been disappointed that what he did achieve has not been appreciated. All the years in Can-Am and Formula 5000, and eight years of F1 as a constructor, he receives no recognition for that. Alright, it was a mid-grid team, but he did win some races. Alan Jones won a Grand Prix.

So Shadow did achieve quite a lot. Not as much as we would have liked, but for what he did achieve I think Don should be acknowledged. If it had not been for him it would never have happened.

IN 1970, when I was racing in the Can-Am with Peter Bryant, who had designed a pretty good car, the Titanium Ti22, Don Nichols asked if I would drive for him. I said, "Don, that's very kind, but no." He said why not? I said, "Because the concept of your car is not correct."

I think that stuck in his mind. He came back and said, "If you won't drive the car because you think it's wrong, what should it be?"

I said, "Well, the first thing you need to do is to hire someone that has knowledge of how to build a racecar that's going to work. Because the one you've got doesn't work. It has too many problems. The best person you can get to do that is Peter Bryant, because he's an itinerant race mechanic. He's had a lot of previous experience about what it takes to make a practical, competitive and reliable racing vehicle."

[Bryant tells it quite differently in his book. He indicates that he was the initiator of the project.]

Well, why I did end up driving for Nichols after I told him a small-wheeled car wasn't right? The facts tell the story. So with Peter, probably like most people's memories of events, what came first, "the Chicken or the Egg?" His book fits how he thought it happened.

I remember saying to Don, "With aerodynamics, the drag coefficient of a racecar is mostly affected by the shadow it makes on the wall behind when you put a light in front of it. So there's no point in having small wheels if you've got a massive big engine and the wing behind the driver."

Don was an entrepreneur. What he did when trying to convince people to support him was based on, "I'm going to do something different, and really exciting, which means it is going to win." That was his *modus operandi*. He didn't want to follow a traditional line, because it wasn't exciting enough to get people to support him.

The difficulty with that approach is, while some people are blinded by it, if you're trying to sell it to someone who knows it's wrong, you're not going to get the right people. People experienced in launching racing programs know that unproven novelty is a disaster.

Motorsport is a year-long business. When you've got a car that is dodgy, you spend all your time firefighting things. Performance and reliability therefore suffer.

WHEN IT WAS decided to include F1 in Shadow's program, Don wanted to continue building the cars in the US. I said, "With all due respect, I think the best place to make racing cars is in the UK." And I gave him all the reasons why.

Taking that step was the right thing for Shadow to do. There's nothing wrong with an American F1 constructor having a car made in the UK. It doesn't take away from the fact that it's owned by an American, and the impetus is American, and rightly displays the Stars & Stripes on the airbox. It's still an American constructor, and the fact that they've used a pool of resources available no other place in the world, with all the experienced personnel and component suppliers, and it's close to so many of the Grands Prix, that is the correct move.

ABOVE Fellow Brit Peter Bryant (left) recruited "Ollie" to debut Shadow's first Can-Am car here at Saint-Jovite in 1971. *Lionel Birnbom*

I told Don that I would recommend Tony Southgate, because he designed a very good car for me at BRM. We would also need a manager to run the operation in the UK, and I said Alan Rees would be very good.

I think Peter Bryant felt as though he was moved sideways. I suppose he was, really, but in motorsport what you try and do is get the best driver, a strong budget, a top designer with previous credentials, fabricators, suppliers and mechanics, a suitable factory fitted out to construct the cars. And that's what we did.

[Peter's book describes a bitter confrontation with you and Don after his wife informed him he'd been passed over without his ever being told.]

Well, that's probably true. I mean, the fact of the matter is I didn't own the company. All I did was drive the car, albeit suggesting and instigating changes involved with getting the job done.

And Peter was not a designer. He was a race mechanic, and a good one, but he was not a designer. He would copy what

ABOVE Winning his fourth 1974 Can-Am in a row here at Mid-Ohio earned Jackie's first series championship, his career high. *Dan R. Boyd*

other people did. And also he wasn't a manager of people. Peter was no longer of any use to Nichols Advanced Vehicle Systems in the change of direction for Shadow goals.

But I suspect Don probably didn't point that out to Peter and handle it very well. He wasn't good at identifying the best people to carry out the tasks required for his ideas. But even if Don had been more diplomatic, it would have still upset Peter that he had been dropped.

Maybe Peter felt he should have come and designed the car in England. Unlikely. He wouldn't have been the right person.

It was not my place to tell him. It was Don who employed Peter, not me.

IN 1973 I drove both F1 and Can-Am. It was a very busy and difficult year, the results were very thin. In F1 George got a couple of points, we both had third-place finishes. We were a very new team.

In Can-Am I was the only driver and the car wasn't good. The Turbo especially, it was very difficult to drive. That also had been the case the year before, when I tested an early version at Riverside. It was Don who wanted a turbocharged car, to match Porsche. His enthusiasm got the better of him, because the technology and the funding and the ability with which to develop your own engine was not in Shadow. They got big truck turbos and stuck them on a normally aspirated engine. Produced fifteen, eighteen hundred horsepower. The lag was horrendous.

The first time I drove it, you'd plant your foot, nothing would happen for a second or so, then suddenly you'd have not only 1,500 horsepower, but more than 1,500 foot pounds of torque and you'd just light up the rear wheels. Everywhere. I even lit up the rear wheels at Riverside in top gear.

Not only that, the torque curve was very peaky. It would come on with an enormous wallop, BANG! Very exciting, but then immediately it would drop away again. The car was a beast. Extremely difficult to drive, and slower than the normally aspirated car. Which wasn't very fast either.

OUR CAN-AM car for 1974 was entirely the opposite. That's because we completely changed our approach. We had demonstrated that a turbo Chev wasn't the way to go, and anyway Porsche had pulled out. At the same time new rules greatly reduced the amount of fuel we had to carry, so Tony's DN4 was quite good, small and light and very, very quick. We had no major competition, really.

Except between ourselves. We were going to run two cars, the other for Peter Revson. I was quite looking forward to that, but you know what happened. George Follmer was brought in, another American, and the competition between us became contentious. Very contentious.

Our speeds in the cars were similar, but in the race there was something different. I think it frustrated him. He's a very competitive guy, good driver. He was a little bit of an angry bear, because I have oodles of that sarcastic English humor, but it didn't go down very well with my American team-mate.

What happened at Mid-Ohio, he tried to intimidate me. He came up the inside and tried to lean on me. But I didn't move. There was a lot of contact and in the end he damaged his car and had to retire. Fortunately, mine didn't get damaged enough to cause a retirement.

It happens. Race drivers are very competitive, selfish

people, and they'll use every tool in the toolbox with which to try and gain an advantage. With George it just got a little too big, and I used to wind him up a little bit.

He was a big guy, and he used to say, "If I get hold of you, you're going to be sorry you said that." When it came to possible physical violence in the paddock I couldn't match him, but I could run quicker than him. It would appear I could even on the track.

George was convinced we had team orders for me to win. We didn't. He wouldn't have complied anyway, but the fact is I won all the rounds in the championship. I can understand his feeling that way. I possess the same competitiveness. To be a competitive racing driver you have to believe in yourself, because as soon as you believe that you're not quick enough, you're not going to win.

So, if you're getting beaten and you have that philosophy that "I'm good, there's no way I can't beat that guy," the only relief that you have with which to maintain that belief is to believe he's got something you haven't got. Absolutely natural.

I ran an F1 team for 20 years, had all the drivers through my fingers. All the best ones believed themselves to be the best in the field. Some dealt with it by doing something about it in the cockpit. Others dealt with it by doing something outside the cockpit, normally complaining of why they hadn't got the upgrade. Why can't I have better equipment than him? That's how it manifests itself.

It's quite natural, and George isn't unlike anybody else, except that he carried the belief to extremes when we did that demonstration thing at Watkins Glen.

Don wanted to have sort of a mini-race, because everybody wanted to see the Follmer-Oliver battle. So we ran this stupid little race and George won, first time he ever beat me. It wasn't important, it was a demonstration. Jean-Pierre Jarier was in a third car, as he was there driving in F1 for Shadow. He came a distant third although he was probably the fastest driver of the three of us.

Afterwards I spoke to Lee Muir, the engine builder, and he said, "We gave him a bigger engine." [Laughs] Because George asked for it. He said, "Why can't I have a big engine like Oliver had the whole time?" I didn't have, obviously, but they made a big engine for him.

But the competition between us both made the championship more interesting. George and I are good mates, now. Whenever we see each other we laugh about it.

FORMULA 5000 is what Don wanted us to do after Can-Am ended. He wanted to keep the shop in Chicago open. But we didn't want to detract from the F1 operation in Northampton, so rather than design a new F5000 chassis the shortcut was to use the F1 chassis.

The problem was, the Dodge engine with its cast-iron block was very heavy, too heavy for the DN5 chassis. The weight distribution wasn't right. The engine was very powerful, traction was very good, so on some circuits I could do well, but you had Unser and Andretti, very good drivers, in Lolas that were designed for the Chevy engine. I was always disadvantaged with corner entry speed.

I noticed particularly with Mario that I just couldn't get into the corner as quickly as he could with the Lola. I just couldn't balance the car. Maybe it was me, I mean Unser and Andretti were very good drivers, but even when Tom Pryce came over to drive the car he couldn't get the hang of it. It kept on swapping ends. You know, he was a good driver.

I think it would have been better if we had had two cars. I would have preferred that, but the budget wouldn't stretch to it.

AFTER UOP went away I wanted to stay in the United States. I already had a house in Chicago. I wanted to build an American F1 team with Don, based both in the USA and in Britain, where the cars were made. That was my ambition. I was looking to expand and maintain the organization with Don. But Don didn't want a partner in the business. So that's where the problem came.

I was still driving, but did a lot more than just drive the cars. All sorts of management matters kept me hopping between the UK and the USA, and other international locations. That was taking a toll on me, honestly. I was finding the money and looking after the sponsors, particularly Tabatip and the Italian, Franco Ambrosio. I raised an awful lot of money to support the F1 team.

I had an inherent ability to present. Don and I would go together, because having a driver with you, a famous race driver with a fair amount of success in other formulae, it was a door-opener. So all the money we raised with Don, we did it together, keeping the team afloat. And I was prodding the organization along in the right direction as well.

I also drove the F1 car when the regular drivers weren't available. Don should have seen in me somebody he didn't want to lose.

ABOVE Franco Ambrosio was a significant Shadow sponsor who gave frustrated Oliver the encouragement he needed to break away and form his own team. *Courtesy of Jackie Oliver*

He wasn't a very open person, he would never talk about what he was doing, but I got the feeling that he was going to move the operation back to the United States and build the cars in Elk Grove. That would have been the wrong thing to do.

I remember saying, "Don, you want an American operation. But whether you're racing in the USA or in Europe, with me or not with me, if you're in F1 the cars need to be based in Northampton. So look after your manufacturing facility there, rather than your base in Chicago."

What finally broke the camel's back was that he started a road car project that was something to do with battery technology. Very forward thinking for the time, but if you're doing the maths, what's going to happen to the F1 team? Northampton was starting to suffer.

I went into the office mid-1977 and just stuck my nose in the accounts books. The money that we were getting for F1 sponsorship, he was siphoning it off to pay for that road car facility as well as the F5000, which didn't have any sponsorship. It wasn't going to the F1 team, which is what the money was raised for. Which I was pretty sore about.

He was entitled to do it. It was his business. He was trying to save his home base, and let the F1 team find its own feet. But it wasn't what I wanted to do.

I STARTED to think, what's going to happen now? I said, "Do you want to sell the Shadow F1 operation?" That was the proposal I made at the British Grand Prix in 1977. He said, "Well, let me think about." So he avoided it.

The reason why I was thinking that way was Franco Ambrosio, our sponsor. He didn't get on with Don. "I don't get this Don guy," he said. He was Italian, but Don didn't speak that language. I did. I used to take Franco to all the interesting locations with others in the sport, and of course there were the girls, because he was having fun and enjoying the whole activity. He was spending millions of dollars personally sponsoring the team. I wasn't driving the cars when I was looking after him at the F1 races.

He said, "You seem to be running the team. You're doing all the work. Why don't you do it on your own?" So I had someone who would back me.

I think by the time we got to the Italian Grand Prix I had already decided that I would start my own team. There was a factory in Milton Keynes and I put a deposit down. I had spoken to Tony Southgate and he said, "You're going to start your own operation? You're out of your mind." I asked if he would come with me. "It's too risky," he said.

Others agreed to come with me, however, most of them in fact. In fairness, they wanted to follow Alan Rees as well.

Bernie Ecclestone saw what was happening and got involved. He rang me up in October. "What are you up to, Oliver?" I told him. "Have you talked with Don? What does he say?" I said he wasn't saying anything. Bernie said, "OK. Why don't you two come and see me. I'll sit you down and see what the result is."

Don came over from the US and the first thing he did was to ask Alan Rees what was going on. Alan told him and Don asked him what he was going to do. Alan said, "Well, what are you going to do?" Don said, "I'm going to carry on."

Alan said, "Well, in that case you really need to think about the funds, because there's no funds here in Northampton anymore. And we've got a lot of debts."

Don says, "What debts have we got?" He didn't know! Alan hadn't told him, not exactly. There were unpaid bills from several suppliers. Some of them had gone to court and obtained writs.

So the whole thing blew up right there and then. I was waiting in the meeting with Bernie, so I got on the phone and said, "Where is Don?" He wasn't coming.

Two weeks after all this, after all of the people had handed in their notice and Alan confirmed he was going to join my operation, Southgate turned up at Shadow and there were only two other people there. He called Don and told him there was no possibility of finishing the car, so he was leaving. I said, "Great, Tony, come on board."

Unfortunately, Tony brought Shadow drawings along with him, and everybody knows what happened then. Fortunately, our solicitor was able to get the court case delayed until we could build our second Arrows car and keep going.

But it could have been different with Don. You know, when you've got an organization with people who have been with you for a long time, if you don't look after them and their ambitions, they'll go away. And that was the mistake he made.

DON'S SHADOW concept was based on the old radio program from the '50s. "Whatever Shadow lurks in the hearts of evil men" or something like that.

The concept was brilliant! Black car, mysterious Shadow figure in the cape; if the car had been more successful, those images from the marketing aspect would have blossomed. Don had the entrepreneurialism, he was a very persuasive individual, very enthusiastic, good person to work with, but the performance of the team was always held back. Without domination, what he created didn't grow as fast as it should have done.

NOT LONG before his death I went to an historic race event at Laguna Seca, and I was sitting at an autograph table when Don approached me. I slipped away and we chatted for a few minutes. He asked me over to his house that evening. I told him that I'd love to come but couldn't, because I had to get on a plane.

So we made up right there and then. I said, "Don, are you all right?" He said, "Yes, Jackie, I couldn't have done it without you."

ABOVE Shadowing his former driver at Dijon in 1977, tall Don Nichols had already lost two others to accident, major sponsorship to corporate reshuffling, and was about to lose crucial manager Oliver to neglect. *Motorsport Images/LAT*

DECLINE **403**

CHAPTER 19
SCRATCHING TO SURVIVE

DN9B (FORMULA 1), 1979

YET ANOTHER harsh winter in the Shadow shop. The drivers departed, so did the design engineer, and the hitherto seemingly hopeful cigarillo manufacturer ended his support except in an occasional minor way.

Don Nichols certainly needed a new car for the new year. Like everyone else's 1978 contender, Shadow's DN9 had followed the lead of Lotus with its type 78 "Wing Car" of the previous year.

But Lotus itself had taken the next step. Its championship-winning 79 had a fully articulated skirt system, making it more of a "tunnel car" able to use all the power of ground effects.

It was time for a Shadow DN11, and John Gentry started making drawings. But Nichols couldn't afford to build it, Gentry left mid-project, and the sadly diminished team had to make do with the old car, unsuccessful though it had been.

One staffer who didn't leave was team manager Jo Ramirez. The longtime premier racing mechanic, veteran of innumerable all-nighters and, often, consequent race victories, stayed in Northampton. So did general manager Bert Baldwin, formerly a tire technician for Goodyear.

Fresh faces included designers Richard Owen and Vic Morris, who picked up the task of upgrading the DN9 of 1978 into a B-model for 1979. Nichols also lured back his first designer, Trevor Harris, for a time.

All this activity and appearance of stability likely provided potential sponsors with a sense of reassurance, and indeed, fresh funding did come in, sufficient to again run two cars.

But not sufficient for their liveries to match. Driving one car for a Dutch tobacco firm named Samson was Dutch driver Jan Lammers, 1978's European Formula 3 Champion. Shadow's familiar number 17 identified this one, but seemed superfluous once the sponsor spiffed it up with one of the most in-your-face flamboyant paint jobs ever seen in motorsport.

ABOVE In the points at last! The very last: Watkins Glen's season finale is where Elio De Angelis finally holds the road in the wet while all about him are losing it, finally splashing home in fourth place. Shadow's DN9B may look like a Lotus, but it isn't. Its new coachwork enfolds a year-old DN9 chassis. *Getty Images/ Bernard Cahier*

LEFT Elio is the youngest driver in this year's series, but is starting to show more promise than most. The rookie from Italy is flanked here by team manager Jo Ramirez (left) and visiting designer Trevor Harris. This garage interior is not identified, but Harris will have left after Silverstone. *Don Nichols collection*

SCRATCHING TO SURVIVE **405**

RIGHT Jan Lammers has a year on De Angelis, making it a pair of Old Shadowmen here, exchanging hard-won life lessons prior to the Austrian GP.
Motorsport Images/Ercole Colombo

The second car's number was no longer 16, which George Follmer brought to the team in 1973. Those digits had escaped to live with a driver for Renault. This year's number 18 identified a young Italian named Elio De Angelis, the most recent winner of that all-important F3 race in Monaco. His father, a multiple champion in powerboat racing, was sufficiently well off to boost his boy's career advancement into F1. At just 21 Elio was the youngest driver in the field that year; his teammate Jan, age 22, was next youngest.

Whatever the terms of the De Angelis family support, it didn't include sponsorship of the car itself. The dull blue-black flanks of Elio's machine were treated as advertising panels, variously displaying occasional temporary brand names, or simply the marque name, or sometimes no name at all.

The quasi-rectangular shapes of those flat flanks made the cars look new, and indeed were part of wholesale aerodynamic changes, but under the skins sat the same DN9 chassis from the year before. Over the winter the team discarded Southgate's original dual-element aerofoils to adopt the same single-wing concept invented by Lotus for its championship-winning type 79 and, naturally, immediately copied by everyone else.

Changing a DN9 into a DN9B involved Lotus-style skirts, the rigid panels that could rise or fall in relation to the heaving chassis, so as to maintain the pressure seal along the bottoms of the body sidepods. That's why the sidepod exteriors had to be rectangular, compared to the more triangular configuration of the Southgate original, which only had angled rubber skirts to block the outside air trying to push in.

Part of the new concept was relocation of the water radiators from their places either side of the engine to abeam the driver's legs, where they now lived inside the leading edges of the now-single side-wings. (This was rather like the Trevor Harris wing atop the "Tiny Tire" Shadow at Saint-Jovite nine years before). The front-end oil radiator now lay exposed on the nosecone.

Just about everybody along the pitlane similarly copied the Lotus 79, and some actually improved on it, making them faster. Shadow did not achieve that level.

Some aero work by Shadow during the season, along with suspension developments like an entirely new Harris-designed rear end introduced at Silverstone, yielded some gains, but not enough to significantly improve results. Too much was lacking on other fronts. But the little team had tried, and it kept on trying. That's what racers do.

SHADOW'S 1978 F1 SEASON

Sweden dropped from the calendar following the tragic double loss of SuperSwede Ronnie Peterson and the death by cancer of Gunnar Nilsson, leaving this year's schedule with only 15 Grands Prix. Doing their bit to beef it up, two

ABOVE The new suspension does seem to make a measurable improvement, but makes for contention between the two drivers. Nor does it do much to reduce drag from the bulky exhaust system.
Trevor Harris collection

LEFT F3 champ Lammers at Buenos Aires for his first F1 race in the Shadow isn't a spectacular success, but a guy has to start somewhere. At this point the color scheme on DN9B no. 17 is serviceable, but wait. Back in Holland the sponsor's ad people have something up their sleeves.
Motorsport Images/LAT

SCRATCHING TO SURVIVE **407**

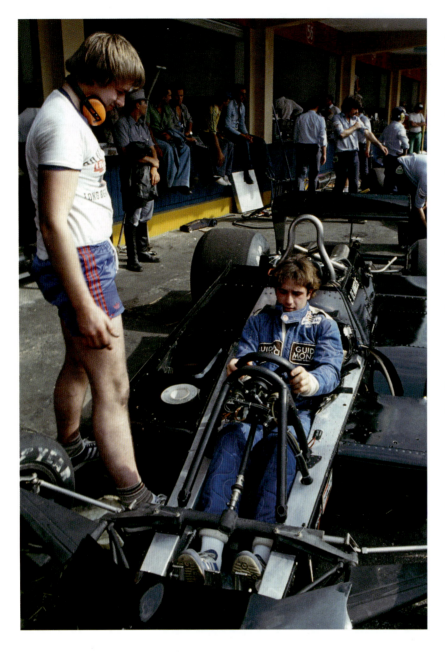

ABOVE Argentina also sees Shadow's other rookie trying out his new ride. This year's much-revised B-model has had a rethink of the DN9 front suspension mountings, no doubt to improve stiffness, but the main mod concerns the downforce aerodynamic system either side of the chassis. *Motorsport Images/ Ercole Colombo*

circuits announced shorter non-championship Formula 1 races, and a third put on a simple time-trial event.

The ensuing season was once again packed to overflowing with noise, color and glamor, drama, excitement, intrigue, thrilling battles in fabulous venues, magnificent performances leading to great triumphs… and of course goodly rations of disappointment and misery.

Shadow's season trended more toward the latter. Racers race to win, and this year any chance of trophies coming back to Northampton was next to nil. But racers race on.

ARGENTINE GP

Buenos Aires, F1 (R1), January 21st, 1979
1st, Jacques Laffite, Ligier JS11
7th, Elio De Angelis, Shadow DN9B
DNF, Jan Lammers, Shadow DN9B, CV joint

On a very hot and humid day in Buenos Aires there was a massive pileup at the first turn, resulting in a red flag, a cleanup, and a restart with five fewer cars.

The Shadowmen escaped trouble the first time, but in the real race Lammers's car broke down with transmission failure, a CV joint specifically. De Angelis kept going and might have finished in the points, but fuel system trouble slowed him at the end.

BRAZILIAN GP

Interlagos, F1 (R2), February 4th, 1979
1st, Jacques Laffite, Ligier JS11
14th, Jan Lammers, Shadow DN9B
15th, Elio De Angelis, Shadow DN9B

Both Shadow drivers crashed in practice, Lammers so heavily he had to switch to the spare car — yes, this struggling little team did manage to have a spare. Both youngsters were able to complete the race.

SOUTH AFRICAN GP

Kyalami, F1 (R3), March 3rd, 1979
1st, Gilles Villeneuve, Ferrari 312T4
DNF, Jan Lammers, Shadow DN9B accident lap 2
DNF, Elio De Angelis, Shadow DN9B, accident lap 16

The good work in Brazil came undone in South Africa, where Lammers again crashed in practice, and then in the race both he and De Angelis crashed — separately. An intra-team collision would have really spoiled the weekend.

UNITED STATES WEST GP

Long Beach, F1 (R4), April 8th, 1979
1st, Gilles Villeneuve, Ferrari 312T4
7th, Elio De Angelis, Shadow DN9B
DNF, Jan Lammers, Shadow DN9B accident damage

Young Jan was the quicker Shadow driver in practice, prompting *Autosport* reporter Jeff Hutchinson to credit the Dutchman's confidence to his youthful training at a skid school in his home town of Zandvoort. Unfortunately his race was ruined by a first-turn shunt that damaged his suspension. Younger Elio avoided the walls and made it to another seventh-place finish.

RACE OF CHAMPIONS (GB)

Brands Hatch, F1 (non-championship), April 15th, 1979
1st, Gilles Villeneuve, Ferrari 312T4
6th, Elio De Angelis, Shadow DN9B

A quick crowd-pleaser of 40 laps, this Easter extravaganza mixed seven contemporary Grand Prix cars with a dozen slightly older F1s now running a local series called Aurora. Shadow brought one car for De Angelis, who faced the likes of two different Lotuses for Mario Andretti (who put one on pole but finished third with several things going wrong), Gilles Villeneuve's Ferrari (which won convincingly) and both Brabham-Alfa drivers, Nelson Piquet (second) and Niki Lauda (fifth).

Rookie De Angelis impressed *Autosport*'s Nigel Roebuck as "a young man of considerable potential, although some of it is hidden by a certain amount of wildness at the moment." But the young Italian kept his DN9B on the island, completing 39 of the 40 laps to finish sixth, just behind Lauda and ahead of the first Aurora competitor — a Fittipaldi driven by Guy Edwards.

As an aside, the car Elio drove here was jet black, lacking any hue of blue, and there is a

BELOW I'm innocent, honest! Jan Lammers in the Samson car (17) gets himself punted out of the Long Beach race at the first turn. After ramming the Shadow, Patrick Tambay's McLaren flies over Niki Lauda's Brabham and sends parts and cars scattering all over the Queen's Hairpin.
Motorsport Images/David Phipps

SCRATCHING TO SURVIVE 409

OPPOSITE Lion at Monaco, where the reliveried Lammers car shows to its most spectacular advantage. Next step would have been to make the race.
Motorsport Images/ Rainer Schlegelmilch

body of thought that it was an "illegal" car flouting F1 rules to its unfair advantage. The car's designer sets the story straight on pages 416–417.

SPANISH GP
Jarama, F1 (R5), April 29th, 1979
1st, Patrick Depailler, Ligier JS11
12th, Jan Lammers, Shadow DN9B
DNF, Elio De Angelis, Shadow DN9B, engine

As usual an interesting race went on up front; as usual, reporters scarcely noticed the Shadows well behind. Once again De Angelis swapped between his two cars in practice, this time due to a gearbox leak. Trouble in his engine didn't surface until the race.

BELGIAN GP
Zolder, F1 (R6), May 13th, 1979
1st, Jody Scheckter, Ferrari 312T4
10th, Jan Lammers, Shadow DN9B
DNF, Elio De Angelis, Shadow DN9B, crash

The Shadow drivers "were both disappointed with their cars," reported the *Autosport* man after practice, but apparently he considered no more about it worth reporting. Life as a backmarker is like that. Happily for the scribe, the race gave him a chance to describe De Angelis assaulting Bruno Giacomelli's Alfa Romeo into a chicane, taking them both out.

In fact there was a Shadow development to be observed. At Trevor Harris's instigation, both cars wore "chimneys," stovepipe-like vertical tubes that were intended to extract air from below the underwings (see pages 445–446).

MONACO GP
Monte Carlo, F1 (R7), May 27th, 1979
1st, Jody Scheckter, Ferrari 312T4
DNQ, Jan Lammers, Shadow DN9B
DNQ, Elio De Angelis, Shadow DN9B

The starting grid was limited to 20 cars and neither Shadow was quick enough. So in terms of this year's history, it's like they didn't even come to the mean streets of Monte Carlo.

Shadow skipped a non-championship, non-racing event the following weekend at Donington. A fundraiser for the Gunnar Nilsson Cancer Foundation, this was a time trial around the iconic circuit between five F1 cars plus a guest appearance by the now-outlawed Brabham BT46B "Fan Car". Jones made best time with a Williams FW07.

RIGHT Sports can look fluid at normal speed, but freeze the action and see the true violence. Lammers bangs his Shadow over a Monaco curb like Ali landing a punch.
Motorsport Images/ Ercole Colombo

FRENCH GP

Dijon, F1 (R8), July 1st, 1979
1st, Jean-Pierre Jabouille, Renault RS10 (turbo)
16th, Elio De Angelis, Shadow DN9B
18th, Jan Lammers, Shadow DN9B

The DN9Bs were shorn of their Harris chimneys at Dijon, after careful real-world testing proved air was going down into them; the wind machine at the UK's MIRA static testing facility had indicated the opposite. Still, the Shadows were slow around this fast, dramatically swooping circuit. Luckily for them, the grid offered more than Monaco's 10 rows, because Lammers needed the 11th, and De Angelis was last qualifier, 24th.

Yet such was the pace of aerodynamic progress in the new ground-effects era that Elio's best lap was faster than Andretti's Dijon pole position two years earlier.

At least the Shadows trailed all the way around to the finish line, while world champ Mario's Lotus didn't. Meanwhile, up front in the spotlights this time was Renault, first manufacturer to win a Grand Prix with a turbocharged engine. That's right, another French victory in France. Much local Burgundy was enjoyed, it's safe to say.

BRITISH GP

Silverstone, F1 (R9), July 14th, 1979
1st, Clay Regazzoni, Williams FW07
11th, Jan Lammers, Shadow DN9B
12th, Elio De Angelis, Shadow DN9B

"Feat of Clay" was the head that *RACECAR* magazine, formerly *Formula*, put atop its story. (No, the editor didn't come up with that one, I blame my boss.) Jeff Hutchinson gave us a stirring account of Regazzoni presenting constructor Frank Williams with his first-ever Grand Prix trophy. We all know what that led to.

Regga himself might have felt a little added

BELOW Make way, turbo coming through. At Dijon for the French GP, French driver Jean-Pierre Jabouille and his French-made, turbocharged Renault RS10 are on their way into F1 history.
Motorsport Images/Ercole Colombo

ABOVE Grudge match, F1 style. Elio is the Shadow works driver and therefore was given the new rear suspension at Silverstone. Jan is the sponsored driver and therefore has the clout to snatch it away for himself. On raceday the young Italian's pursuit of the young Dutchman is something to see. *Motorsport Images/LAT*

satisfaction whenever he whizzed by the cars he'd been wrestling just the year before.

That would be the Shadows, of course, and happily for us here today, Hutch found something interesting to write about them. The faster one split the two Ferraris in qualifying. OK, we're talking about the sixth row here; the flat-12 cars didn't suit this circuit any better than the Shadow did, but whatever straw comes to hand.

"Elio de Angelis' Shadow, normally a backmarker, had split the two Prancing Horses on the grid," wrote our correspondent. "This came as the result of a new rear suspension geometry layout which caused a tense political situation within the team as Jan Lammers struggled on with the standard old car.

"It seemed that Lammers, who does not like playing second fiddle to de Angelis, used his Samson Shag sponsorship as well as good lap times in the old car as a lever to secure a ride in the new car."

So apparently Jan started from the 11th row in the very Harris-modified car that Elio had qualified on the sixth. And look how they finished… Oops, there's a story there too, as Hutchinson added:

"De Angelis finished on the same lap as his Shadow team-mate Lammers despite a stop to replace a cracked wing support strut plus the one-minute penalty assessed for jumping the start. In fact de Angelis failed to beat Lammers by a scant 1.8 seconds…"

Steal my car, will you!

GERMAN GP
Hockenheim, F1 (R10), July 29th, 1979
1st, Alan Jones, Williams FW07
10th, Jan Lammers, Shadow DN9B
11th, Elio De Angelis, Shadow DN9B

This time Jan did his qualifying laps on the new rear suspension and, sure enough, he was faster than Elio, even though the man with the older suspension had the benefit of the one set of stickier Goodyears granted to the first day's faster team member. The Saturday difference was 0.14 second and 20th vs 21st grid places.

The race itself brought no news worth reporting, except that Team Shadow brought both cars to the finish again, and well up on where they started. A close look at the *Autosport* lap chart shows how they did that: simply by staying in the race as many others dropped out, suffering from engine and tire problems on a very hot day.

AUSTRIAN GP
Österreichring, F1 (R11), August 12th, 1979
1st, Alan Jones, Williams FW07
DNF, Jan Lammers, Shadow DN9B, crash
DNF, Elio De Angelis, Shadow DN9B, engine

OK, party over, see you in the paddock. Neither DN9B lasted this time, after Lammers had an accident early, and in the late stages De Angelis had an engine blow.

DUTCH GP
Zandvoort, F1 (R12), August 26th, 1979
1st, Alan Jones, Williams FW07
DNF, Jan Lammers, Shadow DN9B, gearbox
DNF, Elio De Angelis, Shadow DN9B, driveshaft

Jan Lammers would have yearned to show well here at home, literally his home town, but a back-row starting place and a 12th-lap retirement didn't do it. At least his team-mate, his great good friend from Italy, didn't show any better.

ITALIAN GP
Monza, F1 (R13), September 9th, 1979
1st, Jody Scheckter, Ferrari 312T4
DNF, Elio De Angelis, Shadow DN9B, clutch
DNQ, Jan Lammers, Shadow DN9B

Here in his home nation it was Elio De Angelis's turn to start from the back row. At least his great good friend from Holland didn't make the grid at all. This time the one Shadow in the race made it all the way up to 13th place before its clutch broke.

DINO FERRARI GP (I)
Imola, F1 (non-championship), September 16th, 1979
1st, Niki Lauda, Brabham-Alfa Romeo BT48
DNF, Elio De Angelis, Shadow DN9B, spun
DNS, Beppe Gabbiani, Shadow DN9B, engine

While home, Elio motored down the *Autostrada* to Imola, where he joined a goodly throng of his fellow Italian drivers for this fun little extracurricular event. Out of which he spun.

No need to worry about Lammers, though, as his ride for the weekend was in the hands of Beppe Gabbiani. Engine failure kept this poor kid from racing at all.

CANADIAN GP
Montreal, F1 (R14), September 30th, 1979
1st, Alan Jones, Williams FW07
9th, Jan Lammers, Shadow DN9B
DNF, Elio De Angelis, Shadow DN9B, ignition

Whoa, four GP retirements in a row for De Angelis, making seven this year so far. Plus a failure to make a race at all. Only six finishes, only two of them in single digits. What a career-maker of a season.

How was Lammers doing? Mmm, ninth in Canada was his best result to date. Fewer retirements, five, but twice the number of DNQs.

As for Shadow as a constructor, not yet a single point. Nor a grid place higher than 12th — which seemed anomalous, being about twice as far up as the team's customary position.

Little wonder that journos prowling for

ABOVE Last race, last chance, first points. Elio De Angelis makes his desperate little team's roster of heroes for a fine drive at Watkins Glen, shrugging off conditions that defeat nearly everybody else. *Revs Institute for Automotive Research/Geoffrey Hewitt*

stories might pass by the mismatched machines' little encampment and think, nothing to see here, move along.

One chance left.

UNITED STATES EAST GP
Watkins Glen, F1 (R15), October 7th, 1979
1st, Gilles Villeneuve, Ferrari 312T4
4th, Elio De Angelis, Shadow DN9B
DNQ, Jan Lammers, Shadow DN9B

Wet. Dark. Cold. Muddy. Welcome to autumn in New York, some years anyway.

Jan Lammers didn't make the grid again. He could point to illness as some sort of factor, but maybe he was well out of it. It was one of those miserable days that look like speedboat racing, single cars popping into sight trailing roostertails so opaque as to conceal anything that might be behind.

Four cars went out due to accidents in the opening six laps. Then came a seemingly steady litany of woe for many others: gearbox failure; spun, could not restart; collision; engine; engine; accident broken suspension; lost wheel; tire failure… it went on and on. By the weary end of the 59 laps only seven cars were still running.

And fourth among them was a Shadow, Elio De Angelis, F1 rookie, scoring points at last. And still on the leader's lap. "A certain amount of wildness at the moment?" Not at this moment. Fine job, young man.

AS A CONSTRUCTOR, Shadow Cars with its three precious points ranked 10th, two up from the bottom of the list. Next up was Arrows, whose tally was only two points more. Way up front, of course, Ferrari had 113 and was champion by a huge margin over Williams, who scored 75.

World Champion driver Jody Scheckter had contributed 51 of Ferrari's points. With his three, Elio De Angelis shared 15th place with three colleagues. ♠

THE STORY OF SKINNY LIZZIE
BY RICHARD OWEN, DESIGNER

We staggered through 1979. I hadn't gone to South America, but the Ligiers dominated Argentina and Brazil and I think it was this that triggered the idea of a narrower tub.

In the quest to keep up with the Ligiers, the highly unqualified Shadow management led by Don Nichols started calling the technical shots, which unsurprisingly involved much thrashing and little track time. After the cars were back from Brazil there was a gap of some seven or eight weeks, so it was decided to modify a DN9B tub to improve downforce.

Looking back, I suspect we had two main problems: the chassis lacked stiffness, and we were all guessing aerodynamically. With the Lotus 80, even Lotus demonstrated that they didn't really understand what they had appeared to do with the 79.

There were only two racing car designers in the building, Trevor Harris and me. We got on very well. I liked his outside-the-box thinking. Trevor had hot air vents in his Northampton flat and would share with me what aero discoveries he'd made the previous evening with his origami! We tested some of his discoveries in the full-size MIRA wind tunnel in Nuneaton, including the chimneys that we tried for two races. The numbers we got for them at MIRA were quite exciting, but were not born out either by driver feedback or lap time. MIRA's wind tunnel had no moving ground plane, merely a trip on the floor to remove some of the boundary layer. It wasn't really accurate for our purposes.

Don was a good salesman and I can remember a group of Shadow staff standing round a DN9 in the workshop. It may even have been all of us, given that he was about to ask for

LEFT She's been on the diet, now for some exercise. Shadow's slender young maiden and her solicitous attendants prepare for the Race of Champions. Hope burns that her slimmer chassis will give her wings around the corners. *Motorsport Images/Ercole Colombo*

RIGHT De Angelis throws Skinny Lizzie around Druids, trying to save her from the ambitious attention of Desiré Wilson's Tyrrell.
Motorsport Images/LAT

yet another massive effort. We were a small team.

My good friend Mike Lowman, our crew chief, drove this car through to completion with his usual vigour and enthusiasm. Mike is the one who christened it "Skinny Lizzie." I don't think we used an Arrows tub, but it would have been a logical short cut. We narrowed it by about three inches each side.

The notion of slimming the tub to increase tunnel width was all right in itself, but upping the outer skins from 16 gauge to 14 in no way compensated for a tub that was already nearly as stiff as chewing gum. I measured a standard DN9B tub in its manufacturing fixture, and achieved 769 pounds-feet per degree. Barely half the number I would expect even for a spaceframe of similar section.

With a 10-foot lever bolted to the front bulkhead and operated by hand, one could easily see all the inner and outer skins flexing on this shallow bathtub design. And since torsional stiffness goes up as the fourth power of the diameter, it was obvious that Skinny Lizzie wasn't going to be making any gains in this department.

The mods were made very "knife and fork" but the design office would have been needed to draw some parts. I think I did the new rear radius rod pick-ups. The engine cover was modified to suit the narrowing. The venturi tunnels were made wider by adding width to the standard sidepods. The whole thing was hare-brained; the tunnels were blocked by exposing even more of the exhaust primaries.

This was the car taken to Brands Hatch for the Race of Champions. All right, this was not a championship event, but the car was *not* illegal. Where did this come from? It's utter rubbish. How would it be illegal? All the dimensions, such as track width and aero parts, were easily checkable with a tape measure. I suppose we could have installed a 3.9-liter Cosworth DFL "vibrator," but we didn't. What unfair advantage?

Why was it black? More to the point, why were the other ones blue? Shadow race cars should be black! But that dark blue was the base colour of the Lammers Samson-liveried car, so painting the other one the same made it that much easier to make body spares for the two.

Was Skinny Lizzie a good idea? I certainly wasn't consulted. But Don ran on hope and optimism and it was the usual, "Well, if we could but just do these mods we'll bounce to the front of the grid."

CHAPTER 20
THE ORPHANS

DN11 & DN12 (FORMULA 1), 1980

FAILURE HAS FEW friends, but each of us is well acquainted with it. So we understand; understand the bright hopes of those reaching for success, and how hard it is to seize the prize, and how it feels to fall short of our goals.

But hopefully, we also have experienced the resurgence of spirit and energy as, having learned by failing, we pull ourselves together and reach out once more, hopes renewed.

Thus it is that we can look at unsuccessful racing machines like these last Shadows, taking in their forlorn stance today while also seeing the dreams and determination and sheer hard, skillful toil that once, long ago, guided the hands that made them.

In a way, they are emblematic of the life journey of the man responsible for giving them birth.

BY THE END of his dismal 1979 Grand Prix season, Shadowman Don Nichols had little left of the racing organization he created ten years before. Much of the fault lay with him.

Motorsport is an ostentatious, cacophonous, sensationalistic thing, a show hard to ignore and enthralling to its fans, but even the most committed of racewatchers may not fully understand what a war it is. Seeing it from the sidelines or on screen, it often looks like cheery gallantry, a joust amongst gentlemen who give it a jolly good go and then gather convivially for drinks.

And indeed they all do just that. Out of the cars, strolling the pits and paddock, beyond the circuit boundary, even the most hard-nosed of the stars are friendly with each other and welcoming to outsiders. The bitterest grudges incurred on track tend to dissolve into comradely laughter afterward, if sometimes rather long after.

This must be why enthusiasts who grew up on sports car racing, especially, might have presumed it merely a sport. So these innocents might have been jolted — as your scribe confesses he was — by the terse words of championship-

LEFT Proud moment for the persistent Shadowmen as they reveal their newest Grand Prix contender. Unlike the team's recent models, it's an all-new design. And at last Shadows are properly black again. Surely the DN11 must be the magic bullet?
Don Nichols collection

winning team owner Sir Frank Williams, who once said of front-rank Grand Prix drivers: "They're ruthless bastards. They have to be."

A cold, merciless light, but it illuminates truth. We must see, at least at the top levels of professional competition, that "our" sport is not a vehicle of simple pleasure or satisfaction. Teams that win are more like vessels manned by pirates, if you will, marauding the seas of speed in remorseless quest of riches and glory and, above all, winning. That burning desire to be Number 1 seethes white-hot within them all.

Perhaps this viewpoint reveals why not all, but many heroes of the public imagination harbor aspects of character that polite society finds unpalatable. In social circles these darker traits can be kept well hidden, but put such individuals into a racing situation, and what Dan Gurney termed their "track personality" comes out.

Yes, we're talking of The Shadowman. He was assuredly not alone in this, and like his confreres he also had counterbalancing positive qualities. Many memories of Don mention his charming manner at dinner tables, for instance.

But unlike most of his fellow team owners, toward the close of the 1970s Nichols didn't have many friends left. Innumerable were the angry people who hadn't been paid as promised.

Word spreads in racing circles. "The Grand Prix Circus," F1 has been called, and it's equally apt for any series of motorsport, indeed for any such activity. Just as with teams in stick-and-ball leagues, as well as groups of musicians, thespians, journalists and other traveling performers, racers are a tribe of nomads. They go anywhere across the wide world, but wherever they set up their temporary encampment it remains their own established, insular small town. They all know each other, and about each other. Being people, they gossip; being extremely competitive people forever seeking an edge in their enterprise, they talk a lot of shop.

After Nichols's seven years in F1, and ten in racing overall, everyone in the paddock would

THE ORPHANS 419

BELOW DN11 exposed. This recent photo of the first of 1980's Shadows nicely reveals its basic architecture: black-anodized tub, sidepods containing two fluid coolers, swept-back front upper rocker arms actuating inboard coil springs, and steering linkage mounted behind the wheels. Unlike the previous DN9B, the new car tucks its exhaust plumbing up above the arched floors of the sidepods, no longer obstructing venturi tunnel airflow.
Richard Hope

have heard about what he was like to deal with in matters of business.

Once an orphan, he had come full circle in the sense that his racing machines, his "artistic expressions" as we've heard him say, were as he had been as a child. Alone.

Had time come for Shadow to vanish?

DN11

THE TEAM had known before 1979 that it needed a new car, but getting one had to wait until after the end of that disappointing year.

Dubbed the DN11, in concept it naturally followed 1978's all-conquering Lotus 79 "tunnel car." Inside very similar sidepods were venturi-shaped passages to lower the pressure of the airflow, thus generating download and consequently higher tire traction. So vital was the extra adhesion that everything else about the car's layout — Lotus-style sliding skirts to seal in the low underbody pressure, radiator placement, suspension configuration, engine installation — served that goal.

To give the raw data, this car's wheelbase was 109 inches, track widths were 64 front and 67 rear, and its wheel diameters were 13 inches all around. Behind the British-standard Ford-Cosworth DFV engine was the equally ubiquitous Hewland FG300 transaxle.

A distinguishing visual point of this model is its nosepiece, a screwdriver-slender chisel that contained no kind of radiator. Those were all tucked into the broad, squarish, skirted sidepods.

Nichols's design director at that point was engineer John Gentry, who had been with Shadow previously, back in the Tony Southgate days. After stints with Fittipaldi and ATS he returned in 1979 to work on the DN9B. Later that year he started drawing up plans for the DN11. He worked with senior designer Richard Owen, a former BRM and Williams man.

But Gentry has told us that, when he saw there was no money to construct the car, nor even to carry out wind-tunnel evaluation with models, he moved on to a new team called Toleman.

Richard Owen stayed on for a while longer, but finally left as well.

"That left it to basically a committee of designers to finish it. Nobody was committed to the DN11, they just finished it," is the opinion of Californian Dennis Losher. An engineer and vintage racer we have mentioned before, his particular interest in Shadows has led him through a long career of owning and restoring many examples of the marque. He has studied both of Shadow's final F1 models in depth, and at the time of writing was painstakingly bringing a DN12 back to life.

"So the DN11 suffered terribly as a car," Losher continues. "It couldn't qualify for the most part. It was just an awful car.

"The most significant shortcoming was that the chassis would flex too much, enough so that the steering rack would lock on high G-load. Stefan Johansson, one of the drivers, made the statement that, when he would drive the car really hard under high Gs, the steering would just freeze up due to the chassis flex.

"But Gentry was gone, so nobody cared about the 11. It didn't have 'an owner' to make it better, to fix its shortcomings."

Said shortcomings surfaced in January at South America's opening Grands Prix, where neither new driver David Kennedy nor Johansson made it through pre-qualifying in either Argentina or Brazil. We'll come back to these two events, but first let's see how their outcomes drove Shadow's next step.

DN12

DON NICHOLS, a hoarder of the first order, kept original paperwork for nearly all his Shadows, and when he transferred his decrepit old DN12 chassis no. 1 to Dennis Losher its drawings came with it. The new owner/restorer says that "the very first drawing of the 12 was

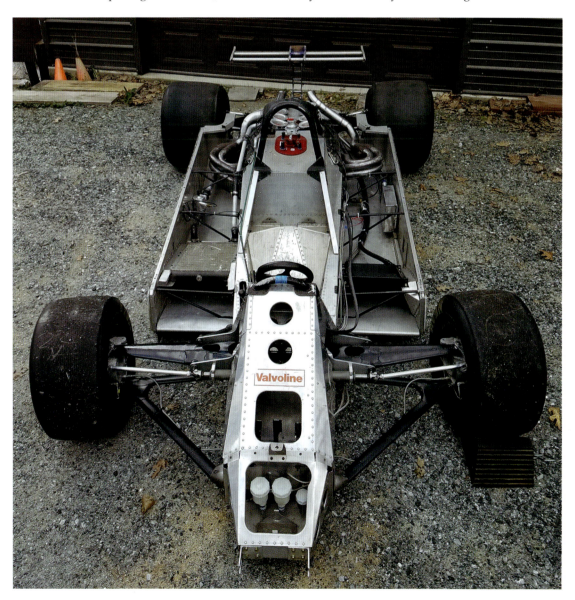

LEFT DN12 exposed. Photographed by its restorer, the first of the pair of the very last Shadow models looks at first glance to be very similar to the DN11 (opposite page). But compare their front suspensions, steering rack locations, relative positions of the larger of their two side radiators (for the engine coolant) and the surface colors of their monocoques. *Dennis Losher*

February 4th, 1980. That was drafted by Vic Morris. It has his name on it, as do pretty much all of them."

Also involved now was Charles "Chuck" Graemiger, an American-born racing mechanic, engineer and entrepreneur based in Lausanne, Switzerland, where he was designing and constructing a line of Cheetah cars.

Continuing Losher's story, "So they started in the first week of February, and lo and behold Shadow rolled that car out in about the third week in April ready for a test. So about 10 or 12 weeks. Which is pretty incredible."

It would have streamlined the workflow that a few components were common to the DN11's. Dennis lists items like the four suspension uprights, which are castings for the front wheels but fabrications at the rear.

But other suspension components are different, and so is the monocoque chassis. "The 12 tub is completely unique to itself," says Losher. Why? Stiffness.

"Morris made sure that in the DN12 the steering rack would never lock up. There are two quarter-inch aluminum plates that are bulkheads to which the steering rack is attached. Those are not going to flex and the steering is never going to bind up." To the same end, the steering rack moved from behind the wheel centerlines, where it lived inside the DN11's monocoque structure, to a "front steer" position on the front of the DN12 tub.

Also, the front suspension rockers were of totally different shape and geometry, and the lower wishbones much more broadly based.

"You can just tell, everything that was a shortcoming for the 11 he fixed in the 12," Losher points out.

The two models really are very different. Photos or real-life comparisons are needed to grasp everything, but expressed in words these are the main ones:

- Front suspensions: while the DN11's top-mounted rocker arm (to actuate the inboard coil springs) swept back as on the familiar DN9, those on the DN12 were perpendicular to the chassis; also, the 12's lower wishbones were much more robust and much more broadly-based on the chassis. The upper-rocker rear suspensions were similar, but their aluminum plate mounting structures differed.
- As mentioned, the 12's steering rack was positioned ahead of the axle line, opposite to its predecessor, and appears to be more solidly mounted.
- Although both monocoque chassis were made of riveted alloy sheeting, otherwise their configurations were very unalike.
- Of the three DN11 monocoques constructed, numbers 2 and 3 were black-anodized as the earliest Shadows had been; the two DN12s were left in their natural state.
- The single water and oil radiators for each car huddled within the sidepods, above the venturi structures — but swapped left to right (water at the DN12 driver's right elbow).
- Where the DN11 bodywork was given a chisel-shaped prow below a rising cowl, the DN12's nosepiece descended straight from the windscreen to an ogive tip, giving the new Shadow the appearance of a large artillery shell.

Another differentiator, minor but interesting: the engine bell housing. Losher: "Vic Morris was also the designer of the DN9B, the 1979 car, and he tried all sorts of things with it. One of them was an integral oil tank in the bell housing. They never raced it on the DN9B, but when he did the DN12 he designed it around having the oil tank/bell housing unit.

"A lot of the stuff he wanted to do on the DN9B he brought back on the DN12. Because they were his babies."

And designers can't stop designing. Shadow needed a second DN12, but when -2 dropped onto its wheels for the first time it was no mere duplicate of -1. In several ways DN12-2 is a different car, Dennis Losher tells us.

"I talked to Bill Wonder, who has chassis -2, and to his son to get their help in restoring mine, but to my amazement there's very little that's interchangeable between the two.

"For example, the front suspension pickup on Bill's chassis is completely different to the one on my chassis. The A-arms are different, the upper rocker is different, even the front-end sway bar is different. None of those are interchangeable.

"I have all the original drawings, so I started making all the little pieces I don't have, but to my amazement a lot of them didn't fit my car. I finally looked very, very closely at the drawings, and there would be little notes: 'this is for 2,' and the other paper would say 'for 1.' So I had to scrutinize the drawings carefully to make sure I had the right one for my car."

Consider that any handmade, one-off item like a racecar is a prototype of the next, because it is the natural way of such work that the build process reveals ways to do it better next time. Especially so when new hands take over.

SHADOW'S 1980 F1 SEASON

FORMULA 1's 1980 season originally offered 16 Grands Prix, but a proposed grand finale in Las Vegas, Nevada, was scrubbed, while poor Spain fell victim to a political tug-of-war at higher levels within Circus Formula 1. The Jarama race ran, but without several teams, and therefore without its championship status.

Remarkably, the laboring but loyal crew at struggling Shadow was able to send two of their new DN11s to January's opening races in South America. At that point the two drivers were two newcomers, Swede Stefan Johansson and Irishman David Kennedy.

It wasn't really worth the effort. As noted earlier, neither man made the top 24 allowed on the starting grid for either race.

ABOVE Young Irishman David Kennedy hurls his black bullet around the Buenos Aires circuit as fast as it will go. Which unfortunately isn't fast enough to make the race. *Motorsport Images/David Phipps*

ARGENTINE GP
Buenos Aires, F1 (R1), January 13th, 1980
1st, Alan Jones, Williams FW07
DNQ, David Kennedy, Shadow DN11
DNQ, Stefan Johansson, Shadow DN11

In the parklike circuit at Argentina's Buenos Aires, Shadow alumnus Alan Jones won pole position aboard his Williams. The last of the two dozen qualifying spots went to Emerson Fittipaldi, still revered as a two-time World Champion but still refusing to give up his family's dream of making good with their own marque. Emmo's best fell short of Jones by all of 5.25 seconds.

Shadow's Kennedy came next, over a second and a half slower than backmarker Fittipaldi's car (ie, 6.8 seconds slower than the Williams on pole) while Johansson was 27th, yet another half second adrift.

If the Shadowmen watched on raceday, they saw Jones take the first victory of a season that would make him and team owner Frank Williams World Champions.

BRAZILIAN GP
Interlagos, F1 (R2), January 27th, 1980
1st, René Arnoux, Renault RE20
DNQ, David Kennedy, Shadow DN11
DNQ, Stefan Johansson, Shadow DN11

ABOVE Replacing disgusted Swede Stefan Johannson for South Africa, England's Geoff Lees does luck into a place on the grid, albeit thanks to bad luck for a French competitor. But Lees won't escape it either.
Motorsport Images/LAT

At the "between-the-lakes" circuit on the outskirts of Sao Paulo, the drivers of the difficult Shadows confronted a blood-curdlingly high-G banked first turn, which opened into a long, downhill straight, which terminated with a heavy braking zone. All of it very bumpy. Not a forgiving place for a car disobedient to the helm at high speeds. The intrepid new Shadowmen missed this show by 9.12 and 10.02 seconds, Kennedy from Johansson.

Oh well, let's hope the boys caught a day or two on the sun-drenched beachfront up at Rio.

SOUTH AFRICAN GP
Kyalami, F1 (R3), March 1st, 1980
1st, René Arnoux, Renault RE20
DNF, Geoff Lees, Shadow DN11, suspension
DNQ, David Kennedy, Shadow DN11

Following a February spent snug and warm inside the Shadow shop in wintry Northampton, the road team broke off working on DN12s to airfreight its DN11s way back down south to summertime. There on Jo'burg's Kyalami circuit one driver finally made it into a race — if only by chance.

Warwickshire lad Geoff Lees had replaced Johansson, but wasn't having any more luck, as he too missed the 24-car grid cutoff — until McLaren's Alain Prost broke his wrist in a practice accident. So what had been the 25th-placed Shadow made the start after all. Not the finish, though. Late in the race new boy Geoff rode through a breakage in his rear suspension.

Poor Kennedy, of course, had to watch his third GP from the wrong side of the pit wall.

UNITED STATES WEST GP
Long Beach, F1 (R4), March 30th, 1980
1st, Nelson Piquet, Brabham BT49
DNQ, Geoff Lees, Shadow DN11
DNQ, David Kennedy, Shadow DN11

The good news: David Kennedy only missed making it into this race by 0.172 second, behind Fittipaldi again. But not much else of positive note came back from California. That made it four very long airline flights for no results on the ground.

Would another month's toil to finally bring the DN12 into the world bring any good news?

BELGIAN GP
Zolder, F1 (R5), May 4th, 1980
1st, Didier Pironi, Ligier JS11/15
DNQ, Geoff Lees, Shadow DN12
DNQ, David Kennedy, Shadow DN11

Kennedy came just 0.15 second short of Fittipaldi this time. Lees debuted the DN12. Newsworthy developments both, but of more portent were the cars' colors. White.

Modest red lettering in Chinese characters that translated to "Theodore Racing" indicated that Don Nichols was handing Shadow over to a gentleman from Hong Kong called Teddy Yip.

Effusively enthusiastic about racing and always genial in public, Yip was a very tough businessman who had built an empire of Asian companies in travel, tourism and related entertainments. Rumors circulated throughout the motorsports community that he operated a luxurious, lively establishment in Macau, where visiting gentlemen a very long way from home might take relief from their loneliness.

Yip set up his Theodore Racing in the 1970s, that is to say in the same timeframe that Don Nichols had started tackling F1. The two certainly would have gotten to know one another later that decade, when Teddy joined the GP Circus by assisting Ensign and Wolf. He also was a backer of David Kennedy.

The outside world says Nichols sold his team to Yip; Don himself told us he handed it over to settle a debt; either way, it comes to the same thing. After almost a decade of trying to storm the ramparts of Fortress Formula 1, the aging American warrior would stand down.

ABOVE Shadow finds sunshine and fresh sea air at Long Beach. But not speed, alas. Neither David Kennedy nor Geoff Lees can qualify. *Courtesy of Richard Hope*

BELOW Maybe painting them white is the charm. The desperately needed DN12 debuts at Zolder — but it's no longer really a Shadow. Nor, sadly, is it meaningfully more competitive than its black predecessor. *Motorsport Images/Rainer Schlegelmilch*

STEFAN JOHANSSON
DRIVER

MY FIRST lap in a Formula 1 car, ever, was the first lap of official practice at the Argentine Grand Prix. Not one lap of testing before.

It was really strange how it came about. I had not driven anything more powerful than a Formula 3 car when Chris Witty took me up to the Shadow factory to see Bert Baldwin, who was team manager at the time. Early in January, I think. It was just to say hello, I was going to do something else, but long story short, I got a call to ask if I could do the Argentine Grand Prix.

A chance to get into a Formula 1 car? I think probably anyone would give their left arm to get in a Formula 1 car, especially at that stage of their career.

So I thought it was going to be a good opportunity, even though it was going to be very difficult to qualify the car in the circumstances and in the conditions the team and the car were in.

They were on the limit in terms of budget. I didn't have to bring any money, but I wasn't getting paid either, obviously. But a free drive, effectively? It was a big gamble, but I felt it wasn't something I could pass up.

We arrived in the paddock in Argentina, and I didn't even have a seat yet. So we molded the seat on the first day, on the Wednesday before the race.

You can imagine, it was a bit much to take in all at once. Every one of my heroes at the time was in the field, and

BELOW Stefan at speed in Argentina — or at the best speed a total F1 rookie can wrest from an untested new vehicle rife with troubles. Its steering behavior, that's the most alarming. *Motorsport Images/LAT*

426 CHAPTER 20

I was doing my best to stay out of their way and trying to get up to speed at the same time. It was a bit of an education, to say the least.

Obviously the car wasn't, by far, the best in the field at the time. So it was really a matter of just trying to keep the thing on the road and not make any stupid mistakes, and gradually build up to speed. We had some mechanical issues, too, so I didn't get a huge amount of running in the practice anyway, and then straight into qualifying.

The car had all sorts of weird issues. I remember the thing was flexing so badly, the steering was locking up in that long right-hander going onto the back straight in Argentina. With the sliding skirts and everything the cars had massive grip, and you couldn't really back out. If you didn't get the radius just right on the turn-in, you were stuck with it. I remember one lap I ended up in a field miles away.

It was the same in Brazil. That's when Interlagos had the long, fast left-hander on the top, like an oval corner. It was so fast. And again, the steering just completely locked up. Whatever you had on the wheel when you turned in, that's what you had the whole frickin' corner. And you're trying to keep your foot in it, you know.

I remember very clearly, the car was just so different in the left- and right-hand corners. After we didn't qualify in Brazil it turned out they had some new wishbones shipped in, but a different geometry, and for whatever reason it ended up on one side of the car. One side had about an inch shorter wheelbase than the other. [Chuckling]

The car was way, way, way off the pace. David Kennedy was my team-mate, and his was the same. The cars didn't qualify in either of the races.

So that's why I decided after Brazil it was probably not the wisest thing in the world to keep going with them. I could see that it wasn't going to be much help in my career. And at the same time I had an offer from Ron Dennis to come back to Project Four and do F3 again. Which is what I did, and we ended up winning the championship.

Nevertheless, having two races with Shadow was a great opportunity for a young guy who was dreaming since he was a kid about racing in F1, so I was very grateful to be given that chance that young.

ABOVE Happily, Johansson will rise above his Shadow experience and enjoy a long career of great achievements. Retired from driving and team ownership, today he's a fine abstract artist in California. *Motorsport Images/David Phipps*

It took almost four years to reestablish myself, to get back in a situation where I could drive in F1 on merit. But it was good.

Funnily enough I never got to meet Don Nichols until years later. I never saw him in South America. But fast forward almost 20 years and I'm running my own sports car team. We were racing up at Laguna Seca and he used to show up. We struck up a pretty good friendship then. It was cool.

I have nothing but fond memories, really.

Derived from a recent interview.

MONACO GP

Monte Carlo, F1 (R6), May 15th, 1980
1st, Carlos Reutemann, Williams FW07B
DNQ, Geoff Lees, Theodore Shadow DN12
DNQ, David Kennedy, Theodore Shadow DN11

Unfortunately for the newly branded Theodore Shadow team, Monaco closed off its starting grid at 20 cars. Had it been the normal 24, the new DN12 would have started its first race. Geoff Lees was 23rd fastest.

SPANISH GP

Jarama, F1 (non-championship), June 1st, 1980
1st, Alan Jones, Williams FW07B
DNF, Geoff Lees, Theodore Shadow DN12, suspension
DNF, David Kennedy, Theodore Shadow DN11, accident

On the original 1980 calendar the Spanish was to have been the seventh World Championship GP. But a political struggle was brewing, not in Spain but between F1's guiding body (known then as FISA) and the group of constructors who built and ran most of the cars (FOCA). It had to do with turbocharging vs. ground effects, or something; exactly what doesn't matter here, except that the outcome was to allow both Shadow-built cars to race for the first time.

That's because several of the top teams pulled out, which rescinded the championship status of the event — and thinned the ranks enough for both Kennedy and Lees to qualify, 20th and 22nd.

Heavy attrition knocked out 16 of the starters, among them Lees (suspension at half distance) and Kennedy (accident after two laps). That Jones boy won again. Not that it mattered.

FRENCH GP

Paul Ricard, F1 (R7), June 29th, 1980
1st, Alan Jones, Williams FW07B
DNQ, Geoff Lees, Theodore Shadow DN12
DNQ, David Kennedy, Theodore Shadow DN12

Dispute resolved, all the cars were back again, and both the white cars with the red Theodore lettering were out of qualifying luck again. Both were DN12s for the first time, not that either brought any obvious benefit. Lees was 25th in qualifying, just over a second slower than Fittipaldi this time. Kennedy was another quarter second back, 27th.

THEODORE RACING entered the DN12s for one more GP, the British on July 13th, but they failed to show up. Mr. Yip stepped back then to regroup for 1981.

So it ended. Shadow was history. That final season's box score: seven GP meetings with two cars each, 13 failures to qualify, one race run to 13th place despite the car not finishing, zero points earned.

What more is to be said?

Oh yes. The following year Geoff Lees, still with Theodore, made it into a non-championship race at Kyalami. His DN12-1, now called a TR2, broke its front suspension on the 11th lap, resulting in chassis damage.

Then it really was all over. ♠

BELOW Lees drives the Theodore Shadow DN12's only race at Jarama. So that's something. But it leads to nothing, not this day.
Motorsport Images/LAT

DAVID KENNEDY
DRIVER

Q: What was it like to find yourself in F1?
Kennedy: Very exciting. You're blinded by the light. When I was racing Formula Ford in Ireland if I'd told anybody that I wanted to go to F1 they would have sent me to the nearest mental asylum. It was like saying you wanted to land on the moon!

Q: What was the Shadow DN11 like?
Kennedy: It was the most beautiful car I'd ever seen. Oh, how looks are deceptive. Being young and naive I thought it was going to be quicker than anything else out there just because it looked so good. But we never really fully understood the car.

Q: How bad was it?
Kennedy: We ran at Silverstone with two sidepod configurations. One of them was so effective that they pulled out of the chassis. But the team kept the ones that didn't pull out. Insane! You wanted the ones that pulled out, you just had to beef them up.

Past the pits at Interlagos the chassis twisted and the steering used to lock. You had to arch your elbow into the monocoque to hold the steering wheel!

The team had big financial problems and didn't know whether it was going to make it from one day to the next. We thought the new DN12 would be the team's saviour. We tested at Nogaro… it was the first time I'd spun on a straight; the engine came apart from the chassis.

Q: You finally started at Jarama after Ferrari, Alfa and Renault withdrew…
Kennedy: I knew the track from my F3 days and understood the technique that worked well around there. I made a really good start and was mixing it with a few of the guys. The problem was that if the car ever got into a sequence of porpoising or bouncing, you just wouldn't get it back. And that's what happened on the second lap, behind a couple of cars and in that disturbed air. The thing started bouncing — and bounced off the circuit. I was so pissed off that I didn't return to the garage. Instead I watched the race to see if I could learn anything.

Q: That Spanish race ultimately lost its championship status so, technically, you never started a GP. Does that frustrate you?
Kennedy: It doesn't bother me in the slightest. F1 led to bigger and better things for me. To have it on my CV helped me make the next step into sports car racing. I was thrilled to have had the experience, but more than anything else I was happy just to have survived.

This interview was published by Motor Sport *in its January 2005 edition under the title "My only Grand Prix." It can be viewed on the magazine's website:* https://www.motorsportmagazine.com/archive/article/january-2005/19/my-only-grand-prix-david-kennedy

LEFT Kennedy, pictured here in Argentina, built on his unsatisfactory start with Shadow to establish a strong record outside F1, including nine 24-hour races at Le Mans, where he scored three class wins with Mazda. *Motorsport Images/David Phipps*

CHAPTER 21
SHADOWMAN'S ACTION ART

AN "ACTIVE ART PIECE." That's how Don Nichols thought of the racecars he was making. "Not only attractive but high performing, and unique, and innovative. Something really innovative in an area where the innovation could be shown and proven, which of course is motor racing."

And who among us does not feel the appeal in that?

The history of motorsport is written around results, which is proper, but the place of aesthetics cannot be ignored. We can admire a winning machine regardless of its appearance — but if it looks good too? "It's beautiful!"

And if it's not a winner? We can still enjoy looking at it.

With racecars it goes deeper than the surface contours. They're all made to be worked on, so their bodywork comes off easily, and it's then we can see their true inner beauty. Inspired concepts. Gracefully minimalistic design. Taut, efficient engineering. Exquisite craftsmanship. Clever details. Tidy assembly. Nice preparation.

The finest competition vehicles are handmade weapons in the tradition of legendary swords of ancient times, where each was the distinctive product of human hands.

Every one carries the soul and pride of its maker. Like those famed blades of old, our era's racing machines are individuals. By birthright each should have its own individual name; many do.

In these remaining pages about Shadow racing cars we celebrate a few special ones that, as we see it, best achieve the artistic vision that the Shadowman had for them.

Don't look at them as winners or losers. We hope you say, "How beautiful."

MK II & MK III (CAN-AM)

ABOVE & BELOW Beautiful Bryant Bookends: the Shadow Mks II and III (left and right) are actually the same basic design of 1971, which was massively revised for 1972. Photographed at Sonoma in 2014, the Mk III is Oliver's original racecar (albeit restored since) then owned by the sadly late Fred Cziska. The smaller Mk II is Dennis Losher's reconstruction atop a chassis built to 1972 spec but not completed at the time. Visually both cars are period correct, and today are with Jim Bartel. *Pete Lyons*

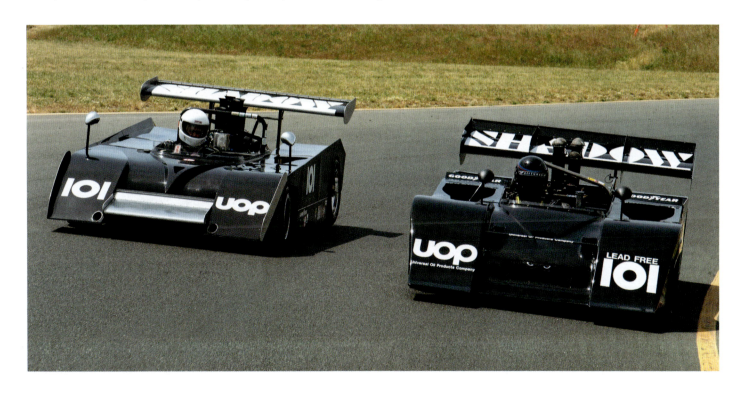

SHADOWMAN'S ACTION ART **431**

DN2 TURBO (CAN-AM)

ABOVE & BELOW BLACK BEAST Against his instincts, Tony Southgate had to make his first Can-Am Shadow big and burly. Not only had it to withstand the brute force of 1,200 projected horsepower, further bulk and weight were added by massive radiators to cool the twin-turbo Big Block Chevrolet and a monstrous amount of fuel to slake its prodigious thirst. *Zach James Todd, courtesy of Canepa*

DN2 TURBO (CAN-AM)

DN2 TURBO (CAN-AM)

ABOVE & BELOW Sisters under their skins, the DN2 has some parts in common with F1's DN1. Not common are the large radiators either side behind the front wheels, and their coolant pipes exterior to the fat chassis. Turbos by the rear tires exhaust laterally, the actual blowers hidden below the bronze-colored pop-off valves. *Zach James Todd, courtesy of Canepa*

DN2 TURBO (CAN-AM)

LEFT Shadow's turbo system took over the entire engine bay. Silvery pipework brings pressurized air into the engine, while exhaust blasts through black headers to spin the turbos either side. The configuration of this restored example may differ from some period photos because many details changed again and again throughout months of experimentation without becoming raceworthy. However, one day it would be airworthy — a "Thunder Engine."
Zach James Todd, courtesy of Canepa

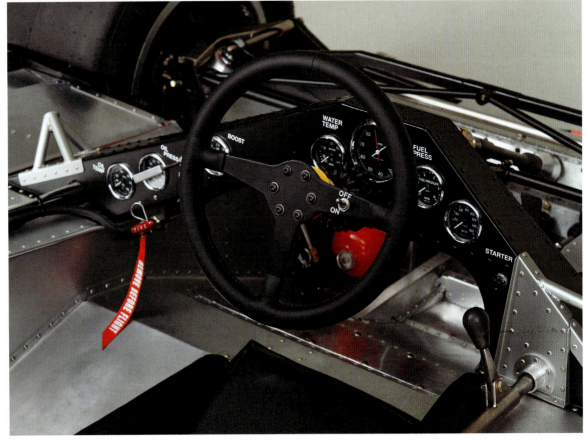

RIGHT How light and delicate the driver's end looks compared to the brutish back. In fact Southgate drew the DN2 straight after his F1, so the Can-Am is very much a DN1 with a two-seater cockpit. And much more fuel tankage, of course.
Zach James Todd, courtesy of Canepa

DN4 (CAN-AM)

RIGHT BLACK BEAUTY. Tony Southgate's second Can-Am Shadow still packs a Big Block, but carries it more gracefully and there's much less mechanical complexity to keep after. Need for less fuel means a narrower monocoque, which opens space for radiators alongside the lucky driver. On the left, a shiny oil cooler lives with the associated circular dry-sump oil tank. She's smaller, lighter and nimbler, and many hard miles of on-track finishing school gave her the refined manners of a racing lady to love. *Jim Bartel collection*

DN4 (CAN-AM)

DN4 (CAN-AM)

THESE PAGES The designer's artistic hand is shown everywhere on the DN4, from Southgate's shovel nose back along the leonine body line to the smooth, spare aerodynamic rear treatment. The round openings in the nosepiece cool the brakes. The front wheels are 13-inchers, two smaller than at the rear (of course the tire brand is not period-correct, nor is the number 102, but both are appropriate for modern vintage racing). "Staggered" induction stacks compensate for a necessary design asymmetry of the Chevy's intake ports, resulting in a smoother torque curve than with equal-length tubes. *Jim Bartel collection*

DN3 (F1)

LEFT Shadow's second F1 model is recognizably a sibling of the first, but distinctively its own machine. The front suspension is more cleanly drawn, a single engine oil cooler in front replaces two in the rear, the chassus sides are now flat and twin water radiators flanking the cockpit are ducted differently.
Courtesy of Andrea Sofia, www.asmonzaracing.com

RIGHT DN3's back end is now familiar F1 practice for the era, with cast magnesium uprights located by twin trailing rods plus a single top transverse link and reversed lower wishbone. As ever, the Ford-Cosworth DFV and Hewland transaxle serve as both powertrain and chassis components.
Courtesy of Andrea Sofia, www.asmonzaracing.com

RIGHT Southgate ventured onto newer ground with the 1975–76 Shadow, designing an inboard-spring, rocker-arm front suspension. Benefits included less unsprung weight on the wheels and, theoretically, less restrictive airflow aft to the radiators. For the first time some fuel lived either side of the cockpit. Note this B-spec DN5 has the stronger instrument panel hoop mandated in 1976.
Courtesy of Andrea Sofia, www.asmonzaracing.com

LEFT But notice as well the innate grace and loveliness of this creature of speed. Hand craftsmanship of such quality is ageless. No matter the passage of years and the advances of technology, each surviving racecar is a work of art testifying to the most advanced understanding and thinking of its time.
Courtesy of Andrea Sofia, www.asmonzaracing.com

DN6 (F5000)

ABOVE & BELOW So sound was Southgate's DN5 concept that he was able to make it serve two further purposes. Here it shouldered the iron burden of a Dodge passenger car engine. Five liters of stock-block torque and power out-muscled the chassis's original 3.0 Cosworth thoroughbred, but the added weight took the fine edge off the F1 handling. *Jim Bartel collection*

DN6 (F5000)

ABOVE & BELOW Bird's eye view of the designer's vision: straightforward chassis of folded aluminum, integrated inboard suspension made of steel, cast-iron engine carried at the best possible point in relation to the rear wheels, simple-looking side radiators the final result of much complex development work… all knitted into a single weapon of combat. *Jim Bartel collection*

DN7 (F1)

ABOVE & BELOW Replacing the DN5's Ford-Cosworth V8 with Matra's V12 made Shadow's single DN7. More power offered hope of better performance, but that was stolen away by more weight, heat and thirst. The French screamer raced only twice, and not for long on either occasion, but her aesthetic appeal seems immortal. *Pete Lyons*

RIGHT By 1979 Southgate was long gone from Shadow, but his last design for them lived on. The DN9 "wing car" of the year before was greatly modified into a DN9B "tunnel car" with entirely different aerodynamics atop the same monocoque chassis. Note the steeply raked rocker arm suspension as well as the leading edge of the inverted wing-cum-radiator fairing behind.
Courtesy of Andrea Sofia, www.asmonzaracing.com

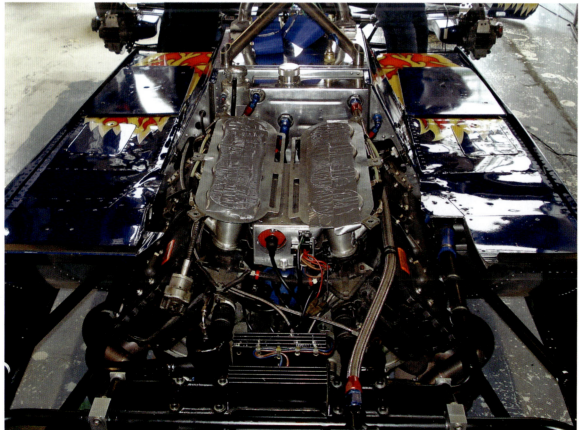

LEFT View from astern shows the "venturi tunnels" either side, upside-down wings enclosed with sideplates to generate not lift but downforce. (In period the tunnels were more efficiently sealed by sliding skirts in the flat outer sides, but vintage racing bodies disallow these.) Here, panels lacking "flame job" paint cover the radiator outlets atop the sidepods.
Courtesy of Andrea Sofia, www.asmonzaracing.com

AFTERWORD
TREVOR HARRIS

FRIEND FOREVER

TEN YEARS AFTER Don Nichols's debacle with his Knee-High Car, the irrepressible dreamer lured back his first designer for help with another car. A Formula 1 car, 1979's troublesome DN9B.

"I was Shadow's chief designer for about six months," Trevor Lee Harris says with a chortle.

But although this second venture ended acrimoniously, as had the first, it would not be the end of their collaboration. Despite frequent moments of stress and long periods of estrangement, these two extraordinary men always seemed gravitationally drawn to one another.

BELOW Trevor Lee Harris, engineering genius and inexhaustible raconteur, at home near the Southern California community called Shadow Hills. Truly. *Pete Lyons*

Creations carry the characters of their creators. Nichols was the man who launched the Shadows, while Harris steered their original course. Both seemed to understand and cherish their bond. Trevor and Don would remain warm and respectful friends throughout the older man's life.

"Don Nichols remains to this day perhaps the most fascinating character I have ever known," Harris says. "The three projects I did with him were all unlikely, rewarding, deeply frustrating — and highly educational!"

GOING F1

"AFTER SAINT-JOVITE in 1970, I felt there was absolutely no hope of continuing the project," Trevor continues. "We had just wrecked the car, we didn't even have the money to buy a spare motor, and we owed Al Bartz on the worn-out engines we had. And my paychecks being a problem was another incentive to leave — a big incentive, I'll tell ya!

"Don was really on his last legs at that point. He was really, legitimately out of money.

"I was so disgusted, and so tired. I had been working day and night, weeks and weeks and weeks. I've never been so worn out. I was completely knackered. I just subtracted myself.

"I never went back to the Santa Ana shop, for instance, and I had a lot of my equipment in that shop. I couldn't bear to go to it. There were years that I didn't want to talk to Don."

Yet racing's ever-flourishing grapevine would have kept Harris aware of his former collaborator's refusal to admit defeat. "One of the things about Nichols, he had a lot of interesting characteristics, but Don would fight to the bitter end to keep something going."

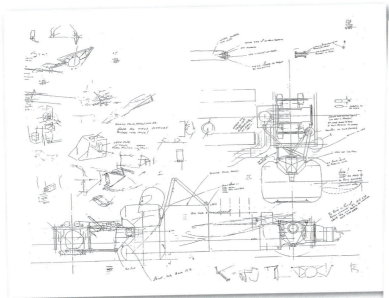

ABOVE LEFT Sketch of a DN9B depicts Harris's new rear suspension concept. A single pivot at the bottom of his fabricated steel upright picks up the apex of a simple wishbone, while the more elaborate linkage needed to keep the wheel aligned is raised above the all-important airflow rushing through the underwing tunnel — similar to his 1970 Mk I Shadow. New geometry also cures a suspension-binding problem. *Trevor Harris collection*

ABOVE RIGHT At Zolder the ever-inventive Trevor Harris poses with his novel "stovepipes" fitted to the Elio De Angelis DN9B. The idea was born of airflow experiments over a heating vent in his Northampton flat. *Trevor Harris collection*

So one day years later Trevor was not unduly surprised to hear a familiar voice in his phone.

"Don said he needed me to run a test. A Formula 1 test. In Europe. I had never worked on an open-wheeler in my life. I said yes immediately."

Late in 1978 Harris found himself in the South of France at a supermodern circuit called Paul Ricard near a Mediaeval hilltop village known as Le Castellet. There he found an underperforming car and a team with problems.

"We had the two youngest drivers in Formula 1, Elio [De Angelis] and Jan [Lammers]. Danny Ongais was there at the test too, and he's a terrific guy but his F1 experience was very limited.

"Someone before me had given one of the cars a new rear suspension, but I was worried about some flimsy details — it broke in transit on the way there! We put the original DN9 suspension back on, but I decided to do a whole new design."

But Trevor himself was reassured. "I found out that a Formula 1 car is just a car like any other. It's not this magical, supernatural thing they think it is. So I felt pretty good about that and agreed to join the team."

"My first F1 race was Argentina at the beginning of 1979. We had a couple of wrecks in practice and worked all-nighters to make the race. The sliding skirts were a pain in the neck, I remember that.

"We had a 'spare car' but it wasn't really ours. Don had that deal with the Interscope guy, Ted Field, and he paid to have that car there just in case Danny Ongais turned up. He never did."

"In Long Beach I ran into an old girlfriend, and wound up taking her to the UK with me. I took her to Brands Hatch. I shouldn't have let Nichols see her. After the race Don called me to his office and said, 'If you're going to have that woman at races, you better think about not working for us.' I wasn't about to ship her home, so I made sure she didn't come into the pits.

"Back in Northampton Don still had the same old shop. The UOP logos were still there, but there was no connection with the company any longer.

"Richard Owen was in the drawing office there — he later went out on his own. We also had Vic Morris, a really good draftsman. He had this huge master drawing of the whole chassis, and used it to keep track of all the modifications.

"I did two main things with the car while I was there. The 'stove-pipes' I put on, or 'chimneys' as they came to be known over there, came from an idea that we could improve the efficiency of the tunnels if we could keep the airflow attached better to the bottom of the wing section. I thought I might be able to suck off the boundary layer. It tends to stagnate as it goes over the curve, so it hurts lift. My vertical tubes were supposed to use the low-pressure air above the car to pull air out from below.

"We took a car over to the full-size MIRA wind tunnel to run tests with the chimneys, and it indicated a marked increase in downforce. But trouble was, that tunnel didn't have a moving ground plane. They had a wooden slat on the floor to 'replicate' the effect, but it turns out it doesn't.

"I found that out at Zolder, where the track got oily and they put down cement powder. The inside of my stove-pipes should have been coated with white stuff. They were clean. So air was not being sucked out in real-world conditions.

"I did more accurate testing later and verified that air was actually going *down* the pipes. They were hurting the downforce!

"What did work was my rear suspension. Halfshafts can vary length with wheel deflection, so shafts and/or CV joints can be made to accommodate plunge. But high torque loads can still make them bind. We measured ours, and at large numbers the suspension locked up. So I redesigned the geometry for zero halfshaft plunge.

"My suspension was tested at Silverstone, back to back with the older car on its original rear suspension, and the new one was seconds a lap quicker. Elio said the car was more stable in high-speed corners, and he qualified ahead of one of the Ferraris.

"Colin Chapman came running over to look at the back of our car to see why it was so quick in the corners.

"I was there even though I'd been fired by that point. That happened right after the previous race at Dijon. I took my girlfriend, and Don found out. He hated women being with the team at races. On Monday I came into work and was introduced to my successor.

"I was in Formula 1 for half a season, enough to know that I really do like open-wheel cars. I would have liked to stay longer,

BELOW Would extracting air from the underside of the ground-effect tunnels lower pressure there to increase downforce on the top? Sure would, said the wind tunnel. Uh, no it won't, said the test track. But subsequently other F1 designers would adopt similar "chimneys."
Motorsport Images/Giorgio Piola

even though it was hard to be in the UK environment, where people weren't really pleased to see an American. Back in California I went to All American Racers and started working for Dan Gurney on his Eagle Indycars — open-wheelers."

NICHOLS'S MILITARY PROJECT

DON NICHOLS's lifelong attachment for the US Army led to a decades-long quest to give his old combat buddies a battlefield weapon he thought they needed: a modernized version of the old Jeeps so universally useful in World War II and subsequently.

In fact the Military thought the same, and there was an ongoing series of government programs to design and refine just such a vehicle.

What was wanted had to be light enough to transport by air directly to the field of combat, small enough to fit through the 58-inch-wide doors of Black Hawk helicopters and Osprey V-22 VTOL planes, traverse rugged terrain of every description as well as cross bodies of water, and operate on universally available diesel fuel.

Crucial factor: such a vehicle must be easily and quickly reconfigurable to suit the vast diversity of planned and unplanned missions that all the various service branches might demand of it. Including medical evacuation.

Versatility was vital. Costs would have to be amortized by meeting the often-contradictory requirements of Air Force, Army, Marine Corps and Naval service.

According to Trevor Harris and Dennis Losher, both of whom would become involved although at different times, Nichols launched serious work soon after dropping out of F1. Harris states that some of his old staff in Northampton produced several prototypes through the early 1980s.

These ranged from a small six-wheeler powered by a Harley-Davidson motorcycle engine, on up through a series of somewhat larger, roomier designs with automobile front-drive powertrains turning four and sometimes six wheels. Their aluminum bodies were watertight, and at least one had a water-jet-drive for amphibious use.

A keynote feature of the most promising concepts: modules of many sorts that would attach to the main body, and could fold inward to make a rectangular package compact enough to slip into an aircraft.

"Shadow Box" was a name that the ever-clever Shadowman came up with for his brand, and he spent an enormous amount of time and money trying to land government contracts so he might transform his dreams into reality. And recoup his dwindling fortune, presumably.

But he had many competitors, much larger ones. Think Boeing. And Northrop-Grumman. The US Military establishment wanted a "Multi-Purpose Utility Vehicle-Reconfigurable" aka "MUV-R", and winning the contract would be a lucrative prize. Nichols found the competition as heated as in professional motorsports.

TREVOR JOINS THE ARMY

"I DID NOT do any engineering on the military vehicles; the Formula 1 Shadow guys in England did it. It was about 1982, I think.

"There were running vehicles made and tested. I saw some up at Don's shop. He was very excited. He showed me videos that ran on local Monterey TV, so there was some buzz at the time.

"Then in '89 the Berlin Wall came down and suddenly there was no longer a need to prepare for war against the Soviet Union. All the funding dried up for these projects.

"But late in the year 2000 Don wanted to resurrect the military vehicles program. I went up to see him. That's when he showed me the existing vehicles. I sat down and did some drawings — not designs for complete vehicles, just concepts.

"Don and his daughter Penny and I formed a sort of emotional venture and went on the road to pitch this thing. She was very good at marketing. She would set up the meetings, and we went everywhere. I think the first was at Quantico, Virginia, the Marine base there. We also went to Fort Bragg, various places in Florida, a lot of bases and military facilities all over.

"We went to Patuxent in Maryland, where the Ospreys were, and they let me crawl all over one with my tape measure. I saw the floor rails and the load ramp in the back weren't strong enough for an ordinary vehicle, so ours had to be light.

"Don and Penny and I were an interesting group. Kind of oddball, right? Our proposal that our vehicle could go into a Black Hawk helicopter met with laughter. Because the doors are in the sides, so how do you turn it 90 degrees to stow it?

So we went to Sikorsky in New York where the Black Hawks were made. Sikorsky engineering liked it, they got eager, they figured out it could be done and they helped to push our program forward.

ABOVE Don and Trevor remember their difficulties with stubbornly concave tread profiles of the original "Tiny Tires" during their 2013 reunion at Nichols's storage cavern in Salinas, CA.
Frame from video by Linda "Freddi" Fredrickson, aka Mrs. Harris

"I never had any experience with the Army or the other services before, but we ran into a lot of very sharp people. I've got a lot of respect for the US military."

Harris did not run out of enthusiasm, but his pocket was draining and no government contracts were in sight. "I told Don respectfully that I couldn't do it anymore, but I could recommend a very capable engineer named Chris Willes. I knew him from several race teams I'd worked with on projects for Nissan. So I believe Chris did the last Shadow Box."

Penny Nichols was forced to leave her father as well, as she explains in her own words a little later in these pages.

To this day, the ever-effusive Trevor Harris retains his good feelings for his sometimes difficult, often enigmatic, but almost always completely compatible late friend Don Nichols. They enjoyed similarly high levels of intellect, they shared an eager interest in new technologies, they both took joyful enthusiasm in creating novel things. They were both Explorers. Adventurers. Risktakers.

"He was a tremendously driven, dedicated American racecar owner and entrepreneur. I really enjoyed the guy. I had a good time with him. A very engaging guy.

"If he had a job for me again I'd probably work for him again." ♠

AFTERWORD
DENNIS LOSHER

OWNER, DRIVER, RESTORER

DENNIS LOSHER, the Shadow superfan who has helped with other elements of this book, credits one of Don Nichols's military vehicle projects for sparking his own long involvement with the racecars.

BELOW Introduced to the Shadowman's world by chance, systems engineer and vintage racer Dennis Losher not only became a custodian and restorer of nearly every model of Shadow racecar, he got caught up in Nichols's "Shadow Box" quest as well. *Pete Lyons*

Over many years, at one time or another this vintage racer and engineer has owned and intimately known at least one example of nearly every Shadow model. He has built up an enormous fund of technical knowledge of the marque, and had a close, longtime relationship with the man who created it.

Losher's 40-year career as a professional systems engineer with a San Francisco-area manufacturing company first brought him into contact with Nichols. Don approached the firm about a business relationship and Dennis was sent to meet and evaluate him.

"It turned out that Don was nothing that [the company] wanted to deal with. But I was interested in racing vintage cars, and he had a warehouse full of them. He had one I really wanted to have," Losher says.

Further conversation brought up a concept Nichols had for "air-transportable" military vehicles.

"Don was passionate about the military, about the special forces. He was convinced they needed small, versatile battlefield vehicles like World War II Jeeps but better. He was so focused on making this happen that he would ignore anything else, financial security, everything.

"He was always fascinated by 'air transportability,' meaning 'how many can we get into a helicopter?' That was the driver. It didn't matter if people couldn't fit into it. I tried to sit in one of his first ones. It was ridiculous.

"Don's vision was never about what the customer wanted. It was about what he wanted. He knew better. I kept trying to tell him, 'Don, if it's not what they asked you for, they're not gonna buy it.' But he never got over that. It was his downfall, for the most part."

Over several years previously, a variety of prototypes had

ABOVE Capt. Donald Robert Nichols, US Army (Rtd.), devoted many of his final years trying to develop small, light, air-transportable military vehicles for his old comrades-in-arms. "Super-Jeeps," one might say. This six-wheeler is one of half a dozen prototypes. *Roger Lemmel*

been designed and constructed to varying degrees, but none had landed any contracts with the government. "He claimed he'd spent his entire fortune on it with no offers. He mentioned leaving F1 with a very large number of dollars, and at one time he did have a very nice home on Seventeen-Mile Drive in Pebble Beach. Then he and his wife moved in with one of their daughters to a little house away from the coast.

"I asked him about the proposals he'd been submitting.

"He said, 'I don't know anything about proposals, what are you talking about?'

"I explained that was what I did — I wrote formal proposals for my employer to get various grants and so on. You had to submit a package outlining what you wanted to do and how you were going to do it, what was your expertise in the field, what team you had in place, how were you financed — all the backup material the government wants to see in the form it wants to see it before they give you money. It's a job I did all the time.

"It seemed to me that Don had been operating as a one-man band. He would come up with an idea and fly all around the country, literally visiting every possible military office he could, trying to sell them on this great idea he had. But all he had were plans, and when it became clear that he had nothing behind him, they never went further with him."

Out of their chance conversation came a bargain: Losher would produce the vital documentation for Nichols's next sales effort, in return for the stored-away old AVS Mk I "Tiny Tire" car that caught the vintage driver's interest.

Losher's professional proposal, plus the political savvy of a local Congressman who lived near Nichols, did the trick. A grant of $1.6 million was duly awarded to Nichols's company for the construction of a prototype. Work began in the middle of 2005 for a contracted period of one year.

The new Shadow Box followed the lead of previous designs, having sufficient room for a few occupants but able to carry diverse additional loads by way of a variety of specialized attachments. All were hinged so they could fold inwards, thus collapsing into a package sufficiently compact for rapid airborne delivery to battlefields.

All four wheels would be driven by a front-mounted powertrain from a small passenger car, a Volkswagen Golf

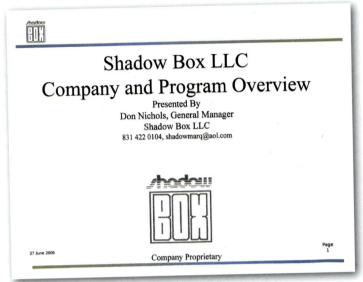

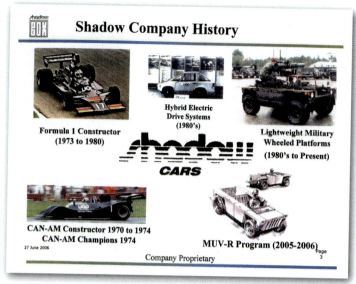

ABOVE Title page of a presentation made up by Losher to help Nichols more effectively lay his proposals before military agencies across the USA. *Don Nichols collection*

ABOVE Entrepreneur Nichols sought to leverage his company's background in international auto racing to bolster his sales pitches to the armed forces. *Don Nichols collection*

BELOW Air transportability illustrated: ferried to the front by VTOL aircraft such as the Bell-Boeing V-22 Osprey, vehicles would be unloaded and unfolded for battlefield action. *Don Nichols collection*

BELOW Shadow's several MUV-R programs offered variants of one basic design, with a front-drive, diesel auto engine powering either four or six wheels under an aluminum "bathtub" made to carry troops, weapons and/or cargo over rough terrain and stretches of water. *Don Nichols collection*

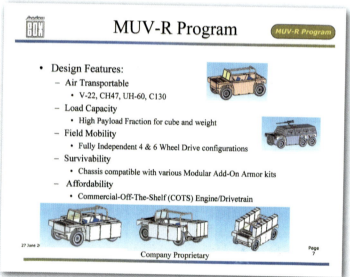

turbo diesel in the case of the prototype. To engineer the installation, Nichols brought in former drag racer and later famed engine builder Robert "Fast Bob" Tarozzi, who had been with Shadow's F5000 Dodge engine program — and whose website incidentally speaks of a secret Shadow plan for an American-made F1 engine!

Chassis engineering was the responsibility of Chris Willes. He made the chassis of aluminum, and all lower orifices were made watertight.

This Shadow Box was not completed before funding ran out. Losher tells us that at the end of the contract the government demanded the vehicle but, amazingly, Nichols parted with enough cash to hang onto it, along with its predecessors.

Don and Dennis continued their barter relationship, Losher exchanging his own expertise for another item from Nichols's stash of old racecars and parts.

"He'd call and say he wanted me to do something, 'but I don't have any money.' That was like a catchphrase with him,

LEFT Earliest prototype is this ATV concept, a rear-engine (Harley-Davidson motorcycle V-twin), single-seat, handlebar-steered 6x6 all-terrain runabout of very small size and limited versatility. *Roger Lemmel*

LEFT Bigger but still a baby, this four-wheeler looks a bit more Jeep-like. *Roger Lemmel*

'I don't have any money.' So I'd talk a car out of him. At one time I owned 11 Shadows."

There was an agreement that these cars would go back to Nichols if, within a stipulated time, he came up with the correct money or could offer equivalent value in another car or needed hardware. Such exchanges were made, but perhaps inevitably, one side or the other came out unsatisfied. Dennis recalls a three-year period when the two would not speak. Yet in the end he and Don were friends once more.

So Losher is one of many people who experienced both sides of the Shadowman's sharp-edged profile. He says these things:

"Don was a risktaker, he wanted to be an entrepreneur. He was inventive and innovative. He would step out of the comfort zone. At an early age he left home to volunteer for the war. He'd get shot, he'd get back up. The vast majority of his friends were killed in combat. He loved the Army, he was dedicated to the Army.

"He loved his family, and always spoke fondly of his daughters and his wife. He could be kindly. His mechanics

AFTERWORD **451**

ABOVE Look vaguely familiar? Not quite finished and still unpainted, this bare aluminum vehicle might strike a chord with racecar enthusiasts. See the doorless, watertight monocoque tub? The little racing steering wheel? The pair of sturdy roll hoops? Why, it even has fold-up panniers to carry its own spares. OK boys, load up the company Osprey and let's go racin'! *Don Nichols collection*

ABOVE Visiting the Wizard's Cave in search of Shadow racecars, one might never have known of the Shadowman's treasured "Super Jeeps" stashed away in obscure corners. *Pete Lyons*

BELOW Don Nichols was never able to sell any of his Military Vehicle programs, but neither could he part with any of his prototypes. *Roger Lemmel*

that I've spoken to all seemed to be very happy with him.

"His business ethics were terrible. Everybody warned me, don't deal with him. So I told him I needed him to sign an agreement. He'd say, 'Oh, a handshake is enough.' I insisted he sign. He'd complain, 'Dennis, you always come out ahead.'

"But there were a lot of good laughs too."

Asked for his thoughts about Shadow's place in motorsport history, Losher was quiet for a moment and then said, "I would call them the best of the rest. They were not Ferrari, McLaren or the Williams of the time, but Tony Southgate's designs were very good. They'd be fast at the start of a season, but for some reason they couldn't carry it through. They would fade through the season. It was a characteristic of Shadow.

"But look at all the opportunities Shadow provided for drivers to show their excellence. Elio De Angelis is probably the best example: Lotus snapped him up after his first year, even though he was under contract for 1980.

"Alan Jones won a race, went on to Williams and eventually became World Champion. Tom Pryce was given a chance to show his brilliance in the Shadow. Jean-Pierre Jarier had had those poles in South America. Stefan Johansson and Geoff Lees had awful times with Shadow, but went on to very good careers. So Nichols provided an opportunity for drivers to show what they had. Shadow was a stepping stone." ♠

AFTERWORD
PENNY NICHOLS

FAMILY BUSINESS

OF DON NICHOLS's eight children, Penny was the only one seriously involved with her father's race team. Beginning while still a teenager and extending into early adulthood, she took on several duties, both at tracks around the world and in the several Shadow shops. In later years she rejoined her father for his venture into military vehicles.

The third and last child of Don's first marriage, she was born near the end of that ten-year relationship in 1956. Thus she never shared her two older sisters' memories of living in Japan; nor in fact did she remember a time when her father lived with the family.

All this added up to give Penny a unique perspective on her already unusual life experiences.

O UR MOM WAS named Alice, and she was a farm girl from Missouri. She married my dad while she was 16 and still in High School. That was probably 1946, when he came out of the military for a while. But he wanted to go back in, and I think he put a lot of pressure on her to come with him.

She told us that she was quite angry that she didn't get to finish High School, but my dad insisted. Our aunt said Mom was very pretty and she could have married any one of the local farmers, but she chose to go with somebody who was a bit more exciting. He was very tall and handsome, and I guess that always has something to do with judgement.

My oldest sister, Donna, was born in 1950. Right after that Dad bought one of the first Jaguar XK120s imported into America. They picked it up in Baltimore, and drove straight across the country. Mom said she didn't get out of the car for two days. She rode across the desert in the passenger seat of this sports car with my six-month-old sister on the floor between her

ABOVE A young woman of ability, will and poise, Penny is the third of Don Nichols's eight offspring, but the only one involved in his racing. It was the family business, as she saw it, but more importantly to her the only way to be close to her dad. She was just 18 when caught mid-race at Mid-Ohio in 1974. *Jim Chambers*

ABOVE Place not named, year unclear, the future unknown. Who cares? Mr. and Mrs. Nichols are young. *Penny Nichols*

BELOW New bride Alice Nichols off on a life of adventure and fun with her soldier-man. Or so she thought. At least her closeness with their three children would remain steadfast. *Penny Nichols*

legs. When they got to California, Dad left by ship for Korea and Mom took the car to the first dealership she could find and sold it for a Buick.

My middle sister, Roberta Ellen, was born in 1953 when they lived in Japan. Mother shipped over not telling her family she was pregnant, and returned with a dark-haired baby girl that at first glance looked like a Japanese baby they could have adopted, but she wasn't.

After Mom remarried we lived on Long Island. I pretty much grew up there. Dad also remarried, to Nancy, and they stayed on in Japan for years with their five children. So we only saw him occasionally, when he would come through New York City. Often my sisters and I would meet him at JFK airport while he was between flights. We'd meet at the old TWA terminal and sit by the planters there with him for a few hours. He always had wonderful stories.

If he had more time he would come by the house and bring us crates full of stuff — dolls from Japan, unusual fabrics, new technology that excited him, all kinds of crazy things. I remember being amazed by the Polaroid camera and instant pictures, and by talk of machines that transmit documents. A fax machine.

He saw the beauty in a lot of different things. He seemed to have loved the Japanese culture. Beautiful scenery. Photography; he loved that, and was actually quite a good photographer.

Sometimes when time permitted we went into New York City. He would take us to Broadway to see whatever play was there. He always had great seats. And we'd go to dinner at Sardi's. There we were, young girls walking around downtown Manhattan. It was very impressive to us as children. So Dad was always kind of an unusual, bigger-than-life character who came and went at different times.

One summer my sister Ellen and I flew out to see him in Los Angeles, and he picked us up at the airport in a Fleetwood stretch limo, that was his normal family car, and took us to the racecar shop in Costa Mesa. We spent a lot of time at the shop, sitting in the back of the car watching television while the mechanics were working on the cars. Or he'd take us to Disneyland in this limo and drop us off with $50 to go and have fun.

I was more interested in the racing than my sisters, partly because I got to spend time with him and travel in his world. Once in the late '60s we went to Bridgehampton on Long Island for a race and we met Bruce McLaren.

I would have been about 14 when I started going to races with my father, to tracks like Watkins Glen, Mid-Ohio, Elkhart Lake, Donnybrooke. Mom would take me to the airport on Thursday

LEFT Waiting to win; that's the hard part. Penny stands above her father and Lynne Oliver, wife of Shadow's soon-to-be champion — if only he makes it through the last laps of Mid-Ohio '74.
Dan R. Boyd

or Friday night, right from school. I would spend the race helping out and sometimes being in the way. I learned timing and scoring — at that time we used windup stopwatches. Later I was given a digital stopwatch by a vendor in exchange for an endorsement. My first deal!

Then, if the race was in California, on Sunday night I would take the "redeye" back to New York. Mom would pick me up and take me straight to school, so I wasn't missing school. And I wasn't allowed to complain!

I came into racing as a family business and not seeing it as a sport. Being on the inside you see it differently. It became my role at the races to do odd jobs, like polishing wheels. Feeding the crew, that was a big job. There were always lots of people to feed and catering to the teams was not the industry it is now, so there were plenty of sandwiches to make. When my sisters came along it was a big help, but I just did whatever needed to be done.

My father would ask me to run errands for him. Like he'd say, "Go over to the Ferrari pit and get so and so and ask him to come over here." Or maybe the mechanics wanted to borrow something from another team, so they'd ask me to go. I was always talking to people or doing something else.

Things are different in racing now, you can't go from one pit to another. I went wherever I wanted to, nobody would really question me. People didn't pay any mind to what I was doing. Dad joked, "She can go undetected." So I often went on a reconnaissance mission, shall we say, but I wasn't spying. I didn't know enough about an engine to be dangerous. I was just looking for people for my father.

Most of the time people were very nice to me. My father always warned me that people were only nice to me to get to him. Perhaps that was true of men as I got older. I mean, who wouldn't want to date a girl whose father owned a racing team?

Personally I didn't want to be a driver. I was only put in the car once to help them get it off the trailer. I have ridden in the racecar with Jackie Oliver around Mid-Ohio, but never assumed that I would be allowed to drive. Dad was quite adamant about the roles of women at racecar driving and it wouldn't even have been considered.

At a party one time, somebody made a comment towards me that, if I had been a boy I would have been a racecar driver. So I know that I was a great disappointment to my father, that I was a girl. Our names show that. My oldest sister, Donna, was expected to be named Donald Robert, same as Dad's two names, until

AFTERWORD 455

ABOVE UOP Shadow is remembered as something of a pioneer of at-track hospitality facilities. It's still all a bit picnic-like here at Dijon in 1974, but Monsieur Nichols is pleased to partake of a *soupçon* of fine French cuisine. *Dan R. Boyd*

ABOVE The Team Tailor tends to a driver's uniform ahead of the Argentine GP at Buenos Aires in 1974. Perhaps an old soldier's skill he never thought he'd employ in civilian life? *Motorsport Images/David Phipps*

she turned out to be a girl. Instead she became Donna Alice, to honor our mother's name.

Then my second sister, she was also supposed to be a boy and she was going to be Robert Allen, but they wound up naming her Roberta Ellen. She's always been called Ellen.

I guess they ran out of boy names by the time I came along, but Dad had his sense of humor and I was Penny Sue Nichols. The joke? "A sou is a French penny," he would explain. In his second family, one of my half sisters was named after the track at Le Mans, and my brother for the track at Sebring.

I spent more time in later years with him, flying out to his house in Pebble Beach with my kids to see their grandfather. But that wasn't the norm.

It's funny: after I left racing and got married I had a son, and one day Dad and I were talking on the phone and he asked, "How old is Ryan now?" "He's 12," I said. "How tall is he going to be?" I said, "Not too tall, his dad's not real tall either." "How much does he weigh?" I said, "No! He is not going to be a racecar driver!" He said, "Well, we could change his name." And I said, "NOOOO!"

Fast forward 25 years and my son is living in New Zealand and getting into doing rally racing and building cars in his spare time. I built a tiny house right next to them so I can go and be with my grandchildren for extended periods.

I have warm memories of our Shadow drivers, especially George Follmer and Brian Redman. Brian would always get up at dinner parties and tell wonderful stories. Vic Elford wasn't around as much, but he was very nice.

And Tom Pryce in F1. We were sitting in one of those big dinner parties one night and all of a sudden there's mashed potatoes in my lap! Tom was across the table with his fork, and without anybody seeing it he just kind of flipped mashed potatoes at me. They would do things to make me laugh. Well, they were bored and we were all just trying to have a good time.

Their relationship with me was quite different from how it would have been with an older woman, because remember, a lot

ABOVE "I say, Don old chap, bowler and brollie? Bit much, wouldn't you agree?" "Ollie, young man, a gentleman always dresses the part. We're launching the next winner of the World Championship, you know." *Courtesy of Jackie Oliver*

ABOVE Gene Hackman, movie star by weekday, Shadow timekeeper this Spanish weekend in 1977. "After the race," Don remembered, "he walked out to the road, flagged down a motorbike and jumped on. Ha ha!" *Courtesy of Jackie Oliver*

of the time I was very young, and the boss's daughter!

I'm still resentful about what happened with Jackie Oliver at the end. I'm probably more resentful than my dad was. But that hurt me, when he took the car design and started another team, because I saw him as my dad's friend and that's something that friends don't do to friends. As an adult I can understand that he wanted what he wanted, but… He's not my favorite person.

As an adult, I sometimes think that had my father not been so stubborn, had he allowed more people like Jackie Oliver to have more of a say in the business, or to own part of it, that breakup might not have happened. I think Jackie very much felt that he had helped build the business and it was owed to him. Not being on the inside I don't really know, but I think it would have helped had my father shared it a bit more.

I don't know that my father was well-liked. I think people always wanted something from him, but maybe that's because he always wanted something from them.

As far as me being his daughter, he didn't make it easy for me. He wanted me there, but I wasn't catered to. I had to work to be there. They didn't even pick me up at the airport.

I flew into Elkhart Lake, Jackie Stewart was on the plane and I had met him a couple of times so I said "hello" to him. He looked at me and he said, "Do you have a way to get to the track? Here, I'll take you. But we have to do a parade first." So we rode through the town in a parade, then he took me to the track and dropped me off.

My dad said, "Did you come into the track with Jackie Stewart?" "Yeah," I said. "Thanks for not sending someone to get me!"

How many kids go for the weekend to see their father and bring an evening gown? Friday night there was always a party for the sponsor. You were at the track all day and then you had to dress up and be ready to go out at night.

Another quite unusual situation: sometimes we would start the weekend at one hotel and end up at another. We'd drive out to the racetrack in the morning, and that night I'd realize

AFTERWORD 457

LEFT For a time in the 2000s, Dad, Daughter and Designer traveled the entirety of the USA trying to make Don's dreams come true. *Penny Nichols*

we were driving to a different hotel. Dad would say, "Well, this one's closer." "Well, my clothes are at the other one!"

I learned to take everything with me in the car. It wouldn't be unusual that we never made it to the hotel and would stay the night in the garage at the track, if they were working on something. If things were bad, Dad would be there.

To me, racing is a depressing sport. I always said, only one person goes home happy — the winning driver.

Back in the '70s racing was extremely dangerous. Often there were accidents and drivers died. We lost two drivers, and I was terribly upset by both. I was in the shop when Peter Revson was killed in South Africa during testing. Dad had been away with his family. This was his first vacation in a long time, he was just away for a couple of days, and I had to find him and call him and tell him. I went with him to the funeral in New York. It was just terribly sad.

And then Tom Pryce, also in South Africa. There were others, before and after, François Cevert, Mark Donohue, too many. It made me constantly apprehensive. I remember one time being out at Riverside and Vic Elford was test-driving the car. I was on the timing stand and I heard the emergency workers call out, "Incident turn 7, Shadow."

I wanted to jump down off the timing stand and run away, but I stayed and into the pitlane came a brown car and it turned out to be our black Shadow just covered in dirt. Vic looked up at me, to let me know he was OK, and shook his hand as if to say, "Whoo, that was close."

I decided I had had enough and wanted to move back to New York. I didn't want to do racing anymore. I wanted to just totally get away from all of it. I didn't want to be part of it, it was just too sad.

But it took many years for me to unwind from the sport. It is a bit addictive, shall we say. I liked the camaraderie, the travel, the working together to do something exciting. When you quit racing, it's a different life. I always think I had to choose to not be in racing, or my whole life could have been very different. What I do now, I'm an admissions adviser for a university. I work online with soldiers all over the world. I can do that wherever I am.

Actually, years later I did go back into racing. After I'd quit I needed to find another career, and because I liked cooking I graduated from culinary school and decided to be a caterer. I worked at that for many years. For six years I did Daytona for Jack Roush as their caterer, and I was on the circuit for the American Le Mans Series.

I would help my dad sometimes too. In the late '90s Dad wanted to start a business with the Technopark in Le Mans, and he asked me to come to Paris to help. He leased a barge on the Seine right across from the Eiffel Tower and he made some contacts with some businesses and teams. Team Courage at that time needed another driver for the 24 Hours of Le Mans, and

Dad contacted Mario Andretti. Mario did drive for them and I remember that with a great lead in the race, the race was lost on the last pitstop.

I assisted my father with his military vehicle "rebranding" project, I was in that all the way. I called every General, head of Special Forces, company or organization I could find to propose the vehicle concepts Dad was pitching. I got us a meeting with a Colonel who had us work with a company that had a "sensor" technology. We traveled all over the US to military bases. We met with Special Forces at MacDill Air Force Base and Camp Pendleton and Lake Washington Shipyards, went to the Pentagon twice; we met with everyone that could help us.

When he could Trevor Harris would come along. Trevor was an enduring friend to my father and to me, and he had agreed to come back and design the military vehicles. I believe he can build anything, and he has an amazing mind and wit.

For fun on long drives Trevor and I would do anything to get under my dad's skin. We would go on and on, always talking about crazy things like the aliens, and we could always get Dad so worked up, so irritated. Sometimes Dad got angry with Trevor, because he wanted to have fun. My father did not have the best sense of humor. He was more serious by nature.

He never drank, never smoked. For a short while he would drink wine, but only in social circles. He did not see the need for human vices.

He had tunnel vision for what he wanted. Nothing around it mattered. He went where he wanted to go when he wanted to go there, his mind uncluttered by "mere mortal needs" as he said; I remember him joking about that. And I think that's what made him very good at what he did. I think it's a difference from men to women, we have to think more circularly.

I don't think the racing itself was so important to him. It was the mechanics of it, designing something that was beautiful and was the fastest and the best. I think that was all his brain was fixed on. It was about building that car or nothing, and I guess it takes that type of thinking to be able to get a project done. He truly loved what he did, loved it.

He had moments when he was a very tender, loving dad, but that was probably just when he couldn't be doing the other. He was stuck with us or whatever, you know! But what always was on his mind was the racing.

I don't think I've ever met anybody quite as tough on me. I think I understood him probably better than many people. He wasn't always endearing. My father was not generous. He was not a saint. He was a male chauvinist; I am told he did not allow women in the motorhome on the F1 circuit — that cracks me up.

I spent a lot of time and money on the military project. I supported that effort financially and ended up losing a great deal of money, which was the source of our disagreement at the end.

I loved my dad, but we didn't always agree. We were very different, politically and otherwise. But he was still my dad.

I visited with him as he got older, trying to help him clean up the shop or do what he needed to do with equipment. He couldn't part with anything, couldn't clean anything up. It was always too hard to let go. He wanted everything. He always had the idea of building a museum, that was very important to him. It never happened.

Whether I was angry with him at the end or not, I said to my sisters, "He's old, we need to be there, Mom would have wanted us to do this." So all three of us went out to California just before Dad died. We camped for four days with him looking after some things, specifically because he wasn't going to be around. It was the right thing to do. ♠

BELOW Don and Nancy Nichols in their modest home on the edge of the Ford Ord military property near Laguna Seca in November, 2015. *Pete Lyons*

AFTERWORD **459**

INDEX

Advanced Vehicle Systems (AVS) 6, 7, 11, 47, 52–54, 62–83, 84, 87, 99, 100–103, 110, 131, 133, 139, 400
   Mk I — see "Shadow cars"
Alexander, Tyler 130, 159
Alfa Romeo 163, 393, 410
All American Racers 163, 446
Allison, Bobby 152, 154–156
Allyson, June 29
Alpine-Renault 255, 301
Ambrosio, Franco 343, 351, 359, 361, 384, 387, 394, 401, 402
Amoco 120
Anderstorp
   Swedish Grand Prix
      1973 181
      1974 220, 222
      1975 276–277
      1976 318
      1977 354–355
      1978 393
Ando, Noriko (Miss Japan) 35
Andretti, Mario 38, 52–54, 172, 228, 229, 292, 299, 300, 302, 304, 305, 306, 307, 308, 326, 330, 348, 350, 354, 355, 359, 362, 363, 364, 365, 379, 380, 389, 390, 391, 392, 393, 394, 396, 397, 401, 409, 412, 459
Armstrong (shock absorbers) 166
Arrows 172, 231, 342, 381, 383, 384–387, 389, 392, 393, 397
   FA1 383, 385–387, 389, 394, 395, 417
   A1 387, 394
Ascari, Alberto 363
ATS (Auto Technisches Spezialzubehör) 420
Austin-Healey 57, 106
Autocourse (English annual book) 342, 350, 360, 361, 362
Automotive News (US weekly magazine) 112
Autosport (English weekly magazine) 87, 88, 98, 140, 142, 144, 150, 167, 201, 204, 224, 233, 234, 247, 266, 267, 296, 300, 327–331, 339, 350, 409, 410
AutoWeek (US weekly magazine) 54, 55, 65, 66, 113, 173, 234
Auto Sport (Japanese monthly magazine) 54, 55, 85
Auto Union 163

Baldwin, Bert 380, 404, 426
Baldwin, John 381
Banks, Henry 38
Bardahl Special 58
Barnard, John 380
Bartel, Jim 431
Bartz, Al 95, 444
Batchelor, Dean 54, 55

Bell-Boeing
   Osprey V-22 446, 450
Beltoise, Jean-Pierre 220
Berra, Yogi 15
Blivet Car Company 111
BMC (British Motor Corporation) 69
Boeing 57, 447
   B-17 55
   Bomarc missile program 57
Bondurant, Bob 29, 31
Bonneville 54, 65
Borth, Don 53, 67, 83, 132
Boyd, Dan R. 300
Boyd, Walt 53, 77–79, 80, 132
Brabham 181, 183, 213, 233, 261, 271, 277, 280, 282, 409
   BT12 260
   BT42 218
   BT44 214, 271
   BT45 313
      BT45B 353, 355
   BT46B ("Fan Car") 393, 394, 410
Brabham, Jack 260
Bradley, Omar 15
Brambilla, Vittorio 277, 283, 284, 348, 364
Brands Hatch 445
   British Grand Prix
      1972 161
      1974 209, 224–226
      1976 318–320
      1978 383, 394
      1980 428
   Race of Champions
      1967 163
      1974 215–216
      1975 10, 11, 272–274, 328
      1976 313–314
      1977 344, 348, 349, 354
      1979 409–410, 416, 417
Brawner Hawk 38
Brezinka, Rainer 118
Bridgehampton, Long Island 58, 454
Brimble, Ray 139, 144, 156
BRM (British Racing Motors) 11, 161, 162, 166, 168, 169, 170, 182, 183, 217, 320, 379, 399, 420
   P153 169
   P154 196, 197
   P160 169
BRM (engines)
   V12 170
Broadley, Eric 107, 168
Brock, Pete 58
Brock Racing Enterprises 99
Brockman, Mike 243
Brown, Warwick 259, 332, 372, 375
Bryant, Peter 7, 86, 90, 104–113, 114, 116, 117, 119, 120, 121, 122, 123, 125, 126, 127, 128, 129, 130, 133, 134–135, 136, 137, 139, 140, 142, 143, 144, 145–146, 147–148, 149–150, 151, 153, 155, 158–159, 169, 196, 341, 398–400, 431

Buenos Aires
   Argentine Grand Prix
      1973 167
      1974 214
      1975 270–271, 272
      1977 342, 343, 344
      1978 388, 389
      1979 407, 408, 416, 445
      1980 421, 423, 426–427
Bührer, Werner 163
Burmah Oil 290
Burness, Bruce 58, 59, 190

Cadillac 114, 117, 120, 170, 171
   Fleetwood 454
Camp Pendleton, California (Marine Corps Base) 459
Can-Am (book by Pete Lyons) 238
Can-Am Challenger (book by Peter Bryant) 104, 107, 139, 159, 399
Cannon, John 38, 332
Carrera Panamericana (Mexican road race) 30, 31, 45
CASC (Canadian Automobile Sport Clubs) 114
Cevert, François 143, 148, 149, 176–177, 189, 192, 458
Chaparral 55, 58, 59, 60, 67, 68, 109, 114, 116, 119, 199, 334, 375, 398
   2E 73
   2H 116
   2J 99, 140, 380, 393
   2K 381
Chapman, Colin 106, 107, 272, 291, 316, 342, 378, 381, 397, 446
Charlotte Motor Speedway, North Carolina
   Can-Am II
      1978 372, 376–377
Cheetah 422
Chevrolet (cars)
   Corvair 45, 59, 61, 71, 91
   Corvette 51, 67, 71, 101
Chevrolet (engines) 57, 59, 100, 292
   Big Block V8 6, 40, 44, 65, 66, 70, 81, 89, 97, 102, 109, 116, 141, 145, 190, 197, 202, 203, 232, 234, 236, 243, 254, 255, 435, 437
      L88 (iron) 69, 74
      ZL1 (aluminum) 66, 74, 109, 117
   Turbocharged 139, 153–155, 172, 196–198, 199, 400, 432, 434
   Flat-six (Corvair) 45, 52
   Small Block V8 39, 42, 52, 292, 293–297, 300, 301, 302, 304, 307, 308, 333, 337, 401
Chrysler 35, 288, 296
   V8 259, 296–297, 333
   B-Block 296

CIA (Central Intelligence Agency) 13, 26, 170
Connor, Tony 246
Copersucar 350
Cordts, John 241, 243
Cosworth 163
   DFV (3-liter V8) 12, 63, 165, 168, 170, 173, 183, 197, 210, 212, 228, 283, 284, 287, 288, 289, 293, 294, 295, 315, 318, 324, 336, 342, 344, 345, 360, 370, 373, 420, 438, 440, 442
   DFL (3.9-liter V8) 417
Courage 458–459
Cranston, Lamont 55
Crown Manufacturing 59

David Bull Publishing 104, 159
Davis, Harry 50
Davis, Gerald "Stump" 297
Daytona International Speedway 34–35, 113, 172, 299
   24 Hours 376
   Daytona 500 35, 458
De Angelis, Elio 405, 406, 408–415, 417, 445, 446, 452
Dean, Tony 98, 118
Dennis, Ron 427
Depailler, Patrick 228, 312, 326, 365, 392
DePalma, Ralph 112
DePalma, Ted 112
Dijon
   French Grand Prix
      1974 172, 224
      1977 355, 403, 412
      1979 412, 446
   Swiss Grand Prix
      1975 284–285
Dioguardi, Nick 158
Dodge 257, 288, 332
   V8 13, 259, 292, 293, 296–297, 304, 306, 307, 309, 333, 334, 336, 367, 368, 369, 370, 371, 373, 401, 440, 450
Donington 410
Donnybrooke, Minnesota 454
   Can-Am
      1971 126–127
      1972 148–150
Donohue, Mark 10, 58, 60, 141, 142, 149, 151, 153, 154, 158, 190, 193, 199, 200, 201, 202, 204, 206, 228, 231, 236, 245–246, 264, 270, 321, 458
Douglas
   C-47 "Dakota" 18, 19
Duckworth, Keith 170, 197
Duesenberg 163

Eagle 7, 38, 61, 108, 110, 136, 159, 163, 168, 293, 381, 446
Eccles, Jim 381
Ecclestone, Bernie 393, 402, 403
Economaki, Chris 261

Edmonton, Alberta, Canada
   Can-Am 253
      1971 127
      1972 150–151
      1973 204
Edwards, Guy 409
Elford, Vic 7, 97–99, 131, 133, 191, 204, 205, 206, 261, 456, 458
Elkhart Lake — see "Road America"
Ensign 11, 320, 353, 388, 396, 425
Excalibur (car) 28, 41

Fendel, Bob 112
Ferrari 53, 57, 106, 163, 176, 180, 181, 216, 224, 243, 246, 270, 275, 276, 277, 280, 284, 285, 286, 311, 316, 320, 323, 326, 344, 345, 347, 348, 350, 354, 359, 360, 363, 364, 367, 381, 396, 397, 409, 413, 415, 446, 452, 455
   312B3 271
   312T2 351
   333SP 172
Ferrari, Enzo 363
FIA (Fédération Internationale de l'Automobile) 32, 68, 164, 264, 310
Field, Frederick "Ted" 388, 445
Firestone 6, 32, 42, 50–51, 53, 59, 70, 71, 73, 78, 80, 82, 85, 86, 87, 90, 96, 98, 99, 102, 105, 119, 166, 210
Firestone, Raymond 85
FISA (Fédération Internationale du Sport Automobile) 428
Fittipaldi, Emerson 10, 176, 177, 184, 185, 187, 192, 224, 226, 228, 229, 271, 274, 284, 285, 286, 350, 423, 425, 428
Fittipaldi (F1 car) 409, 420
Fittipaldi (team) 381
FOCA (Formula One Constructors' Association) 428
Follmer, George 7, 42, 48, 58–59, 60, 74, 76, 79, 80, 87–89, 90, 92–93, 95, 97–98, 101, 102, 103, 133, 142–143, 145, 148, 149, 151, 153, 158, 167, 168, 171, 173–177, 179, 180–182, 185, 186, 188–189, 190–195, 199, 204, 207, 213, 230, 231, 236–250, 252–253, 254–255, 257, 262, 264–265, 369, 372, 376, 400–401, 406, 456
Follmer (book by Tom Madigan) 195
Forbes-Robinson, Elliott 372, 374, 377
Ford 31, 51–52, 53, 165, 381
   G7A 38
   GT40 107
   Model T 17
   Mustang 195
   Ranger pickup 12

460 INDEX

Ford (engines) 66, 70, 107, 163, 172
   V8 51, 292, 333
Ford of Europe Advanced Vehicle Operations 260
Ford-Cosworth
   — see 'Cosworth'
Formula (US monthly magazine) 361, 369, 385, 394, 396, 397, 412
Fort Bragg, North Carolina (army installation) 447
Fort Holabird (National Intelligence Center) 29
France, Bill Jr. 34
France, Bill Sr. 34, 36
Freeman, Bill 377
Fuji International Speedway 28, 31, 33–41, 44, 45
   Indycar
      1966 38
   Can-Am
      1967 39
      1968 38, 44
      1969 38
   Japanese Grand Prix
      1976 41, 310, 325–326, 348, 349, 390
      1977 364–365
FX Bikes 309

Gabbiani, Giuseppe "Beppe" 414
Gable, Clark 29
Ganley, Howden 130, 186
Gardner, Derek 99
Gatorade 125
General Motors (GM) 51, 55, 197, 296, 333
Gentry, John 404, 420, 421
Gethin, Peter 332
Giacomelli, Bruno 409, 410
Girling brakes 132
Goodwood 36, 106, 114
Goodyear 32, 34, 50, 59, 96, 99, 105, 108, 119–120, 121, 122, 125, 126, 128, 129, 134, 146, 166, 183, 193, 207, 210, 213, 235, 242, 246, 311, 380, 381, 404, 414
Goth, Mike 58, 59
Grable, Betty 15
Graemiger, Charles "Chuck" 422
Granatelli, Andy 102
Grand Prix (film) 31
Grands Prix (World Championship)
   Argentine (Buenos Aires)
      1973 167
      1974 214
      1975 11, 270–271, 272
      1977 342, 343, 344
      1978 388, 389
      1979 407, 408, 416, 445
      1980 421, 423, 426–427
   Austrian (Österreichring)
      1973 185
      1974 226
      1975 270, 283–284, 289
      1976 321
      1977 7, 11, 12, 13, 341, 356–361, 372, 378, 384
      1978 394
      1979 406, 414
   Belgian 20
      1967 (Spa-Francorchamps) 163
      1973 (Zolder) 164, 177–179
      1974 (Nivelles) 219, 230
      1975 (Zolder) 276
      1976 (Zolder) 316
      1977 (Zolder) 353–354
      1978 (Zolder) 392
      1979 (Zolder) 410, 445, 446
      1980 (Zolder) 425
   Brazilian
      1973 (Interlagos) 167
      1974 (Interlagos) 165, 214
      1975 (Interlagos) 11, 271–272
      1976 (Interlagos) 310–312
      1977 (Interlagos) 342, 345
      1978 (Jacarepagua) 389
      1979 (Interlagos) 408, 416
      1980 (Interlagos) 421, 423–424, 427
   British
      1972 (Brands Hatch) 161
      1973 (Silverstone) 182–183
      1974 (Brands Hatch) 209, 224–226
      1975 (Silverstone) 268, 269, 279–281
      1976 (Brands Hatch) 318–320
      1977 (Silverstone) 355, 402
      1978 (Brands Hatch) 383, 394
      1979 (Silverstone) 412–413
      1980 (Brands Hatch) 428
   Canadian
      1973 (Mosport) 9, 186–187, 192
      1974 (Mosport) 227–228
      1976 (Mosport) 324
      1977 (Mosport) 363–364, 388
      1978 (Montreal) 374
      1979 (Montreal) 414–415
   Dutch (Zandvoort)
      1973 183–184
      1974 222–224
      1975 269, 277–278
      1976 321–323, 328, 329
      1977 362
      1978 394, 396
      1979 414
   French
      1906 (Le Mans) 355
      1921 (Le Mans) 163
      1973 (Paul Ricard) 181–182
      1974 (Dijon) 172, 224
      1975 (Paul Ricard) 278–279, 328
      1976 (Paul Ricard) 318
      1977 (Dijon) 355, 403, 412
      1978 (Paul Ricard) 394
      1979 (Dijon) 412, 446
      1980 (Paul Ricard) 428
   German
      1973 (Nürburgring) 166, 184–185
      1974 (Nürburgring) 226
      1975 (Nürburgring) 282, 289
      1976 (Nürburgring) 320, 325
      1977 (Hockenheim) 355–356
      1978 (Hockenheim) 394–395
      1979 (Hockenheim) 413–414
   Italian (Monza)
      1967 168
      1973 185
      1974 227
      1975 269, 285–286, 289
      1976 324, 327, 330
      1977 362–363, 402
      1978 382, 396
      1979 414
   Japanese (Fuji) 36
      1976 38, 41, 310, 325–326, 348, 349, 390
      1977 364–365
   Monaco
      1972 168
      1973 165, 179–181
      1974 219–221, 230, 231
      1975 275–276
      1976 316–318
      1977 351–353
      1978 386, 387, 392
      1979 410–411
      1980 428
   South African (Kyalami)
      1973 163, 165, 167, 173–174, 192, 193
      1974 216–217, 230, 236, 262
      1975 11, 272
      1976 312–313
      1977 346–348
      1978 389
      1979 408
      1980 424
   Spanish
      1973 (Montjuich Park) 166, 174–177, 192
      1974 (Jarama) 217–219, 230
      1975 (Montjuich Park) 270, 274–275
      1976 (Jarama) 311, 315–316
      1977 (Jarama) 350–351, 457
      1978 (Jarama) 392–393
      1979 (Jarama) 410
   Swedish (Anderstorp)
      1973 181
      1974 220, 222
      1975 276–277
      1976 318
      1977 354–355
      1978 393
   United States (Watkins Glen)
      1973 188–189, 230
      1974 228–229, 254
      1975 287, 320
   United States East (Watkins Glen)
      1976 324–325
      1977 342, 363
      1978 396
      1979 405, 415
   United States West (Long Beach) 305
      1976 314, 379
      1977 348–350, 366
      1978 391–397
      1979 409, 445
      1980 424
Grands Prix (non-championship)
   Dino Ferrari (Imola)
      1979 414
   Emilio Medici (Brasilia)
      1974 215
   South African (Kyalami)
      1981 428
   Spanish (Jarama)
      1980 423, 428, 429
   Swiss (Dijon)
      1975 284–285
Grant, Jerry 57, 58, 59
Gunn, John 243
Gunnar Nilsson Cancer Foundation 410
Gurney, Dan 7, 46, 78, 79, 86, 90, 92–93, 95, 99, 114, 159, 163, 168, 338, 398, 419, 446
Gurney Eagle — see "Eagle"

Haas, Carl 219, 334, 367, 375
Haas F1 team 7
Haas/Hall F5000 team 302
Hackman, Gene 351, 457
Hall, Jim 58, 59, 60, 73, 99, 109, 114, 116, 119, 230, 308, 375, 380
Harley-Davidson 309, 446, 451
Harlow, Jean 15
Harris, Trevor 6, 7, 32, 42–61, 62–74, 76, 78, 80–83, 84–85, 86, 87, 89, 93, 94–95, 96, 97, 99, 100–101, 102, 104, 105, 108, 109, 110, 131, 132, 139, 159, 161–162, 190, 191, 404, 405, 406, 407, 410, 412, 413, 416, 444–447, 458, 459
   "Car X" 44, 60–61, 68
Hartman, Wayne 46–47, 51, 52, 54, 55, 69, 85, 110
Hasemi, Masahiro 325
Hawthorn, Mike 106
Hayes, Charlie 42, 61
Haywood, Hurley 199
Henry, Alan 267
Hesketh 216, 224, 277 308 347

Hewland (gearboxes) 71, 77, 79, 89, 100–101, 105, 108, 139, 144, 148, 156, 166, 191, 210, 271, 285, 306, 438
   FG300 420
   FG400 210
   FGA400 383
   LG500 72
   TL200 210, 212, 219, 271, 342, 370, 373
Hewland, Mike 72, 89
Hilborn fuel injection 40, 44, 69, 81–82, 100
Hill, Graham 38, 168, 172, 174–175, 176, 177, 179, 180–185, 189, 229, 275, 320, 388
Hill, Phil 163, 396
Hillman, Mike 195, 233, 234, 236, 237, 239, 260–265, 267, 292, 296, 308–309, 332
Hitler, Adolf 20, 22
Hobbs, David 127, 128, 150, 151, 239, 242, 292, 304, 306
Hockenheim
   German Grand Prix
      1977 355–356
      1978 394–395
      1979 413–414
Holbert, Al 374
Honda (engines) 168
Honda, Soichiro 31
Honeywell 111
Hulme, Denny 86, 90, 92–93, 106, 113, 119, 120, 122, 126, 127, 141, 142, 148, 151, 173, 220, 224, 229, 260, 306
Hunt, James 41, 202–204, 216, 224, 228, 255, 256, 257, 274, 277, 278, 310, 311, 312, 316, 318, 324, 326, 330, 344, 345, 347, 350, 355, 359, 360, 364, 385
Hutchinson, Jeff 361, 394, 396, 409, 412, 413
Hutton, Ray 267,

Ickx, Jacky 10, 53–54, 113, 176, 216, 255, 257, 258, 272, 352–353
Imola
   Dino Ferrari Grand Prix
      1979 414
IMSA (International Motor Sports Association) 60, 172, 376, 388
Indianapolis Speedway 34
   Indy 500 38, 53, 66, 78, 80, 163, 236, 348
      1915 112
      1964 260
      1966 168
      1968 168
      1970 102
      1975 262–263
      1980 380
Indianapolis Raceway Park 38, 207

INDEX **461**

Interlagos 429
  Brazilian Grand Prix
    1974 165, 214
    1975 271–272
    1976 310–312
    1977 342, 345
    1979 408, 416
    1980 421, 423–424, 427
International Race of
  Champions (IROC) 234
International Trophy,
  Silverstone
    1974 217
    1975 274
    1976 314–315
    1978 388, 390–391
Interscope 334, 388, 391, 392,
  396, 445
Iso 219
Isooctane fuel 123, 125
Isuzu
  Bellel 31

Jabouille, Jean-Pierre 412
Jacarepagua
  Brazilian Grand Prix
    1978 389
    1979 408
Jackson, Chris 246
Jaguar
  XK120 29, 453
James, Jesse 15
Janesville wagon 15, 16
Japan Auto Federation 80
Jarama
  Spanish Grand Prix
    1974 217–219, 230
    1976 311, 315–316
    1977 350–351, 457
    1978 392–393
    1979 410
    1980 (non-championship)
      423, 428, 429
Jarier, Jean-Pierre 11, 165, 172,
  213, 214, 215, 217–222, 223–
  224, 225–227, 228–229, 236,
  254, 255, 257, 266, 268, 269,
  270–271, 272, 274, 275–283,
  288, 289, 301–302, 310–321,
  323–326, 327, 328, 342, 350,
  363, 372, 374, 375, 376, 397,
  401, 452
Jeep 20, 446, 448
Jenkinson, Denis 348
Johansson, Stefan 421,
  423–424, 426–427, 452
Jones, Alan 7, 11, 12, 177, 259,
  332, 334, 335, 341, 349–351,
  353–367, 368–370, 372, 374,
  375, 384, 397, 398, 410, 423,
  428, 452
Jones, Parnelli 78–79, 80, 195,
  207
Jones, Stan 366
JW Automotive 381
J-Wax 115

Kauhsen, Willi 202
Kawai, Minoru 38
Kemp, Charlie 199, 205,
  206–207

Kennedy, David 421, 423–425,
  427, 428–429
Kent, Washington, USA 58
Kenworth 245
Kerr, Peter 175
Kirby, Gordon 201, 205, 247,
  296, 300
Klausler, Tom 259
Knudsen, Semon "Bunkie"
  51, 52
Koinigg, Helmuth 229
Kojima
  KE007 325
Koni shock absorbers 132
Korean War 24–27, 29, 454
Kroll, Horst 332
Kyalami 208
  South African Grand Prix
    1973 163, 165, 167,
      173–174, 192, 193
    1974 216–217, 230, 236,
      262
    1975 272
    1976 312–313
    1977 346–348
    1978 389
    1979 408
    1980 424
    1981 (non-championship)
      428

Laffite, Jacques 270, 282, 318,
  348, 354–355, 364
Laguna Seca, California 59,
  82–83, 100, 140, 255, 259, 260,
  262, 298, 403, 427, 459
  Can-Am 233, 234, 253
    1971 127–128
    1972 151–153
    1973 204
  Can-Am II
    1978 374, 375
  F5000
    1975 306
Lake Washington Shipyards
  459
Lammers, Jan 404, 406, 407,
  408–415, 417, 445
Land Speed Record 66
Larrousse, Gérard 301
Larson, Fred 81
Lauda, Niki 182, 183, 216, 224,
  228, 270, 276, 286, 287, 310,
  311, 312, 316, 320, 325, 326,
  348, 350, 354, 355, 359, 360,
  362, 363, 365, 390, 393, 409
Le Mans 53, 66, 113, 114, 160,
  172, 210, 255, 257, 258, 288,
  456, 458
  1969 258, 398
  1972 288
  1973 288
  1974 223, 288
  1978 372
Lees, Geoff 424–425, 428, 452
Lewis, Randy 259, 332, 368
Ligier 318, 348, 355, 364, 416
Lincoln 45
  Zephyr 56–57
Lockheed (brakes) 166

Logan, John 112, 253, 261, 290,
  291, 309
Lowman, Mike 114, 115, 133,
  139, 154, 173, 417
Lola 31, 38, 49, 58, 107, 120,
  122, 127, 168, 169, 199, 219,
  243, 255, 260, 293, 299, 302,
  304, 306, 307, 308, 333, 334,
  336, 337, 338, 339, 367, 372,
  374–375, 401
  GT 107
  T70 39, 42, 45, 58, 59, 60, 168,
    190
  T160 40, 44, 61
  T220 90, 92–93
  T260 126
  T310 150, 151
  T333 368, 369, 370
Long Beach, California
  F5000
    1975 305–306, 309
  United States Grand Prix
    West
    1976 314, 379
    1977 348–350, 366
    1978 391–392
    1979 409, 445
    1980 424–425
Losher, Dennis 370, 420–422,
  431, 446, 448–452
Lotus 11, 106, 160, 176, 181,
  182, 192, 216, 224, 229, 270,
  272, 316, 331, 341, 358, 374,
  378, 379, 380, 381, 389, 397,
  409, 452
  Type 19 57
  Type 23 58
  Type 49 197
  Type 72 108, 176, 177
  Type 78 342, 348, 350, 355,
    359, 365, 379–380, 382,
    383, 389, 391, 397, 404
  Type 79 380, 382, 392, 394,
    396, 397, 404, 406, 407,
    412, 416, 420
  Type 80 416
Lucas fuel injection 82, 100,
  155–156, 235
Lunger, Brett 332
Lyons, Lorna 9, 11
Lyons, William 29

Macau 31
MacDill, Florida (Air Force
  Base) 459
MacQueen, Jim 369, 370
Madigan, Tom 48, 195
Maggs, Tony 107
MagnaCharger
  (superchargers) 110
Magnuson, Jerry 53, 110, 132
Man of La Mancha (musical)
  104
March 136, 166, 181, 283, 359,
  379
  732 213
  761 346–347, 348
Martin, Burdie 264
Maserati 57
Mass, Jochen 184, 275, 318, 362

Matra 210, 226, 283–284,
  288–289
  V12 engine 283–284,
    285–286, 287, 288–289,
    318, 355, 442
Mattel
  Hot Wheels 101
Mays, Rex 163
Mazda 99, 133
McCreary, Bill 32
McKitterick, Skeeter 332
McLaren 11, 32, 38, 49, 58, 79,
  82, 86, 90, 107, 119, 120, 122,
  125, 126, 127, 130, 140, 142,
  148, 159, 166, 181, 182, 197,
  198, 199, 213, 214, 226, 229,
  233, 234, 236, 242, 243, 252,
  255, 265, 275, 284, 293, 306,
  311, 312, 318, 326, 344, 345,
  358, 359, 362, 366, 424, 452
  M1A 59
  M6B 90, 92–93, 118
    "McLeagle" 79
  M8 65
    M8A 45
    M8B 74
    M8D 90, 92–93, 118
    M8F 108, 113, 140, 143,
      148, 149, 241
  M20 141, 142, 151, 152, 153,
    156, 237, 238, 239, 246,
    255, 257
  M23 41, 165, 173, 271
  M26 355
McLaren, Bruce 59, 86, 114, 454
Mederer, Jim 53, 78, 85, 86,
  95, 96, 97, 99, 114, 116, 121,
  131–133
Mercedes-Benz 28
Mercury 46
Merzario, Arturo 219, 358,
  359, 360
Meyer, Doug 202, 203, 245,
  295, 297
MG 29
  MGB 101
Michelin 381
Mid-Ohio 79, 454, 455
  Can-Am
    1970 7, 96–99, 103, 104,
      132, 191
    1971 122
    1972 144–146
    1973 201–202
    1974 195, 231, 245–251,
      264, 400, 453, 455
  Can-Am II
    1978 372
  F5000
    1975 304, 308
    1976 337, 338
Mifune, Toshiro 29–31
Miletich, Vel 78
Mini Cooper S 49
Minter, Milt 142, 143, 149
MIRA (Motor Industry
  Research Association) 412,
  416, 445
Mirage 255
Miss World 262

Moneypenny, Charlie 33–34,
  35, 36, 37, 38, 41
Monte Carlo
  Formula 3 race
    1974 222–223
    1975 343
    1978 406
  Monaco Grand Prix
    1972 168
    1973 179–181
    1974 219–221, 230, 231
    1975 275–276
    1976 316–318
    1977 351–353
    1978 386, 387, 392
    1979 410–411
    1980 428
Montezemolo, Luca Di 367
Montjuich Park
  Spanish Grand Prix
    1973 166, 174–177, 192
    1975 270, 274–275
Montreal
  Canadian Grand Prix
    1978 374
    1979 414
Mont-Tremblant — see
  "Saint-Jovite"
Monza 113
  Italian Grand Prix
    1967 168
    1973 185
    1974 227
    1975 269, 285–286, 289
    1976 324, 327, 330
    1977 362–363, 402
    1978 382, 396
    1979 414
Moon, Dean 40, 44, 69, 81
Morris, Vic 404, 422, 445
Mosport, Canada 255, 257, 258,
  259, 338, 367, 368
  Can-Am
    1970 6–7, 83, 84, 85, 86,
      87–93, 94, 95, 101, 102,
      190–191
    1971 113
    1972 136, 140, 141–142
    1973 200–201, 232
    1974 194, 236–240, 242,
      264
  Can-Am II
    1978 374, 375
  Canadian Grand Prix
    1973 9, 186–187, 192
    1974 227–228
    1976 324
    1977 363–364, 388
  F5000
    1975 293, 300
    1976 334–335
Moss, Stirling 36, 37
Motschenbacher, Lothar 90,
  92–93, 120, 242, 243
Motor (English weekly
  magazine) 202
Motor Sport (English monthly
  magazine) 165, 167, 183, 272,
  348, 361, 386, 429
Muir, Dennis 12, 13, 202

Muir, Lee 12, 13, 81–82, 139, 140, 154, 155, 202, 203, 235, 295, 297, 300, 332, 370, 401
Müller, Herbert 243
Murphy, Jimmy 163
Murray, Gordon 213, 393

NASCAR 34, 35, 36, 38, 51, 139, 140, 152, 154, 297, 372
Nippon NASCAR 35
Newman, Paul 377
Nichols Advanced Vehicle Systems — see "Advanced Vehicle Systems"
Nichols, Alice (first wife) 453–454
Nichols, Bob (grandfather) 16–17
Nichols, Don 6–7, 8–13, 14–27, 28–41, 42–55, 56, 61, 62–63, 65, 67, 73, 74, 76, 78, 79, 80, 81, 82, 83, 84, 85, 86, 93, 95, 96–97, 99, 100, 102, 104–105, 107, 108, 110, 111, 113, 114, 116, 117, 118, 119, 120, 121, 130, 131, 132, 133, 134–135, 139, 140, 144, 149, 152, 156, 158–159, 160–163, 168, 169, 170–171, 172, 174, 183, 186, 190, 191, 192, 193, 194, 195, 196, 197, 202, 206, 223, 229, 230, 231, 232, 234, 237, 239, 242, 243, 245, 253, 254, 256, 257, 259, 260, 261, 262, 264, 265, 272, 274, 283, 287, 288, 290–291, 292, 293, 296, 298, 302, 306, 307, 308, 309, 310, 316, 320, 321, 323, 324, 325, 331, 332, 340, 341, 342, 343, 345, 346, 352, 356, 359, 361, 365, 367, 368, 376, 377, 378, 380, 381, 384, 385, 386, 387, 388, 391, 394, 398–403, 404, 406, 416, 417, 418, 419–420, 421, 425, 427, 430, 444–445, 446–447, 448–452, 453–459
Childhood 14–15
Intelligence and counter-intelligence 26–27, 28
Japan, working and living there 28–41, 161
Journalism 23
Military career 17–26
Decorations 20, 21, 24–25
Military vehicles 291, 446–447, 448–452, 459
Wizard's Cave, Salinas 8–13
Nichols, Donna (first daughter) 453, 455–456
Nichols, Ellen (second daughter) 454, 456
Nichols, Fanny (grandmother) 16
Nichols, Guy (father) 16, 17
Nichols, Nancy (second wife) 454, 459
Nichols, Omah (mother) 15
Nichols, Penny (third daughter) 29, 447, 453–459

Nichols, Ray (uncle) 16
Nichols, Ryan (grandson) 456
Nichols, Tom (great-great grandfather) 16
Niemcek, Brad 115, 139
Nilsson, Gunnar 365, 407
Nissan 60, 99, 447
ZX Turbo GTP 60
Nivelles
Belgian Grand Prix
1974 219, 230
Noble, Chuck 53
Nogaro 429
Norma 172
Northrop-Grumman 447
Nunn, Morris "Mo" 388
Nürburgring
1,000Kms
1974 226
German Grand Prix
1973 166, 184–185
1974 226
1975 282, 289
1976 320, 325

Oldsmobile 50, 56, 57, 99, 159
Oliver, Jackie 7, 10, 90, 92–93, 107, 112, 113, 114–116, 118, 119, 120, 121–122, 123, 124, 125, 126–130, 133, 134–135, 136, 138, 140, 141, 142–143, 144, 145–146, 147, 148, 149–150, 151, 152–153, 154, 155, 156, 157, 158, 159, 160–161, 162, 167, 168, 169, 170, 171, 173–175, 177, 179, 180–189, 192–193, 195, 198, 199, 200–202, 204–206, 213, 230, 231, 233, 234, 236–253, 254, 255, 257, 258, 261, 262–265, 267, 292, 293, 296, 298–307, 308, 314, 331, 332–339, 348, 349, 354, 358, 362, 366, 367, 384–385, 386, 387, 394, 397, 398–403, 431, 455, 457
Oliver, Jason (son) 251
Oliver, Lynne (wife) 251, 455
Ongais, Danny 332, 333, 334, 336, 337, 388, 391–392, 396, 445
Ontario Motor Speedway, California 139, 153, 366
Orange County International Raceway (OCIR), California 78–82, 140, 207
Osaka Auto Show 28
Österreichring
Austrian Grand Prix
1973 185
1974 226
1975 270, 283–284, 289
1976 321
1977 7, 11, 12, 13, 341, 356–361, 372, 378, 384
1978 394
1979 406, 414
Owen, Richard 371, 372, 404, 416–417, 420, 445

Pace, Carlos 135, 136, 146, 147, 148, 149, 151, 183, 184, 207, 228, 271, 280, 285, 313
Parnelli (F1 car) 228, 229, 343
Parnelli (team) — see "Vel's Parnelli"
Parsons, Chuck 118
Patrese, Riccardo 352–354, 355–356, 358, 359, 362–365, 384, 386, 389, 392, 393, 394
Patrick, Scooter 237, 238, 239, 240, 242, 243, 245, 246, 252, 253, 255
Patuxent, Maryland (Naval Air Station) 447
Paul Ricard 266, 268, 445
French Grand Prix
1973 181–182
1975 278–279, 328
1976 318
1978 394
1980 428
Penske (F1 car) 228, 229, 350, 388
Penske Racing 7, 11, 60, 141, 145, 149, 150, 198, 199, 231, 245, 250, 264, 265, 343
Penske, Roger 7, 79, 142, 246, 321
Pentagon 29, 459
Pershing, John 15
Pescarolo, Henri 217
Peter Bryant Challenger Award 159
Peterson, Ronnie 11, 175, 182, 184, 224, 228, 262–263, 270, 272, 274, 279, 326, 351, 354, 360, 363, 364, 390, 396, 397, 407
Petty, Richard 35, 297
Phipps, David 288, 347
Phoenix Raceway 61
Phoenix Racing Organization 110, 111, 309, 384
Pilette, Teddy 332
Piola, Giorgio 385, 446
Piquet, Nelson 409
Pocono, Pennsylvania
F5000
1975 299–300, 308
1976 332–333
Porsche 109, 155, 169, 172, 191, 197, 232, 234, 245, 254, 261, 376, 400
906 39
908 98
911 376
914/6 108
917
917L 113
917/10 142, 143, 149, 192, 194
917/10K 137, 141–142, 148, 149, 150, 151, 152, 153, 154, 156, 198, 202, 204, 205, 206–207
917/30 199, 201, 204, 205, 206, 231, 236, 245, 246, 247, 250, 264
936 255, 257

Posey, Sam 332
Posthumus, Cyril 164
Postlethwaite, Harvey 346
Powell, Dick 29
P.R. Reilly team 320
Princess Michiko of Japan 28
Project Four 427
Prophet 372
Prost, Alain 424
Pryce, Tom 10, 11, 222–227, 228–229, 267, 268, 269–270, 271, 272–274, 275–287, 289, 305–306, 309, 310, 343, 344–348, 366, 401, 452, 456, 458
Purley, David 183

Quantico, Virginia (Marine Corps Base) 447
Queen Mary (ocean liner) 305

Race of Champions, Brands Hatch
1967 163
1974 215–216
1975 10, 11, 272–274, 328
1976 313–314
1977 344, 348, 349, 354
1979 409–410, 416, 417
RACECAR (US monthly magazine) 412
Racing Beat 99, 114, 133
Racing History Project, The 159
Ramirez, Jo 381, 404, 405
Rattlesnake Raceway 114, 119, 133, 314
Red Bull 354
Redman, Brian 188–189, 199, 217–220, 222, 246–247, 250, 292, 299, 300, 301, 302, 304, 305, 306, 307, 308, 332, 333, 334, 336, 337, 338, 339, 376, 456
Rees, Alan 193, 223, 263, 267, 268–269, 279, 285, 287, 328, 330–331, 366, 384, 387, 394, 399, 402–403
Regazzoni, Clay 224, 228, 276, 280, 284, 285, 286, 323, 348, 354, 381, 382, 388, 389–397, 412–413
Renault 372, 406
RS10 412
Reventlow, Lance 163
Reventlow Scarab — see "Scarab"
Revson, Peter 38, 90, 92–93, 120, 125, 126, 127, 130, 140, 141, 142, 148, 149, 151, 152, 183, 187, 213, 214, 215, 216, 229, 230, 234, 236, 237, 239, 262, 400, 458
Reutemann, Carlos 214, 224, 228, 271, 274, 277, 282, 330, 344, 345, 350, 397
Richter, Les 253, 262
Rindt, Jochen 108
Rinzler race team 192, 207

Riverside, California 31, 35, 49, 59, 60, 78, 80, 82–83, 100, 122, 123, 125, 139, 262, 349, 367, 458
Can-Am 233, 234, 253
1971 128–130
1972 153–158
1973 204–207, 261, 400
Can-Am II
1977 369–370
1978 375
F5000
1975 306–307
1976 338–339
Road Atlanta, Georgia
Can-Am
1971 121–122, 133
1972 136, 142–143
1973 200–201
1974 240–242
Can-Am II
1978 372
F5000
1975 297, 304–305
Road America, Wisconsin 60, 454, 457
Can-Am
1971 122, 123–126
1972 146–148
1973 202–204
1974 237, 252–253, 265, 291
Can-Am II
1978 373–374, 376, 377
F5000
1975 265, 302–303, 401
1976 309, 332, 333–337, 338, 401
Road & Track (US monthly magazine) 54–55, 65, 84, 85, 100–103, 111, 163, 164
Rodriguez, Pedro 40, 44, 113
Rodriguez, Ricardo 27, 381
Roebuck, Nigel 409
Rogers, Ginger 15
Rolls-Royce 260
Roos, Bertil 220, 222
Rosberg, Keke 377, 391
Roush, Jack 458
Runyan, Robert Miles 309
Rush (film) 310
Rutherford, Johnny 380

SAE (Society of Automotive Engineers) 132
Saint-Jovite, Quebec, Canada 79, 259
Can-Am races
1970 7, 94–95, 103, 104, 107, 142, 406, 444
1971 114–120, 133, 399
Can-Am II
1978 372
Scarab 7, 163
SCCA (Sports Car Club of America) 68, 73, 114, 116, 125, 131, 134, 206, 232, 233, 253, 257, 264, 292, 297, 332, 339, 368, 376, 388

Scheckter, Jody 11, 182, 199, 206–207, 224, 272, 292, 306–307, 313, 315, 318, 323, 348, 355, 356, 360, 415
Schkee 259
Schroder Racing 108
Schuppan, Vern 332, 337, 338
Schweitzer (turbochargers) 154, 202
Sears Point, California 367
  Can-Am II
    1977 368–370
Sebring, Washington 53, 120, 172, 455
Shadow cars
  Mk I (Can-Am) 6–7, 11, 44, 52, 53–55, 62–83, 84–103, 104, 105, 108, 190–191, 204, 207, 235, 323, 398–399, 406, 445, 447, 449
  Mk II (Can-Am) 7, 86, 104–130, 133, 134, 135, 136, 139, 347, 431
  Mk III (Can-Am) 134–159, 169, 341, 431
  Turbo 139, 144, 153–155
  DN1 (F1) 160–189, 192–194, 197, 198, 199, 208, 214, 215, 230, 267, 316, 433
  DN2 (Can-Am) 172, 196–207, 208, 232, 233, 235, 260, 261, 262, 346
    DN2T (Turbo) 196–198, 202, 203, 204–207, 261, 400, 432–434
  DN3 (F1) 208–231, 233, 235, 255, 256, 257, 267, 319–320, 438
    DN3B 271, 272
  DN4 (Can-Am) 7, 172, 194–195, 229, 231, 232–259, 260, 261, 262, 264–265, 292, 294, 323, 338, 374, 400, 435–437
    DN4B 259, 368
  DN5 (F1) 11, 210, 235, 266–287, 289, 293, 294, 296, 305, 308, 311, 316, 327, 328, 336, 340–341, 342, 369, 380, 401, 442
    DN5B 310–321, 324, 326, 340, 343, 344, 345, 439
  DN6 (F5000) 235, 292–309, 333, 369, 401, 440–441
    DN6B 309, 332–339
    DN6C (Can-Am II) 259, 368–371, 372
  DN7 (F1) 210, 283–284, 288–289, 341, 442
  DN8 (F1) 12, 13, 202, 210, 310, 316, 318, 319, 321–331, 340–345, 371, 373, 377, 383
    DN8B 346–356, 359
    "Streamliner" 351, 356
    DN8C 356–365, 372, 388, 389, 391, 397

DN9 (F1) 378–388, 404, 405, 406, 408, 420, 443, 445
  DN9B 404–417, 443, 444–445
  "Skinny Lizzie" 416–417
DN10 (Can-Am II) 13, 259, 370–377
DN11 (F1) 404, 418–429
DN12 (F1) 420–423, 424, 425, 428–429
Shadow Box (military projects) 447, 448–452
Sharp, Hap 59
Shelby, Carroll 29, 35, 38, 159
Shelby Series 1 159
Shinoda, Larry 51, 52
Siffert, Jo 184
Signal Companies 290, 309
Sikorsky 447
  Black Hawk 446, 447
Silverstone 107, 163, 164, 167, 171, 233, 234, 262, 372, 376, 429, 446
  British Grand Prix
    1973 182–183
    1975 268, 269, 279–281
    1977 355, 402
    1979 412–413
  International Trophy
    1973 174
    1974 217
    1975 274
    1976 314–315
    1978 388, 390–391
Simpson, Bill 366
Sonoma, California 431
Southgate, Tony 7, 162–163, 165–167, 168–172, 175, 177, 183, 184, 192, 194, 196–197, 198, 200, 202, 205, 208–210, 217, 230–231, 232–233, 235, 236, 260, 261, 262, 265, 266–269, 288, 289, 293, 296, 307, 308, 316, 323, 331, 340–341, 342, 346, 356, 358, 361, 378, 379, 380, 381, 382, 384–386, 387, 394, 399, 402, 403, 406, 420, 432, 434, 435, 437, 439, 440, 443, 452
Spa-Francorchamps 113
  Belgian Grand Prix
    1967 163
Spellman, Ronnie 139
Spicklemire, Jim 202, 237
Sports Car Graphic (US monthly magazine) 55, 68
Sports Illustrated (US monthly magazine) 38
Spyder 372, 374
Stardust, Las Vegas 39
Stellings, Larry 53, 78, 79, 132
Stengel, Casey 15
Stewart, Jackie 38, 120, 122, 126, 127, 179, 185, 189, 288, 457
Stommelen, Rolf 275, 389, 392, 393, 394, 395
Stone, Ed 332, 336
STP 102

Stroppe, Bill 30–31, 45, 113
Stuck, Hans-Joachim 330, 348, 376, 381, 388, 389–397
Surtees 11, 183, 349, 366
Surtees, John 168, 208, 366
Swanson, B.J. 304

Talladega Superspeedway, Alabama 34
Tamagawa Speedway, Japan 29
Tambay, Patrick 332, 367, 368, 369, 370, 375
Tarozzi, Robert "Fast Bob" 450
Tauranac, Ron 260
Taylor, Simon 386
Team Toro 39
Team Yasuda 40
Tejima, Noritchka "Teji" 85, 86, 87, 91, 99, 133
Telford, Kent 85, 100–103, 111
Terry, Len 107
Tetraethyllead (TEL) 112, 120
Theodore Racing 334, 425, 428
  TR2 428
Timanus, John 125, 131
Titanium Car (Ti22) 86, 90, 92–93, 104, 105, 107, 108, 113, 116, 127, 128, 139, 142, 158, 159, 398
Token 222
Toleman 420
Tony Southgate: From Drawing Board to Chequered Flag (book) 163, 266
Townsend, Randolph 370, 372, 374–377
Toyota 38, 58, 59, 97, 102, 132, 172
  V8 engine 63, 97, 102
Tredway, Ron 24, 25
Trois-Rivières, Quebec, Canada
  Can-Am II
    1978 374
Truman, Harry S. 15
Twain, Mark 15
Tyrrell 11, 99, 176–177, 181, 189, 192, 272, 291, 381
  P34 (six-wheeler) 99, 312, 315, 318, 323, 326, 351, 360, 363, 364, 365
Tyrrell, Ken 288

Universities
  London
    Imperial College 162–163, 196, 266
  Missouri 23
  Nevada 370
  Seattle 46, 56
Unser, Al Jr, 61
Unser, Al Sr, 292, 304, 305, 306, 332, 336–337, 339, 401
Unser, Bobby 38, 292, 308
UOP (Universal Oil Products) 111–113, 118, 120, 123, 125, 126, 127, 130, 132, 133, 140, 144, 145, 149, 150, 152, 153, 154, 158, 160, 161, 163, 165, 173, 182, 184, 189, 199, 201, 204, 214, 220, 229, 232, 234, 253, 254, 261, 262, 265, 270, 280, 282, 283, 285, 287, 290–291, 292, 305, 309, 402, 445
  Divisions
    Automotive Products 291
    Bostrom (seats) 112, 162, 163
    Flexonic (flexible ducting) 112
    Johnson (filters) 112
    Wolverine (titanium tubing) 112
  UOP Honeywell 290
US Air Force 131
US Army 13, 18–26, 28, 29, 161
  101st Airborne Division ("Screaming Eagles") 18, 118
  Pathfinders 18, 19
USAC (United States Auto Club) 38, 140, 292, 297, 332, 366, 388
USRRC (United States Road Racing Championship) 58, 59

van Valkenburgh, Paul 55
Vanderbilt Cup, New York
  1937 163
Vel's Parnelli team 7, 79, 302, 308, 339, 381
Verstappen, Max 354
Villeneuve, Gilles 364, 397, 409
Villiger, Heinrich "Henry" 324, 343, 381
Vintage Motorsport (US monthly magazine) 170
Vintage Racecar (US monthly magazine) 16
Volvo 46
von Rundstedt, Field Marshal Gerd 20, 21
von Trips, Wolfgang 396
Volkswagen (VW) 12, 309
  Golf 449

Wakefield, Ron 66
Wass, Dave 316, 318, 331, 340, 342, 344, 346, 351, 354, 356, 358, 367, 384, 389, 394
Watkins Glen, New York 59, 454
  Can-Am
    1971 122
    1972 135, 138, 143–144
    1973 201
    1974 194, 242–245, 261, 264, 265, 401
  Can-Am II
    1978 372
  F5000
    1975 265, 301–302, 309
    1976 335

United States Grand Prix
  1973 188–189, 230
  1974 228–229, 254
  1975 287, 320
United States Grand Prix East
  1976 324–325
  1977 342, 363
  1978 397
  1979 405, 415
Watson, John 7, 11, 218, 285, 321, 330, 353, 355
Weismann (gearboxes) 105, 108, 137, 139, 142, 143, 144
Weismann, Pete 108, 110, 137
West, Ted 170
Westwood, British Columbia, Canada 57
Wilcox, Pete 110
Wilds, Mike 319–320
Willes, Chris 447, 450
Williams 11, 147, 186, 270, 282, 343, 375, 415, 420, 423, 452
  FW07 410
Williams, Ben 111, 112, 115, 130, 144, 220
Williams, Frank 219, 367, 384, 412, 419, 423
Williamson, Roger 183–184
Willow Springs, California 366
Witty, Chris 267, 426
Wolf 343, 349, 425
  WR1 348, 356, 360
Wonder, Bill 423
World War II 11, 17–25, 29, 55, 153, 446, 448
  Battle of the Bulge 20–22
  D-Day 13, 17–19, 24, 26, 161
  Operation Market Garden 18–20
Wright, Peter 379

Yasuda, Ginji 39, 40
Yip, Teddy 162, 334, 425, 428
Young, Greg 130

Zandvoort 409
  Dutch Grand Prix
    1973 183–184
    1974 222–224
    1975 269, 277–278
    1976 321–323, 328, 329
    1977 362
    1978 394, 396
    1979 414
Zimmermann, John 16
Zink-Urschel Trackburner Special 260
Zolder
  Belgian Grand Prix
    1973 164, 177–179
    1975 276
    1976 316
    1977 353–354
    1978 392
    1979 410, 445, 446
    1980 425
Zorzi, Renzo 343, 344, 345, 347, 348, 350, 351, 365